THE COMPLETE
STEP-BY-STEP
COOK
BOOK

THE COMPLETE
STEP-BY-STEP
COOK
BOOK

MORE THAN 800 RECIPES IN FULL COLOUR

GE

This edition published in 2004
by Greenwich Editions
The Chrysalis Building
Bramley Road, London W10 6SP

ISBN 0 86288 1994

CREDITS
Project managed by: Anne McDowall
Recipes selected by: Hilaire Walden
Typeset by: SX Composing DTP
Printed in China

Half-title page: Asparagus Niçoise (page 35)
Title page: Lemon & Honey Chicken (page 100), Bass with Ginger & Lime (page 72),
Nectarine Meringue Nests (page 382)
Below: Victoria Sponge Cake (page 403)

CONTENTS

Introduction
6

Soups
7

Cold Starters
23

Hot Starters
45

Fish
67

Shellfish
85

Chicken & Turkey
95

Duck & Game
117

Beef & Veal
129

Lamb
149

Pork
163

Vegetarian Main Courses
181

Pasta & Noodles
201

Rice
219

Pizzas
237

Savoury Pies & Pastries
243

Salads
259

Side Dishes
281

Sauces & Salad Dressings
303

Breads & Buns
317

Sweet Pastries
331

Hot Puddings
351

Cold Desserts
371

Large Cakes
395

Small Cakes
408

Biscuits
417

Food for Children
427

Party Pieces
435

Drinks
449

Chocolates & Candies
459

Preserves
465

Mediterranean Ingredients
472

Eastern Ingredients
474

Index
476

INTRODUCTION

The Complete Step-by-Step Cookbook is a unique collection of more than 800 recipes that have been created and written by experienced cookery authors and that are suitable for cooks of all tastes and all levels of abilities and with varying amounts of time and money available. Novice cooks will find instructions for how to make simple recipes such as white sauce or victoria sponge, while experienced cooks and food-lovers of all culinary abilities will find plenty of recipes to inspire and tempt them.

The Complete Step-by-Step Cookbook is both an attractive book and an extremely practical one. Each dish is shown in a full-colour photograph, and clear, concise, step-by-step instructions, accompanied by helpful step-by-step photographs, show how to make it.

The Complete Step-by-Step Cookbook contains authentic recipes from some of the most popular of the World's cuisines, including French, Italian, Spanish, Greek, Turkish, North African, Thai, Vietnamese, Chinese, Japanese, American and British. To help you to find out a little more about some of the ingredients that may be unfamiliar, useful glossaries of Mediterranean and Eastern ingredients (on pages 472–475) give descriptions, preparation, cooking and storing instructions, plus recommendations for suitable substitutes where applicable.

You will find many popular recipes in *The Complete Step-by-Step Cookbook*, whether you are looking for a mouthwatering dish to feed the family for lunch, tea or supper, provide a special meal for friends or serve for a more formal dinner party. There are recipes for every occasion and every type of cooking, from breakfasts to baking, from a festive dinner to a barbecue. Classic dishes – chocolate brownies, English trifle, roast turkey, paella, tiramisu, to name but a few – are accompanied by plenty more unusual ideas that will enable you to extend your repertoire, safe in the knowledge that the recipes will work, and with the reassuring "helping hand" of the step-by-step instructions and photographs.

SOUPS

CLEAR BEETROOT SOUP

VICHYSSOISE

1 onion, coarsely grated
1 large carrot, coarsely grated
450 g (1 lb) raw beetroot, peeled and coarsely grated
parsley sprig
1 bay leaf
1 litre (35 fl oz/4½ cups) chicken stock
1 egg white
juice ½ lemon
salt and pepper
thin strips lemon peel, to garnish

Put vegetables into a saucepan with herbs and stock. Bring to the boil, then cover and simmer for 30 minutes.

Strain soup and return it to rinsed-out pan. To clear soup, bring to the boil. Whisk egg white, then pour into pan and simmer gently for 15 minutes.

Strain soup through a muslin-lined sieve into a bowl. Add lemon juice, then cool and chill. Season the soup before serving and garnish with thin strips of lemon peel.

Serves 4-6.

25 g (1 oz/6 teaspoons) butter
3 leeks, trimmed, sliced and washed
1 shallot, finely chopped
225 g (8 oz) potatoes, sliced
685 ml (24 fl oz/3 cups) light chicken stock
pinch ground mace or grated nutmeg
salt and pepper
150 ml (5 fl oz/⅔ cup) single (light) cream
snipped fresh chives, to garnish

Melt butter in a large saucepan, add leeks and shallot, then cover and cook gently for 10 minutes without browning. Add potatoes, chicken stock and mace or nutmeg.

Bring to the boil, cover and simmer for 20 minutes. Purée in a blender or food processor, then pass through a sieve. Season with salt and pepper.

Set aside to cool, then stir in two-thirds of the cream. Chill until ready to serve. Ladle into bowls, swirl in remaining cream and garnish with snipped chives.

Serves 6.

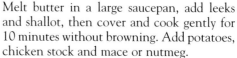

FENNEL & PEAR SOUP

2 fennel bulbs
25 g (1 oz/2 tablespoons) butter
3 ripe pears
850 ml (30 fl oz/3¾ cups) chicken or vegetable
   stock
150 ml (5 fl oz/⅔ cup) crème fraîche or thick sour
   cream
salt and freshly ground black pepper
crème fraîche or thick sour cream and fennel leaves,
   to garnish

Trim fennel, cut lengthways into quarters and coarsely chop. Heat butter in a saucepan, add fennel and cook for 5 minutes, stirring occasionally, until beginning to soften.

Peel pears, cut into quarters and remove cores. Coarsely chop pears and add to pan. Stir in stock, bring to the boil, cover and simmer gently for 15 minutes, until fennel and pears are tender.

Purée soup in a blender or food processor. Return to rinsed-out pan and stir in crème fraîche or thick sour cream and salt and pepper. Chill for at least 2 hours. Garnish with a swirl of crème fraîche or thick sour cream and fennel leaves and serve in chilled bowls, or reheat, garnish and serve hot.

Serves 6.

GAZPACHO

700 g (1½ lb) beefsteak tomatoes
½ Spanish onion, chopped
1 green pepper (capsicum), chopped
1 red pepper (capsicum), chopped
2 cloves garlic, chopped
2 slices firm white bread, crusts removed, broken
   into pieces
300 ml (10 fl oz/1¼ cups) tomato juice
3 tablespoons virgin olive oil
2 tablespoons sherry vinegar
salt and freshly ground black pepper
about 8 ice cubes, to serve
ACCOMPANIMENTS:
1 diced small red pepper (capsicum), 1 diced small
   green pepper (capsicum), 1 diced small onion, 1
   chopped hard-boiled egg and croûtons.

Peel, seed and chop tomatoes. Put in a food processor or blender with remaining soup ingredients, except ice cubes. Mix until smooth. Pour soup through a nylon sieve, pressing down well on contents of sieve. If necessary, thin soup with cold water, then chill well.

Place accompaniments in separate bowls. Adjust seasoning of soup, if necessary, then pour into cold soup bowls. Add ice cubes and serve with accompaniments.

Serves 4.

Variation: Do not sieve the soup if more texture is preferred.

COURGETTE & TOMATO SOUP

25 g (1 oz/6 teaspoons) butter
1 onion, finely chopped
350 g (12 oz) courgettes (zucchini), coarsely grated
1 clove garlic, crushed
550 ml (20 fl oz/2½ cups) vegetable stock
400 g (14 oz) can chopped tomatoes
2 tablespoons chopped fresh mixed herbs, if desired
salt and pepper
55 ml (2 fl oz/¼ cup) double (thick) cream and basil leaves, to garnish

Melt butter in a saucepan, add onion and cook until soft. Add courgettes (zucchini) and garlic and cook for 4-5 minutes.

Add stock and tomatoes with their juice, then bring to the boil, cover and simmer for 15 minutes.

Stir in herbs, if desired, and salt and pepper. Serve the soup in individual bowls, garnished with teaspoonfuls of cream stirred in or floating on the surface and basil leaves.

Serves 4.

CURRIED PARSNIP SOUP

45g (1½ oz/9 teaspoons) butter
1 onion, chopped
1 teaspoon chopped fresh root ginger
1 teaspoon curry powder
½ teaspoon ground cumin
450g (1 lb) parsnips, peeled and chopped
1 potato, chopped
850 ml (30 fl oz/3¾ cups) beef stock
150 ml (5 fl oz/⅔ cup) plain yogurt
salt and pepper
CURRIED CROÛTONS:
½ teaspoon curry powder
squeeze lemon juice
25 g (1 oz/6 teaspoons) butter
2 thick slices bread

Melt butter in a saucepan, add onion and cook gently until soft. Stir in ginger, curry powder and cumin and cook for 1 minute, then add parsnips and potato and stir over a medium heat to coat vegetables with spicy butter. Pour in stock and bring to the boil, then cover and simmer for 30 minutes or until vegetables are very tender. Purée in a blender or food processor, then return to saucepan. Ladle a little soup into a bowl and whisk in yogurt, then pour back into pan.

Add salt and pepper and while reheating, make croûtons. Preheat oven to 200C (400F/Gas 6). Beat curry powder, lemon juice and butter together in a bowl. Spread on bread, then remove crusts and cut into cubes. Place on a baking tray and bake until crisp and golden. Serve with soup.

Serves 4-6.

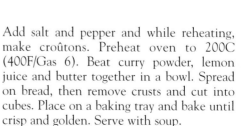

ONION SOUP

85 g (3 oz/¹⁄₃ cup) butter
700 g (1½ lb) large onions, thinly sliced
1 litre (35 fl oz/4½ cups) beef stock
300 ml (10 fl oz/1¼ cups) dry white wine
large pinch of mixed dried herbs
pinch of freshly grated nutmeg
salt and freshly ground black pepper
6 slices French bread
150 g (5 oz/1¼ cups) grated Gruyère cheese
flat-leaf parsley sprigs, to garnish

Heat the butter in a large, heavy saucepan, add the onions, stir to coat with the butter and lay a piece of greaseproof paper on top.

Cook over a very gentle heat, without stirring, for 20-30 minutes, until onions are soft and rich golden brown. Add stock, wine, dried herbs, nutmeg and salt and pepper and bring to the boil. Cover and simmer gently for 45 minutes. Meanwhile, preheat oven to 180C (350F/Gas 4). Arrange bread slices on a baking sheet and bake for 10-15 minutes, until dried but not browned.

Preheat grill. Divide soup among heatproof soup bowls. Float a slice of bread on top and sprinkle with cheese. Grill until cheese is bubbling and golden. Garnish with flat-leaf parsley sprigs and serve immediately.

Serves 6.

ROASTED PEPPER SOUP

6 large tomatoes
70 ml (2½ fl oz/¹⁄₃ cup) olive oil, plus extra for
  greasing
1 clove garlic, chopped
salt and freshly ground black pepper
4 red peppers (capsicum), quartered
1 onion, finely chopped
175 g (6 oz) potatoes, cut into 2 cm (¾ in) cubes
shredded basil leaves, to garnish
BASIL PURÉE:
1 small bunch of basil
2 tablespoons olive oil
1 teaspoon lemon juice

Preheat oven to 190C (350F/Gas 5). Oil two roasting tins. Cut tomatoes in half.

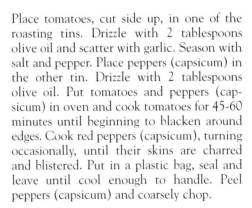

Place tomatoes, cut side up, in one of the roasting tins. Drizzle with 2 tablespoons olive oil and scatter with garlic. Season with salt and pepper. Place peppers (capsicum) in the other tin. Drizzle with 2 tablespoons olive oil. Put tomatoes and peppers (capsicum) in oven and cook tomatoes for 45-60 minutes until beginning to blacken around edges. Cook red peppers (capsicum), turning occasionally, until their skins are charred and blistered. Put in a plastic bag, seal and leave until cool enough to handle. Peel peppers (capsicum) and coarsely chop.

Heat remaining oil in a pan. Add onion and cook, stirring occasionally, for 5 minutes. Add potatoes, peppers (capsicum) and 850ml (30 fl oz/3¾ cups) water. Cover and simmer for 20 minutes. Transfer to a blender or food processor, add tomatoes and purée until smooth. Press through a sieve, return to rinsed-out pan and heat through. Season. Pound basil leaves with a large pinch of salt. Stir in oil and lemon juice. Add a spoonful of basil purée to each bowl, garnish and serve.

Serves 6.

HERBED PEA SOUP

55 g (2 oz/¼ cup) unsalted butter
1 leek, finely chopped
1 small round lettuce, separated into leaves
about 850 ml (30 fl oz/3¾ cups) vegetable or
    chicken stock, or water
several sprigs of chervil
few sprigs of parsley
450 g (1 lb) fresh or frozen peas
salt and freshly ground black pepper
single (light) cream, to garnish

Heat butter in a saucepan, add leek and cook, stirring occasionally, for 5 minutes, until soft. Add lettuce and cook for 1-2 minutes, until leaves have wilted.

Add stock or water, chervil, parsley and fresh peas if using, bring to the boil and simmer for 10 minutes if using fresh peas. If using frozen peas, simmer for 5 minutes, until peas are tender.

Purée soup in a blender or food processor and return to rinsed-out pan. Add salt and pepper and reheat gently without boiling. If soup is too thick, add some boiling stock or water. Swirl in cream and serve.

Serves 4.

CREAM OF MUSHROOM SOUP

55 g (2 oz/¼ cup) butter
350 g (12 oz) mushrooms, finely chopped
25 g (2 oz/½ cup) plain flour
450 ml (16 fl oz/2 cups) chicken stock
150 ml (5 fl oz/⅔ cup) milk
1 tablespoon chopped fresh parsley
3 teaspoons lemon juice
salt and pepper
150 ml (5 fl oz/⅔ cup) single (light) cream
70 ml (2½ fl oz/⅓ cup) double (thick) cream and
    1 tablespoon finely chopped fresh watercress, to
    garnish

Melt the butter in a large saucepan, add mushrooms and cook gently for 5 minutes.

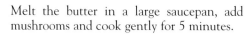
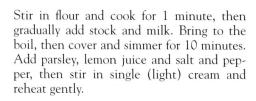

Stir in flour and cook for 1 minute, then gradually add stock and milk. Bring to the boil, then cover and simmer for 10 minutes. Add parsley, lemon juice and salt and pepper, then stir in single (light) cream and reheat gently.

When ready to serve, whip double (thick) cream until holding its shape and stir in watercress. Float a spoonful of the watercress chantilly on each portion, and serve at once.

Serves 4.

CARROT & CORIANDER SOUP

450 g (1 lb) carrots
6 teaspoons olive oil
1 small onion, finely chopped
1 clove garlic, crushed
1 teaspoon coriander seeds, crushed
1 teaspoon ground coriander
850 ml (30 fl oz/3¾ cups) vegetable stock
55 g (2 oz/⅓ cup) sultanas, chopped
salt and pepper
1 tablespoon chopped fresh coriander leaves
SESAME CROÛTONS:
1 thick slice bread, crusts removed
15 g (½ oz/3 teaspoons) butter
3 teaspoons sesame seeds

SOUPE AU PISTOU

115 g (4 oz/½ cup) haricot beans, soaked overnight
1 onion, finely chopped
150 g (5 oz) pumpkin, chopped (optional)
1 stick celery, sliced
2 small leeks, chopped
115 g (4 oz) baby turnips, diced
175 g (6 oz) small green beans, cut into short lengths
150 g (5 oz) shelled broad beans
3 ripe tomatoes, peeled and chopped
55 g (2 oz) fine vermicelli
salt and freshly ground black pepper
PISTOU:
handful of basil leaves
3 cloves garlic
6 tablespoons olive oil
75 g (3 oz/¾ cup) grated Parmesan cheese

Cut 2 carrots into small dice and set aside. Chop remaining carrots. Heat oil in a large saucepan, add onion, garlic and chopped carrots and cook gently for 10 minutes. Stir in crushed and ground coriander and cook for 1 minute. Add 685 ml (24 fl oz/3 cups) of the stock, cover and simmer for 15 minutes, or until the carrots are tender. Meanwhile, put diced carrots in a small saucepan with remaining stock and simmer until tender.

Drain haricot beans. Put in a large saucepan with onion, pumpkin, if using, and 1.7 litres (3 pints/7½ cups) water. Bring to the boil and boil rapidly for 10 minutes. Cover and simmer for 1 hour. Add celery, leeks and turnips and cook for 10-15 minutes. Add remaining ingredients. Cook for 10 minutes until the beans and vegetables are tender.

Purée soup in a blender or food processor, then return to pan. Add diced carrots, sultanas and salt and pepper. Reheat gently while making the croûtons. Toast bread on each side until golden. Cool, then spread with butter and sprinkle over sesame seeds. Return to grill until golden. Cut into small cubes. To serve, stir in chopped coriander and garnish with sesame seed croûtons.

Serves 4.

Meanwhile, make the pistou. Coarsely chop the basil. Using a pestle and mortar, pound the garlic with the basil, then gradually add the oil, stirring until well blended. Stir in Parmesan cheese and 1-2 tablespoons of hot soup. Pour the soup into warmed bowls, spoon a little pistou into each serving, garnish with Parmesan shavings and serve.

Serves 6.

MINESTRONE

2 tablespoons olive oil
55 g (2 oz) lightly smoked streaky bacon, diced
2 large onions, peeled and sliced
2 garlic cloves, skinned and crushed
2 medium carrots, peeled and diced
3 sticks celery, trimmed and sliced
250 g (9 oz/1¼ cups) dried haricot beans, soaked
450 g can chopped tomatoes
2.3 litres (4 pints/10 cups) beef stock
115 g (4 oz) frozen peas
350 g (12 oz) potatoes, peeled and diced
175 g (6 oz) small pasta shapes
225 g (8 oz) green cabbage, thinly sliced
175 g (6 oz) green beans, topped, tailed and sliced
3 tablespoons each chopped fresh parsley and basil
salt and freshly ground pepper

Heat oil in a large saucepan and add bacon, onions, and garlic. Cover and cook gently for 5 minutes, stirring occasionally until soft but not coloured. Add carrots and celery and cook for 2-3 minutes until softening. Drain beans and add to the pan with tomatoes and stock. Cover and simmer for 1-1½ hours until beans are nearly tender.

Add peas and potatoes and cook for a further 15 minutes, then add the pasta, cabbage, beans and chopped parsley and cook for a further 15 minutes. Stir in the basil, adjust seasoning and serve.

Serves 8.

Note: Serve with freshly grated Parmesan cheese, if wished.

BLUE CHEESE & BROCCOLI SOUP

175 g (6 oz) potatoes
25 g (1 oz/2 tablespoons) butter
1 onion, finely chopped
1 litre (35 fl oz/4½ cups) chicken stock
350 g (12 oz) broccoli
salt and freshly ground black pepper
115 g (4 oz) blue cheese such as Roquefort, Danish
  Blue or Gorgonzola
CROÛTONS:
2 thick slices white bread, crusts removed
2 tablespoons sunflower oil
15 g (½ oz/1 tablespoon) butter
1 clove garlic, finely chopped

Peel potatoes and cut into 2.5 cm (1 in) dice.

Heat butter in a saucepan. Add onion and cook, stirring occasionally, for 5 minutes, until soft. Add stock and potatoes, bring to the boil, cover and simmer for 10 minutes. Cut broccoli into flowerets and add to pan. Return to the boil, cover and simmer gently for 10 minutes, until vegetables are tender.

Meanwhile, make croûtons. Cut bread into shapes with a pastry cutter. Heat oil, butter and garlic in a frying pan and fry bread shapes on both sides until golden and crisp. Remove with a slotted spoon and drain on kitchen paper. Purée soup in a blender or food processor. Return to rinsed-out pan, add salt and pepper, then crumble in cheese. Reheat gently without boiling, until cheese has melted. Garnish with croûtons and serve.

Serves 6.

MEDITERRANEAN FISH SOUP

55ml (2 fl oz/¼ cup) olive oil
1 large onion, finely chopped
2 cloves garlic, crushed
1 small fennel bulb, chopped
about 1 kg (2¼ lb) mixed fish and shellfish
2 ripe tomatoes, peeled and chopped
several sprigs parsley, chopped
3 sprigs each thyme and basil
pinch saffron strands
strip orange peel
salt and freshly ground black pepper
about 1 litre (35 fl oz/4½ cups) fish stock

Heat oil in a saucepan, add onion, garlic and fennel and cook for 5 minutes, until soft.

Cut the fish into 4 cm (1½ in) pieces. Add tomatoes, herbs, saffron, orange peel and salt and pepper to saucepan. Lay fish on top and add just enough stock to cover fish. Bring to just on simmering point and cook gently, uncovered, for 8 minutes.

Add shellfish and cook for 5 minutes, until fish and shellfish are tender. Skim any scum from surface of soup and serve.

Serves 4-6

Note: For best results use a selection of white fish such as coley, haddock, cod or whiting. Don't use oily fish such as mackerel as it gives a bitter taste to the soup.

CREAMY FISH SOUP

375 g (12 oz) white fish fillets, skinned
45 g (1½ oz/9 teaspoons) butter
45 g (1½ oz/⅓ cup) plain flour
150 ml (5 fl oz/⅔ cup) single (light) cream
salt
chopped fresh parsley and paprika, to garnish
FISH STOCK:
450 g (1 lb) fish heads, bones and trimmings
1 small onion, quartered
1 carrot, sliced
1 stick celery, chopped
bouquet garni
salt and 6 black peppercorns
1 bay leaf
1 lemon slice

To make stock, place fish bits, vegetables and bouquet garni in a large saucepan. Pour in 1.2 litres (2 pints/5 cups) water and add salt, peppercorns, bay leaf and lemon slice. Bring to the boil over a low heat, skim off any scum that rises to surface, then simmer for 20 minutes. Strain the stock, without pressing, through a muslin-lined colander into a bowl. Measure 850 ml (30 fl oz/3¾ cups) of the stock into a pan (freeze remainder). Add fish fillets and poach until flaking.

Transfer fish to a blender or food processor with a little cooking liquid and purée. Melt butter in a pan, stir in flour and cook for 1 minute without browning. Gradually add remaining cooking liquid, then return to heat and stir until boiling. Simmer for 10 minutes. Then whisk in puréed fish, and cream; season if necessary. Serve garnished with chopped parsley and paprika.

Serves 4-6.

SEAFOOD & COCONUT SOUP

3 stalks lemon grass, cut into 5 cm (2 in) lengths
5 cm (2 in) piece galangal, thinly sliced
5 cm (2 in) piece root ginger, thinly sliced
2 teaspoons finely chopped red chilli
1 litre (35 fl oz/4½ cups) coconut milk
10 kaffir lime leaves
200 g (7 oz) boneless, skinless chicken breast, cut
   into 2.5 cm (1 in) cubes
5 tablespoons fish sauce
juice ½ lime
200 g (7 oz) raw unpeeled jumbo prawns, peeled and
   deveined
200 g (7 oz) firm white fish fillets, cut into 2.5 cm
   (1 in) cubes
small handful each coriander and Thai basil leaves
coriander springs, to garnish

In a saucepan, put lemon grass, galangal, ginger and chilli. Add 2 cups water. Bring to the boil then simmer for 5 minutes. Add coconut milk and lime leaves. Simmer for 10 minutes. Add chicken, fish sauce and lime juice to pan. Poach for 5 minutes. Add prawns and fish. Poach for a further 2-3 minutes until prawns turn pink.

Add coriander and basil to pan. Stir, then ladle into warm soup bowls. Remove and discard lemon grass and lime leaves before eating. Garnish with coriander.

Serves 4.

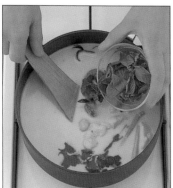

NEW ENGLAND CLAM CHOWDER

two 300 g (10 oz) cans clams
85 g (3 oz) back bacon, rinded and diced
1 onion, finely chopped
450 g (1 lb) potatoes, diced
300 ml (10 fl oz/1¼ cups) fish stock
300 ml (10 fl oz/1¼ cups) milk
150 ml (5 fl oz/⅔ cup) single (light) cream
pinch dried thyme
salt and pepper
fresh thyme leaves or paprika, to garnish

Drain clams, reserving liquid, then chop and set aside.

Put bacon into a saucepan and fry over high heat until fat runs and bacon is lightly browned. Add onion and cook until soft, then add potatoes, liquid from clams, fish stock and milk. Bring to the boil, then cover and simmer for about 20 minutes, or until potatoes are tender.

Stir in cream, clams, thyme and salt and pepper, then reheat for a few minutes: do not boil. Serve garnished with thyme or paprika.

Serves 6.

RICH COUNTRY CHICKEN SOUP

45 g (1½ oz/9 teaspoons) butter
115 g (4 oz) button mushrooms, chopped
45 g (1½ oz/⅓ cup) plain flour
550 ml (20 fl oz/2½ cups) strong chicken stock
550 ml (20 fl oz/2½ cups) milk
350 g (12 oz) cooked skinless chicken, diced
2 egg yolks
150 ml (5 fl oz/⅔ cup) single (thin) cream
salt and pepper
WATERCRESS DUMPLINGS:
115 g (4 oz/1 cup) self-raising flour
pinch dried mixed herbs
55 g (2 oz) shredded suet
1 bunch watercress, trimmed and finely chopped
1 small egg, beaten

Melt butter in a saucepan, add mushrooms and cook gently for 4-5 minutes. Stir in flour, and cook for 1 minute, then gradually add stock and milk. Bring to the boil, stirring constantly, then cover and simmer for 15 minutes. Meanwhile, make dumplings. Sift flour into a bowl, then mix in ½ teaspoon salt, herbs, suet and watercress. Add egg and 3 teaspoons water and mix to a soft dough. Divide into 24 pieces and roll into balls. Bring a pan of water to the boil, drop dumplings into the simmering liquid, cover and simmer for 10 minutes.

Take soup off heat and stir in chicken. Beat egg yolks and cream together, ladle in a little soup and mix quickly, then pour back into pan and heat gently until thickens: do not boil. Add salt and pepper if necessary. Lift dumplings out of water with a slotted spoon and add to the soup just before serving.

Serves 6.

Note: For extra flavour, cook the dumplings in stock instead of water.

CHICKEN & MUSHROOM SOUP

2 cloves garlic, crushed
4 coriander sprigs
1½ teaspoons black peppercorns, crushed
1 tablespoon vegetable oil
1 litre (35 fl oz/4½ cups) chicken stock
5 pieces dried Chinese black mushrooms, soaked in cold water for 20 minutes, drained and coarsely chopped
1 tablespoon fish sauce
115 g (4 oz) chicken, cut into strips
55 g (2 oz) spring onions, thinly sliced
coriander sprigs, to garnish

Using a pestle and mortar or small blender, pound or mix garlic, coriander stalks and leaves and peppercorns to a paste. In a wok, heat oil, add paste and cook, stirring, for 1 minute. Stir in stock, mushrooms and fish sauce. Simmer for 5 minutes.

Add chicken, lower heat so liquid barely moves and cook gently for 5 minutes. Scatter spring onions over surface and garnish with coriander sprigs.

Serves 4.

COCK-A-LEEKIE

2 large chicken joints
1.2 litres (2 pints/5 cups) chicken stock
bouquet garni
4 leeks
12 prunes, soaked for 1 hour and drained
salt and pepper
OATY DUMPLINGS:
115 g (4oz/¾ cup) porridge oats
55 g (2 oz/1 cup) fresh wholemeal breadcrumbs
1 tablespoon chopped fresh herbs
55 g (2 oz/¼ cup) margarine

Put chicken joints into a saucepan with stock and bouquet garni.

Bring to the boil, then cover and simmer for 30 minutes. Remove chicken from pan and leave to cool. Discard bouquet garni and skim off any fat from surface of soup. Trim coarse outer leaves from leeks, then split lengthwise. Wash well, then cut into 2.5cm (1 in) pieces. Add to soup with prunes and simmer for 25 minutes. Cut chicken meat into small pieces and return to soup. Add salt and pepper.

To make dumplings, put oats and bread-crumbs into a bowl and stir in herbs, and salt and pepper. Rub in margarine, then add 6-9 teaspoons cold water and mix to a dough. Divide into small balls, then drop into soup, cover and simmer for 15 minutes, until dumplings are cooked.

Serves 6.

HOT & SOUR PRAWN SOUP

1 teaspoon chopped fresh root ginger
1 tablespoon chopped lemon grass
2-3 small fresh red chillies, seeded and chopped
685 ml (24 fl oz/3 cups) chicken stock
2-3 tablespoons lime juice or vinegar
3 tablespoons fish sauce
1 tablespoon dried shrimps, soaked and rinsed
1 cake tofu, cut into small cubes
25 g (1 oz) bean thread vermicelli, soaked and cut
  into short lengths
2 tablespoons soaked black fungus, coarsely chopped
¼ cucumber, thinly shredded
115-175 g (4-6 oz) cooked peeled prawns
salt and freshly ground white pepper
coriander sprigs, to garnish

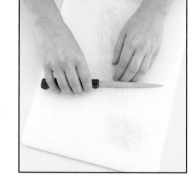

Using a pestle and mortar, pound the ginger, lemon grass and chillies to a fine paste. Bring the stock to a rolling boil in a pan, add the lemon grass mixture with the lime juice or vinegar, fish sauce and soaked shrimps. Bring back to the boil, then add tofu, vermicelli and black fungus. Simmer mixture for about 2 minutes.

Add cucumber and prawns, bring back to boil once more, then season with salt and plenty of pepper. Serve the soup hot (see Note), garnished with coriander sprigs.

Serves 4-6.

Note: This soup must be served piping hot – warm both serving tureen and soup bowls.

HARIRA

6 teaspoons vegetable oil
350 g (12 oz) lean lamb, cut into small cubes
1 onion, sliced
2 teaspoons ground coriander
½ teaspoon ground turmeric
½ teaspoon cayenne
½ teaspoon ground ginger
½ teaspoon ground cumin
225 g (8 oz) tomatoes, peeled and chopped
1 clove garlic, crushed
400 g (14 oz) can chick peas, drained and rinsed
salt and pepper
juice 1 lemon or 2 limes
1 tablespoon chopped fresh coriander
¼ teaspoon ground cinnamon, to garnish

Heat oil in a large saucepan, add cubes of lamb and fry quickly until they are evenly browned all over. Reduce heat, add onion and cook for 5 minutes, stirring constantly. Stir in all spices, except cinnamon for garnish, and cook for 1 minute, then add tomatoes, garlic and 550 ml (20 fl oz/ 2½ cups) water.

Mash three-quarters of the chick peas, add to soup with whole chick peas and salt and pepper. Bring to the boil, cover and simmer for 40 minutes, or until the meat is tender. Just before serving, stir in lemon or lime juice and coriander and simmer for a further 2 minutes. Serve soup sprinkled with cinnamon.

Serves 4-6.

SPICY CHICK PEA POTAJE

225 g (8 oz) chick peas, soaked overnight, then
  drained
4 tablespoons olive oil
1 slice bread, crusts removed
1 Spanish onion, finely chopped
225 g (8 oz) cooking chorizo, thickly sliced
3 beefsteak tomatoes, peeled, seeded and chopped
1 tablespoon paprika
¼-½ teaspoon cumin seeds, finely crushed
450g (1 lb) spinach, trimmed and chopped
3 cloves garlic

Cook chick peas in 1½ times their volume of boiling water for 1½-2 hours until tender.

Meanwhile, heat 2 tablespoons oil in a small frying pan, add bread and fry until golden on both sides. Remove and drain on absorbent kitchen paper. Add onion to pan and cook slowly, stirring occasionally, for 5 minutes. Add chorizo and cook for further 5-10 minutes until onion has softened but not coloured. Stir tomatoes into onion and cook, stirring occasionally, for about 10 minutes.

Heat remaining oil in a saucepan, stir in paprika and cumin, then add spinach. Cook until spinach has wilted. Using a pestle and mortar, pound garlic with a pinch of salt. Add fried bread and pound again. Drain chick peas, reserving liquid. Stir chick peas into spinach with tomato and garlic mixtures, and 175 ml (6 fl oz/¾ cup) chick pea liquid. Cover pan and simmer for about 30 minutes; add more liquid if mixture becomes too dry.

Serves 4.

SCOTCH BROTH

1 kg (2¼ lb) neck of lamb, cut into pieces
1.5 litres (2½ pints/6 cups) light stock
55 g (2 oz/¼ cup) pearl barley
salt and pepper
1 large onion, chopped
2 leeks, trimmed and chopped
2 sticks celery, chopped
1 small turnip, diced
1 large carrot, sliced
bouquet garni
1 tablespoon chopped fresh parsley, to garnish

Put lamb into a large saucepan with stock and slowly bring to the boil. Skim off any scum that rises to surface.

Add barley and salt and pepper, cover and simmer for 2 hours. Lift out lamb and take meat off bones. Discard fat, then return meat to pan.

Add remaining ingredients except parsley to soup and bring back to simmering point. Cover and cook for 30 minutes, or until the vegetables are tender. Discard bouquet garni, season if necessary and serve garnished with chopped parsley.

Serves 6.

MULLIGATAWNY

450 g (1 lb) piece shin of beef
5 cm (2 in) piece fresh root ginger, peeled
2 bay leaves
1 onion, chopped
1 teaspoon turmeric
½ teaspoon chilli powder
2 teaspoons coriander seeds, crushed
2 teaspoons cumin seeds, crushed
8 black peppercorns, crushed
1 small cooking apple, peeled, cored and chopped
1 carrot, sliced
25g (1 oz/2 tablespoons) red lentils, rinsed
2 cloves garlic, chopped
salt
3 teaspoons lemon juice

Put beef into a large saucepan, pour in 1.7 litres (3 pints/7½ cups) water and bring to the boil. Skim surface, then add all remaining ingredients except lemon juice. Cover and simmer very gently for 2½-3 hours, until the beef is tender. Remove beef from the pan and set aside. Sieve soup into a bowl, rubbing vegetables through; discard pulp. Cool, then chill both the meat and stock.

To serve, remove solidified fat from surface of soup, then put into a pan and reheat. Cut beef into small pieces, add to soup with lemon juice and salt if necessary. Simmer for 5 minutes.

Serves 6.

Note: Serve the soup with fried croûtons, adding 3 crushed garlic cloves to the oil.

TUSCAN BEAN SOUP

175 g (6 oz/¾ cup) red kidney beans, soaked
   overnight and drained
175 g (6 oz/¾ cup) haricot beans, soaked overnight
   and drained
2 tablespoons olive oil
1 large onion, finely chopped
2 cloves garlic, crushed
4 sticks celery, thinly sliced
400 g (14 oz) can chopped tomatoes
850 ml (30 fl oz/3¾ cups) vegetable or ham stock
salt and freshly ground black pepper
1 tablespoon chopped fresh marjoram
marjoram sprigs, to garnish

Put kidney beans and haricot beans in a large
saucepan and cover with cold water.

Bring to boil and boil rapidly for 10 minutes.
Cover and simmer for 45 minutes, or until
beans are tender. Drain beans, reserving
cooking liquid. Put half the beans and some
of the cooking liquid in a blender or food
processor and purée until smooth.

Heat oil in a large saucepan. Add onion, garlic and celery and cook gently, stirring occasionally, for 5 minutes, until soft. Stir in bean
purée, tomatoes, stock and beans. Bring to
the boil, cover and simmer for 30 minutes.
Add enough reserved cooking liquid to give
desired consistency. Season with salt and
pepper. Stir in marjoram, garnish with marjoram sprigs and serve.

Serves 6.

MUSHROOM AND BARLEY BROTH

85 g (3 oz/⅓ cup) pot barley, soaked overnight in
   cold water to cover
1 litre (35 fl oz/4½ cups) vegetable stock
15 g (½ oz/¼ cup) dried ceps (mushrooms)
150 ml (5 fl oz/⅔ cup) boiling water
3 tablespoons olive oil
3 shallots, finely chopped
2 teaspoons chopped fresh thyme
350 g (12 oz) mixed fresh mushrooms, sliced
150 ml (5 fl oz/⅔ cup) dry cider
1 bay leaf
1 teaspoon Dijon mustard
salt and pepper

Drain the barley, place in a large pan and add
the stock. Bring to the boil, cover and simmer for 45 minutes. Soak the dried ceps
(mushrooms) in the boiling water for 20
minutes. Drain, reserving liquid, and chop
mushrooms.

Heat the oil in a large pan and fry the
shallots and thyme for 5 minutes. Add the
prepared ceps and fresh mushrooms and stir-
fry over a medium heat for 5 minutes until
golden. Add the cider and boil rapidly until
liquid is almost evaporated. Add the barley
and the cooking liquid, reserved cep (mushroom) liquid, bay leaf and mustard to the pan
and simmer, covered, for 15 minutes. Season
and serve with fresh wholemeal rolls.

Serves 6-8.

SPICED LENTIL SOUP

2 onions
2 cloves garlic
4 tomatoes
½ teaspoon turmeric
1 teaspoon ground cumin
6 cardamom pods
½ cinnamon stick
225 g (8 oz/1¼ cups) red lentils
400 g (14 oz) can coconut milk
1 tablespoon lemon juice
salt and freshly ground black pepper
cumin seeds, to garnish

Finely chop the onions and garlic cloves. Coarsely chop the tomatoes.

Put onions, garlic, tomatoes, turmeric, cumin, cardamom pods, cinnamon stick, lentils and 850 ml (30 fl oz/3¾ cups) water into a large saucepan. Bring to the boil, cover and simmer gently for 20 minutes, or until lentils are soft.

Remove cardamom pods and cinnamon stick then purée lentil mixture in a blender or food processor. Press soup through a sieve and return to rinsed-out pan. Reserve a little coconut milk for garnish and add remainder to pan with lemon juice and salt and pepper. Reheat gently without boiling. Swirl in reserved coconut milk, garnish with cumin seeds and serve.

Serves 6.

DUTCH PEA SOUP

225 g (8 oz) yellow split peas, soaked overnight
bouquet garni
1 bay leaf
225 g (8 oz) back bacon, diced
1 onion, chopped
2 leeks, trimmed and chopped
1 large carrot, chopped
2 sticks celery, chopped
salt and pepper
115 g (4 oz) pieces spicy or garlic sausage, diced
2 tablespoons chopped fresh parsley

Drain peas and put into a large pan with bouquet garni, bay leaf and 1.5 litres (2½ pints/6 cups) water.

Bring to the boil, then cover and simmer for 2 hours, skimming surface if necessary. Add bacon and vegetables, then simmer for a further 1 hour.

Remove bouquet garni and bay leaf and purée the soup in a blender or food processor. Return to pan and add salt and pepper and sausage. Reheat, then stir in parsley and serve.

Serves 6.

COLD STARTERS

TAPÉNADE

ANCHOÏADE

200 g (7 oz) small black olives, pitted
55 g (2 oz) capers
4 anchovy fillets
1-2 cloves garlic, crushed
1 tablespoon Dijon mustard
115 ml (4 fl oz/½ cup) olive oil
1 teaspoon chopped fresh thyme
½-1 teaspoon lemon juice
freshly ground black pepper
8 slices French bread
chopped fresh chives, to garnish

Using a pestle and mortar, pound olives, capers, anchovies, garlic and mustard to a smooth paste.

Work in a little oil, a drop at a time, then gradually add the remaining oil, pounding constantly. Stir in thyme, lemon juice and pepper to taste. If necessary, adjust the consistency by adding more oil (it should be a thick, spreadable paste).

Toast the bread on both sides. Spread with tapénade, garnish with chopped chives and serve.

Serves 4-6.

Note: Tapénade can be kept in a covered container in the refrigerator for several weeks. Serve at room temperature.

2 cloves garlic, crushed
2 x 55 g (2 oz) cans anchovies in olive oil, drained
1½ tablespoons chopped fresh basil
70 ml (2½ fl oz/⅓ cup) olive oil
2-3 teaspoons red wine vinegar
2 teaspoons tomato purée (paste)
freshly ground black pepper

Using a pestle and mortar, pound garlic and anchovies to form a smooth paste.

Pound in basil. Work in a little oil, a drop at a time, then gradually add the remaining oil, pounding constantly.

Stir in vinegar and tomato purée (paste) and season with pepper. Serve with crudités and country bread.

Serves 4-6.

Note: Anchoïade can be stored in the refrigerator in a glass jar. Stir and adjust the level of vinegar and basil to taste before serving.

HUMMUS

TZATZIKI

2 teaspoons cumin seeds
425 g (15 oz) can chick peas, drained
25 g (1 oz/¼ cup) ground almonds
1 clove garlic, crushed
150 ml (5 fl oz/⅔ cup) Greek yogurt
1 tablespoon olive oil
2 teaspoons chopped fresh mint
juice of ½ lemon
salt and freshly ground black pepper
olive oil and cayenne pepper, to garnish
crudités and pitta bread, to serve

Heat a small heavy frying pan and add the cumin seeds. Dry fry, shaking the pan, until the seeds begin to smell aromatic.

Reserve a few cumin seeds for garnish and put the remainder in a food processor or blender. Add the chick peas, ground almonds, garlic, yogurt, olive oil, mint, lemon juice and salt and pepper. Process to form a slightly grainy paste.

Transfer to a serving dish and leave to stand for 30 minutes. Drizzle with a little olive oil and sprinkle with cayenne pepper and the reserved cumin seeds. Serve with crudités and fingers of pitta bread.

Serves 4.

1 cucumber
2½ teaspoons salt
1 clove garlic
1 tablespoon chopped fresh mint
200 g (7 oz) Greek sheeps' milk yogurt
pepper
mint leaves, to garnish
pitta bread, to serve

Peel cucumber and cut into small dice. Place in a colander, sprinkle with 2 teaspoons salt and leave to drain for 1 hour.

Pat cucumber dry with absorbent paper. Crush garlic with remaining salt until creamy.

In a bowl, mix together garlic, chopped mint and yogurt. Season with pepper. Stir in diced cucumber. Transfer to a serving bowl. Garnish with mint leaves and serve at once with pitta bread.

Serves 6.

SOFT CHEESE WITH HERBS

225 g (8 oz/1 cup) well-drained fromage blanc, or
    medium-fat soft cheese
1 tablespoon chopped fresh parsley
1 tablespoon chopped fresh chives
1 tablespoon finely chopped shallot
1 tablespoon olive oil
2 tablespoons dry white wine
1 teaspoon white wine vinegar (optional)
salt and freshly ground black pepper
4 tablespoons crème fraîche or whipping cream
parsley sprigs and fresh chives, to garnish

Beat cheese for 2-3 minutes to lighten it.
Beat in parsley, chives, shallot, oil, wine,
vinegar, if using, and salt and pepper.

Lightly beat crème fraîche or cream and fold
into cheese mixture. Spoon into serving
bowl, cover and chill. Garnish with parsley
sprigs and chives and serve with crudités.

Serves 4.

TARAMASALATA

115 g (4 oz) smoked cod's roe
3 slices white bread, crusts removed
2 cloves garlic, crushed
juice 1 lemon
85 ml (3 fl oz/⅓ cup) olive oil
4 tablespoons yogurt
½ teaspoon paprika
½ small onion, grated
30-40 cherry tomatoes and slivered black olives, to
    serve

Scrape cod's roe from skin and put in a
blender or food processor.

Soak bread in a little water then crumble
into blender or processor. Process until
smooth. With the motor running, add garlic,
lemon juice, olive oil, yogurt and paprika.
Add more lemon juice or olive oil if necessary for flavour or consistency. Finally add
onion.

Cut tops off tomatoes and carefully scoop out
flesh and seeds. Leave upside down on
absorbent kitchen paper for 30 minutes.
Spoon taramasalata into tomatoes. Top each
one with a sliver of black olive.

Serves 6.

HERB & FETA BALLS

PEARS WITH STILTON SAUCE

225 g (8 oz) cream cheese
85 g (3 oz) feta cheese
1 clove garlic, crushed
1 teaspoon chopped fresh parsley
1 teaspoon chopped fresh mint
6 teaspoons sesame seeds, 3 teaspoons finely chopped
  fresh parsley and 3 teaspoons finely chopped fresh
  mint, to garnish
vine leaves, to serve

In a bowl, mix together cream cheese and feta cheese until smooth. Stir in garlic, parsley and mint.

3 large pears
1 tablespoon lemon juice
chervil leaves, to garnish
STILTON SAUCE:
115 ml (4 fl oz/½ cup) crème fraîche
2 tablespoons milk
85 g (3 oz) Stilton cheese
1-2 teaspoons lemon juice
2 teaspoons poppy seeds
salt and freshly ground black pepper

To make the Stilton sauce, put crème fraîche and milk in a saucepan and heat gently. Crumble in Stilton and stir until melted.

Roll cheese into 20 balls. Chill for at least 1 hour. Meanwhile, toast sesame seeds for garnish. Put in a frying pan and heat until seeds are golden brown, stirring frequently. Leave to cool.

Remove pan from heat, stir in lemon juice, poppy seeds and salt and pepper and leave to cool. Cut each pear lengthways in half, keeping stalk intact if possible. Using a small sharp knife, cut out core. Brush lemon juice over cut surfaces.

To serve, mix together chopped parsley and chopped mint for garnish. Roll half cheese balls in herbs and half in toasted sesame seeds. Serve on vine leaves.

Makes 20.

Divide Stilton sauce among six serving plates. Slice each pear half lengthways and arrange on top of sauce, in a fan shape. Garnish with chervil leaves and serve.

Serves 6.

CHEESE & HERB TRIANGLES

115 g (4 oz) feta cheese
115 g (4 oz) cottage cheese
½ egg, beaten
1 tablespoon chopped fresh parsley
1 tablespoon chopped fresh mint
1 tablespoon chopped fresh chives
pepper
4 sheets filo pastry
55 g (2 oz/¼ cup) butter

Crumble feta cheese into a bowl. Add cottage cheese, egg, parsley, mint, chives and pepper. Blend together with a fork.

Preheat oven to 190C (375F/Gas 5). Butter a baking sheet. Lay the sheets of filo in a pile on a work surface. Keep covered while working with one sheet at a time. In a small saucepan, melt butter. Brush one sheet of filo with butter. Cut it into 4 long strips.

Place a teaspoon of filling in one corner of filo strip. Fold a corner of pastry over filling. Turn triangle over and over to the end of the strip. Repeat with remaining pastry. Brush tops of triangles with butter. Bake in the oven for 10-12 minutes until crisp and brown.

Makes 16.

RICOTTA MOULDS

350 g (12 oz/1½ cups) ricotta cheese
1 tablespoon finely chopped flat-leaf parsley
1 tablespoon chopped fresh fennel
1 tablespoon snipped fresh chives
1 tablespoon gelatine
150 ml (5 fl oz/⅔ cups) prepared mayonnaise
salt and freshly ground black pepper
fresh chives, fennel and flat-leaf parsley sprigs, to garnish
PEPPER (CAPSICUM) SAUCE:
2 large red peppers (capsicums), grilled, deseeded and chopped (see page 29)
3 tablespoons extra virgin olive oil
few drops balsamic vinegar
salt and freshly ground black pepper

In a bowl, mix together ricotta and herbs. Oil six 115-150 ml (4-5 fl oz/½ cup) moulds. In a small bowl, soak gelatine in 3 tablespoons cold water for 2 minutes. Place bowl over a saucepan of simmering water, stirring until dissolved. Cool slightly then stir into cheese mixture with mayonnaise and salt and freshly ground black pepper. Divide between moulds and chill until set.

To make sauce, put peppers (capsicums) and oil in a food processor or blender and process until smooth. Add a few drops of balsamic vinegar and season with salt and freshly ground black pepper. Chill until required. To serve, turn out moulds onto individual plates; spoon the pepper (capsicum) sauce around the moulds and garnish with fresh herbs.

Serves 6.

CELERIAC RÉMOULADE

150 ml (5 fl oz/⅔ cup) mayonnaise
2-3 teaspoons Dijon mustard
1 teaspoon lemon juice
salt and freshly ground black pepper
450 g (1 lb) celeriac
2 tablespoons chopped fresh chervil or parsley

Put mayonnaise in a large bowl, add mustard and lemon juice to taste and season with salt and pepper. Peel and coarsely grate celeriac.

Add celeriac to a large saucepan of boiling water and cook for 30-60 seconds. Drain celeriac and rinse under cold running water. Drain again and dry on kitchen paper.

Mix celeriac into mayonnaise. Sprinkle with chervil or parsley and serve.

Serves 4.

Note: Celeriac tastes better if briefly blanched in this way, but it can also be eaten raw.

RED PEPPER VINAIGRETTE

4 red peppers (capsicum)
4 hard-boiled eggs, halved
55 g (2 oz) can anchovies in olive oil, drained
2 tablespoons capers
2 tablespoons chopped fresh flat-leaf parsley
VINAIGRETTE:
2½ tablespoons red wine vinegar
115 ml (4 fl oz/½ cup) olive oil
salt and freshly ground black pepper

Preheat grill. Place whole peppers (capsicum) on grill rack and grill, turning occasionally, until charred and blistered all over.

Leave until cool enough to handle then peel, working over a bowl to catch the juices. Cut in half and discard cores and seeds. Arrange pepper (capsicum) halves on serving plates and pour over juices from bowl.

To make vinaigrette, whisk together vinegar, oil and salt and pepper and pour over peppers (capsicum). Remove egg yolks from whites. Chop egg whites and scatter over peppers (capsicums). Arrange anchovies on top and sprinkle over capers. Sieve egg yolks over peppers (capsicum), sprinkle with chopped flat-leaf parsley and serve.

Serves 4.

LEEKS VINAIGRETTE

12 small leeks
1½ tablespoons chopped fresh parsley
1 hard-boiled egg, chopped
dill sprigs and red pepper (capsicum) strips, to
    garnish
VINAIGRETTE:
1 tablespoon white wine vinegar
½ teaspoon Dijon mustard
salt and freshly ground black pepper
4-5 tablespoons olive oil

Arrange leeks in a steamer, cover and steam
for 6-10 minutes, until tender. Drain on
kitchen paper.

To make vinaigrette, whisk together vinegar,
mustard and salt and pepper. Slowly add oil,
whisking constantly. Transfer leeks to
serving plates, pour over vinaigrette and
leave to cool slightly. Sprinkle over chopped
parsley and egg, garnish with dill sprigs and
red pepper (capsicum) strips and serve.

Serves 4.

MUSHROOMS À LA GRECQUE

2 tablespoons olive oil
1 onion, finely chopped
1 clove garlic, chopped
1 tablespoons coriander seeds
300 ml (10 fl oz/1¼ cups) red wine
1 tablespoon tomato purée (paste)
bouquet garni
450 g (1 lb) button mushrooms
575 g (1¼ lb) ripe tomatoes, peeled, seeded and
    chopped
salt and freshly ground black pepper
flat-leaf parsley sprigs, to garnish

Heat oil in a large frying pan, add the onion
and garlic and cook, stirring occasionally, for
7 minutes, until beginning to colour.

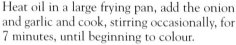

Stir in coriander seeds, wine, tomato purée
(paste) and bouquet garni. Add mushrooms,
tomatoes and salt and pepper.

Bring to the boil then simmer for 10
minutes, until mushrooms are just tender.
Transfer to a bowl and leave to cool. Cover
and chill for several hours. Remove bouquet
garni. Garnish with flat-leaf parsley and
serve.

Serves 4.

Note: A bouquet garni is a bunch of fresh
herbs used to flavour a dish but removed
before serving. The herbs may vary but it
always includes parsley, thyme and a bay leaf.

PRAWN CRYSTAL ROLLS

225 g (8 oz) cooked peeled prawns
115 g (4 oz) cooked pork, coarsely chopped
115 g (4 oz) cooked chicken meat, coarsely chopped
2 tablespoons grated carrot
2 tablespoons chopped water chestnuts
1 tablespoon chopped preserved vegetable
1 teaspoon finely chopped garlic
2 spring onions, finely chopped
1 teaspoon sugar
2 tablespoons fish sauce
salt and freshly ground pepper
10-12 sheets dried rice paper
flour and water paste
fresh mint and coriander leaves
iceberg or leaf lettuce leaves
Spicy Fish Sauce (see page 311)

Cut any large prawns in half. In a bowl, mix prawns, pork, chicken, grated carrot, water chestnuts, preserved vegetable, garlic, onions, sugar, fish sauce, salt and pepper. Fill a bowl with warm water, then dip the sheets of rice paper in the water one at a time. If using large sheets of rice paper, fold in half then place about 2 tablespoons of the filling onto the long end of the rice paper, fold the sides over to enclose the filling and roll up, then seal the end with a little of the flour paste. The roll will be transparent, hence the name crystal.

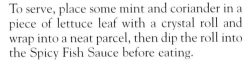

To serve, place some mint and coriander in a piece of lettuce leaf with a crystal roll and wrap into a neat parcel, then dip the roll into the Spicy Fish Sauce before eating.

Serves 4.

MARINATED MUSHROOMS

25 g (1 oz) dried Chinese mushrooms, soaked in hot
   water for 20 minutes
115 g (4 oz) oyster mushrooms
115 g (4 oz) button mushrooms
1 tablespoon sunflower oil
2 tablespoons light soy sauce
2 sticks celery, chopped
2 cloves garlic, thinly sliced
1 whole cinnamon stick, broken
chopped celery leaves, to garnish
MARINADE:
3 tablespoons light soy sauce
3 tablespoons dry sherry
freshly ground black pepper

Drain Chinese mushrooms and squeeze out excess water. Discard stems and thinly slice caps. Slice oyster and button mushrooms. Heat oil in a non-stick or well seasoned wok and stir-fry all the mushrooms for 2 minutes.

Add remaining ingredients except marinade and garnish and stir-fry for 2-3 minutes until just cooked. Transfer to a shallow dish and leave to cool. Mix together marinade ingredients and pour over cooled mushroom mixture. Cover and chill for 1 hour. Discard cinnamon stick, garnish and serve on a bed of bean sprouts and shredded Chinese leaves.

Serves 4.

EGGS & ANCHOVY MAYONNAISE

85 g (3 oz) rocket or other lettuce leaves
4 eggs, hard-boiled, halved
1 teaspoon finely chopped flat-leaf parsley
1 teaspoon snipped fresh chives
DRESSING:
5 anchovy fillets canned in oil, drained
70 ml (2½ fl oz/⅓ cup) prepared mayonnaise
3-4 tablespoons milk
freshly ground black pepper

To make dressing, put anchovy fillets in a small bowl, mash with a fork then blend in mayonnaise, adding milk to give a smooth creamy consistency. Season with freshly ground black pepper.

Arrange salad leaves and eggs on a serving plate. Spoon anchovy mayonnaise over and around eggs and sprinkle with the herbs.

Serves 4.

PRAWN-STUFFED EGGS

4 hard-boiled eggs, peeled
4 tablespoons mayonnaise
55 g (2 oz) peeled prawns, chopped
salt, cayenne pepper and lemon juice, to taste
lettuce leaves, to serve
whole prawns, paprika and parsley sprigs, to garnish

Slice the eggs in half lengthways. Using a teaspoon, scoop the yolks into a small bowl; reserve the white shells.

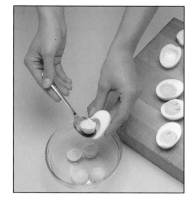

Add the mayonnaise to the bowl and, using a fork, mash with the yolks and prawns. Add salt, cayenne pepper and lemon juice to taste.

Divide the prawn mixture between the egg whites. Arrange on lettuce leaves and garnish with whole prawns, paprika and parsley sprigs.

Serves 4.

FENNEL & DOLCELATTE

3 medium bulbs fennel
1 tablespoon fennel seeds, lightly crushed
4 tablespoons extra virgin olive oil
juice ½ lemon
pinch granulated sugar
salt and freshly ground black pepper
115 g (4 oz) dolcelatte cheese

Trim fennel, reserving green feathery tops. Add whole bulbs to a saucepan of boiling salted water, cook for 5 minutes, then drain. Refresh under cold water, drain well then pat dry with absorbent kitchen paper; set aside. Chop reserved fennel tops and set aside.

In a small frying pan over medium heat, dry-fry fennel seeds for 2-3 minutes to brown and release aroma. Remove from the heat and stir in olive oil, lemon juice, sugar, salt and ground black pepper.

Thinly slice fennel bulbs and arrange in a shallow serving dish. Pour over oil and fennel seed mixture. Crumble cheese and sprinkle over salad with reserved fennel tops. Leave to stand for 30 minutes. Toss lightly before serving.

Serves 4-6.

GINGERED MELONS

½ honeydew melon
½ cantaloupe melon
115 g (4 oz) canned water chestnuts, rinsed
2.5 cm (1 in) piece fresh root ginger, peeled and finely chopped
4 tablespoons dry sherry
4 pieces stem ginger in syrup, sliced
2 tablespoons dried melon seeds

Using a spoon, scoop out the seeds from both melons. Cut in half, peel away skin and thinly slice melon flesh. Slice water chestnuts.

Arrange melon slices on serving plates and top with sliced water chestnuts.

Mix together chopped ginger, dry sherry and stem ginger with its syrup and spoon over melon and water chestnuts. Cover and chill for 30 minutes. Sprinkle with melon seeds and serve.

Serves 4.

GREEN & GOLD ROULADE

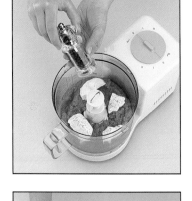

450 g (1 lb) carrots, sliced
115 g (4 oz/½ cup) cream cheese
salt and freshly ground black pepper
sunflower oil, for greasing
450 g (1 lb) frozen chopped spinach
4 eggs, separated
large pinch grated nutmeg
flat-leaf parsley sprigs and carrot ribbons, to garnish
HERB SAUCE:
175 ml (6 fl oz/¾ cup) crème fraîche
1 tablespoon chopped fresh parsley
3 tablespoons chopped fresh chives
chopped fresh chives, to garnish

Cook carrots in a saucepan of boiling salted water for 15 minutes, until tender. Drain.

Purée carrots in a blender or food processor. Add cream cheese and salt and pepper and process until well blended. Set aside.

Preheat oven to 200C (400F/Gas 6). Lightly oil a 33 x 23 cm (13 x 9 in) Swiss roll tin and line with baking parchment. Lightly oil baking parchment. Cook spinach according to directions on packet. Drain well, pressing out as much water as possible. Place in a bowl and leave to cool slightly. Stir in egg yolks, nutmeg and salt and pepper.

In a large bowl, whisk egg whites until soft peaks form, then fold into spinach mixture. Gently spread into prepared tin and bake for 15-20 minutes, until firm.

Meanwhile, make herb sauce. Mix together crème fraîche, parsley and chives, cover and chill until required. Gently reheat carrot mixture without boiling. Turn spinach roll onto a sheet of baking parchment, peel off lining paper and spread spinach roll with carrot mixture.

Roll up by gently lifting baking parchment. Garnish herb sauce with chopped chives. Garnish roulade with flat-leaf parsley and carrot ribbons, slice and serve on warmed plates with herb sauce.

Serves 6.

ASPARAGUS NIÇOISE

AVOCADO & REDCURRANTS

1 tablespoon lemon juice
450 g (1 lb) asparagus spears
225 g (8 oz) cherry tomatoes, halved
12 black olives, pitted and halved
basil sprigs, to garnish
DRESSING:
1 teaspoon Dijon mustard
1 tablespoon white wine vinegar
salt and freshly ground black pepper
70 ml (2½ fl oz/⅓ cup) extra virgin olive oil
1 hard-boiled egg, finely chopped

Add the lemon juice to a saucepan of boiling salted water. Snap the tough ends from the asparagus. Tie the spears in a bundle.

Stand the bundle upright in the pan so that the tips stand out of the water. Cover with a dome of foil and simmer for 10 minutes or until tender. Drain well and leave to cool. Take 16 stalks and cut in half lengthways, cutting as far as the base of the tip so that the tip remains intact. Cut the remaining stalks into 2.5 cm (1 in) lengths and put in a bowl with the tomatoes and olives.

Arrange four asparagus spears on each of four serving plates to make a square, with a tip at each corner and the halved stalks splayed out at right angles. To make the dressing, whisk together the mustard, vinegar and salt and pepper then whisk in the oil. Stir in the chopped hard-boiled egg. Pour the dressing over the tomato and asparagus mixture and toss together. Arrange the mixture in the centre of the asparagus squares. Garnish with basil sprigs and serve.

Serves 4.

3 ripe avocados
redcurrants, to garnish
DRESSING:
175 g (6 oz) redcurrants
2 tablespoons balsamic vinegar
115 ml (4 fl oz/½ cup) light olive oil or sunflower oil
salt and freshly ground black pepper
½-1 teaspoon sugar

To make dressing, purée redcurrants in a blender or food processor. Press through a nylon sieve to remove seeds.

Return redcurrant purée to blender with vinegar. With motor running, gradually pour in oil. Season with salt and pepper and add sugar to taste.

Halve avocados lengthways. Remove stones and peel. Thinly slice flesh lengthways. Fan out slices on serving plates. Stir dressing and pour around avocados. Garnish with redcurrants and serve immediately.

Serves 6.

Note: Be sure to use a nylon sieve as a metal one may taint the flavour of the redcurrants.

CAPONATA

2 aubergines (eggplant)
salt and freshly ground black pepper
115 ml (4 fl oz/½ cup) olive oil
1 onion, finely chopped
1 clove garlic, chopped
4 sticks celery, sliced, leaves reserved for garnish
400 g (14 oz) can chopped tomatoes
2 teaspoons sugar
2 tablespoons balsamic vinegar
1 tablespoon pine nuts, lightly toasted
1 tablespoon capers
12 pitted black olives, halved

Cut aubergines (eggplant) into 5 mm (¼ in) thick slices.

Place aubergines (eggplant) in a colander, sprinkle generously with salt and leave for 1 hour. Preheat oven to 150C (300F/Gas 2). Heat 2 tablespoons olive oil in a saucepan, add onion and garlic and cook, stirring occasionally, for 5 minutes, until soft. Add celery and cook, stirring occasionally, for a further 5 minutes. Stir in tomatoes, sugar and vinegar and bring to the boil. Simmer, uncovered, for 15-20 minutes, until thickened. Season with salt and pepper and stir in pine nuts, capers and olives.

Rinse aubergines (eggplant) thoroughly and pat dry with kitchen paper. Arrange in a shallow ovenproof dish. Spoon a little tomato mixture on to each aubergine (eggplant) slice. Drizzle remaining oil over and around aubergines (eggplant). Cover with foil and cook in oven for 45-60 minutes, until aubergines (eggplant) are tender. Leave to cool. Garnish with celery leaves and serve at room temperature.

Serves 6.

PÂTÉ DE CAMPAGNE

350 g (12 oz) veal or chicken, finely chopped
700 g (1½ lb) fat belly pork, finely chopped
225 g (8 oz) calves' or lambs' liver, finely chopped
25 g (1 oz/2 tablespoons) butter
2 small onions, finely chopped
300 g (10 oz) streaky bacon, chopped
3-4 cloves garlic, finely chopped
2 tablespoons chopped fresh parsley
2 teaspoons herbes de Provence
2 teaspoons freshly ground black pepper
2 teaspoons salt
½ teaspoon ground allspice
115 ml (4 fl oz/½ cup) dry white wine
2 tablespoons brandy

Put veal or chicken, pork and liver into a bowl and mix well. Heat butter in a saucepan and cook onions, stirring occasionally, for 7 minutes, until lightly browned. Add onions to meats with all remaining ingredients and mix well. Cover and leave in a cool place for 2 hours. Preheat oven to 160C (325F/Gas 3).

Pack pâté mixture into a 1.7 litre (3 pints/7½ cup) terrine. Cover with foil. Put into a roasting tin and pour in enough boiling water to come three-quarters of the way up sides of terrine. Bake for 1½ hours. To test if cooked, insert a skewer in centre and count to 5. If skewer feels hot when withdrawn, the pâté is cooked. Remove from roasting tin and let cool. Put weights on top and chill for a few hours. Turn out, slice, and serve.

Serves 10-12.

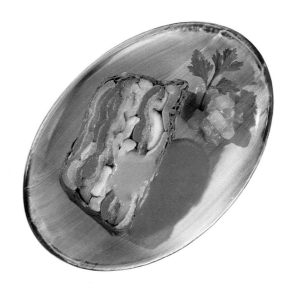

RATATOUILLE TERRINE

10-12 large spinach leaves
salt and freshly ground black pepper
3 yellow peppers (capsicum), quartered
3 red peppers (capsicum), quartered
1 clove garlic, crushed
115 ml (4 fl oz/½ cup) olive oil
2 aubergines (eggplant)
4 courgettes (zucchini)
red and yellow pepper (capsicum) strips and flat-leaf
  parsley sprigs, to garnish
2 tomatoes, peeled, seeded and diced, to serve
TOMATO VINAIGRETTE:
1 large ripe tomato
4 teaspoons balsamic vinegar
115 ml (4 fl oz/½ cup) olive oil

Remove stalks from spinach and rinse leaves thoroughly. Blanch spinach in boiling water for 1 minute. Drain, rinse in cold water and drain again. Spread spinach leaves on a clean tea towel, place another tea towel on top and pat dry. Line a 1 litre (35 fl oz/4½ cup) terrine or loaf tin with cling film. Line terrine with blanched spinach leaves, leaving ends overhanging sides of terrine. Season lightly with salt and pepper.

Preheat grill. Grill and peel peppers (capsicum) (see page 29). Mix together garlic and olive oil. Cut courgettes (zucchini) and aubergines (eggplant) lengthways into 1 cm (½ in) slices. Brush with garlic oil and grill on both sides until soft and beginning to brown.

Put a layer of yellow peppers (capsicum) in base of lined terrine, then add a layer of red peppers (capsicum), followed by layers of aubergine (eggplant), courgettes (zucchini), red pepper (capsicum), aubergine (eggplant), courgettes (zucchini), finishing with a layer of yellow pepper (capsicum). Lightly season each layer with salt and pepper.

Fold overhanging spinach over top of terrine. Cover with cling film. Press down with a weight and chill for 8 hours.

To make tomato vinaigrette, put tomato, vinegar, olive oil and salt and pepper in a blender or food processor and process until smooth. Press through a sieve. Turn terrine onto a serving dish and remove cling film. Garnish with pepper (capsicum) strips. Slice terrine with a very sharp knife, garnish with flat-leaf parsley and serve with tomato vinaigrette and diced tomato.

Serves 6-8.

TUNA PÂTÉ

45 g (1½ oz) butter
4 spring onions, white part only, chopped
2 sticks celery, finely chopped
200 g (7 oz) can tuna in brine, drained
2 tomatoes, skinned, seeded and chopped
2 tablespoons prepared mayonnaise
1 teaspoon lemon juice
1 teaspoon white wine vinegar
salt and freshly ground black pepper
chopped flat-leaf parsley and stoned green olives to
  garnish
crusty bread or toast, to serve

Melt butter in a small frying pan. Add spring onions (scallions) and celery and cook gently for 5 minutes, to soften. Leave to cool.

Put cooled spring onions mixture in a food processor or blender with remaining ingredients and process until fairly smooth. Transfer to a serving dish, cover and refrigerate for at least 30 minutes. Garnish with chopped Italian parsley and stoned green olives and serve with crusty bread or toast.

Serves 4-6.

SMOKED TROUT MOUSSE

575 g (1¼ lb) thinly sliced smoked trout
150 g (5 oz/⅔ cup) cream cheese
150 ml (5 fl oz/⅔ cup) Greek yogurt
juice ½ lemon
salt and freshly ground black pepper
pinch cayenne pepper
tarragon sprigs, to garnish
CUCUMBER VINAIGRETTE:
70 ml (2½ fl oz/⅓ cup) light olive oil
juice ½ lemon
1 tablespoon chopped fresh tarragon
⅛ cucumber, seeded and finely diced

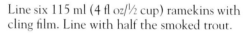

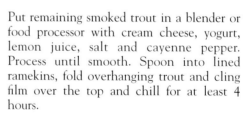

Line six 115 ml (4 fl oz/½ cup) ramekins with cling film. Line with half the smoked trout.

Put remaining smoked trout in a blender or food processor with cream cheese, yogurt, lemon juice, salt and cayenne pepper. Process until smooth. Spoon into lined ramekins, fold overhanging trout and cling film over the top and chill for at least 4 hours.

To make the cucumber vinaigrette, whisk together oil and lemon juice. Stir in tarragon, cucumber and salt and pepper. Turn each mousse out onto a serving plate and remove cling film. Garnish with tarragon sprigs and serve with cucumber vinaigrette.

Serves 6.

POTTED PRAWNS

350 g (12 oz) peeled small prawns
salt
cayenne pepper, to taste
1 teaspoon lemon juice
½ teaspoon ground ginger
175 g (6 oz/¾ cup) butter
3 teaspoons finely chopped fresh chives
chives and lemon slices (optional), to garnish
French bread or buttered toast, to serve

If using thawed frozen prawns, pat dry with absorbent kitchen paper.

Put prawns in a bowl with salt, cayenne pepper, lemon juice and ground ginger. Set aside in a cool place. In a saucepan, melt butter over a very low heat. Pour the clear liquid into a bowl, leaving the milky residue in the pan. Stir in chopped chives. Leave to stand for 20 minutes.

Divide prawns between 6 small ramekin dishes. Spoon chive butter over, pressing prawns down until covered with butter. Chill until firm. Garnish with chives and lemon slices, if wished, and serve with French bread or toast.

Serves 6.

SALMON MILLE FEUILLES

175 ml (6 fl oz/¾ cup) plain yogurt, preferably
  Greek style, chilled
¾ teaspoon chopped fresh dill
salt and pepper
8 sheets filo pastry
melted butter
115 g (4 oz) smoked salmon trimmings, minced
2 tablespoons double (heavy) cream, chilled
1 bunch chives, roughly chopped
12 large slices smoked salmon
dill sprigs, to garnish
lemon wedges, to serve

Mix together half of yoghurt with dill and salt and pepper. Cover and chill. Preheat oven to 220C (425F/Gas 7). Cut twenty-four 7.5 cm (3 in) circles from filo pastry. Lay half the circles on a baking sheet, brush with melted butter, then cover each circle with another. Brush with melted butter and bake for 5 minutes until golden. Transfer to a wire rack to cool. Put salmon trimmings in a blender then, with motor running, slowly pour in cream and remaining yogurt until just evenly mixed. Add chives and pepper to taste.

Cut salmon into twelve 7.5 cm (3 in) circles. Place pastry circle on a plate, spread with a twelfth of the smoked salmon cream, then cover with a smoked salmon circle. Repeat twice more to make one mille feuille. Make 3 more mille feuille in the same way. Chill. Serve garnished with dill sprigs and accompanied by sauce and lemon wedges.

Serves 4.

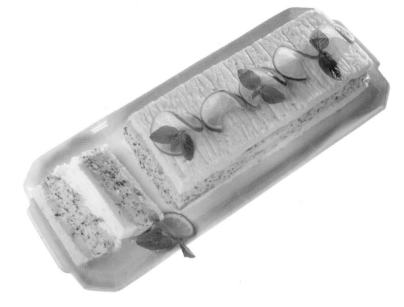

LAYERED FISH TERRINE

450 g (1 lb) salmon, skinned and boned
salt and white pepper
150 ml (5 fl oz/⅔ cup) medium-bodied dry white
  wine
2 small bunches watercress, trimmed
15 g (½ oz/1 tablespoon) butter
1 shallot, finely chopped
450 g (1 lb) firm white fish, such as hake, monkfish
  or cod, skinned, boned and cubed
2 egg whites
210 ml (7½ fl oz/scant 1 cup) double (heavy) cream,
  chilled
lime slices and mint sprigs, to garnish

In a small saucepan, heat butter. Add shallot and cook gently until softened but not browned. Purée shallot with cubed white fish in a food processor. Add egg whites and season with salt and pepper. Mix for 1 minute, then slowly pour in cream. Remove and reserve two thirds of fish mixture. Add watercress to food processor and purée briefly. Chill both mixtures for 30 minutes.

Cut salmon into long strips, put in a dish, season lightly and pour the wine over it. Cover and leave for about 1 hour.

Preheat oven to 180C (350F/Gas 4). Lightly oil a 25 x 9 cm (10 x 3½ in) terrine. Spread half the plain fish mixture in the terrine, then half the salmon strips followed by all the green mixture. Cover this with remaining salmon strips, then remaining white mixture.

Meanwhile, boil a saucepan of lightly salted water, add watercress and blanch for 1 minute. Drain watercress, rinse under cold running water, drain again, then dry on absorbent kitchen paper; set aside.

Cover terrine with foil, place in a roasting tin and pour in enough boiling water to come halfway up sides of terrine. Bake in oven for about 40 minutes until a skewer inserted in centre comes out clean. Transfer terrine to a wire rack to cool, then refrigerate. Serve cut into slices, garnished with lime slices and sprigs of mint.

Serves 4-6.

CHICKEN WITH GREEN SAUCE

450 g (1 lb) cold cooked chicken
mixed salad leaves
SAUCE:
175 g (6 oz) flat-leaf parsley
8 sprigs fresh basil
50 g (1¾ oz) can anchovy fillets in oil, drained
1 shallot, chopped
2 cloves garlic, crushed
3 tablespoons white wine vinegar
1 teaspoon Dijon mustard
15 g (½ oz/¼ cup) fresh white breadcrumbs
115 ml (4 fl oz/½ cup) extra virgin olive oil
freshly ground black pepper

Using a blender or food processor, process
ingredients for sauce, except olive oil, to a
smooth paste. With motor running, slowly
pour in oil to give a thick but pourable consistency.

Slice the chicken and arrange with salad
leaves on a serving plate or individual plates.
Pour sauce over and around chicken.

Serves 4-6.

SPINACH ROULADE

15 g (½ oz/3 teaspoons) garlic and herb-flavoured
  butter
225 g (8 oz) frozen spinach, thawed and drained
salt and pepper
freshly grated nutmeg
2 large eggs, separated
2 tablespoons grated Parmesan cheese
FOR THE FILLING:
4 tablespoons mayonnaise
1 tablespoon creamed horseradish sauce
175 g (6 oz) smoked chicken, finely shredded
1 teaspoon finely grated lemon rind
1 large red pepper (capsicum), deseeded, skinned and
  chopped

Preheat oven to 200C (400F/Gas 6). Grease
a 30 x 23 cm (12 x 9 in) Swiss roll tin and
line with greased greaseproof paper. In a
saucepan, melt the butter, add the spinach
and cook for 1 minute, then season with salt
and pepper and freshly grated nutmeg. Purée
the mixture in a blender or food processor.
Beat in the egg yolks. Stiffly whisk the egg
whites and gently fold into the spinach mixture. Spoon into the prepared tin and level
the surface. Bake in the oven for 7-10
minutes until well risen and springy to the
touch.

Sprinkle the Parmesan over a large piece of
baking parchment. Turn the roulade out onto
the baking parchment, remove the lining
paper, trim the edges and roll up loosely.
Allow to cool. Mix together the mayonnaise,
horseradish, chicken, lemon rind and
chopped pepper (capsicum). Unroll the
roulade, spread with the chicken filling and
re-roll. Serve cut into slices.

Serves 4.

PARMA HAM WITH FIGS

12 paper-thin slices Parma ham
4-6 ripe figs
flat-leaf parsley leaves or mint sprigs to garnish

ITALIAN MEAT PLATTER

115 g (4 oz) mixed thinly sliced salamis
55 g (2 oz) mortadella, thinly sliced
55 g (2 oz) prosciutto or coppa, sliced
55 g (2 oz) bresaola
2 large pickled cucumbers
1 small bunch radishes, trimmed
175 g (6 oz) cherry tomatoes
115 g (4 oz) black or green olives
salad leaves
DRESSING:
5 tablespoons extra virgin olive oil
2 tablespoons lemon juice
1 tablespoon red wine vinegar
1 teaspoon Dijon mustard
salt and freshly ground black pepper

Arrange Parma ham slices on a serving platter or individual plates.

Arrange meats and sausages on a large plate. Slice pickled cucumbers thinly on the diagonal and add to plate with radishes, tomatoes, olives and salad leaves.

Halve or quarter figs lengthwise and arrange beside ham. Serve garnished with parsley leaves or mint sprigs.

Serves 4.

To make dressing mix ingredients together in a small bowl until evenly blended and serve with meats.

Serves 6-8.

Note: Selection of meats can be varied to include your favourite Italian sausages, salamis etc. Serve with crusty bread, bread rolls or bread sticks.

CHICKEN LIVER PÂTÉ

450 g (1 lb) chicken livers
225 g (8 oz/1 cup) unsalted butter
1 clove garlic, crushed
2 tablespoons brandy
2 tablespoons port
salt and pepper
2 tablespoons redcurrant jelly

Soak the livers in cold water for 1 hour, drain and remove the cores. In a frying pan, heat 25 g (1 oz/6 teaspoons) butter, add the livers and fry for 2 minutes, then add the garlic and cook for a further 2-3 minutes until the livers are cooked through, but still pink.

Cut the remaining butter into cubes and add to the pan. Remove the pan from the heat and allow the butter to melt over the livers. Meanwhile, put the brandy and port into a small pan and boil rapidly for about 1½ minutes until the liquid is reduced to a syrup; do not over reduce the liquid as it could burn and ruin the flavour of the pâté.

Add this mixture to the pan of livers, season with salt and pepper and leave the mixture to cool for 15 minutes. Put the liver mixture into a blender or food processor and blend until you have a smooth pâté. Pour into 8 individual ramekins or 1 large serving dish. Melt the redcurrant jelly and pour over the pâté. Chill for at least 3-4 hours before serving.

Serves 8.

PORK & LIVER PÂTÉ

350 g (12 oz) unsmoked streaky bacon slices
225 g (8 oz) pork shoulder, chopped
225 g (8 oz) pigs liver, chopped
225 g (8 oz) pork sausagemeat
1 small onion, chopped
2 cloves garlic, chopped
1 tablespoon chopped fresh thyme
1 tablespoon chopped fresh oregano
3 tablespoons Marsala
salt and freshly ground black pepper
fresh herb sprigs, to garnish

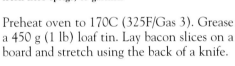

Preheat oven to 170C (325F/Gas 3). Grease a 450 g (1 lb) loaf tin. Lay bacon slices on a board and stretch using the back of a knife.

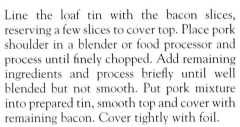

Line the loaf tin with the bacon slices, reserving a few slices to cover top. Place pork shoulder in a blender or food processor and process until finely chopped. Add remaining ingredients and process briefly until well blended but not smooth. Put pork mixture into prepared tin, smooth top and cover with remaining bacon. Cover tightly with foil.

Place loaf tin in a roasting tin half-filled with boiling water. Cook in the preheated oven for 1½-1¾ hours until firm. Remove foil. Cover pâté with greaseproof paper then put a plate or board and a heavy weight on top; leave until cold. Chill overnight. Serve sliced, garnished with fresh herb sprigs.

Serves 6-8.

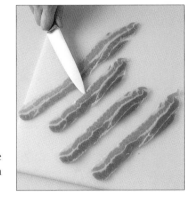

CHICKEN & HAM MOUSSE

175 g (6 oz) cooked chicken, finely minced
115 g (4 oz) cooked ham, finely minced
1 tablespoon lemon juice
1 tablespoon chopped fresh parsley
1 tablespoon chopped fresh chives
150 ml (5 fl oz/²⁄₃ cup) mayonnaise
2 teaspoons powdered gelatine
3 tablespoons chicken stock
150 ml (5 fl oz/²⁄₃ cup) double (thick) cream

In a bowl, mix the chicken with the ham, lemon juice, chopped herbs and mayonnaise.

In a small pan, sprinkle the gelatine over the chicken stock and leave for 5 minutes to soften. Melt very gently over a low heat until gelatine dissolves, then cool and fold into the ham and chicken mixture.

Lightly beat the cream to form soft peaks and then carefully fold into the chicken and ham mixture. Pour the mixture into a 1 litre (35 fl oz/4½ cup) mould and leave to set in the refrigerator for 2-3 hours. Unmould carefully and garnish with fresh herbs. Serve with hot crusty rolls.

Serves 4.

LAYERED COUNTRY TERRINE

8 rashers rindless, smoked streaky bacon
115 g (4 oz) chicken livers
115 g (4 oz) minced pork
115 g (4 oz) herby sausagemeat
1 clove garlic
1 onion, finely chopped
3 tablespoons chopped fresh parsley
25g (1oz/½ cup) fresh white breadcrumbs
55 ml (2 fl oz/¼ cup) brandy
1 small egg, beaten
¼ teaspoon freshly grated nutmeg
1 teaspoon finely grated lemon rind
salt and pepper
2 skinned and boned chicken breasts
1 bay leaf

Preheat oven to 180C (350F/Gas 4). Place the bacon on a board and stretch with the back of a knife. Use 4 rashers to line a 1.2 litre (2 pint/5 cup) loaf tin, reserving 4 rashers for the top. Roughly chop the chicken livers, mix them together with the pork, sausagemeat, garlic, onion and parsley. Soak the breadcrumbs in the brandy, then add to the meat mixture with the egg, nutmeg, lemon rind and seasonings.

Spread one third of the meat mixture over the bacon in the tin. Cut the chicken into very thin slices and layer half over the meat mixture. Cover with half the remaining meat mixture, then cover with the remaining chicken and the rest of the meat mixture. Lay the reserved bacon on top and add the bay leaf. Cover with foil. Stand the terrine in a baking tin three-quarters full of boiling water. Bake for 1½ hours. Allow to cool. Serve with crusty bread, salad and spiced chutney.

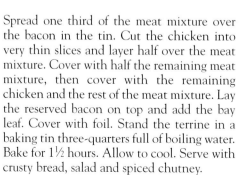

Serves 4-6.

HOT
STARTERS

GOATS' CHEESE SOUFFLÉS

225 ml (8 fl oz/scant cup) milk
1 shallot, finely chopped
1 bay leaf
6 black peppercorns
3 tablespoons butter, plus extra for greasing
45 g (1½ oz/⅓ cup) plain flour
115 g (4 oz) goats' cheese
3 eggs, medium, separated
1 tablespoon chopped fresh chives
salt and freshly ground black pepper
150 ml (5 fl oz/⅔ cup) double (thick) cream
25 g (1 oz/¼ cup) coarsely grated Parmesan cheese
lamb's lettuce and hazelnuts, to garnish

Preheat oven to 180C (350F/Gas 4). Butter six 150 ml (5 fl oz/⅔ cup) ramekins. Put milk, shallot, bay leaf and peppercorns in a saucepan and bring slowly to the boil. Strain into a jug. Melt butter in a saucepan, add flour and cook, stirring, for 1-2 minutes. Remove from heat and gradually stir in milk. Simmer gently for 2-3 minutes. Crumble in goats' cheese and stir until melted. Stir in egg yolks, chives and salt and pepper. Remove from heat. Whisk egg whites until holding soft peaks and fold into cheese mixture.

Spoon into prepared ramekins. Stand dishes in a roasting tin and pour boiling water into tin to come one-third up the sides of ramekins. Bake for 15-20 minutes, until firm. Leave to cool. When ready to serve, preheat oven to 200C (400F/Gas 6). Run a knife round sides of ramekins and turn soufflés into a shallow ovenproof dish. Pour over cream, sprinkle with Parmesan and bake for 10-15 minutes, until golden. Garnish with lamb's lettuce and hazelnuts and serve.

Serves 6.

BAKED EGGS WITH RICOTTA

25 g (1 oz) butter, melted
115 g (4 oz/½ cup) ricotta cheese
2 teaspoons snipped fresh chives
4 eggs
4 tablespoons double (thick) cream
salt and freshly ground black pepper

Preheat oven to 180C (350F/Gas 4). Use butter to grease four individual heatproof dishes. Divide ricotta cheese between dishes, levelling surface with a teaspoon. Sprinkle chives over.

Break an egg into each dish and spoon cream over. Season with salt and freshly ground black pepper.

Place dishes in a shallow baking dish half-filled with warm water. Bake in the pre-heated oven for 10-12 minutes, until cooked as desired. Serve at once.

Serves 4.

FETA & HERB POPOVERS

1 tablespoon sunflower oil
225 ml (8 fl oz/scant cup) milk
15 g (½ oz/1 tablespoon) melted butter
2 eggs, beaten
85 g (3 oz/¾ cup) plain flour
2 teaspoons chopped fresh chives
2 teaspoons chopped fresh parsley
salt and freshly ground black pepper
115 g (4 oz) feta cheese, cut into 24 cubes
flat-leaf parsley and chopped fresh chives, to garnish
MANGO SAUCE:
2 tablespoons mango chutney
175 ml (6 fl oz/¾ cup) Greek yogurt

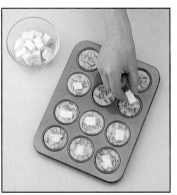

Preheat oven to 220C (425F/Gas 7). Brush the cups in two mini muffin tins with oil and put in the oven to heat. Stir milk and melted butter into eggs. Sift flour into egg mixture and whisk together to make a smooth batter. Stir in chives, parsley and salt and pepper. Fill each muffin cup with batter. Put a cube of feta cheese in the centre of each one and bake in the oven for 20-25 minutes, until risen and golden.

Meanwhile, make mango sauce. Put mango chutney in a bowl, chopping any large pieces of fruit. Stir in yogurt. Arrange popovers on serving plates. Garnish with flat-leaf parsley and chives and serve with mango sauce.

Serves 4-6.

BROAD BEANS & GOAT CHEESE

4 tablespoons extra virgin olive oil
1 onion, chopped
1 kg (2 lbs) fresh broad beans, shelled, or
   350 g (12 oz) frozen broad beans, thawed
1 tablespoon chopped fresh rosemary
salt and freshly ground black pepper
2 heads chicory or 1 head radicchio
225 g (8 oz) goats cheese log, sliced
fresh rosemary sprigs, to garnish

Heat oil in a large frying pan, add onion and cook over a medium heat for about 10 minutes until soft and golden. Stir in beans and rosemary.

Add water to just cover beans and season with salt and freshly ground black pepper. Bring to the boil then cover and simmer for 12-15 minutes, stirring frequently, until beans are very tender and liquid is absorbed.

Preheat grill. Slice chicory or radicchio and stir into hot bean mixture. Lay goats cheese slices over the top. Put frying pan under the hot grill for 2-3 minutes until cheese is browned. Serve hot garnished with rosemary sprigs.

Serves 4-6.

CARROT & GINGER SOUFFLÉS

45g (1½ oz/½ cup) ground almonds, toasted
350 g (12 oz) carrots, trimmed and chopped
1 tablespoon olive oil
1 small onion, finely chopped
2 teaspoons grated fresh root ginger
45 g (1½ oz/9 teaspoons) butter
45 g (1½ oz/9 teaspoons) plain flour
225 ml (8 fl oz/1 cup) milk
55 g (2 oz) Cheshire cheese, grated
3 eggs, separated

Preheat oven to 190C (375F/Gas 5) and lightly oil eight 225 ml (8 fl oz/1 cup) ramekin dishes.

Sprinkle the inside of each ramekin with the ground almonds to coat the sides. Shake out the excess and reserve. Cook the carrots in a pan of boiling water for 15 minutes until soft. Heat the oil in a small pan and gently fry the onion and ginger together for 10 minutes until softened. Drain the carrots and purée with the onion mixture in a blender or food processor until smooth.

Melt the butter in a small pan, stir in the flour and cook for 1 minute. Gradually add the milk, stirring, until thickened. Remove from the heat, stir in the cheese, cool and beat in the egg yolks, carrot purée and the remaining almonds. Stiffly whisk the egg whites and fold in. Spoon into the prepared ramekins, place in a roasting pan and add enough boiling water to come two-thirds of the way up the sides of the dishes. Bake for 30 minutes, then serve at once.

Serves 8.

PARMESAN ASPARAGUS

700 g (1½ lb) asparagus
55 ml (2 fl oz/¼ cup) olive oil
1½ teaspoons coarse sea salt
freshly ground black pepper
2 hard-boiled eggs, chopped
55 g (2 oz) Parmesan cheese

Preheat oven to 180C (350F/Gas 4). Grease an ovenproof dish with a little of the olive oil. Sprinkle with half the salt.

Snap woody ends off asparagus stalks and peel tough skin from bottom 5 cm (2 in) of stalks, if necessary. Arrange asparagus in prepared dish and drizzle over remaining oil. Turn asparagus in oil and sprinkle with remaining salt. Roast for 10-15 minutes, until tender. Transfer to warmed serving plates.

Season with pepper and sprinkle with chopped eggs. Using a vegetable peeler, shave curls of Parmesan over asparagus. Serve immediately with lemon wedges.

Serves 6.

BAKED AUBERGINE LAYERS

2 large aubergines (eggplant)
1 teaspoon salt
2 red peppers (capsicum), peeled (see page 29)
70 ml (2½ fl oz/⅓ cup) olive oil
300 g (10 oz) Mozzarella cheese, thinly sliced
oregano leaves, to garnish
TOMATO SAUCE:
2 tablespoons olive oil
2 cloves garlic, crushed
700 g (1½ lb) plum tomatoes, peeled and chopped
2 teaspoons chopped fresh oregano
salt and freshly ground black pepper

Preheat oven to 180C (350F/Gas 4). Preheat grill. Rinse aubergines (eggplant) well, drain and dry thoroughly with kitchen paper. Brush with 55 ml (2 fl oz/¼ cup) of the olive oil and grill on both sides until soft and beginning to brown.

Cut aubergines (eggplant) into 1 cm (½ in) thick slices. Place in a colander, sprinkle with salt and leave for 1 hour. Cut peppers (capsicum) into thin strips.

Place half the aubergine (eggplant) slices on a baking sheet. Arrange Mozzarella slices on top, cutting to fit if necessary. Top with half the pepper strips. Place remaining aubergine (eggplant) slices on top. Drizzle over remaining olive oil.

To make tomato sauce, heat olive oil in a saucepan. Add garlic and cook for a few minutes until soft. Add tomatoes, oregano and salt and pepper and cook gently, stirring, for 2 minutes, without allowing tomatoes to lose their texture. Keep warm.

Cook in the oven for 3-5 minutes, until heated through, but do not allow Mozzarella to melt. Arrange remaining strips of pepper (capsicum) on top, garnish with oregano leaves and serve with tomato sauce.

Serves 6.

EGG & SPINACH CUPS

225 g (8 oz) spinach
25 g (1 oz/6 teaspoons) butter, diced
25 g (1 oz) dolcelatte cheese, crumbled
115 ml (4 fl oz/½ cup) double (thick) cream
pinch of grated nutmeg
salt and pepper
4 eggs
4 sprigs chervil (optional)

Preheat oven to 190C (375F/Gas 5) and lightly butter 4 ramekin dishes. Wash the spinach and discard any thick stalks.

Place the spinach with only the water that clings to the leaves in a large pan and cook over a medium heat for 1-2 minutes until just wilted. Drain, squeeze out excess liquid and chop finely. Transfer to a bowl and beat in the butter and cheese until melted, then stir in 85 ml (3 fl oz/⅓ cup) cream, the nutmeg and seasoning.

Divide between the ramekin dishes and make a small hollow in the centre of each one. Break an egg into each hollow and spoon over the remaining cream. Place each ramekin in a roasting pan. Pour in enough boiling water to come two-thirds of the way up the sides of the dishes and bake for 20-30 minutes until eggs feel firm to the touch. Garnish each with a chervil sprig, if wished. Serve at once with slices of crisp French bread.

Serves 4.

WATERCRESS CUSTARDS

2 red peppers (capsicums)
2 tablespoons olive oil
115 ml (4 fl oz/½ cup) vegetable stock
15 g (½ oz/3 teaspoons) butter
115 g (4 oz) watercress leaves
3 eggs
200 ml (7 fl oz/¾ cup) double (thick) cream
25 g (1 oz/¼ cup) finely grated Cheddar cheese
1 teaspoon Dijon mustard
salt and pepper

Preheat oven to 200C (400F/Gas 6) and roast the peppers (capsicums) for 20-25 minutes until skins are lightly charred. Transfer to a plastic bag and leave to cool for 30 minutes. Peel the peppers, discard the seeds, reserving any juices. Purée the peppers (capsicums) and juices with the oil and stock to form a smooth sauce. Pass through a sieve into a small pan. Reduce oven temperature to 180C (350F/Gas 4) and grease 6 dariole moulds.

Melt the butter and fry the watercress leaves for 1 minute until just wilted. Purée in a blender or food processor and gradually add the eggs, cream, cheese, mustard and salt and pepper until smooth. Pour into the moulds. Place in a roasting tin and pour in enough boiling water to come two-thirds the way up the sides of the moulds. Bake for 25 minutes until firm in the centre. Leave to rest for 5 minutes, then unmould and serve warm with the reheated pepper sauce.

Serves 6.

ANCHOVY-STUFFED MUSHROOMS

25 g (1 oz) fresh bread without crusts, crumbled
4 tablespoons milk
450 g (1 lb) medium cap mushrooms
115 g (4 oz) green (unsmoked) bacon, finely chopped
4 canned anchovy fillets, finely chopped
1 clove garlic, finely chopped
1 egg, beaten
3 tablespoons finely chopped fresh parsley
pinch chopped fresh oregano
salt and freshly ground black pepper
4 tablespoons dry breadcrumbs
4 tablespoons olive oil
oregano sprigs, to garnish

Preheat oven to 200C (400F/Gas 6). Oil a large baking tray. Put fresh bread in a small bowl, add milk and leave to soak. Remove stalks from mushrooms and chop finely. Put into a bowl with bacon, anchovy fillets, garlic, egg, parsley, oregano and salt and pepper. Squeeze soaked bread dry, add to bacon mixture and mix together well.

Divide bread mixture between open side of mushroom caps, piling mixture into small mounds. Place on baking tray and sprinkle with dry breadcrumbs. Trickle oil over mushrooms. Bake on top shelf of oven for 20-30 minutes until top of stuffing is crisp. Leave to stand for a few minutes before serving, garnished with oregano.

Serves 4-6.

COURGETTE TIMBALES

sunflower oil for greasing
700 g (1½ lb) courgettes (zucchini)
3 eggs, beaten
1 tablespoon chopped fresh basil
115 g (4 oz/½ cup) ricotta cheese
salt and freshly ground black pepper
TOMATO SALSA:
350 g (12 oz) tomatoes, peeled and diced
1 red onion, finely chopped
1 tablespoon chopped fresh basil
1 tablespoon olive oil
1 teaspoon lime juice

To make tomato salsa, mix together tomatoes, onion, basil, olive oil, lime juice and salt and pepper. Chill until required. Oil six 115 ml (4 fl oz/½ cup) ramekins. Trim ends from courgettes (zucchini). Using a vegetable peeler, cut very thin ribbons from two of the courgettes (zucchini). Cut remaining courgettes (zucchini) into slices. Steam ribbons over a saucepan of boiling water for 2 minutes, until soft. Spread on kitchen paper and pat dry. Steam sliced courgettes (zucchini) for 3-5 minutes, until soft. Preheat oven to 200C (400F/Gas 6).

Press out as much moisture as possible from courgette (zucchini) slices and place in a blender or food processor with the eggs, basil, ricotta and salt and pepper. Process to a coarse purée. Line ramekins with courgette (zucchini) strips. Fill with purée, fold over ends of courgette (zucchini) strips and cover with foil. Place ramekins in a roasting tin and pour in 1 cm (½ in) boiling water. Bake for 10-15 minutes, until set. Leave for 5 minutes, turn out and serve with tomato salsa.

Serves 6.

BAKED MUSHROOMS

25 g (1 oz/⅓ cup) desiccated coconut
8 large open cup mushrooms, wiped
85 g (3 oz/⅓ cup) butter, softened
1 clove garlic, crushed
grated zest and juice 1 lime
½ teaspoon grated fresh root ginger
1 tablespoon chopped fresh coriander
salt and pepper

BAKED STUFFED ARTICHOKES

4 large young artichokes
3 tablespoons fresh white breadcrumbs
25 g (1 oz/¼ cup) pecorino cheese, grated
juice 1 lemon
5 tablespoons olive oil
15 g (½ oz) butter
2 tablespoons olive oil
3 slices lean bacon, chopped
1 small onion, finely chopped
2 sticks celery, finely chopped
2 medium courgettes (zucchini), finely chopped
1 clove garlic, crushed
1 tablespoon chopped fresh sage
1 tablespoon chopped flat-leaf parsley
salt and freshly ground black pepper
fresh Italian parsley sprigs to garnish

Preheat oven to 200C (400F/Gas 6). Place the coconut on a baking sheet and bake for 2-3 minutes until browned. Remove from the oven and cool slightly.

Preheat oven to 200C (400F/Gas 6). Cook artichokes in a saucepan of boiling salted water for 30 minutes. Remove and place upside down to drain. Pull away and discard outer leaves and, using a teaspoon, remove central hairy choke. Heat butter and 2 tablespoons olive oil in a saucepan. Add bacon, onion, celery, courgette (zucchini) and garlic and cook gently for 5 minutes, stirring frequently, until vegetables are just soft. Stir in herbs. Purée half the mixture in a food processor or blender. Return to pan. Season with salt and freshly ground black pepper.

Trim the mushrooms, discard the stalks and place in a large roasting tin, trimmed-sides up. Cream the butter, coconut and remaining ingredients together and spread over the inside of the mushrooms. Cover loosely with foil and bake for 15-20 minutes until mushrooms are cooked. Serve hot with fresh bread to mop up the juices.

Serves 4.

Note: For vegans, replace the butter with 85 ml (3 fl oz/⅓ cup olive oil).

Place artichokes close together in an oven-proof dish. Fill centres of artichokes with vegetable mixture. In a small bowl, mix together breadcrumbs and cheese. Pile on top of filling. Sprinkle with lemon juice and remaining 3 tablespoons olive oil. Cover with foil and bake in a preheated oven for 15 minutes. Remove foil. Bake for a further 10 minutes until lightly browned. Serve garnished with Italian parsley sprigs.

Serves 4.

AUBERGINE NAPOLETANA

700 g (1½ lb) medium thin aubergine (eggplant)
salt
115 g (4 oz/1 cup) plain flour
225 ml (8 fl oz/1 cup) groundnut oil
225 ml (8 fl oz/1 cup) olive oil
115 ml (4 fl oz/½ cup) extra virgin olive oil
6 anchovy fillets canned in oil, drained and mashed
1 tablespoon sun-dried tomato paste
3 tablespoons red wine vinegar
8 sprigs flat-leaf parsley
2 cloves garlic
salt and freshly ground black pepper
flat-leaf parsley sprigs, to garnish

Peel aubergines (eggplant) and cut into 2.5 cm (1 inch) slices. Spread out on a large plate and sprinkle with plenty of salt. Leave to stand for 30 minutes then rinse thoroughly under cold running water. Drain and pat dry with absorbent kitchen paper.

Put flour into a large plastic bag. Add aubergine (eggplant) and toss to coat. Remove coated aubergine (eggplant) and discard excess flour.

Preheat groundnut and olive oil together in a saucepan or deep-fat fryer to 190C (375F). Deep-fry aubergines (eggplant) in batches in the hot oil for about 4 minutes until golden brown. Transfer to absorbent kitchen paper to drain. Keep hot.

In a small saucepan, gently warm extra virgin olive oil over a low heat. Stir in anchovies, sun-dried tomato paste and vinegar and simmer, stirring, for 2 minutes.

Finely chop together parsley and garlic. Transfer aubergines (eggplant) to a warmed serving plate. Pour over anchovy sauce and season with salt and freshly ground black pepper. Sprinkle with chopped parsley and garlic and serve immediately garnished with Italian parsley sprigs.

Serves 4-6.

AUBERGINE FRITTERS

2 small aubergines (eggplants)
salt
oil for frying
2 lemons, cut into quarters
BATTER:
115 g (4 oz/1 cup) plain flour
pinch salt
25 g (1 oz/6 teaspoons) butter, melted
1 egg white

To make batter, sift flour and salt into a large bowl. Add melted butter and 175 ml (6 fl oz/ ¾ cup) tepid water, beating to form a smooth thick cream. Leave to stand for 1 hour.

Slice aubergines (eggplants) into 0.5 cm (¼ in) slices. Place in a colander, sprinkle with salt and leave to drain for 30 minutes. In a bowl, whisk egg white until stiff. Fold into batter. Pat aubergine (eggplant) slices dry with absorbent kitchen paper.

In a frying pan, heat 1 cm (½ in) oil. Dip aubergine (eggplant) slices into batter. Fry in batches for 2 minutes, then turn over and fry for a further 2 minutes until crisp and golden on both sides. Keep warm while frying remaining slices. Drain on absorbent paper. Serve at once, with lemon quarters.

Serves 6.

IMAM BAYALDI

2 small aubergines (eggplants)
salt
55 ml (2 fl oz/¼ cup) olive oil
1 large onion, chopped
1 clove garlic, crushed
1 red pepper (capsicum), seeded and chopped
6 teaspoons tomato purée (paste)
55 g (2 oz) sun-dried tomatoes in oil, drained and chopped
½ teaspoon sugar
1 teaspoon wine vinegar
pepper
toasted pine nuts and coriander sprigs, to garnish

Cut aubergines (eggplants) into 0.5 cm (¼ in) slices. Sprinkle with salt and put in a colander to drain for 30 minutes. Preheat oven to 180C (350F/Gas 4). In a frying pan, heat 2 tablespoons olive oil, add onion, garlic and red pepper (capsicum). Cook for about 10 minutes until onion is soft. Add tomato purée (paste), sun-dried tomatoes, sugar, vinegar and pepper.

Wipe aubergine (eggplant) slices dry with absorbent kitchen paper. Arrange slices in a baking tin. Put a teaspoonful of tomato mixture onto each aubergine (eggplant) slice. Drizzle remaining olive oil over and around aubergines (eggplants). Cover dish and bake for 40-50 minutes until aubergines (eggplants) are tender. Serve garnished with toasted pine nuts and sprigs of coriander.

Serves 6.

STUFFED COURGETTE RINGS

85 g (3 oz) bulgar wheat
6 courgettes (zucchini) about 15 cm (6 in) long
3 teaspoons olive oil
1 small onion, finely chopped
2 teaspoons tomato purée (paste)
1 teaspoon chopped fresh mint
salt and pepper
6 teaspoons lemon juice
fresh vine leaves, to serve
fresh herbs, to garnish

Put bulgar wheat in a bowl. Pour in enough boiling water to come well above the wheat. Leave to soak for 1 hour. Drain thoroughly.

Preheat oven to 180C (350F/Gas 4). Cut rounded ends off courgettes (zucchini). With a small apple corer, carefully remove centres from courgettes (zucchini). In a frying pan, heat oil. Cook onion until soft. Remove from heat. Stir in bulgar wheat, tomato purée (paste), mint, salt and pepper. Press stuffing firmly into the hollowed-out courgettes (zucchini).

Place courgettes (zucchini) in an ovenproof dish. Pour over lemon juice and 4 table-spoons water. Cover dish and bake in the oven for 45 minutes or until courgettes (zucchini) are cooked but still firm enough to slice neatly. With a sharp knife, cut cour-gettes (zucchini) into 3 mm (⅛ in) slices. Serve on a plate lined with vine leaves, garnished with fresh herbs.

Serves 6.

GRILLED RADICCHIO

2 large heads of radicchio
6 anchovies in olive oil
2 cloves garlic, cut into slivers
70 ml (2½ fl oz/⅓ cup) olive oil
salt and freshly ground black pepper
115 g (4 oz) Mozzarella cheese, thinly sliced
lemon slices, to garnish

Cut the radicchio lengthways in half. Drain the anchovies, reserving the oil, and chop.

Push the garlic and anchovy pieces between the radicchio leaves. Heat half the olive oil in a flameproof dish. Put the radicchio halves, cut side up, in the dish and cook over a gentle heat for 5 minutes or until the underside of the radicchio softens and begins to brown. Remove from the heat.

Preheat the grill. Season the radicchio with salt and pepper. Drizzle with a little anchovy oil and the remaining olive oil. Arrange the Mozzarella slices on top of the radicchio and grill until the Mozzarella is bubbling and beginning to brown. Garnish with lemon slices and serve immediately.

Serves 4.

GRILLED VEGETABLES

1 red pepper (capsicum)
2 baby courgettes (zucchini)
2 baby aubergines (eggplants)
1 fennel bulb
8 baby sweetcorn
salt and pepper
courgette flowers and basil sprigs, to garnish
MARINADE:
150 ml (5 fl oz/⅔ cup) olive oil
2 cloves garlic, crushed
1 teaspoon chopped fresh parsley
1 teaspoon chopped fresh mint
1 teaspoon chopped fresh oregano

To make marinade, in a bowl mix together olive oil, garlic, parsley, mint and oregano. Cut red pepper (capsicum) into quarters. lengthways. Remove seeds and core. Cut courgettes (zucchini) in half lengthways. Cut aubergines (eggplants) in half lengthways. Cut fennel bulb into quarters. Put pepper (capsicum), courgettes (zucchini), aubergines (eggplants), fennel and sweetcorn into the bowl with the marinade. Leave for at least 1 hour.

Preheat grill or barbecue. Grill vegetables for about 10 minutes, or until tender. Turn them every few minutes and brush with marinade. Season with salt and pepper. Garnish with courgette flowers and basil sprigs.

Serves 4.

Variation: A wide variety of vegetables can be grilled. Try mushrooms, tomatoes, chicory, onions and squashes.

VEGETABLE CROSTINI

1 courgette (zucchini)
1 small aubergine (eggplant)
1 small red pepper (capsicum)
1 small fennel bulb
2 cloves garlic, crushed
1 teaspoon chopped fresh thyme
55 ml (2 fl oz/¼ cup) olive oil
salt and freshly ground black pepper
12 slices ciabatta, toasted
300 g (10 oz) Mozzarella cheese
thyme sprigs, to garnish

Cut courgette (zucchini), aubergine (eggplant) and pepper (capsicum) into 1 cm (½ in) dice. Coarsely chop fennel.

Preheat grill. In a bowl, mix together courgette (zucchini), aubergine (eggplant), pepper (capsicum), fennel, garlic, thyme, oil and salt and pepper. Spread vegetables in a grill pan and grill for 12-15 minutes, turning frequently, until tender and beginning to brown at edges.

Slice Mozzarella and arrange on toasted ciabatta. Pile grilled vegetables on top of Mozzarella. Grill for 2-3 minutes, until cheese is beginning to bubble. Garnish with thyme sprigs and serve at once.

Serves 6.

MUSHROOM BRIOCHES

6 small brioches
70 ml (2½ fl oz/⅓ cup) olive oil
1 clove garlic, crushed
2 shallots, finely chopped
350 g (12 oz) mixed mushrooms, sliced
1 teaspoon Dijon mustard
2 tablespoons dry sherry
1 tablespoon chopped fresh tarragon
150 ml (5 fl oz/⅔ cup) double (thick) cream
salt and freshly ground black pepper
watercress, to garnish

Preheat oven to 200C (400F/Gas 6). Pull tops off brioches and scoop out insides of each brioche to make a hollow case.

Brush insides of brioches with 3 tablespoons of the olive oil. Put on a baking sheet and cook in oven for 10-12 minutes, until crisp. Meanwhile, heat remaining oil in a saucepan, add garlic and shallots and cook, stirring occasionally, for 3 minutes, until soft. Add mushrooms and cook gently, stirring occasionally, for 5 minutes.

Stir in mustard, sherry, tarragon, cream and salt and pepper. Cook for a few minutes until cream reduces and thickens slightly. Fill brioche cases with mushroom mixture, garnish with watercress and serve at once.

Serves 6.

CRISPY WON TONS

1 red pepper (capsicum)
1 carrot
115 g (4 oz) each button mushrooms and bean sprouts
5 spring onions
550 ml (20 fl oz/2½ cups) sunflower oil
1 teaspoon grated fresh root ginger
1 teaspoon sugar
1 teaspoon each soy sauce and sesame oil
2 teaspoons sherry
24 won ton skins
DIPPING SAUCE:
6 tablespoons lime juice
2 teaspoons sugar
1 teaspoon Thai fish sauce
1 teaspoon finely chopped spring onion
1 fresh green chilli, cored, seeded and chopped

To make dipping sauce, mix together lime juice, sugar, fish sauce, spring onion and chilli. Stir until sugar has dissolved. Set aside. Cut pepper (capsicum) and carrot into thin matchsticks. Thinly slice mushrooms. Shred spring onions, reserving a few shreds for garnish. Heat 2 tablespoons sunflower oil in a wok and stir-fry pepper (capsicum), carrot, mushrooms, bean sprouts, spring onions and ginger for 1 minute. Add sugar, soy sauce, sesame oil and sherry and cook, stirring, for 2 minutes. Turn into a sieve and leave to drain and cool.

Put 1 teaspoon vegetable mixture in the middle of each won ton skin. Gather up corners and twist together to seal. In a wok or deep-fat fryer, heat oil to 180C (350F) or until a cube of bread browns in 60 seconds. Fry won tons, a few at a time, for 1-2 minutes, until crisp and golden. Remove with a slotted spoon and drain on kitchen paper. Keep warm while frying remaining won tons. Garnish with reserved spring onion shreds and serve with dipping sauce.

Serves 6.

DIM SUM

300 g (10 oz/2½ cups) plain flour
225 g (8 oz/1 cup) minced pork
3 spring onions, 1 reserved for garnish, 2 chopped, including some green
2 large Chinese cabbage leaves, shredded, plus extra leaves for lining steamer basket
2.5 cm (1 in) piece root ginger, grated
1 tablespoon cornflour
1 tablespoon each light soy sauce and rice wine
2 teaspoons dark sesame oil
½ teaspoon sugar

Sift flour into a bowl. Make a well in centre and slowly pour in 1 cup boiling water. Mix in flour with a fork or chopsticks.

Continue to mix to form a rough dough, adding more flour, if necessary. Cover bowl and leave for 1 minute, to cool. Using your hands, form dough into a soft, loose ball. Knead on a lightly floured surface for about 5 minutes until smooth and elastic. Cover and leave to rest for 30 minutes. In a bowl, combine remaining ingredients using chopsticks or a fork. Set aside.

Divide dough in half. Roll each half to a 23 cm (9 in) cylinder. Using a floured sharp knife, cut each cylinder into 12 thick slices. Cover with a damp cloth.

Roll each slice into a ball then roll out to a 10 cm (4 in) circle, making edges slightly thinner than centre. Place 1 tablespoon filling in centre. Brush edges of circle with a little water.

Lift wrapper around filling, gathering and pinching wrapper to form a purse shape. Put on a tray and cover with a damp cloth. Repeat with remaining dough and filling.

Place some dim sum in a steamer basket lined with cabbage leaves, without crowding dim sum. Cover with a lid. Steam over simmering water for 12-15 minutes until tender but chewy. Garnish with reserved spring onion and serve warm with soy sauce mixed with shredded fresh red chilli for dipping.

Serves 6-8.

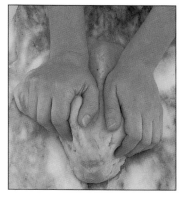

VIETNAMESE SPRING ROLLS

FILLING:
55 g (2 oz) bean thread vermicelli, soaked then cut
   into 1 cm (½ in) pieces
2 tablespoons black fungus, soaked then coarsely
   chopped
225 g (8 oz) minced pork
115 g (4 oz) raw peeled prawns, chopped
1 small onion, finely chopped
2 spring onions, finely chopped
1 teaspoon finely chopped garlic
2 tablespoons fish sauce
salt and freshly ground black pepper
ASSEMBLING AND FRYING:
10-12 sheets dried rice paper
1 egg, beaten
oil for deep-frying

SERVING ACCOMPANIMENTS:
iceberg or Webb's lettuce
fresh mint and coriander leaves
Spicy Fish Sauce, page 311

Separate the lettuce into single leaves and
arrange on a serving platter with the mint
and coriander leaves.

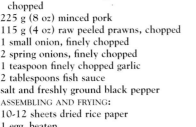

Combine the filling ingredients in a mixing
bowl. Set aside. Soften the rice papers, one
at a time. If using square ones, cut each in
half; if using round ones, leave whole. Place
about 2 tablespoons of the filling at one end
of the paper, fold over and tuck in both sides
and roll over. Seal the end with a little
beaten egg and set aside. Repeat to fill all the
rolls.

Cut the cooked spring rolls in half and
arrange on the platter with the lettuce
leaves, mint and coriander leaves. Place a
saucer of the Spicy Fish Sauce in the centre
for dipping. (The dipping sauce can be
served in individual saucers, if preferred.)

Heat the oil in a wok or deep-fat fryer to
about 180C (350F) and deep-fry the rolls, in
batches, for 5-7 minutes until golden brown.
Remove and drain. (If they are not to be
served at once, they can be kept in a very
low oven for up to 3 hours until needed. Or
they can be par-cooked, cooled and stored in
the refrigerator for several days, then crisped
up just before serving.)

To serve, place half a spring roll with a mint
and coriander leaf on a lettuce leaf, then
wrap it into a neat parcel. Holding it with
fingers, dip into the fish sauce before eating.

Serves 4-6.

Variation: To make vegetarian spring rolls,
substitute 225 g (8 oz) bean sprouts, 115 g
(4 oz) grated carrot and 1 cake tofu for the
pork and prawns.

PARMA HAM BASKETS

CHICKEN LIVER CROSTINI

2 sheets filo pastry, 40 x 30 cm (16 x 12 in)
25 g (1 oz/2 tablespoons) butter, melted
1 tablespoon olive oil
1 red onion, finely chopped
1 teaspoon sugar
150 g (5 oz) Parma ham, coarsely chopped
10 sun-dried tomatoes, coarsely chopped
200 g (7 oz) salad leaves
basil leaves, to garnish
DRESSING:
55 ml (2 fl oz/¼ cup) olive oil
2 teaspoons wine vinegar
salt and freshly ground black pepper

Preheat oven to 190C (375F/Gas 5). Cut filo
pastry into twenty-four 10 cm (4 in) squares.

Lightly brush a 12-cup bun tin with butter.
Brush 12 sheets of pastry with butter. Line
each cup in bun tin with a square of pastry.
Brush remaining sheets of pastry with melted
butter and place on top, arranging them so
that the points are like petals. Bake in the
oven for 10 minutes, until golden. Keep
warm. Heat oil in a saucepan, add onion and
cook, stirring occasionally, for 5 minutes,
until soft. Add sugar and cook for 3 minutes.
Stir in Parma ham and sun-dried tomatoes.
Heat gently to warm through.

To make dressing, put olive oil, wine vinegar
and salt and pepper in a large bowl and
whisk together. Add salad leaves and toss
well. Arrange salad on six serving plates. Fill
tartlet cases with ham mixture. Arrange on
serving plates, garnish with basil leaves and
serve.

Serves 6.

225 g (8 oz) fresh chicken livers
2 tablespoons olive oil
2 medium leeks, white parts only, washed and finely
  chopped
1 stick celery, finely chopped
1 tablespoon balsamic or sherry vinegar
2 tablespoons capers in brine, drained
70 ml (2½ fl oz/⅓ cup) chicken stock
1 tablespoon chopped fresh thyme
salt and freshly ground pepper
12 slices of french bread, toasted on both sides
thyme sprigs, to garnish

Wash livers, removing gristle or discoloured
bits. Dry on absorbent kitchen paper.

Heat olive oil in a non-stick frying pan, add
leeks and celery and cook for 5 minutes until
soft but not coloured. Add chicken livers
and fry them with the vegetables for about 5
minutes. Sprinkle with the vinegar and allow
it to evaporate over the heat.

Stir in the capers, chicken stock and thyme
and bring to the boil. Season well with salt
and pepper. Turn down the heat and simmer
for a further 10-15 minutes until thickened
and creamy, stirring all the time. Spread the
mixture on the warm toasted bread and serve
at once, garnished with thyme sprigs.

Serves 6.

NUTTY GOUJONS

350 g (12 oz) skinned and boned chicken breasts
55 g (2 oz/½ cup) ground almonds
115 g (4 oz/2 cups) fresh white breadcrumbs
2 teaspoons finely chopped freshly parsley
25 g (1 oz/¼ cup) plain flour
salt and pepper
1 large egg, beaten
oil for deep frying
2 tablespoons spiced plum chutney
1 tablespoon mayonnaise
1 teaspoon finely grated orange rind
3 teaspoons orange juice

Cut chicken into thin strips. Mix together
the almonds, breadcrumbs and parsley.

Put the flour, salt and pepper and chicken
into a large polythene bag and shake well.
Dip the chicken strips into the beaten egg,
then roll in the breadcrumb mixture to coat
completely. Chill in the freezer for 15-20
minutes. Half-fill a deep fat pan or fryer with
oil and heat to 190C (375F) or until a cube
of day-old bread browns in 40 seconds. Fry
the chicken strips, a few at a time, for 3-4
minutes until golden. Drain on absorbent
kitchen paper and keep warm while cooking
the remaining goujons.

Mix together the spiced plum chutney,
mayonnaise, orange rind and juice and
spoon into a small dish. Serve the goujons
with the sauce for dipping.

Serves 4.

GARLIC & LEMON PRAWNS

225 g (8 oz) small to medium raw prawns
salt and freshly ground pepper
4 tablespoons olive oil
2 tablespoons sunflower oil
3 large cloves garlic, coarsely chopped
1 dried red chilli pepper, stem and seeds removed,
  chopped
fresh lemon juice
2 tablespoons chopped fresh parsley
crusty bread, to serve

Shell prawns and pat dry on absorbent
kitchen paper. Lay prawns in a dish and
sprinkle lightly with salt.

Heat the oil in a non-stick frying pan, add
garlic and chilli and fry for 1-2 minutes until
garlic is golden. Immediately add prawns and
cook over high heat for 2 minutes until the
prawns are just tender. Add lemon juice to
taste and check the seasoning.

Stir in chopped fresh parsley, then serve the
prawns in ramekins, hot or cold with plenty
of crusty bread.

Serves 4.

PRAWN & FETA PURSES

45 g (1½ oz/3 tablespoons) butter, melted
115 g (4 oz) cooked, peeled prawns, thawed if frozen
175 g (6 oz) feta cheese, crumbled
25 g (1 oz) sun-dried tomatoes, roughly chopped
1 teaspoon chopped fresh chives
1 teaspoon chopped fresh fennel
salt and freshly ground black pepper
6 sheets filo pasty, about 40 x 30 cm (16 x 12 in)
fennels leaves and lemon twists, to garnish

Preheat the oven to 200C (400F/Gas 6).
Brush a baking sheet with melted butter. Dry
the prawns on kitchen paper and roughly
chop.

Mix together the prawns, feta cheese, sun-
dried tomatoes, chives, fennel and salt and
pepper. Cut each sheet of filo pastry into
twelve squares. Brush each square with
melted butter and layer three more squares
on top, arranging them at different angles to
form petals.

Place a spoonful of the prawn mixture in the
middle of the pastry. Pull up the edges of the
pastry and pinch together at the top to form
a purse. Put on the baking sheet and brush
with melted butter. Bake for 10-15 minutes
until golden brown. Garnish with fennel
leaves and lemon twists and serve.

Serves 6.

CHILLI PRAWN BALLS

450 g (1 lb) cooked, peeled prawns, thawed and
  dried, if frozen
1 fresh red chilli, seeded and chopped
3 spring onions, finely chopped
grated rind 1 small lemon
2 tablespoons cornflour
1 egg white, lightly beaten
salt and freshly ground black pepper
strips fresh red chilli, to garnish

Place all the ingredients except the garnish
in a blender or food processor and work to
form a firm dough-like mixture.

Divide the prawn mixture into 12 portions
and form each portion into a smooth ball,
flouring the hands with extra cornflour if
necessary, to prevent sticking.

Bring a wok or large saucepan of water to the
boil, arrange prawn balls on a layer of baking
parchment in a steamer and place over the
water. Cover and steam for 5 minutes or
until cooked through. Garnish with sliced
chilli and serve on a bed of shredded
Chinese leaves and watercress.

Serves 4.

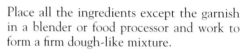

TUNA CROQUETTES

440 g (15½ oz) can tuna in brine
about 200 ml (7 fl oz/scant 1 cup) milk
2 tablespoons olive oil, plus extra for deep frying
¼ Spanish onion, finely chopped
4 tablespoons plain flour
1½ tablespoons finely chopped fresh parsley
2 tablespoons lemon juice
3 eggs, beaten
salt and freshly ground black pepper
175 g (6 oz/3 cups) fresh breadcrumbs
lemon wedges and watercress, to serve

Drain tuna and make up juice to 350 ml (12 fl oz/1½ cups) with milk. Flake tuna; set aside.

Heat 1 tablespoon olive oil in a small saucepan, add onion and cook for about 4 minutes until soft but not coloured. Stir in flour and cook, stirring, for 2 minutes. Remove from heat and slowly stir in half the milk mixture. Return to heat and bring to boil, stirring in remaining milk mixture. Simmer for 8 minutes, stirring occasionally. Off the heat, stir in tuna, parsley, lemon juice, 1 egg and salt and pepper.

Pour into a shallow dish, cool, cover and refrigerate for 2-3 hours. Put remaining eggs and the breadcrumbs into separate bowls. Dip small balls of tuna mixture first in egg then breadcrumbs to coat evenly. Half fill a deep fat fryer with oil and heat to 180C (350F). Fry tuna balls in batches for 2-3 minutes until crisp and golden. Using a slotted spoon, transfer to absorbent kitchen paper to drain. Serve hot with lemon wedges and small sprigs of watercress.

Serves 4.

STUFFED SQUID

750 g–1 kg (1½–2 lb) small squid
4 anchovy fillets, canned in oil, drained
55 g (2 oz) almonds, toasted and chopped, or 6 black olives, stoned and chopped
1 clove garlic, crushed
1½ tablespoons mixed chopped fresh parsley and oregano
1 egg, beaten
1 tablespoon ground almonds
salt and paprika
3 tablespoons olive oil
juice ½ lemon
lemon slices, stoned, sliced black olives and herb sprigs, to garnish

Preheat oven to 180C (350F/Gas 4). To prepare squid, cut off fins. Pull bag and tentacles apart. Remove backbone and any soft innards from bag. Cut head away from tentacles and discard. Rinse bag and tentacles thoroughly under cold running water. Chop tentacles finely and place in a small bowl. Using a fork, mix in anchovies, then chopped almonds or olives, garlic, herbs, egg and ground almonds. Season with salt and paprika.

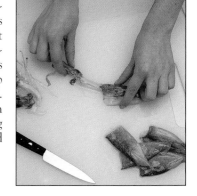

Fill squid with anchovy mixture, secure openings with wooden cocktail sticks, then place in a single layer in a shallow baking dish. Sprinkle with salt and paprika, then pour the oil and lemon juice over the top. Bake for about 30 minutes until tender. Serve garnished with lemon slices, black olives and herbs.

Serves 4–6.

GOUJONS WITH PIQUANT DIP

GRILLED BUTTERFLY PRAWNS

575 g (1¼ lb) firm white fish such as hake, haddock
    or cod, skinned
salt and pepper
1 egg, beaten
55 g (2 oz/1 cup) fresh breadcrumbs
olive oil, for deep frying
lemon wedges and dill sprigs, to garnish
DIP:
150 ml (5 fl oz/⅔ cup) low-calorie mayonnaise
6 tablespoons plain yogurt
3½ tablespoons finely chopped gherkins
2 tablespoons chopped dill
1 tablespoon capers, chopped if large
2 teaspoons Dijon mustard

450 g (1 lb) jumbo (king) prawns
juice 1 lemon
5 tablespoons extra virgin olive oil
½ clove garlic, crushed
2 tablespoons sun-dried tomato paste
pinch cayenne pepper
1 tablespoon chopped fresh basil
salt and freshly ground black pepper
fresh basil leaves to garnish

Remove heads and fine legs from prawns.
Using sharp scissors cut prawns lengthwise
almost in half, leaving tail end intact.

To make dip, beat all ingredients together,
pour into a bowl, cover and chill.

Place in a shallow dish and pour over half of
the lemon juice and 2 tablespoons of the
olive oil. Stir in garlic. Leave for at least 30
minutes. Preheat grill. Arrange prawns in
one layer on a rack and cook under the hot
grill for about 3 minutes until prawns have
curled or 'butterflied' and are bright pink.

Remove bones from fish, then cut flesh into
thin strips. Season pieces, dip in egg then in
breadcrumbs to coat evenly. Half-fill a deep
fat fryer with oil and heat to 180C (350F).
Add fish, in batches if necessary so pan is not
crowded, and fry until crisp and golden.
Drain on absorbent kitchen paper, spear
with cocktail sticks and serve hot, garnished
with lemon wedges and sprigs of dill and
accompanied by the dip.

Serves 4.

In a small bowl, mix together remaining
lemon juice and 3 tablespoons olive oil, the
sun-dried tomato paste, cayenne, basil, salt
and freshly ground black pepper. Either
spoon over prawns or serve separately for
dipping. Garnish prawns with basil sprigs.

Serves 4.

STUFFED MUSSELS

2 kg (4 lb) mussels, scrubbed and trimmed
3 sprigs of thyme
HERB BUTTER STUFFING:
1 shallot, finely chopped
2 cloves garlic, finely chopped
1 tablespoon finely chopped fresh parsley
1 tablespoon finely chopped fresh chives
1 teaspoon chopped fresh chervil
55 g (2 oz/1 cup) breadcrumbs made from stale
  bread
150 g (5 oz/⅔ cup) butter, softened
1-1½ tablespoons lemon juice
salt and freshly ground black pepper
flat-leaf parsley sprigs, to garnish

To make herb butter stuffing, mix together shallot, garlic, herbs and breadcrumbs then beat into butter. Add lemon juice and salt and pepper and set aside. Cover the base of shallow ovenproof serving dishes with a thick layer of coarse sea salt or crumpled foil. Pour 300 ml (10 fl oz/1¼ cups) water into a large saucepan. Bring to the boil, add mussels and thyme, cover tightly and cook over a high heat, for 4 minutes, shaking occasionally, until mussels open.

Preheat oven to 230C (450F/Gas 8). Drain mussels, discarding any that remain closed. Discard top shells of mussels and arrange mussels in dishes on top of salt or foil. Divide herb butter between mussels and bake for 10-12 minutes, until sizzling and golden. Garnish with flat-leaf parsley and serve at once.

Serves 4-6.

CAJUN CRABCAKES

1 small clove garlic, finely chopped
2 tablespoons finely chopped white and green parts
  spring onions
2 tablespoons finely chopped red pepper (capsicum)
1 egg, beaten
1½ tablespoons mayonnaise
450 g (1 lb) fresh white and brown crabmeat,
  chopped
1 tablespoon chopped fresh parsley
115 g (4 oz/2 cups) fresh breadcrumbs
squeeze lemon juice
salt and cayenne pepper
olive oil, for shallow frying
sour cream and chopped chives and crisp green salad,
  to serve

Put garlic, spring onions, pepper (capsicum) and a pinch salt in a mortar or small bowl and crush together using a pestle or end of a rolling pin. Stir in egg, mayonnaise, crabmeat, parsley and about half breadcrumbs to bind together. Add lemon juice, salt and cayenne pepper to taste.

Form crab mixture into 8 cakes 2 cm (¾ in) thick and 6 cm (2½ in) round. Lightly press in remaining breadcrumbs. Chill for 1 hour. In a non-stick frying pan, heat a thin layer oil, add crabcakes in batches and fry for 3-4 minutes on each side until golden. Serve warm with sour cream and chives, and a crisp green salad.

Makes 8.

SPICY KING PRAWNS

2 cloves garlic, crushed
1 small bunch of coriander, finely chopped
juice 2 limes
1 fresh red chilli, cored, seeded and finely chopped
70 ml (2½ fl oz/⅓ cup) sunflower oil
24 large raw prawns
GUACAMOLE:
1 clove garlic, crushed
4 tomatoes, peeled and finely chopped
1 fresh green chilli, cored, seeded and finely chopped
juice 1 lime
2 tablespoons chopped fresh coriander
salt and freshly ground black pepper
1 large ripe avocado

In a shallow non-metallic dish, mix together garlic, coriander, lime juice, chilli and sunflower oil. Add prawns and mix well. Cover and chill for 1-2 hours, turning occasionally. To make guacamole, put garlic, tomatoes, chilli, lime juice, coriander and salt and pepper in a bowl and mix well. Halve avocado lengthways and remove stone. Using a teaspoon, scoop out flesh, taking care to scrape away dark green flesh closest to skin. Mash into tomato mixture. Preheat grill.

Remove prawns from marinade and arrange on grill rack. Grill for 2-3 minutes on each side, basting with marinade. Serve with guacamole and tortilla chips.

Serves 6.

Note: Don't prepare the guacamole more than 30 minutes in advance or the avocado will discolour.

SIZZLING PRAWNS

100 ml (3½ fl oz/scant ½ cup) olive oil
4 cloves garlic, finely crushed
1 small fresh red chilli, seeded and chopped
350 g (12 oz) raw prawns, peeled
sea salt
2 tablespoons chopped fresh parsley
lemon wedges and bread, to serve

Heat oil in 4 individual flameproof earthenware dishes over a high heat. Add garlic and chilli, cook for 1-2 minutes, then add prawns and sea salt.

Cook briskly for 2-3 minutes. Stir in parsley. Serve quickly so the prawns are sizzling in the oil, and accompany with lemon wedges and bread to mop up the juices.

Note: One large dish, or a frying pan, can be used instead of individual dishes.

Serves 4.

FISH

FISH & PESTO PARCELS

2 sheets filo pastry, 25 x 50 cm (10 x 20 in), total
    weight about 55 g (2 oz)
melted butter, for brushing
2 fish fillets, such as turbot or salmon, about 150 g
    (5 oz) each, skinned
55 g (2 oz) cooked peeled prawns, finely chopped
55 g (2 oz) button mushrooms, chopped
5 tablespoons fromage frais or low fat soft cheese
2-3 teaspoons pesto sauce
salt and pepper
mixed salad, to serve

TURBOT PARCELS

2 cloves garlic, unpeeled
2 large red peppers (capsicums)
2 teaspoons balsamic vinegar
1½ teaspoons olive oil
salt and pepper
8 spinach leaves, stalks removed
4 pieces turbot fillets, about 165 g (5½ oz) each
stir-fried mixed peppers, to serve

Preheat grill. Wrap garlic in foil and grill for
5-7 minutes to soften. Grill peppers (capsicums), turning frequently, until evenly
charred and blistered.

Preheat oven to 200C (400F/Gas 6). Butter
a baking sheet. Brush one sheet of pastry
with butter, place the other sheet on top and
brush with butter, then cut in half. Place a
fish fillet in centre of each pastry square. Top
with prawns and mushrooms. Mix together
fromage frais or low fat soft cheese and pesto
sauce and season to taste. Spoon a quarter of
the pesto mixture onto each portion of
mushrooms. Reserve remaining mixture.

Leave peppers (capsicums) until cool enough
to handle, then remove skins. Halve peppers
(capsicums) and remove seeds and white
membrane. Peel garlic and purée with peppers (capsicums), vinegar and oil in a food
processor or blender. Season with salt and
pepper. Add spinach leaves to a saucepan of
boiling water and cook for 30 seconds.
Drain, refresh under cold running water,
then spread out on absorbent kitchen paper
to dry.

Bring together 2 opposite edges of pastry and
fold down over fish. Fold remaining edges
over and tuck ends under fish. Brush with
melted butter and place on baking sheet.
Bake in the oven for 15 minutes until
browned. Using a fish slice, transfer fish to a
warmed serving plate, split open top of
pastry and spoon in remaining pesto mixture. Serve with a mixed salad.

Serves 2.

Season turbot, then wrap each piece in 2
spinach leaves. Place in a steaming basket or
colander and cover. Bring base of steamer or
a saucepan of water to the boil, place basket
or steamer on it and steam for 5-6 minutes.
Heat pepper (capsicum) sauce gently and
serve it with the turbot parcels, accompanied
by stir-fried mixed peppers.

Serves 4.

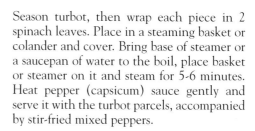

FISH WITH MUSHROOM CRUST

175 g (6 oz) chestnut mushrooms, finely chopped
2 tablespoons lemon juice
2 tablespoons wholegrain mustard
2 firmly packed tablespoons fresh breadcrumbs
3 spring onions, finely chopped
1¼ tablespoons finely chopped fresh parsley
salt and pepper
4 turbot escalopes or fillets, about 150 g (5 oz) each
lemon slices and parsley sprigs, to garnish
courgette (zucchini) and tomato sauté, to serve

Preheat grill. In a bowl, firmly mix together mushrooms, lemon juice, mustard, breadcrumbs, spring onions, 1 tablespoon parsley and seasoning to taste.

Grill turbot, skin-side up, for 2 minutes. Turn fish over, spread with mushroom mixture and pat it in.

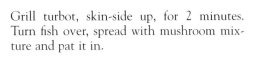

Grill fish until mushroom mixture has set and fish flakes. Sprinkle with remaining chopped parsley. Garnish with lemon slices and sprigs of parsley and serve with courgette (zucchini) and tomato sauté.

Serves 4.

ROAST COD WITH LENTILS

3 tablespoons olive oil
3 shallots, finely chopped
2 cloves garlic, finely crushed
175 g (6 oz) green or brown lentils
3½ teaspoons crushed coriander seeds
300 ml (10 fl oz/1¼ cups) fish stock
300 ml (10 fl oz/1¼ cups) dry white wine
2 tablespoons chopped fresh coriander
700 g (1½ lb) cod fillet, cut into 4 pieces
pinch saffron threads, toasted and crushed
4 tomatoes, peeled, seeded and chopped
salt and pepper
coriander sprigs, to garnish

In a saucepan, heat 1½ tablespoons oil, add 2 shallots and the garlic and cook gently until softened. Stir in lentils and 3 teaspoons coriander seeds. Cook for 2 minutes, stirring, then add stock and wine. Bring to the boil and simmer for 25-45 minutes until lentils are tender. Stir in the chopped coriander. Meanwhile, preheat oven to 230C (450F/Gas 8). Heat 1 tablespoon oil in a non-stick roasting tin and fry cod, skin side down, for 2 minutes. Transfer to oven for 8 minutes.

Heat remaining oil in a saucepan, add remaining shallot and coriander seeds and the saffron and cook gently until softened. Add tomatoes, a little liquid from the lentils and season with salt and pepper. Cook gently for 5 minutes. Drain lentils and season. Serve cod on lentils, garnished with sprigs of coriander and accompanied by the tomato relish.

Serves 4.

YOGURT-TOPPED HALIBUT

FISH GRATINS

2 tablespoons cumin seeds
2 tablespoons coriander seeds
2 large spring onions, chopped
2 cloves garlic, chopped
2 tablespoons chopped fresh mint
2 teaspoons dried dill
150 ml (5 fl oz/⅔ cup) plain yogurt
1 teaspoon paprika
salt and pepper
4 halibut steaks, about 175 g (6 oz) each
mint sprigs, to garnish
red chicory, red onion and mint salad, to serve

Heat a small, heavy frying pan, add cumin and coriander seeds and heat until fragrant.

Tip seeds into a mortar or small bowl and crush with a pestle or end of a rolling pin. Work in spring onions, garlic, mint and dill, then stir in yogurt and paprika. Season with salt and pepper.

Place fish in a single layer in a shallow, heat-proof dish. Spread yogurt mixture over top of each steak, cover dish and leave in a cool place for 2-3 hours. Preheat grill. Grill fish, basting occasionally, for about 10-15 minutes until fish is cooked and a crust has formed on yogurt topping. Garnish with sprigs of mint and serve with red chicory, red onion and mint salad.

Serves 4.

½ teaspoon Dijon mustard
1 tablespoon lemon juice
1 tablespoon olive oil
pinch freshly grated nutmeg
salt and pepper
4 cod or haddock steaks, about 150 g (5 oz) each
85 g (3 oz) sharp Cheshire cheese, finely crumbled,
   or mature Cheddar cheese, thinly sliced
45 g (1½ oz) freshly grated Parmesan cheese
2 tablespoons fine fresh breadcrumbs
paprika
pattypan squash, to serve
basil sprigs, to garnish

Preheat grill. In a small bowl, whisk together mustard and lemon juice using a fork, then gradually whisk in oil. Add nutmeg and season with salt and pepper. Brush one side of fish with mustard mixture, then grill, coated side up, for 2 minutes. Turn fish over, brush top with mustard mixture and grill for 2 minutes.

Cover fish with crumbled or sliced cheese. Mix together Parmesan cheese and bread-crumbs, sprinkle evenly onto fish, then season generously with pepper. Grill until the top is golden and bubbling. Lightly sprinkle with paprika and serve with pattypan squash, garnished with sprigs of basil.

Serves 4.

FISH CAKES

450 g (1 lb) potatoes, boiled
450 g (1 lb) cooked mixed white and smoked fish,
    such as haddock or cod, flaked
25 g (1 oz/2 tablespoons) butter, diced
3 tablespoons chopped fresh parsley
1 egg, separated
salt and pepper
1 egg, beaten
about 55 g (2 oz/1 cup) breadcrumbs made with stale
    bread
olive oil, for frying
lemon wedges and onion and avocado salad, to serve
dill sprigs, to garnish

In a saucepan, gently heat potatoes for a few minutes, shaking the pan occasionally.

Remove pan from heat, mash potatoes, then beat in the fish, butter, chopped parsley and egg yolk. Season with pepper. Transfer to a large bowl and mix well together. Chill if the mixture is soft.

Divide fish mixture into 8 equal portions then, with floured hands, form each portion into a flat cake. In a bowl, beat egg white with the whole egg. Spread out breadcrumbs on a plate. Dip each fish cake in egg, then in breadcrumbs. Heat a thin layer of oil in a frying pan and fry fish cakes for about 3 minutes on each side until crisp and golden. Drain on absorbent kitchen paper and serve hot with lemon wedges and onion and avocado salad, and garnished with sprigs of dill.

Serves 4.

HOT FISH LOAF

45 g (1½ oz/3 tablespoons) butter
2 cloves garlic, crushed
¾ tablespoon plain flour
425 ml (15 fl oz/scant 2 cups) milk
575 (1¼ lb) white fish fillets, such as hake or
    haddock, skinned and chopped
150 ml (5 fl oz/⅔ cup) double (heavy) cream
2 teaspoons anchovy essence
3 eggs plus 1 egg yolk
lemon juice
salt and cayenne pepper
115 g (4 oz) cooked peeled prawns
2 tablespoons chopped fresh basil
lemon wedges and coriander sprigs, to garnish
cheese, tomato or broccoli sauce, to serve (optional)

Preheat oven to 150C (300F/Gas 2). Butter and line base of a 1.6 litre (2¾ pint/6½ cup) terrine or loaf tin. In a saucepan, melt butter, then add garlic and cook for 1 minute. Stir in flour and cook, stirring, for 1 minute, then gradually stir in milk. Bring to the boil, stirring, and simmer for about 3 minutes, stirring occasionally. Pour into a blender, add fish, cream, anchovy essence, eggs and egg yolk. Purée, then add lemon juice and season to taste with salt and cayenne pepper.

Spoon half of fish mixture into terrine or loaf tin. Finely chop prawns, then sprinkle them evenly over the fish with the chopped basil. Spoon remaining fish over the top. Cover terrine or loaf tin tightly with greaseproof paper, place in a roasting tin and pour in enough boiling water to come halfway up sides. Bake for about 1¾ hours. Invert terrine or tin onto a warm serving plate and tilt slightly to drain off juice. Garnish with lemon and coriander and serve with sauce, if wished.

Serves 4-6.

MIDDLE EASTERN MONKFISH

2 cloves garlic
6.25 cm (2½ in) piece fresh root ginger
3 tablespoons olive oil
2½ tablespoons tomato purée (paste)
1½ teaspoons ground cinnamon
1 teaspoon caraway seeds, crushed
salt and pepper
1 kg (2¼ lb) monkfish tail
½ Spanish onion, finely chopped
cous cous and lemon slices, to serve

Finely chop garlic and ginger together. In a small bowl, stir oil into tomato purée (paste), then stir in ginger and garlic, cinnamon and caraway seeds. Season with salt and pepper.

Remove fine skin from monkfish, then spread with spice mixture. Place fish in a shallow dish, cover and leave in a cool place for 1-1½ hours.

Preheat oven to 200C (400F/Gas 6). Cut a piece of foil large enough to enclose fish. Make a bed of chopped onion on foil and place monkfish, and any spice paste left in dish, on onion. Fold foil loosely over fish and seal edges tightly. Bake monkfish for 20-25 minutes. Open foil, baste fish and bake for a further 10-15 minutes. Serve on a bed of cous cous, garnished with lemon slices.

Serves 4.

BASS WITH GINGER & LIME

2 shallots, finely chopped
4 cm (1½ in) piece fresh root ginger, finely chopped
juice 2 limes
4 tablespoons rice wine vinegar
225 ml (8 fl oz/1 cup) olive oil
2 tablespoons Chinese sesame oil
2 tablespoons soy sauce
salt and pepper
6-8 bass fillets, about 175 g (6 oz) and 1 cm (½ in) thick each
leaves from 1 bunch coriander
toasted sesame seeds, to garnish
stir-fried baby corn and sun-dried tomatoes, to serve

In a bowl, mix together first 8 ingredients. Set aside.

Preheat grill. Brush fish lightly with ginger mixture, then grill under a high heat for 2-3 minutes on each side.

Just before serving, reserve a few coriander leaves for garnish, chop remainder and mix into ginger mixture. Spoon some onto serving plates at room temperature and place fish on top. Sprinkle with sesame seeds and garnish with reserved coriander. Serve with stir-fried baby corn and sun-dried tomatoes.

Serves 6-8.

TANDOORI TROUT

seeds from 6 cardamom pods
2 teaspoons cumin seeds
4 tablespoons plain yogurt, preferably Greek style
1 large clove garlic, chopped
2 tablespoons lime juice
2.5 cm (1 in) piece fresh root ginger, chopped
1 teaspoon garam masala
pinch ground turmeric
¼ teaspoon cayenne pepper
salt
1 teaspoon red food colouring (optional)
2 trout, about 300 g (10 oz) each
oil, for brushing
rice with chillies and tomato and onion salad
lemon and lime wedges and coriander sprigs, to
  garnish

Heat a small heavy pan, add cardamom and cumin seeds and heat until fragrant. Tip into a mortar or small bowl and crush with a pestle or end of a rolling pin. Put yogurt, garlic, lime juice, all the spices, cayenne pepper and salt into a blender and mix to a paste. Add food colouring, if using.

With the point of a sharp knife, make 3 deep slashes in each side of the trout. Spread spice mixture over trout, working it into the slashes. Place in a shallow, non-metallic dish, cover and leave to marinate in refrigerator for 4 hours. Preheat grill. Brush grill rack with oil. Sprinkle a little oil over fish and grill for about 7 minutes on each side. Serve with rice with chillies and tomato and onion salad, garnished with lemon and lime wedges and sprigs of coriander.

Serves 2.

GRILLED FISH & CORIANDER

700 g (1½ lb) grey mullet, bream or monkfish fillets
3 tablespoons olive oil
2 cloves garlic, crushed
1½ teaspoons ground toasted cumin seeds
1 teaspoon paprika
1 fresh green chilli, finely chopped
handful coriander leaves, finely chopped
3 tablespoons lime juice
salt
rice, to serve
mint sprigs and lime wedges, to serve

Place fish in a shallow, non-metallic dish. Mix together remaining ingredients, except rice, mint and lime wedges.

Spoon olive oil mixture over fish, cover and leave in a cool place for 3-4 hours, turning occasionally.

Preheat grill. Grill fish for about 4 minutes on each side, basting with coriander mixture occasionally, until flesh flakes when tested with the point of a sharp knife. Serve warm on a bed of rice, garnished with sprigs of mint and lime wedges.

Serves 4.

TROUT WITH ALMONDS

SOLE MEUNIÈRE

salt and freshly ground black pepper
4 trout, about 300 g (10 oz) each, cleaned
70 g (2½ oz/⅓ cup) unsalted butter
55 g (2 oz/½ cup) flaked almonds
2 tablespoons lemon juice
dill sprigs and lemon wedges, to garnish

Season trout inside and out with salt and pepper. Heat 55 g (2 oz/¼ cup) of the butter in a large frying pan.

3 tablespoons plain four
salt and freshly ground black pepper
8 sole fillets, about 75 g (3 oz) each
175 g (6 oz/¾ cup) unsalted butter
juice 2 lemons
2 tablespoons finely chopped fresh parsley
parsley sprigs and lemon wedges, to garnish

Season flour with salt and pepper. Coat fish lightly and evenly in flour and set aside.

Add trout to pan and cook, in batches if necessary, for 12-15 minutes, turning once, until skin is crisp and flesh flakes easily. Drain trout on kitchen paper, transfer to warmed serving plates and keep warm.

Gently heat 115 g (4 oz/½ cup) butter in a small saucepan until if foams. Wring a piece of muslin out in very hot water, use to line a sieve and place over a bowl. Carefully skim foam from surface of butter and pour butter through muslin, to remove white sediment.

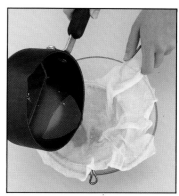

Wipe pan with kitchen paper. Heat remaining butter in pan, add almonds and cook, turning occasionally, until lightly browned. Stir in lemon juice and salt and pepper. Quickly pour over fish, garnish with dill and lemon wedges and serve.

Serves 4.

Heat strained butter in a large frying pan until sizzling. Add fish, in batches, and cook over a moderate heat for 4 minutes on each side, until crisp but not brown. Transfer to warmed serving plates and keep warm. Pour off cooking juices and wipe pan. Add remaining butter to pan and heat until foaming and golden brown. Stir in lemon juice and parsley and immediately pour over fish. Garnish with parsley and lemon wedges and serve.

Serves 4.

TANDOORI TROUT

seeds from 6 cardamom pods
2 teaspoons cumin seeds
4 tablespoons plain yogurt, preferably Greek style
1 large clove garlic, chopped
2 tablespoons lime juice
2.5 cm (1 in) piece fresh root ginger, chopped
1 teaspoon garam masala
pinch ground turmeric
1/4 teaspoon cayenne pepper
salt
1 teaspoon red food colouring (optional)
2 trout, about 300 g (10 oz) each
oil, for brushing
rice with chillies and tomato and onion salad
lemon and lime wedges and coriander sprigs, to
  garnish

Heat a small heavy pan, add cardamom and cumin seeds and heat until fragrant. Tip into a mortar or small bowl and crush with a pestle or end of a rolling pin. Put yogurt, garlic, lime juice, all the spices, cayenne pepper and salt into a blender and mix to a paste. Add food colouring, if using.

With the point of a sharp knife, make 3 deep slashes in each side of the trout. Spread spice mixture over trout, working it into the slashes. Place in a shallow, non-metallic dish, cover and leave to marinate in refrigerator for 4 hours. Preheat grill. Brush grill rack with oil. Sprinkle a little oil over fish and grill for about 7 minutes on each side. Serve with rice with chillies and tomato and onion salad, garnished with lemon and lime wedges and sprigs of coriander.

Serves 2.

GRILLED FISH & CORIANDER

700 g (1½ lb) grey mullet, bream or monkfish fillets
3 tablespoons olive oil
2 cloves garlic, crushed
1½ teaspoons ground toasted cumin seeds
1 teaspoon paprika
1 fresh green chilli, finely chopped
handful coriander leaves, finely chopped
3 tablespoons lime juice
salt
rice, to serve
mint sprigs and lime wedges, to serve

Place fish in a shallow, non-metallic dish. Mix together remaining ingredients, except rice, mint and lime wedges.

Spoon olive oil mixture over fish, cover and leave in a cool place for 3-4 hours, turning occasionally.

Preheat grill. Grill fish for about 4 minutes on each side, basting with coriander mixture occasionally, until flesh flakes when tested with the point of a sharp knife. Serve warm on a bed of rice, garnished with sprigs of mint and lime wedges.

Serves 4.

TROUT WITH ALMONDS

SOLE MEUNIÈRE

salt and freshly ground black pepper
4 trout, about 300 g (10 oz) each, cleaned
70 g (2½ oz/⅓ cup) unsalted butter
55 g (2 oz/½ cup) flaked almonds
2 tablespoons lemon juice
dill sprigs and lemon wedges, to garnish

Season trout inside and out with salt and pepper. Heat 55 g (2 oz/¼ cup) of the butter in a large frying pan.

3 tablespoons plain four
salt and freshly ground black pepper
8 sole fillets, about 75 g (3 oz) each
175 g (6 oz/¾ cup) unsalted butter
juice 2 lemons
2 tablespoons finely chopped fresh parsley
parsley sprigs and lemon wedges, to garnish

Season flour with salt and pepper. Coat fish lightly and evenly in flour and set aside.

Add trout to pan and cook, in batches if necessary, for 12-15 minutes, turning once, until skin is crisp and flesh flakes easily. Drain trout on kitchen paper, transfer to warmed serving plates and keep warm.

Gently heat 115 g (4 oz/½ cup) butter in a small saucepan until if foams. Wring a piece of muslin out in very hot water, use to line a sieve and place over a bowl. Carefully skim foam from surface of butter and pour butter through muslin, to remove white sediment.

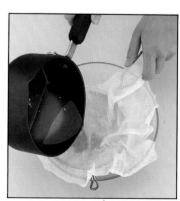

Wipe pan with kitchen paper. Heat remaining butter in pan, add almonds and cook, turning occasionally, until lightly browned. Stir in lemon juice and salt and pepper. Quickly pour over fish, garnish with dill and lemon wedges and serve.

Serves 4.

Heat strained butter in a large frying pan until sizzling. Add fish, in batches, and cook over a moderate heat for 4 minutes on each side, until crisp but not brown. Transfer to warmed serving plates and keep warm. Pour off cooking juices and wipe pan. Add remaining butter to pan and heat until foaming and golden brown. Stir in lemon juice and parsley and immediately pour over fish. Garnish with parsley and lemon wedges and serve.

Serves 4.

TUNA BASQUAISE

SALMON WITH HERB SAUCE

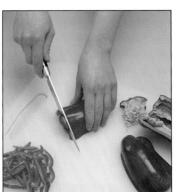

6 slices tuna, about 2.5 cm (1 in) thick
4 cloves garlic
85 ml (3 fl oz/⅓ cup) olive oil
1 large onion, finely chopped
1 large red pepper (capsicum), seeded, cored and thinly sliced
1 green pepper (capsicum), seeded, cored and thinly sliced
400 g (14 oz) tomatoes, peeled, seeded and diced
1 tablespoon sun-dried tomato paste
3 sprigs thyme
1 bay leaf
salt and pepper
parsley sprigs, to garnish

½ onion, chopped
1 carrot, chopped
1 stick celery, chopped
1 lemon, sliced
1.6 kg (3½ lb) salmon
bouquet garni of 2 bay leaves and sprig each rosemary, sage and parsley
175 ml (6 fl oz/¾ cup) dry white wine
salt and pepper
bunch watercress, roughly chopped
3 tablespoons chopped fresh parsley
2 tablespoons chopped fresh chervil
1 tablespoon chopped fresh dill
225 g (8 oz/1 cup) ricotta or low fat soft cheese
lime and lemon slices and herb sprigs, to garnish

Cut slits in tuna. Cut 2 cloves garlic into slivers and insert in slits in tuna. In a large frying pan, heat half the oil, add tuna and cook until lightly browned on both sides. Remove tuna from pan and set aside. Add remaining oil to pan, add onion and peppers (capsicums) and cook over moderate heat, stirring frequently, for about 10 minutes until soft.

Preheat oven to 220C (425F/Gas 7). Place a large piece of foil on a large baking sheet. Make a bed of vegetables and half the lemon slices on the foil. Put salmon on vegetables and add bouquet garni and remaining lemon slices. Fold up foil, pour in wine, season with pepper, then seal edges of foil tightly. Bake in the oven for 1 hour. Remove baking sheet from oven and leave fish to cool completely in foil.

Chop remaining garlic, add to pan, cook for 1 minute, then add tomatoes, tomato paste, thyme and bay leaf. Simmer, uncovered, for 15-20 minutes, stirring occasionally. Return tuna to pan, season with salt and pepper, then cover with buttered greaseproof paper and gook gently for 15 minutes. Serve garnished with sprigs of parsley.

Serves 6.

Strain cooking liquid, then boil it until reduced to about 85 ml (3 fl oz/⅓ cup). Add watercress and herbs and boil until softened. Tip into a blender, add cheese and purée. Season with salt and pepper, pour into a serving bowl or jug and refrigerate. Lift fish onto a rack. Carefully remove skin, fins and fatty line that runs along spine. Transfer to a large serving plate, garnish with lime and lemon slices and sprigs of herbs and serve with sauce.

Serves 6.

MACKEREL WITH MUSTARD

2 tablespoons Dijon mustard
4 tablespoons finely chopped fresh coriander
2 cloves garlic, finely crushed
2-3 teaspoons lemon juice
salt and pepper
4 mackerel, about 300 g (10 oz) each
rolled oats
tomato, fennel and thyme salad, to serve
lemon wedges and coriander sprigs, to garnish

Preheat grill. In a bowl, mix together mustard, coriander, garlic and lemon juice and season with salt and pepper.

Using the point of a sharp knife, cut 3 slashes on each side of the mackerel. Spoon mustard mixture into slashes and sprinkle with a few rolled oats. Wrap each fish in a large piece of foil and fold the edges of the foil together to seal tightly.

Place foil packages under hot grill for 5 minutes. Open foil, turn fish, reseal packages and cook for a further 2-3 minutes. Open foil, place fish under the grill and cook for 2-3 minutes until cooked. Serve with tomato, fennel and thyme salad, garnished with lemon wedges and sprigs of coriander.

Serves 4.

HERRINGS IN OATMEAL

about 1 tablespoon Dijon mustard
about 1½ teaspoons tarragon vinegar
85 ml (3 fl oz/⅓ cup) thick mayonnaise
85 ml (3 fl oz/⅓ cup) plain yogurt
4 herrings, about 225 g (8 oz) each, cleaned and
  heads and tails removed
salt and pepper
1 lemon, halved
115 g (4 oz) medium oatmeal
rice and artichoke heart salad, to serve
lemon wedges and coriander sprigs, to garnish

In a small bowl, beat mustard and vinegar to taste into mayonnaise and yogurt, then spoon into a small serving bowl and chill lightly.

Preheat grill. Place one fish on a board, cut-side down and opened out. Press gently along backbone with your thumbs. Turn fish over and carefully lift away backbone and attached bones.

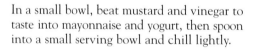

Season with salt and pepper and squeeze lemon juice over both sides of fish, then fold in half, skin-side outwards. Repeat with remaining fish. Coat each fish evenly in oatmeal, pressing it in well but gently. Grill herrings for 3-4 minutes on each side until brown and crisp and flesh flakes easily. Serve hot with the mustard sauce, accompanied by a rice and artichoke heart salad and garnished with lemon wedges and sprigs of coriander.

Serves 4.

MACKEREL & GOOSEBERRIES

450 g (1 lb) gooseberries
1 teaspoon fennel seeds
2 mackerel, about 450 g (1 lb) each, cut into 2 fillets
1 tablespoon olive oil
salt and freshly ground black pepper
1 tablespoon pastis
1 teaspoon sugar
25 g (1 oz/2 tablespoons) butter, diced
parsley sprigs, to garnish

Put gooseberries and fennel seeds in a saucepan with just enough water to cover. Bring to boil then simmer for 7-10 minutes, until very soft.

Meanwhile, preheat grill. With the point of a knife, make three slashes in each mackerel fillet. Season fish, brush with oil on each side and grill for 10 minutes, turning once.

Reserve a few gooseberries for garnish. Press remainder through a nylon sieve into a saucepan, pressing hard to extract all the juice. Add pastis, sugar and salt and pepper and heat gently, gradually beating in butter. Pour sauce over fish, garnish with reserved gooseberries and parsley and serve with steamed vegetables.

Serves 4.

Note: Pastis is an aniseed-flavoured liqueur.

SEA BASS ROASTED WITH FENNEL

1.2 kg (2½ lb) sea bass without head, scaled and gutted
4 rosemary sprigs and 4 oregano sprigs
3 large fennel bulbs
salt and freshly ground black pepper
3 tablespoons olive oil
juice 1 lemon
4 tablespoons chopped fresh oregano and parsley
150 ml (5 fl oz/⅔ cup) dry white wine
8 large green olives, stoned

Preheat oven to 220C (425F/Gas 7). Wash fish inside and out and pat dry on absorbent kitchen paper. Lay it in an oval ovenproof dish. Fill cavity with sprigs of rosemary.

Cut fennel bulbs in half lengthways, cut out core and slice the bulbs thickly. Blanch in boiling salted water for 5 minutes. Drain. Whisk oil, lemon juice, chopped herbs, salt and pepper together in a medium bowl. Stir in the fennel, turning until coated. Spoon the fennel over and around the fish, and pour over any remaining marinade. Spoon the wine over top and scatter with olives.

Bake in oven for 15 minutes, then spoon the cooking juices over the fish and gently stir the fennel around. Bake for a further 15 minutes. Turn off the oven and leave fish for 5 minutes before serving. Garnish with oregano sprigs and serve with mixed rice.

Serves 4.

FISH WITH GINGER

6 tablespoons vegetable oil
1 kg (2¼ lb) whole white fish or single piece, such as cod, bass or red snapper
1 small onion, finely chopped
6 spring onions, thickly sliced
2 cloves garlic, crushed
1 tablespoon grated fresh root ginger
2 teaspoons fish sauce
1½ tablespoons light soy sauce
1 teaspoon crushed palm sugar
1 tablespoon tamarind water (see glossary)
freshly ground black pepper
coriander sprigs, to garnish

Over a medium heat, heat 4 tablespoons oil in a wok. Add fish and fry for about 5 minutes a side until browned and flesh flakes easily when flaked with a knife. Meanwhile, heat remaining oil in a small saucepan over a moderate heat, add onion and cook, stirring occasionally, until browned. When fish is cooked, transfer to absorbent kitchen paper and keep warm.

Stir into wok, spring onions, garlic and ginger. Stir-fry for 2-3 minutes, then stir in fish sauce, soy sauce, palm sugar and tamarind water. Cook for 1 minute, season with black pepper, then pour over fish. Sprinkle over the browned onions and garnish with coriander.

Serves 4.

SKATE WITH BROWN BUTTER

85 g (3 oz/⅓ cup) unsalted butter
2 skate wings, about 225 g (8 oz) each
1 tablespoon chopped fresh parsley
salt and freshly ground black pepper
1 tablespoon lemon juice or white wine vinegar
2-3 teaspoons capers
lemon slices and flat-leaf parsley sprigs, to garnish

Gently melt butter in a small saucepan. Wring a piece of muslin out in very hot water, use to line a sieve and place over a jug. Pour butter through muslin, to remove white sediment. Pour about half of the clear butter into a large frying pan.

Add skate and cook for 4-5 minutes on each side. Drain on kitchen paper then transfer to warmed serving plates. Sprinkle with parsley and salt and pepper and keep warm.

Pour remaining clear butter into a small saucepan and heat until golden brown and nutty smelling. Add lemon juice or vinegar and capers and immediately remove from heat. Pour over skate, garnish with lemon slices and parsley and serve.

Serves 2.

SOLE WITH CHIVE SAUCE

115 g (4 oz/½ cup) firm cottage cheese, drained and
    sieved
grated rind and juice 1 lemon
salt and pepper
100 g (3½ oz) cooked peeled prawns, finely chopped
8 sole or plaice fillets, skinned
225 ml (8 fl oz/1 cup) fish stock
1 small shallot, finely chopped
1 tablespoon dry white vermouth
6 tablespoons dry white wine
175 ml (6 fl oz/¾ cup) double (heavy) cream or
    fromage frais or soft cheese
1½ tablespoons finely chopped fresh chives
prawns and chopped fresh chives, to garnish
broccoli, to serve

Preheat oven to 180C (350F/Gas 4). Oil a
shallow baking dish. Beat together cheese,
lemon rind and juice and season with salt
and pepper. Mix in prawns. Spread on
skinned side of fillets and roll up neatly.
Secure with wooden cocktail sticks. Place
fish in a single layer in dish, pour in stock to
come halfway up the rolls and add chopped
shallot. Cover dish and cook in the oven for
about 20 minutes. Meanwhile, in a small
saucepan, boil vermouth and wine until
reduced by half.

Transfer sole to a warm plate and keep warm.
Add stock and shallot to wines and boil hard
until reduced by three quarters. Stir in
cream, if using, and simmer to a light creamy
consistency. If using fromage frais or soft
cheese, stir in and heat without boiling.
Quickly pour into a blender and mix until
frothy. Add chives and season. Pour some
sauce over fish and serve rest in a warm jug.
Garnish rolls with prawns and chives and
serve with broccoli.

Serves 4.

CAJUN-STYLE RED SNAPPER

2 red snapper, about 575-700 g (1¼-1½ lb) each
25 g (1 oz/2 tablespoons) unsalted butter
2 tablespoons olive oil
SPICE MIX:
1 plump clove garlic
½ onion
1 teaspoon salt
1 teaspoon paprika
½ teaspoon cayenne pepper
½ teaspoon ground cumin
½ teaspoon mustard powder
1 teaspoon each dried thyme and dried oregano
½ teaspoon pepper

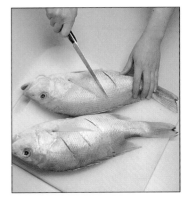

With the point of a sharp knife, cut 3 slashes
on each side of both fish.

To make spice mix, crush together garlic and
onion with salt in a pestle and mortar or in a
bowl using the end of a rolling pin. Stir in
remaining spice mix ingredients. Spread
some spice mix over each fish, making sure it
goes into the slashes. Lay the fish in a shallow dish, cover and leave in a cool place for
1 hour.

In a large frying pan, heat butter and oil until
sizzling. Add fish and fry for about 4 minutes
on each side until fish is cooked and spice
coating has blackened.

Serves 2.

Note: Serve with a colourful selection of
tomato, lemon and lime slices with thyme
and parsley sprigs.

BAKED BASQUE COD

3 tablespoons olive oil
1 small green pepper (capsicum), diced
1 onion, finely chopped
2 tomatoes, peeled (see page 293) and diced
1 clove garlic, crushed
2 teaspoons chopped fresh basil
4 cod fillets, about 175 g (6 oz) each, skinned
juice ½ lemon
salt and freshly ground black pepper
lemon slices, to garnish

Preheat the oven to 190C (375F/Gas 5). Brush four large squares of foil with a little oil.

Mix together the pepper (capsicum), onion, tomatoes, garlic and basil. Put a cod fillet on each piece of foil. Top each fillet with the pepper (capsicum) mixture.

Drizzle with lemon juice and the remaining oil. Season with salt and pepper then fold the foil to make four parcels. Put the parcels on a baking sheet and bake for 20-30 minutes until the fish flakes easily when tested with a knife. Unwrap the foil parcels and transfer the fish, vegetables and cooking juices to warmed serving plates. Garnish with lemon slices and serve.

Serves 4.

FIVE-SPICE SALMON

1 teaspoon sesame oil
3 tablespoons soy sauce
3 tablespoons dry sherry or rice wine
1 tablespoon honey
1 tablespoon lime or lemon juice
1 teaspoon five-spice powder
700 g (1½ lb) salmon fillet, skinned and cut into
    2.5 cm (1 in) strips
2 egg whites
3 teaspoons cornflour
300 ml (10 fl oz/1¼ cups) vegetable oil
6 spring onions, sliced into 5 cm (2 in) pieces
115 ml (4 fl oz/½ cup) light fish or chicken stock or
    water
dash hot pepper sauce (optional)
lime wedges, to garnish

In a shallow baking dish, combine the sesame oil, soy sauce, sherry or wine, honey, lime or lemon juice and five-spice powder. Add salmon strips and toss gently to coat. Leave to stand for 30 minutes. With a slotted spoon, remove the salmon strips from marinade and pat dry with absorbent kitchen paper. Reserve marinade. In a small dish, beat egg whites and cornflour to make a batter. Add salmon strips and toss gently to coat completely.

Heat the vegetable oil in the wok until hot. Add the salmon in batches. Fry for 2-3 minutes until golden, turning once. Remove and drain on absorbent kitchen paper. Pour oil from wok and wipe wok clean. Pour marinade into wok and add spring onions, stock or water and pepper sauce, if using. Bring to the boil and simmer for 1-2 minutes. Add fish and turn gently to coat. Cook for 1 minute until hot. Garnish with lime and serve with noodles.

Serves 4.

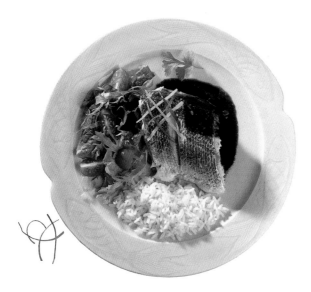

STEAMED FISH

1 whole fish, such as sea bass, grey mullet or
    grouper, weighing about 900 g (2 lb), cleaned and
    scored on both sides at 2.5 cm (1 in) intervals
salt and freshly ground black pepper
1 teaspoon sugar
1 teaspoon chopped fresh root ginger
1 tablespoon each chopped white and green parts of
    spring onions
1 tablespoon fish sauce
2 teaspoons sesame oil
1 tablespoon shredded fresh root ginger
1 tablespoon vegetable oil
1 tablespoon each black bean sauce and soy sauce
2 small fresh red chillies, seeded and shredded
coriander sprigs, to garnish

Rub the fish inside and out with salt and
pepper, then marinate in a shallow dish with
the sugar, ginger, white parts of spring
onions, the fish sauce and sesame oil for 30
minutes. Place fish with marinade in a hot
steamer, or on a rack inside a wok, cover and
steam for 15-20 minutes.

Remove dish from the steamer or wok, place
the ginger and green part of spring onions on
top of the fish. Heat vegetable oil in a small
saucepan, add black bean sauce, soy sauce
and chillies and stir-fry for 30 seconds, then
drizzle it over fish. Garnish with coriander
and serve with rice and a salad.

Serves 4.

Note: If the fish is too big to fit into your
steamer or wok, cut it in half crossways and
re-assemble it on a warmed plate to serve.

GRILLED FLAT FISH

575 g (1¼ lb) flat fish, such as plaice, cleaned
salt and freshly ground black pepper
1 tablespoon vegetable oil, plus extra for brushing
½ teaspoon minced garlic
½ teaspoon chopped fresh root ginger
2 shallots, finely chopped
2-3 small fresh red chillies, seeded and chopped
1 tablespoon chopped spring onion
2 tablespoons fish sauce and 1 teaspoon sugar water
    or lime juice
1 tablespoon tamarind
2-3 tablespoons chicken stock or water
2 teaspoons cornflour

Score both sides of the fish at 2.5 cm (1 in)
intervals and rub with salt and pepper.

Leave the fish to stand for 25 minutes.
Meanwhile, preheat grill. Brush both sides of
fish with oil and grill under the hot grill for
about 4 minutes each side until lightly
brown but not burnt. Place on a warmed
serving dish.

Heat the 1 tablespoon oil in a small pan and
stir-fry the garlic, ginger, shallots, chillies
and spring onion for 1 minute, then add the
fish sauce, sugar, tamarind water or lime juice
and stock or water. Bring to boil and simmer
for 30 seconds. Mix cornflour with 1 tablespoon water and stir into sauce to thicken.
Pour the sauce over the fish. Serve with
carrots and mange tout (snow peas),
garnished with coriander sprigs.

*Serves 2 on its own, or 4-6 with other dishes as
part of a meal.*

LIME GRILLED FISH SKEWERS

350 g (12 oz) monkfish tails, skinned and cut into
  2 cm (¾ in) cubes
350 g (12 oz) trout fillets, skinned and cut into 2 cm
  (¾ in) pieces
2 limes
1 teaspoon sesame oil
large pinch five-spice powder
freshly ground black pepper
pared lime rind, to garnish

Place monkfish and trout in a shallow dish.
Juice one of the limes and grate the rind. Mix
with sesame oil and five-spice powder, pour
over fish, cover and chill for 30 minutes.

Soak 4 bamboo skewers in cold water. Halve
and quarter remaining lime lengthways, and
then halve each quarter in the same way.
Slice each piece of lime in half widthways to
make 16 small pieces.

Preheat grill. Thread monkfish, trout and
lime pieces onto skewers and place on grill
rack. Brush with marinade and season with
black pepper. Grill for 2 minutes on each
side, brushing occasionally with marinade to
prevent drying out. Drain on kitchen paper,
garnish with lime rind and serve with rice,
vegetables and lime wedges.

Serves 4.

SALT & SOUR BAKED TROUT

2 trout, about 300 g (10 oz) each, cleaned
salt and freshly ground black pepper
2 spring onions, finely shredded
1 tablespoon chopped fresh coriander
strips of fresh red chilli, to garnish
SAUCE:
1 clove garlic, finely chopped
1 cm (½ in) piece fresh root ginger, peeled and finely
  chopped
2 tablespoons white rice vinegar
2 tablespoons light soy sauce
2 tablespoons dry sherry
1 teaspoon salt
1 teaspoon chilli powder
2 teaspoons caster sugar

Preheat oven to 180C (350F/Gas 4). Wash
trout and pat dry with kitchen paper. Season
trout inside and out with salt and pepper. Fill
the cavities with spring onion and coriander.
Using a sharp knife, score the flesh lightly in
diagonal lines. Place trout in a non-stick
roasting tin.

Mix together sauce ingredients and pour
over trout. Cover loosely with oiled foil and
bake for 20 minutes, basting halfway
through. Remove foil, baste, and bake,
uncovered for 10 minutes. Skin the trout
and remove flesh from bones to give 4 fillets.
Brush with cooking juices, garnish with
strips of chilli and serve with noodles and
vegetables.

Serves 4.

CRISPY FISH HOTPOT

350 g (12 oz) courgettes (zucchini), thinly sliced
2 red dessert apples, cored and thinly sliced
1 large onion, sliced
175 g (6 oz) small green beans, cut into 2.5 cm
 (1 in) lengths
1 teaspoon dried sage
300 ml (10 fl oz/1¼ cups) fish stock
700 g (1½ lb) cod fillet, skinned and cubed
salt and freshly ground black pepper
350 g (12 oz) potatoes with the skins on, thinly sliced
85 g (3 oz/¾ cup) grated Cheddar cheese

Preheat oven to 190C (375F/Gas 5). Arrange
layers of courgettes (zucchini), apples, onion
and beans in an ovenproof casserole.

Sprinkle with sage and pour in the stock.
Cover and cook in the oven for 30 minutes.
Remove from the oven, arrange the fish on
top and season with salt and pepper.

Arrange the sliced potatoes on top, sprinkle
with cheese and bake for 35-40 minutes,
until the potatoes are tender and the cheese
is melted and golden. Serve.

Serves 4-6.

Variation: Any firm white fish fillets, such as
whiting or haddock, can be used instead of
cod in this recipe.

HADDOCK & SALMON PIE

55 g (2 oz/¼ cup) butter
55 g (2 oz/½ cup) plain flour
300 ml (10 fl oz/1¼ cups) milk
300 ml (10 fl oz/1¼ cups) fish stock
12 shallots
450 g (1 lb) potatoes, diced
2 cloves garlic, crushed
2 tablespoons olive oil
1 tablespoon double (thick) cream
salt and freshly ground black pepper
2 tablespoons wholegrain mustard
4 tablespoons chopped fresh parsley
450 g (1 lb) salmon fillet, skinned and cubed
225 g (8 oz) smoked haddock, skinned and cubed
12 small button mushrooms
1 egg, beaten

Melt the butter in a flameproof casserole,
add the flour and cook over a gentle heat,
stirring, for 2 minutes. Gradually stir in the
milk and fish stock, then add the shallots.
Bring to the boil and simmer for 30 minutes.
Meanwhile, cook the potatoes and garlic in
boiling salted water for 20 minutes, until the
potatoes are tender. Drain. Mash the potatoes and garlic and stir in the olive oil, cream
and salt and pepper. Set aside. Preheat oven
to 200C (400F/Gas 6).

Season the shallot sauce with salt and pepper
and add the mustard and parsley. Add the
salmon, haddock and button mushrooms and
simmer gently for 10 minutes. Pipe or spoon
the potato on top of the fish mixture and
bake for 10 minutes. Take out of the oven
and brush with a little beaten egg. Return to
the oven and bake for 20 minutes, until the
potato is golden. Serve.

Serves 4-6.

GREEK SEAFOOD CASSEROLE

1 tablespoon olive oil
1 onion, chopped
1 clove garlic, crushed
1 stick celery, chopped
grated rind and juice ½ lemon
4 large ripe tomatoes, peeled (see page 293) and
   chopped
2 tablespoons chopped fresh parsley
1 fresh bay leaf
1 teaspoon dried oregano
salt and freshly ground black pepper
350 g (12 oz) monkfish fillet, skinned and cubed
225 g (8 oz) cleaned squid, cut into rings
450 g (1 lb) mussels, cleaned
chopped green olives, to garnish

Heat the olive oil in a flameproof casserole. Add the onion, garlic and celery and cook for 5 minutes until soft. Add the lemon rind and juice, tomatoes, parsley, bay leaf, oregano and salt and pepper. Bring to the boil, cover and simmer for 20 minutes. Add the monkfish to the casserole, adding a little water if necessary. Return to the boil, cover and cook for 3 minutes.

Stir in the squid and place the mussels on top. Return to the boil, cover tightly and cook for 5 minutes until the fish is tender and the mussels have opened. Discard any mussels that remain closed. Garnish with chopped olives and serve.

Serves 4.

CHUNKY FISH CASSEROLE

100 g (3½ oz) pasta shells
3 tablespoons olive oil
2 cloves garlic, finely crushed
85 g (3 oz) button onions, halved
115 g (4 oz) button mushrooms, halved
450 g (1 lb) firm, white fish, such as cod or monkfish
225 g (8 oz) trout fillets
3 tablespoons well-seasoned plain flour
225 g (8 oz) broad beans
115 ml (4 fl oz/½ cup) dry white wine
300 ml (10 fl oz/1¼ cups) fish stock
large bouquet garni
grated rind and juice 1 lemon
150 g (5 oz) cooked peeled prawns or cooked shelled
   mussels or clams
chopped fresh herbs, to garnish

Preheat oven to 180C (350F/Gas 4). Cook pasta in plenty of boiling salted water for three quarters of time recommended on packet. Drain and rinse under cold running water; set aside. In a large frying pan, heat half the oil, add garlic, onions and mushrooms and cook for 3-4 minutes. Using a slotted spoon, transfer to a large, deep baking dish. Meanwhile, skin fish and cut into 2.5 cm (1 in) chunks, then toss in seasoned flour.

Add remaining oil to pan, heat and then add fish, in batches if necessary. Fry for 2-3 minutes, turning pieces carefully. Transfer to dish and add pasta and beans. Stir wine, stock, bouquet garni and lemon rind and juice into pan and bring to the boil. Simmer for a few minutes, then pour into dish. Cover and cook in oven for about 30 minutes. Add prawns, mussels or clams, cover again and cook for about 5 minutes. Garnish with plenty of chopped herbs.

Serves 4.

SHELLFISH

PRAWNS WITH GARLIC

2 tablespoons vegetable oil
5 cloves garlic, chopped
0.5 cm (¼ in) slice fresh root ginger, very finely
  chopped
14-16 large prawns, peeled, tails left on
2 teaspoons fish sauce
2 tablespoons chopped coriander leaves
freshly ground black pepper
lettuce leaves, lime juice and diced cucumber, to
  serve

In a wok, heat oil, add garlic and fry until browned.

Stir in ginger, heat for 30 seconds, then add prawns and stir-fry for 2-3 minutes until beginning to turn opaque. Stir in fish sauce, coriander, 1-2 tablespoons water and plenty of black pepper. Allow to bubble for 1-2 minutes.

Serve prawns on a bed of lettuce leaves with lime juice squeezed over and scattered with cucumber.

Serves 4.

PRAWNS IN COCONUT SAUCE

2 fresh red chillies, seeded and chopped
1 red onion, chopped
1 thick stalk lemon grass, chopped
2.5 cm (1 in) piece galangal, chopped
1 teaspoon ground turmeric
250 ml (8 fl oz/1 cup) coconut milk
14-16 raw Mediterranean (king) prawns, peeled and
  deveined
8 Thai holy basil leaves
2 teaspoons lime juice
1 teaspoon fish sauce
1 spring onion, including some green, cut into fine
  strips

Using a small blender, mix chillies, onion, lemon grass and galangal to a paste. Transfer to a wok and heat, stirring, for 2-3 minutes. Stir in turmeric and 125 ml (4 fl oz/½ cup) water, bring to the boil and simmer for 3-4 minutes until most of the water has evaporated.

Stir in coconut milk and prawns and cook gently, stirring occasionally, for about 4 minutes until prawns are just firm and pink. Stir in basil leaves, lime juice and fish sauce. Scatter over strips of spring onion.

Serves 4.

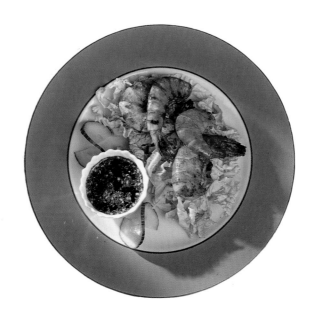

PRAWNS WITH ASIAN SAUCE

700 g (1½ lb) raw jumbo (king) prawns
lime wedges and basil sprigs, to garnish
MARINADE:
handful Thai or ordinary fresh basil, finely chopped
2 tablespoons finely chopped garlic
2 tablespoons finely chopped fresh root ginger
2 tablespoons finely chopped green chillies
2 teaspoons rice wine or medium dry sherry
2½ tablespoons groundnut oil
1 teaspoon Chinese sesame oil
salt and pepper

To make marinade, pound ingredients together in a pestle and mortar or using the end of a rolling pin in a bowl.

Discard legs and heads from prawns then, using strong scissors, cut prawns lengthways in half leaving tail end intact. Remove dark intestinal vein. Rub marinade over prawns, spoon any remaining marinade over them, cover and leave in a cool place for 1 hour.

Preheat grill or barbecue. Cook prawns in a single layer for about 3 minutes until curled, or 'butterflied', and bright pink. Garnish with lime wedges and sprigs of basil. Serve any remaining marinade separately.

Serves 4-6.

SALT & PEPPER PRAWNS

16 uncooked large prawns
1 teaspoon chilli powder
1 teaspoon coarse sea salt
1 teaspoon Szechuan peppercorns, crushed
2 cloves garlic, finely chopped
1 tablespoon groundnut (peanut) oil
DIP:
½ teaspoon Szechuan peppercorns, toasted and ground
2 tablespoons light soy sauce
2 tablespoons dry sherry
1 teaspoon brown sugar

Cut off the heads of the prawns. Use scissors to remove the legs, leaving the shells.

Wash and pat dry with kitchen paper. In a bowl, mix together the prawns, chilli powder, salt, peppercorns and garlic. Heat the oil in a non-stick or well seasoned wok until very hot and stir-fry the prawns for 2-3 minutes until the prawns are pink and cooked through. Drain on kitchen paper.

Mix together ingredients for dip. Serve the prawns immediately with the dip and a salad.

Serves 4

Note: Serve with a rose-bowl of water and lemon slices, to refresh the hands.

PACIFIC PRAWNS

2 tablespoons peanut oil
450 g (1 lb) raw medium prawns, shelled and deveined
2 cloves garlic, finely chopped
2.5 cm (1 in) piece fresh root ginger, peeled and
　finely chopped
2 stalks celery, sliced
1 red pepper (capsicum), sliced
4 spring onions, cut into thin strips
225 g (8 oz) can unsweetened pineapple chunks,
　drained, juice reserved
2 teaspoons cornflour
2 teaspoons soy sauce
1 tablespoon lemon juice
dash hot pepper sauce
150 g (5 oz/1 cup) macadamia nuts, rinsed lightly if
　salted.

Heat the wok until hot. Add 1 tablespoon oil and swirl to coat wok. Add prawns and stir-fry for 2 minutes until prawns turn pink and feel firm to the touch. Remove to bowl. Add remaining oil to the wok. Add garlic and ginger and stir-fry for 30 seconds. Stir in celery, red pepper (capsicum) and spring onions and stir-fry for 3-4 minutes until vegetables are tender but still crisp. Stir in pineapple chunks.

Dissolve the cornflour in the reserved pineapple juice. Stir in the soy sauce, lemon juice and hot pepper sauce. Stir into the vegetable and pineapple mixture and bring to simmering point. Add reserved prawns and macadamia nuts and stir-fry until sauce thickens and prawns are heated through.

Serves 4.

PRAWNS WITH LEMON GRASS

2 cloves garlic, chopped
1 tablespoon chopped coriander
2 tablespoons chopped lemon grass
½ teaspoon black or white peppercorns
3 tablespoons vegetable oil
350-400 g (12-14 oz) raw peeled prawns, cut in half
　lengthways if large
2 shallots or 1 small onion, sliced
2-3 small fresh chillies, seeded and chopped
2-3 tomatoes, cut into wedges
1 tablespoon fish sauce
1 tablespoon oyster sauce
2-3 tablespoons chicken stock or water
coriander sprigs, to garnish

Using a pestle and mortar, pound the garlic, coriander, lemon grass and peppercorns to a paste. Heat oil in a wok or frying pan and stir-fry the spicy paste for 15-20 seconds until fragrant. Add prawns, shallots or onion, chillies and tomatoes and stir-fry for 2-3 minutes.

Add fish sauce, oyster sauce and stock, bring to the boil and simmer for 2-3 minutes. Serve garnished with coriander sprigs.

Serves 4.

LOBSTER WITH BASIL DRESSING

4 lobsters, about 450-575 g (1-1¼ lb) each, cooked
   (see Note)
lamb's lettuce salad and lemon wedges, to serve
DRESSING:
55 g (2 oz) sun-dried tomatoes in olive oil, drained
   and chopped
1 small bunch basil, chopped
4 tablespoons walnut oil
2 tablespoons Spanish sherry vinegar
pepper

To make dressing, chop tomatoes and basil
together. Whisk together oil and vinegar,
then stir in tomatoes and basil. Season with
black pepper.

Using a large heavy knife and working from
head to tail along the back, split lobsters in
half. Remove and discard intestine that runs
through centre to tail, the stomach from
near the head, and the spongy gills.

Brush cut side of lobsters generously with
dressing and set aside for 15 minutes. Preheat
grill. Grill lobster for about 3 minutes. Meanwhile, gently warm remaining dressing in a
small saucepan. Brush lobster with dressing
and serve with lamb's lettuce salad and lemon
wedges. Serve remaining dressing separately.

Serves 4.

Note: If possible, order the lobsters from your
fishmonger and ask for them to be only three
quarters cooked. Use them the same day.

STIR-FRIED PRAWNS

300 g (10 oz) raw peeled prawns
3 tablespoons vegetable oil
1 teaspoon chopped garlic
½ teaspoon chopped fresh root ginger
1 tablespoon chopped spring onion
115 g (4 oz) straw mushrooms, halved lengthways
55 g (2 oz) water chestnuts, sliced
3 tablespoons fish sauce
1 tablespoon sugar
about 2-3 tablespoons chicken stock or water
1 teaspoon chilli sauce (optional)
salt and freshly ground black pepper
coriander sprigs, to garnish

Halve prawns lengthways. Heat oil in a wok
or pan and stir-fry the garlic, ginger and
spring onion for about 20 seconds. Add the
prawns, mushrooms and water chestnuts and
stir-fry for about 2 minutes.

Add fish sauce and sugar, stir for a few times,
then add stock or water. Bring to the boil
and stir for another minute or so. Finally, add
the chilli sauce, if using, and season with salt
and pepper. Garnish with coriander sprigs
and serve at once.

Serves 4.

Variation: This is a standard stir-fry recipe. If
preferred, use different types of fish or meat,
cut into small, thin slices, and cook with
other kind of vegetables.

CURRIED CRAB

SPICY CRAB

700 g (1½ lb) cooked large crab claws, thawed and
  dried, if frozen
1 tablespoon sunflower oil
2 cloves garlic, thinly sliced
1 large green pepper (capsicum), shredded
225 g (8 oz) small broccoli flowerets
5 tablespoons Chinese Vegetable Stock (see glossary)
1 tablespoon Madras curry paste
1 tablespoon light soy sauce
1 teaspoon brown sugar

1 clove garlic, chopped
2 shallots or the white parts of 3-4 spring onions,
  chopped
1 teaspoon chopped fresh root ginger
1 tablespoon chopped lemon grass
2-3 tablespoons vegetable oil
1 teaspoon chilli sauce
1 tablespoon sugar
3-4 tablespoons coconut milk
about 450 ml (16 fl oz/2 cups) chicken stock
3 tablespoons fish sauce
2 tablespoons lime juice or vinegar
meat from 1 large or 2 medium cooked crabs, cut
  into small pieces
salt and freshly ground black pepper
coriander sprigs, to garnish

Wrap the end of a rolling pin in cling film
and tap the main part of the crab claws until
the shell cracks, leaving pincers intact. Peel
away hard shell to expose crab flesh, leaving
shell on pincers. Heat oil in a non-stick or
well seasoned wok and stir-fry crab and garlic for 1-2 minutes until crab is lightly
browned. Drain on kitchen paper and set
aside.

Using a pestle and mortar, pound the garlic,
shallots or spring onions, ginger, and lemon
grass to a fine paste. Heat oil in a clay pot or
flameproof casserole, add the garlic mixture,
chilli sauce and sugar and stir-fry for about 1
minute. Add the coconut milk, stock, fish
sauce and lime juice or vinegar and bring to
the boil.

Mix together remaining ingredients and add
to wok. Simmer gently for 5 minutes, stirring
occasionally. Replace crab and garlic and
cook gently for 2-3 minutes, stirring to coat
crab with sauce. Serve immediately with
rice, vegetables and lemon wedges.

Serves 4.

Add the crab pieces and season with salt and
pepper. Blend well and cook for 3-4 minutes,
stirring constantly, then serve hot, garnished
with coriander sprigs.

Serves 4.

Note: Uncooked crabs can be used for this
dish, but increase the cooking time by about
8-10 minutes.

MALAY CURRIED CLAMS

24 steamer (soft-shell) clams
1 tablespoon vegetable oil
1 tablespoon sesame oil
2 cloves garlic, finely chopped
2.5 cm (1 in) piece fresh root ginger, peeled and
  finely chopped
1 tablespoon fermented black beans, rinsed and
  chopped
3 teaspoons curry paste or 6 teaspoons curry powder
250 ml (9 fl oz/1 cup) light fish or chicken stock
55 ml (2 fl oz/¼ cup) tomato ketchup (sauce)
2 tablespoons oyster sauce
1 tablespoon soy sauce
1 teaspoon Chinese chilli sauce
2 teaspoons cornflour dissolved in 3 tablespoons water
4 spring onions, thinly sliced

With stiff brush, scrub clams well. Cover with cold water and soak for about 1 hour. With a Chinese strainer, carefully remove clams from soaking liquid to a colander. (This leaves any sand or grit on the bottom.) Discard any clams that are not tightly closed. Heat oils in the wok, swirling to mix oils and coat wok. Add garlic, ginger and black beans and stir-fry for 30 seconds until fragrant. Stir in curry paste or powder and cook for 1 minute, stirring constantly.

Stir in clams, fish or chicken stock, tomato ketchup (sauce), oyster sauce, soy sauce and chilli sauce. Bring to the boil, cover and simmer for about 5 minutes until clams open. Stir cornflour mixture and stir into clams with spring onions. Stir until sauce thickens and spring onions turn a bright colour. Discard any unopened clams. Serve immediately with steamed rice or noodles.

Serves 2.

MUSSELS WITH BASIL

700 g (1½ lb) fresh mussels in shell, cleaned,
  bearded and rinsed
1 large clove garlic, chopped
7.5 cm (3 in) piece galangal, thickly sliced
2 stalks lemon grass, chopped
10 Thai holy basil sprigs
1 tablespoon fish sauce
Thai holy basil leaves, to garnish
Spicy Fish Sauce (see page 311), to serve

Place mussels, garlic, galangal, lemon grass, basil sprigs and fish sauce in a large saucepan. Add water to a depth of 1 cm (½ in), cover pan, bring to the boil and cook for about 5 minutes, shaking pan frequently, until mussels have opened; discard any that remain closed.

Transfer mussels to a large warmed bowl, or individual bowls, and strain over cooking liquid. Scatter over basil leaves. Serve with sauce to dip mussels into.

Serves 2-3.

MUSSELS IN TOMATO SAUCE

2 tablespoons olive oil
2 shallots, finely chopped
2 cloves garlic, crushed
150 ml (5 fl oz/⅔ cup) medium-bodied dry white
 wine
250 g (9 oz) tomatoes, peeled, seeded and chopped
finely grated rind 1 lemon
2 tablespoons capers, chopped
3 tablespoons chopped fresh parsley
1.5 kg (3 lb) fresh mussels, cleaned
salt and pepper
crusty bread, to serve

MUSSELS IN WHITE WINE

1 tablespoon olive oil
1 small onion, finely chopped
2 plum tomatoes, peeled, seeded and chopped
pinch chilli powder
500 ml (18 fl oz/2¼ cups) dry white wine
1.3 kg (3 lb) mussels, scrubbed and trimmed
salt and freshly ground black pepper
1 tablespoon chopped fresh flat-leaf parsley

Heat the oil in a large flameproof casserole. Add the onion and cook gently, stirring occasionally, for 5 minutes, until soft. Add the tomatoes, chilli powder and white wine.

In a large saucepan, heat oil, add shallots and garlic and cook gently until softened. Add wine, tomatoes, lemon rind, capers and half the parsley. Bring to the boil.

Bring to the boil. Add the mussels, cover tightly and cook over a high heat, shaking the casserole occasionally, for 3-4 minutes, until the mussels open. Discard any mussels that remain closed.

Add mussels to pan, cover and cook over a high heat for 3-4 minutes or until mussel shells have opened, shaking pan frequently; discard any mussels that remain closed. Season with salt and pepper, transfer to large bowls or soup plates, sprinkle over remaining parsley and serve with crusty bread.

Serves 2-3.

Season with salt and pepper, sprinkle with the parsley and serve.

Serves 4.

Note: Before cooking the mussels, discard any that are open and do not close when tapped sharply.

SCALLOPS WITH CASHEWS

55 ml (2 fl oz/¼ cup) dry sherry or rice wine
3 tablespoons tomato ketchup (sauce)
1 tablespoon oyster sauce
1 tablespoon wine vinegar
1 tablespoon sesame oil
1 teaspoon Chinese chilli sauce (or to taste)
1 tablespoon grated orange zest and 1 tablespoon
   orange juice
1 teaspoon cornflour
1 tablespoon vegetable oil
700 g (1½ lb) queen scallops
2 cloves garlic, finely chopped
4 spring onions, thinly sliced
175 g (6 oz) fresh asparagus, cut into 2.5 cm (1 in)
   pieces
150 g (5 oz) cashew nuts, lightly rinsed

In a medium bowl, combine dry sherry or rice wine, tomato ketchup (sauce), oyster sauce, wine vinegar, sesame oil, chilli sauce, orange zest and juice and cornflour. Heat the wok until hot, add oil and swirl to coat wok. Add scallops and stir-fry for 1-2 minutes until they begin to turn opaque. Remove to a bowl.

Add garlic, spring onions and asparagus and stir-fry for 2-3 minutes, until asparagus is bright green and tender but still crisp. Stir sauce ingredients and pour into the wok. Bring to simmering point. Return scallops to the wok and add the cashews. Stir-fry for 1 minute until scallops are heated through, tossing to coat all ingredients. Serve with rice garnished with strips of orange rind.

Serves 4.

SCALLOPS WITH VEGETABLES

3 tablespoons vegetable oil
1 teaspoon chopped garlic
1-2 small red chillies, seeded and chopped
2 shallots or 1 small onion, chopped
55 g (2 oz) mange tout (snow peas)
1 small carrot, thinly sliced
225 g (8 oz) fresh scallops, sliced
55 g (2 oz) sliced bamboo shoots
2 tablespoons black fungus, soaked and sliced
2-3 spring onions, cut into short sections
2 tablespoons fish sauce
1 teaspoon sugar
about 2-3 tablespoons chicken stock or water
1 tablespoon oyster sauce
salt and freshly ground black pepper
coriander sprigs, to garnish

Heat oil in a wok or pan and stir-fry garlic, chillies and shallots or onion for about 20 seconds. Add the mange tout (snow peas) and carrot and stir-fry for about 2 minutes. Add scallops, bamboo shoots, fungus and spring onions and stir-fry for 1 minute.

Add fish sauce and sugar, blend well and stir for 1 more minute, then add the stock or water. Bring to the boil and stir for a few more seconds. Add oyster sauce and season with salt and pepper. Garnish with coriander sprigs and serve at once.

Serves 4.

STIR-FRIED SCALLOPS

450 g (1 lb) fresh queen scallops, cleaned and
    trimmed
225 g (8 oz) baby sweetcorn
225 g (8 oz) mange tout (snow peas)
1 tablespoon sunflower oil
2 shallots, chopped
1 clove garlic, finely chopped
1 cm (½ in) piece fresh root ginger, peeled and finely
    chopped
2 tablespoons yellow bean sauce
1 tablespoon light soy sauce
1 teaspoon caster sugar
1 tablespoon dry sherry

Wash scallops and dry with kitchen paper.

Slice the baby sweetcorn in half lengthways
and top and tail the mange tout (snow peas).
Heat the oil in a non-stick or well seasoned
wok and stir-fry the shallots, garlic and ginger for 1 minute.

Add scallops, baby sweetcorn and mange
tout (snow peas) and stir-fry for 1 minute.
Stir in remaining ingredients and simmer for
4 minutes or until scallops and vegetables are
cooked through. Serve on a bed of rice.

Serves 4.

THAI CURRIED SEAFOOD

2 tablespoons vegetable oil
450 g (1 lb) sea scallops, cut in half lengthwise
1 onion, chopped
5 cm (2 in) piece fresh root ginger, peeled and finely
    chopped
4 cloves garlic, finely chopped
3 teaspoons curry paste or 6 teaspoons curry powder
1½ teaspoons each ground coriander and cumin
15 cm (6 in) stalk lemon grass, crushed
225 g (8 oz) can chopped tomatoes
115 ml (4 fl oz/½ cup) chicken stock
450 ml (16 fl oz/2 cups) unsweetened coconut milk
12 mussels, scrubbed and debearded
450 g (1 lb) cooked, peeled prawns, deveined
12 crab sticks, defrosted and dried if frozen
chopped fresh coriander and shaved coconut, to garnish

Heat the wok until hot and add 1 tablespoon
oil; swirl to coat wok. Add scallops and stir-
fry for 2-3 minutes until opaque and firm.
Remove to bowl. Add remaining oil to the
wok and add onion, ginger and garlic. Stir-
fry for 1-2 minutes until onion begins to
soften. Add curry paste or powder, coriander,
cumin and lemon grass. Stir-fry for 1-2
minutes. Add the canned tomatoes and the
stock. Bring to the boil, stirring frequently.
Simmer for 5 minutes until slightly reduced
and thickened. Add the coconut milk and
simmer for 2-3 minutes.

Stir mussels into sauce and cook, covered,
for 1-2 minutes, until mussels begin to open.
Stir in prawns, crab sticks cut into 1 cm
(½ in) pieces, and reserved scallops. Cook,
covered, 1-2 minutes more until all mussels
open and seafood is heated through. Remove
the lemon grass stalk and discard any mussels
that have not opened. Serve garnished with
chopped coriander and shaved coconut.
Serve with steamed rice.

Serves 6-8.

CHICKEN & TURKEY

CHICKEN WITH TARRAGON

2 tablespoons finely chopped fresh tarragon
55 g (2 oz/¼ cup) butter, softened
1.5 kg (3½ lb) chicken
salt and freshly ground black pepper
115 ml (4 fl oz/½ cup) dry white wine
55 ml (2 fl oz/¼ cup) double (thick) cream
tarragon sprigs, to garnish

Preheat oven to 200C (400F/Gas 6). Beat tarragon into butter then push butter between chicken breast and skin.

Season chicken with salt and pepper and put in a heavy flameproof casserole. Pour over wine. Cover tightly and cook in oven for 30 minutes. Lower oven temperature to 180C (350F/Gas 4) and cook for 1¼-1½ hours, until chicken is tender.

Transfer chicken to a warmed plate and keep warm. Tilt casserole and spoon off the fat, leaving behind cooking juices. Boil cooking juices to thicken to a light sauce. Reduce heat, stir in cream and simmer to thicken slightly. Carve the chicken, garnish with tarragon sprigs and serve with sauce.

Serves 4.

COQ AU VIN

25 g (1 oz/2 tablespoons) butter
115 g (4 oz) thick-cut smoked streaky bacon, chopped
18 button onions
225 g (8 oz) button mushrooms
olive oil for frying (optional)
6 chicken legs
1 onion, chopped
1 carrot, diced
2 cloves garlic, crushed
1½ tablespoons plain flour
550 ml (20 fl oz/2½ cups) red Burgundy wine
175 ml (6 fl oz/¾ cup) chicken stock
bouquet garni
salt and freshly ground black pepper
chopped fresh parsley, to garnish

Heat butter in a heavy flameproof casserole, add bacon and cook until crisp. Remove with a slotted spoon and drain on kitchen paper. Add button onions to casserole and cook, stirring occasionally, until golden. Remove with a slotted spoon and drain on kitchen paper. Add mushrooms to casserole, adding oil if necessary, and cook until lightly browned. Remove with a slotted spoon and drain on kitchen paper. Add chicken to casserole and cook over a moderately high heat until browned all over. Remove and drain on kitchen paper.

Add chopped onion and carrot to casserole and cook until lightly browned, adding garlic towards end. Sprinkle over flour and cook, stirring, for 2 minutes. Stir in wine and stock and bring to boil. Return all ingredients to casserole, add bouquet garni and salt and pepper, cover and cook very gently for 50-60 minutes. Remove chicken and vegetables, discard bouquet garni and boil sauce to thicken. Return chicken and vegetables to casserole. Garnish with parsley and serve.

Serves 6.

POULET PROVENÇAL

10 cloves garlic
1 tablespoon finely chopped fresh thyme
1 tablespoon finely chopped fresh marjoram
salt and freshly ground black pepper
1.5 kg (3½ lb) chicken, cut into eight
2 tablespoon lemon juice
55 ml (2 fl oz/¼ cup) olive oil
1 sprig of thyme
1 small sprig of rosemary
6 basil leaves, shredded
8 anchovy fillets, drained and chopped
4 beef tomatoes, peeled, seeded and chopped
150 ml (5 fl oz/⅔ cup) dry white wine
24 Niçoise olives
chopped fresh herbs and basil sprigs, to garnish

Crush two garlic cloves and mix with the chopped herbs and a small pinch of salt. Cut small incisions in chicken and insert a little herb mixture into each incision. Rub with lemon juice and pepper and leave in a cool place for 2 hours. Preheat oven to 160C (325F/Gas 3). Heat half the oil in a saucepan. Finely chop remaining garlic and add to pan with thyme, rosemary and basil. Cook, stirring occasionally, for 5 minutes. Stir in anchovy fillets, tomatoes, wine and pepper. Bring to the boil and simmer for 15 minutes.

Heat remaining oil in a heavy, flameproof casserole, add chicken and cook until browned all over. Pour over sauce, cover and cook in the oven for 45 minutes, turning chicken once or twice. Add olives and cook for 15 minutes. Garnish with mixed herbs and basil sprigs and serve.

Serves 4.

Note: Niçoise olives have a special flavour as they are marinated in oil and herbs. If they are not available, use plain black olives.

POULET BASQUAISE

3 red peppers (capsicum)
1.3 kg (3 lb) chicken, cut into eight
salt and freshly ground black pepper
3 tablespoons olive oil
2 onions, thinly sliced
3 cloves garlic, chopped
½ fresh red chilli, cored, seeded and chopped
4 ripe beef tomatoes, peeled, seeded and chopped
bouquet garni
115 g (4 oz) Bayonne or Parma ham, diced
115 ml (4 fl oz/½ cup) dry white wine
chopped fresh parsley, to garnish

Preheat grill. Grill peppers (capsicum), until charred and blistered all over.

Leave peppers (capsicum) until cool enough to handle, then peel. Halve, remove cores and seeds and cut flesh into strips. Season chicken with salt and pepper. Heat oil in a heavy flameproof casserole, add chicken and cook until browned all over. Remove with tongs or a slotted spoon, transfer to a large plate and set aside.

Add onions and garlic to casserole and cook, stirring occasionally, for 5 minutes, until soft. Stir in chilli, tomatoes and bouquet garni and simmer for 15 minutes. Stir in ham, wine and peppers (capsicum). Bring to the boil, add chicken and any juices on plate and season with pepper. Cover tightly and simmer gently for 50-60 minutes. Transfer chicken to warmed serving plates. Boil sauce to thicken, pour over chicken, garnish with chopped parsley and serve.

Serves 4.

CHICKEN CHASSEUR

1 tablespoon olive oil
45 g (1½ oz/3 tablespoons) butter
4 chicken quarters
3 shallots, finely chopped
1 clove garlic, finely chopped
1 tablespoon plain flour
150 g (5 oz) brown cap or shiitake mushrooms, sliced
250 ml (9 fl oz/1 cup) dry white wine
2 beef tomatoes, peeled, seeded and chopped
several sprigs of tarragon and parsley
salt and freshly ground black pepper
tarragon sprigs, to garnish

Heat oil and 25 g (1 oz/2 tablespoons) butter in a heavy flameproof casserole, add chicken and cook until browned all over.

Remove chicken and set aside. Add shallots and garlic to casserole and cook, stirring occasionally, for 5 minutes, until soft. Add flour and mushrooms and cook, stirring, until flour has browned lightly. Stir in wine and tomatoes. Bring to the boil, stirring.

Return chicken to casserole and add herbs and salt and pepper. Cover tightly and cook gently for 50-60 minutes. Remove chicken with a slotted spoon, transfer to warmed serving plates and keep warm. Remove herbs from sauce and discard. Boil sauce to thicken slightly. Lower heat and stir in remaining butter. Pour sauce over chicken, garnish with tarragon sprigs and serve.

Serves 4.

POULET AU VINAIGRE

1 tablespoon oil
15 g (½ oz/1 tablespoon) butter
4 chicken legs
1 onion, finely chopped
bouquet garni
4 ripe tomatoes, peeled, seeded and chopped
300 ml (10 fl oz/1¼ cups) red wine vinegar
2 teaspoons tomato purée (paste)
300 ml (10 fl oz/1¼ cups) chicken stock
salt and freshly ground black pepper
chopped fresh parsley, to garnish

Heat oil and butter in a heavy flameproof casserole. Add chicken and cook until lightly browned all over.

Remove chicken and set aside. Add onion to casserole and cook, stirring occasionally, for 5 minutes, until soft. Return chicken to casserole, add bouquet garni, cover and cook gently for 20 minutes, turning occasionally.

Add tomatoes to casserole, and cook, uncovered, until liquid has evaporated. Combine tomato purée (paste) and vinegar and add to casserole. Simmer until most of liquid has evaporated. Add stock and salt and pepper and simmer until reduced by half. Sprinkle with parsley and serve.

Serves 4.

GARLIC CHICKEN

1 bunch thyme
1.5 kg (3½ lb) chicken
2 heads garlic, separated into cloves but not peeled
salt and freshly ground black pepper
175 ml (6 fl oz/¾ cup) dry white wine
15 g (½ oz/1 tablespoon) butter, diced
thyme sprigs, to garnish

Preheat oven to 200C (400F/Gas 6). Put some thyme sprigs into cavity of chicken. Put chicken into a heavy flameproof casserole just large enough to hold chicken, and tuck remaining thyme sprigs and a few cloves of garlic around it.

Scatter over remaining garlic cloves, season with salt and pepper and pour over wine. Bring to the boil, cover tightly and cook in the oven for 30 minutes. Lower oven temperature to 180C (350F/Gas 4) and cook for 1¼-1½ hours.

Transfer chicken and garlic to a warmed serving plate and keep warm. Discard thyme. Tilt casserole and spoon off fat, leaving behind cooking juices. Boil cooking juices to thicken slightly. Remove from heat and stir in butter. Carve chicken, garnish with thyme sprigs and serve with garlic cloves and sauce.

Serves 4.

Note: Garlic cooked in this way has a mild sweet flavour. To eat, squeeze cloves out of skin and mash into sauce.

CHINESE BARBECUE CHICKEN

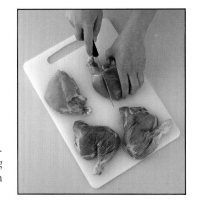

4 chicken quarters, about 225 g (8 oz) each
2 cloves garlic, finely chopped
2.5 cm (1 in) piece fresh root ginger, peeled and finely chopped
4 tablespoons hoisin sauce
2 tablespoons dry sherry
1 teaspoon chilli sauce
1 tablespoon dark soy sauce
1 tablespoon brown sugar
1 tablespoon chopped fresh chives, to garnish

Skin chicken quarters and trim away any fat. Wash and pat dry with kitchen paper. Using a sharp knife, score the top of the quarters in diagonal lines.

Place chicken in a shallow dish. Mix together all the remaining ingredients except the chives and spoon over the prepared quarters. Cover and chill overnight.

Preheat grill or barbecue. Place chicken on grill rack and cook for 20 minutes, turning once, until cooked through. Garnish with chives and serve with rice and salad.

Serves 4.

LEMON CHICKEN

1 egg white
350 g (12 oz) chicken breast, sliced
3 teaspoons cornflour
finely grated rind and juice 1 lemon
2 tablespoons dry sherry
1 teaspoon soy sauce
2 teaspoons clear honey
3 tablespoons vegetable oil
4 spring onions, sliced
55 g (2 oz) mange tout (snow peas), topped and
  tailed
½ red pepper (capsicum), finely sliced
55 g (2 oz) beansprouts

Whisk egg white until frothy. Stir in chicken,
2 teaspoons cornflour and lemon rind.

In another bowl, mix together the remaining
cornflour, sherry, lemon juice, soy sauce and
honey. Put to one side. Heat the oil in a wok
or large frying pan, add the chicken pieces a
few at a time to prevent them sticking
together. Stir-fry for 2 minutes or until the
chicken is cooked through.

Add the spring onions, mange tout (snow
peas), red pepper (capsicum) and beansprouts and continue to stir-fry for a further
1 minute. Add the lemon juice and cornflour
mixture and cook for 1-2 minutes, stirring
until the sauce thickens and coats the
chicken and vegetables.

Serves 4.

STIR-FRIED CHICKEN

225 g (8 oz) chicken fillet, boned and skinned
2 teaspoons cornflour
2 teaspoons fish sauce
salt and freshly ground pepper
2-3 tablespoons vegetable oil
½ teaspoon minced garlic
1 teaspoon finely chopped lemon grass
1 teaspoon chopped fresh root ginger
4-6 dried small red chillies
55 g (2 oz) mange-tout (snow peas), trimmed
½ red pepper (capsicum), cored and cut into cubes
55 g (2 oz) sliced bamboo shoots, drained
1 teaspoon sugar
1 tablespoon rice vinegar
2 tablespoons oyster sauce
½ teaspoon sesame oil

Cut chicken into bite-size slices or cubes.
Mix cornflour with 1 tablespoon water. Place
chicken in a bowl with cornflour paste and
fish sauce. Season with salt and pepper and
leave to marinate for 20-25 minutes. Heat
oil in a wok or frying pan and stir-fry the
garlic, lemon grass, ginger and chillies for 30
seconds. Add the chicken pieces and stir-fry
for about 1 minute until the colour of the
chicken changes.

Add vegetables and cook for 2-3 minutes,
stirring constantly, then add sugar, vinegar,
oyster sauce and 3-4 tablespoons water.
Blend well, bring to boil and add the sesame
oil. Serve at once with flat rice noodles.

Serves 4.

Variation: Use chicken stock instead of the
3-4 tablespoons water.

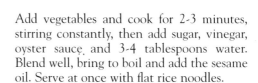

GRILLED CHICKEN DRUMSTICKS

1-2 cloves garlic, chopped
1-2 sticks lemon grass, chopped
2 shallots, chopped
1-2 small red or green chillies, chopped
1 tablespoon chopped fresh coriander
55 ml (2 fl oz/¼ cup) fish sauce
6-8 chicken drumsticks, skinned
lettuce leaves
Spicy Fish Sauce (see page 311), to serve

Using a pestle and mortar, pound garlic, lemon grass, shallots, chillies and coriander to a paste.

In a mixing bowl, thoroughly blend pounded mixture with the fish sauce to a smooth paste. Add drumsticks and coat well with the paste, then cover the bowl, and leave to marinate for 2-3 hours, turning drumsticks every 30 minutes or so.

Prepare barbecue or preheat grill. Cook the drumsticks over barbecue or under the grill for 10-15 minutes, turning frequently and basting with the marinade remaining in the bowl for the first 5 minutes only. Serve hot on a bed of lettuce leaves with the Spicy Fish Sauce as a dip.

Serves 4-6.

CHICKEN & BLACK BEAN SAUCE

1 teaspoon cornflour
4 teaspoons light soy sauce
2.5 cm (1 in) piece fresh root ginger, finely chopped
1 clove garlic, crushed
350 g (12 oz) skinned and boned chicken breasts
1 green pepper (capsicum), deseeded
8 canned water chestnuts, drained
4 spring onions
2 tablespoons vegetable oil
55 g (2 oz/½ cup) cashew nuts
5 tablespoons dry sherry
175 g (6 oz) bottle black bean sauce

In a bowl, mix together the cornflour, soy sauce, ginger and garlic. Slice the chicken into thin strips and coat in the cornflour mixture and leave to stand for 10 minutes. Dice the green pepper (capsicum), cut the water chestnuts in half and slice the spring onions into 2.5 cm (1 in) lengths; set aside.

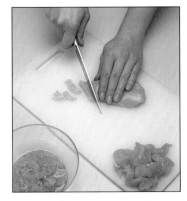

In a wok or large frying pan, heat the oil, add the chicken and stir-fry for 2 minutes, then add the pepper (capsicum), spring onions and water chestnuts and stir-fry for a further 1 minute. Add the cashew nuts, sherry and black bean sauce and stir-fry until sauce thickens.

Serves 4.

PEPPERED CHICKEN SKEWERS

450 g (1 lb) skinless, boneless chicken breasts,
   cubed
1 tablespoon rice wine
1 tablespoon dark soy sauce
grated rind and juice 1 lime
2 teaspoons brown sugar
1 teaspoon ground cinnamon
1 teaspoon sunflower oil
1 teaspoon Szechuan peppercorns, toasted and
   crushed
strips lime rind, to garnish

Place chicken in a shallow dish. Mix together
rice wine, soy sauce, lime rind and juice,
sugar and cinnamon. Pour over chicken.

Cover chicken and chill for 1 hour.
Meanwhile, soak 8 bamboo skewers in cold
water for 30 minutes. Remove chicken
pieces from marinade, reserving marinade,
and thread chicken on to skewers.

Preheat grill. Brush grill rack lightly with oil
and place skewers on rack. Brush with marinade and sprinkle with peppercorns. Grill for
3 minutes, turn, brush again and grill for a
further 2-3 minutes until cooked through.
Drain on kitchen paper. Garnish with lime
rind and serve with wedges of lime and
shredded Chinese leaves.

Serves 4.

CHICKEN FAJITAS

55 ml (2 fl oz/¼ cup) dry white wine
finely grated rind and juice 2 limes
1 tablespoon Worcestershire sauce
2 teaspoons brown sugar
½ teaspoon dried basil
½ teaspoon dried oregano
1 clove garlic, crushed
4 skinned and boned chicken breasts
6 teaspoons vegetable oil
8 spring onions, sliced
1 red pepper (capsicum), deseeded and sliced
1 green pepper (capsicum), deseeded and sliced
8 wheat flour tortillas, warmed gently
150 ml (5fl oz/⅔ cup) thick sour cream
ripe avocado, peeled and chopped

Prepare the marinade for the chicken. In a
bowl, mix together the wine, rind and juice
of the limes, Worcestershire sauce, sugar,
basil, oregano and garlic. Slice the chicken
breast into thin strips and add to the
marinade. Mix well and leave to marinate
for 30-40 minutes, stirring from time to time.
In a pan, heat 2 tablespoons oil and add the
spring onions and peppers (capsicums) and
fry until the onions are starting to colour, but
the vegetables are still crisp. Remove from
the pan and put to one side. Drain the
chicken, reserving the marinade.

Heat the remaining oil, and when very hot,
add the chicken and fry quickly until golden
brown. Remove from the pan with a slotted
spoon; set aside. Add the reserved marinade
to the pan and boil until thickened and
reduced. Return the chicken and peppers
and mix well until all ingredients are coated
in the marinade. Put tortillas on a plate,
place the chicken mixture in the middle,
spoon over some thick sour cream and
chopped avocado. Roll up and serve.

Serves 4.

CHICKEN IN VINEGAR SAUCE

4 boneless chicken breasts, divided into fillets
salt and freshly ground black pepper
85 ml (3 fl oz/⅓ cup) olive oil
12 cloves garlic
1 small onion, finely chopped
about 3 tablespoons sherry vinegar
1 tablespoon paprika
1½ tablespoons chopped fresh oregano
2 tablespoons fresh breadcrumbs
300 ml (10 fl oz/1¼ cups) chicken stock
fresh herbs, to garnish

Season chicken with salt and pepper. Heat oil in a heavy flameproof casserole, add chicken and cook for 10 minutes.

Meanwhile, slice 4 of the garlic cloves. Add sliced garlic to casserole with the onion and cook until chicken is lightly browned all over, about 5 minutes more.

Remove chicken from casserole, stir in vinegar and boil for 2-3 minutes. Pound remaining garlic with a little salt, the paprika and oregano, then stir in bread-crumbs and a quarter of the stock. Pour over chicken, add remaining stock and cook for about 20 minutes until chicken is tender and sauce fairly thick. Adjust seasoning and amount of vinegar, if necessary. Serve garnished with fresh herbs.

Serves 4.

CHICKEN KIEV

115 g (4 oz/½ cup) unsalted butter, softened
3 cloves garlic, crushed
finely grated rind ½ lemon
1 tablespoon chopped fresh parsley
salt and pepper
4 skinned and boned chicken breasts
2 eggs, beaten
175 g (6 oz/3 cups) fresh white breadcrumbs
oil for deep frying

Beat together the softened butter, crushed garlic, grated lemon rind, parsley and salt and pepper. Transfer to a piping bag fitted with a plain 0.5 cm (¼ in) nozzle.

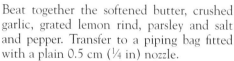

Lay the chicken breasts on a board and insert a sharp knife into the breast to form a pocket. Take the piping bag and pipe the butter into the pocket (do not over-fill or the butter will burst through the flesh). Leave to refrigerate for 25 minutes.

Dip a filled chicken breast into the beaten eggs, then roll in the breadcrumbs. Repeat once more so chicken is well coated. Repeat with the remaining chicken. Half-fill a deep fat pan or fryer with oil and heat to 190C (375F). Lower in the chicken breasts, 2 at a time, and fry for 8-10 minutes or until cooked through and golden brown. Drain on absorbent kitchen paper and serve immediately with a squeeze of lemon.

Serves 4.

ROQUEFORT VERONIQUE

25 g (1 oz/6 teaspoons) butter
1 tablespoon oil
4 skinned and boned chicken breasts
1 leek, trimmed and chopped
2 teaspoons plain flour
175 ml (6 fl oz/¾ cup) milk
70 g (2½ oz) Roquefort cheese
85 ml (3 fl oz/⅓ cup) single (light) cream
150 g (5 oz) seedless green grapes, skinned
chopped fresh parsley, to garnish

In a frying pan, heat the butter and oil and cook the chicken on all sides until golden.

Reduce the heat, stir in the chopped leek, cover and continue cooking for 30 minutes until the juices of the chicken run clear when pierced. Remove the chicken from the pan and set aside on a warmed serving plate.

Sprinkle the flour into the pan and cook for 1 minute, remove from the heat and gradually add the milk. Return to the heat and, stirring, bring to the boil and cook for 2 minutes until thickened. Add the cheese, cream and grapes and cook for a further 5 minutes, stirring all the time. Pour over the chicken and garnish with chopped fresh parsley.

Serves 4.

GRILLED CHICKEN & HERBS

4 chicken breasts, on the bone, about
    175 g (6 oz) each
2 cloves garlic, peeled and sliced
4 sprigs of fresh rosemary
6 tablespoons olive oil
grated rind and juice ½ lemon
2 tablespoons dry white wine
salt and pepper
½ teaspoon Dijon mustard
2 tablespoons balsamic vinegar
1 teaspoon sugar

Make several incisions in the chicken breasts and insert pieces of garlic and rosemary. Place the chicken breasts in a flameproof dish.

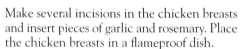

Mix together 2 tablespoons olive oil with the rind and juice of ½ lemon, the white wine and salt and pepper and pour over the chicken breasts and leave to marinate for 45 minutes. Preheat grill.

Place the chicken breast, skin-sides down, in the dish and cook under the hot grill for 5 minutes. Turn over and spoon the marinade over the top and grill for a further 10 minutes until the skin is crisp and brown. Whisk together the mustard, vinegar, sugar, salt and pepper and remaining oil. Add any cooking juices or marinade from the pan and spoon over the chicken to serve.

Serves 4.

TANDOORI CHICKEN

4 chicken leg quarters, skinned
juice 1 lemon
salt
2 teaspoons ground turmeric
2 teaspoons paprika
1 teaspoon garam masala
1 teaspoon ground cardamom
½ teaspoon chilli powder
pinch saffron powder
2 cloves garlic, crushed
2 teaspoons chopped fresh root ginger
1 tablespoon olive oil
200 ml (7 fl oz/¾ cup) natural yogurt

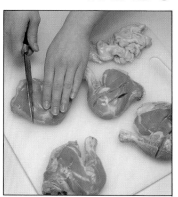

Cut deep diagonal cuts in the chicken flesh.

Sprinkle with lemon juice and a little salt. Mix together all the remaining ingredients and use to coat the chicken quarters, cover and leave in a cool place to marinate for 4 hours or overnight.

Preheat grill and cook chicken for 25 minutes, brushing with any excess marinade and turning frequently until the chicken is tender and juices run clear when chicken leg is pierced with a knife. A slight blackening of the chicken gives an authentic look. Serve with wedges of lemon, boiled rice and an onion salad.

Serves 4.

TIKKA KEBABS

150 ml (5 fl oz/⅔ cup) natural yogurt
1 tablespoon grated fresh root ginger
2 cloves garlic, crushed
1 teaspoon chilli powder
1 teaspoon ground cumin
1 teaspoon turmeric
1 tablespoon coriander seeds
juice 1 lemon
½ teaspoon salt
2 tablespoons chopped fresh coriander
350 g (12 oz) chicken meat, cubed
RAITA:
150 ml (5 fl oz/⅔ cup) natural yogurt
2 teaspoons mint jelly
85 g (3 oz) finely chopped cucumber
2 spring onions, finely chopped

Blend the first 10 ingredients in a blender or food processor until smooth. Pour into a bowl. Stir in the cubed chicken, cover and allow to stand overnight in the refrigerator.

Preheat grill. Thread chicken onto skewers and cook under the hot grill for 15-20 minutes, turning frequently and brushing with any remaining marinade. In a bowl, mix together the raita ingredients. Serve the kebabs on a bed of pilau rice, garnished with sprigs of coriander and lemon wedges. Hand the raita separately.

Serves 4.

CHICKEN & CORN FRITTERS

1 banana
1 egg
85 g (3 oz) cooked chicken, finely chopped
200 g (7 oz) can sweetcorn kernels, drained
2 spring onions, finely chopped
½ teaspoon ground cumin
2 teaspoons chopped fresh coriander
salt and cayenne pepper
85 g (3 oz/¾ cup) self-raising flour
oil for frying

Mash the banana. Mix in the egg, chicken, sweetcorn, spring onions, cumin, coriander, salt and a pinch of cayenne pepper. Add the flour and form a soft batter.

Heat oil in a heavy frying pan or saucepan and add spoonfuls of the mixture, cooking for about 1 minute, turning halfway through cooking, until golden brown.

Remove from the pan with a slotted spoon and drain on absorbent kitchen paper. Serve the fritters warm with a chilli dip or relish.

Serves 4.

CHICKEN WITH SHERRY

4 tablespoons raisins
225 ml (8 fl oz/1 cup) oloroso sherry
3 tablespoons olive oil
1.75 kg (3½ lb) chicken, cut into 8 pieces
1 Spanish onion, finely chopped
1 clove garlic, finely chopped
225 ml (8 fl oz/1 cup) chicken stock
salt and freshly ground black pepper
4 tablespoons pine nuts

In a small bowl, soak raisins in sherry for 30 minutes.

In a flameproof casserole, heat 2 tablespoons oil, add chicken and cook gently until lightly and evenly browned, about 10 minutes. Transfer to absorbent kitchen paper to drain. Add onion and garlic to casserole and cook gently, stirring occasionally, until softened and lightly coloured, about 7 minutes. Strain raisins and set aside.

Stir sherry into casserole. Simmer until reduced by half. Add stock, chicken and seasoning, bring to boil, then simmer gently until chicken is cooked, about 35 minutes. In a small pan, fry nuts in remaining oil until lightly coloured. Drain on absorbent kitchen paper, then stir into casserole with raisins. Transfer chicken to a warm serving dish. Boil liquid in casserole to concentrate slightly. Pour over chicken.

Serves 4.

CHICKEN WITH SALSA VERDE

4 small skinless chicken breasts
8 tablespoons chopped fresh parsley
1 clove garlic, finely chopped
4 tablespoons chopped fresh mint
1 tablespoon finely chopped capers
1 tablespoon finely chopped gherkins
finely grated rind and juice 1 lemon
100 ml (3½ fl oz/⅓ cup) olive oil
salt and freshly ground black pepper

Place chicken breasts in a sauté pan, cover with water and bring to the boil. Simmer very gently for 15-20 minutes until cooked. Allow to cool completely in the water.

In a bowl, mix together the parsley, garlic, mint, capers, gherkins, lemon juice and rind. Gradually beat in olive oil and season to taste. Do not do this in a food processor or the texture will be ruined.

Thickly slice each chicken breast crossways and arrange on a plate, spoon a little salsa verde over it and serve the rest separately. Serve with salad.

Serves 4.

LEMON & CHILLI CHICKEN

1.5 kg (3½ lb) corn-fed or free-range chicken,
* jointed into 8*
4 ripe juicy lemons
8 cloves garlic
1 small red chilli, split, seeds removed, and chopped
1 tablespoon honey
4 tablespoons chopped fresh parsley
salt and freshly ground black pepper

Place chicken joints in a shallow ovenproof baking dish. Squeeze juice from the lemons and pour into a small bowl. Reserve the lemon halves.

Remove skin from 2 of the garlic cloves, crush them and add to lemon juice with the chilli and honey. Stir well and pour mixture over the chicken, tucking the lemon halves around joints. Cover and leave to marinate for at least 2 hours, turning once or twice.

Preheat oven to 200C (400F) Gas 6. Turn the chicken skin side up and place lemon halves cut side down around the joints with the remaining whole garlic. Roast in oven for 45 minutes or until golden brown and tender. Stir in the parsley, taste and season. Garnish with the roasted lemon halves and serve with puréed potatoes.

Serves 4.

MOROCCAN-STYLE CHICKEN

1.3 kg (3 lb) chicken, cut into 8 pieces
4 tablespoons olive oil
grated rind and juice of 1 lemon
1 teaspoon each ground cinnamon, ground ginger
  and ground cumin
½ teaspoon salt
½ teaspoon cayenne pepper (or to taste)
1 onion, chopped
3-4 cloves garlic, finely chopped
1 red pepper (capsicum), diced
1 tomato, peeled, seeded and chopped
250 ml (9 fl oz/1 cup) chicken stock or water
16 stoned prunes
55 ml (2 fl oz/¼ cup) honey
1 large lemon, thinly sliced
toasted almonds and chopped fresh parsley, to garnish

In a large shallow baking dish, combine chicken pieces with 2 tablespoons olive oil, lemon rind and juice, cinnamon, ginger, cumin, salt and cayenne pepper to taste. Work the spices into the chicken pieces, cover and leave to marinate in the refrigerator for 4-6 hours or overnight. Heat the wok until hot. Add 1 tablespoon oil and swirl to coat. Arrange marinated chicken pieces on bottom and side of wok in a single layer and stir-fry for 6-8 minutes, until golden brown. Remove chicken pieces to the cleaned baking dish.

Add remaining oil, onion, garlic and red pepper (capsicum) to wok. Stir-fry for 2-3 minutes. Add tomato and stock or water and bring to simmering point, stirring. Return chicken and marinade to sauce. Simmer, covered, for 35-40 minutes until chicken is tender, adding prunes, honey and lemon slices after 20 minutes cooking. Remove chicken to serving dish, spoon sauce over and sprinkle with almonds and parsley. Serve with cous cous.

Serves 4.

FLEMISH BRAISED CHICKEN

55 g (2 oz/¼ cup) butter
1.8 kg (4 lb) chicken
450 g (1 lb) leeks, sliced
225 g (8 oz) carrots, sliced
½ head celery, chopped
115 g (4 oz) button mushrooms, halved
550 ml (20 fl oz/2½ cups) chicken stock
2 bay leaves
12 small new potatoes
250 ml (9 fl oz/1 cup) dry white wine
70 ml (2½ fl oz/⅓ cup) double (thick) cream
2 egg yolks
flat-leaf parsley sprigs and chopped parsley, to garnish

Melt the butter in a flameproof casserole. Add the chicken and brown all over.

Remove from the casserole. Preheat oven to 200C (400F/Gas 6). Add the leeks, carrots, celery and mushrooms to the casserole and stir well. Cover and cook for 5-10 minutes, until soft. Add the stock and bay leaves. Bring to the boil and add the chicken. Cover and cook in the oven for 30 minutes. Add the potatoes and cook for 30 minutes. Lift out the chicken and remove the vegetables with a slotted spoon. Keep warm.

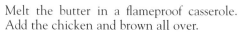

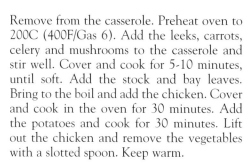

Add the wine to the casserole and bring to the boil. Reduce to a simmer. In a large bowl, mix together the cream and the egg yolks. Pour the simmering stock on to the cream mixture, stirring constantly. Return to the casserole and heat gently. Do not boil. Return the vegetables to the casserole. Carve the chicken, garnish with flat-leaf parsley sprigs and chopped parsley and serve with the vegetables and sauce.

Serves 6.

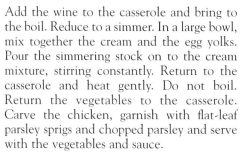

CORIANDER CHICKEN

2 teaspoons sunflower oil
1 clove garlic, finely chopped
1 shallot, finely chopped
350 g (12 oz) lean cooked skinless chicken, diced
1 teaspoon ground coriander
2 teaspoons dark soy sauce
freshly ground black pepper
2 tablespoons chopped fresh coriander
115 g (4 oz) bean sprouts
115 g (4 oz) grated carrot
25 g (1 oz) fresh coriander leaves
2 nectarines, sliced
2 bananas, halved, sliced and tossed in juice
 1 small lemon

Heat oil in a non-stick or well seasoned wok and stir-fry garlic and shallot for 1 minute. Add chicken, ground coriander, soy sauce and black pepper and stir-fry for 2-3 minutes until chicken is lightly browned. Remove from heat and stir in chopped coriander.

Mix together the bean sprouts, grated carrot and coriander leaves. Place on serving plates and top with warm chicken mixture. Arrange nectarine and banana slices around the edge of each salad and serve immediately.

Serves 4.

SPICY CHICKEN WINGS

1 tablespoon light soy sauce
1 tablespoon dry sherry or rice wine
1 kg (2¼ lb) chicken wings, tips removed and wings cut into 2 pieces at joint
1 tablespoon peanut oil
2.5 cm (1 in) fresh root ginger, peeled and chopped
2 cloves garlic, finely chopped
3 tablespoons black beans, coarsely chopped
115 ml (4 fl oz/½ cup) chicken stock
2 tablespoons soy sauce
1 teaspoon Chinese chilli sauce
4-6 spring onions, thinly sliced
175 g (6 oz) thin green beans, cut into 5 cm (2 in) pieces
2 tablespoons chopped peanuts and fresh coriander leaves, to garnish

In a shallow baking dish, combine soy sauce, dry sherry or rice wine and chicken wings. Toss well and leave to stand, covered, 1 hour. Heat the wok until hot. Add peanut oil and swirl to coat wok. Add ginger and garlic and stir-fry for 1 minute. Working in 2 batches if necessary, add chicken wings and stir-fry for 3-5 minutes until golden brown. Stir in black beans, stock, soy sauce and chilli sauce. If working in batches, return all chicken wings to the wok.

Bring to the boil, reduce the heat and cook for 4-6 minutes, stirring frequently. Stir in spring onions and green beans and cook for 2-3 minutes more until chicken is tender and juices run clear. Sprinkle with chopped peanuts and garnish with coriander leaves.

Serves 4-6.

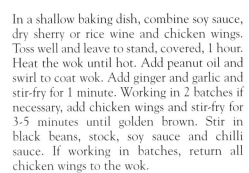

MOZZARELLA CHICKEN

4 skinless, boneless chicken breasts
2 teaspoons pesto
85 g (3 oz) smoked Mozzarella cheese, thinly sliced
4 slices Parma ham
25 g (1 oz/2 tablespoons) butter
85 g (3 oz) shallots, very finely chopped
150 ml (5 fl oz/⅔ cup) dry white wine
1 teaspoon Dijon mustard
salt and freshly ground black pepper
basil sprigs, to garnish

Cut a horizontal slit along each chicken breast to form a pocket. Spread a little pesto in each pocket.

Put the Mozzarella slices into the pockets. Wrap a slice of Parma ham around each chicken breast. Tie with fine string or cotton. Melt the butter in a frying pan, add the shallots and cook gently for 3 minutes until soft. Add the chicken breasts and cook until lightly browned on each side. Pour in the wine. Bring to the boil, cover and simmer for 20 minutes until the chicken is cooked through and tender.

Remove the chicken with a slotted spoon and keep warm. Stir the mustard into the pan. Season with salt and pepper and allow to bubble for 1 minute. Remove the string or cotton from the chicken. With a sharp knife, slice each breast and arrange on warmed serving plates. Pour the sauce over the chicken, garnish with basil sprigs and serve.

Serves 4.

Note: Use plain Mozzarella if the smoked variety is unavailable.

CHICKEN CRUMBLE

1 tablespoon olive oil
450 g (1 lb) skinless, boneless chicken breast, cubed
1 leek, sliced
225 g (8 oz) mushrooms, thinly sliced
115 g (4 oz) frozen peas
450 ml (16 fl oz/2 cups) Greek yogurt
2 teaspoons wholegrain mustard
salt and freshly ground black pepper
55 g (2 oz/⅔ cup) rolled oats
55 g (2 oz/½ cup) wholemeal flour
55 g (2 oz/¼ cup) butter
55 g (2 oz/1 cup) fresh wholemeal breadcrumbs
1 tablespoon grated Parmesan cheese
2 teapoons dried thyme
1 tablespoon sesame seeds
thyme sprigs, to garnish

Heat the oil in a large flameproof casserole. Add the chicken cubes and cook, stirring, until golden on all sides. Add the leek and cook, stirring occasionally, for 10 minutes, until the leek is soft. Preheat oven to 200C (400F/Gas 6). Add the mushrooms and peas to the casserole and cook for 3-5 minutes, until the peas have thawed. Remove from the heat and stir in the Greek yogurt, mustard and salt and pepper.

Put the oats and flour in a bowl and rub in the butter until the mixture resembles breadcrumbs. Stir in the breadcrumbs, Parmesan cheese, thyme and sesame seeds. Sprinkle the mixture evenly over the top of the chicken and bake for 40-45 minutes, until the topping is golden brown. Garnish with thyme sprigs and serve.

Serves 4.

LEMON & CORIANDER CHICKEN

4 chicken thighs, skinned
4 chicken drumsticks, skinned
55 ml (2 fl oz/¼ cup) vegetable oil
5 cm (2 in) piece fresh root ginger, grated
4 cloves garlic, crushed
1 fresh green chilli, seeded and finely chopped
½ teaspoon turmeric
1 teaspoon ground cumin
1 teaspoon ground coriander
salt and cayenne pepper
grated peel and juice 1 lemon
115 g (4 oz) fresh coriander leaves, chopped
coriander leaves and lemon slices, to garnish

APRICOT & CHICKEN CURRY

1.15 kg (2½ lb) chicken joints, skinned
½ teaspoon chilli powder
3 teaspoons garam masala
2.5 cm (1 in) piece fresh root ginger, grated
2 cloves garlic, crushed
125 g (4 oz/1 cup) ready-to-eat dried apricots
2 tablespoons vegetable oil
2 onions, finely sliced
400 g (14 oz) can chopped tomatoes
3 teaspoons sugar
6 teaspoons white wine vinegar
salt

Wash chicken joints and pat dry with absorbent kitchen paper. Heat oil in a large frying pan, add chicken, and fry, stirring frequently, until browned all over. Remove from pan with a slotted spoon and set aside. Add ginger and garlic to pan and fry for 1 minute. Stir in chilli, turmeric, cumin and ground coriander and season with salt and cayenne pepper, then cook for 1 minute more.

Wash chicken and pat dry with absorbent kitchen paper. Cut each joint into 4 pieces and put in a large bowl. Add chilli powder, garam masala, ginger and garlic and toss well to coat chicken pieces. Cover and leave in a cool place for 2-3 hours, to allow chicken to absorb flavours. In a separate bowl, put apricots and 150 ml (5 fl oz/⅔ cup) water and leave to soak for 2-3 hours.

Return chicken to pan, add 125 ml (4 fl oz/ ½ cup) water and lemon peel and juice. Bring to the boil, then cover and cook over a medium heat for 25-30 minutes or until chicken is tender. Stir in chopped coriander, then serve hot, garnished with fresh coriander leaves and lemon slices.

Serves 4.

Variation: Use fresh parsley, or parsley and mint, instead of coriander, if preferred.

Heat oil in a large heavy-based pan and add chicken. Fry over a high heat for 5 minutes or until browned all over. Remove from pan and set aside. Add onions to pan and cook, stirring, for about 5 minutes, until soft. Return chicken to pan with tomatoes and cook, covered, over a low heat for 20 minutes. Drain apricots, add to pan with sugar and vinegar. Season with salt. Simmer, covered, for 10-15 minutes. Serve hot.

Serves 4.

ARABIAN POUSSIN

3 teaspoons olive oil
1 small red onion, finely chopped
225 g (8 oz/1¼ cups) couscous
350 ml (12 fl oz/1½ cups) chicken stock
25 g (1 oz) no-need-to-soak dried apricots, finely
  chopped
15 g (½ oz/2 tablespoons) raisins
grated rind and juice of ½ lemon
25 g (1 oz/¼ cup) toasted pine nuts
1 tablespoon chopped fresh mint
4 poussins
salt and pepper
150 ml (5 fl oz/⅔ cup) dry white wine
2 teaspoons mint jelly

Preheat oven to 180C (350F/Gas 4). In a pan, heat 1 tablespoon oil and gently fry the onion until soft. Put the couscous into a bowl and add 225 ml (8 fl oz/1 cup) of the stock, the fried onion, apricots, raisins and the lemon rind and juice and leave to stand for 15 minutes. Stir in the pine nuts and mint. Loosen the skin around the breast of each poussin and carefully push the stuffing round the meat, securing the skin in place with a wooden cocktail stick. Use any excess stuffing to place under the poussins in a roasting tin.

Brush the poussins with the remaining oil and sprinkle with salt and black pepper. Roast in the oven for 50-60 minutes, basting occasionally. Remove the poussins from the roasting tin and set aside. Pour the remaining stock, wine and mint jelly into the pan and stir together over a high heat, bring to the boil and spoon over the poussins.

Serves 4.

SPICY CHICKEN PATTIES

575 g (1¼ lb) boneless chicken breasts (fillets),
  skinned
85 g (3 oz/1½ cups) fresh breadcrumbs
4 spring onions, finely chopped
3 tomatoes, skinned, seeded and chopped
3 tablespoons chopped fresh coriander
2.5 cm (1 in) piece fresh root ginger, grated
1 clove garlic, crushed
1 teaspoon ground cumin
1 teaspoon garam masala
salt and cayenne pepper
1 egg, beaten
55 ml (2 fl oz/¼ cup) vegetable oil
tomato wedges and spring onion tassels, to garnish

Wash chicken breasts (fillets) and pat dry with absorbent kitchen paper. Finely mince chicken and put into a large bowl with half the breadcrumbs and the onions, tomatoes, coriander, ginger, garlic, cumin, garam masala, salt and cayenne pepper to taste, and egg. Mix thoroughly, then divide into 18 pieces and form into patties. Roll patties in remaining breadcrumbs to coat all over.

Heat oil in a large frying pan. Fry patties in 2 or 3 batches for 10-12 minutes, until crisp and golden brown on both sides and no longer pink in centres. Drain on absorbent kitchen paper. Serve hot, garnished with tomato wedges and spring onion tassels.

Serves 6.

Note: Patties can be prepared up to 12 hours in advance and chilled.

POUSSINS WITH WATERCRESS

4 small oven-ready poussins
watercress sprigs, to garnish
STUFFING:
115 g (4 oz/2 cups) fresh wholemeal breadcrumbs
55 g (2 oz) ready-to-eat dried apricots, chopped
1 small bunch watercress, chopped
55 g (2 oz/½ cup) hazelnuts, chopped
salt and freshly ground black pepper
1 egg yolk
WATERCRESS SAUCE:
1 onion, finely chopped
1 bunch watercress, chopped
115 ml (4 fl oz/½ cup) dry white wine
1 tablespoon chopped fresh tarragon
1 teaspoon lemon juice
55 ml (2 fl oz/¼ cup) Greek yogurt

Preheat oven to 200C (400F/Gas 6). To make the stuffing, mix together the bread-crumbs, apricots, watercress, hazelnuts and salt and pepper. Bind together with the egg yolk. Use to stuff the cavity of each poussin. Place the poussins in a shallow flameproof dish and roast for 50-60 minutes, until cooked through. To test, pierce the thigh with a skewer: if the juices run clear the poussins are cooked. Remove the poussins from the dish and keep warm.

To make the watercress sauce, add the onion to the cooking juices in the dish and cook gently, stirring occasionally, for 5 minutes, until soft. Add the chopped watercress and stir well. Add the white wine, tarragon and lemon juice and heat gently. Stir in the Greek yogurt and season with salt and pep-per. Heat gently to warm through. Pour the sauce on to warmed serving plates and place the poussins on top. Garnish with watercress and serve.

Serves 4.

GINGER TURKEY & CABBAGE

300 ml (10 fl oz/1¼ cups) red wine
2 tablespoons red wine vinegar
115 g (4 oz) sultanas
225 g (8 oz) ready-to-eat dried apricots, halved
2.5 cm (1 in) piece fresh root ginger, peeled and grated
2 cloves garlic, crushed
salt and freshly ground black pepper
4 turkey breast fillets, about 175 g (6 oz) each
½ red cabbage, shredded
flat-leaf parsley sprigs, to garnish

In a large bowl, mix together the red wine, vinegar, sultanas, apricots, ginger, garlic and salt and pepper. Add the turkey.

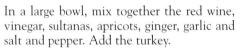

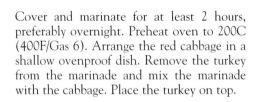

Cover and marinate for at least 2 hours, preferably overnight. Preheat oven to 200C (400F/Gas 6). Arrange the red cabbage in a shallow ovenproof dish. Remove the turkey from the marinade and mix the marinade with the cabbage. Place the turkey on top.

Cook in the oven for 45-50 minutes, until the turkey is tender and cook through. Garnish with flat-leaf parsley and serve.

Serves 4.

CREAMY PAPRIKA TURKEY

55 g (2 oz/4 tablespoons) butter
1 onion, finely chopped
1 teaspoon paprika
250 ml (9 fl oz/1 cup) whipping cream
3 teaspoons Dijon mustard
2 tablespoons chopped fresh dill
salt and freshly ground black pepper
700 g (1½ lb) turkey breast fillets, cut crosswise
    into 2.5 cm (1 in) strips
6 tablespoons seasoned flour
2 tablespoons vegetable oil
225 g (8 oz) tagliatelle or egg noodles
300 g (10 oz) frozen peas
2 teaspoons caraway seeds
fresh dill sprigs, to garnish

Heat wok until hot. Add 1 tablespoon butter and swirl to coat wok. Add onion and stir-fry for 7-8 minutes. Add paprika and cook for 1 minute. Add cream and bring to simmering point; cook for 1-2 minutes until slightly thickened. Add mustard and dill and season. Pour into small bowl; keep warm. Wipe wok clean. Dredge turkey strips in seasoned flour. Heat the wok until hot. Add vegetable oil and 1 tablespoon butter and swirl to coat wok. Add turkey strips, working in batches, and stir-fry for 2-3 minutes. Remove to plate and keep warm.

Cook tagliatelle according to packet directions; drain well. Heat the wok until hot. Add remaining butter, peas and caraway seeds. Stir-fry for 2-3 minutes until peas are tender. Stir in noodles and season. Stir in a spoonful of the reserved sauce and toss to coat noodles. Turn out on to serving plate. Pour remaining sauce and turkey strips into the wok, tossing to coat. Cook for 1 minute. Spoon turkey strips and sauce over noodles. Garnish with dill sprigs.

Serves 4.

TURKEY WITH BROCCOLI

1 tablespoon vegetable oil
450 g (1 lb) boneless turkey cutlets, cut into thin strips
1 tablespoon sesame oil
450 g (1 lb) broccoli, stems and florets cut into
    2.5 cm (1 in) pieces
4 spring onions, cut into 2.5 cm (1 in) pieces
2.5 cm (1 in) piece of fresh root ginger, peeled and
    cut into julienne strips
2 cloves garlic, finely chopped
55 ml (2 fl oz/¼ cup) dry sherry or rice wine
2 tablespoons light soy sauce
2 teaspoons cornflour dissolved in 1 tablespoon water
55 ml (2 fl oz/¼ cup) chicken stock
225 g (8 oz) canned water chestnuts, rinsed and
    sliced
fresh coriander, to garnish

Heat the wok until very hot but not smoking. Add vegetable oil and swirl to coat wok. Add turkey strips and stir-fry for 2-3 minutes until beginning to colour. Remove to a bowl. Add sesame oil to wok. Add broccoli and stir-fry for 2 minutes. Add the spring onions, ginger, and garlic and stir-fry for 2-3 minutes more, until broccoli is tender but still crisp.

Add dry sherry or rice wine and soy sauce and cook for 2 minutes. Stir dissolved cornflour and stir into chicken stock; stir into wok. Stir-fry for 1 minute until sauce bubbles and thickens. Add reserved turkey strips and water chestnuts, tossing to coat, and cook for 1 minute until turkey is heated through. Garnish with coriander and serve with rice and wild rice.

Serves 4.

SZECHUAN TURKEY

450 g (1 lb) lean boneless turkey
1 egg white, lightly beaten
large pinch of salt
1 teaspoon cornflour
1 tablespoon sunflower oil
½ teaspoon Szechuan peppercorns, toasted and
   crushed
225 g (8 oz) Szechuan preserved vegetables,
   shredded
225 g (8 oz) mange tout (snow peas)
115 g (4 oz) canned water chestnuts, rinsed and
   sliced

Skin and trim turkey. Cut into thin strips
about 0.5 cm (¼ in) thick.

Place turkey strips in a bowl and mix with
egg white, salt and cornflour. Cover and chill
for 30 minutes.

Heat the oil in a non-stick or well seasoned
wok and stir-fry turkey with crushed peppercorns for 2 minutes until turkey is just
coloured. Add remaining ingredients and
stir-fry for 3 minutes until just cooked
through. Serve immediately.

Serves 4.

SWEET & SOUR TURKEY

450 g (1 lb) skinless, boneless turkey
1 tablespoon sunflower oil
2 shallots, chopped
2 sticks celery, sliced
2 tablespoons light soy sauce
1 red pepper (capsicum), sliced
1 yellow pepper (capsicum), sliced
1 green pepper (capsicum), sliced
115 g (4 oz) canned bamboo shoots, drained
3 tablespoons plum sauce
2 tablespoons white rice vinegar
1 teaspoon sesame oil
2 tablespoons sesame seeds

Trim away any excess fat from turkey. Cut
into 2.5 cm (1 in) cubes. Heat oil in a non-
stick or well seasoned wok and stir-fry turkey,
shallots and celery for 2-3 minutes until
lightly coloured.

Add soy sauce and peppers (capsicum) and
stir-fry for 2 minutes. Stir in bamboo shoots,
plum sauce and vinegar and simmer gently
for 2 minutes. Stir in sesame oil, sprinkle
with sesame seeds and serve.

Serves 4.

ROAST STUFFED TURKEY

3.6 kg (8 lb) oven-ready turkey with giblets
225 g (8 oz/4¼ cups) soft white breadcrumbs
1 large onion, finely chopped
3 sticks celery, finely chopped
finely grated peel and juice 1 lemon
8 plums, chopped
150 ml (5 fl oz/⅔ cup) red wine
450 g (1 lb/2 cups) chestnut purée
3 teaspoons each of chopped fresh sage, thyme and
  oregano
salt and pepper
450 g (1 lb) rashers fat streaky bacon
55 g (2 oz/½ cup) plain flour

Cover the whole turkey with rashers of streaky bacon to help keep it moist during cooking.

Remove giblets from turkey, place in a saucepan with 550 ml (20 fl oz/2½ cups) water and bring to boil. Cover and simmer for 1 hour. Strain stock into a bowl; reserve liver. In a saucepan, place breadcrumbs, onion, celery, lemon peel and juice, plums and wine. Bring to boil, stirring, and cook for 1 minute. Put chestnut purée, herbs, salt and pepper to taste and turkey liver into a food processor fitted with a metal blade. Process until smooth. Add breadcrumb mixture and process until evenly blended.

Preheat oven to 190C (375F/Gas 5). Cook turkey in the oven for 2 hours, remove from oven; remove bacon if you require it for serving, and cover turkey and tin with thick foil. Return to oven for a further 1-1½ hours until turkey is tender and only clear juices run when pierced with a sharp pointed knife between legs of turkey. Leave to stand in tin for 20 minutes before removing. Remove any skewers or trussing string and place turkey on a warmed serving dish. Chop crispy bacon finely and serve with turkey.

Place ⅓ stuffing into neck end of turkey, pull over flap of skin and secure under turkey with skewers or string. Fill cavity of turkey with remaining stuffing, pull skin over parson's nose and secure with skewers or string. Truss turkey with string, securing wings and legs closely to body, and place in a roasting tin.

To make gravy, blend flour and a little sock together in a pan until smooth. Pour remaining stock into roasting tin, stir well, strain gravy into saucepan with flour mixture. Bring to boil, stirring until thickened; cook for 2 minutes. Season to taste with salt and pepper and pour into a gravy boat. Serve turkey with bread sauce, chipolata sausages, crisp bacon and gravy.

Serves 10.

DUCK &
GAME

DUCK WITH TURNIPS

1.8-2.3 kg (4-5 lb) duck
salt and freshly ground black pepper
1 tablespoon olive oil
250 ml (9 fl oz/1 cup) chicken stock
115 ml (4 fl oz/½ cup) dry white wine
bouquet garni
pinch sugar
575 g (1¼ lb) small turnips, halved or quartered
sage sprigs, to garnish

Season duck generously inside and out with salt and pepper and prick fatty areas of breasts with a fork.

Heat oil in a heavy flameproof casserole, add duck and cook over a low heat, turning, until browned all over. Pour fat from casserole, reserving 2 tablespoons. Add stock, wine and bouquet garni to casserole, cover tightly and cook gently for 30 minutes.

Meanwhile, heat reserved duck fat in a frying pan, add turnips, sprinkle with sugar and cook until browned all over. Add turnips to casserole, baste with cooking liquid and cook, uncovered, for 25 minutes, until duck and turnips are tender. Transfer duck and turnips to a warmed serving plate. Skim fat from sauce then boil sauce to thicken slightly. Season with salt and pepper and remove bouquet garni. Carve duck, garnish and serve with turnips and sauce.

Serves 4.

DUCK WITH ORANGE

2 boneless duck breasts, about 175 g (6 oz) each
salt and freshly ground black pepper
1½ teaspoons chopped fresh thyme
2 oranges
1 teaspoon cornflour
juice 1 lemon
4 tablespoons Cointreau
15 g (½ oz/1 tablespoon) unsalted butter
orange twists and thyme sprigs, to garnish

Using a sharp knife, score skin and fat on duck breasts in a criss-cross pattern, taking care not to cut through flesh. Season with salt and pepper and rub with thyme.

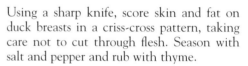

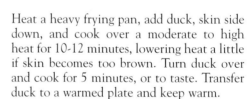

Heat a heavy frying pan, add duck, skin side down, and cook over a moderate to high heat for 10-12 minutes, lowering heat a little if skin becomes too brown. Turn duck over and cook for 5 minutes, or to taste. Transfer duck to a warmed plate and keep warm.

Meanwhile, pare enough rind from oranges to give 1½ tablespoons. Add to a small pan of boiling water and blanch for 2 minutes. Drain, rinse in cold water and set aside. Squeeze juice from oranges. Pour most of fat from frying pan. Stir cornflour into pan then add orange and lemon juice and orange rind. Bring to the boil, stirring, then add Cointreau and salt and pepper. Reduce heat and whisk in butter. Slice duck, arrange on serving plates, pour over sauce, garnish and serve.

Serves 2.

DUCK WITH APPLES & PRUNES

1 tablespoon olive oil
4 boneless duck breasts, about 115 g (4 oz) each
2 cooking apples, peeled, cored and sliced
225 g (8 oz) ready-to-eat prunes
550 ml (20 fl oz/2½ cups) dry cider
salt and freshly ground black pepper

Preheat oven to 200C (400F/Gas 6). Heat the oil in a shallow flameproof dish, add the duck and cook for 3-4 minutes on each side, until browned.

Cover with the apple slices and prunes. Pour the cider over the duck and season with salt and pepper. Bring to the boil, cover with a lid or piece of foil and cook in the oven for 55-60 minutes, until the duck is cooked through. Remove the duck from the dish with a slotted spoon, leaving behind the apples and prunes, and keep warm.

Bring the cooking juices in the dish to the boil and boil for 5 minutes, until the liquid has reduced and thickened. Pour the sauce, apples and prunes over the duck and serve.

Serves 4.

VIETNAMESE ROAST DUCK

1 teaspoon minced garlic
2-3 shallots, finely chopped
2 teaspoons five-spice powder
2 tablespoons sugar
55 ml (2 fl oz/¼ cup) red rice vinegar
1 tablespoon fish sauce
1 tablespoon soy sauce
4 quarter portions duck (2 breasts and 2 legs)
250 ml (9 fl oz/1 cup) coconut milk
salt and freshly ground black pepper
watercress, to serve
coriander sprigs, to garnish

In a bowl, mix garlic, shallots, five-spice powder, sugar, vinegar, fish and soy sauces.

Add duck pieces and leave to marinate for at least 2-3 hours, or overnight in the refrigerator, turning occasionally. Preheat oven to 220C (425F/Gas 7). Remove duck portions from marinade and place, skin-side up, on a rack in a baking tin and cook in the oven for 45 minutes, without turning or basting.

Remove duck and keep warm. Heat the marinade with the drippings in the baking tin, add the coconut milk, bring to boil and simmer for 5 minutes. Season with salt and pepper, then pour sauce into a serving bowl. Serve duck portions on a bed of watercress, garnished with coriander sprigs.

Serves 4-6.

Note: The duck portions can be chopped through the bone into bite-size pieces for serving, if wished.

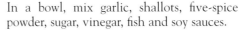

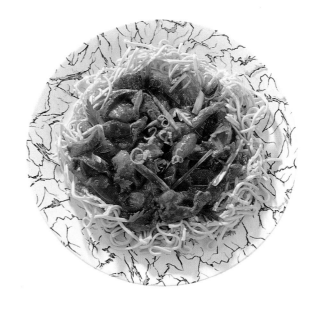

AROMATIC DUCK

2 half or 4 quarter portions of duck (2 breasts and 2 legs)
salt and freshly ground black pepper
1 tablespoon five-spice powder
4-5 small pieces fresh root ginger
3-4 spring onions, cut into short sections
3-4 tablespoons Chinese rice wine or dry sherry
12 sheets dried rice paper, halved if large
fresh mint, basil and coriander leaves
Spicy Fish Sauce (see page 311)

Rub the salt, pepper and five-spice powder all over the duck portions.

In a shallow dish, mix ginger, spring onions and rice wine or sherry, add duck portions and leave to marinate for at least 3-4 hours, turning the duck pieces now and then. Steam the duck portions with marinade in a hot steamer for 2-3 hours. Remove the duck portions from the liquid and leave to cool (the duck can be cooked up to this stage in advance, if wished).

Preheat oven to 230C (450F/Gas 8) and bake the duck pieces, skin-side up, for 10-15 minutes, then pull the meat off the bone. Meanwhile, soften dried rice paper in warm water. Place about 2 tablespoons of meat in each half sheet of rice paper, add a few mint, basil and coriander leaves, roll into a neat bundle, then dip the roll in the Spicy Fish Sauce before eating it.

Serves 4-6.

DUCK WITH PLUMS

2 tablespoons vegetable oil
700 g (1½ lb) duckling breast fillets, skinned and
    excess fat removed, cut crosswise into thin strips
225 g (8 oz) red plums, stoned and thinly sliced
55 ml (2 fl oz/¼ cup) port
6 teaspoons wine vinegar
grated rind and juice 1 orange
2 tablespoons Chinese plum or duck sauce
4 spring onions, cut into thin strips
1 tablespoon soy sauce
3-4 whole cloves
small piece cinnamon stick
½ teaspoon Chinese chilli sauce (or to taste)
fresh parsley and grated orange rind, to garnish

Heat the wok until hot. Add oil and swirl to coat wok. Add duckling breast strips and stir-fry for 3-4 minutes until golden. Remove to a bowl. Add plums, port, wine vinegar, rind and juice of the orange, plum or duck sauce, spring onions, soy sauce, cloves, cinnamon stick and chilli sauce to taste. Bring to simmering point and cook gently for 4-5 minutes until plums begin to soften.

Return duckling strips to wok and stir-fry for 2 minutes until duck is heated through and sauce is thickened. Garnish with parsley and grated orange rind. Serve with noodles or rice tossed with sesame seeds.

Serves 4.

PEKING DUCK

1.8 kg (4 lb) oven-ready duck
1 tablespoon honey
3 tablespoons dark soy sauce
1 tablespoon sesame oil
edible red food colouring, if desired
2 tablespoons water
PANCAKES:
450 g (1 lb/4 cups) plain (all-purpose) flour
225 ml (8 fl oz/1 cup) boiling water
90 ml (3 fl oz/⅓ cup) cold water
1 teaspoon sesame oil
TO SERVE:
hoisin sauce
6 spring onions, cut into long shreds
½ cucumber, cut into long shreds

Place the duck in a colander in the sink. Pour over boiling water; repeat twice. Hang duck overnight in a cold airy place, or place on a rack in the refrigerator. Next morning, in a small bowl, mix together honey, soy sauce, sesame oil and colouring, if used. Place duck on a rack in a roasting tin, making sure the neck opening is closed. Brush evenly with honey mixture and leave for at least 1 hour. Pre-heat oven to 200C (400F/Gas 6)

Stir water into remaining honey mixture and pour through the vent, into the duck. With a meat skewer or wooden cocktail sticks, secure vent. Roast duck, 1½ hours, until juices run clear. Remove duck from oven and leave in a warm place for 10 minutes before carving.

Meanwhile, make the pancakes. Sift flour into a bowl and gradually stir in boiling water; mix well. Stir in cold water to form a ball. On a floured surface, knead until smooth. Return to bowl, cover with a damp cloth and leave for 15 minutes.

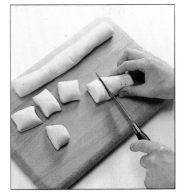

Divide dough in half on a lightly floured surface, roll each half to a long roll 5 cm (2 in) in diameter. Cut into 2.5 cm (1 in) lengths. Flatten each piece with the palm of the hand. Lightly brush tops with sesame oil and place two pieces together, oiled-sides facing. Roll out each pair to 15 cm (6 in) pancakes. Place a dry, non-stick frying pan over a moderate heat and fry each pancake for 20-30 seconds until beginning to bubble. Turn over pancake and cook for a further 10-15 seconds until lightly browned.

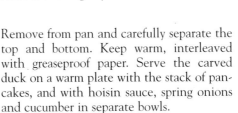

Remove from pan and carefully separate the top and bottom. Keep warm, interleaved with greaseproof paper. Serve the carved duck on a warm plate with the stack of pancakes, and with hoisin sauce, spring onions and cucumber in separate bowls.

Serves 4.

DUCK WITH KIWI FRUIT

2 boneless duck breasts, about 225 g (8 oz) each
1 cm (½ in) piece fresh root ginger, peeled and finely chopped
1 clove garlic, finely chopped
2 tablespoons dry sherry
2 kiwi fruit
1 teaspoon sesame oil
SAUCE:
4 tablespoons dry sherry
2 tablespoons light soy sauce
4 teaspoons clear honey

Skin and trim duck breasts. With a sharp knife, score flesh in diagonal lines. Beat with a meat tenderizer until 1 cm (½ in) thick.

Place duck breasts in a shallow dish and add ginger, garlic and sherry. Cover and chill for 1 hour. Peel and thinly slice kiwi fruit and halve widthways. Cover and chill until required. Preheat grill. Drain duck breasts and place on grill rack. Brush with sesame oil and cook for 8 minutes. Turn and brush again with oil. Cook for 8-10 minutes until tender and cooked through.

Meanwhile, put the sauce ingredients in a saucepan, bring to the boil and simmer for 5 minutes, until syrupy. Drain duck breasts on kitchen paper and slice thinly. Arrange duck slices and kiwi fruit on serving plates. Pour over sauce and serve with rice and vegetables.

Serves 4.

PIGEON WITH CRISP POLENTA

2 tablespoons chopped fresh sage
1 tablespoon chopped fresh rosemary
salt and freshly ground black pepper
115 g (4 oz/scant 1 cup) quick-cook polenta
1 tablespoon olive oil
8 pigeon breasts
pinch of ground allspice
1 quantity Tomato Sauce (see page 307)
rosemary and sage sprigs, to garnish

Bring 550 ml (20 fl oz/2½ cups) water to the boil with chopped herbs, salt and pepper. Sprinkle in the polenta, whisking to prevent lumps forming.

Turn down heat and simmer the polenta for 5-10 minutes, stirring constantly until very thick. Turn out onto a wooden board and shape into a loaf with a spatula. Cool, cover and chill for 1 hour. Preheat the grill. Cut the polenta into 4 thick slices. Brush with some of the olive oil and grill on each side until crisp and golden. Keep warm.

Rub pigeon breasts with the allspice, then brush with a little olive oil. Place skin-side up on grill pan and grill for 4 minutes. Turn over and grill for another 2 minutes. Top each polenta slice with 2 pigeon breasts. Garnish with rosemary and sage sprigs and serve with the fresh tomato sauce.

Serves 4.

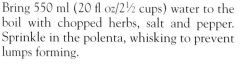

SPICY GRILLED QUAIL

1 clove garlic
salt
1 teaspoon each ground cumin and coriander
½ small onion
1 tablespoon chopped fresh coriander
pinch cayenne pepper
55 ml (2 fl oz/¼ cup) olive oil
8 quail
vine leaves, parsley and lemon slices, to garnish

Put all the ingredients except quail and garnish in a food processor.

Process to make a paste. Spread paste over quail. Cover and leave to marinate in a cool place for 2 hours.

Grill quail for 10-15 minutes, turning frequently, until cooked and slightly charred on the outside. Serve quail on vine leaves, garnished with parsley and lemon slices.

Serves 4.

Variation: Baby poussins or chicken portions can also be cooked in this way.

Note: The grilled quail are particularly good cooked on a barbecue.

PAN-FRIED GUINEA FOWL

1 tablespoon olive oil
2 guinea fowl
115 g (4 oz) streaky bacon, chopped
175 g (6 oz) button mushrooms
175 g (6 oz) shallots
2 tablespoons brandy
250 ml (9 fl oz/1 cup) red wine
550 ml (20 fl oz/2½ cups) chicken stock
3 tablespoons redcurrant jelly
salt and freshly ground black pepper
marjoram sprigs, to garnish

Preheat oven to 180C (350F/Gas 4). Heat the oil in an ovenproof dish. Add the guinea fowl and brown all over.

Cover and cook in the oven for 35-40 minutes. Remove and keep warm. Add the bacon, mushrooms and shallots to the dish and cook, stirring, for 4-5 minutes, until golden brown. Remove with a slotted spoon and keep warm. Add the brandy, wine, stock and redcurrant jelly to the cooking juices and stir well. Bring to the boil, stirring, and boil for 20-25 minutes, stirring occasionally, until the sauce is reduced and thickened.

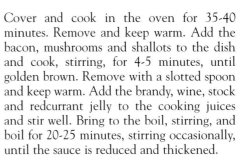

Return the guinea fowl, bacon, mushrooms and shallots to the casserole and season well. Bring to the boil and simmer for 4-5 minutes to warm through. Cut the guinea fowl in half with kitchen scissors or a sharp knife. Garnish with marjoram sprigs and serve.

Serves 4.

PHEASANT IN PARSLEY SAUCE

55 g (2 oz/¼ cup) butter
2 pheasants
85 g (3 oz) fresh parsley
3 onions, thinly sliced
25 g (1 oz/¼ cup) plain flour
300 ml (10 fl oz/1¼ cups) chicken stock
150 ml (5 fl oz/⅔ cup) crème fraîche
salt and freshly ground black pepper
flat-leaf parsley sprigs, to garnish

Preheat oven to 180C (350F/Gas 4). Melt the butter in a large flameproof dish. Add the pheasants and cook until browned all over. Remove and keep warm.

Separate the thick parsley stalks from the leaves and tie the stalks together with string. Chop the leaves and set aside. Add the onions to the dish and cook, stirring occasionally, for 7 minutes, until soft and lightly coloured. Add the flour and cook, stirring, for 1 minute. Gradually add the chicken stock, stirring constantly until smooth. Bring to the boil and add the bundle of parsley stalks. Add the pheasants, cover and cook in the oven for 1 hour.

Remove the pheasants from the dish and keep warm. Remove and discard the parsley stalks. Add the chopped parsley and crème fraîche to the sauce and season with salt and pepper. Heat gently to warm through. Cut the pheasants in half with kitchen scissors. Garnish with flat-leaf parsley sprigs and serve with the parsley sauce.

Serves 4.

GRILLED QUAIL

4 cleaned quail, each split down the backbone and pressed flat
salt and freshly ground black pepper
1 teaspoon minced garlic
1 tablespoon finely chopped lemon grass
1 teaspoon sugar
1 tablespoon fish sauce
1 tablespoon lime juice or vinegar
1-2 tablespoons vegetable oil
lettuce leaves
coriander sprigs, to garnish
Spicy Fish Sauce (see page 311) to serve

Rub the 4 quail all over with plenty of salt and pepper.

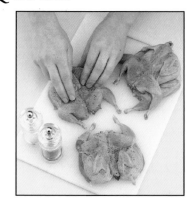

In a mixing bowl, blend garlic, lemon grass, sugar, fish sauce and lime juice or vinegar. Add quail, turning to coat in the mixture, then leave to marinate for 2-3 hours, turning over now and then.

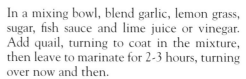

Prepare a barbecue or preheat grill. Brush quail with oil and cook over barbecue or under grill for 6-8 minutes each side, basting with remaining marinade during first 5 minutes of cooking. Serve quail on a bed of lettuce leaves, garnished with coriander sprigs, accompanied by Spicy Fish Sauce for dipping.

Serves 4.

PHEASANT WITH SULTANAS

55 g (2 oz/⅓ cup) sultanas
115 ml (4 fl oz/½ cup) medium sherry
55 ml (2 fl oz/¼ cup) olive oil
1 young pheasant
salt and freshly ground black pepper
25 g (1 oz/¼ cup) pine nuts

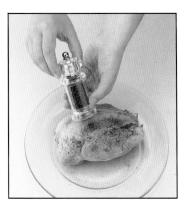

Preheat the oven to 190C (375F/Gas 5). Put the sultanas in a small bowl, add the sherry and leave to soak. Rub 2 tablespoons of the oil over the pheasant and season with salt and pepper.

Put the pheasant in a roasting tin and roast for 30-45 minutes until cooked through and tender. Just before the pheasant is ready, drain the sultanas, reserving the sherry. Heat the remaining oil in a frying pan and cook the pine nuts until golden. Add the sultanas and cook for 1 minute.

Carve the pheasant and arrange on warmed serving plates. Scatter with the pine nuts and sultanas and keep warm. Pour the reserved sherry into the roasting tin and heat, stirring to incorporate any sediment. Pour over the pheasant and serve.

Serves 2-3.

QUAIL WITH FIGS & ORANGES

3 tablespoons olive oil
8 quails
1 onion, thinly sliced
2 sticks celery, thinly sliced
150 ml (5 fl oz/⅔ cup) dry white wine
150 ml (5 fl oz/⅔ cup) hot chicken stock
salt and freshly ground black pepper
2 oranges
4 figs

Preheat the oven to 160C (325F/Gas 3). Heat 2 tablespoons of the olive oil in a heavy casserole. Add the quails and cook until browned all over. Remove and set aside.

Add the onion and celery to the casserole and cook gently for 7 minutes until soft and lightly browned. Replace the quails and pour over the wine and hot stock. Season with salt and pepper. Cover and cook in the oven for 30-40 minutes until the quails are cooked through. Just before the end of the cooking time, preheat the grill. Peel the oranges, removing all the pith and cut each one into four thick slices. Cut the figs in half.

Brush the orange slices with olive oil and grill for 2-3 minutes. Turn, add the figs and grill the cut sides for 2 minutes. Set aside and keep warm. Transfer the quails, onion and celery to a warmed serving dish. Pour over the cooking juices, arrange the oranges and figs around the birds and serve.

Serves 4.

SPANISH PARTRIDGE

2 partridges, halved along backbone
2 tablespoons brandy
salt and freshly ground black pepper
3 tablespoons olive oil
1 Spanish onion, chopped
3 cloves garlic, finely chopped
2 tablespoons plain flour
4 tablespoons red wine vinegar
225 ml (8 fl oz/1 cup) red wine
225 ml (8 fl oz/1 cup) chicken stock
6 black peppercorns
2 cloves
1 bay leaf
2 carrots, cut into short lengths
8 shallots
25 g (1 oz) plain (dark) chocolate, grated

Stir vinegar into casserole and boil for 1-2 minutes. Add wine and boil for 1-2 minutes, then add stock, peppercorns, cloves, bay leaf and partridges. Heat to simmering point, cover tightly and cook gently for 40 minutes. Add carrots and shallots, cover again, and continue to cook gently for 20 minutes.

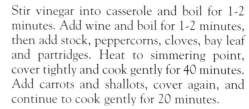

Rub partridges with brandy, salt and pepper and set aside for 30 minutes. Heat oil in a heavy flameproof casserole into which the birds fit snugly. Add onion and fry, stirring occasionally, for 3 minutes. Stir in garlic and cook for 2 minutes.

Transfer partridges, shallots and carrots to a warm dish. If necessary, boil the cooking juices until reduced to 300 ml (10 fl oz/ 1¼ cups), then purée in a blender or food processor.

Sprinkle birds lightly with flour, then fry in casserole for 5 minutes each side. Remove and set aside.

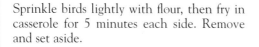

Return juices to casserole, heat gently and stir in chocolate until melted. Return partridges and vegetables to casserole and turn them over in the sauce so they are well coated.

Serves 4.

PROVENÇAL RABBIT

VENISON RAGOÛT

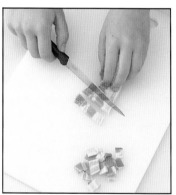

85 g (3 oz) pancetta
2 tablespoons olive oil
1 onion, chopped
4 rabbit portions
1 tablespoon seasoned flour
3 tablespoons tapénade (see below)
400 ml (14 fl oz/1¼ cups) chicken stock
150 ml (5 fl oz/⅔ cup) dry white wine
2 fresh bay leaves
2 sprigs of thyme
salt and freshly ground black pepper
1 small fennel bulb, roughly chopped
black olives and fennel leaves, to garnish

Preheat the oven to 180C (350F/Gas 4).
Roughly chop half the pancetta.

1 tablespoon plain flour
salt and freshly ground black pepper
900 g (2 lb) stewing venison, cubed
1 tablespoon olive oil
1 clove garlic, chopped
300 ml (10 fl oz/1¼ cups) beef stock
1 tablespoon balsamic vinegar
8 juniper berries
8 black peppercorns
4 cloves
400 g (14 oz) can chopped tomatoes
225 g (8 oz) baby carrots, trimmed
115 g (4 oz) button mushrooms
1 tablespoon chopped fresh parsley

Heat half the oil in a flameproof casserole.
Add the onion and chopped pancetta and
cook for 3 minutes. Remove with a slotted
spoon and set aside. Dust the rabbit portions
with the seasoned flour. Heat the remaining
oil in the casserole, add the rabbit and cook
until browned all over. Mix together the
tapénade, stock and wine and pour over the
rabbit. Add the onion, pancetta, bay leaves
and thyme. Season with salt and pepper and
bring to the boil. Cover and cook in the
oven for 45 minutes.

Preheat oven to 180C (350F/Gas 4). Season
the flour with salt and pepper and use to coat
the venison. Heat the oil in a large flameproof casserole. Add the venison, the
remaining seasoned flour and garlic and
cook, stirring, for 4-5 minutes.

Add the fennel and cook for 45 minutes or
until the rabbit is cooked through and
tender. Grill the remaining pancetta until
crisp then snip into small pieces. Scatter the
pancetta over the rabbit. Garnish with olives
and fennel leaves and serve.

Serves 4.

Note: You can make your own tapénade (see
page 24), or buy it ready made, in small jars.

Add the stock, vinegar, juniper berries,
peppercorns, cloves, tomatoes and carrots.
Bring to the boil, cover and cook in the oven
for 1 hour. Add the mushrooms and cook for
15 minutes. Sprinkle with chopped parsley
and serve.

Serves 6-8.

RABBIT STIFADO

6 teaspoons plain flour
salt and pepper
700 g-1 kg (1½-2¼ lb) rabbit joints
70 ml (2½ fl oz/⅓ cup) olive oil
450 g (1 lb) tiny pickling onions, peeled
1 clove garlic, crushed
3 teaspoons tomato purée (paste)
300 ml (10 fl oz/1¼ cups) red wine
300 ml (10 fl oz/1¼ cups) chicken stock
1 bay leaf
2 sprigs thyme
2 slices bread, crusts removed, and 2 tablespoons
  chopped fresh parsley, to garnish

On a plate, mix together flour, salt and pepper. Toss rabbit pieces in seasoned flour. Heat half oil in a frying pan. Fry rabbit pieces until brown on both sides. Transfer to a flameproof casserole. Add onions to frying pan; cook until they begin to brown. Add garlic and tomato purée (paste) to pan and stir in wine and stock. Add bay leaf, thyme, salt and pepper. Add to casserole, cover and cook over a low heat for 1½-2 hours until rabbit is tender.

Cut each slice of bread into 4 triangles. In a frying pan, heat remaining oil and fry bread until golden brown on both sides. Dip one edge of each triangle into chopped parsley. To serve, place rabbit on a shallow plate and arrange onions around edge. Pour the sauce over the rabbit and garnish with fried bread.

Serves 6.

RABBIT IN MUSTARD SAUCE

55 g (2 oz/¼ cup) butter
8 rabbit portions
250 ml (9 fl oz/1 cup) dry white wine
115 g (4 oz) Dijon mustard
1 thyme sprig
salt and freshly ground black pepper
115 ml (4 fl oz/½ cup) Greek yogurt
chopped fresh flat-leaf parsley and thyme sprigs, to
  garnish

Melt the butter in a flameproof casserole. Add the rabbit and cook for 5-10 minutes, turning, until browned all over. Remove with a slotted spoon.

Stir in the wine, mustard, thyme and salt and pepper and bring to the boil. Return the rabbit to the casserole, cover and simmer for 25 minutes. Remove the rabbit with a slotted spoon and keep warm.

Boil the sauce until reduced by half. Remove and discard the thyme sprig and stir in the yogurt. Heat gently to warm through. Garnish the rabbit with chopped parsley and thyme sprigs, pour over the sauce and serve.

Serves 4.

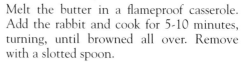

PROVENÇAL RABBIT

VENISON RAGOÛT

85 g (3 oz) pancetta
2 tablespoons olive oil
1 onion, chopped
4 rabbit portions
1 tablespoon seasoned flour
3 tablespoons tapénade (see below)
400 ml (14 fl oz/1¾ cups) chicken stock
150 ml (5 fl oz/⅔ cup) dry white wine
2 fresh bay leaves
2 sprigs of thyme
salt and freshly ground black pepper
1 small fennel bulb, roughly chopped
black olives and fennel leaves, to garnish

1 tablespoon plain flour
salt and freshly ground black pepper
900 g (2 lb) stewing venison, cubed
1 tablespoon olive oil
1 clove garlic, chopped
300 ml (10 fl oz/1¼ cups) beef stock
1 tablespoon balsamic vinegar
8 juniper berries
8 black peppercorns
4 cloves
400 g (14 oz) can chopped tomatoes
225 g (8 oz) baby carrots, trimmed
115 g (4 oz) button mushrooms
1 tablespoon chopped fresh parsley

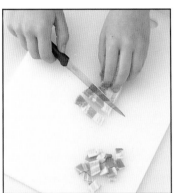

Preheat the oven to 180C (350F/Gas 4). Roughly chop half the pancetta.

Heat half the oil in a flameproof casserole. Add the onion and chopped pancetta and cook for 3 minutes. Remove with a slotted spoon and set aside. Dust the rabbit portions with the seasoned flour. Heat the remaining oil in the casserole, add the rabbit and cook until browned all over. Mix together the tapénade, stock and wine and pour over the rabbit. Add the onion, pancetta, bay leaves and thyme. Season with salt and pepper and bring to the boil. Cover and cook in the oven for 45 minutes.

Preheat oven to 180C (350F/Gas 4). Season the flour with salt and pepper and use to coat the venison. Heat the oil in a large flameproof casserole. Add the venison, the remaining seasoned flour and garlic and cook, stirring, for 4-5 minutes.

Add the fennel and cook for 45 minutes or until the rabbit is cooked through and tender. Grill the remaining pancetta until crisp then snip into small pieces. Scatter the pancetta over the rabbit. Garnish with olives and fennel leaves and serve.

Serves 4.

Note: You can make your own tapénade (see page 24), or buy it ready made, in small jars.

Add the stock, vinegar, juniper berries, peppercorns, cloves, tomatoes and carrots. Bring to the boil, cover and cook in the oven for 1 hour. Add the mushrooms and cook for 15 minutes. Sprinkle with chopped parsley and serve.

Serves 6-8.

RABBIT STIFADO

6 teaspoons plain flour
salt and pepper
700 g-1 kg (1½-2¼ lb) rabbit joints
70 ml (2½ fl oz/⅓ cup) olive oil
450 g (1 lb) tiny pickling onions, peeled
1 clove garlic, crushed
3 teaspoons tomato purée (paste)
300 ml (10 fl oz/1¼ cups) red wine
300 ml (10 fl oz/1¼ cups) chicken stock
1 bay leaf
2 sprigs thyme
2 slices bread, crusts removed, and 2 tablespoons
  chopped fresh parsley, to garnish

RABBIT IN MUSTARD SAUCE

55 g (2 oz/¼ cup) butter
8 rabbit portions
250 ml (9 fl oz/1 cup) dry white wine
115 g (4 oz) Dijon mustard
1 thyme sprig
salt and freshly ground black pepper
115 ml (4 fl oz/½ cup) Greek yogurt
chopped fresh flat-leaf parsley and thyme sprigs, to
  garnish

Melt the butter in a flameproof casserole.
Add the rabbit and cook for 5-10 minutes,
turning, until browned all over. Remove
with a slotted spoon.

On a plate, mix together flour, salt and pepper. Toss rabbit pieces in seasoned flour. Heat
half oil in a frying pan. Fry rabbit pieces until
brown on both sides. Transfer to a flameproof
casserole. Add onions to frying pan; cook
until they begin to brown. Add garlic and
tomato purée (paste) to pan and stir in wine
and stock. Add bay leaf, thyme, salt and
pepper. Add to casserole, cover and cook
over a low heat for 1½-2 hours until rabbit is
tender.

Stir in the wine, mustard, thyme and salt and
pepper and bring to the boil. Return the
rabbit to the casserole, cover and simmer for
25 minutes. Remove the rabbit with a
slotted spoon and keep warm.

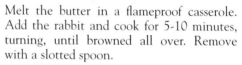

Cut each slice of bread into 4 triangles. In a
frying pan, heat remaining oil and fry bread
until golden brown on both sides. Dip one
edge of each triangle into chopped parsley.
To serve, place rabbit on a shallow plate and
arrange onions around edge. Pour the sauce
over the rabbit and garnish with fried bread.

Serves 6.

Boil the sauce until reduced by half. Remove
and discard the thyme sprig and stir in the
yogurt. Heat gently to warm through.
Garnish the rabbit with chopped parsley and
thyme sprigs, pour over the sauce and serve.

Serves 4.

Beef & Veal

STEAK WITH BÉARNAISE SAUCE

olive oil, for brushing
4 sirloin steaks, about 2.5 cm (1 in) thick
salt and freshly ground black pepper
BÉARNAISE SAUCE:
115 g (4 oz/½ cup) unsalted butter, diced
3 stalks each tarragon and chervil
2 teaspoons chopped shallot
4 black peppercorns, crushed
2 tablespoons dry white wine
2 tablespoons white wine vinegar
2 egg yolks
1 teaspoon each chopped fresh tarragon, parsley and
  chervil

Preheat grill. Oil grill rack, add steaks and
season with black pepper.

Grill for 1-3 minutes on each side, according
to taste. Meanwhile, make sauce. Melt butter in a small saucepan then set aside and
cool slightly. Put tarragon and chervil stalks,
shallot, peppercorns, wine and vinegar in a
small saucepan, bring to the boil and boil
until reduced to 2 teaspoons. Strain.

Put egg yolks in a blender or food processor
with 2 teaspoons water and process briefly to
combine. With motor running at low speed
pour in reduced liquid. With motor still running at low speed, pour in melted butter in a
slow, steady stream, to make a thick sauce.
Add herbs and salt and pepper and serve
immediately with steaks.

Serves 4.

PROVENÇAL BEEF DAUBE

1 large onion, chopped
300 ml (10 fl oz/1¼ cups) red wine
3 cloves garlic, crushed
2 fresh bay leaves
1 sprig thyme
salt and freshly ground black pepper
1 kg (2¼ lb) stewing beef, cubed
2 tablespoons olive oil
175 g (6 oz) streaky bacon, diced
1 tablespoon plain flour
2 tablespoons balsamic vinegar
2 ripe tomatoes, chopped
15 cm (6 in) strip pared orange rind
12 black olives, pitted and halved
300-550 ml (10-20 fl oz/1¼-2½ cups) beef stock

Put the onion, wine, garlic, bay leaves,
thyme and salt and pepper in a large shallow
dish and mix well. Add the beef and stir well
to coat. Cover and leave in a cool place
overnight. Preheat the oven to 160C
(325F/Gas 3). Remove the beef from the
marinade, reserving the marinade, and pat
the beef dry on kitchen paper. Heat the oil in
a flameproof casserole, add the bacon and
cook until golden. Remove with a slotted
spoon and set aside.

Add the beef to the casserole and cook until
browned all over. Sprinkle on the flour and
cook for 1 minute, stirring. Add the reserved
marinade and vinegar. Add the tomatoes,
orange rind and olives. Pour in enough stock
to cover the beef and season with salt and
pepper. Cover tightly and cook in the oven
for 3 hours or until the beef is tender. If
necessary, add more stock during cooking.
Discard the bay leaves, thyme and orange
rind and serve.

Serves 4-6.

SPICY BRAISED BEEF

BOEUF BOURGUIGNON

2 cloves garlic, crushed
½ teaspoon ground cinnamon
¼ teaspoon ground cloves
salt and freshly ground black pepper
1.3 kg (3 lb) beef topside joint
3 tablespoons olive oil
4 onions, thinly sliced
115 ml (4 fl oz/½ cup) red wine
2 tablespoons tomato purée (paste)
450 g (1 lb) spaghetti
1 tablespoon balsamic vinegar

Mix together the garlic, cinnamon, cloves
and salt and pepper. Make incisions in the
beef and push in the garlic mixture.

Leave in a cool place for 1 hour. Heat the oil
in a casserole into which the meat will just
fit. Add the meat and cook, turning, until
browned all over. Remove from the casserole. Add the onions and cook gently until
soft and lightly browned. Replace the meat,
add the wine and enough water to barely
cover. Mix the tomato purée (paste) with a
little water. Stir into the casserole. Season,
cover and simmer, turning the meat frequently, for about 1½ hours until tender.

Bring a large saucepan of salted water to the
boil. Cook the spaghetti according to the
packet instructions until just tender. Drain.
Remove the meat from the casserole and
keep warm. Add the vinegar to the sauce.
Boil briskly until reduced to a smooth glossy
sauce. Slice the beef and arrange on warmed
serving plates. Pour a little sauce over the
beef, stir the remainder into the spaghetti
and serve with the beef.

Serves 6.

1-2 tablespoons olive oil
2 rashers thick-cut streaky bacon, chopped
12 each button onions and button mushrooms
1 kg (2¼ lb) braising steak, cubed
1 large onion, finely chopped
1 carrot, finely chopped
3 cloves garlic, chopped
1 tablespoon plain flour
685 ml (24 fl oz/3 cups) red Burgundy wine
bouquet garni
salt and freshly ground black pepper
chopped fresh parsley, parsley sprigs and bay leaves,
  to garnish

Heat 1 tablespoon oil in a heavy flameproof
casserole and cook bacon for 2-3 minutes.

Remove with a slotted spoon and set aside.
Add button onions to casserole and cook,
stirring occasionally, until browned. Remove
with a slotted spoon and set aside. Add
mushrooms to casserole and cook, stirring
occasionally, until lightly browned, adding
more oil if necessary. Remove with a slotted
spoon and set aside. Add beef to casserole
and cook over a moderately high heat until
browned all over. Remove with a slotted
spoon and set aside.

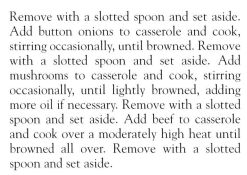

Add chopped onion and carrot to casserole
and cook, stirring occasionally, until beginning to brown. Return bacon and beef to
casserole, add garlic and stir in flour. Stir in
wine, bouquet garni, salt and plenty of pepper. Heat to almost simmering, cover and
cook very gently for 2¾ hours, stirring occasionally. Add reserved onions and mushrooms, cover and cook for 10 minutes, to
warm through. Garnish with parsley and bay
leaves and serve.

Serves 4.

STIR-FRIED BEEF WITH LEEKS

450 g (1 lb) lean rump or sirloin steak
1 tablespoon dark soy sauce
1 teaspoon sesame oil
freshly ground black pepper
1 tablespoon dry sherry
2 teaspoons cornflour
450 g (1 lb) leeks
115 g (4 oz) spring onions
2 teaspoons sunflower oil
2 teaspoons caster sugar
150 ml (5 fl oz/⅔ cup) Chinese Beef Stock (see glossary)
2 tablespoons chopped fresh chives
fresh chives, to garnish

GARLIC BEEF CASSEROLE

1 tablespoon groundnut (peanut) oil
450 g (1 lb) lean stewing beef, trimmed and cut into 2 cm (¾ in) cubes
2 shallots, chopped
4 cloves garlic, thinly sliced
225 g (8 oz) carrots, sliced
175 g (6 oz) baby sweetcorn, halved lengthways
225 g (8 oz) button mushrooms
300 ml (10 fl oz/1¼ cups) Chinese Beef Stock (see glossary)
2 tablespoons dark soy sauce
1 tablespoon rice wine
2 teaspoons five-spice powder
2 tablespoons hoisin sauce
1 teaspoon chilli sauce

Trim any fat from the beef and cut into 2 cm (¾ in) pieces. Place in a bowl and mix in soy sauce, sesame oil, black pepper, sherry and cornflour. Cover and chill for 30 minutes. Trim leeks and discard any coarse outer leaves. Slice thinly and wash well to remove any soil. Trim and shred the spring onions.

Heat oil in a non-stick or well seasoned wok and stir-fry the beef, shallots, garlic, carrots, baby sweetcorn and button mushrooms for 5 minutes. Add remaining ingredients and bring to the boil. Reduce to a simmer, cover and cook gently for 1 hour.

Heat oil in a non-stick or well seasoned wok and stir-fry beef mixture for 1-2 minutes until beef is browned. Add leeks, spring onions and sugar and stir-fry for 3-4 minutes until browned. Pour in the stock and simmer for 5 minutes, stirring occasionally, until thickened. Stir in chopped chives, garnish with chives and serve with noodles.

Serves 4.

Remove from heat and blot surface with kitchen paper to absorb surface fat. Increase the heat and boil for 10 minutes to reduce and thicken the sauce. Serve with rice.

Serves 4.

STIR-FRIED BEEF STEAK

225 g (8 oz) beef steak, cut into small, thin slices,
   about 2.5 cm (1 in) square
¼ teaspoon freshly ground black pepper
1 teaspoon sugar
1 tablespoon fish sauce
2 tablespoons vegetable oil
1 clove garlic, chopped
1 small onion, sliced
1 green pepper (capsicum), cored and cut into cubes
115 g (4 oz) sliced bamboo shoots, drained
1 firm tomato, cut into 8 wedges
2 spring onions, cut into short lengths
2 tablespoons soy or oyster sauce
2 teaspoons cornflour

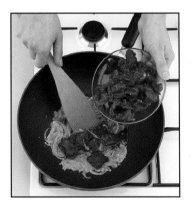

Mix beef with black pepper, sugar and fish
sauce and leave to marinate for 15-20
minutes. Heat oil in a wok or frying pan and
stir-fry garlic and onion for about 1 minute.
Add the beef and stir-fry for 1 minute.

Add the green pepper (capsicum), bamboo
shoots, tomato and spring onions. Continue
stir-frying for 2-3 minutes, then blend in the
soy or oyster sauce. Mix the cornflour with 1
tablespoon water and stir into mixture.
Cook, stirring, until thickened. Serve with
rice noodles.

Serves 4.

SZECHUAN BEEF

450 g (1 lb) lean beef fillet
1 tablespoon sunflower oil
1 clove garlic, finely chopped
1 cm (½ in) piece fresh root ginger, peeled and finely
   chopped
4 spring onions, finely chopped
1 tablespoon hoisin sauce
1 teaspoon Szechuan peppercorns, toasted and
   ground
115 g (4 oz) Szechuan preserved vegetables
1 teaspoon caster sugar
shredded spring onions, to garnish

Trim any fat and silver skin from the beef.
Cut beef into very thin slices.

Heat oil in a non-stick or well seasoned wok
and stir-fry the beef, garlic, ginger and spring
onions for 1 minute until the beef is
browned.

Add remaining ingredients except the garnish and stir-fry for a further 3-4 minutes
until beef is just cooked through. Garnish
with shredded spring onions and serve with
rice.

Serves 4.

BEEF-STUFFED CABBAGE

2 onions
5 tablespoons vegetable oil
3 cloves garlic, crushed
2 fresh green chillies, seeded and chopped
7.5 cm (3 in) piece fresh root ginger, grated
450 g (1 lb) lean minced beef
¼ teaspoon turmeric
2 teaspoons garam masala
1 savoy cabbage
400 g (14 oz) can chopped tomatoes
6 teaspoons lemon juice
salt and pepper
lemon or lime slices, to garnish

Chop 1 onion and slice the other.

Heat 2 tablespoons oil in a heavy-based pan, add chopped onion and cook over a medium heat, stirring, for about 8 minutes, until soft and golden brown. Add garlic, chillies and one-third of the ginger and cook for 1 minute, then remove with a slotted spoon and set aside.

Add beef to pan and cook, stirring, until browned and well broken up. Stir in turmeric and garam masala and cook for 1 minute, then add onion mixture.

Cook, covered, for 20-30 minutes, stirring occasionally, until cooking liquid is absorbed. Leave to cool. Remove core from cabbage with a sharp knife. Cook whole cabbage in boiling salted water for 8 minutes, then drain and rinse in cold water. Leave until cool enough to handle, then carefully peel off 12-16 outside leaves, keeping them whole. Finely shred remaining cabbage.

To make sauce, heat remaining oil in a heavy-based pan, add sliced onion and cook, stirring frequently, for 5 minutes or until soft but not brown. Add shredded cabbage, tomatoes, remaining ginger, lemon juice and 155ml (5 fl oz/⅔ cup) water. Season with salt and pepper. Bring to the boil, then simmer, uncovered, for 5 minutes.

Preheat oven to 190C (375F/Gas 5). Put about 2 tablespoons mince mixture on each cabbage leaf, fold sides in and roll up neatly. Pour a little sauce into base of an ovenproof casserole, add cabbage rolls and pour over remaining sauce. Cover and cook for 40-50 minutes, until cabbage is tender. Serve hot, garnished with lemon or lime slices.

Serves 4.

BEEF WITH TOMATO SAUCE

2 cloves garlic, thinly sliced
1 tablespoon finely chopped fresh thyme
1 tablespoon finely chopped fresh marjoram
700 g (1½ lb) piece chuck steak
2 tablespoons olive oil
SAUCE:
2 tablespoons olive oil
8 cloves garlic, chopped
1 sprig thyme
2 sprigs marjoram
3 sprigs parsley
400 g (14 oz) can chopped tomatoes
8 canned anchovy fillets, chopped
175 ml (6 fl oz/¾ cup) dry white wine
24 small black olives, stones
salt and freshly ground black pepper

To make the sauce, heat oil in a saucepan, add garlic and herbs and cook gently for 5 minutes. Add tomatoes with their juice, then stir in anchovies, wine and olives. Simmer for 15 minutes. Taste and adjust seasoning.

Meanwhile, mix sliced garlic with chopped herbs. Using the point of a sharp knife, cut small slits in beef and push the herb-covered slices of garlic deep into slits. Heat oil in a flameproof casserole, add beef and cook until evenly browned, 10 minutes. Pour over sauce, cover tightly and cook gently for about 1½ hours turning beef occasionally, until it is tender.

Serves 4.

GARLIC BEEF

2 tablespoons olive oil
115 g (4 oz) piece green (unsmoked) bacon, cut into 5 cm (2 in) cubes
1 kg (2¼ lb) chuck steak, cut into 4 cm (1½ in) cubes
1 Spanish onion, chopped
1 head garlic, divided into cloves
225 ml (8 fl oz/1 cup) red wine
2 cloves
bouquet garni of 1 sprig marjoram, 1 sprig thyme, 2 sprigs parsley and 1 bay leaf
salt and freshly ground black pepper

In a heavy flameproof casserole, heat oil, add bacon and cook over a low heat until bacon gives off its fat. Increase heat, add beef and cook for about 5 minutes, stirring occasionally, until browned all over. Using a slotted spoon, transfer beef and bacon to a bowl.

Stir onion and garlic into casserole and cook gently for 6 minutes, stirring occasionally. Stir in wine, cloves, bouquet garni and salt and pepper. Return meat to casserole, cover tightly and cook gently for 2 hours, stirring occasionally, until meat is very tender. Check from time to time to ensure casserole is not drying out.

Serves 6.

BEEF WITH WATER CHESTNUTS

450 g (1 lb) lean rump or sirloin steak
1 tablespoon dark soy sauce
1 tablespoon dry sherry
1 teaspoon chilli sauce
2 teaspoons brown sugar
2 teaspoons cornflour
225 g (8 oz) broccoli
115 g (4 oz) canned water chestnuts, drained
1 tablespoon sunflower oil
salt and freshly ground black pepper
strips of fresh red chilli, to garnish

Trim any fat from the beef and cut into 2 cm
(¾ in) pieces.

Place beef in a bowl, and mix with soy sauce,
sherry, chilli sauce, sugar and cornflour.
Cover and chill for 30 minutes. Meanwhile,
cut the broccoli into small flowerets. Bring a
small saucepan of water to the boil and cook
the broccoli for 3 minutes. Drain and rinse in
cold water. Halve the water chestnuts.

Heat the oil in a non-stick or well seasoned
wok. Add the beef mixture and stir-fry for
2-3 minutes. Add the broccoli and water
chestnuts, season and stir-fry for 3 minutes.
Garnish with strips of red chilli and serve
with noodles.

Serves 4.

SHREDDED BEEF & GINGER

1 tablespoon cornflour
175 ml (6 fl oz/¾ cup) beef stock
175 ml (6 fl oz/¾ cup) dry sherry
2 teaspoons sugar
salt and freshly ground pepper
2 teaspoons olive oil
2 carrots, cut into matchstick strips
5 cm (2 in) piece fresh root ginger, peeled and finely
  chopped
2 garlic cloves, crushed
350 g (12 oz) lean rump steak, cut into thin strips
175 g (6 oz) mange tout (snow peas)

In a bowl, blend cornflour with stock, sherry,
sugar, salt and pepper and set aside. In a large
frying pan or wok, heat oil over high heat
and stir-fry carrots, ginger and garlic for 2
minutes. Add steak and stir-fry for 3 minutes,
until the meat is browned all over and
cooked through. Add mange tout (snow
peas) and stir-fry 1 minute.

Add cornflour mixture and bring to the boil
over high heat, stirring continuously for 1-2
minutes, until sauce is thickened and glossy.
Serve immediately with freshly cooked
fusilli.

Serves 4.

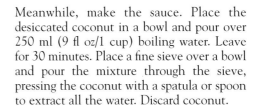

LIGHT BEEF SATAY

450 g (1 lb) lean rump or sirloin steak
MARINADE:
1 shallot, finely chopped
2.5 cm (1 in) piece fresh root ginger, peeled and
   finely chopped
2 cloves garlic, finely chopped
grated rind and juice 1 lime
2 teaspoons garam masala
salt and freshly ground black pepper
1 teaspoon light soy sauce
SAUCE:
6 tablespoons unsweetened desiccated coconut
2 tablespoons crunchy peanut butter
1 tablespoon brown sugar
1 teaspoon sunflower oil
2 cloves garlic, finely chopped
1 fresh red chilli, seeded and chopped
1 tablespoon dark soy sauce
strips fresh red chilli, to garnish

Soak 8 bamboo skewers in cold water to prevent the beef sticking to them. Trim any fat
from the beef and cut into ½ cm (¼ in)
strips. Place in a shallow dish.

Mix together the marinade ingredients and
pour over the beef. Mix well, cover and chill
for 2 hours.

Meanwhile, make the sauce. Place the
desiccated coconut in a bowl and pour over
250 ml (9 fl oz/1 cup) boiling water. Leave
for 30 minutes. Place a fine sieve over a bowl
and pour the mixture through the sieve,
pressing the coconut with a spatula or spoon
to extract all the water. Discard coconut.

Blend coconut water with the peanut butter
and brown sugar. Heat oil in a non-stick or
well seasoned wok and stir-fry garlic and
chilli for 1 minute. Stir in peanut butter mixture and soy sauce and bring to the boil.
Reduce heat and simmer for 10 minutes, stirring occasionally, until thickened. Set aside.

Thread beef strips along each skewer in the
shape of an S. Preheat grill. Cover ends of
skewers with foil to prevent burning. Grill
beef for 3-4 minutes on each side. Drain on
kitchen paper. Reheat peanut sauce. Garnish
with strips of red chilli. Serve the beef
skewers on a bed of rice with the peanut
sauce, lime wedges and a green salad.

Serves 4.

THAI BEEF WITH NOODLES

55 ml (2 fl oz/¼ cup) rice wine or dry sherry
2 tablespoons light soy sauce
2 cloves garlic, finely chopped
2.5 cm (1 in) piece fresh root ginger, peeled and
  finely chopped
½ teaspoon dried crushed chillies
450 g (1 lb) sirloin or fillet steak, 2.5 cm (1 in)
  thick, cut crosswise into 1 cm (½ in) strips
350 g (12 oz) ramen noodles or thin spaghetti
1 tablespoon sesame oil
115 g (4 oz) mange tout (snow peas)
4-6 spring onions, cut into 5 cm (2 in) pieces
2 teaspoons cornflour dissolved in 55 ml (2 fl oz/
  ¼ cup) water
2 tablespoons chopped fresh coriander
fresh coriander leaves and lime slices, to garnish

In a shallow baking dish, combine wine or
sherry, soy sauce, garlic, ginger and chillies.
Add steak, cover and leave to marinate for
30 minutes, turning once. Cook noodles or
spaghetti according to packet directions,
rinse, drain and set aside. Heat wok until
very hot. Add sesame oil and swirl to coat
wok. Remove steak from marinade, scraping
off any ginger and garlic and reserving marinade. Pat steak dry with absorbent kitchen
paper. Add steak to wok and stir-fry for 4-5
minutes, until browned on all sides. Remove
and keep warm.

Add mange tout (snow peas) and spring
onions to any oil remaining in wok and stir-
fry for 1 minute. Stir cornflour mixture and
stir into wok with reserved marinade and
bring to the boil. Add reserved noodles and
beef and chopped coriander. Toss to coat
well. Divide among 4 plates. Garnish with
coriander leaves and lime slices.

Serves 4.

BEEF CURRY

2 tablespoons vegetable oil
3 tablespoons ready-made Red Curry Paste
350 g (12 oz) lean beef, cut into cubes
1 stalk lemon grass, finely chopped
115 g (4 oz) long beans, or green beans, cut into
  4 cm (1½ in) lengths
about 8 pieces dried Chinese black mushrooms,
  soaked, drained and chopped
3 tablespoons roasted peanuts
1 fresh green chilli, seeded and chopped
1 tablespoon fish sauce
2 teaspoons crushed palm sugar
15 Thai mint leaves

In a wok, heat oil, add curry paste and stir for
3 minutes. Add beef and lemon grass and
stir-fry for 5 minutes. Add beans and mushrooms, stir-fry for 3 minutes, then stir in
peanuts and chilli.

Stir for 1 minute, then stir in 4 tablespoons
water, the fish sauce and sugar and cook for
about 2 minutes until beans are tender but
crisp. Transfer to a warmed serving dish and
scatter over mint leaves.

Serves 3-4.

MANGO BEEF WITH CASHEWS

SPICY SESAME BEEF

450 g (1 lb) lean rump or sirloin steak
1 clove garlic, finely chopped
1 tablespoon light soy sauce
1 tablespoon rice wine
1 teaspoon cornflour
salt and freshly ground black pepper
2 ripe mangoes
1 tablespoon sunflower oil
2 tablespoons chopped fresh coriander
25 g (1 oz/¼ cup) unsalted cashew nuts, coarsely
   crushed

Trim any fat from the beef and cut into
0.5 cm (¼ in) strips.

1 tablespoon cornflour
3 tablespoons light soy sauce
450 g (1 lb) rump, sirloin or fillet steak, cut
   crosswise into thin strips
350 g (12 oz) broccoli
2 tablespoons sesame oil
2.5 cm (1 in) piece fresh root ginger, peeled and cut
   into julienne strips
2 cloves garlic, finely chopped
1 fresh chilli, seeded and thinly sliced
1 red pepper (capsicum), thinly sliced
400 g (14 oz) baby corn
115 ml (4 fl oz/½ cup) beef or chicken stock, or
   water
4-6 spring onions, cut into 5 cm (2 in) pieces
toasted sesame seeds, to garnish

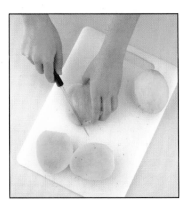

Place in a bowl and mix with garlic, soy
sauce, rice wine, cornflour and seasoning.
Cover and chill for 30 minutes. Peel the
mangoes and slice flesh off the large flat
stone in the centre of each mango. Cut flesh
into thick, even slices, reserving a few small
strips for garnish.

In a bowl, combine cornflour and soy sauce.
Add beef strips and toss to coat well. Leave
to stand for 20 minutes. Cut large flowerets
from the broccoli and divide into small
flowerets. With a swivel-bladed vegetable
peeler, peel the stalk and cut diagonally into
2.5 cm (1 in) pieces. Heat the wok until very
hot. Add sesame oil and swirl to coat. Add
beef strips and marinade and stir-fry for 2-3
minutes until browned.

Heat oil in a non-stick or well seasoned wok
and stir-fry beef mixture for 3-4 minutes
until beef is browned all over. Stir in sliced
mango and cook gently for 2-3 minutes to
heat through. Sprinkle with chopped
coriander and crushed cashews, garnish with
reserved mango and serve on a bed of rice.

Serves 4.

With a slotted spoon, remove beef strips to a
bowl. Add ginger, garlic and chilli to the
wok and stir-fry for 1 minute. Add broccoli,
red pepper (capsicum) and baby corn and
stir-fry for 2-3 minutes until broccoli is
tender but still crisp. Add the stock and stir
for 1 minute until sauce bubbles and
thickens. Add spring onions and reserved
beef strips and stir-fry for 1-2 minutes until
beef strips are heated through. Sprinkle with
sesame seeds and serve with rice or noodles.

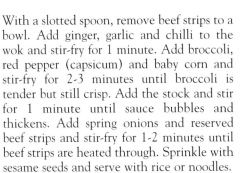

Serves 4.

GINGER BEEF WITH PINEAPPLE

450 g (1 lb) lean rump or sirloin steak
salt and freshly ground black pepper
1 tablespoon ginger wine
2.5 cm (1 in) piece fresh root ginger, peeled and
  finely chopped
1 clove garlic, finely chopped
1 teaspoon cornflour
225 g (8 oz) fresh pineapple
1 tablespoon sunflower oil
2 red peppers (capsicum), thinly sliced
4 spring onions, chopped
2 tablespoons light soy sauce
1 piece stem ginger in syrup, drained and thinly
  sliced

Trim any visible fat from the beef and cut into 0.5 cm (¼ in) strips. Place in a bowl and season. Add the ginger wine, chopped ginger, chopped garlic and the cornflour and mix well. Cover and chill for 30 minutes. Meanwhile, peel and core the pineapple and cut into 2.5 cm (1 in) cubes.

Heat oil in a non-stick or well seasoned wok, add beef mixture and stir-fry for 1-2 minutes until beef is browned all over. Add peppers (capsicum) and stir-fry for a further minute. Add spring onions, pineapple and soy sauce and simmer gently for 2-3 minutes, to heat through. Sprinkle with stem ginger and serve on a bed of noodles.

Serves 4.

DRY-FRIED BEEF STRIPS

2 tablespoons sesame oil
450 g (1 lb) rump or sirloin steak, cut crosswise into
  julienne strips
2 tablespoons rice wine or dry sherry
1 tablespoon light soy sauce
2 cloves garlic, finely chopped
1 cm (½ in) piece fresh root ginger, peeled and finely
  chopped
1 tablespoon Chinese chilli bean paste (sauce)
2 teaspoons sugar
1 carrot, peeled and cut into julienne strips
2 stalks celery, cut into julienne strips
2-3 spring onions, thinly sliced
¼ teaspoon ground Szechuan pepper
cucumber matchsticks, to garnish

Heat the wok until very hot. Add the oil and swirl to coat wok. Add beef and stir-fry for 15 seconds to quickly seal meat. Add 1 tablespoon rice wine or sherry and stir-fry for 1-2 minutes until beef is browned. Pour off and reserve any excess liquid and continue stir-frying until beef is dry.

Stir in soy sauce, garlic, ginger, chilli bean paste, sugar remaining rice wine or sherry and any reserved cooking juices and stir to blend well. Add carrot, celery, spring onions and ground Szechuan pepper and stir-fry until the vegetables begin to soften and all the liquid is absorbed. Garnish with cucumber matchsticks and serve with rice and wild rice.

Serves 4.

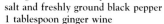

TERIYAKA STEAKS

55 ml (2 fl oz/¼ cup) mirin or dry sherry sweetened
with 1 teaspoon sugar
55 ml (2 fl oz/¼ cup) light soy sauce
1 cm (½ in) piece fresh root ginger, peeled and
minced
1 clove garlic, finely chopped
1 teaspoon sugar
½ teaspoon red pepper sauce (or to taste)
4 sirloin or fillet steaks, cut into strips
2 tablespoons sesame oil
4 spring onions, thinly sliced
fresh coriander leaves, to garnish

In a shallow baking dish, combine mirin or
sweetened dry sherry, soy sauce, ginger, garlic, sugar and red pepper sauce to taste.

Add the steak strips and turn to coat well.
Leave to stand for 1 hour, turning strips once
or twice.

Heat the wok until very hot. Add sesame oil
and swirl to coat. Drain meat, reserving
marinade, and add to wok. Stir-fry for 2-3
minutes until browned on all sides. Pour
over marinade and add spring onions. Cook
for 3-5 minutes until steaks are cooked to
desired doneness and most of marinade has
evaporated, glazing the meat. Garnish with
coriander leaves and serve with marinated
cucumber or daikon (mooli) salad and rice.

Serves 4.

CHILLI BEEF WITH PEPPERS

1 tablespoon cornflour
55 ml (2 fl oz/¼ cup) light soy sauce
1 tablespoon honey or brown sugar
1 teaspoon Chinese chilli sauce
2 tablespoons vegetable oil
450 g (1 lb) rump or sirloin steak, cut crosswise into
thin strips
1 tablespoon sesame oil
2 cloves garlic, finely chopped
1 chilli, seeded and thinly sliced
1 onion, thinly sliced
1 red pepper (capsicum), cut into thin strips
1 green pepper (capsicum), cut into thin strips
1 yellow pepper (capsicum), cut into thin strips

In a small bowl, dissolve the cornflour with
55 ml (2 fl oz/¼ cup) water. Stir in the soy
sauce, honey or sugar and chilli sauce until
blended. Set aside. Heat the wok until very
hot. Add vegetable oil and swirl to coat wok.
Add beef strips and stir-fry for 2-3 minutes
until beef is browned. With a slotted spoon,
remove beef to a bowl.

Add sesame oil to the wok and add garlic and
chilli. Stir-fry for 1 minute until fragrant.
Add onion and pepper (capsicum) strips and
stir-fry for 2-3 minutes until beginning to
soften. Stir cornflour mixture, then stir into
wok and stir until sauce bubbles and begins to
thicken. Add beef strips and any juices and
stir-fry for 1 minute until beef is heated
through. Serve with rice.

Serves 4.

BEEF IN OYSTER SAUCE

3 teaspoons cornflour
1½ tablespoons soy sauce
1½ tablespoons rice wine or dry sherry
450 g (1 lb) rump, sirloin or fillet steak, cut
   crosswise into thin strips
2 tablespoons sesame oil
1 cm (½ in) piece fresh root ginger, peeled and
   chopped
2 cloves garlic, finely chopped
4 stalks celery, sliced
1 red pepper (capsicum), sliced
115 g (4 oz) mushrooms, sliced
4 spring onions, sliced
2 tablespoons oyster sauce
115 ml (4 fl oz/½ cup) chicken stock or water

In a bowl, combine 2 teaspoons of the cornflour with soy sauce and rice wine or sherry.
Add beef strips and toss to coat well. Allow
to stand for 25 minutes. Heat the wok until
very hot. Add oil and swirl to coat wok. Add
beef strips and stir-fry for 2-3 minutes until
browned. With a slotted spoon, remove to a
bowl. Add ginger and garlic to oil remaining
in wok and stir-fry for 1 minute. Add the celery, red pepper (capsicum), mushrooms and
spring onions and stir-fry for 2-3 minutes
until vegetables begin to soften.

Stir in oyster sauce and combine remaining
cornflour with the stock or water, then stir
into the wok and bring to the boil. Add
reserved beef strips and toss beef and vegetables for 1 minute until sauce bubbles and
thickens and beef is heated through. Serve
with rice and wild rice.

Serves 4.

BEEF STROGANOFF

2 tablespoons groundnut oil
800 g (1¾ lb) fillet or boneless sirloin steak, cut
   crosswise into 1 cm (½ in) strips
25 g (1 oz/2 tablespoons) butter
1 onion, thinly sliced
225 g (8 oz) mushrooms, thinly sliced
salt and freshly ground black pepper
1 tablespoon flour
115 ml (4 fl oz/½ cup) beef or veal stock
1 tablespoons Dijon mustard (optional)
250 ml (9 oz/1 cup) sour cream
pinch of cayenne pepper
dill sprigs, to garnish

Heat the wok until very hot. Add oil and
swirl to coat wok. Add half the beef strips.

Stir-fry for 1 minute until just browned and
still rare. With a slotted spoon, remove beef
to a bowl. Allow wok to reheat and add
remaining beef strips. Stir-fry for 1 minute
and turn beef and any juices into bowl. Add
butter to wok, then add onion. Reduce heat
to moderate and stir-fry onion for 3-4
minutes until softened and beginning to
colour. Add mushrooms and increase heat;
stir-fry for 2 minutes until mushrooms and
onions are softened and golden. Add salt and
pepper and stir in flour until well blended.

Add beef stock and bring to the boil, then
simmer for 1 minute until sauce thickens.
Stir in mustard, if using, and gradually add
the sour cream. (Do not allow sour cream to
boil.) Return beef strips and any juices to
sauce and cook gently for 1 minute until beef
is heated through. Sprinkle a little cayenne
pepper over and garnish with dill sprigs.
Serve with rice.

Serves 6.

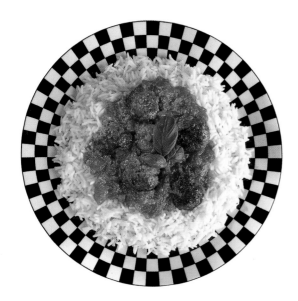

MEATBALLS IN TOMATO SAUCE

55 ml (2 fl oz/¼ cup) milk
1 egg, beaten
½ teaspoon freshly grated nutmeg
55 g (2 oz) white bread
2 onions, finely chopped
2 cloves garlic, crushed
1 teaspoon dried thyme
2 tablespoons chopped fresh parsley
450 g (1 lb) minced beef
1 tablespoon olive oil
400 g (14 oz) can chopped tomatoes
2 tablespoons tomato purée (paste)
salt and freshly ground black pepper
basil leaves, to garnish

BOBOTIE

250 ml (9 fl oz/1 cup) milk
1 thick slice white bread
1 tablespoon olive oil
1 large onion, chopped
1 kg (2¼ lb) minced beef
2 teaspoons apricot jam
55 ml (2 fl oz/¼ cup) lemon juice
85 g (3 oz) seedless raisins
10 ready-to-eat dried apricots
2 tablespoons mild curry powder
12 blanched almonds, roughly chopped
1 teaspoon salt
freshly ground black pepper
6 bay leaves
2 eggs

In a shallow dish, mix together the milk, egg and nutmeg. Add the bread and leave to soak for 5 minutes. In a bowl, mix half the onions and garlic with the thyme, parsley and minced beef. Squeeze the liquid from the bread and add the bread to the beef mixture. Mix well and shape into 30 balls. Heat the oil in a flameproof casserole. Add the meatballs in batches and cook, turning, for about 8 minutes, until browned all over. Remove with a slotted spoon, drain on kitchen paper and keep warm.

Preheat oven to 180C (350F/Gas 4). Put half the milk in a shallow dish, add the bread and leave to soak for 5 minutes. Heat the oil in a flameproof casserole. Add the onion and cook, stirring occasionally, for 5 minutes until soft. Squeeze the milk from the bread and add the bread to the casserole with all the remaining ingredients except the eggs and remaining milk. Mix well then level the surface. Bake for 30 minutes.

Put the remaining onion and garlic in the casserole with the chopped tomatoes, tomato purée (paste) and salt and pepper. Bring to the boil and cook over a medium heat stirring constantly, until reduced and thickened. Add the meatballs and heat gently to warm through. Garnish and serve.

Serves 4.

Beat together the remaining milk and eggs and pour over the meat. Return to the oven and bake for 20-25 minutes, until the custard has set.

Serves 6-8.

Note: This dish is particularly good served with a fruity chutney.

BELGIAN HOTCHPOTCH

225 g (8 oz) brisket of beef, cubed
225 g (8 oz) shoulder of lamb, cubed
85 g (3 oz) belly pork, cubed
500 ml (18 fl oz/2¼ cups) chicken stock
2 bay leaves
salt and freshly ground black pepper
115 g (4 oz) swede, diced
10 small onions
225 g (8 oz) Brussels sprouts
700 g (1½ lb) potatoes, diced
115 g (4 oz) carrots, diced
225 g (8 oz) pork chipolata sausages
150 ml (5 fl oz/⅔ cup) crème fraîche

Put the beef, lamb and pork in a flameproof casserole and pour in the stock.

Add 500 ml (18 fl oz/2¼ cups) water, the bay leaves and 1 teaspoon salt. Bring to the boil, skimming any scum from the surface. Cover tightly and simmer for 2 hours. Add the vegetables and cook for 30 minutes, until the meat is tender. Remove the meat and vegetables from the casserole with a slotted spoon and keep warm. Put the sausages in the casserole and cook for 10 minutes. Remove with a slotted spoon and add to the meat and vegetables.

Bring the sauce to the boil and boil until reduced by one-third. Season with salt and pepper, stir in the crème fraîche and heat gently to warm through. Pour the sauce over the meat and vegetables and serve.

Serves 4-6.

BEEF GOULASH WITH CHILLI

2 tablespoons olive oil
1 onion, sliced
1 clove garlic, crushed
2 teaspoons paprika
700 g (1½ lb) lean stewing beef, cubed
pinch caraway seeds
2 bay leaves
1 tablespoon balsamic vinegar
450 ml (16 fl oz/2 cups) beef stock
salt and freshly ground black pepper
700 g (1½ lb) potatoes, diced
2 green peppers (capsicum), sliced
1 fresh green chilli, cored, seeded and sliced
400 g (14 oz) can chopped tomatoes
2 tablespoons tomato purée (paste)

Heat the oil in a flameproof casserole. Add the onion, garlic and paprika and cook, stirring, for 2 minutes. Add the beef and cook for 3-4 minutes, until the onion is soft and the beef has browned. Add the caraway seeds, bay leaves, vinegar and half the stock. Season with salt and pepper and bring to the boil. Cover and simmer for 1 hour.

Stir in the remaining stock, potatoes, peppers (capsicum), chilli, tomatoes and tomato purée (paste). Bring to the boil, cover and simmer for 30-40 minutes, until the meat and vegetables are tender.

Serves 4.

CHILLI BEEF WITH NACHOS

1 tablespoon olive oil
1 onion, chopped
1 clove garlic, crushed
450 g (1 lb) minced beef
400 g (14 oz) can red kidney beans, drained
1 green pepper (capsicum), chopped
2 tablespoons tomato purée (paste)
2 teaspoons chilli powder
150 g (5 oz) tortilla chips
115 g (4 oz/1 cup) grated mozzarella cheese
1-2 teaspoons paprika

Heat the oil in a flameproof casserole. Add the onion and garlic and cook, stirring occasionally, for 5 minutes, until soft. Add the mince and cook for 6-8 minutes, until brown. Stir in the kidney beans, green peppers (capsicum), tomato purée (paste), chilli powder and 150 ml (5 fl oz/⅔ cup) water. Cover and simmer for 10-15 minutes. Preheat oven to 200C (400F/Gas 6).

Uncover and cook for 5 minutes, until the sauce is reduced and thickened. Arrange the tortilla chips over the top, sprinkle with mozzarella cheese and paprika and cook in the oven for 20 minutes until the cheese is melted and golden. Serve.

Serves 4.

POT ROAST OF BRISKET

1.3 kg (3 lb) brisket of beef
2 leeks, thickly sliced
1 bay leaf
2 parsley stalks
1 celery leaf
450 g (1 lb) carrots, thickly sliced
450 g (1 lb) sweet potatoes, cut into chunks
4 tablespoons cider vinegar
225 g (8 oz) white cabbage, thickly shredded
salt and freshly ground black pepper

Heat a large flameproof casserole, add the brisket and cook, turning, for 3-4 minutes, until browned all over.

Remove from the casserole. Add the leeks and mix into the cooking juices. With a piece of string, tie together the bay leaf, parsley stalks and celery leaf and add to the casserole with the carrots and sweet potatoes. Stir well. Add the vinegar and 115 ml (4 fl oz/½ cup) water. Place the meat on top.

Cover and cook very gently for 2½ hours. Remove the beef from the casserole and keep warm. Remove the vegetables with a slotted spoon and keep warm. Bring the sauce to the boil and add the white cabbage. Season and simmer for 5 minutes. Carve the beef and serve with the vegetables.

Serves 6-8.

DEVILLED STEAKS

1 tablespoon olive oil
4 fillet steaks, about 115 g (4 oz) each
salt and freshly ground pepper
2 tablespoons sherry vinegar
6 tablespoons dry red wine
4 tablespoons strong beef stock
2 cloves garlic, chopped
1 teaspoon crushed fennel seeds
1 tablespoon sun-dried tomato purée
large pinch chilli powder
chopped fresh parsley and parsley sprigs, to garnish

Heat oil in a non-stick frying pan until smoking, then add the steaks.

Cook for 2 minutes, turn over and cook for a further 2 minutes for medium/rare steaks. Cook for a little longer if well-done steaks are preferred. Remove from the pan, season and keep warm while making sauce. Pour vinegar, red wine and stock into the pan and boil for 30 seconds. Stir in garlic and fennel seeds. Whisk in the sun-dried tomato purée and chilli powder, to taste. Simmer until the sauce is syrupy.

Place steaks on warm plates. Pour any juices into the sauce, bring to the boil, taste and season. Pour sauce over the steaks. Garnish with chopped parsley and parsley sprigs and serve with grilled tomatoes and roasted diced potatoes.

Serves 4.

STEAK WITH TOMATO & OLIVES

4 minute steaks, about 115 g (4 oz) each
2 tablespoons olive oil
2 cloves garlic, chopped
1 medium onion, thinly sliced
1 carrot, finely diced
400 g (14 oz) can chopped tomatoes
1 teaspoon balsamic vinegar
½ teaspoon dried oregano
1 tablespoon chopped fresh basil
salt and freshly ground black pepper
12 Greek-style black olives, stoned
basil leaves, to garnish

Lightly brush both sides of the steaks with a little of the olive oil. Set aside.

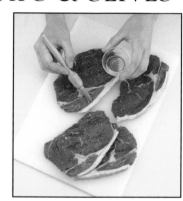

In a non-stick saucepan, heat remaining oil and add garlic. Cook gently until golden. Add onion and carrot and 2 tablespoons water. Cover saucepan and cook gently for 10 minutes until onions are soft, stirring once. Stir in the tomatoes, vinegar, herbs and seasoning, then simmer, uncovered, for 15 minutes until thick and reduced. Stir in the olives and keep warm.

Heat a ridged griddle until smoking and grill steaks for 1 minute per side. Remove to 4 warm plates and season with salt and pepper. Serve with the tomato and olive sauce. Garnish with basil leaves and serve with roasted sliced potatoes and broccoli.

Serves 4.

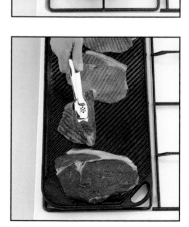

BEEF IN BAROLO WINE

1 kg (2¼ lb) braising beef joint
6 cloves garlic, crushed
1 onion, roughly chopped
1 carrot, chopped
1 stick celery, chopped
2 bay leaves
2 large thyme sprigs
2-3 peppercorns, lightly crushed
2 cloves
2 allspice berries, crushed
115 ml (4 fl oz/½ cup) Barolo wine, or other full-bodied red wine
2 tablespoons tomato purée (paste)
150 ml (5 fl oz/⅔ cup) strong beef stock
salt and freshly ground black pepper

Place meat in a large polythene bag with the garlic, onion, carrot, celery, bay leaves, thyme, peppercorns, cloves, allspice and wine. Shake the bag, seal and refrigerate for several hours or overnight, turning meat occasionally. Next day, preheat oven to 170C (325F) Gas 3. Open bag, remove the meat from marinade and pat dry. Heat oil in a large flameproof casserole and brown the meat all over. Pour in reserved marinade, tomato purée (paste) and stock. Cover tightly and bake in oven for 2-3 hours until beef is tender.

Lift meat out of casserole and keep warm. Skim off any fat, remove bay leaves from the sauce. Purée in a blender or food processor until smooth. Taste and season. The sauce should be quite thick; if it is not, boil to reduce it. Slice the meat thinly and serve with the sauce, accompanied by mange tout and polenta.

Serves 8.

ITALIAN MEATBALLS

6 tablespoons semi-skimmed milk
1 slice bread, crusts removed
700 g (1½ lb) lean minced beef or lamb
6 spring onions, chopped
1 clove garlic, chopped
2 tablespoons freshly grated Parmesan cheese
freshly grated nutmeg
salt and freshly ground pepper
2 tablespoons olive oil
150 ml (5 fl oz/⅔ cup) dry white wine
400 g (14 oz) can chopped tomatoes

Sprinkle milk over the bread in a shallow dish and leave to soak for a few minutes.

Preheat oven to 180C (350F) Gas 4. Put meat in a large bowl and add soaked bread, spring onions, garlic, cheese, nutmeg and salt and pepper to taste. Work together until well mixed and smooth. With wet hands, roll into 30-36 even-sized balls. Heat the oil in a large non-stick frying pan and brown the meatballs in batches, then transfer them to a shallow ovenproof dish. Pour wine and tomatoes into frying pan and bring to boil, scraping up any sediment from the bottom of the pan.

Pour the sauce over the meatballs, cover and bake in oven for 1 hour until tender. Serve with buttered noodles.

Serves 8.

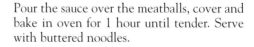

VEAL SCALOPPINE

SALTIMBOCCA

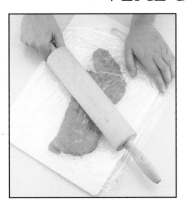

4 veal or turkey escalopes, about 115 g (4 oz) each
2 tablespoons plain flour
salt and freshly ground pepper
3 tablespoons olive oil
3 tablespoons lemon juice
6 tablespoons white wine
2 tablespoons chopped fresh parsley
lemon wedges, to garnish

Trim escalopes of any gristle around edge. Place the escalopes between sheets of plastic film and beat out thinly without tearing. Coat in the flour seasoned with salt and pepper.

Heat the oil in a non-stick frying pan. Add escalopes and fry over brisk heat for about 2 minutes per side, pressing them down with a fish slice to keep them flat. Remove from the pan and keep warm.

Add the lemon juice and wine to the frying pan, stirring and scraping to dislodge any sediment. Boil for 1 minute, then taste and season. Stir in parsley and pour the lemon sauce over escalopes. Garnish with lemon wedges and serve at once, with potatoes and stir-fried vegetables.

Serves 4.

6 veal or turkey escalopes, about 55 g (2 oz) each
8 thin slices of Parma ham
salt and freshly ground pepper
8 fresh sage leaves
1 tablespoon olive oil
25 g (1 oz) butter
70 ml (2½ fl oz/⅓ cup) dry Marsala or sherry
fresh sage leaves, to garnish

Trim escalopes of any gristle around edge. Place between sheets of plastic film and bat out thinly without tearing. Trim Parma ham of any fat and cut to same size as escalopes.

Season each escalope with a little salt. Place a sage leaf on top of each one and cover with a slice of ham. Secure each one through the middle with a wooden cocktail stick, as if taking a large stitch. These are not rolled up.

Heat the oil and butter in a non-stick frying pan and fry the escalopes in batches, on both sides for about 2 minutes until golden and tender. Remove and keep warm. Add the Marsala to the pan, stir and bring to the boil, then boil for 1 minute. Spoon the sauce over escalopes, garnish with sage and serve with green beans and noodles.

Serves 4.

LAMB

TARRAGON LAMB NOISETTES

1 tablespoon olive oil
55 g (2 oz/¼ cup) butter
8 lamb noisettes, about 2.5 cm (1 in) thick
salt and freshly ground black pepper
4 tablespoons brandy
3 tablespoons double (thick) cream
2 tablespoons chopped fresh tarragon
tarragon sprigs and flat-leaf parsley, to garnish

Heat oil and half the butter in a heavy frying pan until sizzling.

Add lamb and cook for 2½-3 minutes on each side, until well-browned but still pink in the centre. Remove with a slotted spoon, transfer to warmed serving plates, season with salt and pepper and keep warm.

Add remaining butter to pan. When melted, add brandy, stirring to dislodge sediment, and bring to the boil. Stir in cream and tarragon and boil until thickened. Season, pour over lamb, garnish with tarragon sprigs and flat-leaf parsley and serve.

Serves 4.

LAMB WITH ROSEMARY

2 kg (4½ lb) leg of young lamb
3 sprigs of rosemary
2-3 cloves garlic, cut into slivers
salt and freshly ground black pepper
55 g (2 oz/¼ cup) butter
150 ml (5 fl oz/⅔ cup) red or white wine

Preheat oven to 230C (450F/Gas 8). Cut small incisions in lamb with the point of a sharp knife.

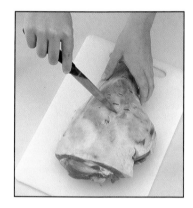

Remove leaves from one rosemary sprig. Insert leaves and garlic slivers into incisions. Season lamb, put the remaining rosemary sprigs on top and dot with butter. Put in a roasting tin and roast for 15 minutes. Lower oven temperature to 180C (350F/Gas 4) and roast for a further 40-60 minutes.

Leave lamb in oven, with door propped open, for 15 minutes, to rest. Remove lamb from roasting tin and transfer to a serving plate. Tilt roasting tin and spoon off most of fat. Add wine, stirring to dislodge sediment. Bring to the boil and simmer briefly. Season with salt and pepper. Carve lamb, garnish with rosemary sprigs and serve with sauce.

Serves 6.

LAMB & FLAGEOLET BEANS

4 lamb shanks about 225 g (8 oz) each
4 cloves garlic, thinly sliced
2 tablespoons olive oil
1 onion, finely chopped
350 g (12 oz/1½ cups) flageolet beans, soaked
  overnight
575 g (1¼ lb) tomatoes, peeled, seeded and chopped
1 tablespoon tomato purée (paste)
150 ml (5 fl oz/⅔ cup) red wine
bouquet garni
salt and freshly ground black pepper
1 small bunch of parsley, chopped
flat-leaf parsley and bay leaves, to garnish

Cut 4 incisions in each lamb shank. Insert a slice of garlic in each incision.

Heat oil in a heavy flameproof casserole, add shanks and cook until browned all over. Remove and set aside. Add onion and remaining garlic to casserole and cook, stirring occasionally, for 5 minutes, until soft but not browned.

Drain and rinse beans and add to casserole with tomatoes, tomato purée (paste), wine, bouquet garni and salt and pepper. Return lamb to casserole, cover tightly and cook gently for 1-2 hours, until lamb and flageolet beans are tender. Discard bouquet garni and stir in parsley. Garnish and serve with béarnaise sauce (see page 130).

Serves 4.

LAMB BOULANGÈRE

2 kg (4½ lb) leg of lamb
4 cloves garlic
salt and freshly ground black pepper
1 kg (2¼ lb) potatoes, fairly thickly sliced
1 Spanish onion, thinly sliced
1 bay leaf
2 sprigs of thyme
about 300 ml (10 fl oz/1¼ cups) veal or vegetable
  stock or water
45 g (1½ oz/3 tablespoons) butter
olive oil for greasing
salt and freshly ground black pepper
flat-leaf parsley, to garnish

Cut small incisions in lamb. Thinly slice two garlic cloves and insert into incisions.

Season lamb and set aside. Preheat oven to 160C (325F/Gas 3). Grease a shallow ovenproof dish with 15g (½ oz/1 tablespoon) butter. Crush remaining garlic. Arrange layers of potatoes, onion, garlic, herbs and salt and pepper in the buttered dish. Add enough stock or water to just cover, dot with remaining butter, cover with foil and bake in the oven for 1 hour.

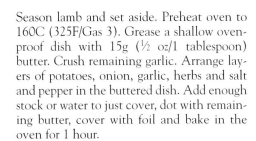

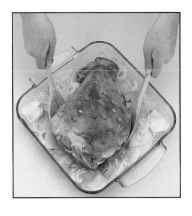

Grease a heavy frying pan with a little oil, add lamb and cook quickly until lightly browned all over. Put lamb on top of potatoes and cover with foil. Increase oven temperature to 190C (375F/Gas 5) and bake lamb and potatoes for 1¼-1½ hours, uncovering 15 minutes before end of cooking time, to brown. Carve lamb, garnish with flat-leaf parsley and serve with potatoes.

Serves 6.

NAVARIN OF LAMB

MOROCCAN LAMB

1 tablespoon olive oil
1 kg (2¼ lb) boneless lamb, cubed
1 onion and 1 large carrot, finely chopped
pinch sugar
2 teaspoons plain flour
115 ml (4 fl oz/½ cup) dry white wine
550 ml (20 fl oz/2½ cups) veal or chicken stock
bouquet garni
salt and freshly ground black pepper
3 ripe tomatoes, peeled, seeded and chopped
3 small turnips, quartered
12 button onions
12 small new potatoes
12 baby carrots, halved or quartered
150 g (5 oz) shelled fresh peas or small broad beans
parsley sprigs, to garnish

115 g (4 oz/1 cup) dried apricots
2 tablespoons olive oil
1 large onion, chopped
1 kg (2¼ lb) boneless shoulder of lamb, cubed
1 teaspoon ground cumin
½ teaspoon each ground coriander and cinnamon
salt and freshly ground black pepper
grated rind and juice ½ orange
1 teaspoon saffron strands
1 tablespoon ground almonds
about 300 ml (10 fl oz/1¼ cups) lamb or chicken
  stock
1 tablespoon sesame seeds
flat-leaf parsley sprigs, to garnish

Cut the apricots in half and put in a bowl.

Heat oil in a heavy flameproof casserole, add lamb and cook until browned all over. Remove with a slotted spoon and set aside. Add chopped onion and carrot and cook, stirring occasionally, for 10 minutes, until browned. Sprinkle over sugar and flour and cook, stirring, until lightly browned. Add wine, stock, bouquet garni and salt and pepper. Add tomatoes and bring to the boil, stirring. Return lamb to casserole, cover tightly and cook gently for 30 minutes.

Cover with 150 ml (5 fl oz/⅔ cup) water and leave to soak overnight. Preheat the oven to 180C (350F/Gas 4). Heat the olive oil in a flameproof casserole. Add the onion and cook gently for 10 minutes until soft and golden. Add the lamb, cumin, coriander, cinnamon and salt and pepper and cook, stirring, for 5 minutes.

Add turnips, onions and potatoes, cover and cook for 20 minutes. Add carrots and cook for 10 minutes. Add peas or beans and cook for 5-7 minutes. Remove meat and vegetables with a slotted spoon, transfer to a warmed plate and keep warm. Boil cooking juices to thicken slightly. Return lamb and vegetables to casserole and turn in sauce. Garnish with parsley and serve.

Add the apricots and their soaking liquid. Stir in the orange rind and juice, saffron, ground almonds and enough stock to cover. Cover and cook in the oven for 1-1½ hours until the meat is tender, adding extra stock if necessary. Heat a frying pan, add the sesame seeds and dry fry, shaking the pan, until golden, Sprinkle the sesame seeds over the meat, garnish with parsley and serve.

Serves 4.

Serves 4-6.

LAMB WITH BLACK OLIVES

4 tablespoons olive oil
700 g (1½ lb) lean lamb, cut into small cubes
115 g (4 oz) piece belly pork, cut into small strips
2 cloves garlic, sliced
½-1 teaspoon chopped fresh oregano
175 ml (6 fl oz/¾ cup) full-bodied white wine
1 fresh red chilli, seeded and finely chopped
12-15 black olives, stoned

Heat oil in a wide, shallow flameproof casserole. Add lamb, pork and garlic and cook over a high heat to seal and brown meat.

In a small saucepan, boil oregano and wine for 2-3 minutes. Stir into casserole, cover and cook gently for 30 minutes.

Stir chilli and olives into casserole. Cover again and cook for about 30 minutes until lamb is tender. If necessary, uncover casserole towards end of cooking time so liquid can evaporate to make a light sauce.

Serves 4.

SPICE-COATED LAMB

4 cloves garlic
¼ teaspoon cumin seeds
1 tablespoon paprika
¼ teaspoon saffron threads, crushed
salt and freshly ground black pepper
700 g (1½ lb) lean boned lamb, cut into 2.5-4 cm (1-1½ in) cubes
3 tablespoons olive oil
150 ml (5 fl oz/⅔ cup) full-bodied dry white wine

Using a pestle and mortar, pound together garlic, cumin, paprika, saffron, salt and pepper.

Put lamb into a bowl, add spice mixture and stir well but gently to coat lamb. Set aside for 30 minutes.

Heat oil in a flameproof casserole, add lamb and cook for 5-7 minutes, stirring occasionally, until lamb has browned. Stir in wine and heat to simmering point. Cover tightly and cook gently for about 30-40 minutes until meat is tender and sauce thickened.

Serves 4.

RED-COOKED LAMB FILLET

450 g (1 lb) lean lamb fillet
3 tablespoons dry sherry
1 cm (½ in) piece fresh root ginger, peeled and finely
 chopped
2 cloves garlic, thinly sliced
1 teaspoon five-spice powder
3 tablespoons dark soy sauce
300 ml (10 fl oz/1¼ cups) Chinese Vegetable Stock
 (see glossary)
2 teaspoons caster sugar
2 teaspoons cornflour mixed with 4 teaspoons water
salt and freshly ground black pepper
shredded spring onions, to garnish

Trim any excess fat and silver skin from lamb
and cut into 2 cm (¾ in) cubes.

Blanch the lamb in a saucepan of boiling
water for 3 minutes. Drain well. Heat a non-
stick or well seasoned wok and add the lamb
with the sherry, ginger, garlic, five-spice powder and soy sauce. Bring to the boil, reduce
heat and simmer for 2 minutes, stirring. Pour
in stock, return to the boil and simmer for 25
minutes.

Add sugar, cornflour mixture and seasoning
and stir until thickened. Simmer gently for 5
minutes. Garnish with shredded spring
onions and serve on a bed of rice.

Serves 4.

STIR-FRIED SESAME LAMB

350 g (12 oz) lean lamb fillet
1 tablespoon sunflower oil
115 g (4 oz) shallots, sliced
1 red pepper (capsicum), sliced
1 green pepper (capsicum), sliced
1 clove garlic, finely chopped
1 tablespoon light soy sauce
1 teaspoon white rice vinegar
1 teaspoon caster sugar
freshly ground black pepper
2 tablespoons sesame seeds

Trim any fat and silver skin from the lamb
fillet. Cut into 0.5 cm (¼ in) cubes.

Heat oil in a non-stick or well seasoned wok
and stir-fry the lamb for 1-2 minutes until
browned. Remove with a slotted spoon and
set aside. Stir-fry shallots, peppers (capsicum) and garlic for 2 minutes until just
soft.

Return lamb to wok with all the remaining
ingredients except the sesame seeds. Stir-fry
for 2 minutes. Sprinkle with sesame seeds
and serve with rice and vegetables.

Serves 4.

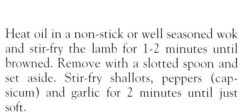

LAMB WITH BLACK OLIVES

4 tablespoons olive oil
700 g (1½ lb) lean lamb, cut into small cubes
115 g (4 oz) piece belly pork, cut into small strips
2 cloves garlic, sliced
½-1 teaspoon chopped fresh oregano
175 ml (6 fl oz/¾ cup) full-bodied white wine
1 fresh red chilli, seeded and finely chopped
12-15 black olives, stoned

Heat oil in a wide, shallow flameproof casserole. Add lamb, pork and garlic and cook over a high heat to seal and brown meat.

In a small saucepan, boil oregano and wine for 2-3 minutes. Stir into casserole, cover and cook gently for 30 minutes.

Stir chilli and olives into casserole. Cover again and cook for about 30 minutes until lamb is tender. If necessary, uncover casserole towards end of cooking time so liquid can evaporate to make a light sauce.

Serves 4.

SPICE-COATED LAMB

4 cloves garlic
¼ teaspoon cumin seeds
1 tablespoon paprika
¼ teaspoon saffron threads, crushed
salt and freshly ground black pepper
700 g (1½ lb) lean boned lamb, cut into 2.5-4 cm (1-1½ in) cubes
3 tablespoons olive oil
150 ml (5 fl oz/⅔ cup) full-bodied dry white wine

Using a pestle and mortar, pound together garlic, cumin, paprika, saffron, salt and pepper.

Put lamb into a bowl, add spice mixture and stir well but gently to coat lamb. Set aside for 30 minutes.

Heat oil in a flameproof casserole, add lamb and cook for 5-7 minutes, stirring occasionally, until lamb has browned. Stir in wine and heat to simmering point. Cover tightly and cook gently for about 30-40 minutes until meat is tender and sauce thickened.

Serves 4.

RED-COOKED LAMB FILLET

450 g (1 lb) lean lamb fillet
3 tablespoons dry sherry
1 cm (½ in) piece fresh root ginger, peeled and finely
  chopped
2 cloves garlic, thinly sliced
1 teaspoon five-spice powder
3 tablespoons dark soy sauce
300 ml (10 fl oz/1¼ cups) Chinese Vegetable Stock
  (see glossary)
2 teaspoons caster sugar
2 teaspoons cornflour mixed with 4 teaspoons water
salt and freshly ground black pepper
shredded spring onions, to garnish

Trim any excess fat and silver skin from lamb
and cut into 2 cm (¾ in) cubes.

Blanch the lamb in a saucepan of boiling
water for 3 minutes. Drain well. Heat a non-
stick or well seasoned wok and add the lamb
with the sherry, ginger, garlic, five-spice powder and soy sauce. Bring to the boil, reduce
heat and simmer for 2 minutes, stirring. Pour
in stock, return to the boil and simmer for 25
minutes.

Add sugar, cornflour mixture and seasoning
and stir until thickened. Simmer gently for 5
minutes. Garnish with shredded spring
onions and serve on a bed of rice.

Serves 4.

STIR-FRIED SESAME LAMB

350 g (12 oz) lean lamb fillet
1 tablespoon sunflower oil
115 g (4 oz) shallots, sliced
1 red pepper (capsicum), sliced
1 green pepper (capsicum), sliced
1 clove garlic, finely chopped
1 tablespoon light soy sauce
1 teaspoon white rice vinegar
1 teaspoon caster sugar
freshly ground black pepper
2 tablespoons sesame seeds

Trim any fat and silver skin from the lamb
fillet. Cut into 0.5 cm (¼ in) cubes.

Heat oil in a non-stick or well seasoned wok
and stir-fry the lamb for 1-2 minutes until
browned. Remove with a slotted spoon and
set aside. Stir-fry shallots, peppers (capsicum) and garlic for 2 minutes until just
soft.

Return lamb to wok with all the remaining
ingredients except the sesame seeds. Stir-fry
for 2 minutes. Sprinkle with sesame seeds
and serve with rice and vegetables.

Serves 4.

LAMB IN GREEN SAUCE

2 tablespoons olive oil
700 g (1½ lb) boneless lamb, cut into pieces
1 Spanish onion, chopped
2 green peppers (capsicums), seeded and chopped
3 cloves garlic, crushed
175 ml (6 fl oz/¾ cup) dry white wine
150 ml (5 fl oz/⅔ cup) water
1½ teaspoons chopped fresh thyme
salt and freshly ground black pepper
1 small round lettuce, sliced
2 tablespoons chopped fresh parsley
2 tablespoons chopped fresh mint
55 g (2 oz) pine nuts
mint sprigs and pine nuts, to garnish

In a flameproof casserole, heat oil, add lamb and fry, stirring occasionally, until evenly browned. Using a slotted spoon, remove lamb and set aside. Stir onion into casserole and cook for about 4 minutes, stirring occasionally, until softened but not browned. Stir in peppers (capsicums) and garlic, cook for 2-3 minutes, then stir in wine. Boil for 1 minute.

Pour in water and bring to the boil. Lower heat so liquid is just simmering, then add lamb, thyme and seasoning. Cover and cook gently for about 1 hour. Stir in lettuce, parsley, mint and pine nuts, cover and cook for a further 10-15 minutes. Serve garnished with sprigs of mint and pine nuts.

Serves 4.

STIR-FRIED MEATBALLS

450 g (1 lb) aubergines (eggplant)
4 tablespoons salt
1 tablespoon sunflower oil
2 tablespoons rice wine
115 g (4 oz) canned bamboo shoots, drained and cut into strips
4 spring onions, finely chopped, to garnish
MEATBALLS:
350 g (12 oz) lean minced lamb
4 spring onions, finely chopped
2 cloves garlic, finely chopped
2 tablespoons chopped fresh chives
salt and ground white pepper
1 teaspoon ground cinnamon
2 teaspoons cornflour
1 egg white

Cut the aubergines (eggplant) into 0.5 cm (¼ in) slices. Layer in a bowl, sprinkling with the salt and set aside for 30 minutes. Mix together ingredients for meatballs. Divide into 24 portions and roll into balls, flouring the hands with extra cornflour. Set aside. Transfer aubergines (eggplant) to a colander and rinse well under cold running water, pressing gently to remove all the salt and bitterness. Drain well and pat dry with kitchen paper.

Heat the oil and rice wine in a non-stick or well seasoned wok and stir-fry aubergines (eggplant) for 2-3 minutes until softened. Add meatballs and gently stir-fry for 5 minutes. Add bamboo shoots and stir-fry for 2 minutes. Remove meatballs and vegetables with a slotted spoon. Garnish with chopped spring onions and serve with salad.

Serves 4.

LAMB WITH ONIONS

700 g (1½ lb) shoulder of lamb, boned
1 teaspoon turmeric
1 teaspoon ground cumin
1 teaspoon ground coriander
2.5 cm (1 in) piece fresh root ginger, grated
2 cloves garlic, crushed
45 ml (1½ fl oz/9 teaspoons) vegetable oil
3 teaspoons caster sugar
4 large onions, sliced into thin rings
450 g (1 lb) potatoes, cut into large chunks
salt and cayenne pepper
1 teaspoon garam masala
rosemary sprigs, to garnish

Wipe lamb, trim and cut into cubes.

Put lamb in a glass or china bowl. Mix together turmeric, cumin, coriander, ginger and garlic and add to lamb. Stir well, then cover loosely and leave in a cool place for 2-3 hours. Heat oil in a heavy-based pan until smoking. Stir in sugar, then add onions and cook over a medium to high heat for 10 minutes, stirring frequently, until a rich brown. Remove onions with a slotted spoon and set aside.

Add lamb to pan and fry until browned all over. Add potatoes and fry, stirring, for 2 minutes. Return onions to pan, add 225 ml (8 fl oz/1 cup) water and season with salt and cayenne pepper. Bring to the boil and simmer, covered, for 1¼ hours, or until lamb is tender, stirring occasionally. Stir in garam masala and serve, garnished with rosemary sprigs.

Serves 4.

SAGE LAMB COBBLER

90 g (2 lb) neck of lamb, boned and cubed
25 g (1 oz/¼ cup) plain flour
1 tablespoon olive oil
1 large onion, chopped
55 g (2 oz/¼ cup) dried peas, soaked overnight
225 g (8 oz) each carrots and swede, diced
500 ml (18 fl oz/2¼ cups) lamb or chicken stock
salt and freshly ground black pepper
large pinch paprika
TOPPING:
225 g (8 oz/2 cups) plain flour
1½ teaspoons baking powder
55 g (2 oz/¼ cup) butter
1 teaspoon dried sage
1 egg
2 tablespoons milk, plus extra for brushing

Preheat oven to 160C (325F/Gas 3). Coat the lamb in the flour. Heat the oil in a flame-proof casserole. Add the lamb and cook until browned all over. Remove and set aside. Add the onion and cook, stirring occasionally, for 7 minutes, until lightly browned. Return the lamb and add the peas, carrots and swede. Pour in the stock and season with salt, pepper and paprika. Bring to the boil, cover and cook in the oven for 2 hours. Sift the flour, baking powder and salt into a bowl. Rub in the butter until the mixture resembles fine breadcrumbs.

Stir in the sage. Add the egg and milk and bind to a soft dough. Knead on a lightly floured urface and roll out to 1 cm (½ in) thick. Using a pastry cutter, cut out 4 cm (1½ in) rounds. Arrange the scones on top of the casserole and brush with milk. Increase the oven temperature to 200C (400F/Gas 6). Return the casserole to the oven and cook, uncovered, for 15-20 minutes, until the scones are risen and golden. Serve.

Serves 6-8.

CURRIED LAMB WITH RAITA

STUFFED AUBERGINES

3 tablespoons olive oil
2 onions, finely chopped
1 cm (½ in) piece fresh root ginger, peeled and grated
3 cloves garlic, crushed
1 teaspoon chilli powder
1½ teaspoons turmeric
1½ teaspoons ground coriander
½ teaspoon each ground cumin and garam masala
450 g (1 lb) lamb fillet, cubed
115 ml (4 fl oz/½ cup) natural yogurt
salt and freshly ground black pepper
mint sprigs, to garnish
RAITA:
300 ml (10 fl oz/1¼ cups) natural yogurt
175 g (6 oz) cucumber, diced
1 tablespoon chopped fresh mint

3 aubergines (eggplants)
salt and pepper
2 teaspoons olive oil
1 onion, finely chopped
450 g (1 lb) minced lamb or beef
2 tomatoes, skinned and chopped
3 teaspoons tomato purée (paste)
3 teaspoons chopped fresh oregano
½ teaspoon ground cinnamon
55 ml (2 fl oz/¼ cup) dry white wine
CHEESE SAUCE:
25 g (1 oz/6 teaspoons) butter
25 g (1 oz/¼ cup) flour
300 ml (10 fl oz/1¼ cups) milk
85 g (3 oz/¾ cup) grated kefalotiri cheese

Heat the oil in a flameproof casserole. Add the onions and cook, stirring occasionally, for 5 minutes, until soft. Add the ginger, garlic, chilli powder, turmeric, coriander, cumin and garam masala and cook, stirring, for 2 minutes. Add the lamb and cook, stirring, for 2 minutes, until browned.

Cut aubergines (eggplants) lengthways, from stalk, sprinkle with salt and leave to drain for 1 hour. In a saucepan, heat oil. Add onion and cook until soft. Add lamb and stir until brown. Add tomatoes, tomato purée (paste), oregano, cinnamon, salt, pepper, wine and 55 ml (2 fl oz/¼ cup) water. Cover and cook gently for 15 minutes. Remove lid and cook until mixture is dry. Dry aubergines (eggplants). Scoop out pulp. Chop half and mix with meat mixture (reserve other half for another dish).

Add the yogurt, 115 ml (4 fl oz/½ cup) water and salt and pepper and stir well. Bring to the boil and simmer gently for 45 minutes. Meanwhile, make the raita. Mix together the yogurt, cucumber and chopped mint. Season with salt and pepper. Chill until required. Garnish the lamb with mint sprigs and serve with the raita.

Serves 4.

Preheat oven to 180C (350F/Gas 4). To make the sauce, in a saucepan, melt butter. Stir in flour; cook for 2 minutes, stirring, over gentle heat. Remove from heat. Gradually stir in milk. Return to heat. Stir until thick and smooth. Cook gently for 5 minutes. Season. Stir in two thirds of cheese. Fill each aubergine (eggplant) shell two thirds full of meat mixture. Top with cheese sauce. Sprinkle with remaining cheese. Bake for 20 minutes until brown.

Serves 6.

BRAISED LAMB & VEGETABLES

450 g (1 lb) firm, yellow-flesh potatoes, cut into
  0.5 cm (¼ in) slices
2 cloves garlic, pounded to a paste
6-8 spring onions, thinly sliced
2 medium-large artichoke bottoms
150 g (5 oz) chestnut mushrooms, chopped
handful parsley, finely chopped
1 tablespoon mixed herbs, chopped
salt and freshly ground black pepper
3 tablespoons olive oil
4 lamb shoulder or loin chops
175 ml (6 fl oz/¾ cup) full-bodied dry white wine

Preheat oven to 190C (375F/Gas 5). In a
bowl, combine potatoes, garlic, spring
onions, artichoke bottoms, mushrooms,
parsley, mixed herbs and seasoning. Place
half the mixture in a heavy flameproof casserole. Heat oil in a frying pan, add lamb and
brown on both sides. Drain on absorbent
kitchen paper, then season and place in
casserole.

Over the heat, stir wine into pan to dislodge
cooking juices, bring to boil and pour over
lamb. Cover with remaining vegetables and
add sufficient water to come almost to the
level of the vegetables. Bring to the boil,
cover and cook in the oven for about 30
minutes. Uncover and cook for a further 1
hour. Add a little water if it seems to be drying out.

Serves 4.

LAMB WITH LEMON & GARLIC

3 tablespoons olive oil
1 kg (2¼ lb) lean, boneless lamb, cut into 2.5 cm
  (1 in) pieces
1 Spanish onion, finely chopped
3 cloves garlic, crushed
1 tablespoon paprika
3 tablespoons finely chopped fresh parsley
3 tablespoons lemon juice
salt and freshly ground black pepper
3 tablespoons dry white wine (optional)

Heat oil in a heavy flameproof casserole, add
lamb and cook, stirring occasionally, until
lightly browned. Do this in batches if necessary so the pieces are not crowded. Using a
slotted spoon, transfer meat to a plate or
bowl and reserve.

Stir onion into casserole and cook for about
5 minutes, stirring occasionally, until softened. Stir in garlic, cook for 2 minutes, then
stir in paprika. When well blended, stir in
lamb and any juices on plate or in bowl, the
parsley, lemon juice and seasoning. Cover
tightly and cook over very low heat for 1¼-
1½ hours, shaking casserole occasionally,
until lamb is very tender. If necessary, add
wine or 3 tablespoons water.

Serves 4-6.

LAMB EN PAPILLOTTE

4 lamb leg steaks, about 175 g (6 oz) each
1 tablespoon Dijon mustard
4 spring onions, sliced
1 teaspoon chopped fresh rosemary
salt and freshly ground black pepper
450 g (1 lb) sweet potatoes, cut into chunks
450 g (1 lb) courgettes (zucchini), thickly sliced
1 tablespoon olive oil
rosemary sprigs, to garnish

Preheat oven to 200C (400F/Gas 6). Cut four large squares of foil and place a lamb steak on each one. Spread the lamb with the mustard and sprinkle with the spring onions and rosemary. Season with salt and pepper.

Bring the foil up over the steaks to make a parcel and twist the edges together to seal. Put the parcels in an ovenproof dish. Arrange the sweet potatoes and courgettes (zucchini) around the parcels.

Drizzle with oil and season with salt and pepper. Cook in the oven for 1 hour, basting and turning the vegetables at least twice. Remove the lamb from the parcels, garnish with rosemary and serve with the vegetables.

Serves 4.

LAMB CHILINDRON

4 tablespoons olive oil
760 g (1½ lb) lean lamb, cubed
salt and freshly ground black pepper
1 Spanish onion, chopped
2 cloves garlic, chopped
3 large red peppers (capsicums), peeled, seeded and cut into strips
4 beefsteak tomatoes, peeled, seeded and chopped
1 dried red chilli, chopped
chopped fresh herbs, to garnish

Heat oil in a flameproof casserole. Season lamb and add to casserole.

Cook, stirring, until evenly browned, then using a slotted spoon, transfer to a bowl. Add onion to casserole and cook for about 4 minutes, stirring occasionally, until softened but not coloured. Stir in garlic, cook for 1-2 minutes, then stir in peppers (capsicums), tomatoes and chilli. Simmer for 5 minutes.

Return lamb, and any juices that have collected in bowl, to casserole. Cover tightly and cook gently for about 1½ hours until lamb is tender. Season if necessary. Serve garnished with chopped herbs.

Serves 6.

LAMB YOGURTLU

2 pitta breads
3 tablespoons olive oil
450 g (1 lb) boneless leg of lamb, cubed
350 g (12 oz) tomatoes, peeled and coarsely chopped
salt and freshly ground black pepper
300 ml (10 fl oz/1¼ cups) Greek yogurt, at room
  temperature
25 g (1 oz/¼ cup) pine nuts
2 tablespoons chopped fresh parsley

Split the pitta breads in half and cut each half into four triangles. Heat half the oil in a frying pan. Add the lamb and cook until browned all over.

Reduce the heat and cook for 10 minutes until cooked through. Remove with a slotted spoon and keep warm. Toast the pitta bread triangles and keep warm. Heat the remaining oil in the frying pan. Add the tomatoes and cook briefly until just softened but still retaining their shape.

Reserve four pitta triangles and put the remainder on warmed serving plates. Pour the tomatoes and their juice over the triangles and season with salt and pepper. Spoon most of the yogurt over the tomatoes. Arrange the lamb on top and spoon over the remaining yogurt. Sprinkle with the pine nuts and chopped parsley, arrange the reserved pitta triangles at the side and serve.

Serves 4.

SOUVLAKIA

2 cloves garlic, crushed
55 ml (2 fl oz/¼ cup) lemon juice
2 tablespoons olive oil
4 tablespoons chopped fresh oregano
salt and freshly ground black pepper
450 g (1 lb) lean lamb fillet, cubed
6 fresh bay leaves, halved
oregano sprigs, to garnish
TOMATO AND OLIVE SALSA:
175 g (6 oz) mixed green and black olives, pitted and
  finely chopped
1 small red onion, finely chopped
4 plum tomatoes, finely chopped
2 tablespoons olive oil

In a shallow dish, mix together the garlic, lemon juice, olive oil, oregano, and salt and pepper. Add the lamb and mix well. Leave in a cool place for 2 hours. To make the salsa, put the olives, onion, tomatoes, olive oil and salt and pepper in a bowl and mix together. Chill until required.

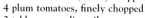

Remove the lamb from the marinade and thread on to skewers, adding the bay leaves to the skewers at regular intervals. Grill over a barbecue or under a hot grill, turning occasionally, for 10 minutes or until the lamb is brown and crisp on the outside and pink and juicy inside. Garnish with oregano sprigs and serve with the tomato and olive salsa.

Serves 4.

SPICED RACK OF LAMB

3 teaspoons plain flour
salt and pepper
2 racks lamb
1 clove garlic, finely chopped
6 teaspoons olive oil
450 g (1 lb) tomatoes, roughly chopped
½ lemon, chopped
1 stick cinnamon
3 cloves
1 small red chilli, seeded and chopped
115 ml (4 fl oz/½ cup) dry white wine
6 teaspoons tomato purée (paste)
lemon slices, to garnish

Preheat oven to 180C (350F/Gas 4). Mix together flour, salt and pepper. Rub over lamb. Press garlic into gaps between bones. In a roasting tin, heat oil. Put lamb, skin side down, in oil to brown. Remove lamb. Add tomatoes, lemon, cinnamon, cloves and chilli to roasting tin. Return lamb, skin side up, to tin.

In a bowl, mix together wine, 115 ml (4 fl oz/ ½ cup) water and tomato purée (paste). Pour over lamb. Cover tin loosely with foil. Cook in the oven for 1 hour. Remove foil and cook for a further 30 minutes until lamb is cooked. Cut lamb into individual chops and keep warm. Place roasting tin on heat and boil liquid to reduce to a thick sauce. Pour over meat. Garnish with lemon slices.

Serves 6.

ROAST LEG OF LAMB WITH WINE

1 kg (2¼ lb) lean leg of lamb
2 tablespoons olive oil
55 g (2 oz) salted anchovies, boned and rinsed
2 cloves garlic, chopped
8 juniper berries
1 tablespoon chopped fresh rosemary
2 tablespoons balsamic vinegar
salt and freshly ground pepper
150 ml (5 fl oz/⅔ cup) dry white wine

Trim lamb of any excess fat. Heat oil in a flameproof casserole in which the lamb will fit snugly. Add the lamb and brown all over. Remove and leave to cool.

In a mortar, pound the anchovies, garlic, rosemary and 4 of the juniper berries to a paste. Stir in vinegar. Make small incisions all over the lamb with a small sharp knife. Spread paste all over lamb, working it into the slits. Season. Replace lamb in casserole, and pour in wine. Crush remaining juniper berries and add to the casserole. Cover and simmer for 1½-2 hours, until very tender, turning lamb every 20 minutes.

Carefully remove lamb from casserole and keep warm. Skim fat from sauce. Add a little water, if necessary, and bring to the boil, scraping the bottom of the pan to mix in the sediment. Serve the sauce with the lamb, accompanied by roast potatoes, carrots and mange tout (snow peas).

Serves 8.

MOUSSAKA

700 g (1½ lb) aubergines (eggplants)
salt and pepper
olive oil
2 onions, finely chopped
700 g (1½ lb) minced lamb or beef
2 tomatoes, peeled and chopped
6 teaspoons tomato purée (paste)
3 teaspoons chopped fresh oregano
1 teaspoon ground cinnamon
115 ml (4 fl oz/½ cup) dry white wine
WHITE SAUCE:
55 g (2 oz/¼ cup) butter
55 g (2 oz/½ cup) plain flour
450 ml (16 fl oz/2 cups) milk
150 ml (5 fl oz/⅔ cup) yogurt
25 g (1 oz/¼ cup) grated kefalotiri cheese

Thinly slice aubergines and put in a colander. Sprinkle with salt and leave to drain for 1 hour. In a saucepan, heat 3 teaspoons oil. Add onions and cook until soft. Add lamb and stir until brown. Add tomatoes, tomato purée (paste), oregano, cinnamon, salt, pepper, wine and 115 ml (4 fl oz/½ cup) water. Cover; cook gently for 30 minutes. Remove lid; cook until mixture is dry. Dry aubergines. Heat 2.5 cm (½ in) oil in a frying pan. Fry aubergines, turning once, until beginning to brown. Drain on absorbent paper. Preheat oven to 180C (350F/Gas 4).

To make sauce, melt butter; stir in flour and cook for 2 minutes over a gentle heat. Remove from heat. Gradually stir in milk and yogurt. Return to heat. Stir until thick and smooth. Cook gently for 5 minutes. Season. Put a layer of aubergine in an oven-proof dish. Cover with half meat then half remaining slices. Cover with remaining mince and aubergine slices. Pour sauce over top. Sprinkle with cheese. Bake for 40 minutes until brown.

Serves 6.

BAKED LAMB WITH VEGETABLES

1 leg of lamb, weighing about 2.25 kg (4½ lb)
3 cloves garlic, cut into slivers
salt and pepper
1 aubergine (eggplant)
700 g (1½ lb) potatoes, peeled
1 large onion, thinly sliced
450 (1 lb) tomatoes, sliced
55 ml (2 fl oz/¼ cup) white wine
1 tablespoon chopped fresh oregano

Preheat oven to 220C (425F/Gas 7). Cut slits in meat and insert slivers of garlic. Rub generously with salt and pepper. Place lamb in a large roasting tin and put in oven.

Reduce heat to 180C (350F/Gas 4) and roast for 1½ hours for slightly pink meat or 2 hours for medium-well done. Meanwhile, slice aubergine (eggplant) into 0.5 cm (¼ in) slices, place in a colander and sprinkle with salt. Leave for 30 minutes, then rinse and pat dry with absorbent kitchen paper.

One hour before the end of cooking time remove any fat from roasting tin and add vegetables. Pour the wine over, season with salt and pepper and sprinkle with oregano. Return to the oven. Turn vegetables over during the cooking time to cook them evenly in juices. Carve lamb into slices, adding any meat juices to vegetables. Serve lamb with the vegetables and meat juices.

Serves 6.

PORK

PORK WITH HERB SAUCE

25 g (1 oz/½ cup) fresh white breadcrumbs
2 tablespoons white wine vinegar
2 cloves garlic
2 canned anchovy fillets, drained
15 g (½ oz/¼ cup) chopped fresh parsley
2 teaspoons capers
1 hard-boiled egg yolk
225 ml (8 fl oz/1 cup) extra virgin olive oil
salt and freshly ground black pepper
4 loin chops, about 2.5 cm (1 in) thick

In a small bowl, soak the breadcrumbs in the white wine vinegar.

Meanwhile, using a pestle and mortar, crush garlic with anchovy fillets, parsley, capers and egg yolk. Squeeze vinegar from breadcrumbs, then mix breadcrumbs into mortar. Stir in oil in a slow trickle to make a creamy sauce. Add black pepper, and salt if necessary. Set aside.

Preheat grill. Grill chops for about 12 minutes each side until lightly browned on both sides and cooked through but still juicy in centre. Season chops and spoon on some of sauce. Serve remaining sauce separately.

Serves 4.

PORK IN CIDER & ORANGE

3 tablespoons olive oil
flour for coating
salt and freshly ground black pepper
750 g (1½ lb) boned and rolled loin of pork
1 small Spanish onion, sliced
300 ml (10 fl oz/1¼ cups) well-flavoured dry cider
juice 1 large juicy orange
rind ¼ orange, cut into fine strips
pinch ground cinnamon
pinch caster sugar (optional)
thin orange slices, parsley sprigs and flaked toasted almonds, to garnish

Heat oil in a heavy flameproof casserole. Put flour on a plate and season with salt and pepper. Roll pork in seasoned flour to coat evenly and lightly. Add to casserole and brown evenly for about 10 minutes. Remove and keep warm. Stir onion into casserole and cook over a low heat for about 20 minutes, stirring occasionally, until very soft and browned. Stir in cider, orange juice and rind strips and cinnamon. Bring to the boil and simmer for 2-3 minutes.

Return pork to casserole, turn it in sauce, cover and cook gently for about 45 minutes until pork is tender. Transfer pork to a serving dish and boil sauce, if necessary, to thicken lightly. Adjust seasoning and level of cinnamon, and add a pinch caster sugar, if desired. Pour sauce over pork and garnish with orange slices, parsley sprigs and toasted flaked almonds.

Serves 4.

SPICED PORK LOIN

THAI PORK CURRY

1 tablespoon paprika
3 cloves garlic, finely crushed
1 teaspoon chopped fresh oregano
½ teaspoon finely crushed cumin seeds
1 bay leaf, crushed
salt
3 tablespoons virgin olive oil
700 g (1½ lb) boned and rolled loin of pork
olive oil for frying
4 tablespoons full-bodied dry white wine
stoned green olives, to serve

In a small bowl, mix together paprika, garlic, oregano, cumin seeds, bay leaf and salt, then stir in olive oil.

Place pork in a non-metallic dish, spoon the marinade mixture over the top, cover and leave in refrigerator for 2-3 days. Return pork to room temperature 30 minutes before cooking.

Cut pork into 4 slices. Heat oil in a frying pan over fairly high heat. Add pork, brown quickly on both sides, then cook more gently for 4-5 minutes a side until cooked through. Transfer slices to a warm serving plate. Stir wine into cooking juices, boil for 2-3 minutes, then pour over pork. Scatter green olives over the top.

Serves 4.

125 ml (4 fl oz/½ cup) coconut cream (see glossary)
1 onion, chopped
1 clove garlic, finely crushed
2 tablespoons ready-made Fragrant Curry Paste
2 teaspoons fish sauce
½ teaspoon crushed palm sugar
350 g (12 oz) lean pork, diced
3 kaffir lime leaves, shredded
25 Thai holy basil leaves
1 long fresh red chilli, seeded and cut into strips, and Thai holy basil sprig, to garnish

In a wok, heat 85 ml (3 fl oz/⅓ cup) coconut cream until oil begins to separate. Stir in onion and garlic and cook, stirring occasionally, until lightly browned. Stir in curry paste and continue to stir for about 2 minutes. Stir in fish sauce and sugar, then pork to coat. Cook for 3-4 minutes.

Add lime and basil leaves and cook for 1 more minute. If necessary, add a little water, but final dish should be dry. Serve garnished with a trail of remaining coconut cream, chilli strips and basil sprig.

Serves 3.

FLORENTINE ROAST PORK

1 kg (2¼ lb) pork loin, boned
2 tablespoons chopped fresh rosemary leaves
2 cloves garlic, chopped
salt and freshly ground black pepper
3 tablespoons olive oil
150 ml (5 fl oz/⅔ cup) dry white wine

Preheat oven to 160C (325F) Gas 3. Using a flat skewer, make deep incisions all over the meat. Mix rosemary and garlic together with plenty of salt and pepper. Push the rosemary mixture into the incisions. Rub any remaining mixture into flap where the bones have been removed.

Season very well and tie up neatly with string. Rub meat all over with olive oil and place in a roasting tin. Pour in white wine and roast in oven for 1½ hours, basting frequently and turning the joint each time. If you have a spit or rotisserie, roast it on the spit, basting frequently.

Transfer pork to a serving dish and keep warm. Skim fat off pan, and add a little water to the juices. Scrape up sediment and bring to a boil, taste and season. Carve the pork into thick slices, garnish with rosemary sprigs and serve with the sauce, carrots and brown lentils.

Serves 6.

BARBECUED SPARE RIBS

2 tablespoons chopped coriander stalks
3 cloves garlic, chopped
1 teaspoon black peppercorns, cracked
1 teaspoon grated kaffir lime peel
1 tablespoon ready-made Green Curry Paste
2 teaspoons fish sauce
1½ teaspoons crushed palm sugar
185 ml (6 fl oz/¾ cup) coconut milk
900 g (2 lb) pork spare ribs, trimmed
spring onion (scallion) brushes, to garnish

Using a pestle and mortar or small blender, pound or mix together coriander, garlic, peppercorns, lime peel, curry paste, fish sauce and sugar. Stir in coconut milk. Place spare ribs in a shallow dish and pour over spiced coconut mixture. Cover and leave in a cool place for 3 hours, basting occasionally.

Preheat a barbecue or moderate grill. Cook ribs for about 5 minutes a side, until cooked through and brown, basting occasionally with coconut mixture. Garnish with spring onion (scallion) brushes.

Serves 4-6.

Note: The ribs can also be cooked on a rack in a roasting tin in an oven preheated to 200C (400F/Gas 6) for 45-60 minutes, basting occasionally.

MARINATED SPICED PORK

1 tablespoon olive oil
1.5 kg (3½ lb) leg of pork, skin and fat removed
115 g (4 oz) brown cap or shiitake mushrooms,
    sliced
thyme sprigs and celery leaves, to garnish
MARINADE:
2 tablespoons olive oil
1 onion, finely chopped
1 carrot, finely chopped
1 stick celery, chopped
450 ml (16 fl oz/2 cups) full-bodied red wine
6 juniper berries, crushed
8 peppercorns, crushed
¼ teaspoon ground allspice
bouquet garni
salt

To make marinade, heat the oil in a heavy
frying pan, add onion and carrot and cook,
stirring occasionally, for 5 minutes. Add
celery and cook, stirring occasionally, until
vegetables are browned. Add wine, juniper
berries, peppercorns, allspice, bouquet garni
and salt. Leave to cool. Put pork in a non-
metallic dish, pour over marinade, cover and
leave in a cool place for 24 hours, turning
pork occasionally. Preheat oven to 180C
(350F/Gas 4). Remove pork and vegetables
with a slotted spoon and drain pork on
kitchen paper. Strain marinade and set aside.

Heat oil in a heavy flameproof casserole just
large enough to hold pork, add pork and
cook until browned all over. Remove and set
aside. Add mushrooms and cook for 5
minutes. Add reserved vegetables and put
pork on top. Pour over marinade. Heat to
almost simmering, cover and cook in oven,
turning occasionally, for 2-2½ hours.
Transfer to a warmed plate. Skim excess fat
from sauce then boil to thicken. Season.
Carve pork, garnish and serve with sauce.

Serves 4-6.

PORK WITH PRUNES

150 g (5 oz) large prunes
550 ml (20 fl oz/2½ cups) dry white wine
45 g (1½ oz/3 tablespoons) butter
4 pork chops
225 g (8 oz) mixed chopped onion, carrot and celery
250 ml (9 fl oz/1 cup) veal or pork stock
bouquet garni
salt and freshly ground black pepper
squeeze lemon juice

Put prunes in a bowl, pour over half the wine
and leave to soak overnight.

Heat 25 g (1 oz/2 tablespoons) butter in a
heavy flameproof casserole, add chops and
cook quickly until browned on both sides.
Remove and set aside. Add vegetables to
casserole and cook, stirring occasionally, for
5-7 minutes, until lightly browned. Stir in
remaining wine, bring to the boil and boil
for 2-3 minutes. Add stock and bring to the
boil. Return chops to casserole, add bouquet
garni and salt and pepper, cover tightly and
cook gently for 45 minutes.

Add prunes and soaking liquid to casserole,
bring to boil, cover and cook for 30 minutes.
Transfer pork and prunes to warmed serving
plates and keep warm. Discard bouquet garni
and boil sauce to thicken slightly. Reduce
heat and gradually stir in remaining butter.
Add lemon juice to taste, pour over pork and
prunes and serve.

Serve 4.

PORK WITH CIDER

25 g (1 oz/2 tablespoons) butter
4 pork chops
1 onion, finely chopped
2 teaspoons Calvados or brandy
300 ml (10 fl oz/1¼ cups) dry cider
1 bay leaf
salt and freshly ground black pepper
2 small cooking apples, peeled, cored and sliced
1 tablespoon lemon juice
2 tablespoons crème fraîche or thick sour cream
salt and freshly ground black pepper
thyme sprigs and leaves, to garnish

Heat butter in a heavy flameproof casserole, add chops and cook quickly until browned on both sides. Remove and set aside.

Preheat oven to 180C (350F/Gas 4). Add onion to casserole and cook, stirring occasionally, for 5 minutes, until soft. Add Calvados or brandy and set alight. When flames die down, stir in cider and bring to the boil. Return chops to casserole, add bay leaf and salt and pepper, cover tightly and cook in oven for 20 minutes.

Toss apples in lemon juice. Add to casserole, cover again and cook for 10-15 minutes. Remove pork and apples from casserole with a slotted spoon, transfer to warmed serving plates and keep warm. Boil cooking liquid until lightly syrupy. Stir in crème fraîche or thick sour cream, pour over pork and apples, garnish with thyme and serve.

Serves 4.

PORK WITH PEARS

6 teaspoons olive oil
2 onions, chopped
1 kg (2.2 lb) boned lean pork, cut into cubes
250 ml (9 fl oz/1 cup) red wine
grated rind ½ orange
½ cinnamon stick
salt and pepper
2 pears
2 teaspoons clear honey
chopped fresh coriander leaves, orange rind strips and pitta bread to garnish

In a flameproof casserole, heat oil. Add onions; cook until soft. Push to side of pan, turn up heat and brown meat in batches.

Add wine, orange rind, cinnamon stick, salt, pepper and 300 ml (10 fl oz/1¼ cups) water. Bring to simmering point, then cover casserole and cook for 1 hour.

Peel, core and slice pears and place on top of meat. Drizzle honey over pears. Cover pan and simmer gently for 30-40 minutes until meat is tender. Garnish with chopped coriander leaves, strips of orange rind and pieces of pitta bread.

Serves 6.

Note: This recipe is traditionally made with quinces. If quinces are available, use them instead of pears.

PORK WITH WATER CHESTNUTS

1½ tablespoons vegetable oil
4 cloves garlic, chopped
2 fresh red chillies, seeded and finely chopped
350 g (12 oz) lean pork, cubed
10 canned water chestnuts, chopped
1 teaspoon fish sauce
freshly ground black pepper
3 tablespoons chopped coriander leaves
6 spring onions, chopped
3-4 spring onion brushes, to garnish

In a wok, heat oil, add garlic and chillies and cook, stirring occasionally, until garlic becomes golden.

Stir in pork and stir-fry for about 2 minutes until almost cooked through. Add water chestnuts, heat for 2 minutes, then stir in fish sauce, 4 tablespoons water and add plenty of black pepper. Stir in coriander and spring onions. Serve garnished with spring onion brushes.

Serves 3-4.

PORK WITH BASIL

250 g (9 oz) thin egg noodles
55 ml (2 fl oz/¼ cup) olive oil
575 g (1¼ lb) pork fillet, cut into shreds
1 red onion, cut lengthwise in half, and thinly sliced
4 tablespoons shredded fresh basil leaves
6 teaspoons balsamic vinegar
3 tablespoons toasted pine nuts
salt and freshly ground black pepper
fresh basil leaves, to garnish

In a large saucepan of boiling water, cook the egg noodles according to the packet directions. Drain and rinse. Turn into a large bowl and toss with 2 tablespoons olive oil. Keep warm.

Heat the wok until very hot. Add remaining olive oil and swirl to coat wok. Add shredded pork and stir-fry for 2-3 minutes until pork is golden. Add red onion and toss with the pork, then stir-fry for 1 minute.

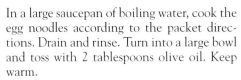

Stir in shredded basil, the balsamic vinegar and pine nuts and toss to mix well. Add noodles to the wok, season to taste and toss with pork mixture. Turn onto shallow serving dish and garnish with basil leaves.

Serves 4.

STIR-FRIED PORK & BEANS

2 tablespoons vegetable oil
6 cloves garlic, chopped
350 g (12 oz) lean pork, finely chopped
350 g (12 oz) long beans or slim green beans
12 water chestnuts
115 g (4 oz) cooked peeled prawns
1 tablespoon fish sauce
½ teaspoon crushed palm sugar
freshly ground black pepper

In a wok, heat oil, add garlic and fry, stirring occasionally, until golden.

Add pork and beans and stir-fry for 2 minutes, then add water chestnuts. Stir for 1 minute.

Add prawns, fish sauce, sugar, plenty of black pepper and about 3 tablespoons water. Bubble for a minute or two, then transfer to a warmed serving plate.

Serves 4.

PORK WITH CHILLI & PEAS

450 g (1 lb) pork fillet, cut crosswise into thin slices
1½ tablespoons soy sauce
6 teaspoons cider vinegar
1 tablespoon vegetable oil
2.5 cm (1 in) piece fresh root ginger, peeled and
  finely chopped
2 cloves garlic, finely chopped
1 fresh red chilli, seeded and thinly sliced
225 g (8 oz) fresh or frozen green peas or sugar snap
  peas
85 g (3 oz) red cabbage or radicchio, thinly shredded

In a small baking dish, sprinkle pork slices with soy sauce and vinegar. Toss to coat well. Leave to stand for 15-20 minutes.

Heat the wok until hot. Add oil and swirl to coat wok. Add pork slices and stir-fry for 2 minutes. Push to one side and add ginger, garlic and chilli; stir-fry for 1 minute to mix.

Add peas or sugar snap peas and red cabbage or radicchio and stir-fry for 2-3 minutes until vegetables are tender but still crisp. Serve with rice and wild rice.

Serves 4.

PORK SATAY

350g (12 oz) lean pork, cubed
juice 1 lime
1 stalk lemon grass, finely chopped
1 clove garlic, chopped
2 tablespoons vegetable oil
SAUCE:
4 tablespoons vegetable oil
85 g (3 oz/½ cup) raw shelled peanuts
2 stalks lemon grass, chopped
2 fresh red chillies, seeded and sliced
3 shallots, chopped
2 cloves garlic, chopped
1 teaspoon fish paste
2 teaspoons crushed palm sugar
300 ml (10 fl oz/1¼ cups) coconut milk
juice ½ lime

Meanwhile, make sauce. Over a high heat, heat 1 tablespoon oil in a wok, add nuts and cook, stirring constantly, for 2 minutes. Using a slotted spoon, transfer to absorbent kitchen paper to drain. Using a pestle and mortar or small blender, grind to a paste. Remove and set aside.

Divide pork between 4 skewers and lay them in a shallow dish. In a bowl, mix together lime juice, lemon grass, garlic and oil. Pour over pork, turn to coat, cover and set aside in a cool place for 1 hour, turning occasionally.

Using a pestle and mortar or small blender, pound or mix lemon grass, chillies, shallots, garlic and fish paste to a smooth paste.

Preheat grill. Remove pork from dish, allowing excess liquid to drain off. Grill, turning frequently and basting, for 8-10 minutes.

Heat remaining oil in wok, add spice mixture and cook, stirring, for 2 minutes. Stir in peanut paste, sugar and coconut milk. Bring to boil, stirring, then adjust heat so sauce simmers. Add lime juice and simmer, stirring, for 5-10 minutes until thickened. Serve in a warmed bowl to accompany pork. Garnish with carrot flowers, and lettuce leaves.

Serves 4.

AFELIA

575 g (1¼ lb) pork fillet
1 teaspoon coriander seeds
1 teaspoon soft brown sugar
salt and pepper
3 teaspoons olive oil
250 ml (9 fl oz/1 cup) red wine
fresh coriander leaves, to garnish

Cut pork into 1 cm (½ in) slices. Place slices between 2 sheets greaseproof paper and beat with a rolling pin to flatten slightly.

In a mortar and pestle, lightly crush coriander seeds with the sugar and salt and pepper to taste. Sprinkle the crushed mixture onto both sides of the pork. Leave in a cool place for at least 30 minutes.

In a frying pan, heat oil. Add pork in batches and brown on both sides. Return pork to pan. Pour in the wine, allow to bubble up for a minute, then reduce heat and cook, uncovered, for 20-30 minutes until pork is tender. The liquid should have reduced to a syrupy consistency. If not, transfer pork to a serving dish and keep hot. Boil liquid until reduced; pour it over the meat and garnish with coriander leaves.

Serves 4.

COCONUT PORK WITH LIME

6 pork escalopes, about 115 g (4 oz) each
1 cm (½ in) piece fresh root ginger, peeled and grated
2 teaspoons ground cumin
1 teaspoon ground coriander
1 teaspoon chilli powder (to taste)
1 teaspoon paprika
½ teaspoon salt
2-3 tablespoons vegetable oil
1 onion, cut lengthwise in half and thinly sliced
3-4 cloves garlic, finely chopped
300 ml (10 fl oz/1¼ cups) unsweetened coconut milk
grated rind and juice 1 large lime
1 small Chinese cabbage, shredded
lime slices and coriander leaves, to garnish

Place escalopes between 2 sheets of greaseproof paper. Pound to a 0.5 cm (¼ in) thickness. Cut into strips. In a large, shallow dish, combine ginger, cumin, coriander, chilli powder, paprika and salt. Stir in pork strips and leave to stand for 15 minutes. Heat wok until very hot. Add half the oil and swirl to coat wok. Add half the pork and stir-fry for 2-3 minutes. Remove to a plate and keep warm. Cook remaining strips using remaining oil. Keep warm. Pour off all but 1 tablespoon oil from the wok.

Add onion and garlic to wok; stir-fry for 2-3 minutes until onion is softened. Slowly add coconut milk. Bring to simmering point but do not boil. Stir in lime rind and juice and shredded cabbage. Simmer gently for 5-7 minutes, stirring frequently, until cabbage is tender and sauce slightly thickened. Add pork and cook, covered, for 1-2 minutes until heated through. Arrange pork and cabbage on plates and garnish with lime slices and coriander. Serve with noodles.

Serves 6.

PORK & PRUNE MEDLEY

450 g (1 lb) pork fillet, cut into thin slices
2 tablespoons soy sauce
6 teaspoons balsamic or cider vinegar
2 tablespoons olive oil
2 courgettes (zucchini), sliced
1 onion, cut lengthwise into 'petals'
1 red pepper (capsicum), cut into thin strips
115 g (4 oz) mushrooms, sliced
115 g (4 oz) mange tout (snow peas)
115 g (4 oz) asparagus, cut into 5 cm (2 in) pieces
55 g (2 oz/½ cup) walnut halves
175 g (6 oz) ready-to-eat prunes, stoned
salt and freshly ground black pepper

INDONESIAN-STYLE PORK

1 tablespoon seasoned flour
575 g (1¼ lb) pork fillet, cut into small cubes
2-3 tablespoons vegetable oil
1 onion, cut lengthwise in half and thinly sliced
2 cloves garlic, finely chopped
2.5 cm (1 in) piece fresh root ginger, peeled and cut
  into julienne strips
½ teaspoon sambal oelek (see Note) or Chinese
  chilli sauce
55 ml (2 fl oz/¼ cup) Indonesian soy sauce or dark
  soy sauce sweetened with 1 tablespoon sugar
coriander leaves, to garnish

In a medium bow, combine seasoned flour and pork cubes and toss to coat well. Shake to remove any excess flour.

In a shallow baking dish, sprinkle pork slices with soy sauce and balsamic or cider vinegar and toss to coat well. Allow to stand for 30 minutes. Heat the wok until hot. Add olive oil and swirl to coat wok. Add pork slices and stir-fry for 3-5 minutes, until golden on all sides. With a slotted spoon, remove to a bowl.

Heat the wok until very hot. Add 2 tablespoons of the oil and swirl to coat wok. Add pork cubes and stir-fry for 3-4 minutes until browned on all sides, adding a little more oil if necessary. Push pork to one side and add onion, garlic and ginger and stir-fry for 1 minute, tossing all the ingredients.

Add courgettes (zucchini), onion, red pepper (capsicum), mushrooms, mange tout (snow peas), asparagus, walnut halves and prunes and stir-fry for 2-3 minutes until well coated with oil. Add 2 tablespoons water to wok and cover wok quickly. Steam for 1-2 minutes until vegetables just begin to soften. Uncover wok, return pork to wok and toss to mix. Season with salt and pepper. Stir-fry for a further 1-2 minutes until pork is heated through.

Serves 4.

Add sambal oelek or chilli sauce, soy sauce and 150 ml (5 fl oz/⅔ cup) water; stir. Bring to the boil, then reduce heat to low and simmer gently, covered, for 20-25 minutes, stirring occasionally, until pork is tender and sauce thickened. Garnish with coriander and serve with fried rice or noodles.

Serves 4.

Note: Sambal oelek is a very hot, chilli-based Indonesian condiment available in specialist or oriental food shops.

RATATOUILLE-STYLE PORK

1 tablespoon olive oil
4 boneless loin pork chops, about 575 g (1¼ lb) and
   2.5 cm (1 in) thick, trimmed of fat
1 onion, coarsely chopped
2 cloves garlic, chopped
1 small aubergine (eggplant), cut into 2.5 cm (1 in)
   cubes
1 red or green pepper (capsicum), diced
2 courgettes (zucchini), thickly sliced
225 g (8 oz) can chopped tomatoes
1 teaspoon chopped fresh oregano or basil leaves or
   ½ teaspoon dried oregano or basil
½ teaspoon dried thyme leaves
salt and freshly ground black pepper
fresh parsley or coriander sprigs, to garnish

Heat the wok until very hot. Add olive oil and swirl to coat. Arrange pork chops on bottom and side of wok, if necessary, in a single layer. Fry for 4-5 minutes until well browned on both sides, turning once and rotating during cooking. Remove to a plate. Add onion and garlic to remaining oil in wok and stir-fry for 1 minute until onion begins to soften. Add the aubergine (eggplant) cubes and diced pepper (capsicum) and stir-fry for 3-5 minutes to brown and soften.

Add courgettes (zucchini), chopped tomatoes and their juice, the fresh or dried oregano or basil, thyme and season with salt and pepper. Stir well and return pork chops to wok, covering them with the ratatouille mixture. Lower the heat and cook, covered, for 6-8 minutes, shaking wok occasionally to prevent sticking. Uncover and cook for 2-3 minutes more to allow sauce to thicken slightly. Garnish with parsley or coriander. Serve with fresh pasta.

Serves 4.

SPICY PORK & LEMON GRASS

1 clove garlic, chopped
2 shallots, chopped
3 tablespoons chopped lemon grass
1 tablespoon sugar
1 tablespoon fish sauce
salt and freshly ground black pepper
350 g (12 oz) pork fillet, cut into small, thin slices
2-3 tablespoons vegetable oil
2-3 sticks celery, thinly sliced
115 g (4 oz) straw mushrooms, halved lengthways
4 small red chillies, seeded and shredded
2 spring onions, shredded
1 tablespoon soy sauce
about 55 ml (2 fl oz/¼ cup) stock or water
2 teaspoons cornflour
coriander sprigs, to garnish

Using a pestle and mortar, pound the garlic, shallots and lemon grass to a paste. Transfer to a mixing bowl and add the sugar, fish sauce, salt and pepper. Blend well, then add the pork slices, turning to coat them with the mixture, and leave to marinate for 25-30 minutes.

Heat oil in a wok or frying-pan and stir-fry pork slices for 2 minutes. Add the celery, straw mushrooms, chillies, spring onions and soy sauce and stir-fry for 2-3 minutes. Use the stock to rinse out the marinade bowl and add to the pork. Bring to the boil. Mix cornflour with 1 tablespoon water and add to sauce to thicken it. Garnish with coriander sprigs and serve at once with a mixture of rice and wild rice.

Serves 4.

STUFFED PORK SHOULDER

1.3 kg (3 lb) shoulder of pork, boned and skinned
450 g (1 lb) potatoes, cut into chunks
450 g (1 lb) swede, cut into chunks
450 g (1 lb) parsnips, cut into chunks
1 tablespoon olive oil
salt and freshly ground black pepper
1 tablespoon cornflour
500 ml (18 fl oz/2¼ cups) vegetable stock
1 tablespoon mango and lime chutney
sage leaves, to garnish
STUFFING:
175 g (6 oz) can corned beef, finely chopped
115 g (4 oz/2 cups) fresh white breadcrumbs
1 onion, finely chopped
1 teaspoon dried sage
1 tablespoon mango and lime chutney

Preheat oven to 180C (350F/Gas 4). Open out the shoulder of pork and flatten. To make the stuffing, mix together the corned beef, breadcrumbs, onion and sage. Add the chutney and bind the mixture together. Spread the stuffing along the centre of the inside of the pork. Roll the pork into a round shape and tie securely with string. Season with salt and pepper. Put in a flameproof dish, cover with a lid or piece of foil and cook in the oven for 2 hours, basting the meat every 45 minutes. Increase the oven temperature to 200C (400F/Gas 6).

Place the potatoes, swede and parsnips around the meat. Drizzle the vegetables with oil and season with salt and pepper. Cook, uncovered, for 45-55 minutes, turning the vegetables occasionally, until tender. Remove the meat and vegetables and keep warm. Add the cornflour and stir into the cooking juices. Gradually add the stock and bring to the boil, stirring. Add the chutney and simmer for 3-4 minutes. Slice the pork, garnish and serve with the vegetables and sauce.

Serves 6-8.

CARAWAY POT ROAST

1 tablespoon olive oil
1.25 kg (2¾ lb) hand of pork, boned
2 large onions, chopped
450 g (1 lb) parsnips, cut into chunks
25 g (1 oz) caraway seeds
½ teaspoon freshly grated nutmeg
salt and freshly ground black pepper
250 ml (9 fl oz/1 cup) chicken stock
250 ml (9 fl oz/1 cup) red wine
thyme sprigs, to garnish

Preheat oven to 180C (350F/Gas 4). Heat the oil in a large flameproof casserole. Add the pork and cook until browned all over.

Remove the meat from the casserole. Add the onions and parsnips and cook, stirring occasionally, for 7 minutes, until golden. Lay the pork on top of the vegetables. Mix together the caraway seeds and nutmeg and sprinkle on top of the pork. Season with salt and pepper. Pour the stock and wine around the pork. Cover tightly and cook in the oven for 2 hours, or until the pork is cooked through and tender. Remove the pork from the casserole and keep warm.

Remove the vegetables from the casserole with a slotted spoon. Bring the sauce to the boil and boil until reduced and thickened. Season with salt and pepper. Slice the meat, garnish with thyme sprigs and serve with the vegetables and sauce.

Serves 6-8.

Note: Hand of pork is quite a fatty cut of meat. Skim any fat from the surface of the sauce before serving, if you prefer.

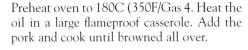

PROVENÇAL PORK CHOPS

2 teaspoons capers, chopped
25 g (1 oz) pitted black olives, chopped
8 sun-dried tomatoes, chopped
55 g (2 oz) can anchovies, drained and chopped
juice 2 lemons
2 cloves garlic, crushed
70 ml (2½ fl oz/⅓ cup) olive oil
4 tablespoons chopped fresh parsley
4 pork loin chops, about 175 g (6 oz) each
basil sprigs, to garnish

Mix together the capers, olives, tomatoes, anchovies and lemon juice. Add the garlic, all but 1 tablespoon of the olive oil, the parsley and season with salt and pepper.

Heat the remaining oil in a flameproof dish. Add the chops and cook for 10 minutes on each side, until cooked through.

Pour the tomato mixture over the chops and bring to the boil. Simmer for 5 minutes. Garnish with basil sprigs and serve.

Serves 4.

PORK WITH APPLE BALLS

2 tablespoons olive oil
4 boneless pork loin chops, about 175 g (6 oz) each
450 g (1 lb) onions, sliced
2 cloves garlic, crushed
12 plum tomatoes, peeled and chopped
150 ml (5 fl oz/⅔ cup) beef stock
55 ml (2 fl oz/¼ cup) red wine vinegar
700 g (1½ lb) crisp eating apples
2 tablespoons lemon juice
salt and freshly ground black pepper

Preheat oven to 180C (350F/Gas 4). Heat the olive oil in an ovenproof casserole. Add the chops and cook for 3 minutes on each side, until browned.

Remove the chops and keep warm. Add the onions to the casserole and cook, stirring occasionally, for 5 minutes, until soft. Add the garlic and tomatoes. Return the chops to the casserole and pour in the stock and red wine vinegar. Bring to the boil. Meanwhile, peel the apples and use a melon baller to cut out ball-shaped pieces. Put the balls into a bowl of water with the lemon juice, to prevent the apple discolouring. Chop the remaining apple and add to the casserole. Cover and cook in the oven for 1 hour.

Remove the chops from the casserole and keep warm. Pour the sauce into a blender or food processor and process for 1 minute. Season with salt and pepper. Return to the pan with the chops and apple balls. Cook gently for 15 minutes, until the apple balls are just tender.

Serves 4.

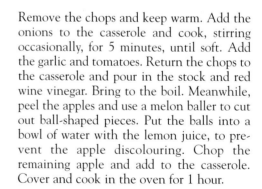

BARBECUE SPARE RIBS

1 kg (2¼ lb) spare ribs
1 large onion, finely chopped
3 cloves garlic, crushed
2 bay leaves
1 teaspoon ground cumin
1 teaspoon mild chilli powder
3 tablespoons cider vinegar
2 tablespoons tomato ketchup
1 tablespoon soy sauce
2 tablespoons clear honey
400 g (14 oz) can chopped tomatoes
salt and freshly ground black pepper

Preheat oven to 200C (400F/Gas 6). Put the spare ribs in a flameproof casserole and cook in the oven for 30 minutes.

Remove the ribs with a slotted spoon and set aside. In a bowl, mix together the onion, garlic, bay leaves, cumin, chilli powder, cider vinegar, tomato ketchup, soy sauce, honey and tomatoes. Season with salt and pepper.

Stir the tomato mixture into the casserole. Bring to the boil and simmer for 5 minutes. Add the ribs, turn to coat with the sauce and cover. Return the casserole to the oven and cook for 30 minutes. Serve.

Serves 4.

Variation: Use 4 spare rib pork chops instead of the spare ribs, if you prefer.

HARVEST CASSEROLE

2 tablespoons olive oil
4 spare rib pork chops
1 large onion, sliced
2 leeks, chopped
1 clove garlic, crushed
225 g (8 oz) parsnips, cut into chunks
225 g (8 oz) carrots, cut into chunks
1 teaspoon dried sage
2 tablespoons plain flour
300 ml (10 fl oz/1¼ cups) beef stock
300 ml (10 fl oz/1¼ cups) apple juice
salt and freshly ground black pepper
2 small eating apples
175 g (6 oz/1½ cups) self-raising flour
85 g (3 oz) shredded suet
1 teaspoon mixed dried herbs

Preheat oven to 160C (325F/Gas 3). Heat the oil in a large flameproof casserole. Add the chops and cook for 2-3 minutes on each side until browned. Remove from the casserole and drain on kitchen paper. Add the onion, leeks and garlic and cook, stirring occasionally, for 5 minutes, until soft. Add the parsnips, carrots and sage and cook for 2 minutes. Add the plain flour and cook, stirring, for 1 minute. Gradually stir in the stock and apple juice. Season with salt and pepper and bring to the boil.

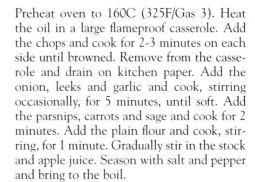

Replace the chops, cover and cook in the oven for 1¼ hours, or until the pork is tender. Meanwhile, core and roughly chop the apples and set aside. Mix together the self-raising flour, suet, herbs and salt and pepper. Add 175 ml (6 fl oz/¾ cup) water and bind to a firm dough. Divide the dough into eight small dumplings. Stir the apples into the casserole. Place the dumplings on top, return to the oven and cook, uncovered, for 20 minutes. Serve.

Serves 4.

FRUITY GAMMON STEAKS

FRAGRANT GAMMON

1 cm (½ in) piece fresh root ginger, peeled and
  grated
2 tablespoons tomato ketchup
1 tablespoon soft brown sugar
1 tablespoon light soy sauce
1 tablespoon malt vinegar
1 tablespoon lemon juice
2 tablespoons olive oil
4 gammon steaks, about 175 g (6 oz) each
1 green pepper (capsicum), chopped
1 red pepper (capsicum), chopped
1 onion, chopped
225 g (8 oz) can pineapple pieces, drained, with 2
  tablespoons juice reserved
1 tablespoon cornflour
watercress, to garnish

1.3 kg (3 lb) piece of gammon
225 g (8 oz) parsnips, halved lengthways
450 g (1 lb) carrots, cut into chunks
450 g (1 lb) swede, cut into chunks
2 sticks celery, cut into chunks
1 tablespoon brown sugar
1 tablespoon red wine vinegar
1 tablespoon black peppercorns
6 cloves
oregano sprigs, to garnish

Put the gammon in a flameproof casserole.
Cover with cold water and leave to soak for
1 hour. Drain and cover with fresh water.

In a bowl, mix together the ginger, tomato
ketchup, brown sugar, soy sauce, vinegar and
lemon juice. Set aside. Heat the oil in a
flameproof dish. Add the gammon steaks and
cook for 5 minutes on each side.

Add the remaining ingredients to the
casserole. Bring to the boil, cover and simmer gently for 1½ hours, until the gammon
is cooked through.

Remove the steaks from the dish and keep
warm. Add the peppers (capsicum) and
onion to the dish and cook, stirring occasionally, for 5 minutes, until soft. Stir in the
tomato ketchup mixture and the pineapple
pieces. Blend the reserved pineapple juice
with the cornflour. Add to the dish and bring
to the boil, stirring. Return the steaks to the
dish and simmer for 5 minutes. Garnish and
serve.

Serves 4.

Lift out the gammon, slice and arrange on
warmed serving plates. Remove the vegetables with a slotted spoon, arrange around the
gammon, garnish with oregano sprigs and
serve.

Serves 6-8.

STUFFED CABBAGE LEAVES

18 large cabbage leaves
2 onions, finely chopped
4 tablespoons finely chopped fresh parsley
2 cloves garlic, crushed
225 g (8 oz) young spinach, shredded
225 g (8 oz) minced pork
450 g (1 lb) pork sausagemeat
25 g (1 oz/¼ cup) plain flour
2 eggs, beaten
salt and freshly ground black pepper
12 rashers streaky bacon
500 ml (18 fl oz/2¼ cups) chicken stock

Blanch the cabbage leaves in boiling water for 2 minutes. Remove and drain.

Preheat oven to 180C (350F/Gas 4). In a large bowl, mix together the onions, parsley, garlic, spinach, pork and sausagemeat. Add the flour and eggs and mix well. Season with salt and pepper. Divide into six portions. Trim the tough central core from each cabbage leaf. Arrange the leaves in six piles of three leaves each.

Divide the portions of filling among the cabbage leaves. Fold each one into a parcel and wrap each one with two rashers of bacon. Put into a flameproof casserole and pour over the stock. Bring to the boil, cover and cook in the oven for 1½ hours. Remove with a slotted spoon, pour over a little of the cooking liquid and serve.

Serves 6.

TOAD IN THE HOLE

115 g (4 oz/1 cup) plain flour
pinch of salt
1 teaspoon mixed dried herbs
1 egg, beaten
300 ml (10 fl oz/1¼ cups) milk
1 tablespoon sunflower oil
1 small onion, chopped
450 g (1 lb) herby sausages

Preheat oven to 200C (400F/Gas 6). In a large bowl, mix together the flour, salt and herbs. Make a well in the centre and add the egg and half of the milk. Beat to a smooth batter. Stir in the remaining milk and mix until smooth.

Heat the oil in a shallow flameproof dish. Add the onion and cook, stirring occasionally, for 3 minutes. Add the sausages and cook until browned all over.

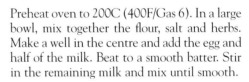

Pour the batter into the dish and cook in the oven for 30 minutes, until the batter is risen and golden. Serve immediately.

Serves 4.

Variation: There are many types of flavoured sausages available. Try using different types to vary this recipe.

SAUSAGE & PEPPERS

2 tablespoons olive oil
700 g (1½ lb) hot, sweet or mixed Italian sausages
2 onions, halved lengthwise, then cut lengthwise into 'petals'
4-6 cloves garlic, finely chopped
1 each large red, green and yellow pepper (capsicum), cut in half lengthwise then into strips
225 g (8 oz) can peeled tomatoes
1 tablespoon fresh shredded oregano or basil or 1 teaspoon dried oregano or basil
½ teaspoon crushed chillies
½ teaspoon dried thyme
½ teaspoon rubbed sage
salt and freshly ground black pepper
fresh oregano or basil leaves, to garnish
Parmesan cheese, to serve

CHINESE SAUSAGE STIR-FRY

2 tablespoons sesame or vegetable oil
225 g (8 oz) Chinese sausage (see Note) or sweet Italian-style sausage, cut diagonally into thin slices
1 onion, cut in half lengthwise and sliced
1 red pepper (capsicum), diced
115 g (4 oz) baby sweetcorn
2 courgettes (zucchini), thinly sliced
115 g (4 oz) mange tout (snow peas)
8 spring onions, cut into 2.5 cm (1 in) pieces
25 g (1 oz) beansprouts, rinsed and drained
25 g (1 oz/¼ cup) cashew nuts or peanuts
2 tablespoons soy sauce
3 tablespoons dry sherry or rice wine

Heat the wok until hot. Add olive oil and swirl to coat wok. Add sausages and cook over moderate heat for 8-10 minutes until sausages are golden brown on all sides, turning and rotating sausages frequently during cooking. Remove sausages to a plate and pour off all but 2 tablespoons oil from the wok. Add onions and garlic and stir-fry for 2 minutes until golden. Add the red, green and yellow pepper (capsicum) strips and stir-fry for 1-2 minutes until just beginning to soften.

Heat the wok until hot. Add sesame or vegetable oil and swirl to coat wok. Add sausage slices and stir-fry for 3-4 minutes until browned and cooked. Add onion, pepper and sweetcorn and stir-fry for 3 minutes. Add courgettes (zucchini), mange tout (snow peas) and spring onions and stir-fry for a further 2 minutes.

Add tomatoes and their liquid, fresh or dried oregano or basil, crushed chillies, thyme, sage, salt and pepper. Stir to break up the tomatoes and mix well. Return sausages to wok and cover with the vegetable mixture. Simmer for 15-20 minutes until vegetables are tender and sauce is thickened. Garnish with fresh oregano or basil leaves and sprinkle with shaved or grated Parmesan cheese. Serve with saffron rice or spaghetti.

Serves 6.

Stir in the beansprouts and nuts and stir-fry for 1-2 minutes. Add soy sauce and dry sherry or rice wine and stir-fry for 1 minute until vegetables are tender but still crisp and sausages slices completely cooked through. Serve with rice or noodles.

Serve 4.

Note: Chinese sausage is available in Chinese groceries and some specialist shops and needs cooking before being used.

VEGETARIAN
MAIN
COURSES

CHICK PEA & PEPPER TORTILLA

2 tablespoons olive oil
1 red onion, chopped
1 red pepper (capsicum), seeded and chopped
2 cloves garlic, crushed
175 g (6 oz/1 cup) cooked chick peas
1 teaspoon ground turmeric
2 tablespoons chopped fresh parsley
4 large eggs
salt and pepper
parsley sprigs, to garnish

In a non-stick frying pan, heat the oil and fry the onion, pepper (capsicum) and garlic for 10 minutes until lightly golden and softened. Add the chick peas, mashing them lightly as you go, then stir in the turmeric and parsley. Stir-fry for 2 minutes. Lightly beat the eggs with salt and pepper and stir into the pan until evenly mixed.

Cook over a medium heat for 5-6 minutes until cooked and browned underneath. Loosen around the edges with a spatula and carefully slip the tortilla out onto a plate. Invert the pan over the tortilla and flip over so that the top is now on the bottom. Cook for a further 3-4 minutes until golden underneath and turn out onto a plate. Allow to cool to room temperature. Garnish with parsley and serve with a tomato salad.

Serves 6.

HAZELNUT CRÊPES & SPINACH

100 g (3½ oz/⅔ cup) plain flour
15 g (½ oz/3 teaspoons) hazelnuts, toasted and finely ground
salt and pepper
1 egg, lightly beaten
300 ml (10 fl oz/1¼ cups) milk
15 g (½ oz/3 teaspoons) butter, melted
175 g (6 oz) trimmed spinach, washed
175 g (6 oz/¾ cup) low-fat cream cheese
1 small clove garlic, crushed
1 tablespoon chopped fresh mixed herbs
2 tablespoons olive oil
1 teaspoon lemon juice
¼ teaspoon freshly grated nutmeg
pinch of chilli powder

Combine the flour, nuts and ½ teaspoon salt in a bowl and gradually beat in the egg, milk and butter to form a thin pouring batter; set aside for 30 minutes. Heat the spinach in a large pan, with just the water from the leaves, for 1 minute until just wilted. Drain well, squeeze out excess water, chop finely and leave to cool. Beat the spinach with the low-fat cheese, garlic, herbs, 1 tablespoon oil, lemon juice, spices and salt and pepper to form a paste.

Brush an omelette pan or small frying pan with a little remaining oil and place over a medium heat. When hot, pour in a little batter, swirl the mixture over the base of the pan and cook for 1-2 minutes until browned underneath. Turn over and cook the other side for 30 seconds, until golden. Transfer to a plate and keep warm. Repeat to make 12 crêpes in total. Spread each one with a little of the spinach and cheese mixture, fold up and serve at once.

Serves 4-6.

GRATIN OF VEGETABLES

115 g (4 oz/²/₃ cup) long-grain rice
3 courgettes (zucchini)
1 red pepper (capsicum)
1 onion
6 ripe tomatoes
2 tablespoons olive oil
2 sprigs fresh thyme
2 sprigs fresh rosemary
2 bay leaves
1 teaspoon dried oregano
1 teaspoon fennel seeds, roasted
150 ml (5 fl oz/²/₃ cup) vegetable stock
85 g (3 oz) Pecorino or vegetarian Cheddar cheese, grated

Preheat oven to 200C (400F/Gas 6). Put the rice into a small pan and cover with cold water. Bring to the boil and cook for 3 minutes, drain well and transfer to a gratin dish. Thickly slice the courgettes (zucchini), roughly chop the pepper (capsicum) and onion and skin, seed and roughly chop the tomatoes.

Place the prepared vegetables in a large bowl, add the oil and stir well until vegetables are coated. Snip in the fresh herbs, add the bay leaves, oregano and fennel seeds, stir and spoon over the rice. Pour over the stock, cover with foil and bake for 40 minutes. Remove the foil, sprinkle over the cheese and return to the oven for a further 10-15 minutes until cheese is melted and all the liquid is absorbed. Brown under a hot grill, if wished, and serve hot.

Serves 6.

MUSHROOM & BEAN CHILLI

4 tablespoons olive oil
1 large aubergine (eggplant), diced
175 g (6 oz) button mushrooms, wiped
1 large onion, chopped
1 clove garlic, chopped
1½ teaspoons paprika
½-1 teaspoon chilli powder
1 teaspoon ground coriander
½ teaspoon ground cumin
900 g (2 lb) tomatoes, skinned and chopped
150 ml (5 fl oz/²/₃ cup) vegetable stock
25 g (1 oz) tortilla chips
1 tablespoon tomato purée (paste)
400 g (14 oz) can red kidney beans
1 tablespoon chopped fresh coriander
salt and pepper

In a large pan, heat 2 tablespoons oil and stir-fry the aubergine (eggplant) for 10 minutes until golden, then remove from the pan with a slotted spoon. Add 1 tablespoon oil to the pan and stir-fry the mushrooms until golden; remove with a slotted spoon. Add the remaining oil to the pan and fry the onion, garlic and spices for 5 minutes. Add the tomatoes and stock and cook, covered, for 45 minutes.

Finely crush the tortilla chips and blend with 4 tablespoons water and the tomato purée (paste). Whisk into the chilli sauce and add the mushroom and aubergine (eggplant). Drain the beans and add to the pan with the coriander. Cover and cook for a further 20 minutes. Season to taste and serve with plain boiled rice and thick sour cream, if wished.

Serves 6.

Note: Check the packet to ensure that the tortilla chips are a vegetarian product.

PARSNIP, PEAR & ALMOND SAUTÉ

12 baby onions
3 tablespoons olive oil
575 g (1¼ lb) baby parsnips, halved or quartered
1 clove garlic, chopped
2 teaspoons chopped fresh thyme
115 ml (4 fl oz/½ cup) dry cider
150 ml (5 fl oz/⅔ cup) vegetable stock
1 tablespoon brown sugar
2 teaspoons wholegrain mustard
2 small pears, cored and thickly sliced
55 g (2 oz/½ cup) blanched almonds, toasted
salt and pepper

BROCCOLI CAPONATA

2 tablespoons olive oil
1 red onion, chopped
1 red pepper (capsicum), seeded and chopped
1 clove garlic, chopped
1 teaspoon chopped fresh thyme
85 ml (3 fl oz/⅓ cup) red wine
450 g (1 lb) tomatoes, skinned, seeded and chopped
150 ml (5 fl oz/⅔ cup) vegetable stock
1 tablespoon red wine vinegar
1 tablespoon brown sugar
450 g (1 lb) broccoli, trimmed and chopped
2 tablespoons tomato purée (paste)
55 g (2 oz/½ cup) stoned green olives
25 g (1 oz/¼ cup) capers, drained
1 tablespoon shredded fresh basil

Place the onions in a small pan, cover with cold water and bring to the boil. Drain, refresh under cold water, peel and cut in half. Heat 2 tablespoons of the oil in a large pan and stir-fry the onions, parsnips, garlic and thyme for 10 minutes until browned all over. Add the cider and boil rapidly for 5 minutes. Blend the stock, sugar and mustard together and stir into the pan. Cover and cook for 10-12 minutes until parsnips are tender.

In a large pan, heat the oil and fry the onion, pepper (capsicum) , garlic and thyme for 6-8 minutes until lightly browned. Add the wine and boil rapidly for 3 minutes. Add the tomatoes, stock, vinegar and sugar. Stir well, then cover and simmer gently for 20 minutes.

Meanwhile, heat the remaining oil and fry the pear slices over a high heat for 1 minute on each side until browned, then remove pears with a slotted spoon. Pour the juices from the parsnips into the pan and boil rapidly for 2-3 minutes until thickened. Pour over the parsnips, add the pears and almonds and heat through. Season to taste and serve at once.

Serves 4.

Steam the broccoli for 5 minutes until almost cooked, add to the tomato mixture with the tomato purée (paste), olives, capers and basil. Cook for a further 3-4 minutes, remove from the heat and leave to cool. Serve at room temperature.

Serves 4.

VEGETABLE & FRUIT CURRY

1½ teaspoons each coriander and cumin seeds
4 tablespoons vegetable oil
1 large onion, chopped
2 carrots, chopped
2 potatoes, diced
3 cloves garlic, crushed, or 1 tablespoon garlic purée
2 teaspoons grated fresh root ginger
1 teaspoon each curry powder and turmeric
450 g (1 lb) ripe tomatoes
450 ml (16 fl oz/2 cups) vegetable stock
115 g (4 oz/1 cup) frozen peas, thawed
1 apple, cored and chopped
1 mango, peeled, stoned and chopped
85 g (3 oz/⅔ cup) cashew nuts, toasted
25 g (1 oz) creamed coconut
1 tablespoon chopped fresh coriander

In a small pan, roast the coriander and cumin seeds until browned and grind in a blender or spice grinder. Heat half the oil in a large pan and fry the onions, carrots and potatoes for 10 minutes until browned. Heat the remaining oil in a small pan and fry the garlic, ginger, ground spices, curry powder and turmeric for 5 minutes. Skin, seed and chop the tomatoes and stir into the spice mixture. Cover and cook for 10 minutes. Stir into the carrot mixture with the stock and simmer gently for 20 minutes.

Add the peas, apple and mango and cook for a further 5 minutes. Grind half the cashew nuts and mix with the creamed coconut. Stir in enough pan juices to form a paste and carefully stir into the curry until evenly combined. Heat through and serve at once, sprinkled with the whole nuts and coriander.

Serves 4-6.

TOMATO & BEAN TIAN

3 tablespoons olive oil
1 red onion, chopped
1 garlic clove, crushed
1 large red pepper (capsicum), seeded and chopped
3 teaspoons chopped fresh thyme
2 teaspoons chopped fresh rosemary
400 g (14 oz) can chopped tomatoes
432 g (15¼ oz) can cannellini beans, drained
25 g (1 oz/½ cup) each fresh breadcrumbs, chopped pine nuts and grated Parmesan cheese or vegetarian Cheddar cheese
2 large courgettes (zucchini), thinly sliced
2 ripe beef tomatoes, thinly sliced
rosemary sprigs, to garnish

Preheat oven to 190C (375F/Gas 5). In a saucepan, heat 2 tablespoons of the oil and fry the onion, garlic, pepper (capsicum), 2 teaspoons thyme and 1 teaspoon rosemary for 5 minutes. Add the tomatoes, cover and cook for 20 minutes. Stir in the beans and transfer to a shallow baking dish.

Mix the breadcrumbs, pine nuts and cheese together and sprinkle half over the tomato layer. Arrange courgettes (zucchini) and beef tomatoes in rows over the top and sprinkle over the remaining crumb mixture. Drizzle over the remaining oil and more herbs, if wished. Cover with kitchen foil and bake for 30 minutes. Remove foil and bake for a further 15-20 minutes until golden. Garnish with rosemary sprigs and serve hot with a crisp green salad.

Serves 4-6.

BUTTERNUT SQUASH CRUMBLE

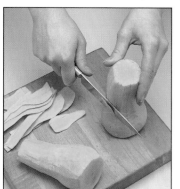

700 g (1½ lb) peeled butternut squash (about 3 small squash)
1 small fennel bulb, about 115 g (4 oz), trimmed
1 clove garlic, crushed
1 tablespoon chopped fresh sage
400 g (14 oz) can chopped tomatoes
150 ml (5 fl oz/⅔ cup) double (thick) cream
salt and pepper
115 g (4 oz/1 cup) wholemeal flour
55 g (2 oz/¼ cup) butter, diced
55 g (2 oz/⅓ cup) macadamia nuts, chopped
25 g (1 oz/¼ cup) grated Parmesan or vegetarian Cheddar cheese

Preheat oven to 200C (400F/Gas 6). Scrape out and discard the squash seeds, cut the flesh into 1 cm (½ in) pieces and place in a large ovenproof dish. Very finely shred the fennel and scatter over the squash with the garlic and sage. Pour in the tomatoes and cream and add a little salt and pepper.

Put the flour in a bowl and rub in the butter until the mixture resembles fine breadcrumbs. Stir in the nuts and cheese and sprinkle the crumble topping over the squash. Cover with foil and bake in the oven for 40 minutes. Remove foil and bake for a further 15-20 minutes until the topping is golden and the squash is tender.

Serves 6.

BREAD & CHEESE PUDDING

550 ml (20 fl oz/2½ cups) milk
1 bay leaf
2 cardamom pods, bruised
15 g (½ oz/3 teaspoons) butter
1 onion, thinly sliced
½ teaspoon chopped fresh thyme
55 g (2 oz/½ cup) drained sun-dried tomatoes, chopped
55 g (2 oz/¼ cup) Mascarpone cheese
225 g (8 oz) vegetarian Double Gloucester cheese, grated
350 g (12 oz) thinly sliced wholemeal bread
3 eggs
pinch of freshly grated nutmeg
salt and pepper

Preheat oven to 200C (400F/Gas 6) and lightly oil a 2 litre (3¾ pint/9 cup) pie dish. Put the milk, bay leaf and cardamom pods into a small pan and heat until almost boiling. Remove from the heat and leave to infuse for 10 minutes; strain into a bowl. Heat the butter and fry the onion and thyme for 10 minutes until soft. Add the tomatoes, remove from the heat, cool slightly and stir in the Mascarpone and one-quarter of the grated cheese.

Spread half the mixture over the base of the dish, top with half the bread and the remaining onion mixture. Sprinkle over half the remaining cheese, top with the rest of the bread. Whisk the eggs, nutmeg and seasonings into the milk and pour into the dish. Sprinkle over the rest of the cheese and place the dish in a roasting tin. Pour in boiling water to come two-thirds of the way up the side of the dish, cover with foil and bake for 30 minutes. Uncover and cook 20 minutes.

Serves 6-8.

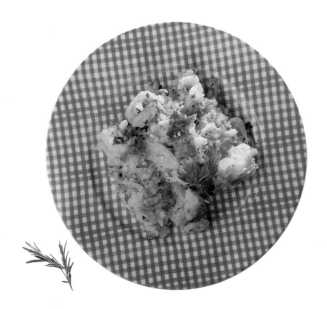

VEGETARIAN HASH POTATOES

575 g (1¼ lb) potatoes, peeled
45 g (1½ oz/9 teaspoons) butter
1 onion, thinly sliced
1 teaspoon chopped fresh sage
1 teaspoon chopped fresh rosemary
85 ml (3 fl oz/⅓ cup) natural yogurt
45 g (1½ oz/⅓ cup) grated Cheddar cheese
1 teaspoon wholegrain mustard
1 teaspoon Worcestershire sauce

Cut potatoes into chunks, place in a pan, cover with cold water and bring to the boil. Cook for 15-20 minutes until cooked. Drain and mash roughly.

Melt 15 g (½ oz/3 teaspoons) butter in a large, non-stick frying pan and fry the onion and herbs for 10 minutes until the onion is soft and golden. Combine the remaining ingredients.

Add the mashed potatoes to the frying pan and stir in the yogurt mixture, flattening the mixture out to sides of the pan. Cook over a high heat for 5-6 minutes until golden underneath. Using a spatula, turn the hash, a little at a time, and brown the other side. Serve straight from pan.

Serves 4.

POTATO CAKES & MANGO SAUCE

225 g (8 oz) potatoes, peeled
115 g (4 oz) butternut squash, peeled
15 g (½ oz/3 teaspoons) butter, diced
1 egg yolk
45 g (1½ oz/⅓ cup) grated Cheddar cheese
1 tablespoon grated onion
2 teaspoons chopped fresh coriander
a little flour seasoned with salt and pepper
1 egg, beaten
115 g (4 oz/¾ cup) Brazil nuts, ground
115 g (4 oz) peeled mango, chopped
1 spring onion, trimmed and chopped
1 small clove garlic, crushed
½ small fresh green chilli, seeded and chopped
juice 1 lime
vegetable oil for deep frying

Cube the potatoes and the squash and cook until tender. Drain, mash well and stir in the butter, egg yolk and cheese until melted. Stir in the onion and coriander and season to taste. Leave until cold. Shape mixture into 8 small rounds and flatten into thin patties. Dust with seasoned flour, dip in the egg and then into the ground nuts to coat the cakes on all sides.

Place all the remaining ingredients, except the oil, in a blender or food processor and purée until fairly smooth; stir in a little water if the sauce is too thick. Heat about 1 cm (½ in) vegetable oil in a non-stick frying pan and fry the potato cakes, in batches, for 2-3 minutes on each side until golden. Change the oil and repeat if necessary. Drain well on absorbent kitchen paper and serve hot with the mango sauce.

Serves 8.

STIR-FRIED SPINACH & TOFU

1 tablespoon olive oil
2 sticks celery, sliced
10 spring onions, sliced
2.5 cm (1 in) piece fresh root ginger, peeled and
    thinly sliced
225 g (8 oz) smoked tofu
175 g (6 oz) mange tout (snow peas)
450 g (1 lb) spinach, roughly torn
1 tablespoon black bean sauce
freshly ground black pepper
2 tablespoons toasted sesame seeds

Heat the oil in a flameproof casserole. Add
the celery, spring onions and ginger and stir-
fry for 3-4 minutes, until soft.

Add the tofu and mange tout (snow peas)
and stir-fry for 2-3 minutes. Gradually add
the spinach and stir-fry for 8-10 minutes,
until wilted and tender.

Stir in the black bean sauce and mix well.
Season with black pepper. Stir in the sesame
seeds and serve.

Serves 4.

POLENTA WITH MUSHROOMS

850 ml (30 fl oz/3¾ cups) vegetable stock
½ teaspoon salt
150 g (5 oz/1 cup) polenta
1 teaspoon chopped fresh thyme
25 g (1 oz/¼ cup) freshly grated Parmesan or
    Cheddar cheese
25 g (1 oz/6 teaspoons) butter
15 g (½ oz/¼ cup) dried ceps (mushrooms)
85 ml (3 fl oz/⅓ cup) boiling water
55 ml (2 fl oz/¼ cup) port
3 tablespoons virgin olive oil
1 clove garlic, crushed
1 shallot, finely chopped
350 g (12 oz) mixed fresh mushrooms, sliced
1 tablespoon chopped fresh parsley

Bring 700 ml (25 fl oz/3¼ cups) of the stock
and the salt to the boil in a pan and immediately whisk in the polenta. Stir, cover and
simmer gently for 25 minutes, stirring frequently. Add the thyme and cook for a
further 5 minutes. Stir in the cheese and butter and pour into a lightly oiled, shallow tin.
Smooth the surface and leave to cool. Soak
the ceps in the boiling water for 20 minutes.
Strain liquid into a pan and chop the ceps.
Add the port and the remaining stock to the
pan and boil until reduced to about 115 ml
(4 fl oz/½ cup). Set aside.

Turn out polenta and cut into 12 triangles,
brush with oil and grill for 8-10 minutes on
each side until golden. Meanwhile, heat the
oil in a large pan and fry the garlic, shallot
and ceps for 5 minutes. Add the fresh sliced
mushrooms and stir-fry for 3-4 minutes until
golden. Add the reduced liquid, cover and
cook for 5 minutes. Add parsley and serve
sauce with the grilled polenta triangles.

Serves 6.

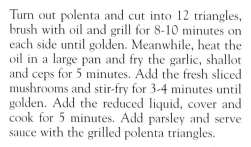

FENNEL & BEAN CASSEROLE

300 g (10 oz/1¼ cups) dried haricot beans, soaked
    overnight
1 tablespoon olive oil
2 onions, chopped
2 cloves garlic, crushed
1 head of celery, sliced
2 fennel bulbs, thinly sliced
2 tablespoons tomato purée (paste)
2 tablespoons chopped fresh oregano
1 tablespoon chopped fresh thyme
2 bay leaves
2 teaspoons each salt and sugar
2 x 400 g (14 oz) cans chopped tomatoes
freshly ground black pepper
6 slices day-old bread, made into crumbs
thyme sprigs, to garnish

Put the haricot beans in a flameproof
casserole. Cover with cold water. Bring to
the boil and boil rapidly for 10 minutes.
Cover and simmer for 1 hour. Drain and set
aside. Heat the oil in the casserole. Add the
onions and garlic and cook, stirring occasionally, for 5 minutes, until soft. Add the
beans, celery, fennel, tomato purée (paste),
half of the oregano, the thyme, bay leaves,
salt, sugar and tomatoes. Season with black
pepper. Cover and simmer for 30 minutes.

Preheat oven to 220C (425F/Gas 7). Mix
together the breadcrumbs and remaining
oregano and scatter over the top of the bean
mixture. Cook for 15-20 minutes, until the
breadcrumbs are golden brown. Garnish
with thyme sprigs and serve.

Serves 4-6.

BAKED EGGS IN NESTS

700 g (1½ lb) waxy potatoes, halved
225 g (8 oz) broccoli flowerets
2 courgettes (zucchini)
2 leeks, thinly sliced
1 tablespoon Worcestershire sauce
salt and freshly ground black pepper
4 eggs

Cook the potatoes in boiling salted water for
5-10 minutes. Add the broccoli and cook for
5 minutes. Drain

Coarsely grate the potatoes. Using a
vegetable peeler, cut the courgettes (zucchini) lengthwise into ribbons. Mix together
the potatoes, broccoli, leeks, courgettes
(zucchini) and Worcestershire sauce. Season
with salt and pepper. Lightly oil a flameproof
casserole and add the vegetable mixture.

Make four wells in the vegetable mixture
and break an egg into each one. Cover and
cook very gently for 10 minutes, until the
eggs have set. Serve immediately.

Serves 2-4.

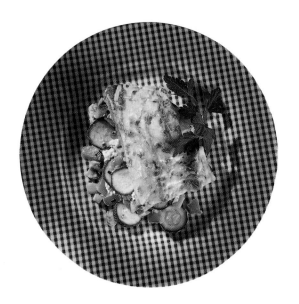

SAVOURY BREAD PUDDING

6 thick slices wholemeal bread
2 courgettes (zucchini), sliced
1 beefsteak tomato, chopped
175 g (6 oz) mushrooms, chopped
400 ml (14 fl oz/1¾ cups) milk
5 eggs, beaten
1 tablespoon chopped fresh chives
salt and freshly ground black pepper
150 g (5 oz/1¼ cups) grated Cheddar cheese
flat-leaf parsley sprigs, to garnish

Preheat oven to 200C (400F/Gas 6). Cut the bread into fingers. Arrange half the fingers in a shallow ovenproof dish.

Spread the courgettes (zucchini), tomatoes and mushrooms over the bread and top with the remaining bread. In a large bowl, mix together the milk and eggs. Add the chives and season with salt and pepper.

Pour the milk mixture over the bread. Sprinkle the cheese over the top and bake for 50 minutes, until the egg mixture has set and the topping is golden brown. Garnish with flat-leaf parsley and serve.

Serves 4.

COURGETTE GOUGÈRE

2 tablespoons olive oil
5 courgettes (zucchini), thinly sliced
300 g (10 oz) button mushrooms
2 leeks, thinly sliced
2 teaspoons wholegrain mustard
300 ml (10 fl oz/1¼ cups) crème fraîche
salt and freshly ground black pepper
CHOUX PASTRY:
55 g (2 oz/¼ cup) butter
225 g (8 oz/2 cups) plain flour
2 eggs, beaten

To make the choux pastry, gently melt the butter in 150 ml (5 fl oz/⅔ cup) water, then bring quickly to the boil. Remove from the heat and immediately stir in the flour.

Beat well until the mixture is smooth and comes away from the sides of the pan. Return to the heat and cook gently, stirring, for 2-3 minutes. Remove from the heat and gradually add the eggs, beating well. Set aside. Preheat oven to 220C (425F/Gas 7). Heat the oil in a flameproof casserole. Add the courgettes (zucchini), button mushrooms and leeks and cook, stirring occasionally, for 6-8 minutes, until tender.

Stir in the mustard and crème fraîche and season with salt and pepper. Put the choux pastry in a piping bag fitted with a plain 1 cm (½ in) nozzle. Pipe small balls of pastry around the edge of the courgette (zucchini) mixture. Bake for 20-30 minutes, until the pastry is risen and golden. Serve.

Serves 4-6.

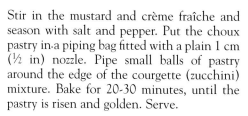

FENNEL & BEAN CASSEROLE

BAKED EGGS IN NESTS

300 g (10 oz/1¼ cups) dried haricot beans, soaked
   overnight
1 tablespoon olive oil
2 onions, chopped
2 cloves garlic, crushed
1 head of celery, sliced
2 fennel bulbs, thinly sliced
2 tablespoons tomato purée (paste)
2 tablespoons chopped fresh oregano
1 tablespoon chopped fresh thyme
2 bay leaves
2 teaspoons each salt and sugar
2 x 400 g (14 oz) cans chopped tomatoes
freshly ground black pepper
6 slices day-old bread, made into crumbs
thyme sprigs, to garnish

700 g (1½ lb) waxy potatoes, halved
225 g (8 oz) broccoli flowerets
2 courgettes (zucchini)
2 leeks, thinly sliced
1 tablespoon Worcestershire sauce
salt and freshly ground black pepper
4 eggs

Cook the potatoes in boiling salted water for
5-10 minutes. Add the broccoli and cook for
5 minutes. Drain

Put the haricot beans in a flameproof
casserole. Cover with cold water. Bring to
the boil and boil rapidly for 10 minutes.
Cover and simmer for 1 hour. Drain and set
aside. Heat the oil in the casserole. Add the
onions and garlic and cook, stirring occasionally, for 5 minutes, until soft. Add the
beans, celery, fennel, tomato purée (paste),
half of the oregano, the thyme, bay leaves,
salt, sugar and tomatoes. Season with black
pepper. Cover and simmer for 30 minutes.

Coarsely grate the potatoes. Using a
vegetable peeler, cut the courgettes (zucchini) lengthwise into ribbons. Mix together
the potatoes, broccoli, leeks, courgettes
(zucchini) and Worcestershire sauce. Season
with salt and pepper. Lightly oil a flameproof
casserole and add the vegetable mixture.

Preheat oven to 220C (425F/Gas 7). Mix
together the breadcrumbs and remaining
oregano and scatter over the top of the bean
mixture. Cook for 15-20 minutes, until the
breadcrumbs are golden brown. Garnish
with thyme sprigs and serve.

Serves 4-6.

Make four wells in the vegetable mixture
and break an egg into each one. Cover and
cook very gently for 10 minutes, until the
eggs have set. Serve immediately.

Serves 2-4.

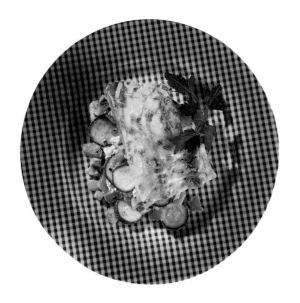

SAVOURY BREAD PUDDING

6 thick slices wholemeal bread
2 courgettes (zucchini), sliced
1 beefsteak tomato, chopped
175 g (6 oz) mushrooms, chopped
400 ml (14 fl oz/1¾ cups) milk
5 eggs, beaten
1 tablespoon chopped fresh chives
salt and freshly ground black pepper
150 g (5 oz/1¼ cups) grated Cheddar cheese
flat-leaf parsley sprigs, to garnish

Preheat oven to 200C (400F/Gas 6). Cut the bread into fingers. Arrange half the fingers in a shallow ovenproof dish.

Spread the courgettes (zucchini), tomatoes and mushrooms over the bread and top with the remaining bread. In a large bowl, mix together the milk and eggs. Add the chives and season with salt and pepper.

Pour the milk mixture over the bread. Sprinkle the cheese over the top and bake for 50 minutes, until the egg mixture has set and the topping is golden brown. Garnish with flat-leaf parsley and serve.

Serves 4.

COURGETTE GOUGÈRE

2 tablespoons olive oil
5 courgettes (zucchini), thinly sliced
300 g (10 oz) button mushrooms
2 leeks, thinly sliced
2 teaspoons wholegrain mustard
300 ml (10 fl oz/1¼ cups) crème fraîche
salt and freshly ground black pepper
CHOUX PASTRY:
55 g (2 oz/¼ cup) butter
225 g (8 oz/2 cups) plain flour
2 eggs, beaten

To make the choux pastry, gently melt the butter in 150 ml (5 fl oz/⅔ cup) water, then bring quickly to the boil. Remove from the heat and immediately stir in the flour.

Beat well until the mixture is smooth and comes away from the sides of the pan. Return to the heat and cook gently, stirring, for 2-3 minutes. Remove from the heat and gradually add the eggs, beating well. Set aside. Preheat oven to 220C (425F/Gas 7). Heat the oil in a flameproof casserole. Add the courgettes (zucchini), button mushrooms and leeks and cook, stirring occasionally, for 6-8 minutes, until tender.

Stir in the mustard and crème fraîche and season with salt and pepper. Put the choux pastry in a piping bag fitted with a plain 1 cm (½ in) nozzle. Pipe small balls of pastry around the edge of the courgette (zucchini) mixture. Bake for 20-30 minutes, until the pastry is risen and golden. Serve.

Serves 4-6.

LEEK STEW WITH DUMPLINGS

700 g (1½ lb) leeks, halved lengthways
350 g (12 oz) potatoes, diced
225 g (8 oz) Jerusalem artichokes, peeled and
  quartered
1 litre (35 fl oz/4½ cups) vegetable stock
salt
fresh chives, to garnish
DUMPLINGS:
115 g (4 oz/1 cup) self-raising flour
55 g (2 oz) vegetable suet
25 g (1oz) chopped fresh chives

Cut the leeks into 7.5 cm (3 in) lengths. Put the leeks, potatoes and artichokes in a large flameproof casserole.

Add the stock and season with salt. Bring to the boil, cover and simmer for 45-60 minutes. Meanwhile, to make the dumplings, put the flour, suet, and chives in a large bowl, season with salt and mix well. Stir in 55 ml (2 fl oz/ ¼ cup) water and bind to a dough. Knead lightly and leave to rest for 5 minutes.

Shape the dough into eight small dumplings. Place the dumplings around the outside of the vegetable mixture. Cover and simmer for 30 minutes. Garnish with chives and serve.

Serves 4.

MOROCCAN CASSEROLE

2 tablespoons olive oil
1 large onion, chopped
1 large aubergine (eggplant), cut into chunks
2 cloves garlic, crushed
1 teaspoon ground cumin
1 teaspoon turmeric
1 teaspoon ground ginger
1 teaspoon paprika
1 teaspoon ground allspice
3 x 400 g (14 oz) cans chopped tomatoes
450 g (1 lb) can chick peas, drained
75 g (3 oz) raisins
1 tablespoon chopped fresh coriander
3 tablespoons chopped fresh parsley
salt and freshly ground black pepper

Heat the oil in a flameproof casserole. Add the onion and cook, stirring occasionally, for 5 minutes, until soft. Add the aubergine (eggplant), cover and cook for 5 minutes. Add the garlic, ground cumin, turmeric, ground ginger, paprika and allspice and cook, stirring, for 1 minute.

Stir in the tomatoes, chick peas, raisins and chopped coriander and parsley. Season with salt and pepper. Bring to the boil and simmer for 45 minutes. Serve.

Serves 4-6.

MIXED VEGETABLE RÖSTI

1 tablespoon olive oil
1 onion, sliced
225 g (8 oz) green beans, trimmed
225 g (8 oz) cauliflower flowerets
4 tomatoes, peeled and quartered
1 tablespoon chopped fresh parsley
salt and freshly ground black pepper
700 g (1½ lb) potatoes, grated
115 g (4 oz/1 cup) grated mozzarella cheese

Heat the oil in a flameproof dish. Add the sliced onion and cook, stirring occasionally, for 5 minutes, until soft. Preheat oven to 200C (400F/Gas 6).

Add the beans, cauliflower and tomatoes and cook, stirring occasionally, for 10 minutes, until tender. Stir in the parsley and season with salt and pepper.

Spread the potatoes over the vegetables and top with cheese. Bake for 30 minutes, until the potatoes are tender and the cheese is melted and golden. Serve.

Serves 4.

Note: Waxy potatoes, such as Maris Piper, should be used for this recipe.

VEGETABLE COBBLER

1 tablespoon olive oil
1 clove garlic, crushed
2 leeks, thinly sliced
2 teaspoons mustard seeds
225 g (8 oz) mushrooms, sliced
225 g (8 oz) broccoli flowerets
175 g (6 oz) fresh or frozen peas
300 ml (10 fl oz/1¼ cups) single (light) cream
large pinch of freshly grated nutmeg
1 teaspoon prepared English mustard
1 tablespoon chopped fresh parsley
200 g (7 oz) puff pastry, thawed if frozen
milk for brushing

Heat the oil in a flameproof casserole. Add the garlic and leeks and cook until soft.

Add the mustard seeds and cook until they start to pop. Add the mushrooms, broccoli and peas. Cover and cook for 8-10 minutes, until tender. Remove from the heat. Stir in the cream, nutmeg, mustard and parsley. Preheat oven to 220C (425F/Gas 7).

Roll out the pastry on a lightly floured surface. Using a pastry cutter, cut out twelve 5 cm (2 in) rounds. Arrange on top of the vegetable mixture. Brush with a little milk and bake for 30-35 minutes, until risen and golden. Serve.

Serves 4-6.

NUT BAKE WITH TOMATOES

25 g (1 oz/2 tablespoons) butter
1 onion, finely chopped
150 g (5 oz) carrot, finely chopped
2 sticks celery, finely chopped
300 g (10 oz/2½ cups) finely chopped mixed nuts
115 g (4 oz/2 cups) fresh wholemeal breadcrumbs
2 teaspoons yeast extract
300 ml (10 fl oz/1¼ cups) hot vegetable stock
2 teaspoons dried thyme
salt and freshly ground black pepper
2 beefsteak tomatoes, sliced
115 g (4 oz/1 cup) grated mature Cheddar cheese

Preheat oven to 180C (350F/Gas 4). Heat the butter in a flameproof casserole.

Add the onion, carrot and celery and cook gently, stirring occasionally, for 10 minutes, until soft. In a large bowl, mix together the nuts and breadcrumbs. Stir in the cooked vegetables. Dissolve the yeast extract in the hot stock and stir into the bowl. Add the thyme and season with salt and pepper. Mix well. Arrange half the tomato slices in the base of the casserole. Sprinkle with half of the grated cheese.

Spread half of the nut mixture on top. Add the remaining tomato slices and cover with the remaining nut mixture. Sprinkle with the remaining grated cheese and bake for 50-60 minutes, until the cheese is melted and golden. Serve.

Serves 4.

SPANISH OMELETTE

2 tablespoons olive oil
1 onion, thinly sliced
350 g (12 oz) potatoes, diced
1 red pepper (capsicum), thinly sliced
1 green pepper (capsicum), thinly sliced
6 eggs, beaten
1 tablespoon chopped fresh parsley
salt and freshly ground black pepper

Heat the oil in a shallow flameproof dish. Add the onion and potatoes and cook, stirring occasionally, for 6-8 minutes, until the potatoes are tender. Stir in the peppers (capsicum) and cook for 2-3 minutes.

Beat together the eggs, parsley and salt and pepper and pour into the dish. Cook gently for 3-4 minutes, until the eggs have set on the bottom. Preheat the grill.

Put the omelette under the grill and cook for 5-6 minutes, until the eggs have set. Cut into wedges and serve hot or at room temperature.

Serves 4.

LENTIL & BEAN CHILLI

1 tablespoon olive oil
1 onion, chopped
1 clove garlic, chopped
175 g (6 oz/¾ cup) green lentils
300 ml (10 fl oz/1¼ cups) vegetable stock
1 teaspoon mild chilli powder
400 g (14 oz) can chopped tomatoes
400 g (14 oz) can red kidney beans in chilli sauce
1 green pepper (capsicum), chopped
salt and freshly ground black pepper
chopped fresh flat-leaf parsley, to garnish

Heat the oil in a flameproof casserole and cook the onion and garlic until soft. Add the lentils, stock, chilli powder and tomatoes.

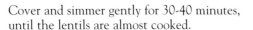

Cover and simmer gently for 30-40 minutes, until the lentils are almost cooked.

Stir in the kidney beans and their sauce and the green pepper (capsicum) and simmer for 10-15 minutes, until the lentils are cooked and the liquid has been absorbed. Season with salt and pepper. Garnish with chopped parsley and serve.

Serves 4.

SWEET PEPPER CHILLI

2 onions
5 large fresh red chillies, cored, seeded and chopped
1 red pepper (capsicum), chopped
1 large clove garlic, chopped
2 tablespoons dry white wine
salt
1 tablespoon olive oil
1 green pepper (capsicum), thinly sliced
1 tablespoon tomato purée (paste)
1 teaspoon ground cumin
200 g (7 oz) can red kidney beans, drained
basil sprigs, to garnish

Roughly chop one of the onions. Put in a food processor with the chillies, red pepper (capsicum), garlic, wine and salt.

Process for 2 minutes. Slice the remaining onion. Heat the oil in a flameproof casserole, add the sliced onion and cook, stirring occasionally, for 5 minutes, until soft. Add the puréed mixture, 2 tablespoons water and the green pepper (capsicum).

Bring to the boil, cover and simmer gently for 30 minutes. Add the tomato purée (paste), cumin and kidney beans. Simmer for 10-15 minutes. Garnish with basil and serve.

Serves 2-4.

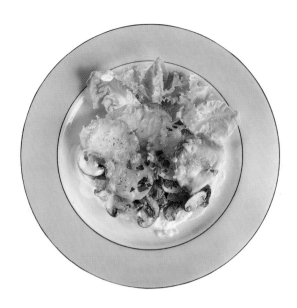

VEGETABLE FRICASSÉE

400 ml (14 fl oz/1¾ cups) vegetable stock
350 g (12 oz) swede, cut into chunks
225 g (8 oz) each carrots and potatoes, cut into chunks
1 leek, sliced
225 g (8 oz) cauliflower flowerets
225 g (8 oz) green beans
55 g (2 oz/¼ cup) butter
55 g (2 oz/½ cup) wholemeal flour
150 ml (5 fl oz/⅔ cup) milk
6 tablespoons chopped fresh parsley
1 teaspoon lemon juice
salt and freshly ground black pepper

Put the stock in a flameproof casserole and bring to the boil. Add the swede, carrots and potatoes.

Return to the boil and cook for 5 minutes. Add the leek, cauliflower and beans and cook for 3-5 minutes. Drain the vegetables, reserving the stock. Heat the butter in the casserole. Add the flour and cook, stirring, for 1 minute. Gradually stir in the milk and 250 ml (9 fl oz/1 cup) of the reserved stock, stirring constantly until smooth.

Reduce the heat, stir in the parsley and lemon juice and season with salt and pepper. Add the vegetables and cook for 4-5 minutes to warm through. Serve.

Serves 4.

MUSHROOM GRATIN

15 g (½ oz/1 tablespoon) butter
1 clove garlic, crushed
900 g (2 lb) potatoes, thinly sliced
175 g (6 oz) chestnut mushrooms, sliced
115 g (4 oz) button mushrooms, sliced
salt and freshly ground black pepper
2 eggs, beaten
150 ml (5 fl oz/⅔ cup) milk
150 ml (5 fl oz/⅔ cup) crème fraîche
175 g (6 oz/1½ cups) grated Gruyère cheese
chopped fresh parsley, to garnish

Preheat oven to 200C (400F/Gas 6). Rub an ovenproof dish with the butter and garlic. Add half the potatoes and the mushrooms.

Top with the remaining potatoes. Season generously with salt and pepper. Mix together the eggs, milk and crème fraîche and pour over the vegetables. Bake for 1 hour.

Sprinkle the cheese over the top and bake for 25 minutes, until the cheese is melted and golden. Garnish with parsley and serve.

Serves 4.

MIXED VEGETABLE CURRY

3 tablespoons vegetable oil
1 onion, sliced
1 teaspoon ground cumin
1 teaspoon chilli powder
2 teaspoons ground coriander
1 teaspoon turmeric
225 g (8 oz) potatoes, diced
175 g (6 oz) cauliflower flowerets
115 g (4 oz) green beans, sliced
175 g (6 oz) carrots, diced
4 tomatoes, skinned and chopped
300 ml (10 fl oz/1¼ cups) hot vegetable stock
onion rings, to garnish

Heat oil in a large saucepan, add onion and fry for 5 minutes, until softened. Stir in cumin, chilli powder, coriander and turmeric and cook for 2 minutes, stirring occasionally. Add potatoes, cauliflower, green beans and carrots, tossing them in the spices until coated.

Add tomatoes and stock and cover. Bring to the boil, then reduce heat and simmer for 10-12 minutes or until vegetables are just tender. Serve hot, garnished with onion rings.

Serves 4.

Variation: Use any mixture of vegetables to make a total of 750 g (1½ lb) – turnips, swedes, courgettes (zucchini), aubergines (eggplant), parsnips and leeks are all suitable for this curry.

FRESH HERB FRITTATA

6 eggs
2 egg whites
2 spring onions, trimmed and chopped
115 g (4 oz/½ cup) cottage cheese
25 g (1 oz/½ cup) fresh chopped mixed herbs
25 g (1 oz/1 cup) rocket
salt and pepper
olive oil

Whisk the eggs and the egg whites together until thoroughly mixed and stir in the spring onions, cheese and herbs. Roughly chop the rocket and add to mixture together with the seasonings.

Preheat grill. Heat about 4 teaspoons oil in a non-stick frying pan and pour in the egg mixture, swirling to reach the edges of the pan. Cook, stirring, over a medium-low heat for about 3 minutes until eggs are beginning to set.

Place pan under the hot grill and cook for a further 2-3 minutes until set and lightly golden. Turn out onto a plate, cut into wedges and serve warm or cold with a tomato and olive salad.

Serves 2-4.

LENTIL-STUFFED PEPPERS

115 g (4 oz/⅔ cup) red split lentils
55 ml (2 fl oz/¼ cup) vegetable oil
4 green or red peppers (capsicums)
1 teaspoon cumin seeds
2 onions, finely chopped
2 green chillies, seeded and chopped
2.5 cm (1 in) piece fresh root ginger, grated
3 teaspoons ground coriander
salt and pepper
2 tablespoons chopped fresh coriander
coriander leaves, to garnish

Wash lentils, then soak in cold water for 30 minutes.

Heat half the oil in a frying pan and fry peppers (capsicums) for 3-5 minutes, until golden brown on all sides. Drain on absorbent kitchen paper and leave to cool. Add remaining oil to pan, then add cumin seeds and fry until just beginning to pop. Add onions and chillies and fry, stirring, for 8 minutes, until onions are soft and golden brown. Stir in ginger and ground coriander. Drain lentils and add to pan with 300 ml (10 fl oz/1¼ cups) water and stir well.

Cook, covered, over low heat for 15-20 minutes, until tender and liquid has been absorbed. Season with salt and pepper and add fresh coriander. Preheat oven to 180C (350F/Gas 4). Cut tops from peppers (capsicums) and remove seeds. Stuff peppers (capsicums) with lentil mixture and replace tops. Stand in an ovenproof dish and cook for 15-20 minutes, until soft. Serve hot, garnished with coriander leaves.

Serves 4.

SZECHUAN PANCAKES

225 g (8 oz/2 cups) plain flour
2 teaspoons sesame oil
strips of fresh green and red chilli and celery leaves, to garnish
FILLING:
2 tablespoons cornflour
1 teaspoon Szechuan peppercorns, toasted and ground
large pinch of salt
225 g (8 oz) fresh bean curd, drained and cut into 2 cm (¾ in) cubes
1 tablespoon sunflower oil
2 cloves garlic, finely chopped
2 tablespoons light soy sauce
175 g (6 oz) preserved Szechuan vegetables, shredded

Sieve flour into a bowl and, using chopsticks or a fork, mix in 150 ml (5 fl oz/⅔ cup) boiling water, to form a firm dough. Knead on a lightly floured surface until smooth. Divide dough into 8 and roll out each portion to form a 15 cm (6 in) diameter pancake. Heat a non-stick frying pan. Lightly brush the pancakes on each side with oil and cook in frying pan for 1-2 minutes on each side. Drain on kitchen paper, layer between sheets of baking parchment and keep warm.

Place cornflour, peppercorns and salt on a plate and toss bean curd in the mixture until well coated. Heat oil in a non-stick or well seasoned wok and stir-fry bean curd and garlic for 2-3 minutes until browned. Add soy sauce and Szechuan vegetables and stir-fry for 3 minutes. Place a little bean curd mixture on each pancake and fold pancake over the filling. Garnish and serve.

Serves 4.

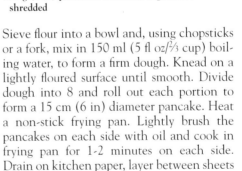

CURRIED CHICK PEAS

175 g (6 oz/1 cup) dried chick peas
2 tablespoons vegetable oil
1 small onion, finely chopped
2.5 cm (1 in) piece fresh root ginger, grated
2 cloves garlic, crushed
½ teaspoon turmeric
1 teaspoon ground cumin
1 teaspoon garam masala
½ teaspoon chilli powder
salt
2 tablespoons chopped fresh coriander

Wash chick peas well, then put them in a bowl, cover with cold water and leave to soak overnight.

Drain chick peas, then put in a saucepan with 500 ml (16 fl oz/2 cups) fresh cold water. Bring to the boil for 10 minutes, then reduce heat and simmer, partially covered, for 1 hour. In a separate pan, heat oil, add onion and fry for about 8 minutes, until soft and golden brown.

Add ginger, garlic, turmeric, cumin, garam masala and chilli powder and fry for 1 minute. Stir in chick peas and their cooking water and season with salt. Bring to the boil, then simmer, covered, for 20 minutes, until chick peas are very tender but still whole. Serve hot, sprinkled with chopped fresh coriander.

Serves 4.

BEAN & CORN CHILLI

2 teaspoons sunflower oil
2 onions, sliced
2 garlic cloves, crushed
1-2 teaspoons hot chilli powder
1 teaspoon ground cumin
1 teaspoon ground coriander
3 sticks celery, sliced, leaves reserved for garnish
175 g (6 oz) mushrooms, sliced
150 ml (5 fl oz/⅔ cup) vegetable stock
2 x 225 g (8 oz) cans sweetcorn, drained
425 g (15 oz) can each borlotti or pinto beans and
   red kidney beans, rinsed and drained
400 g (14 oz) can crushed tomatoes
2 tablespoons tomato purée (paste)
salt and freshly ground pepper

In a large saucepan, heat oil and cook the onions and garlic for 5 minutes. Add chilli powder, cumin, coriander, celery and mushrooms and cook for 5 minutes, stirring occasionally.

Add stock, sweetcorn, borlotti or pinto beans, kidney beans, tomatoes, tomato purée (paste), salt and pepper and mix well. Bring slowly to the boil, reduce heat, cover and simmer for 30 minutes, stirring occasionally. Garnish with the reserved celery leaves and serve with freshly cooked tagliatelle.

Serves 6.

CHEESY STUFFED TOMATOES

8 tomatoes
2 tablespoons vegetable oil
1 small onion, finely chopped
1 clove garlic, crushed
2.5 cm (1 in) piece fresh root ginger, grated
1 teaspoon ground cumin
½ teaspoon turmeric
½ teaspoon cayenne pepper
2 teaspoons ground coriander
salt
115 g (4 oz/½ cup) fresh Indian cheese or natural fromage frais
25 g (1 oz/¼ cup) Cheddar cheese, grated
1 tablespoon chopped fresh coriander

Cut a slice from the top of each tomato. Scoop out centres and discard seeds, then chop pulp and reserve. Turn tomatoes upside down on absorbent kitchen paper and leave to drain. Heat oil in a small frying pan, add onion and fry for 5 minutes, stirring occasionally, until soft. Stir in garlic and ginger and fry for 1 minute. Stir in cumin, turmeric, cayenne pepper and ground coriander. Season with salt and fry for 1 minute more.

Stir in tomato pulp and cook, uncovered, for about 5 minutes, until thick. Preheat oven to 190C (375F/Gas 5). Stir fresh cheese or fromage frais and half the Cheddar into spice mixture and spoon into tomato shells. Sprinkle remaining Cheddar over the tops and place on a baking tray. Cook for 10-15 minutes, until tops are golden brown and tomatoes soft. Sprinkle with chopped coriander and serve hot.

Serves 4.

FASOULIA

55 ml (2 fl oz/¼ cup) olive oil
1 clove garlic, crushed
3 large tomatoes, skinned and chopped
225 g (8 oz) dried haricot beans, soaked overnight
1 bay leaf
1 sprig thyme
salt and pepper
onion rings and thyme sprigs, to garnish

In a large saucepan, heat oil. Add garlic and tomatoes. Cook for a few minutes until tomatoes soften.

Drain beans and add to pan. Pour in boiling water to come 2.5 cm (1 in) above top of beans. Add bay leaf and thyme. Cover pan and simmer for 1-1¼ hours until beans are tender.

The liquid should have reduced to form a thick sauce. If not, simmer uncovered for a few minutes. Season with salt and pepper. Transfer beans to a serving dish. Serve garnished with onion rings and sprigs of thyme.

Serves 4.

STUFFED AUBERGINES

2 aubergines (eggplants), about 225 g (8 oz) each
2 cloves garlic, finely chopped
2 stalks lemon grass, chopped
2 tablespoons vegetable oil
1 small onion, finely chopped
175 g (6 oz) chicken breast meat, finely chopped
2 teaspoons fish sauce
25 Thai holy basil leaves
freshly ground black pepper
Thai holy basil leaves, to garnish

Preheat grill. Place aubergines (eggplants) under grill and cook, turning as necessary, for about 20 minutes until evenly charred.

Meanwhile, using a pestle and mortar, pound together garlic and lemon grass; set aside. Heat oil in a wok, add onion and cook, stirring occasionally, until lightly browned. Stir in garlic mixture, cook for 1-2 minutes, then add chicken. Stir-fry for 2 minutes. Stir in fish sauce, basil leaves and plenty of black pepper.

Using a sharp knife, slice each charred aubergine (eggplant) in half lengthwise. Using a teaspoon, carefully scoop aubergine (eggplant) flesh into a bowl; keep skins warm. Using kitchen scissors, chop flesh. Add to wok and stir ingredients together for about 1 minute. Place aubergine (eggplant) skins on a large warmed plate and divide chicken mixture between them. Garnish with basil leaves.

Serves 4.

SPICY TOFU

vegetable oil for deep-frying
2 cakes tofu, cut into small cubes
1 clove garlic, chopped
2 shallots, chopped
2-3 small red chillies, seeded and chopped
2 leeks, sliced
about 15 g (½ oz) black fungus, soaked and cut into small pieces
salt and freshly ground black pepper
½ teaspoon sugar
1 tablespoon rice vinegar
1 tablespoon crushed black bean sauce
about 55 ml (2 fl oz/¼ cup) stock or water
2 teaspoons cornflour
½ teaspoon sesame oil
chopped spring onions, to garnish

Heat oil in a wok or deep-fat fryer and deep-fry the tofu cubes until browned on all sides. Remove and drain. Pour off the excess oil, leaving about 1 tablespoon in the wok, stir-fry the garlic, shallots, and chillies for about 30 seconds, then add the leeks and stir-fry for 2-3 minutes.

Add tofu, black fungus and salt and pepper. Stir-fry for 1 minute, then blend in sugar, vinegar, black bean sauce and stock or water. Bring to boil and simmer for 1-2 minutes. Mix cornflour with 1 tablespoon water and stir into mixture. Add sesame oil and serve garnished with chopped spring onions.

Serves 4.

Note: For a non-vegetarian dish, add about 175 g (6 oz) chopped beef with the leeks in step 2, and increase seasonings by half.

PASTA & NOODLES

BUCATINI SICILIANA

350 g (12 oz) bucatini
4 tablespoons olive oil
1 onion, chopped
2 cloves garlic, chopped
2 teaspoons capers
2 tablespoons sun-dried tomato paste
freshly ground black pepper
4 teaspoons pine nuts
25 g (1 oz/½ cup) fresh breadcrumbs
1 tablespoon chopped fresh parsley
2 teaspoons chopped black olives

Bring a large saucepan of salted water to the boil. Add the pasta and cook according to the packet instructions until just tender.

Meanwhile, heat 3 tablespoons of the oil in a frying pan. Add the onion and garlic and cook gently for 5 minutes until soft. Add the capers, tomato paste, 70 ml (2½ fl oz/⅓ cup) of the water from the saucepan of pasta, black pepper and heat gently. Heat the remaining oil in a frying pan. When hot, add the pine nuts and breadcrumbs and cook, stirring, until crisp and golden. Stir in the parsley.

Drain the pasta and return to the pan. Add the caper mixture and toss to coat. Transfer to a warmed serving dish, sprinkle with the breadcrumb mixture and chopped olives and serve immediately.

Serves 4.

Note: Bucatini is a long, thin, tubular type of pasta. If it is unavailable, spaghetti can be used instead.

PASTA WITH BROCCOLI

450 g (1 lb) broccoli
350 g (12 oz) trumpet-shaped pasta, eg campanelle
70 ml (2½ fl oz/⅓ cup) olive oil
2 cloves garlic, finely chopped
6 anchovies in olive oil, drained and chopped
½ fresh red chilli, cored, seeded and finely chopped
salt and freshly ground black pepper
Parmesan cheese, to serve

Divide the broccoli into small flowerets and slice the stalks. Bring a large saucepan of salted water to the boil, add the broccoli flowerets and stalks and cook for 3-5 minutes until just tender.

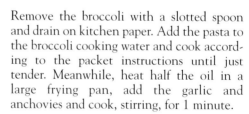

Remove the broccoli with a slotted spoon and drain on kitchen paper. Add the pasta to the broccoli cooking water and cook according to the packet instructions until just tender. Meanwhile, heat half the oil in a large frying pan, add the garlic and anchovies and cook, stirring, for 1 minute.

Add the chilli and cook for 1 minute. Gently stir in the broccoli and season with salt and pepper. Drain the pasta and add to the broccoli mixture. Stir in the remaining olive oil and cook, stirring, for 1 minute. Transfer to a warmed serving dish. Use a vegetable peeler to shave the Parmesan cheese on top of the pasta and serve.

Serves 4.

SPAGHETTI WITH GARLIC

5 tablespoons olive oil
salt and freshly ground pepper
2 cloves garlic, finely chopped
1 red chilli, seeded and chopped
400 g (14 oz) dried spaghettini or spaghetti
2 tablespoons chopped fresh parsley

Heat oil in a medium saucepan. Add garlic and a pinch of salt and cook very gently until golden, stirring all the time. Do not allow the garlic to become too brown or it will taste bitter. Add chopped chilli and cook for 1 minute.

Bring a large pan of salted water to the boil and cook pasta according to manufacturer's instructions until *al dente* (tender but firm to the bite). Drain well.

Toss pasta with the warm, not sizzling, garlic and chilli oil and add plenty of black pepper and the parsley. Serve immediately.

Serves 6.

PASTA CARBONARA

115 g (4 oz) smoked lean streaky bacon or pancetta
 in a piece
1 clove garlic, finely chopped
300 g (10 oz) dried spaghetti or other ribbon pasta
3 eggs, beaten
salt and freshly ground pepper
3 tablespoons freshly grated Parmesan cheese

Cut bacon into dice and place in a medium saucepan with the garlic. Place over the heat and fry in its own fat until brown. Keep warm.

Bring a large saucepan of salted water to boil and cook pasta according to manufacturer's instructions until *al dente* (tender but still firm to the bite). Drain well. Quickly turn the spaghetti into the pan with the bacon.

Stir in eggs, a little salt, lots of pepper and half the cheese. Toss well to mix. The eggs should lightly cook with the heat from the spaghetti. Serve in warm bowls with the remaining cheese.

Serves 4.

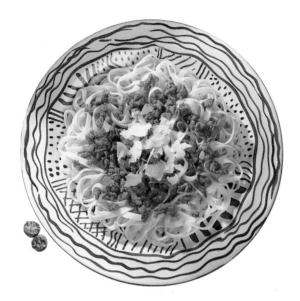

PASTA BOLOGNESE

75 g (3 oz) pancetta or bacon in a piece, diced
1 medium onion, finely chopped
1 medium carrot, finely diced
1 celery stick, finely chopped
225 g (8 oz) lean minced beef
115 g (4 oz) chicken livers, trimmed and chopped
1 medium potato, grated
2 tablespoons tomato purée (paste)
115 ml (4 fl oz/½ cup) white wine
200 ml (7 fl oz/1 cup) beef stock or water
salt and freshly ground pepper
freshly grated nutmeg
400 g (14 oz) dried spaghetti, fettuccine or tagliatelle
freshly grated Parmesan cheese, to serve (optional)

Heat a saucepan and add pancetta. Cook in its own fat for 2-3 minutes until browning. Add onion, carrot and celery and brown them. Stir in minced beef and brown over high heat, breaking it up with a wooden spoon. Stir in the chicken livers and cook them for 2-3 minutes.

Add potato, tomato purée (paste), mix well and pour in wine and stock. Season with salt, pepper and nutmeg. Bring to boil, half-cover and simmer for 35 minutes until reduced and thickened, stirring occasionally. Meanwhile, cook pasta in boiling salted water until tender. Drain well and toss with sauce. Serve with Parmesan cheese, if liked.

Serves 6.

PASTA NAPOLETANA

900 g (2 lb) fresh ripe red tomatoes, or two 400 g
   (14 oz) cans plum tomatoes with juice, chopped
1 medium onion, finely chopped
1 medium carrot, finely diced
1 stick celery, diced
150 ml (5 fl oz/⅔ cup) dry white wine (optional)
parsley sprig
salt and freshly ground pepper
pinch sugar
1 tablespoon chopped fresh oregano
350 g (12 oz) dried pasta of your choice
freshly grated Parmesan cheese, to serve (optional)

Put vegetables, wine, parsley, seasoning and sugar in a medium saucepan.

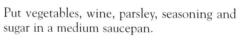
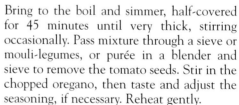

Bring to the boil and simmer, half-covered for 45 minutes until very thick, stirring occasionally. Pass mixture through a sieve or mouli-legumes, or purée in a blender and sieve to remove the tomato seeds. Stir in the chopped oregano, then taste and adjust the seasoning, if necessary. Reheat gently.

Bring a large pan of salted water to the boil and cook pasta according to manufacturer's instructions until *al dente* (tender but firm to the bite). Drain well and toss with the hot sauce. Serve at once, with grated Parmesan cheese if wished.

Serves 4.

PENNE WITH LEEKS & RICOTTA

450 g (1 lb) young leeks, washed and trimmed
2-3 tablespoons hazelnut oil
1 clove garlic, sliced
350 g (12 oz/4 cups) dried penne or other pasta
  shells
olive oil
225 g (8 oz/1 cup) ricotta cheese
4 tablespoons milk
45 g (1½ oz/⅓ cup) freshly grated Pecorino or
  Parmesan cheese
2 tablespoons mixed chopped fresh herbs
½ teaspoon grated lemon zest
½ teaspoon lemon juice
salt and pepper

Preheat oven to 220C (425F/Gas 7). Pat the leeks dry. Cut into thick slices, place in a roasting tin with 2 tablespoons oil and the garlic and roast for 25 minutes until lightly browned. After 10 minutes, bring a large pan of water to the boil, add the pasta, a little olive oil and return to the boil. Lower heat and simmer gently for 10 minutes until pasta is *al dente* (just cooked but with a firm bite).

Meanwhile, place all the remaining ingredients in a small pan and stir over a low heat until melted. Heat through for 5 minutes without boiling. Strain the pasta, stir in a little more hazelnut oil and toss with the cooked leeks. Carefully stir in the melted cheese mixture, season to taste and serve at once.

Serves 4.

VEGETARIAN SPAGHETTI

2 tablespoons hazelnut oil
55 g (2 oz/1 cup) fresh breadcrumbs
350 g (12 oz) dried spaghetti
85 ml (3 fl oz/⅓ cup) virgin olive oil
2 cloves garlic, sliced
grated zest 1 lemon
1½ teaspoons chopped fresh rosemary
450 g (1 lb) small courgettes (zucchini), thinly sliced
45 g (1½ oz/⅓ cup) drained sun-dried tomatoes in
  oil, sliced
2 tablespoons capers, drained
juice ½ lemon
salt and pepper

In a large non-stick frying pan, heat the hazelnut oil and stir-fry the breadcrumbs over a medium heat for 3-4 minutes until evenly browned. Remove from heat and set aside. Cook the spaghetti in a pan of boiling water, with a little added olive oil, for 8-10 minutes until *al dente* (just cooked but with a firm bite).

Heat 1 teaspoon olive oil in a large frying pan, add the garlic, lemon zest and rosemary and fry for 30 seconds until beginning to brown. Add the courgettes (zucchini) and stir-fry for 3-4 minutes until golden. Add the tomatoes and capers and cook for a further 1 minute. Stir in the lemon juice and seasonings. Drain the pasta, add the remaining olive oil and toss until well coated. Serve at once topped with the courgettes (zucchini) and breadcrumbs.

Serves 4.

MACARONI WITH AUBERGINES

450 g (1 lb) aubergines (eggplants), cut into 0.5 cm
 (¼ in) matchstick strips
salt
450 g (1 lb) macaroni
3 tablespoons olive oil
3 cloves garlic, finely chopped
450 g (1 lb) plum or beefsteak tomatoes, peeled,
 seeded and chopped
1 fresh chilli, seeded and chopped
115 g (4 oz) Italian salami, cut into julienne strips
85 g (3 oz) black olives
2 tablespoons capers, rinsed and drained
4 tablespoons chopped fresh basil or oregano
115 g (4 oz) feta cheese, crumbled
25 g (1 oz/¼ cup) Parmesan cheese, grated
herb sprigs, to garnish

Place aubergine (eggplant) strips in a
colander and sprinkle with salt. Toss to mix,
then leave to stand, on a plate, for 1 hour.
Rinse under cold running water and pat dry
with absorbent kitchen paper. In a large
saucepan of boiling water, cook macaroni
according to packet directions. Drain and set
aside.

Heat wok until very hot. Add olive oil and
swirl to coat. Add aubergine (eggplant) and
stir-fry for 3-5 minutes until browned. Drain
on absorbent kitchen paper. Add garlic,
tomatoes and chilli and stir-fry for 2 minutes
until juices are absorbed. Add salami, olives,
capers, basil or oregano, aubergine (eggplant) and macaroni and toss to coat well.
Stir fry for 1-2 minutes to heat through. Add
feta cheese and toss. Sprinkle with Parmesan
cheese, garnish and serve hot.

Serves 6.

TAGLIATELLE WITH BEETROOT

115 g (4 oz/½ cup) butter, softened
2 tablespoons chopped fresh chives
1 teaspoon grated lemon zest
2 tablespoons walnut oil
1 large onion, thinly sliced
1 teaspoon sugar
2 teaspoons balsamic vinegar
450 g (1 lb) cooked beetroot, diced
450 g (1 lb) fresh tagliatelle
salt and pepper
small bunch fresh chervil, chopped

Cream the butter, chives and lemon zest
together, and chill for 1 hour.

In a non-stick frying pan, heat the oil and fry
the onion over a medium heat for 15
minutes until evenly golden. Add the sugar,
vinegar and beetroot and stir in three-
quarters of the chive butter. Cover and cook
gently for 4-5 minutes.

Cook the pasta in boiling water for 3-4
minutes until *al dente* (just cooked but with a
firm bite). Drain well, season with salt and
plenty of freshly ground black pepper and stir
in the remaining chive butter to thoroughly
coat the pasta. Toss with the beetroot and
onion mixture and serve at once, sprinkled
with the chervil.

Serves 4.

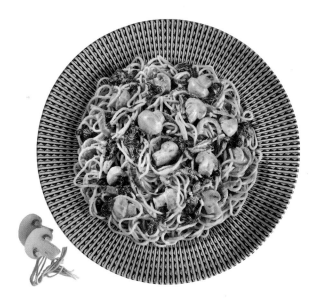

NOODLES WITH SPINACH

2 tablespoons olive oil
1 red onion, thinly sliced
300 g (10 oz) button mushrooms, halved
350 g (12 oz) spinach, roughly torn
225 g (8 oz) thread egg noodles
225 g (8 oz/1 cup) soft cheese with garlic and herbs
salt and freshly ground black pepper

Heat the oil in a flameproof casserole. Add the onion and cook, stirring occasionally, for 5 minutes, until soft. Add the mushrooms and spinach and cook, stirring occasionally, for 10-15 minutes, until the spinach is wilted and the mushrooms tender.

Meanwhile, put the noodles in a large bowl and cover with boiling water. Leave for 4-5 minutes, until tender. Drain. Add the garlic and herb cheese to the spinach mixture and heat gently, stirring, until melted.

Add the noodles to the vegetables and cheese, season with salt and pepper and mix well. Serve

Serves 4.

SEAFOOD LASAGNE

2 tablespoons olive oil
1 leek, thinly sliced
225 g (8 oz) mushrooms, thinly sliced
225 g (8 oz) haddock fillet, skinned and cubed
115 g (4 oz) cooked, peeled prawns
300 g (10 oz) cod fillet, skinned and cubed
2 tablespoons lemon juice
salt and freshly ground black pepper
4 eggs, beaten
55 g (2 oz/½ cup) freshly grated Parmesan cheese
500 ml (18 fl oz/2¼ cups) Greek yogurt
6 sheets fresh lasagne
225 g (8 oz) mozzarella cheese, sliced

Heat the oil in a large flameproof dish and add the leek and mushrooms.

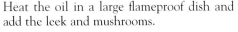

Cook gently for 10 minutes, stirring occasionally, until soft. Add the haddock, prawns, cod, lemon juice and salt and pepper and cook, stirring, for 5 minutes. Preheat oven to 180C (350F/Gas 4). Mix together the eggs, Parmesan cheese and yogurt. Stir into the fish mixture. Remove two-thirds of the fish mixture from the dish.

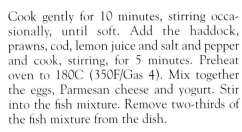

Cover the fish mixture in the dish with two sheets of lasagne. Cover them with half the remaining mixture then two more sheets of lasagne. Reserve a ladleful of the liquid from the fish mixture and spread the remaining mixture over the lasagne. Cover with two sheets of lasagne and pour the reserved liquid over the top. Cover with the cheese and bake for 40-50 minutes, until the topping is golden and the pasta is tender. Serve.

Serves 6-8.

FIDEUA

3-4 tablespoons olive oil
250 g (9 oz) raw Dublin Bay prawns
250 g (9 oz) raw prawns
salt
250 g (9 oz) monkfish fillet, cut into pieces
1½ teaspoons paprika
225 g (8 oz) beefsteak tomatoes, peeled, seeded and
  chopped
1.3 litres (2¼ pints/5½ cups) fish stock
2 cloves garlic
1 tablespoon chopped fresh parsley
6-8 saffron threads, finely crushed
250 g (9 oz) spaghettini, broken into lengths
lemon wedges and parsley sprigs, to garnish

Add more oil to pan, if necessary. Stir in paprika, cook 30-60 seconds, then add tomatoes. Cook gently for about 5 minutes, stirring occasionally. Add stock and bring to the boil.

Heat 3 tablespoons oil in a large paella pan or large frying pan, add Dublin Bay prawns, cook 1 minute then add prawns and sprinkle over a little salt. Fry shellfish on both sides for 2-3 minutes, then remove and set aside.

Pound garlic, parsley and saffron together. Stir in a little hot stock, then stir into pan and boil for 2 minutes. Add spaghettini and boil until pasta has absorbed most of the stock and is just tender.

Add monkfish to pan and cook for a few minutes until lightly browned all over. Remove and set aside.

Nestle monkfish and shellfish in the spaghettini, heat for 1-2 minutes, then remove from heat, cover pan and leave to stand for 5 minutes. Garnish with lemon wedges and parsley and serve from pan if a paella pan has been used.

Serves 4.

SNAPPER WITH CAPELLINI

1 tablespoon olive oil
55 g (2 oz/¼ cup) unsalted butter
450 g (1 lb) red snapper or sea bass fillets, cut into
  2.5 cm (1 in) strips
salt and freshly ground black pepper
225 g (8 oz) mushrooms, quartered
2 cloves garlic, finely chopped
150 ml (5 fl oz/⅔ cup) dry white wine
2 tomatoes, peeled, seeded and chopped
juice 1 lemon
1 tablespoon tomato purée (paste)
4 spring onions, thinly sliced
2 tablespoons thinly shredded fresh basil
450 g (1 lb) capellini or thin spaghetti
fresh basil sprigs, to garnish

Heat the wok until hot. Add oil and swirl to coat wok. Add half the butter and swirl to mix with oil. Add snapper or bass strips and gently stir-fry for 1-2 minutes until just firm. Season with salt and pepper and, with a slotted spoon, remove to a bowl. Stir mushrooms into remaining oil and butter in the wok, then add garlic and stir-fry for 1 minute. Add white wine and stir to deglaze any bits stuck to wok. Bring to the boil and simmer for 1 minute.

Add chopped tomatoes, lemon juice, tomato purée (paste), spring onions and basil, stirring frequently. Whisk in remaining butter in small pieces to thicken and smooth sauce. Return fish to sauce and cook gently for 1 minute until heated through. Meanwhile, in a large saucepan of boiling water, cook capellini or spaghetti according to directions. Drain and divide among 4 plates. Top with fish strips and sauce and garnish with fresh basil sprigs.

Serves 4.

SPAGHETTI MARINARA

225 g (8 oz) spaghetti
1 tablespoon olive oil
1 small onion, finely chopped
1 clove garlic, crushed
115 g (4 oz) button mushrooms, sliced
½ red or green pepper (capsicum), seeded and finely
  diced
300 ml (10 fl oz/1¼ cups) passata (sieved tomatoes)
200 g (7 oz) can pink salmon, drained
115 g (4 oz) cooked peeled prawns
pinch dried oregano
salt and pepper

Put the spaghetti into a pan of boiling, salted water and cook until tender; drain.

Meanwhile, heat the oil in a saucepan, add the onion, garlic, mushrooms and pepper (capsicum) and cook for 3-4 minutes. Add the passata and simmer for 2-3 minutes. Remove the bones and skin from salmon, then flake and add to the sauce with the prawns. Add the oregano and season to taste.

Return the drained spaghetti to the pan, pour over the sauce and toss together to heat through and mix before serving.

Serves 4.

TUNA, TOMATO & PENNE

2 tablespoons olive oil
1 onion, chopped
2 cloves garlic, finely chopped
800 g (28 oz) can peeled tomatoes
1 tablespoon tomato purée (paste)
1 tablespoon chopped fresh oregano or 1 teaspoon
    dried
55 g (2½ oz/⅓ cup) sun-dried tomatoes in oil,
    drained and chopped
salt and freshly ground black pepper
350 g (12 oz) penne or rigatoni
55 g (2½ oz/⅓ cup) black olives, coarsely chopped
2 tablespoons capers, drained
200 g (7 oz) can light tuna, drained
2 tablespoons chopped fresh parsley
Parmesan cheese, to garnish

Heat the wok until hot. Add the oil and swirl to coat wok. Add onion and garlic and stir-fry for 1-2 minutes until beginning to soften. Add the tomatoes, stirring to break up the large pieces. Stir in the tomato purée (paste), oregano and sun-dried tomatoes. Bring to the boil and simmer for 10-12 minutes until sauce is slightly thickened. Season with salt and pepper. Meanwhile, in a large saucepan of boiling water, cook penne according to packet directions.

Stir black olives, capers and tuna into the sauce. Drain pasta and add to sauce, stirring gently to mix well. Stir in chopped parsley and serve immediately from the wok, or spoon into 4 soup plates. Using a swivel-bladed vegetable peeler, shave flakes of Parmesan over each serving. Alternatively, grate Parmesan over each serving.

Serves 4.

PENNE, VODKA & TOMATOES

450 g (1 lb) penne or rigatoni
2 tablespoons olive oil
1 onion, finely chopped
2 cloves garlic, finely chopped
400 g (14 oz) can plum tomatoes
½ teaspoon crushed dried chillies
115 g (4 oz) thinly sliced ham
115 ml (4 fl oz/½ cup) vodka
250 ml (9 fl oz/1 cup) whipping cream
55 g (2 oz/½ cup) Parmesan cheese, grated
4 tablespoons chopped fresh parsley
salt and freshly ground black pepper

Cook penne or rigatoni according to packet directions.

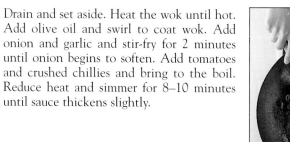

Drain and set aside. Heat the wok until hot. Add olive oil and swirl to coat wok. Add onion and garlic and stir-fry for 2 minutes until onion begins to soften. Add tomatoes and crushed chillies and bring to the boil. Reduce heat and simmer for 8–10 minutes until sauce thickens slightly.

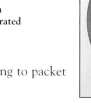

Add ham and vodka and simmer for a further 5 minutes. Add cream and half the grated Parmesan and simmer for 3 minutes. Stir in penne or rigatoni and parsley and toss to coat pasta. Season with salt and pepper and cook for 1–2 minutes to heat through. Serve hot with the remaining Parmesan sprinkled over the top. Garnish with extra parsley, if wished.

Serves 4–6.

PASTITSIO

225 g (8 oz) macaroni
6 teaspoons olive oil
1 onion, chopped
1 clove garlic, crushed
450 g (1 lb) minced steak
300 ml (10 fl oz/1¼ cups) stock
2 teaspoons tomato purée (paste)
½ teaspoon ground cinnamon
1 teaspoon chopped fresh mint
salt and pepper
55 g (2 oz/¼ cup) butter
55 g (2 oz/½ cup) plain flour
450 ml (16 fl oz/2 cups) milk
115 ml (4 fl oz/½ cup) yogurt
175 g (6 oz/1½ cups) grated kefalotiri cheese

In a pan of boiling water, cook macaroni for 8 minutes until tender. Drain, rinse with cold water and set aside. Preheat oven to 190C (375F/Gas 5). In a frying pan, heat oil, add onion and garlic and cook until soft. Add mince and stir until browned. Stir in stock, tomato purée (paste), cinnamon, mint, salt and pepper. Cook gently for 10-15 minutes until sauce is reduced.

In a saucepan, melt butter. Stir in flour; cook for 1 minute. Gradually stir in milk and yogurt; cook gently for 5 minutes. Stir in half cheese. Season. Mix macaroni into cheese sauce. Spread half macaroni mixture over base of a large gratin or soufflé dish. Cover with meat sauce; top with remaining macaroni. Sprinkle remaining cheese over top. Bake for 45 minutes until browned.

Serves 4-6.

RAINBOW MACARONI & CHEESE

115 g (4 oz/¾ cup) macaroni
15 g (½ oz/6 teaspoons) plain flour
15 g (½ oz/3 teaspoons) butter
300 ml (10 fl oz/1¼ cups) milk
salt and pepper
55 g (2 oz) frozen peas
55 g (2 oz) frozen sweetcorn
1 tomato, diced
85 g (3 oz/¾ cup) grated Gouda or Edam cheese
25 g (1 oz/½ cup) wholemeal breadcrumbs

Half-fill a saucepan with water and bring to the boil. Add 1 teaspoon salt, then stir in the macaroni and cook for 7 minutes until tender. Drain.

Put the flour, butter and milk into a medium saucepan and cook over a medium heat, whisking all the time until thickened. Season with a little salt and pepper, turn the heat to low and add the peas, sweetcorn, diced tomato and 55 g (2 oz/½ cup) of the cheese. Stir and cook for 2 minutes.

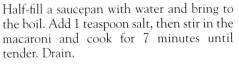

Mix the macaroni into the sauce and heat through. Spoon the mixture into 4 small ovenproof dishes or 1 large one. Mix the breadcrumbs with the remaining cheese and sprinkle on top. Place under a hot grill for 3-4 minutes to brown. Serve immediately.

Serves 4.

PASTA PRIMAVERA

450 g (1 lb) tagliatelle, linguine or thin spaghetti
2-4 tablespoons olive oil
225 g (8 oz) asparagus, cut into 5 cm (2 in) pieces
225 g (8 oz) broccoli florets, cut into small florets
2 yellow or green courgettes (zucchini), sliced
115 g (4 oz) mange tout (snow peas), cut in half if large
2-4 cloves garlic, finely chopped
400 g (14 oz) can chopped tomatoes
25 g (1 oz/2 tablespoons) butter
115 g (4 oz) frozen peas
4-6 tablespoons shredded fresh basil or chopped fresh
    dill
grated Parmesan, to serve

In the wok or a large saucepan, cook pasta according to packet directions.

Drain, turn into a large bowl, toss with 1 tablespoon olive oil and set aside. Heat the wok until hot. Add remaining oil and swirl to coat wok. Add asparagus and broccoli and stir-fry for 4-5 minutes until tender but still crisp. Remove to a bowl. Add courgettes (zucchini) and mange tout (snow peas) and stir-fry for 1-2 minutes until tender but still crisp. Remove to the bowl. Add garlic to oil remaining in wok and stir-fry for 1 minute. Stir in chopped tomatoes and their juice and simmer for 4-6 minutes until slightly thickened.

Stir butter into tomato sauce and add reserved vegetables, frozen peas, basil or dill and reserved pasta. Toss to coat well. Stir and toss for 2-3 minutes to heat through. Serve with grated Parmesan cheese.

Serves 4-6.

LAMB STEAKS WITH PASTA

4 thick lamb leg steaks
salt and pepper
2 cloves garlic, sliced
400 g (14 oz) can chopped tomatoes
70 ml (2½ fl oz/⅓ cup) olive oil
3 teaspoons chopped fresh marjoram
3 teaspoons chopped fresh parsley
315 g (10 oz) orzo (rice-shaped pasta)
salad leaves, to serve

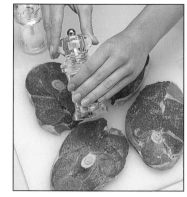

Preheat oven to 200C (400F/Gas 6). Season meat with salt and pepper. Place in a large roasting tin.

Scatter garlic over meat. Add 150 ml (5 fl oz/⅔ cup) water and tomatoes. Stir in olive oil, salt, pepper, marjoram and parsley. Cook for 40 minutes, basting from time to time and turning pieces of lamb over.

Add 300 ml (10 fl oz/1¼ cups) boiling water and the pasta. Stir in more salt and pepper. Cook for a further 40 minutes until pasta is cooked. If necessary, add more hot water. Serve with salad leaves.

Serves 6.

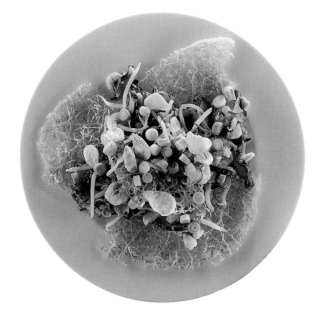

CRISPY NOODLES

175 g (6 oz) rice vermicelli
6 pieces dried Chinese black mushrooms
115 g (4 oz) lean pork
115 g (4 oz) chicken breast
vegetable oil, for deep frying
2 eggs
4 cloves garlic, finely chopped
3 shallots, thinly sliced
1 fresh red chilli, seeded and sliced
1 fresh green chilli, seeded and sliced
6 tablespoons lime juice
1 tablespoon fish sauce
1 tablespoon crushed palm sugar
45 g (1½ oz) cooked peeled shrimps
115 g (4 oz) beansprouts
3 spring onions, thickly sliced

Soak vermicelli in water for 20 minutes, then drain and set aside. Soak mushrooms in water for 20 minutes, then drain, chop and set aside. Cut pork and chicken into 2.5 cm (1 in) strips or small dice. Set aside.

For garnish, heat 2 teaspoons oil in a wok. In a small bowl, beat eggs with 2 tablespoons water, then drip small amounts in batches in tear shapes onto wok. Cook for 1½-2 minutes until set. Remove using a fish slice or thin spatula. Set aside.

Add more oil to wok until there is sufficient for deep frying. Heat to 190C (375F). Add vermicelli in batches and fry until puffed, light golden brown and crisp. Transfer to absorbent kitchen paper. Set aside.

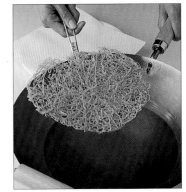

Pour off oil leaving 3 tablespoons. Add garlic and shallots and cook, stirring occasionally, until lightly browned. Add pork, stir-fry for 1 minute, then mix in chicken and stir for 2 minutes. Stir in chillies, mushrooms, lime juice, fish sauce and sugar.

Bubble until liquid becomes very lightly syrupy. Add shrimps, beansprouts and noodles, tossing to coat with sauce without breaking up noodles. Serve with spring onions scattered over and garnished with egg 'tears'.

Serves 4.

THAI FRIED NOODLES

3 tablespoons vegetable oil
4 cloves garlic, crushed
1 tablespoon fish sauce
3-4 tablespoons lime juice
1 teaspoon crushed palm sugar
2 eggs, beaten
350 g (12 oz) rice vermicelli, soaked in water for 20
  minutes, drained
115 g (4 oz) cooked peeled shrimps
115 g (4 oz) beansprouts
4 spring onions, sliced
2 tablespoons ground dried shrimps, finely chopped
  roasted peanuts, coriander leaves and lime slices, to
  garnish

In a wok, heat oil, add garlic and cook, stirring occasionally, until golden. Stir in fish sauce, lime juice and sugar until sugar has dissolved. Quickly stir in eggs and cook for a few seconds. Stir in noodles to coat with garlic and egg, then add shrimps, 85 g (3 oz) beansprouts and half spring onions.

When noodles are tender, transfer contents of wok to a warmed serving dish. Garnish with remaining beansprouts and spring onions, dried shrimps, peanuts, coriander leaves and lime slices.

Serves 4.

PORK & NOODLE PARCELS

3 cloves garlic, chopped
4 coriander roots, chopped
175 g (6 oz) lean pork, minced
1 small egg, beaten
2 teaspoons fish sauce
freshly ground black pepper
about 55 g (2 oz) egg thread noodles (1 'nest')
vegetable oil, for deep frying
Spicy Fish Sauce (see page 311), to serve
coriander sprig, to garnish

Using a pestle and mortar or small blender, pound or mix together garlic and coriander roots. In a bowl, mix together pork, egg, fish sauce and pepper, then stir in garlic mixture.

Place noodles in a heatproof sieve and dip in boiling water for 5 seconds if fresh, about 2 minutes if dried, until separated. Remove and rinse immediately in cold running water. Form pork mixture into approximately 12 balls. Neatly and evenly wind 3 or 4 strands of noodles around each ball to cover completely.

In a wok, heat oil to 180C (350F). Using a slotted spoon, lower 4-6 balls into oil and cook for about 3 minutes until golden and pork is cooked through. Using a slotted or draining spoon, transfer to absorbent kitchen paper to drain. Keep warm while cooking remaining balls. Serve hot with Spicy Fish Sauce. Garnish with coriander sprig.

Makes about 12 parcels.

CRAB & AUBERGINE NOODLES

PORK & PRAWN NOODLES

225 g (8 oz) brown and white crab meat
175 g (6 oz) dried egg thread noodles
3 tablespoons vegetable oil
1 aubergine (eggplant), about 225 g (8 oz), cut into
    about 5 x 0.5 cm (2 x ¼ in) strips
2 cloves garlic, very finely chopped
1 cm (½ in) slice galangal, finely chopped
1 fresh green chilli, seeded and finely chopped
6 spring onions, sliced
1 tablespoon fish sauce
2 teaspoons lime juice
1½ tablespoons chopped coriander leaves

In a bowl, well mash brown crab meat.
Roughly mash white meat. Set aside.

Add noodles to a saucepan of boiling salted
water and cook for about 4 minutes until just
tender. Drain well. Meanwhile, in a wok,
heat 2 tablespoons oil, add aubergine (eggplant) and stir-fry for about 5 minutes until
evenly well coloured. Using a slotted spoon,
transfer to absorbent kitchen paper; set
aside.

Add remaining oil to wok, heat, then one by
one stir in garlic, galangal, chilli, finally
spring onions. Add noodles, toss together for
1 minute, then toss in crab meats and
aubergine (eggplant). Sprinkle over fish
sauce, lime juice and coriander, and toss to
mix. Garnish with coriander sprig.

Serves 4.

200 g (7 oz) bean thread noodles
6 dried Chinese black mushrooms
2 tablespoons vegetable oil
350 g (12 oz) lean pork, very finely chopped
115 g (4 oz) cooked peeled large prawns
3 red shallots, finely chopped
4 spring onions, including some green, sliced
3 slim inner celery stalks, thinly sliced
55 g (2 oz) dried shrimps
2 tablespoons fish sauce
5 tablespoons lime juice
1½ teaspoons crushed palm sugar
2 fresh red chillies, seeded and chopped
15 g (½ oz) coriander leaves, chopped
whole cooked prawns and coriander, to garnish

Soak noodles in cold water for 15 minutes.
Soak mushrooms in water for 30 minutes.
Drain and chop. In a wok, heat oil, add pork
and stir-fry for 2-3 minutes until cooked
through. Using a slotted spoon, transfer to
absorbent kitchen paper. Add noodles to a
saucepan of boiling water and boil for 5
minutes. Drain well and set aside.

Cut each prawn into 3 and place in a bowl.
Add shallots, spring onions, celery, mushrooms, noodles, pork and dried shrimps; toss
together. In a small bowl, mix together fish
sauce, lime juice and sugar. Pour into bowl,
add coriander leaves and toss ingredients
together. Serve garnished with whole prawns
and coriander sprigs.

Serves 4.

NOODLES WITH CHOP SUEY

1 tablespoon groundnut (peanut) oil
2 cloves garlic, finely chopped
1 green pepper (capsicum), thinly sliced
1 red pepper (capsicum), thinly sliced
225 g (8 oz) shallots, chopped
225 g (8 oz) courgettes (zucchini), cut into
  matchstick strips
225 g (8 oz) carrots, cut into matchstick strips
115 g (4 oz) bean sprouts
2 teaspoons caster sugar
2 tablespoons light soy sauce
4 tablespoons Chinese Vegetable Stock (see glossary)
salt and freshly ground black pepper
225 g (8 oz) egg noodles

Heat the oil in a non-stick or well seasoned
wok and stir-fry garlic, green and red peppers
(capsicums), shallots, courgettes and carrots
for 2-3 minutes until just softened. Add all
remaining ingredients except noodles, bring
to the boil, reduce the heat and simmer for
6-7 minutes.

Meanwhile, bring a large saucepan of water
to the boil, add the noodles and cook for 5
minutes until just tender. Drain well and
transfer to warmed serving plates. Top with
the vegetable mixture and serve.

Serves 4.

COLD SPICY NOODLES

450 g (1 lb) soba (buckwheat) noodles or
  wholewheat spaghetti
2 tablespoons sesame oil
2 cloves garlic, finely chopped
1 green pepper (capsicum), thinly sliced
115 g (4 oz) mange tout (snow peas), sliced
115 g (4 oz) daikon (mooli), thinly sliced
2 tablespoons light soy sauce
3 teaspoons cider vinegar
3-6 teaspoons Chinese chilli paste or sauce
2 teaspoons sugar
70 ml (2½ fl oz/⅓ cup) peanut butter or sesame paste
8-10 spring onions, thinly sliced
toasted chopped peanuts or toasted sesame seeds, to
  garnish
cucumber matchsticks, to serve (optional)

In a large saucepan of boiling water, cook
noodles or spaghetti according to packet
directions. Drain and rinse well. Drain again
and toss with 1 tablespoon sesame oil. Set
aside. Heat the wok until very hot. Add
remaining sesame oil and swirl to coat. Add
garlic and stir-fry for 5-10 seconds. Add pepper (capsicum), mange tout (snow peas) and
daikon. Stir-fry for 1 minute until fragrant
and brightly coloured.

Stir in soy sauce, vinegar, chilli paste or
sauce, sugar, peanut butter or sesame paste
and 55 ml (2 fl oz/¼ cup) hot water. Remove
from heat. Stir until peanut butter or sesame
paste is diluted and smooth, adding a little
more water, if necessary. Add reserved
noodles and toss to coat. Turn into a large
shallow bowl and allow to cool. Before
serving, toss again, adding spring onions and
sprinkling with peanuts or sesame seeds.
Serve with cucumber, if wished.

Serves 4-6.

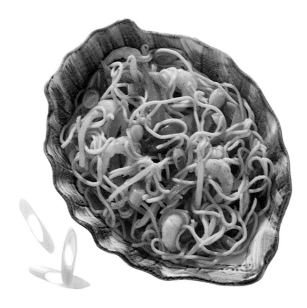

SINGAPORE NOODLES

225 g (8 oz) thin round egg noodles
55 ml (2 fl oz/¼ cup) vegetable oil
2 cloves garlic, chopped
2.5 cm (1 in) piece fresh root ginger, peeled and
  finely chopped
1 fresh chilli, seeded and chopped
1 red pepper (capsicum), thinly sliced
115 g (4 oz) mange tout (snow peas), sliced if large
4-6 spring onions, finely sliced
175 g (6 oz) peeled cooked prawns, defrosted if
  frozen
115 g (4 oz) beansprouts, trimmed, rinsed and dried
70 ml (2½ fl oz/⅓ cup) tomato ketchup (sauce)
1 teaspoon chilli powder
1-2 teaspoons chilli sauce

In a large saucepan of boiling water, cook the noodles according to packet directions. Drain and toss with 1 tablespoon of the oil. Set aside. Heat the wok until hot. Add remaining oil and swirl to coat the wok. Add garlic, ginger and chilli and stir-fry for 1 minute. Add red pepper (capsicum) and mange tout (snow peas) and stir-fry for 1 minute.

Add spring onions, prawns and beansprouts and stir in the tomato ketchup (sauce), chilli powder, chilli sauce and 115 ml (4 fl oz/ ½ cup) water. Bring to the boil. Add noodles and toss. Stir-fry for 1-2 minutes until coated with sauce and heated through. Turn into large shallow serving bowl and serve at once.

Serves 4.

NOODLES WITH BROCCOLI

450 g (1 lb) wet rice noodles
225 g (8 oz) broccoli
2 tablespoons vegetable oil
3 cloves garlic, finely chopped
225 g (8 oz) lean pork, finely chopped
4 tablespoons roasted peanuts, chopped
2 teaspoons fish sauce
½ teaspoon crushed palm sugar
1 fresh red chilli, seeded and cut into thin slivers, to
  garnish

Remove wrapping from noodles and immediately cut into 1 cm (½ in) strips; set aside. Cut broccoli diagonally into 5 cm (2 in) wide pieces and cook in a saucepan of boiling salted water for 2 minutes. Drain, refresh under cold running water and drain well; set aside.

In a wok, heat oil, add garlic and fry, stirring occasionally, until golden. Using a slotted spoon, transfer to absorbent kitchen paper; set aside. Add pork to wok and stir-fry for 2 minutes. Add noodles, stir quickly, then add broccoli and peanuts and stir-fry for 2 minutes. Stir in fish sauce, sugar and 3 tablespoons water. Stir briefly and serve garnished with reserved garlic and chilli slivers.

Serves 4.

CHOW MIEN

3 tablespoons soy sauce
2 tablespoons dry sherry or rice wine
1 teaspoon Chinese chilli paste or sauce
1 tablespoon sesame oil
6 teaspoons cornflour
350 g (12 oz) skinned and boned chicken breasts,
  cut into shreds
225 g (8 oz) Chinese long egg noodles or linguine
2 tablespoons vegetable oil
2 stalks celery, thinly sliced
175 g (6 oz) mushrooms
1 red or green pepper (capsicum), thinly sliced
115 g (4 oz) mange tout (snow peas)
4-6 spring onions
115 ml (4 fl oz/½ cup) chicken stock or water
115 g (4 oz) beansprouts, trimmed and rinsed

In a shallow baking dish, combine the soy
sauce, sherry or rice wine, chilli paste or
sauce, sesame oil and cornflour. Add the
shredded chicken and toss to coat evenly.
Allow to stand 20 minutes. In a large
saucepan of boiling water, cook the egg
noodles or linguine according to the packet
directions. Drain and set aside.

Heat wok until hot. Add oil and swirl to coat
wok. Add celery, mushrooms and pepper. Stir-
fry for 2-3 minutes until vegetables begin to
soften. Add mange tout and spring onions
and stir-fry for 1 minute. Remove to a bowl.
Add chicken and marinade to wok. Stir-fry
for 2-3 minutes until chicken is cooked. Add
stock, bring to the boil, then add noodles or
linguine and reserved vegetables and
beansprouts. Toss and stir-fry for 1-2 minutes
until sauce thickens and noodles are hot.

Serves 4-6.

BEAN & MUSHROOM NOODLES

175 g (6 oz) black-eye beans
175 g (6 oz) vermicelli rice noodles
1 tablespoon sunflower oil
2 cloves garlic, finely chopped
2 shallots, finely chopped
2 teaspoons fermented black beans
25 g (1 oz) dried Chinese mushrooms, soaked in hot
  water for 20 minutes, drained and caps sliced
115 g (4 oz) button mushrooms, sliced
115 g (4 oz) oyster mushrooms, sliced
3 tablespoons light soy sauce
salt and freshly ground black pepper
4 tablespoons chopped fresh chives

Place black-eye beans in a saucepan, cover
with water and bring to the boil. Cover and
simmer for 45 minutes until just softened.
Drain and rinse in cold water. Bring a large
saucepan of water to the boil. Turn off heat
and add noodles. Loosen with chopsticks or
2 forks and leave to soak for 3 minutes. Drain
well and rinse in cold water.

Heat oil in a non-stick or well seasoned wok
and stir-fry garlic, shallots, black beans and
mushrooms for 2-3 minutes. Add black-eye
beans and stir-fry for 1 minute. Add the soy
sauce, seasoning and noodles, mix well and
cook gently for 2-3 minutes to warm
through. Stir in chives, transfer to serving
plates and serve with salad.

Serves 4.

RICE

CHICKEN BIRYANI

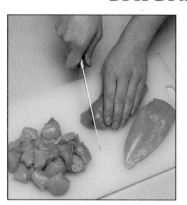

8 tablespoons vegetable oil
1 stick cinnamon
8 cloves
6 cardamom pods, bruised
2.5 cm (1 in) piece fresh root ginger, finely chopped
700 g (1½ lb) skinned and boned chicken, cubed
2 cloves garlic, crushed
1 teaspoon chilli powder
300 ml (10 fl oz/1¼ cups) natural yogurt
150 ml (5 fl oz/⅔ cup) chicken stock
pinch of saffron strands
4 tablespoons boiling water
350 g (12 oz/2¼ cups) basmati rice
4 tablespoons sultanas
4 tablespoons flaked almonds
1 onion, sliced

Preheat oven to 190C (375F/Gas 5). In a flameproof casserole, heat 4 tablespoons oil and add the spices and fry for 15 seconds. Add the chicken, garlic and chilli and fry for 4 minutes. Add the yogurt, 1 tablespoon at a time, stirring between each addition until yogurt is absorbed by the spices. Add the stock and simmer for 20-25 minutes. Transfer to a bowl. Soak the saffron in the boiling water and put to one side. Wash the rice under cold running water until the water runs clear, then cook in boiling, salted water for 3 minutes and drain.

Put 2 tablespoons oil in the casserole, spoon in a layer of rice, sprinkle with a little of the saffron water and cover with a layer of chicken. Repeat, ending with a layer of rice. Add any cooking juices left from the chicken, cover tightly and cook in the oven for 25-30 minutes. In a pan, heat the remaining oil and fry the sultanas and almonds until golden; remove. Fry the onions until crisp and golden. Sprinkle the biryani with the almonds, onions and sultanas.

Serves 4.

RICE WITH ASPARAGUS & NUTS

55 g (2 oz/¼ cup) butter
1 small onion, finely chopped
1 clove garlic, crushed
225 g (8 oz/1¼ cups) long-grain rice, washed well in cold water
450 ml (16 fl oz/2 cups) vegetable stock
225 g (8 oz) asparagus spears, trimmed
45 g (1½ oz/9 teaspoons) pine nuts
2 tablespoons chopped fresh sage
salt and pepper

Heat 15 g (½ oz/3 teaspoons) of the butter in a saucepan and fry the onion and garlic for 5 minutes. Add rice and stir-fry for 1 minute until transparent and glossy and pour in the stock. Bring to the boil, stir once, cover and cook gently for 12 minutes.

Steam the asparagus for 3 minutes, refresh under cold water, drain and dry well and coarsely chop. Heat the remaining butter in a large pan and stir-fry the pine nuts over a medium heat for 3-4 minutes until golden. Add the sage and asparagus and stir in the cooked rice. Season and heat through, stirring, for 2 minutes and serve at once.

Serves 6.

JAMBALAYA

1 tablespoon olive oil
15 g (½ oz/3 teaspoons) butter
350 g (12 oz) skinned and boned chicken meat
175 g (6 oz) chorizo sausage
1 onion, thinly sliced
2 cloves garlic, sliced
1 red pepper (capsicum), sliced
1 yellow pepper (capsicum), sliced
1 green pepper (capsicum), sliced
115 g (4 oz) mushrooms, sliced
150 g (5 oz/1 cup) long-grain rice
½ teaspoon ground allspice
300 ml (10 fl oz/1¼ cups) chicken stock
150 ml (5 fl oz/⅔ cup) white wine
115 g (4 oz) large cooked peeled prawns
lime wedges and whole prawns, to garnish

In a large frying pan or paella pan, heat the oil and butter. Cut the chicken into thick strips and fry until well browned, then remove from the pan and set aside. Cut the chorizo into chunks and fry for 1 minute, stirring well, then using a slotted spoon, remove from the pan and add to the chicken. Fry the onion and garlic until slightly softened, add the peppers (capsicums), mushrooms, rice and allspice and cook for a further 1 minute.

Pour in the stock and wine and bring to the boil, return the chicken and chorizo to the pan and simmer, uncovered, for 15-20 minutes until the liquid is absorbed and the rice tender. Stir in the prawns, cook for a further 5 minutes, then season to taste. Serve garnished with wedges of lime and whole prawns.

Serves 4.

KEDGEREE

575 g (1¼ lb) smoked haddock (finnan haddie) or salmon
115 g (4 oz/generous ½ cup) long grain rice
2 tablespoons lemon juice
150 ml (5 fl oz/⅔ cup) single (light) or sour cream
pinch of freshly grated nutmeg
cayenne pepper
2 hard-boiled eggs, peeled and chopped
55 g (2 oz/4 tablespoons) butter, diced
2 tablespoons chopped fresh parsley
parsley sprigs and sliced hard-boiled eggs, to garnish

Poach fish just covered by water for about 10 minutes. Lift fish from cooking liquid, discard bones and skin and flake flesh. Measure fish cooking liquid to twice volume of rice; top up with water if necessary. Bring to the boil, add rice, stir, then cover and simmer for about 15 minutes until rice is tender and liquid absorbed. Meanwhile, preheat oven to 180C (350F/Gas 4) and butter a baking dish.

Remove rice from heat and stir in lemon juice, cream, fish, nutmeg and a pinch of cayenne. Gently fold in eggs. Turn into dish, dot with butter and bake for about 25 minutes. Stir chopped parsley into kedgeree and garnish with parsley sprigs and sliced hard-boiled egg. Sprinkle a little cayenne pepper over the top, if wished.

Serves 4.

SHRIMP PASTE RICE

300 g (10 oz) long-grain rice
2 tablespoons shrimp paste
2.5 cm (1 in) piece fresh root ginger, peeled and
   grated
1 tablespoon peanut oil
1 teaspoon sesame oil
2 spring onions, very finely chopped

Cook rice in plenty of boiling water for about 15 minutes until tender but just firm to the bite. Drain then rinse with boiling water.

Meanwhile, in a bowl, mix together shrimp paste, ginger, peanut oil and sesame oil. Transfer rice to a warmed serving bowl and stir in paste mixture. Sprinkle with finely chopped spring onions.

Serves 4.

GREEN FRIED RICE

150 g (5 oz) long-grain rice
3 eggs, beaten
4 tablespoons vegetable oil
225 g (8 oz) spring greens, ribs removed and finely
   sliced
1 clove garlic, finely chopped
4 spring onions, finely chopped
115 g (4 oz) ham, shredded

Cook rice in plenty of boiling water for 15 minutes until tender but still firm to the bite. Drain and rinse with boiling water. Use eggs to make an omelette; cut it into thin strips.

In a wok, heat 1 tablespoon vegetable oil, add greens and fry for 1 minute; remove and keep warm. Add remaining oil to the wok, add garlic and spring onions and stir-fry for 1 minute, then stir in the rice. When mixed thoroughly, stir in ham, greens, omelette slices and salt.

Serves 4.

CRAB FRIED RICE

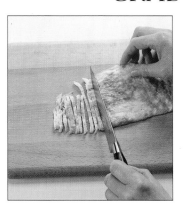

150 g (5 oz) long-grain rice
3 eggs, beaten
85 g (3 oz) can crabmeat
2 tablespoons vegetable oil
175 g (6 oz) beansprouts
1 tablespoon light soy sauce
6 spring onions, finely chopped
1 teaspoon sesame oil

Cook rice in plenty of boiling water for 15 minutes until tender but still firm to the bite. Drain and rinse with boiling water.

In a bowl mix together eggs and crabmeat with its liquid. Use to make an omelette then cut it into strips.

In a wok, heat vegetable oil, add beansprouts and fry for 1 minute. Remove from wok and keep warm. Add rice to wok and stir-fry for 3 minutes. Stir in soy sauce and cook for a further 2 minutes. Stir in beansprouts, omelette strips and spring onions, and cook for 2-3 minutes. Serve sprinkled with sesame oil.

Serves 4.

VEGETABLE FRIED RICE

150 g (5 oz) long-grain rice
4 tablespoons vegetable oil
2 cloves garlic, finely chopped
1 cm (½ in) piece fresh root ginger, peeled and grated
1 tablespoon Chinese winter pickle
6 tomatoes, seeded and chopped
1 large red pepper (capsicum), seeded and diced
6 dried black winter mushrooms, soaked in hot water from 25 minutes, drained, squeezed and diced
55 g (2 oz) cooked peas, or frozen peas, thawed
115 g (4 oz) cucumber, diced
2 tablespoons light soy sauce

Cook rice in plenty of boiling water for 15 minutes until tender but still firm to the bite. Drain and rinse with boiling water.

In a wok, heat oil, add garlic and ginger, fry for 30 seconds then add pickle, tomatoes, pepper (capsicum) and mushrooms, peas and cucumber. Stir-fry for 4 minutes then stir in soy sauce. Add rice, mix well and heat through for 2-3 minutes.

Serves 4.

EGG FRIED RICE

150 g (5 oz) long-grain rice
3 eggs, beaten
2 tablespoons vegetable oil
1 clove garlic, finely chopped
3 spring onions, finely chopped
115 g (4 oz) cooked peas, or frozen, thawed
1 tablespoon light soy sauce
1 teaspoon sea salt

Cook rice in plenty of boiling water for 15 minutes until tender but still firm to the bite. Drain and rinse with boiling water.

In a small saucepan, cook eggs over a moderately low heat, stirring until lightly scrambled. Remove and keep warm.

In a wok, heat oil, add garlic, spring onions and peas and stir-fry for 1 minute. Stir in rice to mix thoroughly, then add soy sauce, eggs and salt. Stir to break up egg and mix thoroughly.

Serves 4.

YANGCHOW FRIED RICE

150 g (5 oz) long-grain rice
3 tablespoons peanut oil
2 medium onions, finely sliced
3 slices fresh root ginger, peeled and finely chopped
115 g (4 oz) pork tenderloin, minced
1 tablespoon light soy sauce
1 teaspoon brown sugar
½ teaspoon sea salt
2 eggs, beaten
3 dried black winter mushrooms, soaked in hot
  water for 25 minutes, drained and squeezed
2 large tomatoes, peeled, seeded and chopped
55 g (2 oz) cooked peas, or frozen peas, thawed

Cook rice in plenty of boiling water for 15 minutes until tender but still firm to the bite. Drain and rinse with boiling water.

In a wok, heat oil, add onion and ginger and stir-fry for 2 minutes. Stir in pork, continue stirring for 3 minutes until crisp then add soy sauce and sugar. Stir-fry for 1 minute, then stir in rice. Remove to a warmed dish and keep warm. Pour eggs into wok, season with salt and pepper, then cook stirring for 2-3 minutes until just beginning to set. Stir in mushrooms, tomatoes and peas. Cook for 2-3 minutes, then stir in rice mixture.

Serves 4.

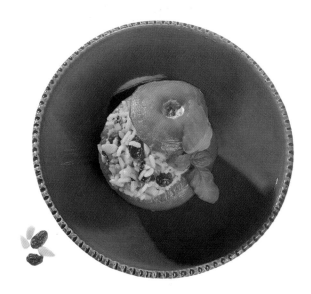

MEXICAN RICE

350 g (12 oz) long-grain rice
2 tablespoons sunflower oil
1 large onion, chopped
2 cloves garlic, finely chopped
4-6 fresh hot red or green chillies
300 g (10 oz) tomatoes, blanched, peeled, seeded and
   chopped
1 litre (35 fl oz/4 cups) chicken stock
salt and pepper
55 g (2 oz) cooked peas, or frozen peas, thawed
fresh coriander sprigs, to garnish

Put the rice into a bowl, cover with boiling water and leave for 30 minutes. Drain. Leave in a sieve for about 1 hour until dry. Heat the oil in a heavy frying pan. Over a low heat, stir in the rice until all the grains are well coated with oil. Add onion, garlic and chillies. Cook for about 4 minutes until the onion is transparent and the rice is golden. Add the tomatoes and stock, season with salt and pepper, cover and simmer for 20-30 minutes or until the liquid has been absorbed and the rice is tender and fluffy; add peas 5 minutes before end of cooking.

If softer rice is preferred, stir in a little more stock after 20 minutes and continue cooking until additional liquid has been absorbed. Transfer to a warmed serving dish and garnish with coriander.

Serves 6-8.

RICE-FILLED TOMATOES

4 ripe beefsteak tomatoes
salt and freshly ground black pepper
150 g (5 oz) cooked rice
1 tablespoon pine nuts
1 tablespoon raisins, soaked in hot water
1 celery stick, finely chopped
2 tablespoons chopped fresh basil
2 teaspoons balsamic vinegar
2 tablespoons olive oil

Preheat oven to 170C (325F/Gas 3). Slice a lid off tomatoes; reserve. Scoop out flesh and sprinkle insides of tomatoes with salt. Invert and drain on kitchen paper for 15 minutes.

Sieve tomato pulp and mix into the cooked rice with pine nuts, raisins, celery and half the basil. Season well and use this to fill the tomatoes. Replace lids and place tomatoes in an oiled shallow ovenproof dish. Bake in oven for 45 minutes.

Whisk the vinegar with the oil. Remove the tomatoes from the oven, take off the lids and drizzle each one with the oil and vinegar. Replace the lids and leave to cool. Serve at room temperature, garnished with the rest of the basil.

Serves 4.

SWEET SAFFRON RICE

225 g (8 oz/1½ cups) basmati rice
1 teaspoon saffron threads
3 tablespoons boiling water
3 tablespoons vegetable oil
6 cloves
6 green cardamom pods, bruised
7.5 cm (3 in) cinnamon stick
85 g (3 oz/½ cup) raisins
3 tablespoons sugar
salt
parsley sprigs, to garnish

Place rice in a sieve and wash under cold running water until water runs clear.

Put rice in a bowl with 550 ml (20 fl oz/ 2½ cups) water and soak for 30 minutes. Put saffron in a small bowl, add boiling water and leave to soak for 5 minutes. Heat oil in a heavy-based saucepan, add cloves, cardamom pods and cinnamon and fry for 1 minute. Drain rice and reserve the soaking water. Add rice to the pan and fry for 2-3 minutes, until opaque and light golden.

Stir in reserved water, saffron and its soaking water, raisins and sugar and season with salt. Bring to the boil, then lower the heat and simmer, covered, for 12-15 minutes, stirring once or twice, until liquid is absorbed and rice is very tender. Serve hot, garnished with parsley.

Serves 4.

Note: The whole spices in the rice are not meant to be eaten.

LEEK & MUSHROOM PILAF

15 g (½ oz/¼ cup) dried ceps (mushrooms)
pinch saffron strands
150 ml (5 fl oz/⅔ cup) boiling water
225 g (8 oz/1¼ cups) basmati rice
450 ml (16 fl oz/2 cups) vegetable stock
2 tablespoons olive oil
3 large leeks, trimmed
115 g (4 oz) fresh mushrooms, wiped
salt and pepper
whole or chopped chives, to garnish

Place the ceps and saffron in a small bowl and pour over the boiling water. Leave to soak for 10 minutes.

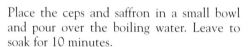

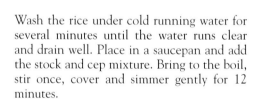

Wash the rice under cold running water for several minutes until the water runs clear and drain well. Place in a saucepan and add the stock and cep mixture. Bring to the boil, stir once, cover and simmer gently for 12 minutes.

Meanwhile, heat the oil and fry the leeks for 3 minutes, then add the fresh mushrooms and stir-fry for a further 3 minutes; keep warm. As soon as the rice is cooked, stir it into the pan and heat through for 1-2 minutes. Season, garnish with chives and serve at once.

Serves 6.

MUSHROOM & RICE PATTIES

185 g (6 oz/1¼ cups) long-grain rice
1 tablespoon sunflower oil
55 g (2 oz) onion, very finely chopped
185 g (6 oz) mushrooms, finely chopped
55 g (2 oz/½ cup) grated Cheddar cheese
salt and pepper
flour
vegetables, to serve

Cook the rice in a pan of boiling, salted water until very tender. Drain well, then put into a bowl and mash to break up the grains. Preheat oven to 200C (400F/Gas 6).

Heat the oil in a medium saucepan, add the onion and mushrooms and cook until all the liquid has evaporated from the mushrooms. Stir into the rice with the cheese and season with salt and pepper.

With floured hands, form the mixture into 8 patty shapes and place them on a well greased baking sheet. Bake for 15-20 minutes until golden. Serve with lightly cooked vegetables.

Serves 4.

Variation: Serve with salad and a relish, if preferred.

FRANKFURTER RISOTTO

2 tablespoons sunflower oil
1 large onion, chopped
225 g (8 oz/1½ cups) long-grain rice
1 red or green pepper (capsicum), seeded and chopped
450 ml (16 fl oz/2 cups) hot chicken stock
200 g (7 oz) can tomatoes
8 frankfurters
115 g (4 oz) frozen peas
salt and pepper
tomato slices or wedges, to garnish

Heat the oil in a large saucepan, add the onion and cook until the onion softens. Add the rice and pepper (capsicum) and cook for 1 minute, stirring all the time.

Pour in the stock. Sieve the tomatoes and add the purée to the pan. Bring to the boil, then lower the heat, cover and simmer for 15-20 minutes, or until the rice is tender and all the liquid has been absorbed.

Cut the frankfurters into 1 cm (½ in) long pieces and add to the risotto with the peas; season with salt and pepper. Stir the mixture together over a low heat for about 3 minutes. Garnish with tomato and serve hot.

Serves 4.

BLACK-EYED BEANS & RICE

WOK-STYLE PAELLA

225 g (8 oz) dried black-eyed beans
3 teaspoons lemon juice
6 teaspoons olive oil
1 large onion, finely chopped
1 clove garlic, crushed
85 g (3 oz/½ cup) long-grain rice, rinsed and drained
salt and pepper
2 teaspoons white wine vinegar
chopped fresh herbs and green olives, to garnish

Wash and drain beans, place in a saucepan; cover with cold water. Bring to the boil and boil for 2 minutes.

Drain, discarding water. Return beans to pan; cover with fresh water to come well above surface of beans. Add lemon juice. Bring to boil; cover and boil for 20-30 minutes until beans are tender.

In another saucepan, heat oil, add onion and garlic and cook until soft. Add rice, stir to coat with oil, then add 175 ml (6 fl oz/¾ cup) water and season with salt. Bring to the boil; cover pan and simmer for 10-15 minutes until rice is tender and water absorbed. Drain beans and mix with rice. Add vinegar, salt and pepper. Heat together for 2 minutes. Serve garnished with chopped herbs and olives.

Serves 4-6.

2 tablespoons olive oil
450 g (1 lb) Spanish chorizo sausage or hot, Italian-style sausage, cut into 2.5 cm (1 in) slices
450 g (1 lb) skinned and boned chicken breasts, cut into 2.5 cm (1 in) strips
1 onion, chopped
2-3 cloves garlic, finely chopped
1 green or red pepper (capsicum), diced
400 g (14 oz) can Italian-style tomatoes
450 g (1 lb/2⅔ cups) long-grain rice
½ teaspoon crushed dried chillies
½ teaspoon dried thyme
1 teaspoon crushed saffron threads
225 g (8 oz) green beans, cut into 2.5 cm (1 in) pieces
225 g (8 oz) cooked peeled prawns (optional)
parsley sprigs and lime or lemon wedges, to garnish

Heat wok until hot. Add oil and swirl to coat wok. Add chorizo or Italian sausage and stir-fry for 4-5 minutes until golden. Remove to a plate. Add chicken pieces to oil in wok and stir-fry for 3-4 minutes until golden. Remove to the plate.

Add onion, garlic and pepper to wok. Stir-fry for 3-4 minutes. Add tomatoes, rice, 450 ml (16 fl oz/2 cups) water, chillies, thyme and saffron. Boil, add the sausage and reduce heat to low. Cover wok and cook gently for 20-30 minutes until rice is tender. Add chicken and green beans. Cook, covered, for 5-7 minutes more. Add prawns and fluff with a fork. Cook, uncovered, for 2-3 minutes. Garnish and serve.

Serves 6-8.

RICE & BLACK BEANS

2 tablespoons olive oil
1 Spanish onion, chopped
2 cloves garlic, chopped
115 g (4 oz) bacon, chopped
1 small red pepper (capsicum), chopped
1 teaspoon paprika
300 g (10 oz) beefsteak tomatoes, peeled, seeded and chopped
salt and freshly ground black pepper
225 g (8 oz) risotto rice
herb sprigs, to garnish
BEANS:
225 g (8 oz) black beans, soaked overnight and drained
½ Spanish onion
2 cloves garlic, crushed

To prepare the beans, put them in a saucepan with onion and garlic. Cover with plenty of water, bring to the boil, then simmer for 1½-2 hours until just tender. Meanwhile, in a saucepan, heat oil, add chopped onion, garlic, bacon and red pepper (capsicum) and cook, stirring occasionally, until bacon begins to brown. Stir in paprika for 30-60 seconds, then stir in tomatoes and cook for about 5 minutes, stirring occasionally. Season well.

Stir rice and 450 ml (16 fl oz/2 cups) water into pan with tomato mixture. Bring to the boil, stir, then simmer gently for about 25 minutes until liquid is absorbed and rice tender. Drain beans. Discard onion and garlic. Stir the beans into the rice mixture. Adjust seasoning and serve garnished with sprigs of herbs.

Serves 4-6.

SPICED RICE & PEPPERS

4 tablespoons olive oil
225 g (8 oz) long-grain rice
2 cloves garlic
salt
1 teaspoon each cumin and coriander seeds
3 tablespoons tomato purée (paste)
2 teaspoons paprika
1 teaspoon chilli powder
pinch saffron threads, crushed and dissolved in 2 tablespoons boiling water
550 ml (20 fl oz/2½ cups) boiling chicken or vegetable stock or water
3-4 red peppers (capsicums), peeled, halved lengthways and seeded
extra virgin olive oil, to serve (optional)
chopped fresh herbs, to garnish

Heat oil in a paella pan or wide, heavy-based shallow saucepan. Stir in rice, then stir-fry for 2-3 minutes. Meanwhile, using a pestle and mortar, grind together garlic, salt, cumin and coriander seeds, then stir in tomato purée (paste), paprika, chilli and saffron liquid. Stir into rice. Stir in stock or water. Bring to boil, then cover and simmer for about 7 minutes.

Arrange peppers (capsicums) around sides of pan. Simmer for 7-10 minutes until rice is tender and plump, and liquid absorbed. Remove from heat and leave for 5 minutes. Trickle extra virgin oil over peppers (capsicums), if desired, and garnish with chopped herbs.

Serves 4.

RICE WITH CHICK PEAS

350 g (12 oz) chick peas, soaked overnight and
    drained
olive oil, for frying
3 cloves garlic, finely chopped
225 g (8 oz) risotto rice
550 ml (20 fl oz/2½ cups) chicken stock, or water
1 quantity Tomato Sauce (see page 307)
chopped fresh herbs, to garnish

Simmer chick peas in plenty of water for 1½-
2 hours until just tender.

Meanwhile, prepare the rice. Heat 2 tablespoons oil in a saucepan, add garlic and fry
for 2 minutes. Stir in rice, stir-fry for 3-4
minutes, then stir in 300 ml (10 fl oz/1¼
cups) stock or water. Simmer for 10 minutes,
then add another 300 ml (10 fl oz/1¼ cups)
stock or water. Continue cooking for 10-12
minutes until liquid is absorbed and rice
tender. Cover and keep warm.

Drain chick peas. Heat about 1 cm (½ in)
layer of oil in a frying pan, add chick peas
and fry, stirring frequently, until golden
brown. Stir into rice, then transfer to a
warmed serving dish. Pour Tomato Sauce
over chick peas and rice. Garnish with herbs
and serve.

Serves 4.

ASIAN-STYLE FRIED RICE

250 g (9 oz/1½ cups) long-grain rice
2 tablespoons vegetable oil
2 cloves garlic, finely chopped
1 fresh red chilli, seeded and chopped
1 cm (½ in) piece fresh root ginger, peeled and
  minced
2 tablespoons light soy sauce
1 teaspoon sugar
2 teaspoons nam pla (fish sauce)
½ teaspoon turmeric
4-6 spring onions, thinly sliced
450 g (1 lb) cooked peeled small prawns
225 g (8 oz) can unsweetened pineapple chunks,
  juice reserved
3-4 tablespoons chopped fresh coriander

In a large saucepan of boiling water, cook the
rice for 15-17 minutes until just tender.
Drain in a colander and rinse under cold
running water until cold. Set aside. Heat the
wok until hot. Add vegetable oil and swirl to
coat wok. Add garlic, chilli and ginger and
stir-fry for 1 minute. Add soy sauce, sugar,
nam pla (fish sauce), turmeric and spring
onions, stirring to dissolve sugar.

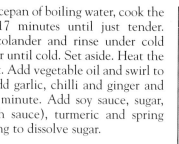

Stir in reserved rice, prawns and pineapple
chunks, tossing to mix. Stir-fry for 3-4
minutes until rice is heated through, adding
a little reserved pineapple juice if rice begins
to stick. Stir in coriander, turn into serving
bowl and serve at once.

Serves 4-6.

RICE, PRAWNS & TOFU

175 g (6 oz/³⁄₄ cup) long-grain white rice
3 tablespoons vegetable oil
3 cloves garlic, chopped
1 small onion, chopped
115 g (4 oz) cake tofu, drained and cut into about 1
  cm (½ in) cubes
2 small fresh red chillies, seeded and finely chopped
1 tablespoon fish sauce
175 g (6 oz) peeled prawns
1 shallot, thinly sliced
chilli flower, prawns in their shells and coriander
  leaves, to garnish

CHICKEN & MUSHROOM RICE

175 g (6 oz/³⁄₄ cup) long-grain white rice
2 tablespoons vegetable oil
1 small onion, finely chopped
2 cloves garlic, finely chopped
2 fresh red chillies, seeded and cut into slivers
225 g (8 oz) chicken breast meat, finely chopped
85 g (3 oz) bamboo shoots, chopped or cut into
  matchstick strips
8 pieces dried Chinese black mushrooms, soaked for
  30 minutes, drained and chopped
2 tablespoons dried shrimps
1 tablespoon fish sauce
about 25 Thai holy basil leaves
Thai holy basil sprig, to garnish

Cook rice. In a wok, heat oil, add garlic and onion and cook, stirring occasionally, for 3-4 minutes until lightly browned. Add tofu and fry for about 3 minutes until browned. Add chillies and stir-fry briefly. Stir in fish sauce and rice for 2-3 minutes, then stir in prawns.

Cook rice. In a wok, heat oil, add onion and garlic and cook, stirring occasionally, until golden. Add chillies and chicken and stir-fry for 2 minutes.

Add shallot, stir quickly to mix, then transfer to a warmed serving plate. Garnish with chilli flower and prawns in their shells and scatter coriander leaves over rice mixture.

Serves 4.

Stir in bamboo shoots, mushrooms, dried shrimps and fish sauce. Continue to stir for 2 minutes, then stir in rice and basil. Serve garnished with basil sprig.

Serves 4.

STEAMED CHICKEN & RICE

1 teaspoon sugar
1 teaspoon sesame oil
1 tablespoon fish sauce
2 teaspoons chopped garlic
300 g (10 oz) chicken thigh meat, boned and
   skinned, cut into bite-size pieces
3 tablespoons vegetable oil
4 shallots, finely chopped
450 g (1 lb/2½ cups) long grain rice
550 ml (20 fl oz/2 cups) chicken stock
8 dried Chinese mushrooms, soaked and cut into
   small pieces
115 g (4 oz) canned straw mushrooms, drained
1 tablespoon each soy sauce and oyster sauce
2 spring onions, chopped
coriander sprigs, to garnish

In a bowl, mix sugar, sesame oil, fish sauce
and half the garlic and season with salt and
freshly ground black pepper. Add chicken
and leave to marinate for 25-30 minutes.
Heat about 2 tablespoons vegetable oil in a
clay pot or flameproof casserole and stir-fry
the remaining garlic and half of the chopped
shallots for about 1 minute. Add the rice and
stir-fry for about 5 minutes, then add the
stock. Stir and bring to the boil, then reduce
the heat to very low, cover and cook gently
for 8-10 minutes.

Heat remaining oil in a wok or saucepan and
stir-fry remaining shallots until opaque. Add
chicken pieces and stir-fry for 2-3 minutes.
Add mushrooms and soy sauce and continue
stirring for about 5 minutes. Uncover the
rice and fluff up with a fork. Spoon chicken
and mushroom mixture on top of the rice,
add oyster sauce and spring onions, cover
and cook for a further 5 minutes. Garnish
with coriander sprigs and serve at once.

Serves 4-6.

SEAFOOD FRIED RICE

225 g (8 oz/1 cup) long grain rice
3 tablespoons vegetable oil
1 clove garlic, chopped
2 shallots, chopped
115 g (4 oz) small cooked peeled prawns
115 g (4 oz) crab meat, flaked
salt and freshly ground black pepper
2-3 eggs, beaten
2 tablespoons fish or soy sauce
chopped spring onions, to garnish

The day before, cook the rice, then refrigerate it, so that it is cold and dry when
required.

Heat about 1 tablespoon oil in a wok or
frying-pan and stir-fry the garlic and shallots
for about 30 seconds, then add the prawns
and crab meat with salt and pepper. Stir-fry
for 2-3 minutes, remove from pan and set
aside.

Heat remaining oil in the pan and lightly
scramble beaten eggs. When just beginning
to set hard, add the rice and stir-fry mixture
for 2-3 minutes. Add prawns and crab meat
with the fish or soy sauce and blend well.
Garnish with chopped spring onions and
serve at once.

Serves 4.

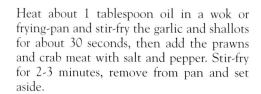

GREEN RICE

300 g (10 oz/1¼ cups) long grain white rice, rinsed
800 ml (28 fl oz/3½ cups) Chinese Vegetable Stock
  (see glossary)
225 g (8 oz) small broccoli flowerets
225 g (8 oz) fresh spinach, tough stalks removed
1 tablespoon groundnut (peanut) oil
2 cloves garlic, finely chopped
1 fresh green chilli, seeded and chopped
1 bunch spring onions, finely chopped
225 g (8 oz) frozen peas
2 tablespoons light soy sauce
salt and freshly ground black pepper
4 tablespoons chopped fresh chives
fresh chives, to garnish

SPICY FRIED RICE

175 g (6 oz/¾ cup) long-grain white rice
2 tablespoons vegetable oil
1 large onion, finely chopped
3 cloves garlic, chopped
2 fresh green chillies, seeded and finely chopped
2 tablespoons ready-made Thai Red Curry Paste
55 g (2 oz) lean pork, very finely chopped
3 eggs, beaten
1 tablespoon fish sauce
55 g (2 oz) cooked peeled prawns
finely sliced red chilli, shredded coriander leaves and
  spring onion brushes, to garnish

Place rice and stock in a large saucepan, bring to the boil, reduce heat and simmer gently for 25 minutes until the rice is cooked and the liquid has been absorbed. Blanch the broccoli in a saucepan of boiling water for 2 minutes. Drain and set aside. Blanch the spinach in a saucepan of boiling water for a few seconds until just wilted. Drain well, shred and set aside.

Cook rice. In a wok, heat oil, add onion, garlic and chillies and cook, stirring occasionally, until onion has softened. Stir in curry paste and continue to stir for 3-4 minutes. Add pork and stir-fry for 2-3 minutes. Stir in rice to coat with ingredients, then push to sides of wok.

Heat oil in a non-stick or well seasoned wok and stir-fry garlic, chilli, spring onions and broccoli for 1 minute. Add cooked rice, spinach, frozen peas and soy sauce. Season well and cook gently for 5 minutes. Stir in chopped chives. Garnish with chives and serve with a mixed salad.

Serves 4.

Pour eggs into centre of wok. When just beginning to set, mix evenly into the rice, adding fish sauce at the same time. Stir in prawns, then transfer to a shallow, warmed serving dish. Garnish with chilli, coriander and spring onion brushes.

Serves 4.

LEMON VEGETABLE RICE

juice 2 lemons
2 tablespoons caster sugar
vegetable stock (see method)
300 g (10 oz/1½ cups) long-grain rice
½ teaspoon salt
1 cinnamon stick
5 whole cloves
25 g (1 oz/6 teaspoons) butter
1 teaspoon cumin seeds
1 small onion, thinly sliced
2 small courgettes (zucchini)
55 g (2 oz/⅓ cup) cashew nuts, toasted
2 tablespoons chopped fresh mint

Mix the lemon juice and sugar together in a measuring jug. Make up to 550 ml (20 fl oz/2½ cups) with vegetable stock. Pour into a saucepan, add the rice, salt, cinnamon and cloves, bring to the boil, stir once and cook gently for 10 minutes until all the liquid is absorbed. Remove from the heat, cover with a tight-fitting lid and leave to sit undisturbed for a further 10 minutes.

In a small frying pan, melt the butter and stir-fry the cumin seeds for 1-3 minutes until they start to pop. Add the onion and fry for 5 minutes. Cut the courgettes (zucchini) into thin slices and add to the pan with the cashew nuts and mint. Stir-fry for 2-3 minutes until courgettes (zucchini) are tender, then stir in the rice. Heat through for 1 minute and serve.

Serves 4-6.

ASPARAGUS RISOTTO

1.2 litres (2 pints/5 cups) vegetable stock
450 g (1 lb) thin asparagus
85 g (3 oz/⅓ cup) butter
1 onion, finely chopped
350 g (12 oz/1½ cups) risotto rice
pinch saffron strands
juice 1 lemon
salt and freshly ground black pepper
flat-leaf parsley and strips lemon rind, to garnish

In a large saucepan, heat stock until boiling. Keep at simmering point over a low heat. Cut tips off asparagus and set aside.

Snap woody ends off asparagus stalks and peel off any tough skin. Cut stalks into 5 cm (2 in) lengths. In a large heavy saucepan, heat 25 g (1 oz/2 tablespoons) of the butter. Add the onion and cook, stirring occasionally, for 5 minutes, until soft. Add rice and asparagus stalks and cook, stirring, for 2-3 minutes. Add a ladleful of hot stock and cook gently, stirring frequently, until stock is absorbed. Continue to stir in stock in this way, one ladleful at a time.

When rice begins to look creamy, add saffron, lemon juice and salt and pepper. Continue adding stock and stirring until risotto is thick and creamy and rice is tender but not sticky. Meanwhile, put asparagus tips in a steamer and steam for 5 minutes, or until tender. Just before serving, add asparagus tips and remaining butter to risotto and stir gently to combine. Garnish with parsley and lemon rind and serve.

Serves 6.

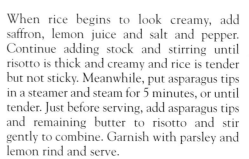

VEGETABLE BIRYANI

2 tablespoons sunflower oil
450 g (1 lb) onions, sliced
300 g (10 oz) carrots, diced
115 g (4 oz) potatoes, diced
2.5 cm (1 in) piece fresh root ginger, peeled and grated
2 cloves garlic, crushed
1 tablespoon hot curry paste
1 teaspoon turmeric
½ teaspoon ground cinnamon
225 g (8 oz/1 cup) long grain rice
1 litre (35 fl oz/4½ cups) hot vegetable stock
115 g (4 oz) cauliflower flowerets
salt and freshly ground black pepper
115 g (4 oz) frozen peas
55 g (2 oz/½ cup) toasted cashew nuts
2 tablespoons chopped fresh coriander

Heat half the oil in a large flameproof casserole. Add half the onions and cook, stirring occasionally, for 10-15 minutes, until crisp and golden. Remove with a slotted spoon, drain on kitchen paper and set aside. Heat the remaining oil in the casserole and add the carrots, potatoes and remaining onions. Stir in the ginger, garlic, curry paste, turmeric and cinnamon and cook, stirring for 5 minutes.

Add the rice and stir for 1 minute. Pour in the stock and bring to the boil. Stir in the cauliflower and salt and pepper. Cover and simmer gently for 15 minutes. Stir in the peas, cashews and coriander. Cover and cook for 5 minutes until the rice is tender and the liquid has been absorbed. Scatter the reserved onions over the top and serve.

Serves 4.

SUN-DRIED TOMATO RISOTTO

55 g (2 oz/¼ cup) butter
1 tablespoon olive oil
2 red onions, chopped
12 sun-dried tomatoes, chopped
3 teaspoons pesto sauce
225 g (8 oz/1 cup) risotto rice
1 litre (35 fl oz/4½ cups) vegetable stock
225 g (8 oz) mushrooms, sliced
salt and freshly ground black pepper
55 g (2 oz) Parmesan cheese
chopped fresh flat-leaf parsley, to garnish

Heat the butter and oil in a flameproof casserole. Add the onions and cook, stirring occasionally, for 5 minutes, until soft.

Add the sun-dried tomatoes and pesto sauce and cook for 3-4 minutes. Add the rice and cook, stirring, for 1 minute. Stir in about one-third of the stock and simmer gently, stirring occasionally, until most of the liquid has been absorbed.

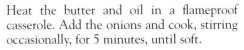

Stir in the mushrooms and season with salt and pepper. Add half of the remaining stock and simmer, stirring occasionally. When most of the liquid has been absorbed, stir in the remaining stock and simmer gently until all the liquid has been absorbed and the rice is tender and creamy. Using a vegetable peeler, shave curls of Parmesan cheese over the risotto, sprinkle with parsley and serve.

Serves 2-4.

SUMMER RISOTTO

450 ml (16 fl oz/2 cups) chicken stock
115 g (4 oz) sugar snap peas
115 g (4 oz) asparagus, cut into 5 cm (2 in) lengths
115 g (4 oz) green beans, cut into 5 cm (2 in) lengths
115 ml (4 fl oz/½ cup) dry white wine
1 tablespoon olive oil
4 spring onions, chopped
1 clove garlic, crushed
225 g (8 oz/1¼ cups) risotto rice
4 sun-dried tomatoes in oil, drained
25 g (1 oz/¼ cup) grated Pecorino cheese
55 g (2 oz) Parma ham, roughly chopped
salt and freshly ground black pepper
Pecorino shavings and basil sprigs, to garnish

Put the stock in a saucepan and bring to the boil. Add the sugar snap peas, asparagus and green beans and cook for 3 minutes. Remove with a slotted spoon and set aside. Add the wine to the stock and bring to a simmer. Heat the olive oil in a large saucepan. Add the spring onions and garlic and cook gently for 5 minutes until soft. Add the rice and cook, stirring, for 2 minutes. Add a ladleful of the simmering stock and cook, stirring, until absorbed. Continue adding the stock, a ladleful at a time, as it is absorbed, stirring frequently.

Roughly chop the sun-dried tomatoes. When the rice has been cooking for 15 minutes, add the sugar snap peas, asparagus, beans, tomatoes and any remaining stock. Cook, stirring, until the rice is tender and creamy. Stir in the grated Pecorino and Parma ham and season with salt and pepper. Garnish with Pecorino shavings and basil and serve.

Serves 4.

Note: Pecorino is a hard cheese from Italy. Replace it with Parmesan if it is unavailable.

SPINACH RISOTTO CAKE

pinch saffron strands
700 ml (25 fl oz/3¼ cups) hot vegetable stock
55 g (2 oz/¼ cup) butter
1 large onion, finely chopped
1 clove garlic, crushed
225 g (8 oz/1⅓ cups) risotto rice
225 g (8 oz) spinach, washed and trimmed
2 eggs, lightly beaten
55 g (2 oz/¼ cup) mascarpone cheese or thick sour cream
25 g (1 oz/¼ cup) grated vegetarian Cheddar cheese
1 tablespoon chopped fresh tarragon
pinch grated nutmeg
salt and pepper

Soak the saffron strands in the hot stock for 10 minutes. Melt the butter in a large frying pan and fry the onion and garlic for 10 minutes. Add rice and stir-fry for 2 minutes. Add a little stock, simmer until absorbed and continue adding stock gradually until completely absorbed and rice is tender – about 25 minutes. Preheat oven to 200C (400F/Gas 6) and lightly oil a 20 cm (8 in) spring-release tin.

Cook the spinach in a large pan with only the water that clings to the leaves until just wilted. Drain well and squeeze out excess liquid; chop finely. Beat all the remaining ingredients together until combined and stir into the cooked rice with the spinach. Transfer to the prepared tin, smooth the surface and bake for 30 minutes until risen.

Serves 8.

PIZZAS

PIZZA MARGHERITA

15 g (½ oz) fresh yeast, 15 ml (1 tbsp) dried active
  baking yeast, or 7 g (¼ oz) sachet easy-blend yeast
pinch sugar
350 g (12 oz) strong plain white bread flour, plus
  extra for dusting
3 tablespoons olive oil
½ teaspoon salt
8 tablespoons passata
115 g (4 oz) half-fat mozzarella cheese, thinly sliced
pinch of dried oregano
fresh basil leaves, shredded
salt and freshly ground black pepper

In a bowl, cream fresh yeast with sugar and
whisk in 250 ml (9 fl oz/1 cup) warm water.
Leave for 10 minutes until frothy. For dried
yeasts, follow the packet instructions. Sift
flour into a large bowl and make a well in
centre. Pour in yeast mixture, oil and salt.
Mix together with a round-bladed knife,
then hands until the dough comes together.
Tip out onto a floured surface and knead for
10 minutes until smooth and elastic. Place
dough in a clean oiled bowl, cover with a
damp tea towel and leave to rise for about 1
hour until doubled in size.

Preheat oven to 240C (475F/Gas 9). Knock
back dough and roll out, or stretch with your
fingers, to a 30 cm (12 in) circle on a large
floured baking sheet. Spread passata over the
dough, avoiding the edges. Scatter cheese,
herbs, salt and pepper over the surface.
Drizzle with oil. Bake for 10-15 minutes until
golden and crisp. Serve with salad.

Serves 4.

ONION & ANCHOVY PIZZA

15 g (½ oz) fresh yeast, 15 ml (1 tbsp) dried active
  baking yeast, or 7 g (¼ oz) sachet easy-blend yeast
pinch sugar
350 g (12 oz/3 cups) strong plain white bread flour
1 tablespoon olive oil
½ teaspoon salt
TOPPING:
1 tablespoon olive oil and sunflower oil, mixed
900 g (2 lb) red onions, thinly sliced
2 tablespoons freshly squeezed lemon juice
2 tablespoons chopped fresh oregano and rosemary
8 anchovy fillets in oil, drained, rinsed and sliced
  lengthways if wished, or 6 anchovies in salt, boned
  and rinsed
10 black olives, stoned
rosemary sprigs, to garnish

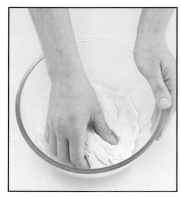

In a bowl, cream fresh yeast with sugar and
whisk in 250 ml (9 fl oz/1 cup) warm water.
Leave 10 minutes. Use dried yeast, according
to packet instructions. Sift flour into a bowl
and make well in centre. Pour in yeast, oil
and salt; mix until dough comes together.
On a floured surface, knead 10 minutes until
smooth. Place in a clean oiled bowl, cover
with damp tea towel and leave to rise until
doubled in size. To make topping, heat oil in
a pan and stir in onions and lemon juice.
Cover and cook over gentle heat until
onions are soft. Add chopped herbs.

Preheat oven to 240C (475F/Gas 9). Knock
back dough and stretch out to 30 cm (12 in)
circle on a floured baking sheet. Spread
onions evenly over the dough and scatter
with anchovy fillets and olives. Bake in oven
for 10-15 minutes until crisp and golden,
scattering the rosemary sprigs over the top
for the last 3 minutes. Serve with salad.

Serves 6.

AUBERGINE PIZZA

350 g (12 oz) aubergine (eggplant)
1 clove garlic, crushed
1 tablespoon lemon juice
1 tablespoon chopped fresh parsley
salt and freshly ground black pepper
1 quantity pizza dough (opposite)
350 g (12 oz) tomatoes, sliced
150 g (5 oz) chorizo sausage, sliced
115 g (4 oz) feta cheese, crumbled
1 tablespoon roughly chopped fresh oregano
1 tablespoon olive oil
oregano leaves, to garnish

Preheat the oven to 180C (350F/Gas 4).
Pierce the aubergine (eggplant) all over with
a skewer and put on a baking sheet.

Bake for 30 minutes until soft. Halve the
aubergine (eggplant) and scoop the soft flesh
into a bowl. Stir in the garlic, lemon juice,
parsley and salt and pepper and leave to cool.
Roll out the pizza dough to fit a Swiss roll tin
30 x 22.5 cm (12 x 9 in). Put the dough in
the tin and pinch up the edges to form a rim.
Spread the aubergine purée over the dough.

Arrange the tomato slices on top and season
with salt and pepper. Arrange the chorizo
over the tomatoes. Sprinkle with the feta
cheese and oregano. Leave for 15 minutes.
Preheat the oven to 200C (400F/Gas 6).
Drizzle the pizza with the olive oil and bake
for 20 minutes. Cut into squares, garnish
with oregano leaves and serve.

Makes 12 squares.

Note: The aubergine purée can be made in
advance. It also makes a delicious dip.

ROASTED PEPPER PIZZA

1 tablespoon sun-dried tomato paste
2 large red and 1 large yellow pepper (capsicum),
  peeled (see page 29) and cut into strips
3 cloves garlic, finely chopped
1 tablespoon roughly chopped fresh parsley
salt and freshly ground black pepper
1 tablespoon olive oil
PIZZA DOUGH:
175 g (6 oz/1½ cups) strong white bread flour
¼ teaspoon salt
1 teaspoon easy-blend dried yeast
1 tablespoon olive oil

To make the pizza dough, sift the flour and
salt into a warmed bowl. Stir in the yeast.

Make a well in the centre and stir in the
olive oil and about 115 ml (4 fl oz/½ cup)
tepid water to form a soft dough – you may
need to add more water. Turn on to a well
floured surface and knead for 5 minutes until
smooth and elastic. Put in an oiled bowl,
cover and leave in a warm place for 1 hour
until doubled in size. Turn on to a floured
surface and knead again for 2-3 minutes.

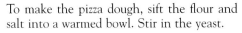
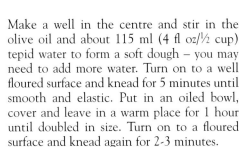

Roll out the dough to a circle approximately
25 cm (10 in) in diameter and put on a
lightly oiled baking sheet. Pinch up the
edges to form a rim. Spread the sun-dried
tomato paste over the dough. Arrange the
pepper (capsicum) strips on top. Sprinkle
with the chopped garlic and parsley and season with salt and pepper. Leave for 20
minutes. Preheat the oven to 200C/400F/
Gas 6. Drizzle the pizza with oil and bake for
15-20 minutes. Cut into wedges and serve.

Serves 2-4.

PEPPER PIZZETTES

PIZZA DOUGH:
450 g (1 lb/4 cups) strong plain flour
pinch salt
15 g (½ oz) packet dried yeast
1 teaspoon granulated sugar
200 ml (7 fl oz/scant cup) warm water
2 tablespoons extra virgin olive oil
fresh herb sprigs to garnish
TOPPING:
2 red or yellow peppers (capsicums)
3 tablespoons sun-dried tomato paste
4 tablespoons capers in wine vinegar, drained
2 tablespoons chopped fresh oregano
salt and freshly ground black pepper

Sieve flour and salt into a large mixing bowl. In a small bowl, mix yeast, sugar and warm water. Leave for 10-15 minutes, until frothy. Stir oil into yeast then gradually beat into flour using a wooden spoon to give a soft, but not wet, dough. Turn onto a floured surface; knead for 5 minutes until smooth and elastic. Put into an oiled mixing bowl, cover and leave in a warm place for 35-40 minutes until doubled in size.

Preheat grill. Cook whole peppers (capsicums) under the hot grill for about 10 minutes, turning occasionally, until evenly blistered and charred. Transfer to a plastic bag for a few minutes, then peel away and discard skins. De-seed peppers (capsicums) and cut into strips. Set aside.

Preheat oven to 230C (450F/Gas 8). Oil two baking sheets. Turn dough onto a lightly floured surface. Knead gently then cut into 16 equal pieces. Roll each piece into a small oval about 5 mm (¼ inch) thick.

Transfer to the baking sheets and prick dough with a fork. Divide sun-dried tomato paste, reserved peppers (capsicums), capers and oregano between dough ovals. Season with salt and freshly ground black pepper. Bake in the preheated oven for 8-10 minutes, until golden. Serve hot or warm garnished with herb sprigs.

Makes 16 pizzettes.

Variations:
Red onion and Gorgonzola Replace above topping with 115 g (4 oz) crumbled Gorgonzola cheese; ½ red onion, chopped and 2 tablespoons chopped fresh thyme.

Prawn and fennel Instead of the peppers (capsicums), capers and herbs use 1 small fennel bulb, brushed with olive oil, roasted at 180C (350F/Gas 4) for 35-40 minutes, then cooled and chopped, 115 g (4 oz) peeled prawns and 2 teaspoons fennel seeds.

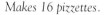

PIZZA SWIRLS

225 g (8 oz/2 cups) strong white flour
pinch salt
1 sachet easy blend dried yeast
200 ml (7 fl oz/1 cup) warm water
150 ml (5 fl oz/⅔ cup) passata (sieved tomatoes)
2 tablespoons tomato purée (paste)
1 clove garlic, crushed
1 teaspoon dried oregano
200 g (7 oz) can tuna, drained and mashed
1 red or green pepper (capsicum), seeded and chopped
1 small onion, finely chopped
85 g (3 oz/⅔ cup) grated Mozzarella cheese

Sift the flour and salt into a bowl, add the yeast and warm water. Mix to a soft dough.

Turn the dough onto a lightly floured work surface and knead for 10 minutes. Roll out to a rectangle about 40 x 20 cm (16 x 8 in). Mix the passata, tomato purée (paste), garlic and oregano together and spread over the dough. Mix the tuna with the pepper (capsicum) and onion and spoon over the dough; scatter the cheese over the top.

Roll up from a long side, then cut into 1 cm (½ in) slices. Place slices, cut side up, on greased baking sheets and leave in a warm place for 15 minutes. Meanwhile, preheat oven to 190C (375F/Gas 5). Bake the pizza swirls for 15 minutes until golden brown. Serve warm.

Makes about 25-30.

POTATO PIZZA

450 g (1 lb) potatoes, peeled
25 g (1 oz/6 teaspoons) butter
55 g (2 oz/½ cup) plain wholemeal flour
salt
TOPPING:
1 tablespoon olive oil
1 small onion, sliced
200 g (7 oz) can chopped tomatoes
1 tablespoon tomato purée (paste)
½ teaspoon dried basil
55 g (2 oz) button mushrooms, sliced
55 g (2 oz) sliced pizza pepperoni
½ green pepper (capsicum), seeded and cut into thin
  strips

Preheat oven to 200C (400F/Gas 6). Cut the potatoes into even pieces, put into a pan of water and boil until tender. Drain well, mash, then beat in the butter and flour; season with salt. Turn on to a greased baking sheet and spread out to an even round about 20 cm (8 in) in diameter. Bake in the oven for about 10 minutes until the edge of the pizza begins to crisp.

Meanwhile, heat the oil in a small saucepan, add the onion and cook over a medium heat until soft. Stir in the tomatoes, tomato purée (paste) and basil and simmer for 5 minutes until thickened. Spread over the potato base. Arrange the mushrooms over the sauce, then the pepperoni. Place the pepper (capsicum) strips in a criss-cross pattern over the pizza; then bake in the oven for 20 minutes. Serve hot, cut into wedges.

Serves 3-4.

DOLCELATTE PIZZAS

55 g (2 oz/½ cup) stoned black olives
1 clove garlic, chopped
1 teaspoon chopped fresh thyme
1 tablespoon olive oil
1 quantity pizza dough (see page 239)
45 g (1½ oz/9 teaspoons) butter
2 red onions, thinly sliced
½ teaspoon fennel seeds
1 teaspoon chopped fresh rosemary
85 g (3 oz/½ cup) dolcelatte cheese
grated zest 1 lemon

Purée olives, garlic, thyme and oil in a blender or food processor to a smooth paste.

Make up the pizza dough (see page 239), cover and leave to rise in a warm place for 30 minutes. Melt the butter and fry the onions over a low heat for 20-25 minutes until golden. Leave to cool. Preheat oven to 230C (450F/Gas 8) and place a baking sheet or pizza stone on the top shelf.

Divide the pizza dough in 4 and roll each piece out on a lightly floured surface to a 12.5 cm (5 in) round. Spread over the olive paste and onion mixture. Sprinkle over the fennel seeds and rosemary and crumble over the cheese. Sprinkle over the lemon zest and transfer the pizzas to the hot baking sheet. Cook for 10-12 minutes until bubbling and golden. Serve the pizzas hot with a tomato and green salad.

Serves 4.

GRILLED VEGETABLE PIZZA

225 g (8 oz/1⅔ cups) strong plain flour
½ teaspoon fast action dried yeast
½ teaspoon salt
100 ml (3½ fl oz/½ cup) warmed water
1 tablespoon olive oil
TOPPING:
1 red pepper (capsicum), quartered and seeded
1 small courgette (zucchini), sliced
1 small aubergine (eggplant), sliced
1 small onion, thinly sliced
6 large ripe tomatoes, quartered and seeded
2 tablespoons shop-bought pesto sauce
salt and pepper
150 g (5 oz) Mozzarella cheese, grated

Mix the flour, yeast and salt together, make a well in the centre and work in the water and oil to form a stiff dough. Knead for 5 minutes, place in an oiled bowl, cover and leave to rise in a warm place for 30 minutes until doubled in size. Preheat oven to 230C (450F/Gas 8) and place a pizza plate or baking sheet on the top shelf. Preheat grill. Brush the pepper (capsicum), courgette (zucchini), aubergine (eggplant) and onion slices with a little oil and grill until charred on all sides.

Grill the tomato quarters, skin side up, until blistered. Peel and discard the skin and mash the flesh with the pesto sauce and salt and pepper. Roll out dough to a 23-25 cm (9-10 in) round. Spread over the tomato mixture and arrange the grilled vegetables over the top. Sprinkle over the cheese and transfer to the hot pizza plate or baking sheet. Bake for 25-30 minutes until bubbling and golden.

Serves 4.

SAVOURY PIES & PASTRIES

LEEK TART

55 g (2 oz/¼ cup) butter
4 leeks, halved lengthways and thinly sliced
salt and freshly ground black pepper
4 egg yolks
250 ml (9 fl oz/1 cup) milk or single (light) cream
leaves from 4 sprigs of tarragon, finely chopped
3 tablespoons freshly grated Parmesan cheese
  (optional)
PASTRY:
175 g (6 oz/1½ cups) plain flour
85 g (3 oz/⅓ cup) butter, diced
1 egg yolk

Heat butter in a large saucepan, add leeks and salt and pepper and cook over a low heat, stirring occasionally, for 10 minutes, until soft.

Leave leeks to cool. To make pastry, mix together flour and salt and pepper. Add butter and rub in until mixture resembles fine breadcrumbs. Stir in egg yolk and enough cold water to bind to a firm but not dry dough. Cover and chill for 30 minutes. Thinly roll out pastry on a lightly floured surface and line a 20 cm (8 in) flan tin. Prick base with a fork and line with foil or greaseproof paper. Fill with baking beans and chill for 20 minutes. Preheat oven to 200C (400F/Gas 6).

Bake pastry case for 10 minutes. Remove beans and foil or paper for a further 10 minutes. Lower oven temperature to 180C (350F/Gas 4). Mix together egg yolks, milk or cream, tarragon, salt and pepper and Parmesan cheese, if using. Arrange leeks in pastry case and pour over egg mixture. Bake for 30-40 minutes, until lightly set and golden. Serve warm or cold.

Serves 4-6.

TURKEY & BROCCOLI FLANS

175 g (6 oz/1⅓ cup) plain wholemeal flour
pinch salt
85 g (3 oz/⅓ cup) butter or margarine
2 tablespoons oil
225 g (8 oz) turkey breast meat
175 g (6 oz) broccoli
55 g (2 oz/½ cup) grated Gouda cheese
3 eggs
300 ml (10 fl oz/1¼ cups) milk
salt and pepper

In a bowl, mix together the flour, and salt, then rub in the butter until the mixture resembles breadcrumbs. Mix to a dough with 1 tablespoon oil and 3 tablespoons water.

Divide the dough into 6, roll each piece out and use to line six 10 cm (4 in) quiche tins. Place on 2 baking sheets. Preheat oven to 190C (375F/Gas 5). Cut the turkey into small dice. Heat the remaining oil in a non-stick pan and sauté the turkey for 4-5 minutes until white all over. Set aside.

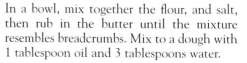

Trim the broccoli into tiny flowerets and blanch in boiling water for 2 minutes; drain well. Divide the cheese between the pastry cases, then add the turkey and broccoli. Beat the eggs and milk together, season and pour into the flan. Bake in the oven for 25-30 minutes until set. Remove from the tins and serve warm or cold.

Makes 6.

SALAMI PUFFS

175 g (6 oz) puff pastry
8 slices Italian salami
25 g (1 oz/¼ cup) grated Cheddar cheese
beaten egg, to glaze
lamb's lettuce or parsley sprigs, to garnish

Preheat oven to 200C (400F/Gas 6). On a floured surface, roll out pastry 0.3 cm (⅛ in) thick. Using a 10 cm (4 in) fluted cutter, cut out 8 circles of pastry.

Lay a slice of salami in the middle of each pastry circle. Put a little cheese on each slice of salami.

In a bowl, beat egg and brush around edges of pastry. Fold pastry circle in half and press edges firmly to seal. Brush each puff with beaten egg. Bake in the oven for 15 minutes until well risen and golden brown. Serve garnished with lamb's lettuce or parsley.

Makes 8.

SPANAKOPITTA

150 ml (5 fl oz/⅔ cup) olive oil
1 onion, finely chopped
1 clove garlic, crushed
450 g (1 lb) frozen chopped spinach, thawed and
    well drained
2 tablespoons chopped fresh coriander
½ teaspoon freshly grated nutmeg
115 g (4 oz) feta cheese, crumbled
115 g (4 oz/1 cup) curd cheese
salt and freshly ground black pepper
8 sheets filo pastry, about 40 x 30 cm (16 x 12 in)
coriander leaves, to garnish

Preheat the oven to 190C (375F/Gas 5). Brush a 30 x 23 cm (12 x 9 in) baking tin with oil.

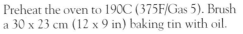
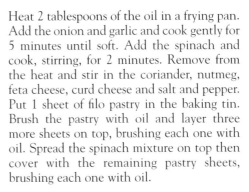

Heat 2 tablespoons of the oil in a frying pan. Add the onion and garlic and cook gently for 5 minutes until soft. Add the spinach and cook, stirring, for 2 minutes. Remove from the heat and stir in the coriander, nutmeg, feta cheese, curd cheese and salt and pepper. Put 1 sheet of filo pastry in the baking tin. Brush the pastry with oil and layer three more sheets on top, brushing each one with oil. Spread the spinach mixture on top then cover with the remaining pastry sheets, brushing each one with oil.

Trim the overhanging pastry then tuck in the edges to seal. Brush the top with oil. With a sharp knife, cut through the top layers to mark 16 squares. Bake in the oven for 30 minutes until golden brown and crisp. Leave in the tin for 10 minutes, then cut into the marked squares. Garnish with coriander leaves and serve hot or warm.

Makes 16 squares.

COULIBIAC

55 g (2 oz) long grain rice
salt and pepper
350 g (12 oz) spinach, stalks removed, torn
pinch freshly grated nutmeg
85 g (3 oz/6 tablespoons) butter
1 onion, finely chopped
200 ml (7 fl oz/scant 1 cup) milk
450 g (1 lb) salmon fillets
2 tablespoons plain flour
4 tablespoons sour cream
1½ tablespoons chopped fresh parsley
1½ tablespoons chopped fresh chives
2 hard-boiled eggs, coarsely chopped
4 large sheets filo pastry

Heat 25 g (1 oz/2 tablespoons) butter in a saucepan, stir in flour for 1 minute, then slowly pour in reserved milk, stirring. Bring to the boil, stirring, and simmer for about 4 minutes, stirring occasionally. Remove from heat, cool slightly then fold in salmon, cream, herbs, eggs and seasoning. Cool completely.

In a saucepan, bring 150 ml (5 fl oz/⅔ cup) water to boil, add rice and salt, stir, then return to boil. Cover and cook for 12-15 minutes until rice is tender and water absorbed. Meanwhile, wash but do not dry spinach, put into a saucepan and heat until there is no visible liquid. Tip into a colander and press out surplus liquid. Season with salt, pepper and nutmeg. Leave to cool.

Preheat oven to 200C (400F/Gas 6). Butter a baking sheet. Melt remaining butter. Cut pastry in half. Lay one sheet on baking sheet, brush lightly with melted butter, then repeat with 3 more sheets pastry; keep remaining pastry covered with damp cloth.

In a pan, heat 25 g (1 oz/2 tablespoons) butter, add onion and fry until softened but not coloured. Stir into rice with pepper. Cool. Pour milk into a shallow pan, add salmon, bring to boil, then poach for 10-15 minutes until only just cooked. Drain and reserve milk. Skin and flake fish.

Spoon rice onto pastry, leaving a 2.5 cm (1 in) border. Cover with spinach, then fish mixture. Lay a sheet of pastry over filling, brush with butter, then repeat with remaining pastry. Press edges together, then bake in the oven for about 25 minutes until pastry is crisp and golden.

Serves 4-6.

CRAB & RICOTTA TARTS

PASTRY:
225 g (8 oz/2 cups) plain flour
pinch salt
115 g (4 oz) butter, diced
FILLING:
225 g (8 oz) crabmeat
225 g (8 oz/1 cup) ricotta cheese
3 spring onions, finely chopped
2 whole eggs plus 1 yolk
2 tablespoons chopped flat-leaf parsley
few drops Tabasco (hot pepper sauce)
salt and freshly ground black pepper
mixed salad leaves, to serve
flat-leaf parsley sprigs, to garnish

Preheat oven to 200C (400F/Gas 6). Sieve flour and salt into a mixing bowl; rub in butter until mixture resembles breadcrumbs. Stir in about 4 tablespoons cold water to make a firm dough. Turn onto a floured surface; knead gently until smooth. Use to line four 10 cm (4 inch) tartlet tins. Prick bases with a fork; chill for 20 minutes. Line pastry cases with greaseproof paper and fill with baking beans. Bake in the preheated oven for 15 minutes, removing beans and paper after 10 minutes.

Remove tartlet cases from oven and turn temperature to 180C (350F/Gas 4). Mix filling ingredients together in a bowl. Spoon into tartlet cases. Bake in the oven for about 20 minutes until set and golden brown. Serve warm or cold with a few mixed salad leaves and garnish with Italian parsley sprigs.

Serves 4.

GOAT CHEESE & FIG TART

200 g (7 oz/1¾ cups) plain flour
pinch salt
115 g (4 oz/½ cup) butter
1 egg yolk
2 tablespoons iced water
1 tablespoon olive oil
1 large onion, thinly sliced
2 teaspoons chopped fresh thyme
½ teaspoon fennel seeds
4 fresh figs
115 g (4 oz/½ cup) soft goat cheese
25 g (1 oz/¼ cup) freshly grated Parmesan cheese
150 ml (5 fl oz/⅔ cup) thick sour cream
1 large egg, lightly beaten

Preheat oven to 200C (400F/Gas 6). Sift the flour and salt into a bowl and rub in the butter until mixture resembles fine breadcrumbs. Make a well in the centre and work in the egg yolk and water to form a soft dough. Knead on a floured surface, wrap and chill for 30 minutes. Roll out thinly and use to line a 23 cm (9 in) tart tin. Prick the base and chill for 20 minutes. Line with foil and baking beans and bake blind for 10 minutes; remove foil and beans and bake for a further 10-12 minutes until crisp and golden.

Heat the oil and fry the onions, thyme and fennel for 10 minutes. Chop 2 figs, add to the pan and remove from the heat. Beat the goat cheese, Parmesan, cream and egg together until smooth. Spread the onion mixture into tart case and spoon in the cheese mixture. Slice the remaining figs and arrange around the outside of the tart. Bake for 25 minutes until risen and set. Leave to cool and serve warm or cold.

Serves 8.

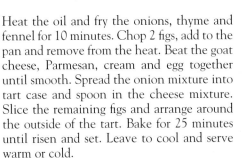

PRAWN & FETA TARTS

175 g (6 oz) peeled cooked prawns
115 g (4 oz) feta cheese
fresh basil leaves, to garnish
PASTRY:
175 g (6 oz/1½ cups) plain flour
½ teaspoon salt
9 teaspoons olive oil
1 egg, beaten
TOMATO SAUCE:
6 teaspoons olive oil
1 onion, chopped
1 clove garlic, crushed
200 g (7 oz) can chopped tomatoes
3 teaspoons chopped sun-dried tomato
2 teaspoons chopped fresh basil
salt and pepper

To make the pastry, sift flour and ½ teaspoon salt into a bowl. With a fork, mix in olive oil, egg and 1-2 teaspoons water to make a firm dough. Knead lightly, wrap in plastic wrap and chill for 1 hour. Make tomato sauce. Heat oil in a frying pan, add onion and garlic; cook until soft. Add tomatoes and sun-dried tomato. Cook for 5-10 minutes until sauce is very thick. Stir in basil, salt and pepper. Preheat oven to 200C (400F/Gas 6).

On a floured surface, roll out pastry thinly. Line four 10 cm (4 in) loose-bottom flan tins with pastry and press a piece of foil into each. Bake in the oven for 10 minutes. Remove foil; cook for a further 5 minutes. Divide prawns between pastry cases. Crumble cheese over. Spread tomato sauce over cheese and prawns. Bake for 5 minutes. Serve garnished with basil leaves.

Serves 4.

SEAFOOD PARCELS

85 g (3 oz/⅔ cup) butter
25 g (1 oz/¼ cup) flour
150 ml (5 fl oz/⅔ cup) milk
6 teaspoons lemon juice
1 clove garlic, crushed
1 tablespoon each chopped fresh mint, chopped fresh coriander and chopped fresh parsley
pinch cayenne pepper
pinch paprika
½ teaspoon ground cumin
salt
85 g (3 oz) cooked mussels
55 g (2 oz) cooked peeled prawns
55 g (2 oz) cooked squid or white fish
6 sheets filo pastry

Preheat oven to 190C (375F/Gas 5). In a saucepan, melt 25 g (1 oz/6 teaspoons) butter. Stir in flour, then gradually add milk. Stirring, heat sauce until thick. Stir in lemon juice, garlic, mint, coriander, parsley, cayenne, paprika, cumin and salt. Add mussels, prawns and squid or white fish.

Melt remaining butter. Brush over 1 sheet filo pastry, place another sheet on top and butter it. Repeat with 2 more layers of pastry. Cut into 12 squares. Butter remaining 2 sheets of pastry. Place one on top of the other. Cut in half. Pile the 4 sheets together; cut into 6 squares. Place some filling in middle of each square. Draw pastry up and pinch together to form pouches. Bake for 30 minutes or until brown and crisp.

Makes 18.

GOAT CHEESE TARTS

1-2 teaspoons extra virgin olive oil
25 g (1 oz) butter
115 g (4 oz/2 cups) soft white breadcrumbs
1 tablespoon sesame seeds
175 g (6 oz/¾ cup) soft goats cheese
4 sun-dried tomatoes in oil, drained
4 fresh basil leaves
1 teaspoon finely chopped fresh mint
salt and freshly ground black pepper
mixed salad leaves to garnish, if desired

Use olive oil to grease four 7.5-10 cm (3-4 inch) tartlet tins.

Preheat oven to 200C (400F/Gas 6). Melt butter in a small saucepan and stir in bread-crumbs and sesame seeds. Divide between prepared tartlet tins, pressing firmly into base and sides. Bake in the preheated oven for 12-15 minutes until crisp and light golden. Carefully remove tartlets from tins and place on a baking sheet.

Divide goats cheese between tartlets and top each with a sun-dried tomato. Season with salt and freshly ground black pepper. Return to oven for 8-10 minutes to heat through. Serve hot or warm with a basil leaf and a sprinkling of chopped mint on each tart. Garnish with mixed salad leaves, if desired.

Serves 4.

LEEK & CHEESE PIE

450 g (1 lb) leeks, chopped
1 teaspoon salt
55 g (2 oz/¼ cup) butter
2 large onions, sliced
2 bunches spring onions, sliced
115 g (4 oz/1 cup) crumbled feta cheese
2 eggs, beaten
freshly ground black pepper
2 tablespoons olive oil
8 sheets filo pastry
55 g (2 oz/¼ cup) melted butter

Put the leeks into a colander, sprinkle with salt and leave for 30 minutes. Squeeze dry.

Heat the butter in a flameproof dish. Add the onions and spring onions and cook, stir-ring occasionally, for 3-5 minutes, until soft but not coloured. Remove from the heat and leave to cool for 10 minutes. Preheat oven to 200C (400F/Gas 6). Add the leeks, feta cheese and eggs to the onion mixture, season with black pepper and mix well.

Crumple the sheets of filo pastry and arrange on top of the leek mixture. Brush with melted butter and bake for 30-35 minutes, until the pastry is golden brown. Serve.

Serves 4-6.

FAMILY CHICKEN PIE

700 g (1½ lb) chicken pieces
1 large onion, thickly sliced
85 ml (3 fl oz/⅓ cup) dry white wine
200 ml (7 fl oz/¾ cup) chicken stock
1 bouquet garni and salt and pepper
25 g (1 oz/6 teaspoons) butter
175 g (6 oz) button mushrooms, halved
25 g (1 oz/¼ cup) plain flour
225 g (8 oz) can sweetcorn kernels
2 tablespoons chopped fresh parsley
1 teaspoon lemon juice
4 tablespoons double (thick) cream
1 kg (2¼ lb) potatoes
115 ml (4 fl oz/½ cup) hot milk
85 g (3 oz/¾ cup) grated Cheddar cheese
25 g (1 oz) salted potato crisps, crushed

CHICKEN & HAM PIE

25 g (1 oz/6 teaspoons) butter
225 g (8 oz) sweetcure ham, cut into 2.5 cm (1 in)
    cubes
350 g (12 oz) skinned and boned chicken, cut into
    2.5 cm (1 in) cubes
1 onion, chopped
225 g (8 oz) leeks, trimmed and sliced
175 g (6 oz) button mushrooms, sliced
25 g (1 oz/¼ cup) plain flour
300 ml (10 fl oz/1¼ cups) chicken stock
150 ml (5 fl oz/⅔ cup) single (light) cream
finely grated rind ½ lemon
salt and pepper
225 g (8 oz) shortcrust pastry
2 tablespoons grated Parmesan cheese
milk for glazing

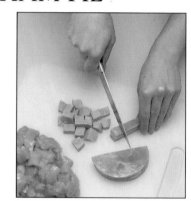

Place the chicken, onion, wine, stock and bouquet garni in a large pan and bring to the boil. Reduce the heat and simmer for 25-30 minutes until the chicken is tender. Drain the liquid and reserve for the sauce. Discard the bouquet garni and remove skin and bones from the chicken; coarsely chop the flesh. Melt the butter in a pan and gently fry the mushrooms, then stir in the flour and cook for 1 minute. Add the reserved poaching liquor and onion.

Preheat oven to 200C (400F/Gas 6). In a pan, melt the butter, add the ham and chicken and cook for 2-3 minutes. Remove from the pan and reserve. Add the vegetables and cook for 2-3 minutes until starting to soften. Return the ham and chicken to the pan, stir in the flour and cook for 1-2 minutes until vegetables are starting to soften. Remove from the heat and gradually add the chicken stock and the cream. Return to the heat and, stirring, cook for 2 minutes until thickened. Add the lemon rind and season with salt and pepper.

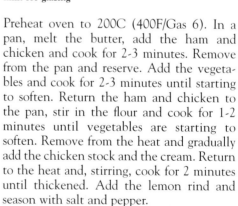

Return to the heat and bring to the boil, stirring continuously. Stir in the chicken, sweetcorn, parsley, lemon juice and cream and season to taste with salt and pepper. Cook the potatoes and mash with the milk and 55 g (2 oz/½ cup) of the cheese and season to taste. Preheat grill. Spoon the chicken mixture into a flameproof dish and cover with creamed potato. Mix the crisps with the remaining cheese. Sprinkle over the potato crisps and grill until golden.

Transfer the chicken and ham mixture to a 1 litre (35 fl oz/4½ cup) pie dish. Mix the pastry with the Parmesan, then roll out on a floured surface 2.5 cm (1 in) larger than the pie dish. Cut off a 2.5 cm (1 in) strip to fit the edge of the dish. Brush the edge with a little water, then cover with the pastry lid. Pinch the edges together to seal and brush the pie with milk to glaze. Bake in the oven for 25-30 minutes or until the pastry is golden brown.

Serves 4.

Serves 4.

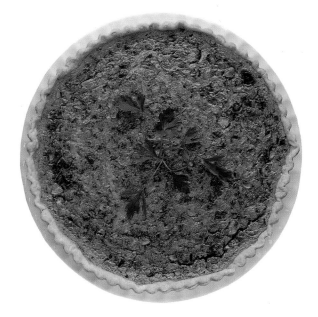

MUSHROOM TART

PASTRY:
225 g (8 oz/2 cups) plain flour
pinch salt
115 g (4 oz) butter, diced
flat-leaf parsley sprigs to garnish
FILLING:
25 g (1 oz) dried ceps (porcini)
25 g (1 oz) butter, diced
1 medium onion, finely chopped
115 g (4 oz) button mushrooms, chopped
2 tablespoons finely chopped flat-leaf parsley
1 tablespoon sun-dried tomato paste
4 tablespoons single (light) cream
3 large eggs
25 g (1 oz/¼ cup) freshly grated Parmesan cheese
salt and freshly ground black pepper

Melt butter in a medium saucepan. Add onion and button mushrooms and cook gently for 5 minutes to soften. Stir in ceps (porcini), parsley and sun-dried tomato paste. Cook for a further 2 minutes then stir in cream. Continue to cook over a low heat for 8-10 minutes until liquid is reduced by half. Remove from heat and allow to cool.

To make pastry, sieve flour and salt into a mixing bowl, add butter and rub in until mixture resembles breadcrumbs. Stir in 4-5 tablespoons cold water to make to a firm dough. Wrap in plastic wrap and put in refrigerator while preparing filling.

Roll out dough and use to line the flan ring. Prick base with a fork. Line pastry case with greaseproof paper and cover with baking beans. Bake 'blind' in the preheated oven for 25 minutes, removing beans and paper for last 5 minutes. Turn oven temperature to 190C (375F/Gas 5).

Preheat oven to 200C (400F/Gas 6). Grease a 23 cm (9 in) flan ring. Put dried ceps (porcini) in a small bowl. Cover generously with warm water and leave to soak for 20 minutes. Drain and rinse to remove any grit. Dry briefly on absorbent kitchen paper then chop finely and set aside.

Beat eggs in a large jug or bowl. Stir in Parmesan and cooled mushroom mixture. Season with salt and freshly ground black pepper then pour into pastry case. Bake for about 20 minutes until set. Serve warm or cold garnished with parsley sprigs.

Serves 8.

RED PEPPER & ONION TART

225 g (8 oz/2 cups) strong flour
salt and freshly ground black pepper
1 teaspoon easy-blend yeast
150 ml (5 fl oz/⅔ cup) milk
1 egg yolk
4 tablespoons olive oil
450 g (1 lb) Spanish onions, halved and sliced
4 red peppers (capsicums), seeded and sliced
4 yellow peppers (capsicums), seeded and sliced
handful thyme, oregano and parsley sprigs
16-20 canned anchovy fillets, drained

Sift flour and salt into a bowl. Stir in yeast.

Stir milk into egg yolk then slowly pour into flour, stirring constantly. Beat for 5-10 minutes, until dough comes cleanly away from bowl.

Turn dough onto a lightly floured surface and knead until smooth and elastic. Form into a ball, place in an oiled bowl, cover and leave in a warm place for about 1 hour, until doubled in volume.

Meanwhile, heat 3 tablespoons oil in a large non-stick frying pan, add onions, peppers (capsicums) and herbs and cook over a moderate heat, stirring occasionally, for 20-25 minutes, until vegetables are soft but not browned. Add a few tablespoons water if necessary to prevent browning. Season and set aside.

Preheat oven to 240C (475F/Gas 9). On a lightly floured surface, punch down and flatten dough. Roll out to a 30 cm (12 in) circle. Curl up edge to make a lip. Carefully transfer to an oiled baking tray. Prick well.

Spread vegetable mixture over dough, arrange anchovy fillets on top, trickle over remaining oil and bake for 25-30 minutes, until the dough is well risen, crisp and golden. Serve warm.

Serves 6.

VEGETABLE FILO PARCELS

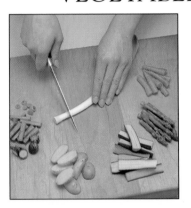

4 small new potatoes, halved
8 baby carrots, trimmed
8 baby courgettes (zucchini), halved
8 asparagus tips, trimmed
1 baby leek, trimmed and sliced into 8
55 g (2 oz/¼ cup) butter, softened
1 tablespoon chopped fresh mint
¼ teaspoon ground cumin
pinch of cayenne pepper
salt and pepper
4 large sheets filo pastry
85 ml (3 fl oz/⅓ cup) olive oil

Preheat oven to 190C (375F/Gas 5) and place a baking sheet on the middle shelf.

Cook the potatoes in boiling water for 6-8 minutes until almost cooked. Blanch the remaining vegetables for 2-3 minutes, depending on the size, until almost tender. Drain all the vegetables, plunge into cold water, allow to cool, then drain and dry thoroughly. Cream together the butter, mint, spices and salt and pepper. Take one large sheet of pastry and using a 25 cm (10 in) plate or saucepan lid as a template, carefully cut out a circle; repeat to make 4 in total. Brush liberally with oil.

Take a quarter of the vegetables and place a small pile on one side of the pastry circle. Dot with the mint butter and fold the other side of pastry over the filling, pressing the edges together well. Brush a little oil along the edge and turn over a bit at a time to ensure filling is totally enclosed. Repeat to make 4 parcels and transfer to the heated baking sheet. Carefully brush over remaining oil and bake for 12-15 minutes until pastry is golden. Serve immediately.

Serves 4.

MUSHROOM & CHEESE PIES

1 kg (2¼ lb) ready-made puff pastry
7 g (¼ oz) dried ceps (mushrooms)
150 ml (5 fl oz/⅔ cup) boiling water
2 tablespoons olive oil
115 g (4 oz) aubergine (eggplant), diced
225 g (8 oz) mixed mushrooms, wiped and finely chopped
1 clove garlic, crushed
1 teaspoon chopped fresh thyme
2 tablespoons tomato purée (paste)
salt and pepper
45 g (1½ oz) vegetarian goat cheese, diced
1 egg, beaten
1 tablespoon milk

Roll out the pastry into two 23 x 32.5 cm (9 x 13 in) rectangles and cut six 10 cm (4 in) squares from each one. Cover and leave to rest for 30 minutes. Place ceps in a bowl, pour over the boiling water and leave to soak for 20 minutes. Drain, reserve stock and chop and reserve ceps. Heat 1 tablespoon oil in a large pan, stir-fry the aubergine (eggplant) for 3-4 minutes, add the ceps, fresh mushrooms, garlic and thyme and stir-fry for a further 3 minutes. Add the reserved cep liquid and boil rapidly for 3 minutes. Stir in the tomato purée (paste) and seasonings; cool.

Preheat oven to 220C (425F/Gas 7). Spread a large spoonful of the mushroom mixture in the centre of 6 pastry squares, leaving a narrow border around the edges. Top with the diced cheese. Dampen the edges with a little water and top with the remaining pastry. Press edges together to seal and cut a small slit in the top of each pie. Beat the egg and milk together and brush over each pie. Transfer to a baking sheet and cook for 15-18 minutes until puffed and golden.

Serves 6.

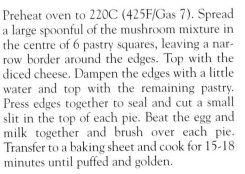

WINTER VEGETABLE PIE

175 g (6 oz/1¼ cups) self-raising flour
salt
115 g (4 oz/½ cup) hard white vegetable fat, divided
   into 4
2 tablespoons chopped fresh mixed herbs
4-5 tablespoons iced water
175 g (6 oz) baby onions, halved
1 clove garlic, chopped
575 g (1¼ lb) prepared mixed winter vegetables
   (carrots, turnips, parsnips, cauliflower flowerets)
115 g (4 oz) button mushrooms, wiped
2 tablespoons olive oil
150 ml (5 fl oz/⅔ cup) red wine
350 ml (12 fl oz/1½ cups) vegetable stock (see
   Note)
2 tablespoons tomato purée (paste)

Sift the flour with 1 teaspoon salt and finely
rub in one-quarter of the fat. Stir in half the
herbs and work in enough iced water to form
a soft dough. Knead lightly, wrap and chill
for 30 minutes. Roll out pastry to a rectangle
about 1 cm (½ in) thick, dot the top two-
thirds with one-third of the remaining fat.
Bring the bottom third of pastry up into the
middle and the top third down over this.
Press edges to seal, cover and chill for 30
minutes. Repeat the process twice and chill
for a final 30 minutes.

Preheat oven to 200C (400F/Gas 6). Fry
onions, garlic and the vegetables in the oil
for 10 minutes. Add the wine and boil for 5
minutes. Add the stock and tomato purée
(paste) and simmer for 20 minutes. Transfer
to a 1.2 litre (2 pint/5 cup) pie dish.

Roll pastry out to a 0.5 cm (¼ in) rectangle,
cut out a pie top a little larger than the dish.
Cut remaining pastry into strips, dampen
and press around edge of dish. Dampen edge
of pastry, place pastry lid over pie and press
edges to seal. Bake in the oven for 30
minutes.

Serves 6.

Note: To make your own stock, fry 1 roughly
chopped onion and 1 trimmed and sliced
leek in 2 teaspoons olive oil until softened.
Add 2 chopped carrots, 1 diced large potato
and 2 sliced sticks celery and fry for a further
5 minutes.

Add 4 roughly chopped ripe tomatoes, 115 g
(4 oz) quartered mushrooms, 55 g (2 oz/
⅓ cup) rice, 2 sprigs parsley, 2 sprigs thyme,
1 bay leaf, 1 teaspoon salt, 6 white peppercorns and 1.2 litres (2 pints/5 cups) water.
Bring to the boil, cover and simmer gently
for 30 minutes. Strain through a fine sieve.

POTATO & ONION TART

200 g (7 oz/1¾ cup) plain flour
pinch of salt
100 g (3½ oz) unsalted butter, diced
1 egg yolk
2 tablespoons iced water
FILLING:
450 g (1 lb) waxy potatoes
25 g (1 oz/6 teaspoons) butter
2 large onions, thinly sliced
1 teaspoon chopped fresh rosemary
½ teaspoon caraway seeds
200 ml (7 fl oz/1 cup) low-fat fromage frais
25 g (1 oz/¼ cup) grated Cheddar cheese
freshly grated nutmeg

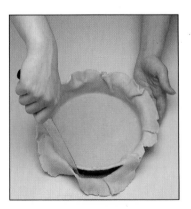

Preheat oven to 200C (400F/Gas 6). Sift the flour and salt into a large bowl and rub in the butter until mixture resembles fine breadcrumbs. Make a well in the centre, work in the egg yolk and water to form a soft dough. Knead on a floured surface, wrap and chill for 30 minutes. Roll out thinly and use to line a deep 23 cm (9 in) fluted flan tin. Prick the base, then chill for 20 minutes. Line with foil and baking beans and bake blind for 10 minutes; remove beans and foil and bake for a further 10-12 minutes until crisp.

Increase oven temperature to 230C (450F/ Gas 8). Cook the potatoes for 15 minutes until just tender. Allow to cool, carefully peel and cut into very thin slices. Melt the butter and fry the onions, rosemary and caraway seeds for 10 minutes until golden. Spread the onion mixture over pastry case and arrange the potato slices over the top. Beat the remaining ingredients together, spread over the potatoes and bake at the top of the oven for 15 minutes until golden.

Serves 6-8.

OLIVE & MOZZARELLA PUFFS

55 g (2 oz/½ cup) stoned green olives
25 g (1 oz) Mozzarella cheese
2 teaspoons chopped fresh parsley
½ teaspoon chopped fresh sage
pinch chilli powder
225 g (8 oz) ready-made puff pastry, thawed if frozen
1 egg
salt

Preheat oven to 220C (425F/Gas 7) and lightly oil a baking sheet. Very finely chop the olives and cheese and mix with the herbs and chilli powder to form a paste. Set aside.

Roll out the pastry thinly and stamp out 8 rounds, using a 10 cm (4 in) fluted pastry cutter. Place a heaped teaspoon of olive mixture in the centre of each round. Lightly dampen the edges of pastry, fold in half to form semi-circles, pressing edges together well to seal. Transfer to the baking sheet.

Beat the egg with a little salt and brush over pastries. Cut 2 small slashes in each one and bake for 12-15 minutes until puffed up and golden. Serve warm or cold with a salad garnish.

Serves 8.

Note: These make ideal buffet party nibbles. Make up double quantity of the filling, cut pastry into small rounds to make bite-sized appetizers.

RATATOUILLE IN OLIVE TARTS

4 tablespoons olive oil
1 onion, chopped
1 clove garlic, crushed
1 aubergine (eggplant), diced
1 courgette (zucchini), diced
1 red pepper (capsicum), diced
3 tomatoes, peeled (see page 293) and chopped
1 teaspoon dried herbes de Provence
salt and freshly ground black pepper
mint sprigs and endive leaves, to garnish
PASTRY:
225 g (8 oz/2 cups) plain flour, sifted
115 g (4 oz/½ cup) butter
25 g (1 oz) black olives, pitted and roughly chopped
1 egg, beaten
1 tablespoon olive oil

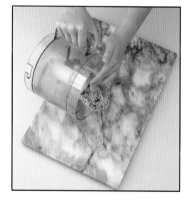

To make the pastry, put the flour, butter and a pinch of salt in a food processor and process until the mixture resembles fine breadcrumbs. Add the olives and, with the motor running, add the egg and olive oil and process until the mixture forms a ball. Remove from the food processor. Wrap in cling film and chill for 30 minutes.

Preheat the oven to 200C (400F/Gas 6). Heat 2 tablespoons of the olive oil in a frying pan. Add the onion and garlic and cook gently for 5 minutes until soft. Add the aubergine (eggplant), courgette (zucchini) and pepper (capsicum) and cook for 5 minutes.

Stir in the tomatoes, herbes de Provence and salt and pepper. Cover and cook for 10 minutes, stirring occasionally. Uncover and cook for 15 minutes until the vegetables are tender but not too soft.

Meanwhile, prepare the pastry cases. Thinly roll out the pastry on a lightly floured surface. Cut into six circles of pastry to fit six 10 cm (4 in) flan tins. Line the tins with the pastry, prick all over with a fork and press a square of foil into each one.

Bake the flan cases for 15 minutes, then remove the foil and bake for a further 10-15 minutes until the pastry is crisp. Reheat the ratatouille, if necessary, and spoon into the pastry cases. Drizzle with the remaining olive oil, garnish and serve.

Serves 6.

CHICKEN PASTIES

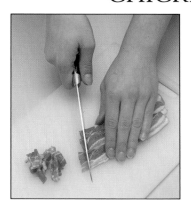

350 g (12 oz/3 cups) plain flour
salt and pepper
85 g (3 oz/⅓ cup) butter
85 g (3 oz/⅓ cup) solid vegetable fat
1 tablespoon fresh chopped thyme
1 tablespoon vegetable oil
½ onion, chopped
55 g (2 oz) rindless streaky bacon, chopped
1 carrot, peeled and diced
1 large potato, peeled and diced
350 g (12 oz) chicken breast, minced
85 g (3 oz) mushrooms, chopped
½ tablespoon plain flour
150 ml (5 fl oz/⅔ cup) chicken stock
beaten egg or milk for brushing

Preheat oven to 190C (375F/Gas 5). Sift the flour and a pinch of salt into a bowl, add fats and rub in finely until mixture resembles breadcrumbs. Add the chopped thyme and 3 tablespoons iced water and mix together to form a dough. Wrap in cling film and refrigerate for 30 minutes. Heat the oil in a frying pan and add the onion, bacon, carrots and potato and fry for 2-3 minutes until the onion starts to soften. Add the chicken and mushrooms and fry for a further 3-4 minutes. Add the flour and cook for 1 minute.

Gradually add the stock, return to the heat and, stirring, cook for 2 minutes until the sauce thickens. Season and leave to cool. On a floured surface, roll out the pastry and cut out eight 15 cm (6 in) rounds. Place 2 tablespoons of the cold mixture in the centre of each round, brush the edges with a little beaten egg or milk and fold the pastry over to enclose the filling. Pinch the edges together to seal. Glaze with egg or milk and place on a baking sheet. Bake for 20-25 minutes until golden.

Serves 4.

MINCED MEAT FINGERS

3 teaspoons pine nuts
55 ml (2 fl oz/¼ cup) olive oil
1 onion, finely chopped
350 g (12 oz) lean minced beef
1 teaspoon ground cinnamon
1 tablespoon chopped fresh parsley
salt and pepper
6 sheets filo pastry
1 quantity Tzatziki (see page 25), to serve

In a frying pan, heat pine nuts until golden. Remove from pan and set aside.

Heat 6 teaspoons oil in frying pan, add onion and cook until soft. Stir in beef and cook, stirring, for a few minutes until brown all over. Add cinnamon, parsley, pine nuts, salt and pepper. Cook for a further 10 minutes, then leave to cool.

Preheat oven to 180C (350F/Gas 4). Cut each sheet of filo pastry into 3 long strips. Brush strips with remaining oil. Spread 1 teaspoon of filling in a line on one end of each strip, leaving a small margin on either side. Roll over twice and fold long sides over the edge, then continue rolling to make a tube. Place fingers on a baking sheet. Bake in the oven for 20-30 minutes until crisp and golden. Serve with Tzatziki.

Makes 18.

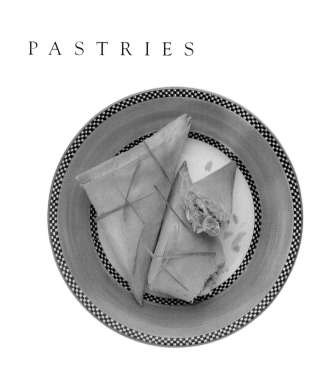

LAMB PARCELS

12 vine leaves, preserved in brine
55 ml (2 fl oz/¼ cup) olive oil
juice ½ lemon
2 cloves garlic, crushed
3 teaspoons chopped fresh marjoram
salt and pepper
6 sheets filo pastry
55 g (2 oz/¼ cup) butter, melted
6 thin lamb steaks or pieces of lamb fillet
shredded nasturtium flowers and mint, to garnish

Soak vine leaves in water for 1 hour. In a saucepan of boiling water, cook vine leaves for 5 minutes. Drain and dry on a tea towel.

In a bowl, mix together olive oil, lemon juice, garlic, marjoram, salt and pepper. Place lamb in a dish, pour marinade over and leave in a cool place for 1 hour.

Preheat oven to 190C (375F/Gas 5). Brush each sheet of filo pastry with butter. Lay a vine leaf in middle of one end of each sheet. Place a lamb steak on top, then cover with another vine leaf. Fold sides of pastry over lamb and roll up to form neat parcels. Place on a baking sheet. Bake in the oven for 20-30 minutes until pastry is golden and crisp. Serve garnished with shredded nasturtium flowers and mint.

Serves 6.

CRAB & GINGER TRIANGLES

200 g (7 oz) can crabmeat, drained
6 spring onions, finely chopped
2.5 cm (1 in) piece fresh root ginger, peeled and
  grated
2 teaspoons soy sauce
salt and pepper
6 large sheets filo pastry about 35 cm (14 in) square
85 g (3 oz/⅓ cup) butter, melted
spring onion slivers or tassels, to garnish

In a bowl, mix together crabmeat, spring onions, ginger, soy sauce and salt and pepper. Set aside.

Preheat oven to 180C (350F/Gas 4). Lightly grease a baking sheet. Work with 1 sheet of pastry at a time, keeping the rest covered with a damp cloth. Cut sheet of pastry in half. Brush each half with melted butter and fold in half lengthways. Brush pastry all over with melted butter. Put a portion of crab mixture in 1 corner of 1 strip of pastry. Fold pastry and filling over at right angles to make a triangle and continue folding in this way along strip of pastry to make a triangular parcel.

Repeat with remaining pastry and crab mixture. Brush each parcel with melted butter. Bake in the oven for 20-25 minutes until crisp and golden brown. Serve warm, garnished with spring onion slivers or tassels.

Makes 12.

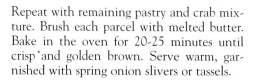

SALADS

TROPICAL SALAD

3 pink grapefruit
1 large papaya
3 avocados
3 tablespoons olive oil
2 teaspoons pink peppercorns, lightly crushed
salt

Cut rind from pink grapefruit, removing white pith at the same time. Hold grapefruit over a bowl to catch juice and cut between membranes to remove segments.

Peel papaya, cut in half and scoop out seeds with a teaspoon. Cut flesh into thin slices. Halve avocados lengthways, remove stones and peel. Cut flesh into thin slices.

Arrange grapefruit segments, papaya slices and avocado slices on serving plates. Mix together 2 teaspoons reserved grapefruit juice, the olive oil, crushed peppercorns and salt. Drizzle over fruit and serve at once.

Serves 6.

TUNISIAN ORANGE SALAD

4 small oranges
1 daikon (mooli)
mint sprigs, to garnish
DRESSING:
1 tablespoon lemon juice
2 teaspoons orange-flower water
1 teaspoon caster sugar
4 tablespoons olive oil
salt and freshly ground black pepper
1 tablespoons chopped fresh mint

Cut the peel off the oranges, removing all the pith. Thinly slice the oranges.

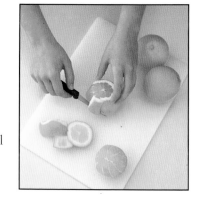

Peel the daikon (mooli) and thinly slice. Arrange the orange and daikon (mooli) slices on a large serving plate. To make the dressing, whisk together the lemon juice, orange-flower water, sugar, olive oil and salt and pepper.

Pour the dressing over the orange and daikon (mooli) slices. Sprinkle with chopped mint and chill. Garnish with mint sprigs and serve.

Serves 4.

Note: A daikon (mooli) is a large white radish. If it is unavailable, this salad is also delicious made with sliced fennel.

GRILLED PEPPER SALAD

SPINACH SALAD

1 large red pepper (capsicum)
1 large green pepper (capsicum)
1 large yellow pepper (capsicum)
1 small red onion, sliced
16 black olives
2 teaspoons chopped fresh basil
2 teaspoons chopped fresh thyme
DRESSING:
3 tablespoons extra virgin olive oil
1 tablespoon red wine vinegar
1 clove garlic, finely chopped
pinch granulated sugar
salt and freshly ground black pepper

2 red peppers (capsicum)
about 115 g (4 oz) young spinach leaves
1 head chicory
1 ripe pear
85 g (3 oz) Gorgonzola cheese
DRESSING:
3 tablespoons extra virgin olive oil
1 tablespoon lemon juice
1 clove garlic, crushed
2 tablespoons chopped flat-leaf parsley
salt and freshly ground black pepper

To make dressing, mix all ingredients together in a small bowl, or shake together in a screw-top jar. Set aside. Preheat grill. Place whole peppers (capsicum) under hot grill for about 10 minutes, turning occasionally, until skins are evenly blistered and charred. Transfer peppers to a plastic bag for a few minutes, then peel away and discard skins.

Preheat grill. Put peppers (capsicums) under the hot grill and cook for about 10 minutes, turning occasionally, until skins are evenly blistered and charred. Transfer peppers (capsicums) to a plastic bag for a few minutes, then peel away and discard skins. Remove and discard seeds then cut peppers (capsicums) into strips. Place in a salad bowl.

Cut peppers in half, discard seeds and cut into strips. Place in salad bowl with onions and olives. Shake dressing and pour over salad. Toss gently to mix and sprinkle over herbs.

Serves 4.

Tear spinach leaves into bite-sized pieces; slice the chicory. Peel, core and slice pear. Add spinach, chicory and pear to salad bowl. Mix dressing ingredients together in a small bowl or put in a screw-top jar and shake until blended. Pour over salad and toss to mix. Crumble Gorgonzola over and serve immediately.

Serves 4-6.

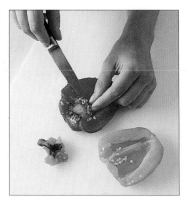

BEAN & ONION SALAD

350 g (12 oz) French beans, topped and tailed
1 onion, thinly sliced
2 tablespoons capers in vinegar, drained
6 tablespoons extra virgin olive oil
juice 1 lemon
½ teaspoons hot red pepper flakes
pinch granulated sugar
salt and freshly ground black pepper
2 teaspoons chopped flat-leaf parsley
1 teaspoon chopped fresh mint

Cook beans in boiling salted water for 3-4 minutes so they remain crisp. Drain and refresh under cold running water. Drain well. Place in a bowl with onion and capers.

Put olive oil, lemon juice and red pepper flakes, sugar, salt and ground black pepper, in a small bowl or screw-top jar. Beat or shake together to mix well.

Add dressing and herbs to salad, mix well.

Serves 4-6.

ASPARAGUS & EGG SALAD

1 kg (2¼ lb) asparagus
7 eggs, hard-boiled
6 tablespoons olive oil
2 tablespoons white wine vinegar
2 small pickled gherkins, finely chopped
salt and freshly ground black pepper
chopped flat-leaf parsley and sprigs, to garnish

Snap off and discard woody ends of asparagus stems. Using a small, sharp knife, scrape stems, rinse then tie into small bundles using string.

Stand bundles upright in a deep pan of boiling salted water so tips are above water. Cover, making a dome of foil, if necessary. Boil for 15 minutes until tips are just tender. Drain, refresh under cold running water, drain, untie bundles and leave to cool.

Finely chop four hard-boiled eggs and place in a bowl. Using a wooden spoon stir in oil, vinegar and gherkins. Season with salt and ground black pepper. Set aside. Quarter remaining eggs and arrange with asparagus around edge of a serving plate. Pour egg sauce into centre and sprinkle with chopped flat-leaf parsley. Garnish with flat-leaf parsley sprigs.

Serves 4-6.

TOMATO & RED ONION SALAD

4 beefsteak tomatoes, sliced
4 sun-dried tomatoes packed in oil, drained and
  chopped
1 red onion, chopped
salt and freshly ground black pepper
3 tablespoons extra virgin olive oil
2 tablespoons oil from the sun-dried tomatoes
2 tablespoons red wine vinegar
pinch granulated sugar
4 tablespoons chopped mixed fresh herbs, such as
  basil, oregano, parsley, chives, dill and coriander
fresh herb sprigs, to garnish

Layer tomatoes, sun-dried tomatoes and onion in a shallow serving dish. Season with salt and freshly ground black pepper.

Mix together remaining ingredients, except garnish, in a small bowl then pour over the salad. Serve garnished with fresh herb sprigs.

Serves 4-6.

CAULIFLOWER INSALATA

1 cauliflower
55 g (2 oz) stoned green olives, halved
55 g (2 oz) stoned black olives, halved
2 tablespoons capers in wine vinegar, drained
1 red pepper (capsicum) packed in wine vinegar
  drained and chopped
5 anchovy fillets, canned in oil, drained and halved
  crosswise
6 tablespoons extra virgin olive oil
1 tablespoon white wine vinegar
salt and freshly ground black pepper
3 small carrots

Break the cauliflower into flowerets.

Cook cauliflower in boiling salted water for 4-5 minutes until crisp. Drain and refresh under cold running water. Drain and leave to cool. Put cauliflower, olives, capers, red pepper (capsicum) and anchovies into a serving bowl. Add oil and vinegar and season with salt and freshly ground black pepper. Toss gently and chill for at least 30 minutes.

Using a potato peeler, remove long thin shreds from carrots. Place shreds in a bowl of iced water for 10 minutes to curl and crisp. Drain well and add to salad. Toss lightly then serve.

Serves 6.

TRICOLOR SALAD

1 avocado
1 tablespoon lemon juice
2 large beefsteak tomatoes
175 g (6 oz) mozzarella cheese
salt and freshly ground black pepper
few drops balsamic vinegar
4 tablespoons extra virgin olive oil
6 basil leaves, shredded
fresh basil sprigs, to garnish

Stone and peel avocado, slice thinly and
brush with lemon juice.

Arrange tomatoes, mozzarella and avocado
on a large serving plate. Sprinkle over salt
and freshly ground black pepper.

Sprinkle balsamic vinegar, oil and basil over
salad. Serve garnished with fresh basil sprigs.

Serves 4-6.

COURGETTE & TOMATO SALAD

about thirty 5 cm (2 in) long courgettes (zucchini),
   total weight about 450 g (1 lb)
350 g (12 oz) small tomatoes, sliced
4 spring onions, white part only, sliced
1 tablespoon chopped fresh Italian parsley
DRESSING:
5 tablespoons extra virgin olive oil
3 tablespoons white wine vinegar
2 cloves garlic, chopped
1 tablespoon chopped fresh thyme
1 teaspoon clear honey
salt and freshly ground black pepper

Add courgettes (zucchini) to a saucepan of
boiling salted water and cook for 3 minutes.
Drain well. Using a small, sharp knife, cut a
long lengthwise slit in each courgette
(zucchini) and place in a serving dish.

To make dressing, mix ingredients together
in a small bowl, or shake together in a screw-
top jar. Pour over hot courgettes (zucchini)
and leave until completely cold. Add
tomatoes, spring onions and parsley to dish.
Toss to mix. Adjust seasoning before serving.

Serves 6.

AUBERGINE & OLIVE SALAD

450 g (1 lb) aubergines (eggplant), diced
salt
10 tablespoons light olive oil
2 onions, chopped
1 clove garlic, chopped
4 sticks celery, sliced
2 small courgettes (zucchini), sliced
1 tablespoon chopped fresh rosemary
400 g (14 oz) can chopped plum tomatoes
1 tablespoon sun-dried tomato paste
2 teaspoons sugar
85 ml (3 fl oz/⅓ cup) red wine vinegar
175 g (6 oz) stoned mixed olives, halved
2 tablespoons capers in wine vinegar, drained
salt and freshly ground black pepper
flat-leaf parsley sprigs, to garnish

Put aubergines (eggplants) in a colander; sprinkle with plenty of salt and leave to drain for 30-40 minutes. Rinse thoroughly to remove salt, drain and pat dry on absorbent kitchen paper. Heat 4 tablespoons of the oil, in a frying pan over a high heat. Add aubergines (eggplant) and fry for 4-5 minutes until evenly browned. Transfer aubergines (eggplants) to absorbent kitchen paper. Heat remaining oil in a large frying pan. Stir in onions and garlic and fry gently for 5 minutes to soften.

Add celery, courgettes (zucchini) and rosemary and cook for a further 5 minutes. Stir in tomatoes, sun-dried tomato paste, sugar and vinegar and cook, stirring frequently, for 10 minutes until vinegar has evaporated. Transfer to a serving dish. Set aside to cool, then add reserved aubergines (eggplant), olives and capers. Season with salt and freshly ground black pepper and toss well. Chill. Serve garnished with Italian parsley sprigs.

Serves 4-6.

ORIENTAL CARROT SALAD

350 g (12 oz) carrots, scrubbed
3 tablespoons peanut oil
½ teaspoon sesame oil
1 teaspoon grated fresh root ginger
1 small clove garlic, sliced
1 dried red chilli, seeded and crushed
2 tablespoons lemon juice
1 teaspoon sugar
55 g (2 oz/⅓ cup) raw peanuts, toasted and chopped
salt and pepper
coriander leaves, to garnish

Finely grate the carrots and place in a large bowl.

Heat 1 tablespoon peanut oil with the sesame oil and fry the ginger, garlic and chilli until just turning golden. Whisk in the remaining oil, lemon juice and sugar and remove from the heat.

Pour the dressing over the carrots, add the nuts and toss well until evenly combined. Cover and leave to marinate for 30 minutes. Stir again, season to taste and serve garnished with coriander leaves.

Serves 4.

LETTUCE & EGG SALAD

12 quail eggs or 3 hen eggs
6 Little Gem lettuces
85 g (3 oz/3 cups) watercress
3 spring onions, trimmed
25 g (1 oz) Parmesan or Cheddar cheese
25 g (1 oz) chervil, roughly shredded
DRESSING:
3 tablespoons virgin olive oil
2 teaspoons Champagne vinegar
salt and pepper

Cook the quail eggs for 3 minutes or the hen eggs for 12 minutes, then plunge immediately into cold water. Peel and then cut into halves or quarters.

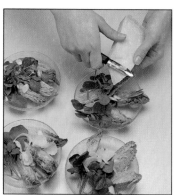

Trim and discard the outer leaves of the lettuces and cut each lettuce into quarters. Discard any thick stalks from the watercress, then wash and pat dry. Thinly slice the spring onions. Divide the lettuce quarters, watercress and onions between 4 serving plates, and using a potato peeler, shave a little Parmesan or Cheddar over each. Sprinkle with the chervil and garnish each salad with the cooked eggs.

Blend the dressing ingredients together until combined, pour the dressing over the salads and serve at once.

Serves 4.

ANCHOVY & PARMESAN SALAD

2 tablespoons olive oil
50 g (1¾ oz) can anchovies in olive oil
1 clove garlic
pinch cayenne pepper
4 slices white bread
250 g (9 oz) mixed salad leaves
55 g (2 oz) Parmesan cheese
DRESSING:
1 tablespoon balsamic vinegar
1 teaspoon Dijon mustard
55 ml (2 fl oz/¼ cup) olive oil
freshly ground black pepper

Preheat oven to 190C (375F/Gas 5). Brush a baking sheet with half the olive oil.

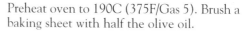

Drain anchovies, reserving oil. Using a pestle and mortar, or in a blender or food processor, pound together anchovies, garlic, cayenne pepper and remaining olive oil. Remove crusts from bread. Spread one side of each slice of bread with anchovy paste. Cut bread into 1 cm (½ in) cubes and arrange, paste side up, on baking sheet. Bake for 8-10 minutes, until crisp. Leave to cool.

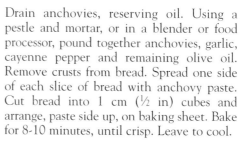

To make dressing, in a large bowl, mix together vinegar, mustard, olive oil, reserved oil from anchovies and pepper. Add salad leaves and toss to coat thoroughly. Arrange salad leaves on serving plates. Scatter anchovy croûtons over salad leaves. Using a vegetable peeler, shave curls of Parmesan cheese over salads and serve.

Serves 6.

ROQUEFORT SALAD

55 g (2 oz/½ cup) walnut pieces
2 bunches watercress
115 g (4 oz) Roquefort cheese
DRESSING:
1 tablespoon red wine vinegar
½-1 teaspoon Dijon mustard
4 tablespoons olive oil
salt and freshly ground black pepper

To make dressing, whisk together vinegar and mustard then slowly pour in oil, whisking constantly. Season with salt and pepper and set aside.

Preheat grill. Spread walnut pieces on a baking sheet and grill, turning occasionally, until crisp and evenly browned.

Put watercress in a serving bowl, crumble over Roquefort cheese and sprinkle with toasted walnuts. Whisk dressing, pour over salad, toss and serve.

Serves 4.

PANZANELLA SALAD

8 thick slices day-old Italian bread
10 plum tomatoes
½ small cucumber
½ small red onion
55 g (2 oz/½ cup) stoned black olives
2 tablespoons chopped fresh basil
grated zest 1 lemon
55 ml (2 fl oz/¼ cup) virgin olive oil
2 teaspoons balsamic vinegar
salt and pepper
lemon slices and basil sprigs, to garnish

Cut the bread into small cubes, place in a shallow dish and pour over enough water to lightly moisten. Set aside for 30 minutes.

Squeeze out all the excess water and crumble bread into a large bowl. Chop the tomatoes, cucumber, onion and olives into dice and add to the bread, with the basil and lemon zest. Stir well.

Whisk the oil and vinegar together, pour over the salad. Season and toss well until evenly combined. Cover and chill for at least 30 minutes, allowing the salad to return to room temperature before serving, garnished with lemon slices and basil sprigs.

Serves 4-6.

WARM SPINACH SALAD

450 g (1 lb) young spinach leaves
6 rashers thick-cut streaky bacon, cut into strips
2 slices bread, crusts removed
4 tablespoons olive oil
4 teaspoons red wine vinegar
1 teaspoon Dijon mustard
salt and freshly ground black pepper

Put spinach in a serving bowl. Heat a non-stick frying pan, add bacon and dry-fry until crisp and brown. Remove with a slotted spoon and drain on kitchen paper.

Cut bread into cubes. Heat 1 tablespoon oil in frying pan, add bread and fry over a moderately high heat until crisp and golden. Remove and drain on kitchen paper. Add to spinach with bacon.

Stir vinegar and mustard into frying pan and bring to boil. Add remaining oil and salt and pepper. Heat through and pour over salad. Toss and serve immediately.

Serves 4.

VEGETARIAN CAESAR SALAD

2 tablespoons mayonnaise
1 tablespoon vodka
1 tablespoon lime juice
1 teaspoon Worcestershire sauce or 2 drops Tabasco
150 ml (5 fl oz/⅔ cup) light olive oil
1 tablespoon chopped fresh mint
1 tablespoon chopped fresh parsley
½ teaspoon ground cumin
¼ teaspoon chilli powder
1 small clove garlic, crushed
two 1 cm (½ in) slices day-old bread
2 Cos lettuces
115 g (4 oz/¾ cup) grated Cheshire cheese

Preheat the oven to 190C (375F/Gas 5). Blend the mayonnaise, vodka, lime juice, Worcestershire sauce or Tabasco together and whisk in 85 ml (3 fl oz/⅓ cup) oil, a little at a time, until thickened slightly. Stir in half the herbs and set aside. Mix remaining oil and herbs, the spices and garlic together and brush over both sides of the bread. Place on a wire rack or trivet and bake for 10-12 minutes. Turn bread and continue cooking for a further 10-12 minutes until crisp and golden on both sides. Cool slightly and cut into cubes.

Just before serving, wash the lettuce, discarding the outer leaves, and dry well. Place in a large bowl, stir in the croûtons and cheese, add the dressing and toss well until evenly coated.

Serves 4.

SPANISH VEGETABLE SALAD

2 Spanish onions, unpeeled
450 g (1 lb) small aubergines (eggplants)
2 red peppers (capsicums)
3 firm but ripe beefsteak tomatoes
8 cloves garlic
10 g (⅓ oz) cumin seeds
juice 1 lemon
4 tablespoons virgin olive oil
3 tablespoons white wine vinegar
salt
2 tablespoons finely chopped fresh parsley (optional)

Preheat oven to 180C (350F/Gas 4). Place onions on a baking sheet and bake for 10 minutes. Add aubergines (eggplants).

Bake for another 10 minutes, then add peppers (capsicums). Bake for 10 minutes before adding tomatoes and 6 of the garlic cloves and cooking for a further 15 minutes, until all vegetables tender. If necessary, remove any cooked vegetables from oven. When vegetables are cool enough to handle, peel them with your fingers.

Cut core and seeds from peppers (capsicums) then cut flesh into strips. Halve tomatoes, discard seeds then slice flesh. Slice aubergines (eggplants) into strips, onions into rings. Arrange in a serving dish. Using a pestle and mortar, pound to a paste the roasted and the raw garlic and the cumin seeds. Beat in lemon juice, oil and vinegar. Add salt to taste. Pour over vegetables and sprinkle with parsley, if desired. Serve warm or cold.

Serves 4.

VEGETABLE SALAD

450 g (1 lb) potatoes, unpeeled
1 large carrot, peeled and halved or quartered
55 g (2 oz) peas
115 g (4 oz) green beans
2 tablespoons chopped Spanish onion
1 small red pepper (capsicum), peeled, seeded and chopped
4 small pickled gherkins, chopped
1½ tablespoons capers
8-12 black or anchovy-stuffed olives
150 ml (5 fl oz/⅔ cup) mayonnaise
1 hard-boiled egg, sliced
chopped fresh parsley, to garnish

Boil potatoes in their skins until tender. Cool, peel, then cut into dice. Boil carrot, peas and beans. Dice carrot and cut beans into short lengths.

Put potatoes, carrot, peas and beans into a bowl and stir in onion, pepper (capsicum), gherkins, capers, olives and mayonnaise while vegetables are still warm. Leave to cool. Arrange hard-boiled egg and chopped parsley on top before serving.

Serves 4.

SALADE NIÇOISE

225 g (8 oz) small green beans
1 crisp lettuce
4 ripe beef tomatoes, cut into wedges
1 red pepper (capsicum), chopped
3 hard-boiled eggs, quartered
200 g (7 oz) can tuna in olive oil, drained
leaves from small bunch of flat-leaf parsley, coarsely
   chopped
16 pitted black olives
6-8 anchovy fillets, halved lengthways
DRESSING:
8 tablespoons olive oil
2 teaspoons wine vinegar
1-2 cloves garlic, crushed
salt and freshly ground black pepper

Halve beans and cook in a saucepan of boiling salted water for 10 minutes, until tender. Drain, rinse in cold water and drain again. Leave to cool. Tear lettuce leaves and arrange on a large serving plate with beans, tomatoes, pepper (capsicum), eggs and tuna.

Scatter over parsley and olives. Arrange anchovies on top in a lattice pattern. To make dressing, whisk together olive oil, vinegar, garlic and salt and pepper. Pour over salad and serve.

Serves 4.

FRUITY CHEESE COLESLAW

1 red apple
3 teaspoons lemon juice
175 g (6 oz) white cabbage, finely shredded
2 sticks celery, finely sliced
115 g (4 oz) green grapes
115 g (4 oz) black grapes
55 g (2 oz) Cheddar cheese
55 g (2 oz) Gouda Cheese
2 tablespoons sunflower oil
2 tablespoons fromage frais or natural yogurt
1 teaspoon clear honey

Core the apple, cut apple into small chunks and toss in the lemon juice.

Lift the apple from the juice (reserving juice) and add to the cabbage and celery in a bowl. Cut the grapes in half, remove the pips and add to the salad. Cut the cheeses into small cubes and add to the other ingredients.

Mix the reserved lemon juice with the oil, fromage frais and honey and whisk until smooth, then fold into the salad.

Serves 4-6.

SQUID SALAD

450 g (1 lb) small or medium squid, prepared
300 ml (10 fl oz/1¼ cups) dry white wine
1 shallot, chopped
strip lemon peel
1 clove garlic, chopped
1 red onion, chopped
4 tablespoons chopped fresh mixed herbs such as
  basil, tarragon and flat-leaf parsley
DRESSING:
5 tablespoons extra virgin olive oil
2 tablespoons lemon juice
1 teaspoon balsamic vinegar
½ teaspoon Dijon mustard
Salt and freshly ground black pepper
Fresh herb sprigs to garnish

If squid are very small leave whole, otherwise slice flesh into rings. Put wine, shallot, lemon peel and garlic into a medium saucepan. Bring to the boil and cook for 1 minute. Add squid, in batches if necessary, and cook for 5-7 minutes until firm but still tender. Using a slotted spoon, remove to a serving dish and leave to cool.

Add onion and herbs to squid and toss to mix. To make dressing, mix ingredients together in a small bowl until evenly blended or shake together in a screw-top jar. Pour over salad and toss to mix. Chill for at least 30 minutes before serving garnished with fresh herb sprigs.

Serves 4.

MINTED SEAFOOD SALAD

150 ml (5 fl oz/⅔ cup) dry white wine
1 shallot, chopped
5 whole black peppercorns
450 g (1 lb) shelled scallops, fresh or frozen and
  thawed
450 g (1 lb) cooked large prawns
4 sticks celery
2 medium carrots
about 16 whole fresh mint leaves
½ teaspoon finely grated lemon peel
DRESSING:
juice 2 lemons
115 ml (4 fl oz/½ cup) extra virgin olive oil
1 tablespoon white wine vinegar
2 tablespoons chopped flat-leaf parsley
salt and freshly ground black pepper

Put white wine, shallot, peppercorns and 70 ml (2½ fl oz/⅓ cup) water in a shallow saucepan. Heat until boiling then add scallops. Lower the heat and poach for 5-6 minutes, until scallops are just firm and opaque. Using a slotted spoon transfer scallops to absorbent kitchen paper to drain and cool. Discard cooking liquid. Slice scallops in half horizontally. Put in a serving dish. Peel prawns and add to dish.

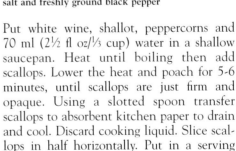

Cut celery and carrots into thin matchsticks and add to seafood with mint leaves and lemon peel. Toss lightly to mix. To make dressing mix ingredients together in a small bowl until evenly blended or put in a screw-top jar and shake until blended. Pour over salad and toss. Cover and refrigerate for 30 minutes before serving.

Serves 4-6.

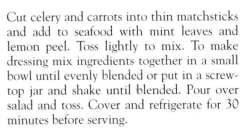

CRAB & AVOCADO SALAD

350 g (12 oz) dressed crab
1 tablespoon lime juice
grated rind 1 lime
1 tablespoon chopped fresh coriander
salt and freshly ground black pepper
2 ripe avocados
250 g (9 oz) mixed salad leaves
lime slices and coriander leaves, to garnish
LIME DRESSING:
1 tablespoon lime juice
70 ml (2½ fl oz/⅓ cup) olive oil
1 tablespoon chopped fresh coriander
½ teaspoon caster sugar

TUNA SALAD

3 small carrots, thickly sliced
225 g (8 oz) potato, diced
200 g (7 oz) can tuna in olive oil, drained and
  chopped
50 g (1¾ oz) can anchovy fillets in oil, drained and
  chopped
about 12 stoned black olives, halved
2 tablespoons capers in wine vinegar, drained
2 eggs, hard-boiled, quartered
4 tablespoons extra virgin olive oil
juice 1 small lemon
1 clove garlic, crushed
salt and freshly ground black pepper
1 tablespoon chopped flat-leaf parsley and sprigs, to
  garnish

Mix together crab, lime juice, lime rind, coriander and salt and pepper. Halve avocados lengthways, remove stones and peel. Cut flesh into 1 cm (½ in) cubes.

Cook carrots in a saucepan of boiling salted water for 4 minutes until tender. Cook potato in a separate pan of boiling salted water for about 7 minutes until tender. Drain and refresh both vegetables under cold running water. Drain and allow to cool completely.

To make lime dressing, in a large bowl, mix together lime juice, olive oil, coriander, sugar and salt and pepper. Put salad leaves into bowl and toss to coat thoroughly. Arrange salad leaves on serving plates. Put a spoonful of crab mixture in centre of each plate. Arrange diced avocado around crab mixture. Garnish with slices of lime and coriander leaves and serve.

Serves 6.

Put carrots and potatoes with tuna, anchovies, olives, capers and eggs into a large serving dish. Mix olive oil, lemon juice, garlic and salt and pepper together in a small bowl or put in a screw-top jar and shake until blended. Pour over salad and toss lightly to mix then garnish with chopped flat-leaf parsley and parsley sprigs.

Serves 4.

MORTADELLA SALAD

225 g (8 oz) piece mortadella
1 small red onion, sliced
½ yellow pepper (capsicum) packed in wine vinegar, drained
½ red pepper (capsicum) packed in wine vinegar, drained
3 small pickled gherkins, sliced
6 radishes, sliced
12 stoned green olives, halved
6 leaves Cos lettuce
DRESSING:
4 tablespoons extra virgin olive oil
2 tablespoons red wine vinegar
1 teaspoon Dijon mustard
1 tablespoon chopped flat-leaf parsley
salt and freshly ground black pepper

Cut mortadella into 1.5 cm (½ in) dice and place in a bowl with the onion. Cut red and yellow peppers (capsicum) into strips and add to bowl with gherkins, radishes and olives.

To make dressing mix ingredients together in a small bowl until evenly mixed or shake together in a screw-top jar. Pour over salad and toss to mix. Tear lettuce leaves into pieces and arrange on a serving plate. Arrange salad on top and serve at once.

Serves 4-6.

SPICY THAI SALAD

2 teaspoons sesame oil
2 red chillies, deseeded and chopped
1 clove garlic, crushed
juice 1 lime
2 teaspoons brown sugar
1 tablespoon fish sauce
1 stem lemon grass, chopped
2 tablespoons shredded fresh basil
225 g (8 oz) cooked chicken, shredded
55 g (2 oz) rice noodles
4 spring onions, sliced into matchstick strips
1 large carrot, cut into matchstick strips
1 yellow pepper (capsicum), cut into matchstick strips
3 Chinese leaves, shredded
2 tablespoons dry roasted peanuts, chopped

In a small pan, heat the oil and quickly fry the chillies and garlic, then remove from the heat and stir in the lime juice, sugar, fish sauce, lemon grass and basil. Pour mixture over the shredded chicken and allow to stand for 30 minutes.

Cook the rice noodles according to the packet instructions, then drain, rinse well in cold water and drain well again. Mix together the noodles, onions, carrot, pepper (capsicum) and Chinese leaves. Spoon over the chicken and sauce and sprinkle with the chopped peanuts.

Serves 4.

CHICKEN SATAY SALAD

2 tablespoons dry sherry
4 tablespoons crunchy peanut butter
2.5 cm (1 in) piece fresh root ginger, finely chopped
2 tablespoons hoisin sauce
3 teaspoons lemon juice
2 tablespoons dark soy sauce
150 ml (5 fl oz/⅔ cup) chicken stock or water
4 tablespoons sunflower seeds
2 teaspoons sesame oil
2 tablespoons vegetable oil
salt and pepper
1 Cos lettuce, washed and broken into leaves
115 g (4 oz) beansprouts
115 g (4 oz) cooked green beans
4 skinned and boned chicken breasts

MEXICAN CHICKEN SALAD

115 g (4 oz/⅔ cup) canned kidney beans, drained
115 g (4 oz/⅔ cup) canned chick peas, drained
1 red pepper (capsicum), sliced
3 Little Gem lettuces, shredded
3 teaspoons ready made English mustard
2 teaspoons sugar
2 tablespoons red wine vinegar
150 ml (5 fl oz/⅔ cup) olive oil
salt and pepper
4 teaspoons paprika
2 teaspoons cayenne pepper
1 teaspoon chilli powder
4 skinned and boned chicken breasts, cut into strips
2 tablespoons vegetable oil

Mix together the sherry, peanut butter, ginger, hoisin sauce, 2 teaspoons of the lemon juice and 1 tablespoon of the soy sauce. Mix well, then beat in the stock or water. Put the sunflower seeds in a pan over a high heat. Stir constantly and after about 1 minute the seeds should start to turn golden. Still stirring, add the remaining soy sauce; it will instantly evaporate and coat the seeds. Tip the seeds onto a saucer and leave to cool. Mix together the sesame oil, 1 tablespoon vegetable oil, the remaining lemon juice and salt and pepper.

Mix together the kidney beans, chick peas, red pepper (capsicum) and shredded lettuce and arrange on 4 serving plates. In a bowl, whisk together the mustard, sugar and vinegar and slowly drizzle in the olive oil, whisking well all the time to make a dressing the consistency of runny mayonnaise. Season with salt and pepper and set aside.

Put the lettuce leaves and beansprouts into a bowl, pour over the salad dressing and toss gently. Arrange the leaves and beans on 4 serving plates. Slice chicken into thin strips. In a frying pan, heat the remaining 1 tablespoon vegetable oil and add the chicken. Stir-fry over a high heat until the chicken starts to brown. Lower the heat and pour over the peanut butter mixture; stir until the sauce is simmering and thick. Spoon over the salad leaves and sprinkle with the sunflower seeds.

Mix the paprika, cayenne pepper and chilli powder together on a plate. Add the strips of chicken and toss until evenly coated in the mixture. Heat the vegetable oil in a frying pan and fry the coated chicken for 2-3 minutes or until cooked. Spoon the chicken over the salad and pour over the salad dressing. Serve immediately.

Serves 4.

Serves 4.

CORONATION CHICKEN

1 tablespoon olive oil
1 small onion, diced
2 teaspoons mild curry paste
200 g (7 oz) can chopped tomatoes
55 ml (2 fl oz/¼ cup) white wine
2 tablespoons hot mango chutney, chopped if
  necessary
2 teaspoons apricot jam
2 teaspoons lemon juice
150 ml (5 fl oz/⅔ cup) mayonnaise
150 ml (5 fl oz/⅔ cup) Greek yogurt
450 g (1 lb) cooked chicken
350 g (12 oz/2 cups) cooked, long-grain rice
1 red pepper (capsicum), diced
2 tablespoons chopped fresh mint
3 tablespoons prepared vinaigrette

In a small saucepan, heat the oil and fry the onion gently without browning until the onion is soft. Stir in the curry paste, tomatoes and wine, bring to the boil and simmer gently for 15 minutes. Add the chutney, jam and lemon juice and cook for a further 5 minutes until thick and syrupy.

Remove from the heat and strain into a small bowl; set aside to cool. When completely cold, stir in the mayonnaise and yogurt and mix well. Cut the chicken into large pieces and stir into the sauce. Combine the rice, pepper (capsicum), mint and vinaigrette and spoon onto a large serving dish and pile the chicken in the centre.

Serves 4.

CHICK PEA SALAD

350 g (12 oz/1½ cups) chick peas, soaked overnight
1 tablespoon finely chopped fresh parsley
1½ teaspoons finely chopped fresh tarragon
4 spring onions, finely chopped
sliced spring onion and flat-leaf parsley, to garnish
DRESSING:
2 cloves garlic, finely chopped
1 tablespoon red wine vinegar
2-3 teaspoons Dijon mustard
salt and freshly ground black pepper
4 tablespoons olive oil

Drain and rinse chick peas. Put in a saucepan and cover with cold water.

Bring to the boil. Cover pan and simmer for 1-1½ hours, until chick peas are tender. Meanwhile, make dressing. Mix together garlic, vinegar, mustard and salt and pepper. Slowly pour in the oil, whisking constantly.

Drain chick peas and immediately toss with dressing, parsley, tarragon and spring onion. Garnish with spring onion slices and flat-leaf parsley and serve warm.

Serves 4.

MEDITERRANEAN POTATO SALAD

450g (1 lb) new potatoes
115 g (4 oz) French beans, trimmed
115 g (4 oz) trimmed fennel
25 g (1 oz/¼ cup) stoned olives
2 tablespoons capers, drained
2 tablespoons chopped fresh chives
2 teaspoons chopped fresh tarragon
55 ml (2 fl oz/¼ cup) virgin olive oil
juice ½ lemon
2 eggs
400 g (14 oz) can artichoke hearts, drained and
    halved

POTATO SALAD

700 g (1½ lb) new potatoes
4-5 mint leaves, chopped
1 tablespoon chopped fresh chives
½ shallot, finely chopped
mint sprigs, to garnish
DRESSING:
1 tablespoon wine vinegar
2 teaspoons Dijon mustard
salt and freshly ground black pepper
3 tablespoons olive oil

Cook potatoes in a saucepan of boiling salted water for 15 minutes, until tender.

Cook the potatoes in a pan of lightly salted boiling water for 10-12 minutes until just cooked. Drain and place in a large bowl. Blanch the beans in boiling water for 1-2 minutes until just tender, drain and refresh under cold water; pat dry. Very thinly slice the fennel and halve the olives. Add to the potatoes with the beans, capers and herbs. Stir in the oil and lemon juice and set aside until potatoes are cold.

Meanwhile, make dressing. Whisk together vinegar, mustard and salt and pepper. Slowly pour in oil, whisking constantly.

Hard-boil the eggs, plunge into cold water and peel. Roughly chop and add to the salad with the artichoke hearts. Toss well and serve at once.

Serves 4-6.

Drain potatoes thoroughly, cut into halves or quarters, if necessary, then immediately toss with dressing, herbs and shallot. Leave to cool. Garnish with mint sprigs and serve.

Serves 4.

THREE BEAN SALAD

85 g (3 oz) dried flageolet beans
85 g (3 oz) dried red kidney beans
2 sprigs thyme
450 g (1 lb) fresh broad beans, podded
1 small onion, finely chopped
red pepper (capsicum) rings, to garnish
DRESSING:
115 ml (4 fl oz/½ cup) olive oil
juice 1 lemon
1 tablespoon chopped fresh mint
1 tablespoon chopped fresh parsley
salt and pepper

Put the flageolet and the kidney beans in 2 separate bowls.

Cover with water to come well above top of beans. Leave to soak for at least 6 hours. Drain. Put flageolet and kidney beans in 2 separate saucepans each with a sprig of thyme. Cover with water. Bring to the boil and boil briskly for 10 minutes. Cover pans and simmer for 1-1½ hours until beans are tender. In a pan of boiling water, cook broad beans for 5-10 minutes until tender. Drain all the beans and put into a bowl.

To make the dressing, in a bowl, mix together oil, lemon juice, mint, parsley, salt and pepper. Pour dressing over warm beans. Add chopped onion and mix well. Leave until cold, then transfer to a serving dish. Serve the salad garnished with rings of red pepper (capsicum).

Serves 6.

LENTIL SALAD

225 g (8 oz/1¼ cups) green lentils
55 ml (2 fl oz/¼ cup) olive oil
1 onion, finely chopped
3 tomatoes, peeled and chopped
salt and pepper
1 tablespoon chopped fresh parsley
2 tablespoons lemon juice
onion rings, chopped fresh parsley and lemon slices, to garnish

Put lentils in a bowl, cover with cold water and leave to soak for 3-4 hours. Drain well.

In a large saucepan, heat half the oil, add onion and cook until soft. Add tomatoes, cook for 1 minute, then add lentils. Cover with water, cover pan and simmer gently for 30 minutes, adding water if necessary, until lentils are tender and all water has been absorbed. The lentils should still be holding their shape.

Add salt, pepper, parsley, lemon juice and remaining oil to lentils. Mix carefully, then transfer to a serving dish and leave to cool. Serve garnished with onion rings, chopped parsley and lemon slices.

Serves 4-6.

PEA TABBOULEH

225 g (8 oz/1¼ cups) bulgar wheat
150 ml (5 fl oz/⅔ cup) olive oil
1 clove garlic, crushed
1 tablespoon red wine vinegar
1 tablespoon chopped fresh coriander
1 tablespoon chopped fresh mint
1 teaspoon ground coriander
½ teaspoon ground cumin
115 g (4 oz) sugar snap peas, trimmed
115 g (4 oz/1 cup) frozen peas, thawed
1 large ripe peach, stoned and chopped
1 red onion, finely chopped
salt and pepper

Cover the bulgar wheat with plenty of cold water and leave to soak for 30 minutes. Drain well and squeeze out excess liquid. Mix together the oil, garlic, vinegar, herbs and spices and pour over the bulgar, stir well, cover and set aside for 30 minutes.

Cook the sugar snap peas in boiling water for 2 minutes and the peas for 1 minute. Drain both and refresh under cold water. Pat all the peas dry. Stir into the bulgar wheat with the peaches, onion and seasonings.

Serves 4-6.

COUS COUS SALAD

115 g (4 oz/⅔ cup) quick-cook cous cous
1 fresh red chilli
225 g (8 oz) cherry tomatoes
1 bunch spring onions
4 tablespoons extra virgin olive oil
2 tablespoons lemon juice
4 tablespoons chopped fresh parsley
4 tablespoons chopped fresh coriander
salt and freshly ground black pepper
salad leaves, to serve

Put the cous cous in a bowl and pour over 150 ml (5 fl oz/⅔ cup) cold water. Leave for 30-60 minutes until the water has been completely absorbed.

Meanwhile, cut the chilli in half and remove the core and seeds. Finely chop the chilli. Cut the cherry tomatoes in half and slice the spring onions. Gently fluff up the cous cous with a fork.

Add the olive oil, lemon juice, parsley, coriander and salt and pepper to the cous cous. Gently stir in the chilli, tomatoes and spring onions. Leave for 1 hour. Line a serving dish with salad leaves, pile the cous cous in the centre and serve.

Serves 4.

WILD & BROWN RICE SALAD

115 g (4 oz/1 cup) wild rice
salt
175 g (6 oz/1¼ cups) brown rice
55 g (2 oz/⅔ cup) pecan nuts
6 spring onions, trimmed
55 g (2 oz/⅓ cup) dried cherries, cranberries or
  raisins
2 tablespoons chopped fresh coriander
1 tablespoon chopped fresh parsley
DRESSING:
100 ml (3½ fl oz/⅓ cup) olive oil
2 teaspoons raspberry vinegar
¼ teaspoon clear honey or sugar
salt and pepper

Cook the wild rice in a pan of lightly salted boiling water for 35-40 minutes until just tender. Cook the brown rice in a pan of lightly salted boiling water for 25 minutes or until just tender. Drain well and place both rices in a large bowl. Meanwhile, preheat oven to 220C (400F/Gas 6).

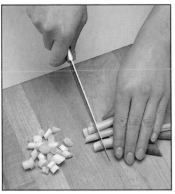

Roast the nuts in the oven for 5-6 minutes until browned; cool and coarsely chop. Set aside. Chop the spring onions and add to the rice with the dried fruit and herbs and stir well. Blend the dressing ingredients well together and pour over the salad, stir once, cover and leave rice to cool. Just before serving, toss in the roasted nuts and season to taste.

Serves 4-6.

WARM PASTA SALAD

225 g (8 oz) mixed mushrooms, wiped
25 g (1 oz/¼ cup) drained sun-dried tomatoes in oil,
  sliced
115 ml (4 fl oz/½ cup) olive oil
2 cloves garlic, chopped
grated zest 1 lemon
1 tablespoon lemon juice
2 tablespoons chopped fresh mint
225 g (8 oz/2½ cups) dried penne
2 ripe tomatoes, skinned, seeded and chopped
salt and pepper

Thinly slice the mushrooms and place in a large bowl with the sun-dried tomatoes.

Heat 1 tablespoon oil and sauté the garlic for 1 minute until starting to turn golden. Remove the pan from the heat and stir in the remaining oil, lemon zest, juice and mint, pour half over the mushrooms and reserve the rest. Stir mushrooms until well coated, cover and set aside to soften for several hours.

Cook the pasta in lightly salted, boiling water for 10 minutes until *al dente* (just cooked). Drain well, toss with the remaining dressing and stir into the marinated mushrooms with the fresh tomatoes. Season with salt and pepper.

Serves 4.

Note: Use a selection of button, field, oyster and shiitake mushrooms.

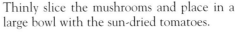

SESAME NOODLE SALAD

200 g (7 oz) fine rice noodles
1 carrot
4 spring onions, sliced
1 tablespoon toasted sesame seeds
coriander sprigs, to garnish
SESAME DRESSING:
5 teaspoons sesame paste
5 teaspoons sesame oil
5 teaspoons soy sauce
2 tablespoons rice vinegar
1 teaspoon sugar
1 teaspoon grated fresh root ginger
salt and freshly ground black pepper

Soak noodles as directed on packet, until soft. Drain and set aside.

Cut carrot into 2.5 cm (1 in) long matchsticks. Blanch in boiling water for 1 minute. Drain, rinse in cold water, drain again and set aside.

To make sesame dressing, in a large bowl, mix together sesame paste, sesame oil, soy sauce, rice vinegar, sugar, ginger and salt and pepper. Add noodles and toss to coat thoroughly. Stir in carrot and spring onion. Sprinkle with sesame seeds, garnish with coriander sprigs and serve at once.

Serves 6.

Variation: Add cooked, peeled prawns or diced ham before serving.

TORTELLONI SALAD

350 g (12 oz) green, cheese- or meat-filled tortelloni
115 ml (4 fl oz/½ cup) olive oil
2 cloves garlic, finely chopped
225 g (8 oz) asparagus, cut into 5 cm (2 in) pieces
175 g (6 oz) broccoli, cut into small flowerets
1 yellow pepper (capsicum), thinly sliced
175 g (6 oz) jar marinated artichoke hearts, drained
1 red onion, thinly sliced
2 tablespoons capers
3-4 tablespoons black olives
9 teaspoons red wine vinegar
3 teaspoons Dijon mustard
salt and freshly ground black pepper
3 tablespoons shredded fresh basil or parsley

In a large saucepan of boiling water, cook tortelloni according to packet directions. Drain and rinse. Drain again and toss with 1 tablespoon olive oil. Set aside. Heat wok until hot. Add 2 tablespoons olive oil to wok and swirl to coat. Add garlic, asparagus and broccoli and stir-fry for 4-5 minutes until vegetables are tender but still crisp. Add pepper (capsicum) and stir-fry for 1 minute. Remove vegetables to a large bowl and toss with reserved tortelloni, artichoke hearts, red onion, capers and olives. Allow to cool to room temperature.

In a small bowl, whisk together the wine vinegar, mustard, and salt and pepper to taste. Slowly whisk in remaining olive oil until creamy. Pour the dressing over the tortelloni and vegetables. Add the shredded basil or parsley and toss gently to mix well. Serve at room temperature.

Serves 4-6.

SIDE DISHES

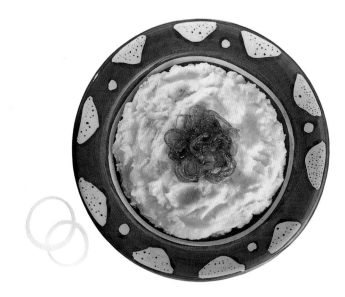

GARLIC & OLIVE OIL MASH

1 small garlic bulb
450 g (1 lb) floury potatoes, cut into chunks
55 ml (2 fl oz/¼ cup) milk
5 tablespoons extra virgin olive oil
salt and freshly ground black pepper
2 onions, finely sliced
1 tablespoon balsamic vinegar
1 tablespoon extra virgin olive oil, to serve

Preheat the oven to 200C (400F/Gas 6). Cut the top off the garlic bulb. Wrap the garlic loosely in foil and cook in the oven for 20-30 minutes until soft.

Cook the potatoes in a saucepan of boiling salted water for 15-20 minutes until soft. Drain thoroughly and return to the pan. Heat the milk until warm. Squeeze the soft garlic cloves out of their skins and add to the potatoes. Mash the potatoes. Gradually stir in 4 tablespoons of the oil, alternating with the milk, until the potatoes reach the desired consistency. Season with salt and pepper.

Meanwhile, heat the remaining oil in a frying pan. Add the onions and cook slowly, stirring frequently, for 20 minutes or until soft and golden brown. Stir in the balsamic vinegar. Top the potatoes with the fried onions, drizzle with olive oil and serve.

Serves 4.

GARLIC-ROASTED POTATOES

900 g (2 lb) new potatoes
12 unpeeled shallots
12 unpeeled cloves garlic
1 tablespoon chopped fresh sage
1 tablespoon chopped fresh thyme or rosemary
4 tablespoons hazelnut or olive oil
salt and pepper

Preheat oven to 200C (400F/Gas 6). Wash and dry the potatoes and halve any large ones. Trim the shallots, removing any dirt that may be trapped in the root ends and combine with the potatoes, garlic and herbs.

Put the oil into a roasting tin and place in the oven for 5 minutes until hot and starting to smoke. Add the potato and shallot mixture (taking care not to splash the hot oil) and stir until the potatoes, shallots, garlic and herbs are well coated.

Return to the oven and cook for 50-60 minutes until roasted and golden, turning from time to time to brown evenly. Transfer to a hot serving dish and serve at once.

Serves 6.

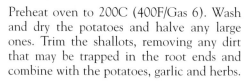

POTATOES WITH CHORIZO

4 tablespoons olive oil
115 g (4 oz) chorizo, chopped
700 g (1½ lb) potatoes, coarsely chopped
1 Spanish onion, chopped
1 red pepper (capsicum), chopped
350 g (12 oz) beefsteak tomatoes, peeled, seeded and
   chopped
salt and freshly ground black pepper
chicken or veal stock, or water, to cover
mint sprigs, to garnish

Heat oil in a flameproof casserole. Add chorizo and cook, stirring occasionally, until fat runs. Remove chorizo.

Add potatoes and onion and cook, stirring occasionally, for 5 minutes. Stir in red pepper (capsicum), fry for 5 minutes, then add tomatoes and return chorizo to pan. Season with salt and pepper.

Just cover with stock or water and simmer for about 15 minutes until potatoes are tender and most of the liquid has been absorbed. Garnish with mint sprigs and serve.

Serves 4.

POTATOES FORESTIÈRE

375 g (12 oz) mixed mushrooms
450 g (1 lb) potatoes
olive oil for greasing
leaves from a bunch of parsley or basil
4 cloves garlic, crushed
salt and freshly ground black pepper
flat-leaf parsley sprigs and basil leaves, to garnish

Thinly slice mushrooms and potatoes. Preheat oven to 180C (350F/Gas 4).

Generously oil an ovenproof dish that will hold potatoes and mushrooms in a layer no more than 4 cm (1½ in) deep. In a large bowl, toss together mushrooms, potatoes, parsley or basil, garlic and salt and pepper.

Spread potato mixture into dish in an even layer and bake for about 45 minutes, until potatoes are tender, turning mixture halfway through. Leave to stand for a couple of minutes. Garnish with flat-leaf parsley and basil and serve.

Serves 4.

GRATIN SAVOYARD

1 kg (2¼ lb) potatoes
175 g (6 oz/1½ cups) grated Gruyère cheese
freshly grated nutmeg
salt and freshly ground black pepper
about 250 ml (9 fl oz/1 cup) chicken or vegetable
   stock
55 g (2 oz/¼ cup) butter, plus extra for greasing
flat-leaf parsley sprigs, to garnish

Slice potatoes very thinly, keeping them in a bowl of cold water before slicing. Preheat oven to 200C (400F/Gas 6).

Grease a shallow ovenproof dish with butter. Layer potatoes in dish, sprinkling each layer with cheese, nutmeg and salt and pepper, and finishing with a layer of cheese.

Pour over enough stock to come almost to the top of potatoes. Dot with butter. Bake for 10 minutes. Lower oven temperature to 180C (350F/Gas 4) and bake for 50 minutes, until potatoes are tender and top is golden, and adding more stock if potatoes start to become dry. Garnish with parsley and serve.

Serves 4.

PURÉED GINGER CARROTS

900 g (2 lb) carrots, scrubbed
150 ml (5 fl oz/⅔ cup) vegetable stock
2 tablespoons hazelnut oil
1 large onion, chopped
1 clove garlic, chopped
2 teaspoons grated fresh root ginger
1 teaspoon ground cumin
pinch freshly grated nutmeg
salt and pepper
mint sprigs, to garnish

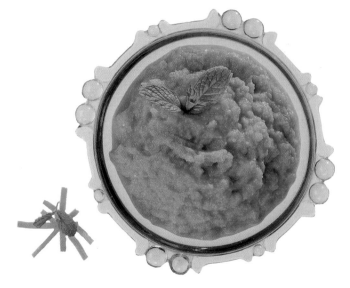

Roughly chop the carrots and place in a large pan with the stock. Bring slowly to the boil, cover and simmer gently for 20 minutes until carrots are cooked.

Heat 1 tablespoon oil and fry the onion, garlic, ginger and cumin for 5 minutes until soft. Transfer to a blender or food processor, add the cooked carrots and their juices and purée until smooth. Pass through a food mill or fine sieve if the purée is not completely smooth.

Beat in the remaining oil, freshly grated nutmeg and salt and pepper to taste and serve hot, garnished with mint.

Serves 6.

Note: This purée can easily be made ahead of time. To reheat, place in an ovenproof dish, cover with foil and bake in the oven for 20 minutes at 200C (400F/Gas 6). Or microwave on medium for 6-8 minutes until hot.

CAROTTES VICHY

450 g (1 lb) young carrots, thinly sliced diagonally
small pinch of bicarbonate of soda
salt
25 g (1 oz/2 tablespoons) unsalted butter
2 teaspoons sugar
1 tablespoon finely chopped fresh chervil or parsley
chervil sprigs, to garnish

Put carrots in a heavy saucepan and add enough water to just cover. Add bicarbonate of soda and a little salt.

Bring to the boil then simmer, uncovered, stirring occasionally, until carrots are tender and nearly all the water has evaporated.

Add the butter and sugar and cook, shaking pan frequently, until carrots are lightly coated with glaze. Sprinkle with chervil or parsley, garnish with chervil sprigs and serve.

Serves 4.

GLAZED BABY ONIONS

575 g (1¼ lb) pickling onions
55 g (2 oz) unsalted butter
1 tablespoon caster sugar
salt and freshly ground black pepper
100 ml (3½ fl oz/⅓ cup) chicken or vegetable stock

Peel onions by plunging them into boiling water for 1 minute, then drain well and refresh under cold running water and peel off the skins.

Melt the butter in a heavy non-stick pan and add onions in a single layer. Sprinkle the sugar over them and add salt and pepper to taste. Cover and cook over very gentle heat for 20-30 minutes until the onions are tender and caramelized, shaking pan often.

Add the stock, bring to the boil and simmer without the lid for 5 minutes or until the sauce is syrupy. Serve immediately.

Serves 4.

TOMATO & AUBERGINE GRATIN

1 medium aubergine (eggplant)
salt and freshly ground pepper
450 g (1 lb) ripe red tomatoes
150 ml (5 fl oz/⅔ cup) olive oil
3 tablespoons freshly grated Parmesan cheese

Using a sharp knife, slice the aubergine (eggplant) into 3 mm (⅛ in) slices. Sprinkle with salt and place in a colander to drain for 30 minutes. Rinse well and pat dry with absorbent kitchen paper.

Preheat oven to 200C (400F/Gas 6). Halve tomatoes through the middle. Heat oil in a frying pan and fry the aubergine (eggplant) slices in batches until golden brown. Drain on absorbent kitchen paper.

Arrange the tomato halves and aubergine (eggplant) slices haphazardly in a shallow ovenproof dish. Season with salt and pepper and sprinkle with Parmesan cheese. Bake in the oven for 10-15 minutes until browned. Cool slightly and serve warm.

Serves 6.

HERBY PEAS

2 tablespoons olive oil
1 onion, finely chopped
2 cloves garlic, chopped
225 g (8 oz) shelled peas
115 ml (4 fl oz/½ cup) dry white wine
bouquet garni of 2 sprigs parsley, 1 sprig thyme and
  1 bay leaf
8 saffron threads
salt and freshly ground black pepper
mint sprigs and strips of peeled red pepper
  (capsicum), to garnish

In a flameproof casserole, heat oil, add onion and cook for about 5 minutes, stirring occasionally, until soft but not coloured. Add 1 clove garlic, cook for 1 minute, then stir in peas, wine and bouquet garni. Heat until simmering, then cover and cook gently for about 15 minutes until peas are tender. Discard bouquet garni.

Using a pestle and mortar, crush together remaining garlic, the saffron and a pinch salt to make a smooth paste. Stir in a little of the cooking liquid, then stir mixture into peas. Add black pepper and cook for a few more minutes. Serve garnished with mint sprigs and strips of red pepper (capsicum).

Serves 4.

TOMATOES WITH GARLIC CRUST

OKRA & TOMATOES

6 slices stale bread
55 g (2 oz) anchovies in oil, drained
6 cloves garlic, finely chopped
3 tablespoons chopped fresh parsley
salt and freshly ground pepper
700 g (1½ lb) small plum tomatoes
3 tablespoons olive oil
extra chopped fresh parsley, to garnish

450 g (1 lb) small okra
55 ml (2 fl oz/¼ cup) olive oil
1 small onion, chopped
1 small leek, chopped
450 g (1 lb) tomatoes, peeled (see page 293) and
  chopped
25 g (1 oz) sun-dried tomatoes, chopped
1 clove garlic, crushed
1 tablespoon lemon juice
1 teaspoon sugar
salt and freshly ground black pepper
oregano leaves, to garnish

Preheat oven to 220C (425F/Gas 7). Tear up bread and place in a food processor with anchovies. Blend bread to crumbs, then dry-fry in a frying pan until crumbs are golden. Stir in garlic, parsley, salt and pepper.

Cut the stalks off the okra but do not pierce the pods. Wash the pods, drain and pat dry.

Halve tomatoes around middle and place cut side up, close together in a single layer in a shallow roasting tin or dish. Sprinkle the breadcrumb mixture evenly over tomatoes and drizzle with olive oil.

Heat the oil in a large frying pan. Add the onion and leek and cook for 7 minutes until softened and lightly coloured. Add the okra and turn carefully to coat in the oil. Cook for 5 minutes.

Bake in oven for about 20 minutes until crust is golden and tomatoes are soft. The tomatoes will slightly disintegrate under the crust. Garnish with more chopped parsley and serve at once.

Serves 6.

Add the tomatoes, sun-dried tomatoes, garlic, lemon juice, sugar and salt and pepper. Cover the pan and simmer for 10 minutes. Remove the lid and cook for 10 minutes or until the okra is tender and the sauce reduced and thickened. If the sauce reduces too quickly, add a little water. Garnish with oregano leaves and serve hot or warm.

Serves 4.

FENNEL & PARMESAN GRATIN

4 small fennel bulbs
3 tablespoons lemon juice
55 g (2 oz/4 tablespoons) unsalted butter
1 tablespoon olive oil
55 g (2 oz) freshly grated Parmesan cheese
salt and freshly ground black pepper
25 g (1 oz/¼ cup) toasted flaked almonds

Trim feathery fronds from fennel and reserve. Cut fennel lengthways into quarters.

Add fennel and lemon juice to a saucepan of boiling salted water and cook for 15 minutes, until fennel is tender but still crisp. Drain, place on kitchen paper and drain thoroughly.

Preheat oven to 200C (400F/Gas 6). Arrange fennel in a single layer in an oven-proof dish, dot with butter, sprinkle with olive oil and cheese, season with plenty of black pepper and bake, uncovered, for 20-25 minutes until golden. Sprinkle with almonds, garnish with reserved fennel fronds and serve.

Serves 4.

COURGETTE GRATIN

1 kg (2¼ lb) courgettes (zucchini), sliced
85 g (3 oz/⅓ cup) butter
450 g (1 lb) ripe tomatoes, peeled, seeded and chopped
2 cloves garlic, chopped
2 tablespoons chopped fresh basil or parsley
salt and freshly ground black pepper
55 g (2 oz/1 cup) fresh breadcrumbs
4-5 tablespoons finely grated Gruyère cheese
basil sprigs, to garnish

Put courgettes (zucchini) in a colander, sprinkle generously with salt and leave for 1 hour. Rinse well, drain and dry thoroughly with kitchen paper.

Preheat oven to 200C (400F/Gas 6). Heat 55 g (2 oz/¼ cup) butter in a frying pan, add courgettes (zucchini) and cook, stirring occasionally, for 7 minutes, until browned. Remove with a slotted spoon and set aside.

Add tomatoes, garlic, basil or parsley and salt and pepper to frying pan, bring to the boil and simmer gently until thickened. Stir in courgettes (zucchini). Turn into a shallow ovenproof dish. Mix together breadcrumbs and cheese and sprinkle over courgettes, (zucchini). Dot with remaining butter and bake for 25 minutes. Garnish with basil sprigs and serve.

Serves 4-6.

FENNEL SICILIANO

3 fennel bulbs
55 g (2 oz/1 cup) fresh breadcrumbs
25 g (1 oz/¼ cup) pine nuts
25 g (1 oz/¼ cup) raisins
1 teaspoon chopped fresh thyme
25 g (1 oz/¼ cup) grated Parmesan cheese
4 tablespoons olive oil
salt and freshly ground black pepper
fennel leaves, to garnish

Preheat the oven to 190C (375F/Gas 5). Trim the fennel and discard the outer leaves, if necessary. Quarter the bulbs and thinly slice.

Bring a saucepan of salted water to the boil. Add the fennel and simmer for 3-5 minutes until just soft. Drain thoroughly. Brush an ovenproof dish with olive oil and arrange the fennel slices in it in an even layer.

Mix together the breadcrumbs, pine nuts, raisins, thyme, Parmesan, olive oil and salt and pepper. Sprinkle the mixture over the fennel, making sure the raisins are beneath the surface. Bake for 20-30 minutes, until golden. Garnish with fennel leaves and serve.

Serves 4.

BEANS IN TOMATO SAUCE

6 tablespoons olive oil
2 cloves garlic, chopped
1 small onion, finely chopped
2 sprigs fresh sage
1 kg (2¼ lb) broad beans, shelled
400 g (14 oz) can chopped plum tomatoes
1 tablespoon sun-dried tomato paste
salt and freshly ground black pepper
fresh sage leaves to garnish

Heat oil in a large, heavy-based saucepan. Add garlic, onion and sage and cook gently for 4-5 minutes to soften.

Stir in beans, tomatoes and sun-dried tomato paste and bring to the boil. Lower the heat, cover and cook for 20 minutes, stirring frequently, until beans are tender. Discard sage sprigs and season with salt and ground black pepper. Serve hot garnished with sage leaves.

Serves 4-6.

GREEN BEANS WITH ONION

450 g (1 lb) green beans
9 teaspoons olive oil
2 onions, chopped
1 clove garlic, crushed
4 teaspoons tomato purée (paste)
1 tablespoon chopped fresh oregano
salt and pepper
finely chopped red pepper (capsicum) or oregano
  sprig, to garnish

Top and tail beans. In a large saucepan, heat oil. Add onions and garlic. Cook for 5-10 minutes until soft.

Mix the tomato purée (paste) with 175 ml (6 fl oz/¾ cup) water. Put beans in pan with onion. Pour tomato mixture over them, then add more water, if necessary, to just cover the beans.

Add oregano, salt and pepper. Cover pan and simmer for 15-20 minutes until beans are tender. Remove lid and boil to reduce the liquid. Serve garnished with chopped red pepper (capsicum) or a sprig of oregano.

Serves 4.

SPINACH WITH RAISINS

55 g (2 oz) raisins
1 kg (2¼ lb) spinach
3 tablespoons olive oil
1 clove garlic, finely chopped
3 tablespoons pine nuts
salt and freshly ground black pepper
croûtons, to serve

Put raisins into a small bowl, cover with boiling water and leave to soak.

Wash spinach, shake off surplus water but do not dry the leaves. Put into a large saucepan, cover and cook until spinach wilts. Uncover and cook until excess moisture has evaporated. Chop coarsely. Drain raisins.

Heat oil in a frying pan, add garlic and pine nuts and fry, stirring occasionally, until beginning to colour. Stir in spinach and raisins, add salt and pepper and cook over low heat for 5 minutes. Serve with croûtons sprinkled over the top.

Serves 4.

BROAD BEANS WITH DILL

1 kg (2¼ lb) fresh broad beans
55 ml (2 fl oz/¼ cup) olive oil
1 onion, finely chopped
1 clove garlic, crushed
2 tablespoons chopped fresh dill
salt and pepper
dill sprigs, to garnish
yogurt, to serve

Shell broad beans. In a saucepan, heat oil. Add onion and garlic and cook gently until just beginning to colour.

Add beans and cook gently for 2-3 minutes. Add enough hot water to just cover beans, stir in chopped dill and season with salt and pepper. Cook, covered, for 10 minutes or until beans are tender.

When beans are tender, remove lid and cook briskly until liquid has almost evaporated. Garnish with sprigs of dill and serve with yogurt.

Serves 6.

BROAD BEANS & ARTICHOKES

700 g (1½ lb) broad beans, shelled
400 g (14 oz) can artichoke hearts
3 teaspoons olive oil
1 teaspoon cornflour
3 teaspoons lemon juice
1 tablespoon chopped fresh parsley
salt and pepper
chopped fresh parsley, to garnish

In a saucepan of boiling water, cook beans for 10 minutes or until tender. Drain, reserving 55 ml (2 fl oz/¼ cup) of the water.

Drain and rinse artichoke hearts; cut in half. In a saucepan, heat olive oil. Add broad beans and artichokes. In a bowl, mix cornflour and lemon juice and stir into reserved cooking water. Stir parsley, salt and pepper into cornflour mixture.

Pour cornflour mixture over beans and artichokes. Bring to the boil and cook until sauce is slightly thickened. Serve with more parsley scattered over the top.

Serves 6.

SZECHUAN AUBERGINE

450 g (1 lb) small aubergines (eggplants), cut into
   2.5 cm (1 in) cubes or thin slices
salt
2 tablespoons groundnut oil
2 cloves garlic, finely chopped
2.5 cm (1 in) piece fresh root ginger, peeled and
   finely chopped
3-4 spring onions, finely sliced
2 tablespoons dark soy sauce
3-6 teaspoons chilli bean paste or sauce or 1
   teaspoon crushed dried chillies
1 tablespoon yellow bean paste (optional)
2 tablespoons dry sherry or rice wine
3 teaspoons cider vinegar
1 tablespoon sugar
chopped fresh parsley, to garnish

Place aubergine (eggplant) cubes in a plastic
or stainless steel colander or sieve, placed on
a plate or baking sheet. Sprinkle with salt
and leave to stand 30 minutes. Rinse
aubergine (eggplant) under cold running
water and turn out onto layers of absorbent
kitchen paper; pat dry thoroughly. Heat wok
until very hot. Add oil and swirl to coat wok.
Add garlic, ginger and spring onions and stir-
fry for 1-2 minutes until spring onions begin
to soften. Add aubergine (eggplant) and stir-
fry for 2-3 minutes until softened and beginning to brown.

Stir in remaining ingredients and 150 ml
(5 fl oz/⅔ cup) water and bring to the boil.
Reduce the heat and simmer for 5-7 minutes
until aubergine (eggplant) is very tender,
stirring frequently. Increase heat to high and
stir-fry mixture until the liquid is almost
completely reduced. Spoon into serving dish
and garnish with parsley.

Serves 4-6.

COURGETTES WITH GINGER

2 tablespoons vegetable oil
small piece fresh root ginger, peeled and sliced
1 teaspoon minced garlic
450 g (1 lb) courgettes (zucchini), peeled and cut
   into small wedges
1 small carrot, sliced
2-3 tablespoons stock or water
55 g (2 oz) straw mushrooms, halved lengthways
1 tomato, sliced
2 spring onions, cut into short lengths
salt and freshly ground pepper
½ teaspoon sugar
1 tablespoon fish sauce

Heat oil in a wok or frying pan and stir-fry
ginger and garlic for about 30 seconds until
fragrant. Add the courgettes (zucchini) and
carrot and stir-fry for about 2 minutes, then
add the stock or water to create steam, and
continue stirring another 1-2 minutes.

Add straw mushrooms, tomato and spring
onions with salt, pepper and sugar, blend
well and cook for a further 1-2 minutes.
Sprinkle with fish sauce and serve at once.

Serves 4.

Variation: Other fresh delicate vegetables,
such as asparagus, mange tout (snow peas),
green peppers (capsicums) or cucumber can
all be cooked in the same way.

BROCCOLI & TOMATOES

900 g (2 lb) ripe tomatoes
3 tablespoons olive oil
1 clove garlic, crushed
2 teaspoons lemon juice
1 teaspoon hot chilli sauce
1 teaspoon balsamic vinegar
450 g (1 lb) broccoli
25 g (1 oz/¼ cup) stoned black olives, sliced
25 g (1 oz/¼ cup) pine nuts, toasted
1 tablespoon chopped fresh parsley
15 g (½ oz/¼ cup) Parmesan shavings

Place the tomatoes in a large heatproof bowl and pour over boiling water to cover.

Leave for 1 minute, then drain, refresh under cold water and pat dry. Skin and discard the skins and seeds and finely chop the flesh. Heat the oil in a large saucepan, add the tomatoes, garlic, lemon juice, chilli sauce and vinegar. Bring to the boil, cover and cook for 10 minutes. Uncover, increase the heat and cook until slightly reduced and thickened.

Meanwhile, trim the broccoli and steam for 5 minutes. Add to the sauce with the olives, nuts and parsley and stir well until combined. Transfer to a warmed serving dish, sprinkle over the Parmesan shavings and serve at once.

Serves 4.

BROCCOLI WITH CHILLIES

450 g (1 lb) broccoli
olive oil
2 cloves garlic, sliced
2 dried red chillies, seeded and crushed
salt

Cut thick broccoli stems in half or thirds lengthways. Add all of broccoli to a saucepan of boiling salted water, boil for 2 minutes, then drain and rinse under cold running water.

Heat olive oil in a heavy-based frying pan sufficiently large to hold broccoli in a single layer. Add garlic and chillies to pan. Cook over a moderate heat until sizzling, 3-4 minutes.

Add broccoli, turn to coat in oil then reduce heat to very low. Pour in 115 ml (4 fl oz/ ½ cup) water, add salt and cover tightly. Cook very gently for about 20 minutes, turning broccoli carefully 2 or 3 times, until broccoli is very tender. If necessary, uncover and boil off excess liquid. Serve hot or warm.

Serves 4.

SPICY CAULIFLOWER

55 g (2 oz/¼ cup) whole almonds
1 large cauliflower, divided into flowerets
55 g (2 oz/4 tablespoons) butter
1 onion, finely chopped
½ teaspoon chilli powder
½ teaspoon turmeric
3-4 tablespoons lemon juice
55 g (2 oz/½ cup) dried breadcrumbs
salt and freshly ground black pepper
lime wedges and parsley sprigs, to garnish

Heat the wok until hot. Add the almonds and stir-fry over a moderate heat until browned on all sides. Remove to a plate. When cool, chop almonds coarsely.

Half-fill the wok with water and over high heat bring to the boil. Add the cauliflower pieces and simmer for 2 minutes. Drain and rinse; set aside. Wipe wok dry and return to heat. Add butter to wok and swirl until melted. Add the onion, chilli powder and turmeric and stir-fry for 2-3 minutes until softened.

Add the blanched cauliflower pieces and lemon juice and stir-fry for 3-4 minutes until tender but still crisp. Add the breadcrumbs and chopped almonds and toss until cauliflower pieces are well coated. Season with salt and pepper. Turn into a serving dish and serve hot, garnished with lime wedges and parsley.

Serves 4-6.

GINGERED BRUSSELS SPROUTS

3 tablespoons vegetable oil
1 onion, cut lengthwise in half and thinly sliced
1-2 cloves garlic, finely chopped
2.5 cm (1 in) piece fresh root ginger, peeled and cut into julienne strips
1 kg (2¼ lb) Brussels sprouts, washed, trimmed and shredded
1 tablespoon crystallized ginger, chopped, or 1 piece stem ginger in syrup, chopped
salt and cayenne pepper

Heat the wok until hot. Add oil and swirl to coat wok. Add onion, garlic and ginger and stir-fry for 1 minute. Add remaining oil. Stir in the shredded sprouts and crystallized or stem ginger and stir-fry for 2-3 minutes.

Add 2 tablespoons water and cook, covered, for 2-3 minutes, stirring once or twice. Uncover and add 1 tablespoon water if sprouts seem too dry. Stir in salt and cayenne pepper and turn into a serving dish.

Serves 4-6.

MUSHROOM CURRY

500 g (1 lb) button mushrooms
2 fresh green chillies, seeded
2 teaspoons ground coriander
1 teaspoon ground cumin
½ teaspoon chilli powder
2 cloves garlic, crushed
1 onion, cut into wedges
155 ml (5 fl oz/⅔ cup) Coconut Milk (see glossary)
salt
30 g (1 oz/6 teaspoons) butter or ghee
bay leaves, to garnish

Wipe mushrooms and trim stalks, then set aside.

Put chillies, ground coriander, cumin, chilli powder, garlic, onion, coconut milk and salt to taste in a blender or food processor fitted with a metal blade and blend until smooth.

Melt butter in a saucepan, add mushrooms and fry for 3-4 minutes, until golden brown. Pour over spicy coconut milk and simmer, uncovered, for 10 minutes or until mushrooms are tender. Serve hot, garnished with bay leaves.

Serves 4.

PEPPERS WITH CAULIFLOWER

55 ml (2 fl oz/¼ cup) vegetable oil
1 large onion, sliced
2 cloves garlic, crushed
2 green chillies, seeded and chopped
1 cauliflower, cut into small flowerets
½ teaspoon turmeric
1 teaspoon garam masala
1 green pepper (capsicum)
1 red pepper (capsicum)
1 orange or yellow pepper (capsicum)
salt and pepper
1 tablespoon chopped fresh coriander, to garnish

Heat oil in a large saucepan, add onion and fry over a medium heat for 8 minutes or until soft and golden brown. Stir in garlic, chillies and cauliflower and fry for 5 minutes, stirring occasionally. Stir in turmeric and garam masala and fry for 1 minute.

Reduce heat, add 55 ml (2 fl oz/¼ cup) water and cook, covered, for 10-15 minutes, until cauliflower is almost tender. Cut peppers (capsicums) in half lengthwise, remove stalks and seeds, then slice peppers (capsicums) finely. Add to pan and cook for a further 3-5 minutes, until softened. Season with salt and pepper. Serve hot, garnished with chopped coriander.

Serves 4.

AUBERGINES IN SPICY SAUCE

450 g (1 lb) aubergines (eggplant), cut into small
 strips, rather like potato chips
2-3 tablespoons vegetable oil
1 clove garlic, chopped
2 shallots, finely chopped
salt and freshly ground black pepper
½ teaspoon sugar
2-3 small hot red chillies, seeded and chopped
2 tomatoes, cut into wedges
1 tablespoon soy sauce
1 teaspoon chilli sauce
1 tablespoon rice vinegar
about 115 ml (4 fl oz/½ cup) vegetarian stock
2 teaspoons cornflour
½ teaspoon sesame oil
coriander sprigs, to garnish

Stir-fry the aubergines (eggplants) in a dry
wok or frying pan for 3-4 minutes until soft
and a small amount of natural juice has
appeared. Remove and set aside. Heat the oil
and stir-fry garlic and shallots for about 30
seconds. Add the aubergines (eggplants),
salt, pepper, sugar and chillies and stir-fry for
2-3 minutes.

Add the tomatoes, soy sauce, chilli sauce,
vinegar and stock, blend well and bring to
the boil. Reduce heat and simmer for 3-4
minutes. Mix cornflour with 1 tablespoon
water and stir into sauce to thicken it. Blend
in sesame oil, garnish and serve at once.

Serves 4.

Variation: For non-vegetarians, fish sauce or
shrimp paste can be used instead of soy
sauce. Chicken stock can be used instead of
the vegetarian stock.

CAULIFLOWER & COCONUT

1 cauliflower
2 tablespoons light olive oil
1 teaspoon sesame oil
1 red chilli, seeded and sliced
1 cm (½ in) piece fresh root ginger, peeled and finely
 chopped
2 shallots, thinly sliced
25 g (1 oz/⅓ cup) desiccated coconut
1 tablespoon light soy sauce
1 teaspoon sherry vinegar

Trim and discard the cauliflower leaves and
cut out the central core. Cut flowerets into
bite-sized pieces and steam for 5-6 minutes
until just tender.

Meanwhile, heat 1 tablespoon olive oil and
the sesame oil in a non-stick frying pan and
fry the chilli, ginger and shallots for 5
minutes until softened.

Add the coconut and stir-fry over a medium
heat for 3-4 minutes until golden. Stir in the
cauliflower, remaining oil, soy sauce and
vinegar and serve hot or warm.

Serves 4.

STIR-FRIED VEGETABLES

2 tablespoons vegetable oil
1 clove garlic, chopped
1 teaspoon chopped fresh root ginger
1 carrot, sliced
115 g (4 oz) baby corn cobs, halved
1-2 young leeks, sliced
1-2 bok choy (Chinese cabbage), cut into small
   pieces
115 g (4 oz) mange tout (snow peas)
115 g (4 oz) bean sprouts
salt and freshly ground black pepper
1 tablespoon soy sauce
2 teaspoons cornflour
½ teaspoon sesame oil (optional)

SPICED CABBAGE

14 black peppercorns
2 tablespoons coconut cream (see glossary)
2 shallots, chopped
115 g (4 oz) lean pork, very finely chopped
about 450 g (1 lb) white cabbage, finely sliced
300 ml (10 fl oz/1¼ cups) coconut milk
1 tablespoon fish sauce
1 fresh red chilli, seeded and very finely chopped

In a wok, heat peppercorns for about 3 minutes until aroma changes. Stir in coconut cream, heat for 2-3 minutes, then stir in shallots.

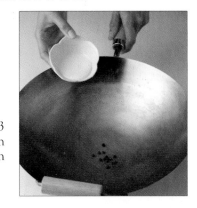

Heat oil in a wok or frying-pan and stir-fry garlic and ginger for about 30 seconds. Add the carrot, baby corn, leeks, bok choy and mange tout (snow peas) and stir-fry for about 2 minutes.

Stir-fry for a further 2-3 minutes, then stir in pork and cabbage. Cook, stirring occasionally, for 3 minutes, then add coconut milk and bring just to the boil. Cover and simmer for 5 minutes.

Add bean sprouts and continue stir-frying for 1 minute. Add salt, pepper and soy sauce and stir-fry for a further 2 minutes. Mix cornflour with 1 tablespoon water and stir into the gravy to thicken it. Finally blend in sesame oil, if using, then serve vegetables hot or cold.

Serves 4-6.

Variation: Fish or oyster sauce can be used instead of soy sauce for non-vegetarians.

Uncover and cook for about 10 minutes until cabbage is tender but retains some bite. Stir in fish sauce. Serve sprinkled with chilli.

Serves 4-5.

POLENTA WITH VEGETABLES

salt and freshly ground black pepper
115 g (4 oz/scant 1 cup) polenta
15 g (½ oz/1 tablespoon) butter
1 small aubergine (eggplant), thinly sliced
1 courgette (zucchini), thinly sliced
115 ml (4 fl oz/½ cup) olive oil
1 red pepper (capsicum), quartered
basil sprigs, to garnish

Put 550 ml (20 fl oz/2½ cups) water in a saucepan and bring to the boil. Add a pinch of salt then pour in the polenta in a fine, steady stream, stirring vigorously with a wooden spoon.

Simmer gently for 5-10 minutes, stirring frequently, until the polenta is thick and no longer grainy. Remove the pan from the heat and stir in the butter and black pepper. Turn the polenta on to an oiled baking sheet or wooden board and spread out to a thickness of 0.5-1 cm (¼-½ in). Cool, cover and chill for 1 hour. With a 6-7.5 cm (2½-3 in) pastry cutter, cut into eight circles. Preheat the grill. Brush the aubergine (eggplant) and courgette (zucchini) with oil and grill until browned on both sides. Keep warm.

Grill the pepper (capsicum) quarters and peel (see page 29). Keep warm. Brush the polenta circles with oil and grill for 3-4 minutes on each side until browned and crisp. Place a polenta circle on each of four serving plates and arrange the vegetable slices on top. Season with salt and pepper and top with a polenta circle. Garnish with basil and serve.

Serves 4.

MIXED VEGETABLES

2-3 tablespoons vegetable oil
350 g (12 oz) bok choy (Chinese leaves), cut into
  large pieces
4-6 dried Chinese mushrooms, soaked and sliced
55 g (2 oz) bean thread vermicelli, soaked and cut
  into short lengths
55 g (2 oz) dried bean curd sticks, soaked and cut
  into short sections
55 g (2 oz) dried lily buds, soaked
115 g (4 oz) sliced bamboo shoots, drained
115 g (4 oz) broccoli flowerets
salt and freshly ground black pepper
2 tablespoons soy sauce
½ teaspoon sesame oil
coriander sprigs, to garnish

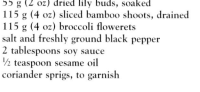

Heat oil in a clay pot or flameproof casserole and stir-fry the bok choy for 2-3 minutes.

Add the soaked mushrooms, vermicelli, bean curd sticks, lily buds, bamboo shoots and broccoli and stir-fry for 2 minutes, then add salt, pepper, soy sauce and some of the mushroom soaking water. Bring to boil, cover and simmer for 2-3 minutes. Blend in the sesame oil. Serve hot straight from the pot, garnished with coriander sprigs.

Serves 4-6.

BAKED MIXED VEGETABLES

450 g (1 lb) aubergines (eggplants), thinly sliced
salt and freshly ground black pepper
150 ml (5 fl oz/²⁄₃ cup) olive oil
3 cloves garlic, crushed
450 g (1 lb) beefsteak tomatoes, peeled, seeded and chopped
1 tablespoon tomato purée (paste)
2 Spanish onions, thinly sliced
1 green pepper (capsicum), sliced
1 red pepper (capsicum), sliced
450 g (1 lb) potatoes, boiled and sliced
25 g (1 oz/½ cup) fresh breadcrumbs

Sprinkle aubergine (eggplant) slices with salt and leave in a colander for 30 minutes. Rinse under cold running water and dry well on absorbent kitchen paper. Meanwhile, in a saucepan, heat 1 tablespoon oil, add garlic and fry gently without browning. Add tomatoes, tomato purée (paste) and salt and pepper. Cover and simmer for 15 minutes. Preheat oven to 200C (400F/Gas 6). In a frying pan, heat 4 tablespoons oil.

Add onions and peppers (capsicums); cook gently for 15 minutes. Using a slotted spoon, remove from pan; set aside. Add remaining oil to pan. Add aubergine (eggplant) slices in batches; fry until golden. Drain on absorbent kitchen paper. Layer all the vegetables in a baking dish; season each layer and moisten with the tomato sauce. Finish with tomato sauce. Sprinkle with breadcrumbs. Bake for about 20 minutes until golden.

Serves 4-6.

VEGETABLES IN SPICY SAUCE

2-3 tablespoons vegetable oil
1 cake tofu, cut into small cubes
½ teaspoon minced garlic
2 shallots, sliced
1 tablespoon curry powder
2 tablespoons soy sauce
1 tablespoon chopped lemon grass
1 tablespoon chopped fresh root ginger
1 teaspoon chilli sauce (optional)
250 ml (9 fl oz/1 cup) coconut milk
½ teaspoon salt
1 tablespoon sugar
2 small carrots and 1 onion, sliced
115-175 g (4-6 oz) cauliflower flowerets
225 g (8 oz) green beans, trimmed and cut in half
2 firm tomatoes, cut into wedges

Heat oil in a wok or large fry-pan and fry the tofu until browned on all sides. Remove and drain. Stir-fry the garlic and shallots in the same oil for about 1 minute, then add curry powder, soy sauce, lemon grass, ginger and chilli sauce, if using, and continue cooking for a further 1 minute. Add the coconut milk, salt and sugar and bring to the boil.

Add the carrots, onion, cauliflower, beans and tofu and stir-fry for 3-4 minutes, then add the tomatoes. Blend well and cook for a further 2 minutes. Serve at once.

Serves 4-6.

Variation: For non-vegetarians, either fish sauce or oyster sauce can be used instead of soy sauce for this dish.

PEPERONATA

2 green peppers (capsicums)
1 red pepper (capsicum)
700 g (1½ lb) tomatoes, peeled, seeded and roughly
  chopped
85 ml (3 fl oz/⅓ cup) olive oil
1 onion, roughly chopped
1 clove garlic, crushed
pinch granulated sugar
salt and freshly ground black pepper
1 tablespoon chopped flat-leaf parsley

Preheat grill. Put peppers (capsicums) under the hot grill and cook for about 10 minutes, turning occasionally, until skins are evenly blistered and charred.

Transfer to a plastic bag for a few minutes then peel away and discard skins. Cut peppers (capsicums) in half, discard seeds and cut into strips. Heat oil in a large frying pan. Add onion and garlic and cook gently for 3 minutes to soften.

Stir in tomatoes and sugar and cook gently for 10-12 minutes until thickened. Increase heat if necessary. Add pepper (capsicum) strips and simmer gently for 5 minutes until peppers are soft. Season with salt and freshly ground black pepper and serve hot sprinkled with chopped flat-leaf parsley.

Serves 4.

CHAR-GRILLED ARTICHOKES

70 ml (2½ fl oz/⅓ cup) olive oil
1 clove garlic, crushed
2 tablespoons chopped fresh parsley
salt and freshly ground black pepper
6 baby artichokes
flat-leaf parsley sprigs, to garnish
RED PEPPER (CAPSICUM) SAUCE:
1 tablespoon olive oil
1 small onion, chopped
2 red peppers (capsicum), diced
250 ml (9 fl oz/1 cup) vegetable stock

Mix together the olive oil, garlic, parsley and salt and pepper. Set aside.

To make the red pepper (capsicum) sauce, heat the oil in a saucepan. Add the onion and cook for 5 minutes until soft. Add the red peppers (capsicum) and cook over a low heat for 5 minutes. Pour in the stock, bring to the boil and simmer for 10 minutes. Push through a sieve or purée in a food processor or blender. Season with salt and pepper.

Trim the bases of the artichokes and remove any tough outer leaves. Cut the artichokes in half lengthways and immediately brush with the seasoned oil. Preheat a ridged grill pan, add the artichokes and cook over a medium heat for 10 minutes, turning once, until browned on both sides. Reheat the sauce. Drizzle the artichokes with the remaining seasoned oil, garnish with parsley and serve with the red pepper (capsicum) sauce.

Serves 3-4.

RATATOUILLE

2 aubergines (eggplant), sliced
3 courgettes (zucchini), sliced
3-4 tablespoons olive oil
1 Spanish onion, very thinly sliced
3 cloves garlic, crushed
2 large red peppers (capsicum), thinly sliced
4 ripe beef tomatoes, peeled, seeded and chopped
leaves from a few sprigs of thyme, marjoram and
    oregano
salt and freshly ground black pepper
2 tablespoons each chopped fresh parsley and basil

Put aubergine (eggplant) and courgette (zucchini) in a colander, sprinkle generously with salt and leave for 1 hour.

Rinse well, drain and dry thoroughly with kitchen paper. Heat 2 tablespoons oil in a heavy flameproof casserole, add aubergine (eggplant) and cook, stirring occasionally, for a few minutes. Add 1 tablespoon oil, the onions and garlic and cook, stirring occasionally, for 2-3 minutes. Add peppers (capsicum) and cook, stirring occasionally, for 1-2 minutes.

Add courgettes (zucchini) to casserole with more oil if necessary. Cook, stirring occasionally, for 2-3 minutes, then add tomatoes, thyme, marjoram and oregano. Season lightly with salt and pepper, cover and cook very gently for 30-40 minutes, stirring occasionally. Stir in parsley and basil and cook, uncovered, for 5-10 minutes, until liquid has evaporated. Serve warm or cold.

Serves 4.

COURGETTES WITH CHEESE

700 g (1½ lb) courgettes (zucchini)
6 teaspoons olive oil
1 large onion, chopped
1 teaspoon chopped fresh mint
2 eggs
175 g (6 oz/1½ cups) grated kefalotiri cheese
¼ teaspoon freshly grated nutmeg
salt and pepper

Preheat oven to 180C (350F/Gas 4). Trim courgettes (zucchini) ends, then cut into 1 cm (½ in) slices. Put courgette (zucchini) slices into a steamer above boiling water. Cook in batches, if necessary. Steam for a few minutes until just tender.

In a frying pan, heat oil, add onion and cook until soft. Mix courgettes (zucchini) and mint with the softened onion, then put in an ovenproof dish.

In a bowl, beat eggs with cheese, nutmeg, salt and pepper, then pour over the courgettes (zucchini). Bake in the oven for 20 minutes or until top is lightly browned.

Serves 4.

Variation: This dish may also be made with marrow instead of courgettes.

FUNGHETTO

225 g (8 oz) aubergine (eggplant), diced
225 g (8 oz) courgettes (zucchini), thinly sliced
15 g (½ oz) dried ceps (porcini)
25 g (1 oz) butter
4 tablespoons olive oil
2 cloves garlic, crushed
225 g (8 oz) button or oyster mushrooms, or a
  mixture, sliced
2 tablespoons fresh rosemary leaves
2 tablespoons chopped flat-leaf parsley
salt and freshly ground black pepper
fresh rosemary sprigs, to garnish

Put aubergine (eggplant) and courgette (zucchini) in a colander.

Sprinkle with plenty of salt and leave to drain for 30 minutes. Rinse thoroughly to remove salt and drain on absorbent kitchen paper. Put dried ceps (porcini) in a small bowl. Cover with warm water and set aside for 20 minutes. Strain, reserving 3 tablespoons soaking liquor. Rinse ceps (porcini) thoroughly and chop.

Heat butter and oil in a large, heavy frying pan. Add garlic and sauté for 1 minute. Add aubergine (eggplant) and courgette (zucchini), mushrooms, ceps (porcini) and rosemary. Sauté for 3-4 minutes. Stir in reserved soaking liquor and the parsley, lower heat and cook for 20-25 minutes until vegetables are soft and liquid evaporated. Season with salt and ground black pepper and garnish with rosemary sprigs.

Serves 4-6.

COURGETTES WITH GARLIC

6 medium-sized courgettes (zucchini)
225 ml (8 fl oz/1 cup) corn or groundnut oil
225 ml (8 fl oz/1 cup) olive oil
2 cloves garlic, chopped
70 ml (2½ fl oz/⅓ cup) red wine vinegar
1-2 tablespoons chopped fresh dill
salt and freshly ground black pepper
12 fresh mint leaves

Preheat oven to 190C (375F/Gas 5). Using a potato peeler and pressing fairly firmly, peel along the lengths of courgettes (zucchini) to remove long, thick 'ribbons'. Divide between two baking sheets and bake in the preheated oven for 20 minutes until just tender.

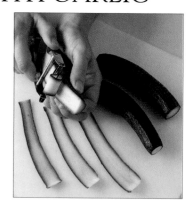

Transfer courgettes (zucchini) to absorbent kitchen paper to drain for 30 minutes. Half-fill a saucepan or deep-fat fryer with the oils and heat to 190C (375F). Line a baking sheet with absorbent kitchen paper. Fry courgette (zucchini) slices in batches in the hot oil for 2-3 minutes until a light golden brown. Using a slotted spoon, transfer to prepared baking sheet to drain. When all courgettes (zucchini) are cooked and drained transfer to a serving dish.

Add garlic, red wine vinegar, chopped dill and salt and freshly ground black pepper to courgettes (zucchini). Toss gently to mix. Cover and leave in refrigerator for at least 2 hours. Serve sprinkled with mint leaves.

Serves 6.

SAUCES & SALAD DRESSINGS

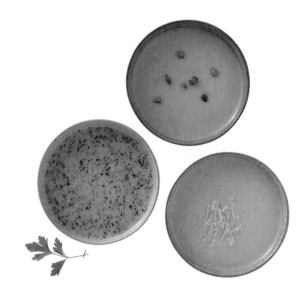

BASIC WHITE SAUCE

25 g (1 oz/6 teaspoons) butter
25 g (1 oz/¼ cup) plain flour
300 ml (10 fl oz/1¼ cups) milk
salt and pepper

In a saucepan, melt butter over a low heat. Stir in flour and cook for 1 minute, stirring.

Remove pan from heat and gradually stir or whisk in the milk. Bring slowly to the boil, stirring or whisking, and continue to cook until the mixture thickens.

Simmer gently for 3 minutes. Remove pan from heat and season with salt and pepper. Serve with meat, poultry, fish or vegetables.

Makes 300 ml (10 fl oz/1¼ cups).

WHITE SAUCE VARIATIONS

CHEESE SAUCE
Follow the recipe for Basic White Sauce. Before seasoning with salt and pepper, stir in 55 g (2 oz/½ cup) grated Cheddar cheese and 1 teaspoon prepared mustard. Serve with fish, poultry, ham, vegetables or egg dishes.

PARSLEY SAUCE
Follow the recipe for Basic White Sauce. After seasoning with salt and pepper, stir in 2 tablespoons finely chopped fresh parsley. Serve with fish, ham or bacon.

CAPER SAUCE
Follow the recipe for Basic White Sauce. Before seasoning with salt and pepper, stir in 2 tablespoons capers and 2 teaspoons vinegar from the jar of capers. Reheat gently before serving. Serve with lamb.

TARRAGON SAUCE

25 g (1 oz/6 teaspoons) butter
25 g (1 oz/¼ cup) plain flour
300 ml (10 fl oz/1¼ cups) chicken stock
150 ml (5 fl oz/⅔ cup) milk
2 tablespoons tarragon vinegar
few sprigs tarragon
2 teaspoons smooth mustard
55 g (2 oz/½ cup) Cheddar cheese
salt and pepper

In a saucepan, melt butter over a low heat. Stir in flour and cook for 1 minute, stirring. Remove pan from heat and gradually stir or whisk in stock, milk and vinegar.

Bring slowly to the boil, stirring or whisking, and continue to cook until the mixture thickens. Simmer gently for 3 minutes. Chop the tarragon finely.

Stir the tarragon into the sauce with the mustard, cheese and salt and pepper and reheat gently, but do not allow the mixture to boil. Serve with chicken or turkey.

Makes 550 ml (20 fl oz/2½ cups).

BÉCHAMEL SAUCE

1 small onion or shallot
1 small carrot
½ stick celery
1 bay leaf
6 black peppercorns
several stalks parsley
300 ml (10 fl oz/1¼ cups) milk
25 g (1 oz/6 teaspoons) butter
25 g (1 oz/¼ cup) plain flour
salt and pepper

Slice the onion or shallot and carrot. Chop the celery roughly. Put vegetables and flavourings in a saucepan with milk and bring slowly to the boil.

Remove pan from heat, cover and set aside to infuse for 30 minutes. Strain into a jug, reserving the milk. In a saucepan, melt butter over a low heat. Stir in flour and cook for 1 minute, stirring.

Remove pan from heat and gradually stir or whisk in flavoured milk. Bring slowly to the boil, stirring or whisking, and continue to cook until the mixture thickens. Simmer gently for 3 minutes. Remove pan from heat and season with salt and pepper. Serve with poultry, fish, vegetables or egg dishes.

Makes 300 ml (10 fl oz/1¼ cups).

SPICY COURGETTE SAUCE

2 courgettes (zucchini)
1 green pepper (capsicum)
1 small onion
1 clove garlic
25 g (1 oz/6 teaspoons) butter
1 teaspoon ground coriander
½ teaspoon ground cumin
½ teaspoon ground chilli powder
¼ teaspoon cayenne pepper
¼ teaspoon turmeric
150 ml (5 fl oz/⅔ cup) vegetable stock
salt and pepper

Trim the courgettes (zucchini) and grate them coarsely.

Seed and chop pepper (capsicum) finely. Chop onion finely and crush garlic. In a saucepan, melt butter over a low heat. Add courgettes (zucchini), pepper (capsicum), onion and garlic and cook for 5 minutes, stirring.

Stir in spices, stock and salt and pepper and mix well. Bring slowly to the boil, cover and simmer for 25 minutes, stirring occasionally. Remove pan from heat and set aside to cool. Once cool, purée mixture in a blender or food processor until smooth. Return the sauce to a saucepan. Reheat gently and adjust the seasoning before serving. Serve with seafood, fish or meat.

Makes 500 ml (18 fl oz/2¼ cups).

BROCCOLI & CHEESE SAUCE

225 g (8 oz) broccoli
3 teaspoons cornflour
150 ml (5 fl oz/⅔ cup) dry white wine
1 clove garlic
150 g (5 oz) soft cheese
salt and pepper

Trim broccoli and cook in a saucepan of boiling water for 10 minutes until tender. Drain, reserving 2 tablespoons of the cooking liquid. Cool the broccoli, then purée with reserved liquid in a blender or food processor until smooth. Set the puréed broccoli aside.

In a saucepan, blend cornflour with wine. Crush garlic and add to the wine mixture. Bring slowly to the boil, stirring continuously, until the mixture thickens. Simmer gently for 3 minutes.

Remove pan from heat and stir in soft cheese, puréed broccoli and salt and pepper, mixing well. Reheat gently and adjust the seasoning before serving. Serve hot or cold with poultry, beef or fish.

Makes 550 ml (20 fl oz/2½ cups).

HERBY YELLOW PEPPER SAUCE

2 yellow peppers (capsicums)
½ green chilli
1 tablespoon chopped mixed fresh herbs, such as
   parsley, thyme, rosemary and chives
300 ml (10 fl oz/1¼ cups) vegetable stock
6 teaspoons medium white wine
salt and pepper
3 teaspoons cornflour

Seed and chop peppers (capsicums) and chilli finely. Put peppers (capsicums), chilli, herbs, stock, wine and salt and pepper into a saucepan and mix well.

Bring slowly to boil, cover and simmer gently for 10 minutes, stirring occasionally. Remove pan from heat and set aside to cool. Once cool, purée the mixture in a blender or food processor until smooth. Return sauce to a saucepan. In a small bowl, blend cornflour with 2 tablespoons water.

Stir cornflour mixture into pepper sauce and heat gently until sauce thickens, stirring continuously. Simmer gently for 3 minutes. Remove pan from heat and adjust the seasoning before serving. Serve with lamb or vegetables such as asparagus, broccoli or sweetcorn.

Makes 500 ml (18 fl oz/2¼ cups).

TOMATO SAUCE

2 tablespoons olive oil
½ Spanish onion, finely chopped
½ clove garlic, chopped
1 red pepper (capsicum), chopped
900 g (2 lb) beefsteak tomatoes, peeled, seeded and
   chopped
sugar or tomato purée (paste), (optional)
salt and freshly ground black pepper

Heat oil in a frying pan, add onion and cook slowly for 5 minutes.

Stir in garlic and pepper (capsicum) and continue to cook slowly for a further 10 minutes, stirring occasionally.

Stir tomatoes into pan. Simmer gently for 20-30 minutes, stirring occasionally, until thickened. Add sugar or tomato purée (paste), if desired, and season with salt and pepper. Mix in a blender or food processor, or pass through a non-metallic sieve, if desired.

Serves 4-6.

GOOSEBERRY SAUCE

450 g (1 lb) gooseberries
finely grated rind and juice 1 orange
25 g (1 oz/6 teaspoons) butter
25 g (1 oz/2 tablespoons) soft brown sugar
¼ teaspoon ground nutmeg

Place gooseberries in a saucepan with orange rind and juice and 150 ml (5 fl oz/⅔ cup) water, mixing well. Bring the mixture slowly to the boil, cover saucepan and simmer gently for 5-10 minutes until the gooseberries are cooked, stirring occasionally.

Remove the pan from the heat and set aside to cool. Once cool, purée the gooseberries in a blender or food processor until smooth. Return the mixture to a saucepan.

Stir in butter, sugar and nutmeg. Bring slowly to the boil, stirring, and simmer gently for 1 minute. Serve with oily fish such as mackerel.

Makes 500 ml (18 fl oz/2¼ cups).

MINTY APPLE SAUCE

1 small onion
450 g (1 lb) cooking apples
small bunch fresh mint
25 g (1 oz/5 teaspoons) caster sugar

Chop onion finely. Peel, core and slice apples. Put onion and apples in a saucepan with 2 tablespoons water.

Cover saucepan and heat mixture gently until the apples and onion are soft. Remove pan from heat and mash the apples and onion lightly.

Chop mint finely and add to saucepan with the sugar, mixing well. Reheat sauce gently until the sugar has dissolved. Serve hot or cold with lamb or pork.

Makes 400 ml (14 fl oz/1¾ cups).

PLUM SAUCE

350 g (12 oz) red dessert plums
finely grated rind and juice 1 orange
55 g (2 oz/¼ cup) caster sugar
½ teaspoon ground cinnamon
3 teaspoons brandy

Halve and stone plums. Place plums in a saucepan with 150 ml (5 fl oz/⅔ cup) cold water.

Bring slowly to the boil, cover and simmer until the plums are soft. Remove pan from heat and set aside to cool. Once cool, purée the plums and juice in a blender or food processor until smooth.

Return the sauce to a saucepan and stir in orange rind, orange juice, sugar, cinnamon and brandy, mixing well. Reheat the sauce gently before serving. Serve with lamb, pork or beef.

Makes 550 ml (20 fl oz/2½ cups).

Note: The sauce may be served cold, if preferred.

SWEET & SOUR SAUCE

225 g (8 oz) carrots
6 spring onions
1 clove garlic
2.5 cm (1 in) piece fresh root ginger
2 teaspoons olive oil
225 g (8 oz) unsweetened apple purée
450 ml (16 fl oz/2 cups) beef stock
150 ml (5 fl oz/⅔ cup) red wine
3 tablespoons lemon juice
6 teaspoons clear honey
6 teaspoons light soy sauce
salt and pepper
3 teaspoons cornflour

Grate carrots coarsely and chop onions finely. Peel and crush garlic. Peel and grate or chop ginger finely. In a saucepan, heat oil for 1 minute. Add carrots, spring onions, garlic and ginger and cook for 5 minutes, stirring. Stir in the apple purée, stock, red wine, lemon juice, honey, soy sauce and salt and pepper and mix well. Bring slowly to the boil, cover and simmer gently for 1 hour, stirring occasionally. Remove pan from heat and press the sauce through a nylon sieve. Discard pulp and return the sauce to a saucepan.

In a small bowl, blend cornflour with 1 tablespoon water. Stir cornflour mixture into sauce and bring slowly to the boil, stirring continuously. Simmer gently for 3 minutes and adjust the seasoning before serving. Serve with lamb, pork, fresh vegetables or mixed beans.

Makes 680 ml (24 fl oz).

CURRY SAUCE

1 onion
1 clove garlic
2 teaspoons sunflower oil
225 g (8 oz) potatoes
225 g (8 oz) can chopped tomatoes
300 ml (10 fl oz/1¼ cups) vegetable stock
3 teaspoons curry powder
1 teaspoon ground bay leaves
salt and pepper
55 g (2 oz/⅓ cup) sultanas

Chop onion finely and crush garlic. In a saucepan, heat oil for 1 minute. Add onion and garlic and cook for 5 minutes, stirring.

Peel and grate potatoes coarsely. Add potatoes, tomatoes, stock, curry powder, ground bay leaves and salt and pepper to the saucepan and mix well. Bring slowly to the boil, cover and simmer gently for 30 minutes, stirring occasionally. Remove pan from the heat and set aside to cool. Once cool, purée the sauce in a blender or food processor until smooth.

Return the sauce to a saucepan and add the sultanas. Reheat gently and adjust the seasoning before serving. Serve with vegetables or egg dishes.

Makes 800 ml (28 fl oz/3½ cups).

Variation: The sultanas can be added with the potatoes and tomatoes and puréed, if preferred.

BARBECUE SAUCE

2 garlic cloves
225 g (8 oz) can pineapple in fruit juice
225 g (8 oz) can chopped tomatoes
3 tablespoons cider vinegar
6 teaspoons soft brown sugar
6 teaspoons mango chutney
2 teaspoons Worcestershire sauce
½ teaspoon smooth mustard
½ teaspoon mixed spice
few drops Tabasco sauce
salt and pepper
3 teaspoons cornflour

Peel and crush garlic cloves and chop pineapple roughly.

Put garlic and pineapple in a saucepan with the tomatoes, vinegar, sugar, chutney, Worcestershire sauce, mustard, mixed spice, Tabasco sauce and salt and pepper and mix well. Bring slowly to the boil, cover and simmer gently for 10 minutes, stirring occasionally. Remove pan from heat and set aside to cool. Once cool, purée the sauce in a blender or food processor until smooth. Return the sauce to a saucepan.

In a small bowl, blend cornflour with 1 tablespoon water. Stir cornflour mixture into sauce and bring slowly to the boil, stirring continuously. Simmer gently for 3 minutes and adjust the seasoning before serving. Serve with barbecued or grilled meats such as steaks, chops or chicken portions.

Makes 400 ml (14 fl oz/1¾ cups).

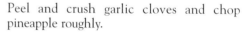

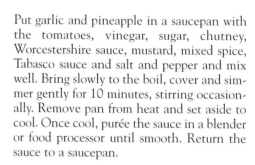

SPICY FISH SAUCE

2 cloves garlic
2 small red or green chillies, seeded and chopped
1 tablespoon sugar
2 tablespoons lime juice
2 tablespoons fish sauce

SALSA FRESCA

4 large, ripe, firm tomatoes, roughly chopped
1 tablespoon finely chopped fresh coriander
½ small onion, finely chopped
2 fresh green chillies, finely chopped
juice ½ lemon
½ teaspoon salt
1 teaspoon freshly ground black pepper

Using a pestle and mortar, pound garlic and chillies until finely ground. If you do not have a pestle and mortar, just finely mince the garlic and chillies.

Mix all the ingredients together and leave for 15 minutes before serving. Serve as an accompaniment to any bean, rice or meat dish.

Makes 315 ml (10 fl oz).

Place mixture in a bowl and add sugar, lime juice, fish sauce and 2-3 tablespoons water. Blend well. Serve in small dipping saucers.

Serves 4.

Note: This sauce is known as nuoc cham. You can make a large quantity of the base for later use by boiling the lime juice, fish sauce and water with sugar in a pan. It will keep for months in a tightly sealed jar or bottle in the refrigerator. Add freshly minced garlic and chillies for serving.

Note: The relish does not keep long, so if there is any left, fry it in a little oil and serve as a sauce for hot Mexican dishes.

MELBA SAUCE

450 g (1 lb) raspberries
115 g (4 oz/¾ cup) icing sugar
9 teaspoons medium white wine
1 teaspoon arrowroot

APRICOT SAUCE

225 g (8 oz) dried apricots
55 g (2 oz/¼ cup) caster sugar
300 ml (10 fl oz/1¼ cups) dry white wine

Put raspberries in a saucepan with 2 table-spoons water. Cover and cook raspberries gently until they are soft. Remove pan from heat and set aside to cool.

Chop apricots roughly. Place sugar in a saucepan with 150 ml (5 fl oz/⅔ cup) water. Heat mixture gently until sugar has dissolved.

Once cool, strain raspberries through a nylon sieve, discarding pips. Sift icing sugar and place in saucepan with raspberry sauce and wine, mixing well. Heat the sauce gently until sugar has dissolved, then bring to the boil. Remove pan from heat. In a small bowl, blend arrowroot with 1 tablespoon water.

Stir in apricots and wine, mixing well. Bring slowly to the boil, cover and simmer gently for 20 minutes, stirring occasionally. Remove pan from heat and set aside to cool.

Stir arrowroot mixture into raspberry sauce. Reheat gently until sauce thickens, stirring continuously. Serve hot or cold with peaches, low fat ice cream or sorbet.

Makes 535 ml (19 fl oz/2⅓ cups).

Once cool, purée the mixture in a blender or food processor until smooth. Return the sauce to a saucepan and reheat gently before serving. Serve with baked puddings, crêpes or baked fruit such as baked pears.

Makes 550 ml (20 fl oz/2½ cups).

HOT LEMON SAUCE

DARK CHOCOLATE SAUCE

juice and grated peel 3 lemons
85 g (3 oz/⅓ cup) butter
85 g (3 oz/⅓ cup) caster sugar
1 rounded teaspoon cornflour

175 g (6 oz) plain (dark) chocolate
115 ml (4 fl oz/½ cup) strong black coffee or water
55 g (2 oz/¼ cup) caster sugar

Put lemon juice and peel in a saucepan with butter and sugar. Stir over gentle heat until butter has melted and sugar dissolved.

Break chocolate into pieces and put in the top of a double boiler or a bowl set over a saucepan of simmering water. Add the coffee or water and sugar.

Mix cornflour to a smooth paste with a little water and stir into the pan. Bring the sauce to the boil, stirring constantly.

Stir over medium heat until the chocolate has melted and the sauce is smooth and creamy. Serve hot or cold.

Serves 4-6.

Simmer 1 to 2 minutes, stirring all the time. Keep warm until ready to serve.

Serves 4-6.

Note: Serve with Austrian Cheesecake (see page 380), if desired.

Note: Serve Dark Chocolate Sauce Chocolate Profiteroles (see page 390) or Mixed Chocolate Terrine (see page 391) or with vanilla ice cream.

THOUSAND ISLAND DRESSING

55 g (2 oz) gherkins
2 tablespoons chopped red pepper (capsicum)
2 tablespoons chopped green pepper (capsicum)
300 ml (10 fl oz/1¼ cups) mayonnaise
4 tablespoons low fat plain yogurt
6 teaspoons tomato ketchup (sauce)
1 tablespoon chopped fresh parsley
salt and pepper

Chop gherkins finely. In a bowl, mix together gherkins and red and green pepper (capsicum).

Stir in mayonnaise, yogurt, tomato ketchup (sauce), parsley and salt and pepper and mix thoroughly. Cover and leave in a cool place for 30 minutes before serving, to allow the flavours to develop.

Serve with a fresh mixed seafood salad.

Makes 600 ml (21 fl oz/2¾ cups).

Variation: Add two cold hard-boiled eggs, mashed or finely chopped, to the dressing.

MILD CURRY MAYONNAISE

6 spring onions
15 g (½ oz/3 teaspoons) butter
6 teaspoons mango chutney
3 teaspoons mild curry powder
3 teaspoons desiccated coconut
300 ml (10 fl oz/1¼ cups) mayonnaise
150 ml (5 fl oz/⅔ cup) low fat plain yogurt
salt and pepper

Trim and chop spring onions finely. In a saucepan, melt butter over a low heat. Add spring onions and cook for 5 minutes, stirring.

Remove pan from heat and stir in chutney, curry powder and coconut, mixing well. Set aside to cool.

Once cool, mix with mayonnaise, yogurt and salt and pepper. Cover and leave the sauce in a cool place for 30 minutes before serving, to allow the flavours to develop. Serve with potato salad or coleslaw.

Makes 500 ml (18 fl oz/2¼ cups).

HERBY CHEESE DRESSING

1 clove garlic
225 g (8 oz) low fat soft cheese
150 ml (5 fl oz/⅔ cup) sour cream
2 tablespoons chopped fresh mixed herbs, such as
   parsley, chives, rosemary and thyme
1 tablespoon lemon juice
salt and pepper

Peel and crush garlic. Put garlic, soft cheese, cream, herbs, lemon juice and salt and pepper in a bowl.

Whisk ingredients together until thoroughly mixed. Cover and leave the dressing in a cool place for 30 minutes before serving, to allow the flavours to develop.

Adjust the seasoning before serving. Serve with fresh salad leaves, raw or cooked vegetables, pasta salad or beef salad.

Makes 350 ml (12 fl oz/1½ cups).

ORANGE CINNAMON DRESSING

150 ml (5 fl oz/⅔ cup) unsweetened orange juice
6 tablespoons white wine vinegar
12 teaspoons sunflower oil
finely grated rind and juice 1 orange
1 teaspoon ground cinnamon
salt and pepper

Put orange juice, vinegar, oil, orange rind and squeezed juice, cinnamon and salt and pepper in a bowl and whisk the ingredients together until thoroughly mixed.

Alternatively, place all the ingredients in a clean jam jar. Screw top on jar and shake until all the ingredients are thoroughly mixed.

Adjust the seasoning before serving. Serve with fresh salad leaves, pasta salad, cooked or raw vegetables or cold sliced pork.

Makes 300 ml (10 fl oz/1¼ cups).

Variation: Use all freshly squeezed orange juice for extra flavour.

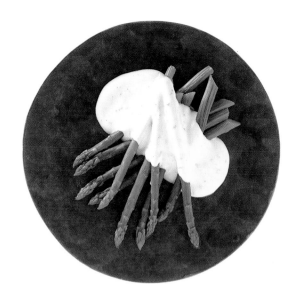

CORIANDER & LIME DRESSING

150 ml (5 fl oz/²⁄₃ cup) white grape juice
6 tablespoons white wine vinegar
12 teaspoons sunflower oil
2 tablespoons chopped fresh coriander
finely grated rind 1 lime
juice 2 limes
1 teaspoon caster sugar
salt and pepper

Put grape juice, vinegar, oil, coriander, lime rind, lime juice, sugar and salt and pepper in a bowl.

Whisk ingredients together until thoroughly mixed. Alternatively, put all the ingredients in a clean jam jar. Screw top on jar and shake until all the ingredients are thoroughly mixed.

Adjust the seasoning before serving. Serve with fresh salad leaves, fish or cold sliced meats.

Makes 350 ml (12 fl oz/1½ cups).

Variation: In place of the lime rind and juice, use lemon or orange rind and a mixture of chopped fresh herbs, such as parsley, thyme and basil.

FRESH TARRAGON DRESSING

175 g (6 oz) low fat soft cheese
150 ml (5 fl oz/²⁄₃ cup) single (light) cream or low fat yogurt
2 tablespoons chopped fresh tarragon
1 tablespoon tarragon vinegar
salt and pepper

Put soft cheese and cream in a bowl and mix well.

Stir in tarragon, vinegar and salt and pepper, mixing well. Cover and leave the dressing in a cool place for 30 minutes before serving, to allow the flavours to develop. Adjust the seasoning before serving.

Serve with asparagus or hot or cold sliced meats such as chicken or turkey.

Makes 325 ml (11 fl oz/1⅓ cups).

Variation: Use semi-skimmed milk in place of the cream or yogurt, for a lower calorie/lower fat dressing.

BREAD & BUNS

CHAPATI

150 g (5 oz/1¼ cups) plain flour
150 g (5 oz/1¼ cups) wholewheat flour
salt
55 g (2 oz/¼ cup) butter or ghee, melted, for serving

Sift flours and salt together into a mixing bowl and tip in any bran caught in sieve. Mix in about 175 ml (6 fl oz/¾ cup) water to make a soft dough.

Knead dough on a lightly floured surface for about 5 minutes, until smooth and pliable, then, with wet hands, knead dough for 1 minute more to make it extra smooth. Wrap in plastic wrap and chill for 30 minutes. Divide dough into 12 pieces and roll each out on a lightly floured surface to a 12.5 cm (5 in) round.

Heat a griddle or heavy-based frying pan on a medium heat and cook dough rounds, 1 at a time, floury side down, for 1-2 minutes, until beginning to bubble on surface. Turn over and cook second side for ½-1 minute, pressing with a folded dry cloth during cooking to make them puff up. Wrap each chapati in a dry cloth as soon as it is ready. Serve them warm, brushed with melted butter or ghee.

Makes 12.

NAAN

450 g (1 lb/4 cups) plain flour
1 teaspoon baking powder
½ teaspoon bicarbonate of soda
salt
1 egg, beaten
6 tablespoons natural yogurt
45 g (1½ oz/9 teaspoons) butter or ghee, melted
about 225 ml (8 fl oz/1 cup) milk
3 teaspoons poppy seeds

Sift flour, baking powder and bicarbonate of soda together into a mixing bowl. Season with salt.

Stir in egg, yogurt and 25 g (1 oz/6 teaspoons) butter or ghee. Gradually mix in enough milk to make a soft dough. Cover bowl with a damp cloth and put in a warm place for 2 hours. Preheat oven to 200C (400F/Gas 6). Knead dough on a lightly floured surface for 2-3 minutes, until smooth, then divide dough into 8 pieces.

Roll each piece into a ball, then roll out to make ovals about 15 cm (6 in) long, pulling ends to stretch dough into shape. Brush ovals with water and place wet-side down on greased baking trays. Brush dry side with melted butter or ghee and sprinkle with poppy seeds. Bake for 8-10 minutes, until puffy and golden brown. Serve at once.

Makes 8.

TOMATO & ONION BREAD

450 g (1 lb/4 cups) strong plain flour
pinch salt
15 g (½ oz) packet dried yeast
1 teaspoon granulated sugar
200 ml (7 fl oz/scant 1 cup) warm water
4 tablespoons extra virgin olive oil
1 onion, finely chopped
1 clove garlic, crushed
115 g (4 oz) sun-dried tomatoes preserved in oil, drained
9 large fresh basil leaves
freshly ground black pepper
milk to glaze
1 teaspoon coarse sea salt

Oil a baking sheet. Heat remaining oil in a frying pan, add onion and garlic and cook for 3 minutes, to soften. Remove from the heat and set aside. Turn dough onto a lightly floured surface and cut in half. Roll out to give two identical rectangles about 23 x 30 cm (9 x 12 in). Transfer one piece to the baking sheet and prick surface with a fork.

Sieve flour and salt into a large mixing bowl. In a small bowl mix yeast, sugar and warm water. Leave for 10-15 minutes until frothy.

Spread reserved onion mixture over pricked dough, leaving a 1.5 cm (½ in) border around edge. Top with sun-dried tomatoes and basil leaves and season with freshly ground black pepper. Moisten edges of dough with a little cold water and cover with second rectangle of dough.

Oil a mixing bowl. Stir 3 tablespoons of the olive oil into yeast mixture then, using a wooden spoon, gradually mix into flour to give a soft, but not wet, dough. Turn onto a lightly floured surface and knead for 5 minutes until smooth and elastic. Put into the oiled bowl, cover and leave in a warm place for 35-40 minutes until doubled in size.

Preheat oven to 230C (450F/Gas 8). Crimp edges of the dough to seal and using a sharp knife mark a lattice pattern on the surface. Brush the dough with a little milk to glaze and sprinkle with the coarse sea salt. Leave to rise for 25 minutes. Bake in the preheated oven for about 25 minutes until golden brown and the underside is firm and lightly coloured. Serve warm or cold, on its own as part of the antipasti.

Makes 1 large loaf.

WALNUT BREAD

15 g (½ oz) sachet dried yeast
150 ml (5 fl oz/⅔ cup) warm milk
1 tablespoon clear honey
350 g (12 oz/3 cups) strong plain flour
350 g (12 oz/3 cups) plain wholemeal flour
1½ teaspoons salt
25 g (1 oz) butter, diced
150 g (5 oz/1¼ cups) walnuts, chopped
2 teaspoons fennel seeds, lightly crushed
½ teaspoon grated nutmeg
milk to glaze

In a small bowl or jug mix yeast with warm milk and honey. Leave for 10-15 minutes until frothy.

Sieve flours and salt into a large mixing bowl. Rub in butter until mixture resembles breadcrumbs. Stir in walnuts, 1 teaspoon of the fennel seeds and the grated nutmeg.

Using a wooden spoon, stir yeast liquid into flour mixture with sufficient warm water to form a soft, but not wet, dough.

Oil a mixing bowl. Turn dough out onto a lightly floured surface and knead for 5 minutes until elastic. Put into an oiled mixing bowl, cover and leave in a warm place for 35-40 minutes until doubled in size. Turn onto a lightly floured surface and knead again for 5 minutes.

Preheat oven to 220C (425F/Gas 7). Oil a deep 15 cm (6 inch) round cake tin. Divide dough into seven equal sized pieces and shape into balls. Arrange in the cake tin. Brush tops with milk and sprinkle with remaining 1 teaspoon fennel seeds. Leave in a warm place for 25 minutes then bake in the oven for about 45 minutes until the top is well browned and the bottom sounds hollow when tapped.

Turn bread onto a wire rack and leave to cool. Serve as part of the antipasti.

Makes 1 large loaf.

Note: This bread is delicious served with cheese and fish dishes, for soaking up olive oil dressings and is particularly good toasted.

FOCACCIA

450 g (1 lb/4 cups) strong plain flour
pinch salt
15 g (½ oz) packet dried yeast
225 ml (8 fl oz/1 cup) warm milk
1 teaspoon granulated sugar
4 tablespoons extra virgin olive oil, plus extra for
  brushing
2 teaspoons fresh rosemary leaves
coarse sea salt

Sieve flour and salt into a large mixing bowl. In a small bowl, mix together yeast, milk and sugar. Leave for 10-15 minutes, until frothy.

Stir in oil then gradually beat into flour mixture using wooden spoon to give a soft, but not wet, dough; add a little more warm milk if necessary. Turn dough onto a floured surface; knead for 5 minutes until smooth and elastic. Place in an oiled bowl, cover and leave in a warm place for about 40 minutes until doubled in size. Turn onto a floured surface and knead for 5 minutes.

Preheat oven to 230C (450F/Gas 8). Oil a baking sheet. Roll dough to a large circle about 1.5 cm (½ in) thick and transfer to the baking sheet. Brush with olive oil and sprinkle over rosemary and sea salt, pressing in lightly. With a clean finger make deep indentations over surface of dough. Leave to rise for 25 minutes. Bake in the preheated oven for 20-25 minutes until golden. Brush again with olive oil. Serve warm.

Makes 1 loaf.

SAVOURY PASTIES

1 quantity Pizza Dough recipe (see page 239)
vegetable oil for deep frying
flat-leaf parsley sprigs to garnish
FILLING:
3 tablespoons sun-dried tomato paste
2 tablespoons olive paste (see page 437), or buy
  ready-made)
175 g (6 oz) mozzarella cheese, thinly sliced
salt and freshly ground black pepper
1 egg white, lightly beaten

Make pizza dough and put to rise for 30 minutes until doubled in size.

Turn dough onto a lightly floured surface and roll out to 5 mm (¼ inch) thickness. Stamp out circles using a 10 cm (4 inch) plain round biscuit cutter. Spread a little sun-dried tomato paste and olive paste onto each round of dough. Cut mozzarella slices in half and put a piece on each dough circle. Season with salt and ground black pepper.

Brush edges of dough with a little egg white then fold dough over filling to make half-moon shapes, pressing edges to seal. Half-fill a deep-fat frying pan with oil. Preheat to 180C (350F). Deep fry a few pasties at a time, in the hot oil for 2-3 minutes, turning once, until golden. Using a slotted spoon, transfer to absorbent kitchen paper to drain. Serve hot garnished with flat-leaf parsley sprigs.

Makes about 12.

LEEK & BACON KNOTS

1 leek, finely chopped
55 g (2 oz/¼ cup) butter
175 g (6 oz) streaky bacon, chopped
225 g (8 oz/2 cups) strong plain white flour
225 g (8 oz/2 cups) plain wholemeal flour
1 teaspoon salt
1 teaspoon caster sugar
2 teaspoons easy blend dried yeast
150 ml (5 fl oz/⅔ cup) tepid milk
175 ml (6 fl oz/¾ cup) tepid water
beaten egg and sesame seeds, to garnish

Put leek and half the butter in frying pan. Cook until leek is soft. Remove from pan. Gently cook bacon in frying pan until fat

begins to run. Continue cooking until just beginning to turn crisp. Leave to cool. Sift white flour into a bowl. Stir in wholemeal flour, salt, sugar and yeast. Rub in remaining butter. Stir in leek and bacon and make a well in centre. Pour in milk and tepid water. Stir until a soft dough is formed. Turn out onto a floured surface and knead for about 10 minutes until smooth. Put in an oiled bowl, cover and leave in a warm place until doubled in size.

Grease 2 baking sheets. Turn dough onto a floured surface; knead for 3-4 minutes until smooth. Divide into 12 pieces and roll each into a sausage about 30 cm (12 in) long. Tie each one in a knot and place on baking sheets. Cover with plastic wrap and leave in a warm place until doubled in size. Preheat oven to 220C (425F/Gas 7). Brush rolls with egg and sprinkle with sesame seeds. Bake in the oven for 15 minutes until golden.

Makes 12.

CHEESE BUNS

800 g (1¾ lb/7 cups) strong white bread flour
1 sachet easy blend dried yeast
2 teaspoons salt
2 teaspoons caster sugar
6 teaspoons olive oil
sesame seeds, to decorate
CHEESE FILLING:
350 g (12 oz) kefalotiri cheese, grated
115 g (4 oz) haloumi cheese, finely grated
3 teaspoons plain flour
1 teaspoon baking powder
1 teaspoon chopped fresh mint
¼ teaspoon freshly grated nutmeg
4 eggs, beaten

To make the filling, place cheeses in a bowl. Add flour, baking powder, mint and nutmeg to cheese. Stir in most of beaten egg to make a stiff paste. To make the dough, sift flour into a bowl. Stir in yeast, salt and sugar. Add oil and 425 ml (15 fl oz/scant 2 cups) tepid water. Mix together, then turn dough onto a floured surface and knead for 10 minutes until smooth and elastic. Divide into 16 pieces; roll out each piece to a 10 cm (4 in) circle.

Place a little filling in centre of each circle. Pull dough up on 3 sides to make a tricorn shape, with filling showing in centre. Pinch corners together well. Place on oiled baking sheets, cover with oiled plastic wrap and leave in a warm place until doubled in size. Preheat oven to 230C (450F/Gas 8). Brush buns with remaining beaten egg. Scatter with sesame seeds. Bake for 12-15 minutes until golden brown.

Makes 16.

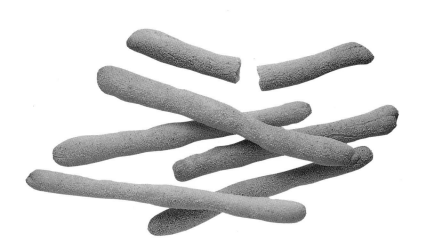

GRISSINI

450 g (1 lb) strong plain flour
½ teaspoon salt
25 g (1 oz) grated Parmesan or provolone cheese
7 g (¼ oz) dry yeast
1 teaspoon granulated sugar
300 ml (10 fl oz/1¼ cups) warm water
2 tablespoons extra virgin olive oil plus extra for oiling
85 g (3 oz/1 cup) polenta (corn meal)

Sieve flour and salt in a large mixing bowl. Stir in cheese. In a small bowl mix yeast, sugar and warm water. Leave for 10-15 minutes until frothy.

Stir olive oil into frothy yeast liquid then beat into flour using a wooden spoon to give a soft dough. Turn onto a floured surface and knead for 5 minutes until smooth and elastic. Lightly oil a baking sheet. Roll out dough to a large rectangle and transfer to prepared baking sheet. Brush the surface with a little oil, cover loosely and leave in a warm place for 35-40 minutes until doubled in size.

Preheat oven to 230C (450F/Gas 8). Oil 2 more baking sheets. Cut dough into 24 equal pieces. Sprinkle polenta on work surface. Using your hands, roll each piece of dough to a thin stick about 23 cm (9 in) long.

Arrange slightly apart on the baking sheets and bake in the preheated oven for 15-20 minutes until golden and crisp. Cool on wire racks. Serve warm or cold as part of the antipasti.

Makes 24.

Variation: Replace polenta with 85 g (3 oz) sesame seeds.

OLIVE BREAD

70 ml (2½ fl oz/⅓ cup) olive oil
1 onion, finely chopped
800 g (1¾ lb/7 cups) strong white bread flour
1 sachet easy blend dried yeast
2 teaspoons salt
225 g (8 oz/1⅓ cups) black olives, stoned and
  chopped

In a frying pan, heat oil. Add onion and cook until soft. Leave to cool. Sift flour into a large bowl. Stir in yeast and salt. Add 6 teaspoons oil and 425 ml (15 fl oz/scant 1 cup) tepid water. Mix together, then turn dough onto a floured surface.

Knead dough thoroughly for 10 minutes until smooth and elastic. Knead in 3 teaspoons oil, the fried onion and chopped olives. Cut dough in half and shape into 2 round loaves. Place on lightly oiled baking sheets.

Cover with oiled plastic wrap and leave in a warm place for 1 hour or until doubled in size. Preheat oven to 180C (350F/Gas 4). Brush with a little of the oil. Bake loaves for 30-40 minutes until base of each sounds hollow when tapped. Brush tops of loaves with remaining oil. Return to the oven for 2 minutes, then transfer to wire racks to cool.

Makes 2 loaves.

PITTA BREAD

800 g (1¾ lb/7 cups) strong white bread flour
1 sachet easy blend dried yeast
2 teaspoons salt
6 teaspoons olive oil

Sift flour into a large bowl. Stir in yeast and salt. Add oil and 425 ml (15 fl oz/scant 2 cups) tepid water. Mix together, then turn dough out onto a floured surface.

Knead dough thoroughly for 10 minutes until smooth and elastic. Cut into 12 equal pieces. Roll each piece into a ball, then roll out to an oval shape 18 cm (7 in) long. Place on floured trays; cover with a cloth; leave in a warm place for 1 hour or until puffed up to double the original size.

Preheat oven to 240C (475F/Gas 9). Oil 2 baking sheets and place in the oven to heat up. Place 3 pitta breads on each baking sheet and sprinkle with water. Bake in the oven for 5 minutes until puffed up and lightly browned. Remove from baking sheets and wrap in a cloth while baking remaining bread.

Makes 12.

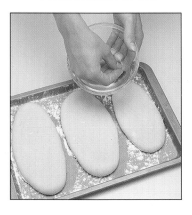

PISSALADIÈRE

55 ml (2 fl oz/¼ cup) olive oil, plus extra for
  brushing
1 kg (2¼ lb) Spanish onions, thinly sliced
1 large clove garlic, crushed
salt and freshly ground black pepper
50 g (1¾ oz) can anchovies in olive oil
12 large pitted black olives, halved
1 teaspoon herbes de Provence
basil sprigs, to garnish
BASE:
225 g (8 oz/2 cups) strong white flour
1 teaspoon herbes de Provence
1 teaspoon easy-blend yeast

Heat oil in a large, heavy frying pan, add
onions, garlic and salt and pepper and cook
gently, stirring occasionally, for 25-30
minutes, until onions are well reduced, soft
and golden. Leave to cool.

Meanwhile, make base. Stir together flour,
herbs, yeast and salt and pepper. Slowly stir
in about 175 ml (6 fl oz/¾ cup) tepid water
to bind to a smooth dough.

Turn dough on to a lightly floured surface
and knead well until firm and elastic. Lightly
oil a 33 x 23 cm (13 x 9 in) Swiss roll tin.
Roll out dough to fit tin and use to line tin,
pushing dough up sides and into corners.

Brush with oil, cover and leave for 30
minutes until dough has risen and is lightly
puffy. Preheat oven to 220C (425F/Gas 7).

Spread onions over dough. Drain anchovies,
reserving oil. Cut anchovies lengthways in
half and arrange in lattice pattern on top of
onions. Arrange olives on top, sprinkle with
herbs and drizzle over anchovy oil. Bake on
top shelf of oven for 20-25 minutes. Cut into
squares, garnish with basil sprigs and serve
warm or cold.

Serves 4-6.

SPANISH COUNTRY BREAD

225 g (8 oz/2 cups) strong flour
2 teaspoons salt, preferably coarse
3 teaspoons easy-blend dried yeast
oil for brushing
cornmeal for sprinkling

Sift flour and salt into a large bowl, stir in yeast and form a well in centre. Slowly pour 175 ml (6 fl oz/¾ cup) tepid water into well, stirring with a wooden spoon, to make a dough. Beat well until dough comes away from sides of bowl.

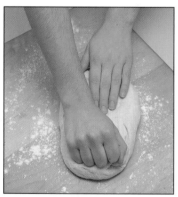

Turn dough onto a lightly floured surface and knead for 10-15 minutes until smooth and elastic; add a little more flour if dough is sticky. Put dough in an oiled bowl, cover and leave in a warm place until doubled in volume, about 2½ hours. Lightly sprinkle a baking sheet with cornmeal. Turn dough onto lightly floured surface, punch down then roll to a rectangle about 15 x 40 cm (6 x 16 in). Roll up like a Swiss roll and pinch seam to seal.

Place roll, seam-side down, on baking sheet. Using a very sharp knife, make 3 diagonal slashes on roll at equal distances. Brush top lightly with water. Leave in a warm place until doubled in volume, about 1 hour. Preheat oven to 230C (450F/Gas 8) and place a pan of water in the bottom. Brush loaf again with water and bake for 5 minutes. Remove pan of water. Brush loaf once more with water. Bake for about 20 minutes until loaf sounds hollow underneath.

Makes 1 loaf.

CHEESE & CHIVE PLAIT

450 g (1 lb/4 cups) strong plain white flour
1 teaspoon salt
1 teaspoon caster sugar
1½ teaspoons easy blend dried yeast
25 g (1 oz/6 teaspoons) butter
115 g (4 oz/1 cup) coarsely grated Cheddar cheese
3 tablespoons chopped fresh chives
4 spring onions, chopped
150 ml (5 fl oz/⅔ cup) tepid milk
175 ml (6 fl oz/¾ cup) tepid water
beaten egg, to glaze

Sift flour into a bowl. Stir in salt, sugar and yeast. Rub in butter.

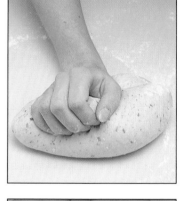

Stir in cheese, chives and spring onions and make a well in the centre. Mix milk with the tepid water and pour into the well. Mix until a soft dough is formed. Turn dough onto a lightly floured surface. Knead for about 10 minutes until smooth and elastic. Place in an oiled bowl, cover and leave in a warm place for about 1 hour, until doubled in size. Preheat oven to 220C (425F/Gas 7). Turn dough out onto a floured surface and knead for about 3 minutes.

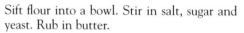

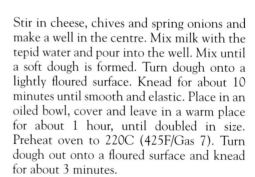

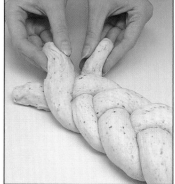

Divide dough into 3 pieces. Roll each one out to a rope shape and plait together, pinching ends to seal. Place on a baking sheet, cover with oiled plastic wrap and leave in a warm place for about 45 minutes until doubled in size. Brush with beaten egg and bake in the oven for 20 minutes. Reduce temperature to 180C (350F/Gas 4) and bake for a further 15 minutes until golden brown and the base sounds hollow when tapped. Serve loaf warm or cold.

Makes about 10 slices.

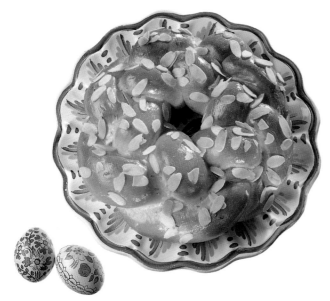

EASTER BREAD

800 g (1¾ lb/7 cups) strong white bread flour
1 sachet easy blend dried yeast
55 g (2 oz/¼ cup) caster sugar
2 teaspoons caraway seeds
115 g (4 oz/½ cup) butter, melted
2 eggs, beaten
225 ml (8 fl oz/1 cup) warm milk
1 egg, beaten, for glazing
6 teaspoons flaked almonds, to decorate

Sift flour into a large bowl. Stir in yeast, sugar and caraway seeds. Stir in butter, eggs and milk. Mix together, then turn dough out onto a floured surface.

Knead dough thoroughly for 10 minutes until smooth and elastic. Cut dough in half and divide each half into 3 pieces. Roll each piece into a rope 50 cm (20 in) long. Plait 3 ropes, then shape plait into a ring, pressing the ends together firmly. Repeat with remaining 3 ropes. Place the 2 rings on oiled baking sheets. Cover with a cloth and leave in a warm place for 1 hour or until doubled in size. Preheat oven to 190C (375F/Gas 5).

Brush loaves with beaten egg. Scatter flaked almonds over the top. Bake for 40 minutes or until loaves are lightly browned and sound hollow when tapped on the bases. Leave on wire racks to cool. Serve sliced and buttered.

Makes 2 loaves.

Note: Traditionally these loaves have red dyed eggs tucked into the braids before baking.

PARATHA

225 g (8 oz/2 cups) plain flour
225 g (8 oz/2 cups) wholewheat flour
salt
½ teaspoon onion seeds
½ teaspoon celery seeds
225 g (8 oz/1 cup) butter or ghee, melted
celery leaves, to garnish

Sift flours and salt to taste together into a mixing bowl and tip in any bran caught in the sieve. Stir in onion and celery seeds, then mix in about 155 ml (5 fl oz/⅔ cup) water to form a fairly soft dough.

Knead dough on a lightly floured surface for 5 minutes or until pliable and smooth. Wrap in plastic wrap and chill for 30 minutes. Divide dough into 10 pieces and roll each out to a 12.5 cm (5 in) round. Brush 1 side of each round with butter or ghee, then fold in half with buttered side inside. Brush top side with butter and fold in half again to make a triangle.

Roll out on a lightly floured surface until straight sides measure about 12.5 cm (5 in). Heat a griddle or heavy-based frying pan and brush with butter or ghee. Cook 2 or 3 at a time for 1 minute, then brush with butter, turn over and cook 1-2 minutes more. Stack on a plate and cover with a cloth while cooking remainder. Serve warm, garnished with celery leaves.

Makes 10.

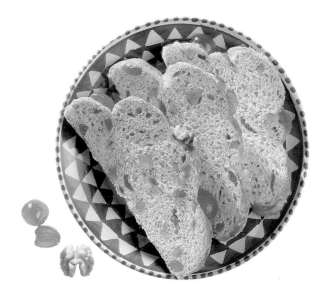

CARAWAY KUGELHOPF

225 g (8 oz/2 cups) plain flour
55 g (2 oz/¼ cup) caster sugar
2 teaspoons easy blend yeast
6 teaspoons caraway seeds
55 ml (2 fl oz/¼ cup) tepid water
115 g (4 oz/½ cup) unsalted butter, melted
3 eggs, beaten
icing sugar, to finish

Grease a 20 cm (8 in) kugelhopf mould. Sift flour into a bowl. Stir in sugar, yeast and caraway seeds.

Make a well in the centre; stir in water, butter and eggs. Beat vigorously until smooth. Cover bowl with plastic wrap and leave in a warm place until doubled in size. Stir mixture and turn into prepared mould. Cover with plastic wrap and leave to rise again until doubled in size.

Preheat oven to 200C (400F/Gas 6). Remove plastic wrap. Bake kugelhopf in the oven for 20 minutes. Lower the temperature to 190C (375F/Gas 5) and bake for a further 10 minutes until well risen and golden brown. Leave in the tin for 10 minutes, then remove to a wire rack. Dust lightly with icing sugar. Serve with butter while still slightly warm.

Makes 8-10 slices.

CHERRY NUT BREAD

350 g (12 oz/3 cups) strong plain white flour
½ teaspoon salt
1 teaspoon sugar
2 teaspoons easy blend dried yeast
55 g (2 oz/¼ cup) butter
55 g (2 oz/⅓ cup) glacé cherries, chopped
55 g (2 oz/½ cup) chopped walnuts
150 ml (5 fl oz/⅔ cup) tepid milk
70 ml (2½ fl oz/⅓ cup) tepid water
1 egg, beaten
TOPPING:
85 g (3 oz/½ cup) icing sugar, sifted
25 g (1 oz/2 tablespoons) glacé cherries
25 g (1 oz/⅓ cup) walnut halves

Grease and flour a baking sheet. Sift flour into a bowl. Stir in salt, sugar and yeast. Rub in butter and add chopped cherries and walnuts. Make a well in centre. Pour in milk, tepid water and egg. Mix to a soft dough. Turn onto a floured surface and knead for 10 minutes until smooth. Put in an oiled bowl, cover and leave in a warm place until doubled in size. Turn dough onto a floured surface, knead lightly and divide into 5 pieces. Roll each out to a rope 30 cm (12 in) long.

Plait 3 ropes together and place on prepared baking sheet. Twist the remaining 2 ropes together and place on top. Cover with oiled plastic wrap. Leave in a warm place until doubled in size. Preheat oven to 220C (425F/Gas 7). Bake bread in oven for 10 minutes; reduce heat to 190C (375F/Gas 5); bake for a further 20 minutes. Cool. Mix icing sugar with enough water to give a runny icing; drizzle over loaf. Decorate top with glacé cherries and walnut halves.

Makes about 12 slices.

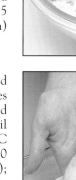

CHELSEA BUNS

225 g (8 oz/2 cups) strong plain white flour
2 teaspoons easy blend dried yeast
1 teaspoon caster sugar
½ teaspoon salt
6 teaspoons unsalted butter
115 ml (4 fl oz/½ cup) tepid milk
1 egg, beaten
FILLING:
55 g (2 oz/¼ cup) unsalted butter, softened
55 g (2 oz/⅓ cup) soft light brown sugar
115 g (4 oz/¾ cup) mixed dried fruit
1 teaspoon mixed spice
85 g (3 oz/½ cup) icing sugar, to finish

Butter a 17.5 cm (7 in) square cake tin. Sift flour into a bowl. Stir in yeast, caster sugar and salt. Rub in butter. Make a well in the centre. Pour in the tepid milk and egg. Beat vigorously to make a soft dough. On a floured surface, knead dough for 5-10 minutes until smooth. Put dough in an oiled bowl, cover and leave in a warm place for about 1 hour until doubled in size. Turn dough out onto a floured surface. Knead lightly; roll out to a rectangle 30 x 22.5 cm (12 x 9 in).

Spread with softened butter and sprinkle with brown sugar, fruit and spice. Roll up from a long side and cut into 9 pieces. Place in tin, cut sides up. Cover with oiled plastic wrap. Leave in a warm place for 45 minutes until well risen. Preheat oven to 190C (375F/Gas 5). Bake in oven for 30 minutes until golden. Leave to cool in tin for 10 minutes, then transfer, in one piece, to a wire rack to cool. Mix icing sugar with enough water to make a thin glaze. Brush over buns.

Makes 9.

LEMON & CURRANT BRIOCHES

225 g (8 oz/2 cups) strong plain white fluor
2 teaspoons easy blend dried yeast
½ teaspoon salt
3 teaspoons caster sugar
55 g (2 oz/⅓ cup) currants
grated rind 1 lemon
6 teaspoons tepid water
2 eggs, beaten
55 g (2 oz/¼ cup) unsalted butter, melted
beaten egg, to glaze

Butter 12 individual brioche tins. Sift flour into a bowl; stir in yeast, salt, sugar, currants and lemon rind.

Make a well in the centre. Pour in water, eggs and melted butter and beat vigorously to make a soft dough. Turn onto a lightly floured surface and knead for 5 minutes until smooth and elastic. Put dough in an oiled bowl; cover and leave in a warm place for 1 hour until doubled in size. Turn out onto a lightly floured surface, re-knead and roll into a rope shape. Cut into 12 equal pieces. Shape three-quarters of each piece into a ball and place in prepared tins.

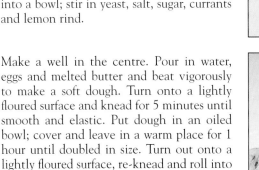

With a floured finger, press a hole in centre of each. Shape remaining pieces of dough into a little plug and press into holes, flattening the top slightly. Place tins on a baking sheet. Cover with oiled plastic wrap and leave in a warm place until dough comes almost to top of tins. Preheat oven to 220C (425F/Gas 7). Brush brioches with beaten egg. Bake in the oven for 15 minutes until golden brown. Serve warm with butter and jam.

Makes 12.

CRUMPETS

450 g (1 lb/4 cups) strong plain white flour
1 teaspoon salt
1 teaspoon caster sugar
2 teaspoons easy blend dried yeast
550 ml (20 fl oz/2½ cups) tepid milk
150 ml (5 fl oz/⅔ cup) tepid water
oil, for cooking
butter, to serve

Sift flour into a bowl. Stir in salt, sugar and yeast.

Make a well in the centre of flour and pour in the tepid milk and water. With a wooden spoon, gradually work flour into liquid, then beat vigorously to make a smooth batter. Cover bowl with a cloth and leave in a warm place for about 1 hour or until mixture has doubled in size.

Thoroughly grease a heavy frying pan or griddle and several crumpet rings. Arrange as many rings as possible in the pan. Heat the pan and pour in enough of the mixture to half fill each ring. Cook crumpets for 5-6 minutes until bubbles appear and burst on the surface. Remove rings and turn crumpets over. Cook on other side for a further 2-3 minutes. Serve crumpets hot, generously buttered.

Makes about 16.

DEVONSHIRE SPLITS

55 g (2 oz/¼ cup) unsalted butter
6 teaspoons caster sugar
150 ml (5 fl oz/⅔ cup) milk
450 g (1 lb/4 cups) strong plain white flour
2 teaspoons easy blend dried yeast
½ teaspoon salt
FILLING:
115 g (4 oz/⅓ cup) strawberry jam
300 ml (10 fl oz/1¼ cups) double (thick) cream, whipped
TO FINISH:
icing sugar, for dusting

In a saucepan, heat butter, sugar, milk and 150 ml (5 fl oz/⅔ cup) water until butter has melted and sugar dissolved. Leave liquid until tepid. Sift flour into a bowl. Stir in yeast and salt. Make a well in the centre, pour in liquid and mix vigorously to a soft dough. Turn onto a floured surface and knead until smooth. Place in an oiled bowl, cover and leave in a warm place until the mixture has doubled in size. Preheat oven to 220C (425F/Gas 7). Grease 2 baking sheets.

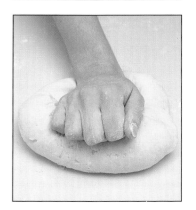

Turn dough out onto a floured surface. Divide into 16 pieces. Knead each piece lightly and shape into a ball. Place on baking sheets, flattening each ball slightly. Cover with oiled plastic wrap and leave in a warm place for about 40 minutes until well risen. Bake in the oven for about 15 minutes until bases sound hollow when tapped. Cool on a wire rack. Split and fill with jam and cream. Dust lightly with icing sugar.

Makes 16.

SWEET PASTRIES

PECAN PIE

1 quantity Shortcrust Pastry (see page 336)
3 eggs
300 g (10 oz/2 cups) soft brown sugar
1 tablespoon clear honey
25 g (1 oz/6 teaspoons) butter, melted
2 tablespoons whipping cream
pinch salt
175 g (6 oz/1½ cups) pecan nuts, roughly chopped
icing sugar, to serve, if desired

Preheat the oven to 190C (375F/Gas 5). Use the pastry to line a 25 cm(10 in) flan tin and bake blind as directed on page 336. Leave oven at 190C (375F/Gas 5).

In a large bowl, whisk eggs and brown sugar together until pale and thick. Stir in honey, butter, whipping cream and salt and mix together thoroughly. Fold in pecan nuts.

Pour mixture evenly into baked pastry case and bake in the oven for 20 minutes. Lower oven temperature to 160C (325F/Gas 3) and cook for a further 45-50 minutes, until set. Serve warm, or allow to cool and serve chilled. Dust with icing sugar, if desired.

Serves 6.

Note: Substitute walnuts for pecans in this pie if you prefer, or if you have difficulty in obtaining pecan nuts.

ORANGE MERINGUE PIE

1 quantity Shortcrust Pastry (see page 336)
45 g (1½ oz/12 teaspoons) cornflour
300 ml (10 fl oz/1¼ cups) water
25 g (1 oz/6 teaspoons) butter
juice and grated peel 2 small oranges
juice and grated peel 1 small lime
2 eggs, separated
175 g (6 oz/¾ cup) caster sugar

Preheat oven to 190C (375F/Gas 5). Use the pastry to line a 25 cm (10 in) flan tin and bake blind as described on page 336. Lower oven to 160C (325F/Gas 3).

In a bowl, mix cornflour to a smooth paste with a little of the water. Stir in remaining water, then pour into a saucepan and add butter. Bring to the boil, stirring constantly. Simmer for 2-3 minutes, still stirring, then remove from heat. Beat in fruit juices and grated peel, egg yolks and one-third of the sugar. Spoon into flan case and cool slightly.

In a large bowl, whisk egg whites until stiff but not dry, add half remaining sugar and whisk again until mixture holds its shape. Fold in rest of sugar, then spoon or pipe meringue on top of flan, to cover filling and pastry. Bake in the oven for 20-30 minutes, until meringue is set and lightly golden. Serve warm or cold.

Serves 6-8.

TARTE AU CITRON

3 eggs
1 egg yolk
150 g (5 oz/¾ cup) caster sugar
grated rind and juice 3 lemons
grated rind and juice 1 orange
70 g (2½ oz/½ cup) icing sugar
thinly pared rind 1 lemon
icing sugar, for dusting
lemon twists and chervil sprigs, to decorate
PÂTE SUCRÉE:
200 g (7 oz/¾ cup) plain flour
pinch of salt
4 tablespoons caster sugar
115 g (4 oz/½ cup) unsalted butter, softened
2 egg yolks

Prick base of pastry case with a fork, line with greaseproof paper or foil and fill with baking beans. Put flan tin on a baking sheet and bake for 10-12 minutes. Lower oven temperature to 190C (375F/Gas 5). Remove paper and beans and bake for 5 minutes, until golden. Transfer tin to a wire rack and leave to cool. Leave oven on.

To make pâte sucrée, sift flour and salt onto a marble slab or a work surface and make a well in centre. Put sugar, butter and egg yolks into well and pinch them together to form a paste, then lightly draw in the flour, adding about 1 tablespoon cold water to make a soft but firm dough. Cover and chill for 2 hours.

Mix together eggs, egg yolk, caster sugar and lemon and orange rind and juice. Return flan tin to baking sheet and ladle in filling. Bake for 25-30 minutes, until set. Transfer tin to a wire rack, cool slightly, then remove outer ring of flan tin. Leave tart to cool completely.

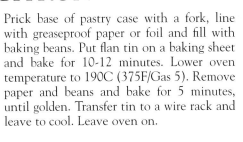

Roll out pastry on a lightly floured surface and line a 23.5 cm (9½ in) loose-bottomed fluted flan tin, pressing pastry well into sides and base. Run rolling pin over top of tin to cut off excess pastry. Chill for 20 minutes. Preheat oven to 200C (400F/Gas 6).

Put icing sugar and 150 ml (5 fl oz/⅔ cup) water in a small pan and heat gently, stirring, until dissolved. Boil for 2 minutes then add pared lemon rind and simmer until glassy. Remove with a slotted spoon and leave to cool on greaseproof paper. Just before serving, dust tart thickly with sifted icing sugar and scatter over candied lemon rind. Garnish with lemon twists and chervil sprigs and serve with cream, if liked.

Serves 6-8.

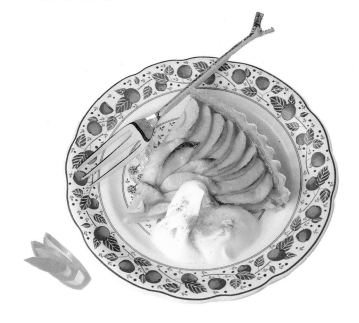

RED FRUIT TART

23.5 cm (9½ in) loose-bottomed fluted flan tin lined
  with pâte sucrée (see page 333)
about 26 each raspberries, halved strawberries and
  pitted cherries
3 tablespoons red fruit jam
1 teaspoon lemon juice
raspberries and raspberry leaves, to decorate
CRÈME PÂTISSIÈRE:
150 ml (5 fl oz/⅔ cup) milk
150 ml (5 fl oz/⅔ cup) single (light) cream
1 vanilla pod
3 egg yolks
55 g (2 oz/¼ cup) sugar
1 tablespoon plain flour
1½ tablespoons cornflour
15 g (½ oz/1 tablespoon) unsalted butter

To make crème pâtissière, put milk, cream
and vanilla pod in a saucepan and heat
gently to simmering point. Remove from
heat, cover and leave for 30 minutes. Whisk
egg yolks and sugar until pale and very thick.
Stir in flour and cornflour. Remove vanilla
pod from milk and return to the boil. Slowly
pour into egg mixture, whisking constantly.
Return to pan and bring to boil, whisking.
Simmer for 2-3 minutes. Remove from heat,
stir in butter and pour into a bowl. Leave to
cool, stirring occasionally. Cover and chill.
Preheat oven to 200C (400F/Gas 6).

Prick pastry case with a fork, line with
greaseproof paper or foil and fill with baking
beans. Bake for 10-12 minutes. Lower oven
temperature to 190C (375F/Gas 5). Remove
paper and beans and bake for 8-10 minutes.
Cool on a wire rack. Fill pastry case with
crème pâtissière and arrange fruit on top. Put
jam and lemon juice in a pan and heat
gently, to soften. Pass through a sieve and
brush over fruit. Leave to cool, decorate and
serve.

Serves 6.

FRENCH APPLE TART

115 g (4 oz/1 cup) plain flour
1 teaspoon caster sugar
85 g (3 oz/⅓ cup) butter
1 kg (2¼ lb) cooking apples
grated rind and juice 1 lemon
4 tablespoons apricot jam
225 g (8 oz) eating apples

Preheat oven to 180C (350F/Gas 4). Sift
flour into a bowl and mix in the sugar. Rub
in 55 g (2 oz/¼ cup) of the butter until mixture resembles breadcrumbs. Add enough
water to make a soft dough. On a lightly
floured surface, roll out the dough.

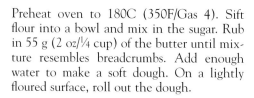

Use dough to line a 20 cm (8 in) loose-
bottomed flan tin. Prick base of pastry all
over with a fork. Bake blind in oven for 10
minutes. Peel, core and slice cooking apples
and place in a saucepan with remaining butter and 2 tablespoons water. Cover and cook
gently for 15 minutes, until apples are soft.
Add grated lemon rind and 3 tablespoons
jam. Cook for a further 15 minutes until
purée has thickened. Spoon apple purée into
flan case and leave to cool. Peel, core and
slice eating apples thinly.

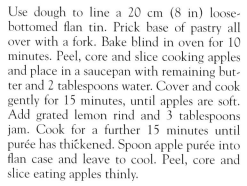

Arrange in an overlapping circle around
edge of flan and in the centre. Brush with
lemon juice. Bake in oven for 30-40 minutes
until light brown on top. Warm remaining
jam and brush over flan to glaze. Serve warm
or cold with custard or cream sprinkled with
cinnamon.

Serves 6.

FIG & ORANGE TART

225 g (8 oz/1½ cups) no-soak dried figs, chopped
juice 2 oranges
70 g (3 oz/¾ cup) butter, diced
2 eggs, beaten
2 tablespoons pine nuts
icing sugar, for dusting
orange slices, to decorate
PASTRY:
150 g (5 oz/1¼ cups) plain flour
85 g (3 oz/⅓ cup) butter
2 tablespoons icing sugar
1 egg yolk

To make the pastry, sift the flour into a bowl. Rub in the butter until the mixture resembles fine breadcrumbs.

Stir in the icing sugar. Add the egg yolk and 1 teaspoon of water. Stir with a knife to form a smooth dough. Knead lightly, wrap in cling film and chill for 30 minutes. On a lightly floured surface, roll out the dough to fit a 20 cm (8 in) loose-bottomed flan tin. Line the flan tin with the pastry and chill again for 20-30 minutes. Preheat the oven to 190C (375F/Gas 5). Prick the pastry all over with a fork then line with foil and fill with baking beans. Bake blind for 10-15 minutes until the pastry has set.

Remove the baking beans and foil and bake for a further 10-15 minutes until firm and golden brown. Put the figs and orange juice in a saucepan. Cook for 5-10 minutes, stirring, until thickened. Remove from the heat, add the butter and stir until melted. Beat in the eggs. Pour the mixture into the flan case and scatter with the pine nuts. Bake for 15 minutes until just set. Dust with icing sugar, decorate with orange slices and serve warm or cold.

Serves 6.

PLUM-CUSTARD TART

450 g (1 lb) plums or damsons
55 g (2 oz/½ cup) plain flour
55 g (2 oz/½ cup) wholemeal plain flour
55 g (2 oz/¼ cup) butter
300 ml (10 fl oz/1¼ cups) milk
2 eggs
55 g (2 oz/¼ cup) caster sugar
few drops almond essence

Preheat oven to 180C (350F/Gas 4). Wash and drain plums or damsons; set aside. Sift flours into a bowl and rub in butter until mixture resembles breadcrumbs.

Add enough water to make a soft dough. On a lightly floured surface, roll out pastry and use to line a 20 cm (8 in) flan dish. Prick base of pastry with a fork. Bake blind in oven for 10 minutes. Place plums or damsons in base of pastry case.

In a bowl, beat together milk, eggs, sugar and almond essence. Pour over plums or damsons. Bake in oven for 45 minutes until custard is set and golden. Serve warm or cold.

Serves 6.

Note: Almond essence is strong in flavour – use it sparingly.

TARTE TATIN

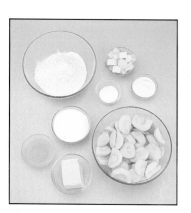

115 g (4 oz/½ cup) unsalted butter, softened
115 g (4 oz/½ cup) caster sugar
about 1.3 kg (3 lb) firm, well-flavoured apples, such
  as Cox's, peeled, cored and cut into wedges
juice 1 lemon
strips lemon rind and mint sprigs, to decorate
SHORTCRUST PASTRY:
225 g (8 oz/2 cups) plain flour
1 tablespoon caster sugar
130 g (4½ oz/½ cup) butter, diced
2-3 tablespoons crème fraîche or milk

To make pastry, combine flour and sugar in a bowl. Add butter and rub in until mixture resembles fine breadcrumbs. Add enough crème fraîche or milk to bind to a dough. Form into a ball, cover and chill for at least 30 minutes.

Spread butter over base of a heavy 23.5 cm (9½ in) cake tin or ovenproof frying pan. Sprinkle over sugar and arrange apples on top, rounded-side down.

Sprinkle with lemon juice and cook over a moderately high heat, shaking tin or pan occasionally, for 20-30 minutes, until apples are lightly caramelized. If a lot of juice is produced, pour it off into a saucepan, boil to a thick syrup and pour back over apples.

Preheat oven to 220C (425F/Gas 7). Roll out pastry on a lightly floured surface until slightly larger than tin or pan. Lay pastry on top of apples, tucking edge of pastry down side of tin or pan.

Prick pastry lightly with a fork and put tin or pan on a baking sheet. Bake for 20 minutes, until pastry is golden. Turn tart onto a warmed serving plate, decorate with lemon rind and mint sprigs and serve with cream.

Serves 6-8.

Note: Be careful when turning out the tart as the syrup will be very hot and can burn.

PRUNE & ALMOND TART

225 g (8 oz) prunes
4 tablespoons brandy
225 g (8 oz) shortcrust pastry, thawed if frozen
115 g (4 oz/½ cup) unsalted butter, softened
115 g (4 oz/½ cup) icing sugar
3 eggs, beaten
55 g (2 oz/½ cup) plain flour
115 g (4 oz/½ cup) ground almonds
55 g (2 oz/½ cup) flaked almonds

Put the prunes and brandy in a bowl and leave to soak overnight. Roll out the pastry on a lightly floured surface and use to line a 27 cm (10½ in) flan dish.

Trim the pastry and prick the base all over with a fork. Drain the prunes and arrange in the pastry case. Preheat oven to 200C (400F/Gas 6). In a bowl, beat together the butter and icing sugar. Beat in the eggs and fold in the flour and ground almonds. Spread the mixture evenly over the prunes.

Sprinkle the flaked almonds over the top. Bake for 40-45 minutes, until the filling is risen and golden brown. Serve warm.

Serves 6-8.

TIA MARIA CHOUX RING

1 quantity Choux Pastry (see page 343)
6 teaspoons plain flour
6 teaspoons cornflour
55 g (2 oz/¼ cup) caster sugar
300 ml (10 fl oz/1¼ cups) milk
3 egg yolks
150 ml (5 fl oz/⅔ cup) whipping cream
coffee essence
2 teaspoons Tia Maria
115 g (4 oz/¾ cup) icing sugar

Preheat oven to 220C (425F/Gas 7). Put pastry in a piping bag fitted with a 1 cm (½ in) plain nozzle.

Pipe a double 20 cm (8 in) ring onto a paper-lined baking sheet. Bake ring in the oven for 20 minutes. Lower the temperature to 180C (350F/Gas 4); bake for a further 10-15 minutes until golden brown and hollow. Split horizontally; cool on a wire rack. Sift flour and cornflour into a bowl. Stir in sugar and 2 tablespoons milk. Stir to form a thick paste. Whisk in egg yolks. In a saucepan, heat remaining milk to just below boiling point. Pour onto egg mixture, stirring constantly.

Strain mixture back into saucepan and cook gently, stirring constantly, until thickened. Cover closely with plastic wrap and leave until cold. In a bowl, stiffly whip cream and fold into custard. Stir in 2 teaspoons coffee essence and the Tia Maria. Sandwich choux rings together with coffee filling. In a bowl, mix together sifted icing sugar, few drops coffee essence and about 3 teaspoons water. Spoon over cake and leave to set.

Serves 8.

NUTTY FILO FINGERS

115 g (4 oz/1¼ cups) ground hazelnuts
55 g (2 oz/¼ cup) granulated sugar
3 teaspoons orange flower water
85 g (3 oz/⅓ cup) unsalted butter
6 large sheets filo pastry
caster sugar, for dusting

Preheat oven to 180C (350F/Gas 4). Grease 2 baking sheets. In a bowl, mix together ground hazelnuts, granulated sugar and orange flower water.

In a saucepan, melt butter. Cut each sheet of pastry into 4 rectangles. Pile on top of each other and cover with a tea-towel to prevent drying out. Working with one filo rectangle at a time, brush the pastry with melted butter.

Spread a teaspoon of filling along one short end. Fold long sides in, slightly over filling. Roll up from filling end. Place on one of the prepared baking sheets with seam underneath; brush with melted butter. Repeat with remaining pastry and filling. Bake in the oven for 20 minutes or until very lightly coloured. Transfer to wire racks to cool; sprinkle with caster sugar.

Makes 24.

FRUITY FILO PARCELS

1 eating apple
2 teaspoons lemon juice
2 kiwi fruit
1 peach
55 g (2 oz/⅓ cup) raisins
1 teaspoon ground mixed spice
8 sheets filo pastry
55 g (2 oz/¼ cup) butter, melted
1 tablespoon icing sugar
strawberry slices, to decorate (optional)

Preheat oven to 200C (400F/Gas 6). To prepare filling, peel, core and coarsely grate apple into a bowl and sprinkle with lemon juice to prevent discoloration.

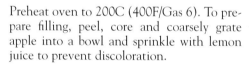
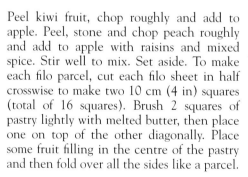

Peel kiwi fruit, chop roughly and add to apple. Peel, stone and chop peach roughly and add to apple with raisins and mixed spice. Stir well to mix. Set aside. To make each filo parcel, cut each filo sheet in half crosswise to make two 10 cm (4 in) squares (total of 16 squares). Brush 2 squares of pastry lightly with melted butter, then place one on top of the other diagonally. Place some fruit filling in the centre of the pastry and then fold over all the sides like a parcel.

Place seam-edge downwards onto a greased baking sheet and brush lightly with melted butter. Repeat with remaining pastry squares and filling, to make 8 parcels. Bake in oven for 30 minutes until golden brown and crisp. Sprinkle with sifted icing sugar just before serving and decorate with a few slices of strawberry, if wished. Serve hot or cold.

Makes 8.

MANGO & LYCHEE TURNOVERS

3 teaspoons cornflour
3 teaspoons sugar
3 tablespoons unsweetened orange juice
1 teaspoon lemon juice
1 teaspoon ground nutmeg
1 mango
10 lychees
8 sheets filo pastry
55 g (2 oz/¼ cup) butter, melted
1 tablespoon icing sugar

Preheat oven to 200C (400F/Gas 6). In a saucepan, blend cornflour and sugar with 3 tablespoons water. Add orange juice, lemon juice and nutmeg and mix well.

Heat gently over a low heat until mixture thickens, stirring all the time. Simmer sauce for 3 minutes, then allow to cool. Peel, stone and roughly chop mango and lychees. Add fruit to cooled sauce, mixing well. To make each turnover, cut each filo sheet in half crosswise to make two 10 cm (4 in) squares (total of 16 squares). Brush 2 squares of pastry lightly with melted butter and place one on top of the other. Place some filling in the centre of the pastry, fold diagonally in half and press edges to seal.

Place on a greased baking sheet and brush lightly with melted butter. Repeat with remaining pastry squares and filling to make 8 turnovers. Bake in oven for 30 minutes, until golden brown and crisp. Dust with sifted icing sugar and serve immediately with ice cream, if desired.

Makes 8.

KADAIFI

115 g (4 oz/1 cup) finely chopped walnuts
115 g (4 oz/1 cup) finely chopped almonds
55 g (2 oz/¼ cup) caster sugar
½ teaspoon ground cinnamon
400 g (14 oz) kadaifi pastry (see Note)
55 g (2 oz/¼ cup) butter
SYRUP:
225 g (8 oz/1 cup) granulated sugar
3 teaspoons lemon juice
3 teaspoons orange flower water

Preheat oven to 180C (350F/Gas 4). Butter a baking tray. In a bowl, mix together walnuts, almonds, sugar and cinnamon.

Tease pastry out to a rectangle 45 x 37.5 cm (18 x 15 in). Cut into 18 pieces measuring 12.5 x 7.5 cm (5 x 3 in). Place 1 tablespoon of nut mixture on short end of each rectangle of pastry. Roll up, enclosing filling. Place rolls on the baking tray. In a small saucepan, melt butter, then pour it over the rolls. Bake in the oven for 25-30 minutes until golden and crisp. Leave to cool for 15 minutes.

To make the syrup, put sugar, the lemon juice and 300 ml (10 fl oz/1¼ cups) water in a saucepan. Heat gently until sugar has dissolved, then boil for 5 minutes until slightly thickened. Add orange flower water, then pour syrup over pastry rolls.

Makes 18.

Note: Kadaifi is a white shredded raw pastry available from delicatessens and Greek shops. It has to be teased into shape rather than rolled.

CHEESE & HONEY TRIANGLES

225 g (8 oz/1 cup) cream cheese
6 teaspoons set aromatic honey
1 egg yolk
55 g (2 oz/¼ cup) butter
6 sheets filo pastry
icing sugar, for dusting

Preheat oven to 190C (375F/Gas 5). Butter a baking sheet. In a bowl, beat together cream cheese, honey and egg yolk.

In a small saucepan, melt butter. Brush a sheet of filo pastry with melted butter. Cover with a second sheet of pastry and brush with butter. Cover with a third sheet of pastry. Cut pastry layers in half across. Cut each half into 4 strips across. Repeat with remaining 3 sheets of pastry.

Place a spoonful of cream cheese mixture on corner of pastry strip. Fold pastry and filling over at right angles to make a triangle and continue folding in this way along strip of pastry to form a neat triangular parcel. Place on baking sheet and brush with melted butter. Repeat with remaining pastry strips and filling. Bake in the oven for 10 minutes until crisp. Dust lightly with icing sugar.

Makes 16.

WALNUT PASTRIES

300 g (10 fl oz/2½ cups) plain flour
175 g (6 oz/¾ cup) butter
85 g (3 oz/⅓ cup) icing sugar
1 egg yolk
9 teaspoons caster sugar
115 g (4 oz/1 cup) walnuts, coarsely chopped
85 g (3 oz/½ cup) chopped mixed citrus peel
¼ teaspoon freshly grated nutmeg
9 teaspoons rosewater
icing sugar, for coating

Sift flour into a bowl. Rub in butter until mixture resembles breadcrumbs.

Sift in icing sugar and stir. Mix in egg yolk and a little water to make a firm dough. Chill for 30 minutes. Preheat oven to 180C (350F/Gas 4). Butter a baking sheet. To make the syrup, in a saucepan, put caster sugar and 100 ml (3½ fl oz/⅓ cup) water. Heat gently until sugar has dissolved. Bring to the boil and boil for a few minutes until syrup has reduced and thickened slightly.

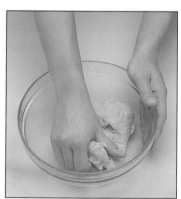

In a bowl, mix together walnuts, chopped mixed citrus peel and nutmeg. Moisten with the syrup. On a floured surface roll out pastry. Cut out 10 cm (4 in) circles. Place a teaspoon of walnut mixture on each circle. Fold in half, pressing edges together. Bake in the oven for 20-30 minutes until pale golden. Brush with rosewater. Coat liberally with icing sugar.

Makes about 20.

SERPENT CAKE

12 sheets filo pastry, about 40 x 30 cm (16 x 12 in)
85 g (3 oz/⅓ cup) unsalted butter, melted
icing sugar, for dusting
ground cinnamon, to decorate
ALMOND PASTE:
225 g (8 oz/2 cups) ground almonds
115 g (4 oz/¾ cup) icing sugar
grated rind and juice ½ orange
55 g (2 oz/¼ cup) softened butter

To make the almond paste, mix together the ground almonds, icing sugar, orange rind, orange juice and butter. Cover and chill for 30 minutes, until firm.

Preheat the oven to 180C (350F/Gas 4). Dust a work surface with icing sugar. Divide the almond paste into three and roll each piece into a sausage 50 cm (20 in) long. Brush two sheets of filo pastry with melted butter and place side by side, with the long sides overlapping slightly. Place two more buttered sheets on top. Lay a roll of almond paste along one of the long sides and roll up. Brush with butter and roll into a tight coil. Place the coil on a baking sheet.

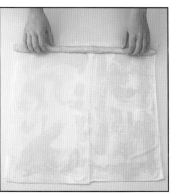

Make two more rolls in the same way. Join them to the coil, continuing the shape and sealing the joins with water. Bake for 20-30 minutes until crisp and golden. Invert on to another baking sheet and return to the oven until crisp. Invert on to a serving dish and leave to cool. Dust with icing sugar. Decorate with stripes of ground cinnamon and serve.

Serves 6.

Note: This cake does not keep well and is best eaten on the day it is made.

CANDIED FRUIT TARTS

225 g (8 oz/1 cup) ricotta cheese
3 egg yolks
55 g (2 oz/¼ cup) caster sugar
1 tablespoon brandy
grated rind 1 lemon
1 tablespoon lemon juice
115 g (4 oz/⅔ cup) crystallized fruit, finely chopped
icing sugar, for dusting
mint sprigs, to decorate
PASTRY:
175 g (6 oz/1½ cups) plain flour
85 g (3 oz/⅓ cup) butter
85 g (3 oz/⅓ cup) white vegetable fat

To make the pastry, sift the flour into a bowl. Add the butter and vegetable fat.

Rub in the butter and vegetable fat until the mixture resembles fine breadcrumbs. Stir in 2 tablespoons of cold water and use a knife to mix to a smooth dough. Knead lightly, wrap in cling film and chill for 30 minutes. Preheat the oven to 180C (350F/Gas 4). On a lightly floured surface, roll out the pastry until 3 mm (⅛ in) thick. Cut out four circles to fit four 10 cm (4 in) flan tins.

Put the ricotta cheese, egg yolks, caster sugar, brandy and lemon rind and juice in a bowl. Beat together until smooth then stir in the crystallized fruit. Divide the mixture among the pastry cases. Bake for 30-40 minutes or until the filling is set and golden. Leave to cool. Dust with icing sugar, decorate with mint sprigs and serve cold.

Serves 4.

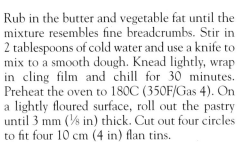

MAIDS OF HONOUR

1½ quantities Shortcrust Pastry (see page 336)
115 g (4 oz) cottage cheese
55 g (2 oz/¼ cup) softened butter
55 g (2 oz/¼ cup) caster sugar
grated rind and juice ½ lemon
25 g (1 oz/¼ cup) ground almonds
½ teaspoon grated nutmeg
2 teaspoons brandy
55 g (2 oz/⅓ cup) currants
caster sugar, for sprinkling

Roll out pastry and use to line 12 tartlet tins. Chill for 30 minutes.

Preheat oven to 190C (375F/Gas 5). Sieve cottage cheese into a bowl. Add butter and beat until well blended. Add sugar, lemon rind and juice, ground almonds, nutmeg and brandy. Mix thoroughly. Stir in currants.

Spoon mixture into prepared pastry cases. Bake in the oven for 20-30 minutes until risen and golden brown. Sprinkle with caster sugar. Transfer to a wire rack to cool.

Makes 12.

PALMIERS

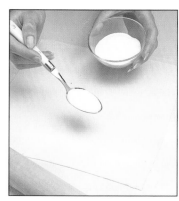

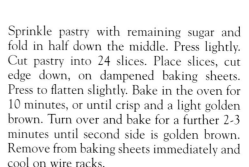

225 g (8 oz) puff pastry, thawed if frozen
55 g (2 oz/¼ cup) caster sugar
extra sugar, for rolling out
FILLING:
115 ml (4 fl oz/½ cup) double (thick) cream
4 teaspoons red jelly (such as redcurrant jelly)

Preheat oven to 220C (425F/Gas 7). On a surface dredged with caster sugar, roll out pastry to a 30 cm (12 in) square and sprinkle with half the sugar. Fold sides of pastry into the middle, sprinkle with half remaining sugar and fold sides into the middle again.

Sprinkle pastry with remaining sugar and fold in half down the middle. Press lightly. Cut pastry into 24 slices. Place slices, cut edge down, on dampened baking sheets. Press to flatten slightly. Bake in the oven for 10 minutes, or until crisp and a light golden brown. Turn over and bake for a further 2-3 minutes until second side is golden brown. Remove from baking sheets immediately and cool on wire racks.

In a bowl, whip cream until holding soft peaks. Spread a little jelly on 12 of the palmiers. Spread cream over jelly and top with remaining 12 palmiers.

Makes 12.

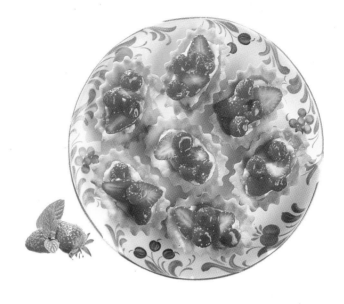

RASPBERRY ÉCLAIRS

CHOUX PASTRY:
55 g (2 oz/¼ cup) unsalted butter or margarine
70 g (2½ oz/⅓ cup) plain flour, sifted
2 eggs, beaten
FILLING:
175 ml (6 fl oz/¾ cup) double (thick) cream
3 teaspoons icing sugar
175 g (6 oz) raspberries
ICING:
115 g (4 oz/¾ cup) icing sugar, sifted
2 teaspoons lemon juice
pink food colouring (optional)

Preheat oven to 220C (425F/Gas 7). In a saucepan, melt butter or margarine, add 150 ml (5 fl oz/⅔ cup) water and bring to the boil. Add flour, all at once, and beat thoroughly until mixture leaves the side of the pan. Cool slightly, then vigorously beat in eggs, one at a time. Put mixture into a piping bag fitted with a plain 1 cm (½ in) nozzle and pipe twenty to twenty four 7.5 cm (3 in) lengths onto dampened baking sheets. Bake in the oven for 10 minutes. Reduce temperature to 190C (375F/Gas 5) and bake for 20 minutes until golden.

Slit the side of each éclair and leave on wire racks to cool. Make filling, whip cream and icing sugar in a bowl until thick, put in a piping bag fitted with a 0.3 cm (⅛ in) plain nozzle and pipe into each éclair. Put a few raspberries in each éclair. Make icing, mix icing sugar with lemon juice and enough water to make a smooth paste. Add pink colouring, if desired. Spread icing over éclairs and leave to set.

Makes 20-24.

SUMMER FRUIT TARTLETS

PASTRY:
200 g (7 oz/1¾ cups) plain flour, sifted
55 g (2 oz/½ cup) ground almonds
85 g (3 oz/½ cup) icing sugar, sifted
115 g (4 oz/½ cup) butter
1 egg yolk
3 teaspoons milk
FILLING:
225 g (8 oz) cream cheese
caster sugar, to taste
350 g (12 oz) fresh summer fruits, such as red and
  blackcurrants, raspberries and wild strawberries
redcurrant jelly, heated, to glaze

In a bowl, mix together flour, ground almonds and icing sugar. Rub in butter until mixture resembles breadcrumbs. Add egg yolk and milk; work in with a palette knife, then with fingers, until dough binds together. Wrap dough in plastic wrap and chill for 30 minutes. Preheat the oven to 200C (400F/Gas 6). On a floured surface, roll out pastry thinly and use to line 12 deep tartlet or individual brioche tins; prick bases.

Press a piece of foil into each tartlet, covering the edges. Bake in the oven for 10-15 minutes until light golden brown. Remove foil and bake for a further 2-3 minutes. Transfer to a wire rack to cool. To make filling, mix cream cheese and caster sugar together in a bowl. Put a spoonful of filling in each pastry case. Arrange fruit on top, brush with glaze and serve at once.

Makes 12.

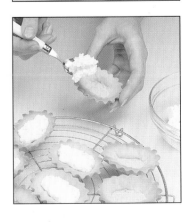

INDIVIDUAL PEAR PUFFS

225 g (8 oz) puff pastry, thawed if frozen
2 large, ripe eating pears
1 egg yolk
1 tablespoon milk
caster sugar, for sprinkling
Poire William liqueur, if desired

Preheat oven to 220C (425F/Gas 7). Roll out pastry to a rough rectangle, about 0.5 cm (¼ in) thick. Using a pear (halved, if easier) as a guide, cut out a pastry pear shape, 1 cm (½ in) larger than the pear.

Cut directly round pear, leaving a pear-shaped 'frame'. Roll out solid pear shape to same size as frame, dampen edges with water and fit frame on top. Press edges together lightly, then 'knock up' using a blunt knife. Make 3 more pastry pear shapes in same way. Peel and halve pears. Scoop out cores with a teaspoon, then cut across into thin slices. Fit neatly into pastry shapes.

Place pear puffs on baking sheet. Beat egg yolk with milk in a small bowl and brush edges of pastry with this. Bake in the oven for 15-20 minutes, until pears are tender and pastry edges are puffed up and golden. Remove from oven, sprinkle with caster sugar and place under a hot grill for 1 minute. Transfer to serving plates. Heat liqueur, if using, in a small saucepan, set alight and pour, flaming, over puffs. Serve at once.

Serves 4.

STRAWBERRY MILLE-FEUILLE

375 g (13 oz) puff pastry, thawed if frozen
450 g (1 lb) fresh strawberries
300 ml (10 fl oz/1¼ cups) whipping cream
1-2 drops vanilla essence
caster sugar, to taste
5 tablespoons redcurrant jelly

Preheat oven to 220C (425F/Gas 7). Roll out the pastry to a thin rectangle and cut it into 3 even sections.

Place sections on baking sheets and prick all over with a fork. Bake in the oven for 15-20 minutes, until golden brown and crisp. Cool on a wire rack. When cold, trim edges with a very sharp knife to make even. Reserve trimmings. Cut half of the strawberries in half – choose even-sized ones for this. Slice remainder. In a bowl, whip cream fairly stiffly and flavour with vanilla essence and sugar. Fold sliced strawberries into cream.

Put a pastry slice onto a serving plate and spread with half the cream mixture. Lay another slice on top and spread with remaining cream mixture. Top with third slice. Put redcurrant jelly and 2 tablespoons water into a small saucepan and heat gently until jelly has dissolved. Brush top slice with a little jelly and arrange halved strawberries on top. Brush with remainder of jelly. Crush reserved pastry trimmings and press into sides of slice with the blade of a knife.

Serves 6-8.

MINCEMEAT JALOUSIE

375 g (13 oz) puff pastry, thawed if frozen
1 tablespoon milk
1 tablespoon caster sugar
MINCEMEAT:
2 eating apples
2 bananas
juice and grated peel ½ lemon and 1 orange
55 g (2 oz) grapes
85 g (3 oz/⅔ cup) currants
85 g (3 oz/½ cup) raisins
85 g (3 oz/½ cup) sultanas
25 g (1 oz/¼ cup) almonds, roughly chopped
25 g (1 oz/⅓ cup) walnuts, roughly chopped
25 g (1 oz/⅓ cup) raw cane sugar
2 tablespoons brandy
45 g (1½ oz/9 teaspoons) butter, melted

To make the mincemeat, peel and chop apples and bananas. In a large bowl, quickly toss prepared fruit in lemon juice. Halve and seed grapes and add to fruit with orange juice and lemon and orange peel. Add currants, raisins and sultanas. Add nuts to mixture with sugar and brandy. Mix everything together well, then stir in melted butter. You only need one-third of this quantity for the jalousie, but it is not worth making a smaller amount. Use the remainder for mince pies.

Preheat oven to 220C (425F/Gas 7). Roll out pastry to a 30 x 12.5 cm (12 x 5 in) rectangle. Cut pastry in half, to two 15 x 12.5 cm (6 x 5 in) rectangles.

Put one pastry half on a dampened baking sheet and spread mincemeat on top to within 2.5 cm (1 in) of edges. Moisten edges with water. Roll out remaining pastry to 2.5 cm (1 in) larger all round than other piece. Fold in half lengthwise and make cuts down from folded edge, 1 cm (½ in) apart to within 2.5 cm (1 in) of edge. Open and lifting carefully, place over mincemeat and pastry.

Press edges of pastry together and 'knock up' sides using a blunt knife. Chill jalousie for 30 minutes. Brush lightly with milk and sprinkle with caster sugar. Bake in the oven for 30-35 minutes, until pastry is puffed up and golden.

If the pastry starts to brown too quickly, cover it with foil.

Serves 6.

Note: Serve the jalousie with 250 ml (8 fl oz/ 1 cup) whipping cream, whipped with 1 tablespoon brandy and 1 tablespoon caster sugar.

The mincemeat can be made in advance and stored in a rigid plastic container in the refrigerator for up to 5 days.

CLEMENTINE TARTLETS

1 quantity Shortcrust Pastry (see page 336)
juice 2 oranges and 1 lemon
425 g (15 oz/2 cups) caster sugar
4 clementines
2 eggs, plus 2 extra yolks
115 g (4 oz/½ cup) butter, softened
1 heaped tablespoon ground almonds
2-3 tablespoons Grand Marnier or Cointreau

Preheat the oven to 190C (375F/Gas 5). Use the pastry to line six 12.5 cm (5 in) tartlet tins and bake blind for 10-15 minutes as described on page 336. Leave oven temperature at 190C (375F/Gas 5).

Put orange and lemon juice into a saucepan with 250 g (9 oz/1¼ cups) sugar. Set over a medium heat until sugar has dissolved, then boil syrup for 15 minutes. Peel clementines, cut into slices and add to syrup. Simmer gently for 2-3 minutes. Remove clementines to a plate with a slotted spoon and boil syrup until very thick and syrupy. Set aside. In a bowl, beat eggs, extra yolks and remaining sugar together until well mixed. Beat in butter, almonds and liqueur.

Divide mixture between tartlets and bake for about 8 minutes, until set and golden. Set aside to cool. When cold, brush tartlets with a little thick syrup and arrange clementine slices on top (halve the slices for a daintier effect, if preferred). Brush with a little more syrup, then chill until required.

Serves 6.

Variation: Use strawberries or blackberries instead of clementines, but immerse in syrup for a few seconds only.

FRANGIPANE TARTS

SHORTCRUST PASTRY:
115 g (4 oz/1 cup) plain flour
pinch salt
55 g (2 oz/¼ cup) butter or margarine
FILLING:
6 teaspoons apricot jam
55 g (2 oz/¼ cup) butter
55 g (2 oz/¼ cup) caster sugar
1 egg
½ teaspoon almond essence
3 teaspoons plain flour, sifted
55 g (2 oz/½ cup) ground almonds
TOPPING:
25 g (1 oz/¼ cup) flaked almonds
6 teaspoons apricot jam

Preheat oven to 190C (375F/Gas 5). Sift flour and salt into a bowl. Rub in fat until mixture resembles breadcrumbs. Add 1-2 tablespoons water to bind mixture to a soft dough. On a floured surface, roll out pastry thinly and use to line 12 tartlet tins. Put a little apricot jam in the base of each pastry shell. To make filling, beat butter and sugar in a bowl until creamy. Mix egg and almond essence together; add to creamed mixture with flour and ground almonds. Mix well to form a smooth paste.

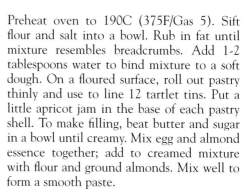

Spoon mixture into pastry cases. Arrange a few flaked almonds on top of each one. Bake in the oven for 15-20 minutes until golden. To make topping, heat jam with 2 teaspoons cold water in a saucepan. Bring to the boil; sieve and reheat. Brush over hot tarts. Transfer tarts to a wire rack to cool.

Makes 12.

PEAR & DATE SLICES

450 g (1 lb) pears
85 g (3 oz/⅓ cup) caster sugar
1 teaspoon ground cinnamon
115 g (4 oz/⅔ cup) dried dates, chopped
12 sheets filo pastry
55 g (2 oz/¼ cup) butter, melted
6 teaspoons clear honey, warmed

Preheat oven to 150C (300F/Gas 2). Peel, core and slice pears. Place in a saucepan with 2 tablespoons water. Cover and cook over a low heat until just softened. Add sugar, cinnamon and dates, mix well and cool slightly. Trim filo pastry sheets into sheets measuring 27.5 x 17.5 cm (11 x 7 in).

Place one sheet of pastry in the base of a 27.5 x 17.5 cm (11 x 7 in) baking tin. Brush lightly with melted fat. Place another sheet of pastry on top, brush lightly with melted butter and repeat with another 2 sheets pastry. Place half the fruit mixture on top. Place 4 sheets of pastry on top of fruit, brushing each sheet lightly with melted fat.

Repeat with remaining fruit mixture and pastry sheets, brushing each sheet with melted fat. Cut through the layers to make 12 slices. Bake in oven for 1-1½ hours until golden brown on top. Spoon warm honey evenly over the slices. Allow to stand for 5 minutes, then serve with low fat custard or cream.

Makes 12.

APRICOT & HAZELNUT GALETTE

85 g (3 oz/½ cup) hazelnuts, skinned
85 g (3 oz/⅓ cup) butter, softened
85 g (3 oz/⅓ cup) caster sugar
115 g (4 oz/1 cup) plain flour
225 g (8 oz) fresh apricots, halved and stoned
300 ml (10 fl oz/1¼ cups) whipping cream
icing sugar for dusting

Preheat oven to 180C (350F/Gas 4). Lightly grease 2 baking sheets. Toast hazelnuts under a medium grill to brown evenly. Reserve 8 nuts, then grind remainder finely in a coffee grinder or food processor.

In a bowl, beat butter and two-thirds sugar together until light and fluffy. Fold in ground nuts and flour, then beat to a firm dough. Knead lightly on a lightly floured surface, then wrap in foil and chill for 30 minutes. Unwrap, cut in half and roll each piece out to a 17.5-20 cm (7-8 in) diameter circle. Carefully place on the greased baking sheets and bake in the oven for about 20 minutes, until golden. Cut one circle into 8 wedges and cool all pastry on a wire rack.

Poach apricots gently in 3 tablespoons water and remaining sugar, until just soft. Cool. In a bowl, whip cream stiffly. Transfer pastry circle to a serving plate and spread with half the cream. Remove apricots from pan with a slotted spoon and arrange over cream. Top with pastry sections and dust with icing sugar. Pipe a rosette onto each section with remaining cream and decorate with hazelnuts. Serve within 1 hour.

Serves 8.

347

RASPBERRY & APPLE STRUDEL

225 g (8 oz) cooking apples
225 g (8 oz) raspberries
55 g (2 oz/¼ cup) caster sugar
55 g (2 oz/½ cup) chopped mixed nuts
1 teaspoon ground cinnamon
8 sheets filo pastry
55 g (2 oz/¼ cup) butter
1 tablespoon icing sugar

Preheat oven to 190C (375F/Gas 5). Peel, core and slice apples. Place in a saucepan with raspberries and 2 tablespoons water. Cover and cook gently until just soft. Stir in sugar and cool. Add nuts and cinnamon and mix well.

Place one sheet of pastry on a sheet of baking parchment and brush lightly with melted fat. Place another sheet of pastry on top and layer all 8 sheets of pastry on top of one another, brushing each one lightly with melted butter. Spoon fruit mixture over pastry leaving a 2.5 cm (1 in) border uncovered all around edge. Fold these edges over fruit mixture.

With a long side towards you, using baking parchment, roll up strudel. Carefully place it on a greased baking sheet, seam-side down. Brush it lightly with melted butter. Bake in oven for about 40 minutes until golden brown. Dust with sifted icing sugar.

Serves 8.

LEMON CUSTARD SLICES

225 g (8 oz) puff pastry, thawed if frozen
FILLING:
25 g (1 oz/3 tablespoons) cornflour
55 g (2 oz/¼ cup) caster sugar
150 ml (5 fl oz/⅔ cup) milk
juice 1 lemon
grated rind ½ lemon
1 egg yolk
115 ml (4 fl oz/½ cup) double (thick) cream
TO DECORATE:
85 g (3 oz/½ cup) icing sugar, sifted
2 kiwi fruit, peeled and sliced

Preheat oven to 230C (450F/Gas 8). On a floured surface, roll pastry out thinly to a rectangle 30 x 25 cm (12 x 10 in). With a sharp, floured knife, cut pastry into 8 rectangles. Prick all over with a fork. Place pastry slices on a dampened baking sheet. Bake in the oven for 10-15 minutes until well risen and golden brown. Transfer to a wire rack to cool. Split slices in half.

To make filling, smoothly blend cornflour with sugar and milk in a saucepan; boil, stirring, until mixture thickens. Stir in lemon juice and rind. Beat in egg yolk. Cover and leave to cool. Beat in cream. Mix icing sugar with about 6 teaspoons water to make a smooth paste. Spread over one side of 8 pastry slices. Leave to set. Spread custard over remaining pastry slices. Top with iced slices. Decorate with kiwi fruit.

Makes 8.

CREAM CHEESE STRUDEL

70 g (2½ oz/¾ cup) hazelnuts
225 g (8 oz) cream or curd cheese
2 tablespoons caster sugar
1 egg
grated peel 1 lemon
5 sheets filo pastry, thawed if frozen
55 g (2 oz/¼ cup) butter, melted
BLACKCURRANT SAUCE:
225 g (8 oz) fresh or frozen blackcurrants
55 g (2 oz/¼ cup) sugar
2 tablespoons crème de cassis

Preheat oven to 200C (400F/Gas 6). Grease a baking sheet. Toast hazelnuts to brown evenly. Cool, then chop.

In a bowl, beat cheese with sugar, egg and lemon peel until smooth. Beat in hazelnuts. Place a sheet of pastry on greased baking sheet, keeping remainder covered with a damp tea towel. Brush with melted butter and place another sheet on top. Layer all 5 sheets of pastry on top of one another, brushing each one with melted butter.

Spoon cheese mixture in a line down centre of pastry and fold short ends over the filling. Roll up pastry, round filling, and turn it on baking sheet, so join is underneath. Brush top with butter and bake for 25-30 minutes, until golden brown and flaky. To make sauce, cook blackcurrants, sugar and 55 ml (2 fl oz/¼ cup) water over medium heat until currants are tender. Drain, reserving juice. Push currants through a sieve. Stir in liqueur and enough juice to desired consistency. Cool.

Serves 4-6.

NECTARINE BAKLAVA

10 sheets filo pastry, thawed if frozen
150 g (5 oz/⅔ cup) butter, melted
200 g (7 oz/1¾ cups) chopped mixed nuts
1½ teaspoons ground cinnamon
8 tablespoons caster sugar
juice and grated peel 2 lemons
1 tablespoon orange flower water
4 nectarines
icing sugar, to decorate

Preheat oven to 180C (350F/Gas 4). Cut pastry sheets in half, and each half into 4.

Working quickly, brush one cut sheet of pastry with melted butter. Line 8 individual 10 cm (4 in) Yorkshire pudding tins with one piece of pastry each. Brush 3 more cut sheets with butter and lay the pieces in the tins, so each tin has 4 pieces overlapping each other at different angles. Mix nuts, cinnamon and half the sugar, and spread half this mixture over pastry. Cover with 2 more layers of pastry, brushed with butter, then top with remaining nut mixture. Cover with rest of pastry, brushed with butter.

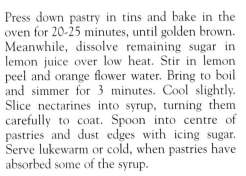

Press down pastry in tins and bake in the oven for 20-25 minutes, until golden brown. Meanwhile, dissolve remaining sugar in lemon juice over low heat. Stir in lemon peel and orange flower water. Bring to boil and simmer for 3 minutes. Cool slightly. Slice nectarines into syrup, turning them carefully to coat. Spoon into centre of pastries and dust edges with icing sugar. Serve lukewarm or cold, when pastries have absorbed some of the syrup.

Serves 8.

APRICOPITTA

1 kg (2¼ lb) fresh apricots
seeds from 5 cardamom pods
115 g (4 oz/½ cup) caster sugar
¼ teaspoon vanilla essence
85 g (3 oz/⅓ cup) butter, melted
12 sheets filo pastry
3 egg whites, for dusting
45 g (1½ oz) demerara sugar
115 g (4 oz/1¼ cups) ground almonds
icing sugar

Put apricots in a bowl. Cover with boiling water. Leave for 2 minutes, then drain. Cover with cold water, leave for 2 minutes and drain again.

Peel skins off apricots. Cut in half and remove stones. Put apricots in a saucepan with cardamom seeds, caster sugar and vanilla essence. Cook gently until apricots are soft. In a blender or food processor, purée the apricots. Preheat oven to 190C (375F/Gas 5). Brush a small roasting tin with melted butter. Brush a sheet of pastry with butter and lay it in tin. Repeat with 3 more pastry layers. Spread apricot purée on pastry. Cover with 4 more layers of buttered pastry.

In a bowl, whisk egg whites until stiff. Whisk in demerara sugar. Fold in ground almonds. Spread meringue on pastry. Cover gently with 4 more sheets buttered pastry. Tuck top layer of pastry down sides. With a sharp knife, cut diamond shapes in pastry, down to meringue layer. Dust with icing sugar, then bake in oven for 40-50 minutes until browned and crisp. Serve warm or cold, cut into diamonds, and dusted with more sugar.

Serves 6-8.

BAKLAVA

115 g (4 oz/1 cup) blanched almonds
115 g (4 oz/1 cup) walnuts
55 g (2 oz/⅓ cup) shelled pistachio nuts
55 g (2 oz/⅓ cup) soft brown sugar
1 teaspoon ground cinnamon
¼ teaspoon freshly grated nutmeg
55 g (2 oz/¼ cup) butter
8 sheets filo pastry
SYRUP:
225 g (8 oz/1 cup) granulated sugar
1 tablespoon lemon juice
1 tablespoon orange flower water

To make syrup, in a saucepan, heat sugar, 150 ml (5 fl oz/⅔ cup) water and the lemon juice until sugar dissolves. Boil gently for 5 minutes until syrupy. Add orange flower water and boil for a further 2 minutes. Leave to cool completely. In a food processor, process one third of all nuts until finely chopped. Coarsely chop the remainder. In a bowl, mix together nuts, brown sugar, cinnamon and nutmeg. Butter a large baking tin. Preheat oven to 180C (350F/Gas 4). In a saucepan, melt butter.

Cut pastry sheets in half across. Brush one halved sheet with butter and place on bottom of baking tin. Repeat with 3 more sheets. Spread one third of nut mixture over the top, then repeat the layers twice more, ending with a layer of pastry. With a sharp knife, cut top layer of pastry into diamonds. Bake in oven for 30-40 minutes until crisp and golden. Pour cold syrup over the top. When cold, trim edges and cut into diamond shapes.

Makes about 20.

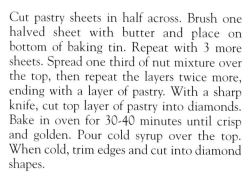

HOT PUDDINGS

ROAST FIGS

12 figs
3 tablespoons caster sugar
1 tablespoon orange juice
55 g (2 oz/⅔ cup) walnut halves
1 tablespoon clear honey
Greek yogurt, to serve

Preheat the oven to 200C (400F/Gas 6). Butter a shallow flameproof dish. Put the figs side by side in the dish.

Sprinkle with 2 tablespoons of the sugar and the orange juice. Bake for 20 minutes, basting from time to time with the cooking juices. Add the walnuts and sprinkle with the remaining sugar.

Reduce the oven temperature to 150C (300F/Gas 2) and bake for a further 10 minutes. Remove the figs and walnuts with a slotted spoon and arrange on a serving dish. Add the honey to the cooking juices and warm through over a low heat. Spoon the syrup over the figs and serve warm or cold with Greek yogurt.

Serves 4.

AMARETTI-STUFFED PEACHES

4 large peaches
55 g (2 oz) amaretti biscuits
1 egg yolk
4 teaspoons caster sugar
25 g (1 oz/2 tablespoons) softened butter
250 ml (9 fl oz/1 cup) sweet white wine
toasted flaked almonds and vine leaves, to decorate

Preheat the oven to 190C (375F/Gas 5). Butter an ovenproof dish. Cut the peaches in half and remove the stones.

Scoop out a little flesh from each peach half and place in a bowl. Crush the amaretti biscuits and add to the bowl. Stir in the egg yolk, caster sugar and butter and mix well. Put some filling in each peach half, forming it into a smooth mound.

Put the peaches in the dish and pour in the wine. Bake in the oven for 30-40 minutes until the peaches are tender and the filling is firm. Transfer to serving plates, sprinkle with toasted almonds and decorate with vine leaves. Spoon around the baking juices and serve.

Serves 4.

Note: Be careful not to bake the peaches for too long – they should retain their shape.

PINEAPPLE ALASKA

1 large ripe pineapple with leaves
1-2 tablespoons kirsch
1 litre (35 fl oz/4½ cups) vanilla ice cream
3 egg whites
175 g (6 oz/¾ cup) caster sugar
1 tablespoon caster sugar for sprinkling

Cut pineapple and leafy 'plume' in half lengthwise. Using a grapefruit knife, cut out flesh. Discard core, then cut flesh into chunks and put into a bowl. Sprinkle with kirsch, cover with plastic wrap and chill overnight with pineapple shells.

Put pineapple chunks back into shells and pack ice cream on top. Put in freezer for about 2 hours, until very firm. Meanwhile, preheat oven to 200C (400F/Gas 6). Just before serving, whisk egg whites in a bowl until stiff. Whisk in half the sugar, whisking for 1 minute more. Fold in remaining sugar.

Pile this meringue over ice cream, making sure it is completely covered. Make small peaks in meringue with a flat-bladed knife. Place pineapple shells on a baking sheet and sprinkle with the 1 tablespoon caster sugar. Bake in the oven for about 8 minutes, until meringue is browned. Serve immediately.

Serves 6.

Variation: Try making this dessert using a fruit sorbet instead of ice cream.

RED BERRY SOUFFLÉ

25 g (1 oz/6 tablespoons) butter
115 g (4 oz/½ cup) caster sugar, plus 1 extra tablespoon
225 g (8 oz) mixed soft red fruits, fresh or frozen, thawed if frozen
1 tablespoon Fraise liqueur or crème de cassis
5 egg whites
icing sugar, to serve

Preheat oven to 180C (350F/Gas 4). Use the butter to grease a 1 litre (35 fl oz/4½ cup) soufflé dish or 6 individual dishes, then dust out with 1 tablespoon caster sugar.

Purée fruit, liqueur and remaining caster sugar together in a blender or food processor. Turn into a bowl. In a separate bowl, whisk egg whites until stiff, but not dry. Fold 1 tablespoon into fruit purée, then tip purée onto whites and fold together carefully, using a metal spoon.

Spoon mixture into prepared soufflé dish, place on a baking sheet and bake in the oven for 25-30 minutes for the large soufflé; 15-20 minutes for the individual soufflés, until risen and just set. Dust with a little icing sugar and serve immediately.

Serves 6.

CRUNCHY PEACHES

6 peaches
4 tablespoons maraschino or similar cherry liqueur
300 ml (10 fl oz/1¼ cups) whipping cream
55 g (2 oz/⅓ cup) demerara sugar

Blanch peaches in boiling water for 1 minute. Drain and peel off skin. Cut flesh into thick slices. Discard stones.

Place peach slices in a shallow heatproof dish, filling dish evenly. Pour liqueur over slices. In a bowl, whip cream stiffly and place spoonfuls on top of peaches. Gently spread cream evenly. Cover dish with plastic wrap and refrigerate for at least 4 hours.

Just before serving, heat grill to very high. Remove plastic wrap from dish and spoon sugar evenly over top of cream. Place under the grill until sugar has dissolved and caramellized. Serve the peaches immediately.

Serves 6.

Note: Liqueurs are expensive, but there is no point in skimping for this dish – you need to add enough liqueur to make sure the flavour comes through.

FIGS WITH CINNAMON CREAM

9 large ripe figs
55 g (2 oz/¼ cup) unsalted butter
4 teaspoons brandy
15 g (½ oz/3 teaspoons) brown sugar
almond flakes, to decorate
CINNAMON CREAM:
150 ml (5 fl oz/⅔ cup) double (thick) cream
1 teaspoon ground cinnamon
1 tablespoon brandy
2 teaspoons clear honey

Prepare the cinnamon cream. Combine all the ingredients in a small bowl, cover and refrigerate for 30 minutes to allow time for flavours to develop.

Preheat grill. Halve the figs and thread onto 6 skewers. Melt the butter in a small pan and stir in the brandy.

Brush the figs with the brandy butter and sprinkle with a little sugar. Place under a hot grill for 4-5 minutes until bubbling and golden. Whip the cinnamon cream until just holding its shape, decorate with almond flakes, and serve with the grilled figs.

Serves 6.

BANANAS WITH RUM & LIME

55 g (2 oz/4 tablespoons) butter
55 g (2 oz/¼ cup) light brown sugar
½ teaspoon ground cinnamon
4 bananas, peeled and cut diagonally into 1 cm
  (½ in) slices
70 ml (2½ fl oz/⅓ cup) light rum
grated rind and juice 1 lime or lemon
2 tablespoons chopped almonds, toasted
shavings of fresh coconut or toasted shredded
  coconut, to garnish (optional)

Heat the wok until hot. Add the butter and
swirl to melt and coat wok. Stir in sugar and
cinnamon and cook for 1 minute until sugar
melts and mixture bubbles.

Add banana slices and stir-fry gently for 1-2
minutes, tossing to coat all pieces and heat
through. Add rum and, with a match, light
rum to ignite. Shake wok gently until flames
subside.

Add rind and juice of the lime or lemon and
toasted almonds, and stir in gently. Spoon
into dessert dishes and garnish with fresh or
toasted coconut.

Serves 4.

TOFFEE PEARS & PECANS

4 dessert pears, cut lengthwise in half and cored
6 teaspoons lemon juice
70 g (2½ oz/5 tablespoons) butter
70 g (2½ oz/about ½ cup packed) brown sugar
1 teaspoon ground cinnamon
½ teaspoon ground ginger
85 g (3 oz/1 cup) pecan halves
250 ml (9 fl oz/1 cup) double (heavy) or whipping
  cream
few drops vanilla essence

Cut pear halves into 0.5 cm (¼ in) thick
slices. Sprinkle with the lemon juice.

Heat the wok until hot. Add 2 tablespoons
butter and 3 tablespoons brown sugar and
swirl to melt and coat wok. Stir until sugar
melts and bubbles. Add pear slices, cinnamon, ginger and pecans and stir-fry gently
for 4-6 minutes until pear slices are tender
but still crisp. Remove pear slices and pecans
to a shallow serving bowl.

Add remaining butter and sugar and stir for
2 minutes until sugar dissolves and sauce
boils and bubbles. Stir in cream and bring to
the boil. Simmer for 2-3 minutes until sauce
thickens. Remove from heat, stir in vanilla
essence and pour over pear slices and pecans.
Cool slightly before serving or serve at room
temperature.

Serves 4-6.

BLACKBERRY & APPLE COBBLER

450 g (1 lb) cooking apples
225 g (8 oz) blackberries
85 g (3 oz/⅓ cup) caster sugar
225 g (8 oz/2 cups) self-raising flour
pinch of salt
2 teaspoons ground mixed spice
45 g (1½ oz/9 teaspoons) butter
about 150 ml (5 fl oz/⅔ cup) milk

Preheat oven to 220C (425F/Gas 7). Peel, core and slice apples and place in a saucepan with blackberries and 2 tablespoons water. Cover pan and cook gently until just soft. Add 55 g (2 oz/¼ cup) sugar and put in a 1.5 litre (50 fl oz/6⅔ cup) ovenproof dish.

Sift flour into a bowl with salt and mixed spice. Rub in butter until mixture resembles breadcrumbs, then stir in remaining sugar. Add enough milk to bind dough. Roll out dough on a lightly floured surface and cut out twelve 5 cm (2 in) scones.

Place scones around edge of dish on top of fruit, overlapping them slightly. Brush scones with a little milk. Bake in oven for 15-20 minutes until scones are well risen and brown. Serve with custard (see page 359).

Serves 6.

CHERRY CLAFOUTI

700 g (1½ lb) stoned black cherries, fresh or frozen, thawed if frozen
85 g (3 oz/¾ cup) plain flour
pinch salt
3 eggs
85 g (3 oz/⅓ cup) caster sugar
450 ml (16 fl oz/2 cups) milk
1 tablespoon cherry brandy or kirsch
icing sugar, to serve

Preheat oven to 200C (400F/Gas 6). Drain the cherries, if thawed. Butter a 1.25 litre (40 fl oz/5 cup) pie dish and put cherries in it.

Sift flour and salt together onto a plate. In a large bowl, beat eggs with sugar until creamy, then fold in flour. Warm milk slightly in a saucepan over a low heat and stir into egg mixture with cherry brandy or kirsch. Beat well to make batter smooth, then pour the batter over the cherries.

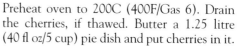

Bake in the oven for 30 minutes, until batter is set and golden. Serve warm, dusted with icing sugar.

Serves 6.

Note: Fresh cherries can taste a little bland when cooked. Add 1-2 drops almond essence to improve the flavour, if desired.

# PEAR & CINNAMON CRUMBLE	# BAKED DEMELZA APPLES

PEAR & CINNAMON CRUMBLE

2 x 400 g (14 oz) cans pear halves in fruit juice
3 teaspoons caster sugar
2 teaspoons ground cinnamon
150 g (5 oz/1¼ cups) plain wholemeal flour
55 g (2 oz/¼ cup) soft brown sugar
85 g (3 oz/⅓ cup) butter

Preheat oven to 200F (400F/Gas 6). Drain pears, reserving juice, and chop roughly. Mix caster sugar with 1 teaspoon cinnamon and mix with pears.

In a bowl, mix together remaining cinnamon, flour and brown sugar. Rub in butter until mixture resembles bread crumbs.

In a 1.2 litre (2 pint/5 cup) ovenproof dish, layer crumble mixture and pear mixture, pouring pear juice over fruit, finishing with a crumble layer. Bake in oven for 30 minutes until golden brown on top. Serve hot or cold with custard (see page 359) or cream.

Serves 6.

BAKED DEMELZA APPLES

55 g (2 oz/⅓ cup) mixed raisins and sultanas
5 tablespoons ginger wine, Madeira or sweet sherry
4 large cooking apples
85 g (3 oz/¾ cup) toasted, flaked almonds
1-2 tablespoons marmalade
chilled whipped cream, to serve

Preheat oven to 180C (350F/Gas 4). Put raisins and sultanas into a small bowl and add ginger wine, Madeira or sherry. Leave to soak for several hours.

Wash and dry apples, but do not peel. Remove core using an apple corer and score a line around each apple. Stand the apples in an ovenproof dish. Drain dried fruit, reserving liquid. Mix fruit with almonds and marmalade in a bowl, then fill the apple cavities with this mixture, pushing it down firmly. Pour strained liquid over apples.

Bake the apples in the oven for 45-60 minutes, until soft. Pile a spoonful of whipped cream on top of each apple and serve immediately.

Serves 4.

RICE PUDDING WITH PEACHES

850 ml (30 fl oz/3¾ cups) full-fat milk
6 cardamom pods
115 g (4 oz/½ cup) short grain rice
55 g (2 oz/½ cup) pistachio nuts, chopped
115 g (4 oz/½ cup) soft brown sugar
55 g (2 oz/¼ cup) butter, diced
2 egg yolks
400 g (14 oz) can peach halves, drained

Put the milk in a flameproof casserole. Add the cardamom pods, bring to the boil and simmer gently for 5 minutes. Remove the cardamom pods. Stir in the rice.

Return to the boil and simmer gently, stirring frequently, for 15-20 minutes, until the rice is tender and most of the liquid has been absorbed. Remove from the heat and stir in the pistachio nuts, half the brown sugar, butter and egg yolks. Leave to cool slightly. Preheat oven to 160C (325F/Gas 3).

Remove half the mixture from the casserole and set aside. Arrange the peaches on top of the rice in the casserole and cover with the remaining rice. Bake for 25 minutes. Preheat grill. Sprinkle the pudding with the remaining sugar and grill until the sugar melts and turns a deep golden brown. Serve.

Serves 6-8.

SAUCY LIME PUDDING

55 g (2 oz/¼ cup) unsalted butter, plus extra for
  greasing
55 g (2 oz/¼ cup) caster sugar
grated rind and juice 3 limes
2 eggs, separated
55 g (2 oz/½ cup) self-raising flour
300 ml (10 fl oz/1¼ cups) milk

Preheat oven to 160C (325F/Gas 3). In a large bowl, beat together the butter, sugar and lime rind until light and fluffy. Stir in the egg yolks and carefully fold in the flour. Stir in the milk and lime juice.

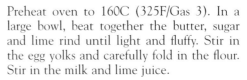

Whisk the egg whites until they form stiff peaks. Fold in to the lime mixture. Lightly butter an ovenproof dish.

Pour the lime mixture into the dish and bake for 40-50 minutes, until risen and golden. Serve warm.

Serves 4-6.

BREAD & FRUIT PUDDING

115 g (4 oz/³⁄₄ cup) sultanas and currants, mixed
8 slices thin white bread, buttered
25 g (1 oz/2 tablespoons) candied fruit, chopped
caster sugar for sprinkling
CUSTARD:
1 egg yolk
300 ml (10 fl oz/1¼ cups) milk
150 ml (5 fl oz/²⁄₃ cup) single (light) cream
1 vanilla pod
caster sugar for sprinkling

Put sultanas and currants into a bowl and cover with water. Leave to swell. Preheat oven to 180C (350F/Gas 4). Grease a 1 litre (35 fl oz/4½ cup) pie dish.

Cut crusts from bread and sandwich 4 slices together. Cut into 6 pieces and place in prepared pie dish. Drain fruit and scatter over bread with chopped candied fruit. Top with remaining bread, butter side up.

Put egg yolk in a medium bowl. Put milk, cream, vanilla pod and sugar into a saucepan and bring almost to boiling point. Pour over egg, stir, then strain into pie dish, pouring down sides so top slices of bread are not soaked. Stand for 30 minutes, then sprinkle with caster sugar and place in a roasting tin. Pour in boiling water to come halfway up sides of dish and bake in the oven for 45-50 minutes, until top is golden brown.

Serves 4.

QUEEN OF PUDDINGS

500 ml (18 fl oz/2¼ cups) milk
55 g (2 oz/¼ cup) butter
115 g (4 oz/2 cups) cake crumbs
grated rind 1 lemon
grated rind 1 orange
55 g (2 oz/¼ cup) caster sugar
4 egg yolks, beaten
2 egg whites, whisked
55 g (2 oz) strawberry jam
115 g (4 oz) strawberries, sliced
icing sugar, for dusting
MERINGUE:
2 egg whites
55 g (2 oz/¼ cup) caster sugar

Preheat oven to 160C (325F/Gas 3). Put the milk and butter in an ovenproof casserole and heat gently until the butter melts. Stir in the cake crumbs and lemon and orange rind. Add the sugar and egg yolks. Fold in the egg whites. Put the casserole in a deep roasting tin and pour in enough boiling water to come halfway up the sides of the casserole. Bake for 45-50 minutes, until set. Mix together the jam and strawberries and spread over the top of the pudding.

To make the meringue, beat the egg whites until they form stiff peaks. Fold in the sugar. Put the mixture in a piping bag and pipe in a trellis pattern on top of the pudding. Dust with icing sugar and bake (out of the roasting tin) for 30 minutes. Serve warm.

Serves 4-6.

MANGO WITH STICKY RICE

225 g (8 oz/1¼ cups) sticky rice, soaked overnight
  in cold water
250 ml (8 fl oz/1 cup) coconut milk
pinch salt
2-4 tablespoons sugar, to taste
2 large ripe mangoes, peeled and halved
3 tablespoons coconut cream (see glossary)
mint leaves to decorate

Drain and rinse rice thoroughly. Place in a
steaming basket lined with a double thickness of muslin. Steam over simmering water
for 30 minutes. Remove from heat.

In a bowl, stir together coconut milk, salt
and sugar to taste until sugar has dissolved.
Stir in warm rice. Set aside for 30 minutes.

Thinly slice mangoes by cutting lengthwise
through flesh to the stone. Discard the
stones. Spoon rice into a mound in centre of
serving plates and arrange mango slices
around. Pour coconut cream over rice.
Decorate with mint leaves.

Serves 4.

SUMMER FRUIT GRATIN

2 large peaches, peeled and sliced
55 g (2 oz) raspberries
115 g (4 oz) strawberries, sliced
55 g (2 oz) redcurrants and blueberries or
  blackcurrants
2 tablespoons kirsch or Cointreau (optional)
2 tablespoons caster sugar
300 ml (10 fl oz/1¼ cups) crème fraîche or double
  (thick) cream
85-115 g (3-4 oz) soft brown sugar

Divide the fruit between four heatproof serving dishes. Sprinkle with kirsch or
Cointreau, if using, and caster sugar.

Whip crème fraîche or cream until it forms
soft peaks. Spread over fruit and chill for at
least 1 hour.

Preheat grill to very hot. Sprinkle a thick
even layer of brown sugar over crème fraîche
or cream. Grill until sugar is bubbling and
caramelized. Serve immediately.

Serves 4.

ZABAGLIONE

4 egg yolks
70 g (2½ oz) vanilla sugar
115 ml (4 fl oz/½ cup) Marsala
sponge fingers, to serve

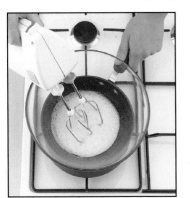

With an electric whisk, whisk the egg yolks and sugar together in a large heatproof bowl until pale and fluffy. Place bowl over a pan of gently simmering water. Mix in the Marsala.

Start whisking slowly. Gradually whisk faster until the mixture doubles in volume and becomes very thick and glossy. Take care not to overheat or the mixture will scramble.

Spoon the Zabaglione into heatproof glasses or ramekins and serve immediately with sponge fingers.

Serves 6.

Note: To make vanilla sugar, simply store a vanilla pod in a jar of sugar and leave for at least 2-3 weeks for it to flavour the sugar.

CARAMEL SESAME BANANAS

4 bananas
juice 1 lemon
115 g (4 oz) caster sugar
2 tablespoons sesame seeds
mint sprigs and lemon slices, to decorate

Peel bananas and cut into 5 cm (2 in) pieces. Place in a bowl, pour over the lemon juice and stir well to coat.

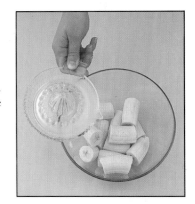

Place sugar and 4 tablespoons water in a saucepan and heat gently, stirring, until the sugar dissolves. Bring to the boil and cook for 5-6 minutes until the mixture caramelizes and turns golden brown. Drain bananas well and arrange on a layer of baking parchment.

Drizzle the caramel over the bananas, working quickly as the caramel sets within a few seconds. Sprinkle with the sesame seeds. Allow to cool for 5 minutes, then carefully peel away from paper, decorate and serve.

Serves 4.

Note: Tossing the banana in lemon juice prevents it from turning brown.

LECHE FRITA

about 3 tablespoons caster sugar
3 eggs
55 g (2 oz/½ cup) plain flour
225 ml (8 fl oz/1 cup) whipping cream
225 ml (8 fl oz/1 cup) milk
few drops vanilla essence
100 g (3½ oz/1 cup) cake crumbs, preferably lemon
vegetable oil, for deep frying

Lightly flour a baking sheet. In a bowl, beat together sugar and 2 eggs until pale. Gradually stir in flour.

In a heavy, preferably non-stick, saucepan, heat cream, milk and vanilla essence to boiling point. Slowly pour into the bowl, stirring. Return to heat and cook gently, stirring, until thickened; do not allow to boil. Pour onto baking sheet to make an even layer about 1 cm (½ in) thick, then leave to cool. Cover and refrigerate for at least 1 hour. Cut cold custard mixture into approximately 2.5 cm (1 in) squares, rectangles or diamonds.

Beat remaining egg, then dip shapes first in beaten egg, then in the crumbs. Half fill a deep fat fryer or pan with vegetable oil and heat to 190C (375F). Add coated shapes in batches and cook for about 1½ minutes until golden and crisp on outside; keep an eye on temperature of the oil to make sure that it does not drop as the cubes should cook very quickly. Using a slotted spoon, transfer to absorbent kitchen paper, drain quickly and serve immediately.

Serves 4-6.

SOUFFLÉ OMELETTE

3 eggs, separated
1 tablespoon single (light) cream
2 teaspoons caster sugar
15 g (½ oz/3 teaspoons) butter
6 teaspoons raspberry jam
icing sugar, to decorate

Preheat oven to 200C (400F/Gas 6). In a bowl, beat egg yolks, cream and sugar lightly. In a separate larger bowl, whisk egg whites until stiff. Add yolk mixture to whisked whites and carefully fold together.

Melt butter in an omelette pan over medium heat and pour soufflé mixture into pan. Spread it evenly and cook for about 1 minute, until brown underneath. Put pan in oven for 5 minutes, until top is set. Meanwhile, heat 2 skewers either in a gas flame or under a very hot grill until they are red hot and glowing.

In a small saucepan, warm jam slightly. Remove omelette from oven and quickly spread with jam. Fold over and transfer to a serving plate. Sift icing sugar thickly over omelette, then holding the skewers with thick oven gloves, mark a criss-cross pattern in the icing sugar by pressing the skewers into it. Cut omelette in half and serve.

Serves 2.

APPLE PANCAKES

115 g (4 oz/1 cup) plain flour
pinch salt
250 ml (8 fl oz/1 cup) milk and water, mixed
2 eggs
1 tablespoon oil
3 well-flavoured eating apples
2 teaspoons lemon juice
1 tablespoon brandy
2 teaspoons caster sugar

In a food processor fitted with a metal blade, process flour and salt, ½ of milk and water and eggs. Blend well, add remaining milk and water and oil and blend again. Leave to stand for 30 minutes. Process again before using.

Peel and core apples and slice very finely onto a plate. Sprinkle with lemon juice and brandy. Heat a 15-17.5 cm (6-7 in) heavy-based frying pan and grease lightly. Pour in 1 tablespoon batter and roll pan to spread it evenly. Put a few apple slices over pancake, then spoon a little more batter over apple. Cook for 2-3 minutes, until batter is almost set. Hold pan under a hot grill to finish cooking batter.

Turn pancake out onto a plate and serve as soon as possible, sprinkled with a little caster sugar. Continue until all the batter is used.

Serves 4.

Note: Mixing water with the milk helps to lighten pancake batter. Beer or cider can be used instead of milk.

PEKING APPLES

4 crisp eating apples
115 g (4 oz/1 cup) plain (all-purpose) flour
1 egg
115 ml (4 fl oz/½ cup) water
SYRUP:
1 tablespoon vegetable oil
6 tablespoons brown sugar
2 tablespoons golden syrup
2 tablespoons water
iced water, to set

In a large bowl, stir the egg and water into the flour to make a thick batter. Peel, core and thickly slice apples. Dip each apple slice in the batter to evenly coat; allow excess to drain off. In a wok, heat oil until smoking. Add apple pieces in batches and deep-fry for 3 minutes until golden brown. Using a slotted spoon, remove to absorbent kitchen paper to drain.

To make syrup, in a small saucepan, gently heat oil, water and sugar, stirring until sugar has dissolved. Simmer for 5 minutes, stirring. Stir in golden syrup and boil for 5-10 minutes until hard and stringy. Reduce heat to very low. Dip each piece of apple into syrup to coat then place in ice cold water for a few seconds. Remove to a serving dish. Repeat with remaining apple. Serve immediately.

Serves 4.

FRUIT FRITTERS

4 cooking or crisp tart eating apples
2-3 tablespoons calvados or cognac
3 tablespoons caster sugar
115 g (4 oz/1 cup) plain flour
pinch of salt
2 eggs, separated
150 ml (5 fl oz/⅔ cup) milk
1 tablespoon oil
oil, for deep frying
icing sugar, to decorate

Peel, core and cut apples into rings.

In a shallow dish, mix calvados or cognac with half the sugar. Add apples, turning them over to coat. Leave to macerate for 30 minutes. Sift flour and salt into a large bowl and mix in remaining sugar. Make a well in centre and drop in egg yolks. Using a wooden spoon, draw flour into yolks while gradually adding milk. Beat to a smooth batter, then leave to stand for 30 minutes. In a separate bowl, whisk egg whites until stiff and fold into batter with 1 tablespoon oil.

Heat oil for deep frying to 195C (385F). Drain fruit and dip each ring into batter to coat. Deep fry a few at a time, turning once, until puffed up and golden brown. Drain the fritters on absorbent kitchen paper and serve hot, sprinkled with a little icing sugar.

Serves 4.

Variations: Use pineapple, pears or bananas in place of apples, soaking them in an appropriate liqueur for 30 minutes.

FRUIT-FILLED WHITE CRÊPES

3 egg whites, lightly beaten
4 tablespoons cornflour
1 teaspoon sunflower oil
mint sprigs, to decorate
FILLING:
4 slices fresh pineapple, peeled, cored and chopped
2 kiwi fruit, peeled and quartered
½ mango, peeled, stoned and sliced
½ papaya, peeled, seeded and chopped
2 tablespoons dry sherry
1 tablespoon brown sugar
1 whole cinnamon stick, broken
2 star anise

Place all the filling ingredients in a non-stick or well seasoned wok and mix gently. Bring to the boil, reduce heat and simmer very gently for 10 minutes. Remove and discard cinnamon stick and star anise. Set aside. Meanwhile, make the crêpes. Put the egg whites and cornflour in a jug and stir in 8 teaspoons water, mixing well to form a smooth paste.

Brush a non-stick or well seasoned crêpe pan with a little oil and heat. Pour in a quarter of the mixture, tilting the pan to cover the base. Cook for 1 minute on one side only, until set. Drain on kitchen paper, layer with baking parchment and keep warm whilst making the remaining 3 crêpes. Lay crêpes cooked-side up, fill with the fruit and fold crêpes over the filling. Decorate and serve.

Serves 4.

MINCEMEAT CRÊPE GÂTEAU

1 quantity Pancakes (see page 363)
375 g (12 oz) mincemeat (see Note)
1 eating apple
1 tablespoon brandy
grated peel 1 orange
juice ½ lemon
125 g (4 oz/1 cup) slivered almonds
4 tablespoons apricot jam, sieved

Make and cook pancakes as described on page 363. Preheat oven to 180C (350F/Gas 4). Put mincemeat into a saucepan. Peel, core and chop apple and add to pan.

Heat through, stirring from time to time, until apple is tender. Remove from heat and stir in brandy, orange peel, lemon juice and three-quarters of the almonds. Put a pancake on a greased ovenproof dish and spread with a little mincemeat mixture. Layer up gâteau, alternating pancakes and mincemeat, ending with a pancake.

Warm apricot jam in a small saucepan and pour over gâteau. Sprinkle with remaining almonds and place in oven for 15 minutes. Serve at once, cut in wedges, like a cake.

Serves 6.

Note: The mincemeat recipe on page 345 is not thick enough for this recipe. Use a good quality commercially prepared one.

HOT ORANGE CAKE

115 g (4oz/½ cup) butter, softened
115 g (4 oz/½ cup) caster sugar
2 large eggs, separated
115 g (4 oz/1 cup) self-raising flour
juice and grated peel 3 small oranges
250 ml (8 fl oz/1 cup) double (thick) cream
icing sugar, for dusting
fresh orange segments

Preheat oven to 180C (350F/Gas 4). Well grease a deep 20 cm (8 in) non-stick cake tin. In a large bowl, cream butter and sugar until light and fluffy. Beat egg yolks into mixture with 1 tablespoon flour and juice and grated peel of 1 orange.

In a separate bowl, whisk egg whites until stiff, but not dry. Fold into mixture with remaining flour and spoon into the prepared cake tin. Bake in the oven for 20-30 minutes, until golden brown and springy to touch.

While cake is cooking, whip cream stiffly in a bowl with remaining orange juice and peel. Leave cake in tin for 2-3 minutes, then turn out and cut in half horizontally. Working quickly, spread bottom with cream, cover with top half. Dust thickly with icing sugar and arrange orange segments on top. Serve the cake at once.

Serves 6.

Note: The cream will melt into the hot cake, so serve as quickly as possible.

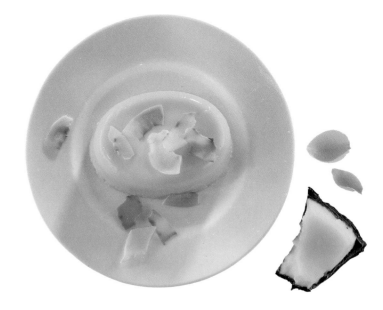

APRICOT PUDDING

400 g (4 oz) can apricot halves in fruit juice
6 glacé cherries
100 g (3½ oz/7 tablespoons) butter
100 g (3½ oz/½ cup) soft brown sugar
2 eggs, beaten
225 g (8 oz/2 cups) self-raising flour
5 tablespoons milk

Preheat oven to 180C (350F/Gas 4). Drain apricots and halve cherries. Place cherries, cut side down, over the base of a greased 1.5 litre (50 fl oz/6⅔ cup) ovenproof dish and place apricot halves on top.

In a bowl, cream together butter and sugar until light and fluffy. Gradually add beaten eggs, beating well after each addition. Fold in flour and milk to give a soft dropping consistency.

Spread mixture over apricots. Bake in oven for 45 minutes until well risen and golden brown. Turn out onto a warmed serving dish and serve with ice cream.

Serves 8.

COCONUT CUSTARD

3 eggs
2 egg yolks
450 ml (16 fl oz/2 cups) coconut milk
85 g (3 oz/⅓ cup) caster sugar
few drops rosewater or jasmine essence
toasted coconut, to decorate

Preheat the oven to 180C (350F/Gas 4). Place 4 individual heatproof dishes in a baking tin.

In a bowl, stir together eggs, egg yolks, coconut milk, sugar and rosewater or jasmine essence until sugar dissolves. Pass through a sieve into dishes. Pour boiling water into baking tin to surround dishes.

Cook in oven for about 20 minutes until custards are lightly set in centre. Remove from baking tin and allow to cool slightly before unmoulding. Serve warm or cold. Decorate with coconut.

Serves 4.

CABINET PUDDING

55 g (2 oz/⅓ cup) raisins
2 tablespoons rum, brandy or water
300 g (10 oz) chocolate or plain sponge cake
115 g (4 oz/½ cup) caster sugar
115 g (4 oz/1 cup) chopped mixed nuts
4 eggs
450 ml (16 fl oz/2 cups) milk
25 g (1 oz/¼ cup) flaked almonds
RASPBERRY SAUCE:
225 g (8 oz) fresh or frozen raspberries
2 tablespoons lemon juice
55-85 g (2-3 oz/¼-⅓ cup) sugar
70 ml (2½ fl oz/⅓ cup) Framboise liqueur or water

Soak raisins in rum, brandy or water for at least 1 hour.

Preheat oven to 180C (350F/Gas 4). Lightly butter a 1.2 litre (2 pint/5 cup) pie dish. Roughly break up sponge cake and put into prepared pie dish. Add raisin and soaking liquid, then sprinkle with just over one-quarter of sugar and all chopped mixed nuts. In a bowl, beat eggs with remaining sugar and whisk in milk. Pour into pie dish. Scatter with flaked almonds.

Put pie dish into a roasting tin and add enough boiling water to come halfway up sides. Bake in the oven for 1-1½ hours, until lightly set. To make sauce, put all ingredients into a saucepan and bring slowly to boil. Simmer for a few minutes, then rub through a sieve.

Serves 6.

Note: Stale, leftover sponge is ideal for this pudding, or ratafias can be used in place of sponge cake, if preferred.

COFFEE BRULÉE

8 egg yolks
115 g (4 oz/½ cup) caster sugar
250 ml (9 fl oz/1 cup) full-fat milk
500 ml (18 fl oz/2¼ cups) double (thick) cream
1 teaspoon coffee essence
55 g (2 oz/¼ cup) caster sugar
summer berries, to decorate

In a large bowl, beat together the egg yolks and sugar until light and foamy.

Put the milk, cream and coffee essence in a flameproof casserole. Heat gently but do not boil. Remove from the heat and leave to cool. Preheat oven to 150C (300F/Gas 2). Pour the milk mixture on to the egg yolk mixture and stir well. Pour into a large jug and allow the froth to rise to the surface. Skim off the froth. Pour the mixture back into the casserole.

Put a piece of greaseproof paper in a roasting tin. Put the casserole on top of the paper. Pour enough boiling water into the tin to come halfway up the sides of the casserole. Bake for 45 minutes, until the mixture has set. Leave to cool then chill. To make the topping, preheat the grill. Sprinkle the top of the custard with the sugar and grill until the sugar melts and turns a deep golden brown. Decorate with summer berries and serve.

Serves 6.

SPOTTED DICK

115 g (4 oz/1 cup) self-raising flour
9 teaspoons cornflour
1 teaspoon baking powder
115 g (4 oz/½ cup) caster sugar
115 g (4 oz/½ cup) butter, softened
juice and grated peel 1 orange
2 eggs
115 g (4 oz/¾ cup) sultanas
55 g (2 oz/⅓ cup) chopped mixed citrus peel
1 quantity Raspberry Sauce (see page 367), to serve

Butter an 850 ml (30 fl oz/3¾ cup) pudding bowl or a 20 cm (8 in) ring mould. Sift flour, cornflour and baking powder onto a plate.

In a large bowl, cream sugar, butter and grated orange peel until light and fluffy. In a separate bowl, beat eggs with orange juice, then beat this gradually into butter mixture with 1 tablespoon flour mixture. Fold in remaining flour with sultanas and citrus peel. The mixture should be a soft, dropping consistency (if it is too stiff, add a little milk).

Spoon mixture into prepared bowl or mould and cover top with a piece of buttered foil, pleated in middle. Tie securely with string round rim of bowl or mould and place in saucepan of gently boiling water to come halfway up sides. Steam for 1½–2 hours. Turn out and serve warm with Raspberry Sauce.

Serves 6.

Note: Wash fruit before using in a pudding or cake to remove the coating of oil or sugar.

STEAMED FRUIT DUMPLINGS

1 small banana, chopped
grated rind and juice 1 small lemon
25 g (1 oz) dried mango or dried apricots, chopped
55 g (2 oz) stoned dates, chopped
25 g (1 oz) ground almonds
large pinch ground cinnamon
12 round wuntun skins
1 egg white, lightly beaten
2 teaspoons icing sugar
strips of dried mango and date and mint sprigs, to decorate

Place the banana, lemon rind and juice, mango, dates, almonds and cinnamon in a food processor and blend until smooth.

Divide the fruit mixture between the wuntun skins, placing it in the centre of each one. Brush the edge of the wuntun skins with egg white, fold in half to form crescent shapes and press edges together to seal.

Bring a wok or large saucepan of water to the boil. Place dumplings on a sheet of baking parchment in a steamer and place over the water. Cover and steam for 10 minutes until soft. Dust with icing sugar, decorate and serve.

Serves 4.

HOT CHOCOLATE SOUFFLÉ

2 tablespoons caster sugar
125 g (4 oz) plain (dark) chocolate
2 tablespoons brandy or coffee
4 eggs, separated, plus 2 extra whites
icing sugar, to serve
Dark Chocolate Sauce (see page 313), to serve

Preheat oven to 200C (400F/Gas 6). Butter a 1 litre (35 fl oz/4½ cup) soufflé dish and dust out with 1 tablespoon caster sugar. Break chocolate into pieces and put into a double boiler or a bowl set over a saucepan of simmering water with the brandy or coffee.

Set over medium heat and stir until smooth. Take care not to overheat the chocolate or it will lose its gloss and become very thick and difficult to combine with other ingredients. Remove from heat and beat in egg yolks with remaining caster sugar. In a bowl, whisk egg whites until stiff but not dry. Fold 1 table-spoon into chocolate mixture, then scrape into egg whites and quickly fold together using a metal spoon.

Pour into prepared soufflé dish, place on a baking sheet and bake in the oven for 15-18 minutes, until risen and just set. Serve immediately, dusted with icing sugar.

Serves 4.

LEMON BELVOIR PUDDING

115 g (4 oz/½ cup) butter, softened
115 g (4 oz/½ cup) caster sugar
2 large egg yolks
150 g (5 oz/2½ cups) fresh breadcrumbs
juice and grated peel 2 lemons
scant 1 teaspoon baking powder
lemon peel strips and icing sugar, to decorate
Hot Lemon Sauce (see page 313), to serve

Butter a 1 litre (35 fl oz/4½ cup) charlotte mould thoroughly. In a large bowl, cream butter and sugar until light and fluffy.

Beat in egg yolks and breadcrumbs. When well mixed, stir in lemon juice and grated peel and baking powder. Spoon into pre-pared mould and cover top with a piece of foil, pleated in the middle. Tie securely with string round mould, then place in a saucepan with enough gently boiling water to come halfway up sides.

Steam for 45-60 minutes. Check water in pan from time to time and add more boiling water as necessary. Turn out pudding and decorate with strips of lemon peel. Dust with icing sugar and serve hot with Hot Lemon Sauce.

Serves 4.

ROUND CHRISTMAS PUDDING

450 g (1 lb/3 cups) mixed dried fruit
55 g (2 oz/⅓ cup) chopped prunes
45 g (1½ oz/⅓ cup) chopped glacé cherries
55 g (2 oz/½ cup) chopped almonds
45 g (1½ oz/¼ cup) grated carrot
45 g (1½ oz/¼ cup) grated cooking apple
finely grated peel and juice 1 orange
3 teaspoons black treacle (molasses)
85 ml (3 fl oz/⅓ cup) stout
3 teaspoons brandy plus extra for serving
1 egg
55 g (2 oz/¼ cup) butter, melted
55 g (2 oz/⅓ cup) dark soft brown sugar
¾ teaspoon ground allspice
55 g (2 oz/½ cup) plain flour
55 g (2 oz/1 cup) soft white breadcrumbs

In a large mixing bowl, put mixed fruit, prunes, cherries, almonds, carrot, apple, orange peel and juice, treacle, stout and the brandy. Mix well together. Stir in egg, butter, sugar, allspice, flour and breadcrumbs until well blended. Cover; leave in a cool place until ready to cook. Use a buttered round Christmas pudding mould, measuring 12.5 cm (5 in) in diameter, or a rice steaming mould, lined with double thickness foil. Fill each half of mould with mixture. Place two halves together, securing mould tightly.

Half-fill a saucepan with water, bring to the boil and place mould carefully into pan so that water comes just below join of mould. Cover and cook very gently for 6 hours. Cool in mould; turn out and wrap in foil until required. To re-heat pudding: unwrap and replace in mould. Cook as before for 2-3 hours. Turn onto a serving plate, decorate with holly, spoon over warmed brandy and set alight. Serve with Brandy Butter, see opposite.

Serves 8.

SULTANA & CARROT PUDDING

115 g (4 oz/½ cup) butter
85 g (3 oz/½ cup) soft brown sugar
2 eggs, beaten
175 g (6 oz/1½ cups) self-raising flour, sifted
115 g (4 oz) carrots, peeled and coarsely grated
55 g (2 oz/⅓ cup) sultanas
3 tablespoons milk

In a bowl, cream together butter and sugar until light and fluffy. Gradually add beaten eggs, beating well after each addition.

Using a metal spoon, fold in sifted flour, carrots, sultanas and milk, mixing gently to combine. Place mixture in a greased 1.2 litre (2 pint/5 cup) pudding basin and level the surface.

Cover with a double layer of greased grease-proof paper and secure with string. Place in a saucepan of gently boiling water to come halfway up sides of basin. Steam for 1½ hours. To serve, turn out carefully onto a plate and serve with custard (see page 359) or cream.

Serves 8.

COLD
DESSERTS

PEARS WITH CHOCOLATE SAUCE

CARAMEL ORANGES

115 g (4 oz/½ cup) ricotta cheese
55 g (2 oz/½ cup) ground hazelnuts
2 tablespoons clear honey
2 small egg yolks
seeds from 1 cardamom pod, crushed
4 large pears
CHOCOLATE SAUCE:
115 g (4 oz) plain chocolate
45 g (1½ oz/9 teaspoons) unsalted butter
2 tablespoons brandy
2 tablespoons thick sour cream

4 large oranges, scrubbed
115 g (4 oz/½ cup) caster sugar
300 ml (10 fl oz/1¼ cup) orange juice
1 tablespoon orange liqueur

Cream together the ricotta cheese, hazelnuts, honey, egg yolks and crushed cardamom seeds.

Remove the rind from the oranges, then remove pith as you would an apple, being careful not to leave any of the white pith behind. Cut the rind into fine needleshreds.

Preheat oven to 190C (375F/Gas 5). Cut a thin slice from the base of each pear and using a corer or small spoon, carefully scoop out the core as far up inside the pear as possible, without damaging the flesh. Fill cavities with the ricotta mixture, pressing in well; smooth the bases flat. Peel the pears and place in a small roasting tin. Cover with foil and bake for 45-50 minutes until pears are cooked.

Slice each orange horizontally into rounds and re-form into oranges with the help of a cocktail stick. Place in a serving dish. Put the sugar into a heavy-based pan and add 55 ml (2 fl oz/¼ cup) of the orange juice. Heat gently to allow the sugar to melt and dissolve slowly, then boil until it turns a rich golden brown. Remove from heat and add the remaining orange juice, taking care as it will splutter.

Just before pears are cooked, place the chocolate, butter, brandy and thick sour cream in a small pan and heat gently until melted, stir well and keep warm. Transfer the cooked pears to serving plates, slice in half to reveal filling and pour over the sauce. Serve immediately.

Serves 4.

Set on the heat again, add the needleshreds and stir until caramel has dissolved. Bring to the boil and boil until reduced and syrupy. Cool, then stir in the liqueur. Pour mixture over the oranges and serve.

Serves 4.

MELON & CHILLED BERRIES

350 g (12 oz) mixed fresh berries (raspberries,
 strawberries, blackberries, blueberries)
115 ml (4 fl oz/½ cup) Muscat dessert wine
1 teaspoon chopped preserved stem ginger
2 teaspoons stem ginger syrup (from jar)
1 teaspoon shredded fresh mint
2 small Cantaloupe or Charentais melons
mint leaves, to decorate

FRUIT & ELDERFLOWER CREAM

115 ml (4 fl oz/½ cup) double (thick) cream
115 ml (4 fl oz/½ cup) fromage frais
2 tablespoons elderflower syrup
1 small ripe mango
1 small ripe papaya
1 large ripe peach
1 large apple
115 g (4 oz) strawberries
115 g (4 oz) bunch seedless grapes
freshly grated nutmeg and fresh lemon balm or mint,
 to decorate

Wash and dry the berries and hull and halve
as necessary. Place in a bowl and pour over
the wine, ginger, ginger syrup and mint. Stir
well, cover and chill for 2 hours.

Whip the double (thick) cream and gently
fold in the fromage frais and elderflower
syrup, cover and chill until required.

Peel the mango, cut down either side of the
stone and cut the flesh into thin slices. Peel
and halve the papaya, scoop out and discard
the seeds and cut flesh into thin strips. Halve
and stone the peach and cut into thin
wedges. Quarter and core the apple and cut
into thin wedges. Hull and halve the strawberries.

With a sharp knife, cut the melons in half,
cutting into the flesh in a zig-zag pattern all
the way around the centre of each fruit to
form attractive edges. Carefully scoop out
and discard the seeds and fill each hollow
with a large spoonful of the chilled berries.
Pour in the juices, decorate with mint leaves
and serve with crème fraîche or mascarpone
cheese.

Serves 4.

Arrange all the prepared fruit and the grapes
on a large platter and place the bowl of
elderflower dip in the centre. Sprinkle over a
little nutmeg and serve the fruit decorated
with the lemon balm or mint.

Serves 8.

Note: Use any fruit liqueur such as crème
de cassis or crème de peche as an alternative
to elderflower syrup, if wished. Sprinkle
lemon juice over the fruit if not serving
immediately.

CLEMENTINE & DATE SALAD

PEARS IN RED WINE

8 clementines
2 teaspoons orange-flower water
115 g (4 oz/¾ cup) dates
25 g (1 oz/¼ cup) pistachio nuts
clementine leaves, to decorate

Peel the clementines. Cut them into slices, reserving any juice.

4 firm Williams or Comice pears, peeled, with stalks
 left on
4 cloves
8 prunes
550 ml (20 fl oz/2½ cups) red wine
1-2 tablespoons sugar
1½ cinnamon sticks
1 vanilla pod
2 tablespoons crème de cassis
orange slices and bay leaves, to decorate

Preheat oven to lowest setting. Stud pears with cloves and put into a large heavy casserole with prunes.

Arrange the clementine slices on serving plates. Pour over the reserved juice and sprinkle with the orange-flower water.

Put wine, sugar, cinnamon sticks and vanilla into a saucepan and bring to the boil over a low heat, stirring until sugar has dissolved. Pour over pears, cover and bake for 3 hours, turning and basting pears twice.

Remove the stones from the dates. Chop the dates. Roughly chop the pistachio nuts. Scatter the dates and nuts over the clementines. Decorate with clementine leaves and serve.

Serves 4-6.

Transfer pears and prunes to a dish, standing pears upright. Remove vanilla pod. Add cassis to cooking liquid and boil rapidly until lightly syrupy. Pour sauce over pears and leave to cool. Chill before serving. Slice pears and arrange on serving plates. Decorate with orange slices and bay leaves and serve.

Serves 4.

APRICOT DESSERT

225 g (8 oz/1¾ cups) ready-to-eat dried apricots
225 g (8 oz/1 cup) caster sugar
250 ml (8 fl oz/1 cup) whipping cream
55 g (2 oz/⅓ cup) blanched almonds, chopped and
  toasted

Put apricots in a saucepan with 250 ml
(8 fl oz/1 cup) water and bring to the boil,
then simmer, covered, for about 25 minutes
or until very soft.

Meanwhile, put sugar and 450 ml (16 fl oz/
2 cups) water in a heavy-based saucepan and
heat gently, stirring occasionally, until sugar
has dissolved. Bring to the boil and boil for 3
minutes or until syrupy. Drain apricots and
purée in a blender or food processor fitted
with a metal blade. Add syrup and process
again.

Pour mixture into a bowl and leave to cool,
then chill for at least 1 hour. Whip cream
until holding soft peaks, fold half into
apricot purée, leaving it slightly marbled,
and spoon into serving dishes. Chill for 30
minutes, then top with remaining cream and
scatter with chopped almonds.

Serves 4-6.

RHUBARB MERINGUE

450 g (1 lb) rhubarb, sliced
4 bananas, sliced
55 g (2 oz/¼ cup) soft brown sugar
½ teaspoon ground cinnamon
grated rind and juice 3 oranges
MERINGUE:
3 egg whites
175 g (6 oz/¾ cup) caster sugar

Preheat oven to 180C (350F/Gas 4). Put the
rhubarb and bananas in an ovenproof dish.
Sprinkle with brown sugar, cinnamon and
orange rind. Pour over the orange juice,
making sure the fruit is evenly coated.

Cover with a lid or piece of foil and bake for
15-20 minutes, until the fruit is tender.
Meanwhile, to make the meringue, beat the
egg whites until they form stiff peaks. Fold in
the caster sugar.

Put the meringue in a piping bag and pipe
over the fruit. Return to the oven and cook
for 20 minutes, until the meringue is crisp
and golden. Serve warm or cold.

Serves 4-6.

Note: If you prefer, you can simply spoon the
meringue over the fruit.

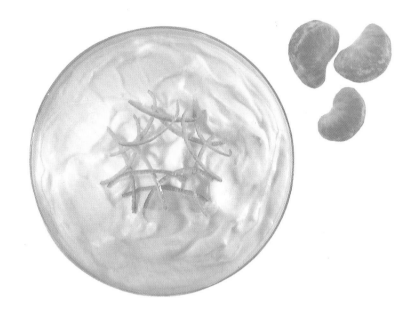

TANGERINE SYLLABUB

grated peel and juice 3 tangerines
grated peel and juice 1 lemon
85 g (3 oz/⅓ cup) caster sugar
85 ml (3 fl oz/⅓ cup) cream sherry
300 ml (10 fl oz/1¼ cups) double (thick) cream
extra grated peel, to decorate, if desired

Put tangerine and lemon peel and both juices into a bowl with sugar and sherry and leave to infuse in a cool place for at least 1 hour.

In a large bowl, whip the cream while gradually pouring in the infused mixture. Keep whipping until mixture is thick enough to form soft peaks.

Pour mixture into a glass serving bowl or individual glasses and chill for at least 2 hours before serving. Decorate with extra peel, if desired.

Serves 4-6.

Note: Use a sharp grater to grate the peel of tangerines, otherwise the peel tends to tear. Warm citrus fruits slightly before squeezing and they will yield more juice.

SUMMER PUDDINGS

450 g (1 lb) redcurrants and blackcurrants, mixed
juice ½ orange
115 g (4 oz/½ cup) caster sugar
225 g (8 oz) raspberries
12-16 slices thin white bread
extra raspberries, if desired, and whipping cream, to
  serve

Put currants into a saucepan with orange juice and sugar and cook over a low heat, stirring occasionally, until juicy and just tender. Gently stir in raspberries, then set aside to cool.

Cut crusts from bread. From 6 slices, cut circles the same size as the top of small ramekin dishes or dariole moulds. Use remaining bread to line 6 ramekin dishes or dariole moulds, overlapping bread to line dishes completely. Strain fruit, reserving juices, and spoon fruit into bread-lined dishes, pressing down quite firmly. Cover with bread circles. Pour some of the reserved juice into dishes to soak bread. Put a small weight on top of each pudding.

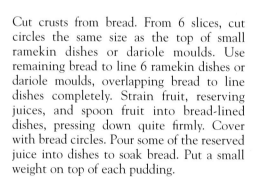

Chill puddings and remaining juice, for several hours or overnight. When ready to serve, turn puddings out onto individual plates and spoon a little of the reserved juices around them. Top with the extra raspberries, if desired. Whip cream lightly and dot a small amount in the juice and serve the remaining cream separately.

Serves 6.

MIXED CURRANT SENSATION

115 g (4 oz) blackcurrants
115 g (4 oz) redcurrants
115 g (4 oz) white currants
3 teaspoons thick honey
3 teaspoons powdered gelatine
400 ml (14 fl oz/1¾ cups) ready-made cold custard
300 ml (10 fl oz/1¼ cups) single (light) cream
25 g (1 oz/¼ cup) mixed chopped nuts

Reserve a few currants for decoration. Put remaining currants in a saucepan with honey and 2 tablespoons water. Heat gently until just soft. Leave to cool completely.

Sprinkle gelatine over 3 tablespoons water in a small bowl and leave for 2-3 minutes to soften. Place bowl in a saucepan of hot water and stir until dissolved. Cool. Place currants and juice, gelatine, custard and cream in a blender or food processor and purée until well mixed.

Pour mixture into individual serving dishes and leave to set in the refrigerator. When ready to serve, sprinkle chopped nuts over each dessert and decorate with the reserved currants. Serve chilled.

Serves 6.

Note: Desserts set more quickly if placed in a container full of cold water and ice cubes.

DRIED FRUIT SALAD

150 ml (5 fl oz/⅔ cup) orange juice
55 g (2 oz/⅓ cup) soft brown sugar
1 tablespoon orange liqueur
350 g (12 oz/2¼ cups) mixed dried fruit, eg apricots, peaches, dates, figs, pears
55 g (2 oz/⅓ cup) raisins
55 g (2 oz/¼ cup) blanched almonds
1 tablespoon chopped pistachio nuts
Greek yogurt and ground cinnamon, to serve

Put the orange juice in a saucepan and heat until warm. Add the sugar and heat, stirring, until dissolved.

Remove from the heat and stir in the orange liqueur and 175 ml (6 fl oz/¾ cup) cold water. Add the mixed fruit, raisins and orange juice mixture. Turn the fruit in the liquid. Transfer to a bowl and add more water, if necessary, to cover.

Cover the bowl and leave in a cool place for 24 hours. Add the almonds and pistachio nuts and stir to mix with the fruit. Serve with Greek yogurt, sprinkled with cinnamon.

Serves 4.

GOOSEBERRY YOGURT SNOW

350 g (12 oz) gooseberries
85 g (3 oz/⅓ cup) caster sugar
425 ml (15 fl oz/1¾ cups) Greek yogurt
mint sprigs, to decorate

Place gooseberries in a saucepan with 2 tablespoons water. Cook gently until soft.

Stir sugar into gooseberries and leave to cool. Purée cooled gooseberries, juice and yogurt in a blender or food processor until smooth.

Pour mixture into 6 serving dishes and chill in the refrigerator before serving. To serve, decorate with mint sprigs.

Serves 6.

Variation: Bottled gooseberries in syrup may be used instead of fresh gooseberries – omit 55 g (2 oz/¼ cup) caster sugar and blend gooseberries with remaining sugar and yogurt.

MANGO MOUSSE

400 g (14 oz) can mangoes
juice ½ lemon
1-2 tablespoons caster sugar
3 teaspoons powdered gelatine
300 ml (10 fl oz/1¼ cups) whipping cream
fresh mango slices and lemon peel strips, to decorate

Drain mangoes well and purée flesh with lemon juice in a blender or food processor. Pour into a bowl and sweeten to taste with caster sugar.

Sprinkle gelatine over 5 tablespoons water in a small bowl and leave to soften for 2-3 minutes. Stand bowl in a saucepan of hot water and stir until gelatine has dissolved. Stir into purée, then put in a cool place until on point of setting. In a bowl, whip cream lightly and fold into mango mixture.

Pour mixture into a glass serving bowl or individual glasses and chill until set. Decorate with fresh mango slices and lemon peel just before serving.

Serves 4.

Note: When folding whipped cream and/or egg whites into gelatine mixtures, it is essential that the base mixture is on the point of setting. If folded in too soon, the mixture will separate out to jelly on the bottom and froth on top.

RICOTTA & COFFEE DESSERT

350 g (12 oz) ricotta cheese, at room temperature
350 g (12 oz) cream cheese, at room temperature
1 tablespoon rum
2 tablespoons brandy or Tia Maria
few drops of vanilla essence
2 tablespoons espresso ground Italian roast coffee
3 tablespoons icing sugar
150 ml (5 fl oz/²⁄₃ cup) whipping cream
55 g (2 oz) chocolate shavings, to decorate

Sieve ricotta and mascarpone together, then beat with a wooden spoon. Do not attempt to do this in a food processor.

Beat in the rum, brandy, vanilla and ground coffee. Taste and add icing sugar. Carefully spoon mixture into small freezerproof dishes or demi-tasse cups, piling the mixture high. Place in freezer for 30 minutes and transfer to the refrigerator to soften slightly for about 10 minutes before serving it. The dessert should be only just frozen or very chilled.

Just before serving, whisk the whipping cream to soft peaks and spoon a blob on top of each dessert, then sprinkle with chocolate flakes. Place on saucers and serve at once.

Serves 6.

MINTY CHOCOLATE MOUSSE

175 g (6 oz) plain (dark) chocolate
300 ml (10 fl oz/1¼ cups) double (thick) cream
1 egg
pinch salt
few drops peppermint essence
TO DECORATE:
mint leaves
1 small egg white
caster sugar
grated chocolate

Break chocolate into small pieces and put into a blender or food processor fitted with a metal blade.

Heat cream in a small saucepan until almost boiling. Pour over chocolate and blend for 1 minute. Add egg, salt and peppermint essence and blend for 1 minute more. Pour into individual ramekin dishes or chocolate cups and refrigerate overnight.

To make the decoration, wash and dry mint leaves. Lightly whisk egg white in a shallow bowl and dip in mint leaves to cover. Dip them into caster sugar, shake off any excess and leave to harden on greaseproof paper. Place on each mousse just before serving and sprinkle with grated chocolate.

Serves 4-6.

Note: Peppermint essence has a very strong flavour; use it sparingly.

FEATHER-LIGHT TIRAMISU

3 tablespoons very strong cold espresso coffee
few drops vanilla essence
1 tablespoon brandy or rum
100 g (3½ oz/⅓ cup) vanilla sugar (see page 361)
2 egg whites
225 g (8 oz) cream cheese
115 ml (4 fl oz/½ cup) crème fraîche
18 sponge fingers
55 g (2 oz) bitter (dark) chocolate, grated

In a bowl, mix together coffee, vanilla and brandy. In another bowl, beat sugar and cream cheese together. Whisk crème fraîche until just holding its shape and fold into the cream cheese mixture.

In a clean bowl, whisk the egg whites until forming soft peaks, then fold into the cheese and cream mixture.

Break half the sponge fingers into pieces and place on the bottom of 6 glasses. Drizzle with half the coffee mixture. Spoon on half the cream mixture and sprinkle with half the grated chocolate. Repeat with remaining ingredients, finishing with grated chocolate. Chill until firm and serve within 1 day.

Serves 6.

AUSTRIAN CURD CHEESECAKE

55 g (1 oz/¼ cup) butter softened
130 g (4½ oz/⅔ cup) caster sugar
250 g (9 oz) curd cheese, sieved
2 eggs, separated
55 g (2 oz/½ cup) ground almonds
55 g (2 oz/⅓ cup) fine semolina
juice and grated peel 1 small lemon
icing sugar, for dusting
Raspberry Sauce (see page 367) or Hot Lemon Sauce (see page 313), to serve

Preheat oven to 190C (375F/Gas 5). Butter a 20 cm (8 in) cake tin and dust out with flour. In a large bowl, cream butter, sugar and cheese until soft and fluffy.

Beat egg yolks into mixture, then fold in almonds, semolina and lemon juice and peel. In a separate bowl, whisk egg whites stiffly and carefully fold into the cheese mixture.

Turn mixture into prepared tin and bake in the oven for about 50 minutes, until golden brown and springy to touch. Cool for 20 minutes in tin, then turn out and dust with icing sugar. Serve warm or cold, with Raspberry or Hot Lemon Sauce.

Serves 6.

Note: For a pretty pattern, place a doily on the cake, then dust with icing sugar. Remove doily and serve.

RICE & FRUIT MOULD

100 g (3½ oz/½ cup plus 1 tablespoon) pudding rice
850 ml (30 fl oz/3¾ cups) milk
caster sugar, to taste
grated peel and juice 1 orange
3 teaspoons powdered gelatine
250 g (8 oz) mixed fresh fruit, such as grapes,
  bananas and strawberries
2 tablespoons whipping cream
2 egg whites
Raspberry Sauce (see page 367), to serve

Wash rice, put in saucepan with milk and simmer for 40-60 minutes, until creamy. Sweeten rice with caster sugar and stir in grated orange peel.

Sprinkle gelatine over orange juice in a small bowl and leave to soften for 2-3 minutes. Stand bowl in saucepan of hot water and stir until gelatine has dissolved. Stir into rice. Leave to cool. To prepare fruit, halve and seed grapes, finely slice bananas and cut strawberries into quarters. Reserve a few pieces for decoration and fold remainder into rice. In a bowl, whip cream lightly.

In a separate bowl, whisk egg whites stiffly. Fold cream, then egg whites into rice mixture. Turn into a glass serving bowl or a lightly oiled ring mould and chill until set. Turn out of mould, if using, decorate with reserved fruit and serve with the sauce.

Serves 4-6.

Note: Turn moulded puddings out onto a wet serving plate. The pudding will then slide easily over the plate, so it can be centred.

PORT JELLY

550 ml (20 fl oz/2½ cups) ruby port
peel and juice ½ orange
peel and juice 1 lemon
85 g (3 oz/⅓ cup) caster sugar
1 cinnamon stick
5 teaspoons powdered gelatine
FROSTED FRUIT:
1 egg white
small bunches redcurrants and/or seedless grapes
caster sugar

Put port into a saucepan. Using a vegetable peeler, peel the orange half and the lemon thinly and add to port with lemon juice and squeezed lemon shell.

Add sugar and cinnamon stick and heat gently until sugar has dissolved. Leave to infuse for 20 minutes. Sprinkle gelatine on to squeezed orange juice in a small bowl and leave to soften for 2-3 minutes. Stand bowl in a saucepan of hot water and stir until gelatine has dissolved. Stir into port, then strain the mixture through a fine sieve into a wetted 740 ml (26 fl oz/3¼ cup) mould.

Place jelly in refrigerator to set. To make frosted fruit, lightly whisk egg white in shallow dish. Wash and dry fruit, dip into egg white and then into caster sugar to coat thoroughly. Put on a sheet of greaseproof paper to dry. When ready to serve, turn jelly out onto a serving dish and decorate with the frosted fruit.

Serves 4-6.

NECTARINE MERINGUE NESTS

3 egg whites
175 g (6 oz/¾ cup) caster sugar
115 g (4 oz/½ cup) soft cheese
150 ml (5 fl oz/⅔ cup) fromage frais
3 nectarines
115 g (4 oz) blackcurrants
6 teaspoons apricot jam

Preheat oven to 150C (300F/Gas 2). Line a large baking sheet with non-stick baking parchment. In a large bowl, whisk egg whites stiffly. Gradually add sugar, beating well after each addition, until mixture is stiff and glossy.

Spoon meringue into a piping bag fitted with a star nozzle and pipe meringue in six 10 cm (4 in) rounds onto the lined baking sheet, leaving a gap between them. Pipe remaining meringue in stars around the edge of each round to form an attractive border. Bake meringue nests in oven for 1-1½ hours until crisp on the outside. Cool on a wire rack. In a bowl, stir together soft cheese and fromage frais, mixing well. Peel and stone nectarines and slice thinly. Top and tail blackcurrants, wash and drain.

In a saucepan, gently heat apricot jam with 1 tablespoon water until warm. To fill each meringue nest, place some cheese mixture in the nest. Top with sliced nectarines and blackcurrants, then brush with warmed jam to glaze. Refrigerate until ready to serve.

Serves 6.

LEMON ORANGE CUPS

4 large oranges
grated rind 1 lemon
150 ml (5 fl oz/⅔ cup) double (heavy) cream
115 g (4 oz/½ cup) soft cheese
julienne strips lemon and orange rind, to decorate

Cut each orange in half crosswise. Remove flesh and chop finely, then place in a bowl. Drain shells upside down on a wire rack.

Mix lemon rind and chopped orange flesh together. Whip cream lightly and mix with soft cheese. Add cheese mixture to chopped oranges and stir gently to mix. Thinly slice base off each orange shell so that they will sit level.

Fill all the shells with orange and cheese mixture and place on a serving plate. Any cheese mixture left over can be served separately alongside desserts. Chill in the refrigerator until ready to serve. Decorate with lemon and orange rind before serving.

Serves 8.

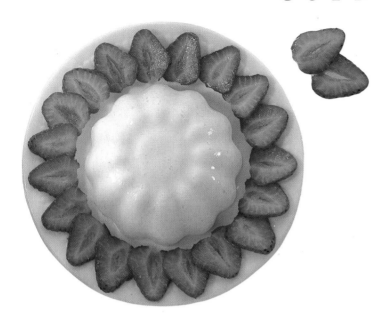

STRAWBERRY MILK JELLY

450 ml (16 fl oz/2 cups) strawberry-flavoured
　drinking yogurt
3 teaspoons powdered gelatine
225 g (8 oz) strawberries

Pour yogurt into a bowl and chill.

Sprinkle gelatine over 3 tablespoons water in a small bowl and leave to soften for 2-3 minutes. Stand the bowl in a saucepan of hot water and stir until the gelatine has dissolved. Whisk into chilled yogurt, then pour into a dampened 550 ml (20 fl oz/2½ cup) mould. Leave to set.

When ready to serve, slice strawberries. Turn out mould onto a serving plate and surround with strawberries.

Serves 4.

Note: For a softer texture jelly, increase quantity of yogurt to 550 ml (20 fl oz/ 2½ cups), but set in a bowl rather than a mould.

Variation: The jelly can be made in individual moulds, if preferred.

ENGLISH TRIFLE

1 egg, plus 2 egg yolks
25 g (1 oz/5 teaspoons) caster sugar
300 ml (10 fl oz/1¼ cups) milk
few drops vanilla essence
20 sponge fingers
6 teaspoons Madeira
3 teaspoons brandy
6 teaspoons raspberry jam
225 g (8 oz/1½ cups) raspberries, thawed if frozen
300 ml (10 fl oz/1¼ cups) double (thick) cream
16 ratafias and angelica leaves, to decorate

In a bowl, whisk egg, egg yolks and sugar until well blended. Bring milk and vanilla essence to the boil in a saucepan; pour onto eggs in bowl, stirring thoroughly. Rinse out saucepan and strain custard back into saucepan. Stirring continuously, cook over a gentle heat until thick, but do not boil. Leave until cold. Dip one sponge finger at a time into Madeira and brandy mixed together, spread with some jam and sandwich together with another dipped sponge finger. Place in a glass dish.

Repeat with remaining sponge fingers, Madeira, brandy and jam to cover base of dish. Pour remaining Madeira and brandy over top; cover with ⅔ raspberries. In a bowl, whip cream until softly peaking and fold ⅔ into cold custard. Pour over sponges and raspberries in bowl. Place remaining cream in a piping bag fitted with a star nozzle. Decorate trifle with piped cream, ratafias, angelica leaves and remaining raspberries. Chill.

Serves 8.

COEURS À LA CRÈME

225 g (8 oz) ricotta or cottage cheese
25 g (1 oz/5 teaspoons) caster sugar
1 teaspoon lemon juice
300 ml (10 fl oz/1¼ cups) double (thick) cream
2 egg whites
fresh fruit or Raspberry Sauce (see page 367) double
   (thick) cream, to serve

ORANGE CARAMEL CREAM

115 g (4 oz/½ cup) granulated sugar
3 eggs
8 teaspoons caster sugar
300 ml (10 fl oz/1¼ cups) milk
3 teaspoons sweet orange oil
1 orange
fresh herbs, to decorate

Line 8 heart-shaped moulds with muslin.
Press cheese through a sieve into a bowl. Stir
in sugar and lemon juice.

Preheat oven to 180C (350F/Gas 4). Warm 4
china ramekin dishes or 4 dariole moulds. Put
granulated sugar and 3 tablespoons water into
a small saucepan and place over a low heat to
dissolve sugar. Increase heat and boil steadily,
without stirring, to a rich brown caramel.

In a separate bowl, whip cream until stiff.
Stir into cheese mixture. Whisk egg whites
until stiff, then fold into the cheese mixture.

Divide between the dishes or moulds, tip-
ping them to cover bottom and sides with
caramel. Set aside. In a bowl, beat eggs and
caster sugar together. Heat milk until almost
boiling, then pour over egg mixture, beating
all the time. Stir in orange oil.

Spoon into moulds, place on 2 plates and
leave to drain overnight in the refrigerator.
To serve, unmould on to individual plates
and gently remove the muslin. Serve the
hearts with fresh fruit with cream handed
separately, or with whipped cream and
Raspberry Sauce.

Serves 8.

Note: To add extra colour, decorate with
sprigs of redcurrants and blackcurrants.

Strain mixture into dishes or moulds. Grate
orange peel finely, divide between dishes and
stir in. Place dishes in a roasting tin, pour in
boiling water to come halfway up the sides,
then bake in the oven for about 20 minutes,
until set. Cool in the dishes, then chill until
required. Turn out onto serving plates, and
decorate with segments cut from the grated
orange and herb leaves.

Serves 4.

APPLE CHARLOTTE

700 g (1½ lb) eating apples
grated peel 1 lemon
85 g (3 oz/½ cup) brown sugar
115 g (4 oz/½ cup) butter
150 g (5 oz/2½ cups) coarse fresh breadcrumbs
apple slices and mint sprigs, to decorate

CHARLOTTE RUSSE

16 sponge fingers
3 teaspoons powdered gelatine
4 egg yolks
85 g (3 oz/⅓ cup) caster sugar
550 ml (20 fl oz/2½ cups) whipping cream
1 vanilla pod, split open
300 ml (10 fl oz/1¼ cups) thick sour cream
175 g (6 oz) fresh raspberries
whipped cream, to decorate

Peel, core and slice apples. Put into a saucepan with grated lemon peel, 55 g (2 oz/ ⅓ cup) of the sugar and 25 g (1 oz/6 teaspoons) of the butter. Simmer, covered, over a low heat until soft. Beat until pulpy.

Line the base of 1 litre (35 fl oz/4½ cup) charlotte mould with greaseproof paper. Stand sponge fingers, pressing against each other, round sides of mould and trim to fit.

Melt remaining butter in a frying pan and fry breadcrumbs until golden brown, stirring constantly to prevent burning. Stir in remaining sugar and leave to cool.

Sprinkle gelatine over 3 tablespoons of water in a small bowl, and leave to soften for 2-3 minutes. In a bowl, whisk egg yolks and sugar together until thick and mousse-like. Put 350 ml (12 fl oz/1½ cups) whipping cream in a saucepan with vanilla pod and bring almost to boiling point. Strain over egg mixture, stirring well. Pour back into saucepan and stir over low heat until mixture has thickened slightly. Do not boil.

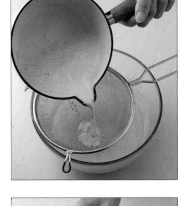

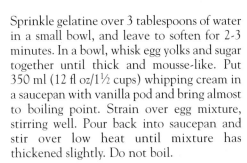

Spoon half the apple mixture into 4 glasses and cover with half the crumb mixture. Top with remaining apple and crumbs. Chill in the refrigerator for 2 hours before serving. Decorate with apple slices and sprigs of mint.

Serves 4.

Strain into clean bowl and add soaked gelatine. Stir until dissolved. Cool, then stand bowl in larger bowl of iced water and stir until mixture thickens. Whip remaining cream with sour cream and fold into mixture. Pour into prepared mould, cover with plastic wrap and refrigerate overnight. When ready to serve, turn out onto serving plate, remove greaseproof paper and decorate with the raspberries and whipped cream. Tie a ribbon round pudding.

Serves 6-8.

PETITS POTS AU CHOCOLAT

550 ml (20 fl oz/2½ cups) single (light) cream or milk
1 vanilla pod
butter for greasing
1 egg
5 egg yolks
3 tablespoons caster sugar
225 g (8 oz) plain chocolate, chopped
1 tablespoon instant coffee granules
whipped cream and chocolate shavings, to decorate

Put cream or milk and vanilla pod into a small saucepan and bring to the boil over a low heat. Cover, remove from heat and leave to infuse for 15 minutes.

Preheat oven to 150C (300F/Gas 2). Butter individual custard pots or ramekins and put in a roasting tin. Put egg, egg yolks and sugar in a large bowl and whisk together until thick and pale. Remove vanilla pod from cream or milk and return to the boil.

Remove milk from heat, add chocolate and coffee and stir until dissolved. Stir into egg mixture. Strain into pots. Pour boiling water into roasting tin to come halfway up sides of pots and bake for about 1 hour, until very lightly set. Transfer pots to a wire rack and leave to cool. Chill. Decorate with whipped cream and chocolate shavings and serve.

Serves 6-8.

OEUFS À LA NEIGE

3 eggs, separated
115 g (4 oz/½ cup) caster sugar
2 egg yolks
450 ml (16 fl oz/2 cups) milk
1½-2 tablespoons Cointreau or orange flower water or rose water
strips of orange rind and mint sprigs, to decorate

Whisk egg whites until stiff but not dry. Gradually whisk in half the sugar until mixture is stiff and shiny. Meanwhile, bring a large frying pan of water to the boil.

Lower heat beneath pan so water is barely simmering. Float dessertspoonfuls of egg white onto water, a few at a time so they are not crowded, and poach for 2-3 minutes, turning halfway through. Remove with a slotted spoon, transfer to a tilted tray and leave to drain. Whisk all 5 egg yolks with remaining sugar until thick and pale. Put milk into a saucepan and bring to the boil.

Stir a little milk into egg yolk mixture then, over a low heat, stir back into milk. Cook gently, stirring, until thickened slightly: do not boil. Leave to cool, stirring occasionally. Just before serving, add Cointreau or flower water and pour custard into shallow serving bowls. Float meringues on top, decorate with orange rind and mint sprigs and serve.

Serves 4-6.

PEACH TRIFLE

6 teaspoons strawberry jam
5 trifle sponge cakes
400 g (14 oz) can peach slices in fruit juice
6 teaspoons sweet sherry
15 g (½ oz) packet sugar-free strawberry jelly
  crystals
3 teaspoons cornflour
3 teaspoons sugar
pinch salt
3 egg yolks
450 ml (16 fl oz/2 cups) milk
150 ml (5 fl oz/⅔ cup) double (heavy) cream, lightly
  whipped
fresh fruit, to decorate

Spread jam on cakes; cut into fingers.

Place fingers in base of a glass serving dish. Drain peaches, reserving juice. Mix together peach juice and sherry and pour over sponge cakes. Arrange peach slices on top. Dissolve jelly crystals in 300 ml (10 fl oz/1¼ cups) boiling water, then make up to 550 ml (20 fl oz/2½ cups) with cold water. Cool and then pour jelly over sponge cakes. Chill in the refrigerator until set. Meanwhile, blend cornflour, sugar, salt and egg yolks with 3 tablespoons of the milk. In a saucepan, heat remaining milk, bring to the boil, then pour onto blended mixture, stirring well.

Return mixture to pan and bring to the boil, stirring, until thick. Boil for 1 minute. Pour into a basin to cool, cover with a damp cloth. When cool, spread it over the jelly. Top with cream; decorate with fruit.

Serves 6.

Variation: Sprinkle chopped nuts over the top.

RASPBERRY ROULADE

175 g (6 oz/1⅔ cups) hazelnuts
5 eggs, separated
150 g (5 oz/⅔ cup) caster sugar
icing sugar
300 ml (10 fl oz/1¼ cups) whipping cream
350 g (12 oz) raspberries
115 ml (4 fl oz/½ cup) double (thick) cream

Heat oven to 180C (350F/Gas 4). Line a swiss roll tin with double thickness foil and oil thoroughly. Grind hazelnuts finely in a coffee grinder or food processor.

In a large bowl, whisk egg yolks with sugar until thick and mousse-like. Fold in ground hazelnuts. In a separate bowl, whisk egg whites until stiff but not dry. Fold carefully into nut mixture, then pour into prepared tin and spread evenly. Bake in the oven for 15-20 minutes, until risen and firm to touch. Cover immediately with a damp tea towel and leave overnight. The next day, turn out onto a sheet of foil thickly dusted with icing sugar. Peel off foil.

In a bowl, whip whipping cream to stiff peaks. In a separate bowl, lightly crush half the raspberries, then fold into cream. Spread mixture over roulade. Reserve 6 raspberries, and dot remainder over the cream, then roll up the roulade using the foil to help. Transfer to a serving plate. Whip double (thick) cream thickly and use to pipe 6 large rosettes along the top of the roulade. Top each cream rosette with a raspberry.

Serves 6.

GÂTEAU GRENOBLE

55 g (2 oz/⅓ cup) hazelnuts, skinned
4 eggs, separated, plus 1 extra white
130 g (4½ oz/½ cup plus 3 teaspoons) caster sugar
85 g (3 oz) plain (dark) chocolate
225 g (8 oz/2½ cups) walnuts, finely chopped
150 ml (5 fl oz/⅔ cup) whipping cream

Preheat oven to 150C (300F/Gas 2). Butter a 1 kg (2¼ lb) loaf tin very well. Grind hazelnuts in a coffee grinder or food processor. In a large bowl, beat egg yolks together, then gradually beat in all but 3 teaspoons of the sugar, until mixture is light and fluffy.

Melt chocolate in top of a double boiler or bowl set over a saucepan of simmering water, then stir into yolk mixture with hazelnuts and walnuts. In a large bowl, whisk egg whites until stiff, but not dry. Sprinkle in remaining sugar and whisk again until mixture is glossy. Fold 2-3 tablespoons into chocolate mixture.

Carefully fold remaining egg white into mixture – this is quite hard to do as chocolate mixture is very stiff; keep cutting and folding until it is incorporated. Pour into prepared tin and place in a roasting tin. Add boiling water to come halfway up tin, cover and bake in the oven for 1½ hours. Cool. When ready to serve, whip cream stiffly. Turn dessert out onto a serving dish and decorate with piped whipped cream.

Serves 6.

SPIKY COFFEE-BRANDY CAKE

1 quantity of Victoria Sponge mixture (see page 403)
2 tablespoons brandy
3 teaspoons caster sugar
300 ml (10 fl oz/1¼ cups) hot strong black coffee
300 ml (10 fl oz/1¼ cups) whipping cream
3 teaspoons icing sugar
55 g (2 oz/½ cup) split almonds, toasted

Preheat oven to 180C (350F/Gas 4). Bake cake in a 550 ml (20 fl oz/2½ cup) greased pudding bowl and leave to cool in the bowl.

When cake is cold, stir in brandy and caster sugar into hot coffee and pour over cake (still in bowl). Put a saucer over the bowl and refrigerate overnight.

About 2 hours before serving, run a knife around edges of cake, then turn out onto a serving plate. In a bowl, whip cream with icing sugar until very stiff and spread evenly over cake, covering completely. Refrigerate. Immediately before serving, stick toasted almonds into surface of cream all over cake.

Serves 4-6.

Variation: For a special occasion, pipe rosettes of cream all over the cake, then decorate with almonds and flowers.

VINE FRUITS GÂTEAU

4 eggs
115 g (4 oz/½ cup) caster sugar
115 g (4 oz/1 cup) plain flour
225 ml (8 fl oz/1 cup) double (heavy) cream
115 g (4 oz) black grapes
½ small cantaloupe melon
2 kiwi fruit
1 tablespoon icing sugar

Preheat oven to 190C (375F/Gas 5). Grease a 20 cm (8 in) deep cake tin. Place eggs and sugar in a large bowl and whisk until thick, pale and creamy. Sift flour over mixture and fold in gently, using a metal spoon.

Pour mixture into prepared tin, tilting tin to level surface. Bake in oven for 25-30 minutes until well risen and firm to touch. Turn out and cool on a wire rack. In a bowl, whisk cream until stiff. To prepare fruit, halve and seed grapes. Peel, seed and dice melon, and peel and slice kiwi fruit. In a bowl, gently mix fruit together. To assemble gâteau, cut the sponge cake across into 3 layers. Place one slice on a serving plate, cut-side up. Spread one third of the cream over base, then arrange some fruit on top.

Place a sponge cake on top and spread this with another third of cream. Arrange fruit on top. Place remaining sponge cake slice on top, cut-side down. Spread or pipe remaining cream over top and arrange remaining fruit decoratively over cream. Dust fruit with sifted icing sugar and serve immediately.

Serves 10.

COCONUT LAYER CAKE

55 g (2 oz/½ cup) plain flour
440 ml (14 fl oz/1⅔ cups) coconut milk (see glossary)
6 egg yolks, beaten
115 g (4 oz/½ cup) caster sugar
seeds from 4 green cardamom pods, crushed
pinch freshly grated nutmeg
115 g (4 oz/½ cup) butter, melted
natural yogurt and slices of banana, to serve

Put flour into a mixing bowl, whisk in coconut milk, egg yolks, sugar, cardamom seeds and nutmeg, then leave batter to stand for 30 minutes.

Preheat oven to 220C (425F/Gas 7). Butter and base-line a 15 cm (6 in) soufflé dish. Add 3 teaspoons butter to dish and heat in oven for 5 minutes. Pour in 5-6 tablespoons of batter and bake for 10-15 minutes, until firm to touch and lightly browned. Continue adding another 3 layers, brushing cooked layer with butter before adding batter, then cooking each layer for 10-15 minutes.

Put soufflé dish in a roasting tin half-filled with boiling water, then continue adding final 3 layers in same way as before. When last layer is cooked, remove dish from oven and leave to cool. Run a knife around edge of dish to loosen cake and turn out onto a serving plate. Serve warm, with yogurt and sliced bananas.

Serves 4-6.

CHOCOLATE CHERRY SLICE

175 g (6 oz) plain (dark) chocolate
4 eggs
55 g (2 oz/¼ cup) caster sugar
45 g (1½ oz/¼ cup) plain flour
FILLING:
200 g (7 oz/1 cup) unsweetened marron purée
115 g (4 oz) plain (dark) chocolate, melted
300 ml (10 fl oz/1¼ cups) double (thick) cream
9 teaspoons Morello cherry jam
175 g (6 oz/1 cup) fresh or canned cherries, stoned
  and halved

Preheat oven to 190C (375F/Gas 5). Line a
32.5 x 22.5 cm (13 x 9 in) Swiss roll tin with
non-stick paper.

Melt chocolate in a bowl over a pan of hand-
hot water. Whisk eggs and sugar until pale
and thick enough to leave a trail. Stir in
chocolate; sift in flour and fold in gently.
Transfer to tin, shake to level and bake in
the oven for 20-25 minutes until firm to
touch. Cover with a damp tea towel; leave
until cold. To make filling, put marron purée
and chocolate in a food processor fitted with
a metal blade. Process until puréed. Fold in
⅔ cream. Stiffly whip remaining cream;
place in a piping bag fitted with a small star
nozzle.

Turn cake out of tin; remove paper. Trim
edges and cut into 3 short strips across width.
Spread 2 strips of cake with jam, then cover
with ⅓ marron mixture. Arrange ⅓ cherry
halves on each; stack layers together on a
serving plate with remaining cake layer on
top. Spread top and sides with remaining
marron mixture and pipe cream around top
edge. Decorate with remaining cherry
halves. Chill.

Serves 10.

CHOCOLATE PROFITEROLES

CHOUX PASTRY:
55 g (2 oz/¼ cup) butter, cubed
70 g (2½ oz/⅝ cup) plain flour, sifted
2 eggs, beaten
TO SERVE:
300 ml (10 fl oz/1¼ cups) whipping cream
hot Dark Chocolate Sauce (see page 313)

Preheat oven to 200C (400F/Gas 6). Line 2
baking sheets with silicone paper. Put butter
and 150 ml (5 fl oz/⅔ cup) water into a
saucepan and set over a medium heat. When
butter has melted, bring to boil; remove from
heat. Add flour and beat until mixture leaves
sides of pan.

Beat in eggs gradually until mixture is
smooth and shiny (do this in a food processor for speed and ease). Put mixture into a
piping bag and pipe walnut-sized blobs onto
prepared baking sheets. Bake in the oven for
20-25 minutes, until brown, puffed up and
just crisp on the outside. Make a small hole
in side of each profiterole; this allows steam
to escape and helps keep them crisp.

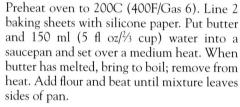

Cool profiteroles on a wire rack. When ready
to serve, whip cream stiffly. Enlarge hole in
side of each profiterole and pipe cream into
them. Serve profiteroles with the hot sauce
poured over them.

Serves 4.

MIXED CHOCOLATE TERRINE

WHITE CHOCOLATE MOUSSE:
250 g (9 oz) white chocolate
1½ teaspoons powdered gelatine
1 good tablespoon liquid glucose
2 egg yolks
150 ml (5 fl oz/⅔ cup) double (thick) cream
150 ml (5 fl oz/⅔ cup) thick sour cream
DARK CHOCOLATE MOUSSE
175 g (6 oz) plain (dark) chocolate
4 tablespoons strong black coffee
2 teaspoons powdered gelatine
115 g (4 oz/½ cup) butter, cut into cubes
2 egg yolks
300 ml (10 fl oz/1¼ cups) whipping cream

To make dark chocolate mousse, melt chocolate with coffee in the top of a double boiler or a bowl set over a pan of simmering water. Sprinkle gelatine over 3 tablespoons water in a small bowl and leave to soften for 2-3 minutes. Stand bowl in a pan of hot water and stir until gelatine has dissolved. Stir into chocolate with butter and beat until butter has melted and everything is well mixed. Leave to cool, then beat in egg yolks. In a bowl, whip cream lightly and fold into chocolate mixture.

Line a 1 kg (2¼ lb) loaf tin with plastic wrap to overlap edges. To make the white chocolate mousse, break the white chocolate into small pieces and set aside. Sprinkle gelatine over 2 tablespoons water in a small bowl and leave to soften for 2-3 minutes. Put 3 tablespoons water in a saucepan with glucose and bring to the boil. Remove from heat and stir in gelatine until dissolved. Add chocolate and beat mixture until chocolate has melted and is smooth.

Pour dark chocolate mixture over set white chocolate mouse in terrine. Return to refrigerator until set, then cover with overlapping plastic wrap and place in the refrigerator overnight.

Beat in egg yolks, one at a time. In a bowl, whip the creams together lightly and fold into the chocolate mixture. Pour the chocolate into the loaf tin and refrigerate until set.

When ready to serve, unfold plastic wrap from top of mousse and turn out onto a serving dish. Carefully peel off plastic wrap and serve terrine cut in slices.

Serves 8-10

Note: Decorate the terrine with whipped cream and grated chocolate, and serve with Dark Chocolate Sauce (see page 313) if desired. Either mousse can be served as a dessert on its own and will serve 4 people.

KIWI WATER ICE

6 kiwi fruit
1 tablespoon lemon juice
115 g (4 oz/½ cup) caster sugar
4 ripe passion fruit

Peel kiwi fruit and place in a blender or food processor with lemon juice. Blend until smooth and then set aside.

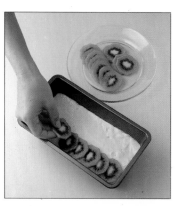

Place caster sugar in a saucepan with 300 ml (10 fl oz/1¼ cups) water. Bring slowly to the boil and boil gently for 10 minutes. Add kiwi purée, mix well and allow to cool. Put cooled mixture into a chilled, shallow plastic container. Cover and freeze for 1½-2 hours or until the mixture is mushy in consistency. Turn into a chilled bowl.

Cut each passion fruit in half and scoop out flesh. Add to kiwi water ice. Beat with a fork or whisk until smooth. Return mixture to container, cover and freeze until firm. Transfer to the refrigerator for about 15 minutes before serving to soften. Serve in individual dishes, accompanied by sweet biscuits.

Serves 6.

BANANA & RUM ICE CREAM

450 g (1 lb) bananas
300 ml (10 fl oz/1¼ cups) single (light) cream
300 ml (10 fl oz/1¼ cups) low fat plain yogurt
9 teaspoons rum
5 tablespoons clear honey
25 g (1 oz/¼ cup) walnuts, chopped

Peel bananas, place in a large bowl and mash with a fork.

Add cream, yogurt, rum, honey and walnuts and beat well to mix. Pour mixture into a chilled, shallow plastic container. Cover and freeze for 1½-2 hours or until the mixture is mushy in consistency. Turn into a chilled bowl and beat with a fork or whisk until smooth.

Return mixture to container, cover and freeze until firm. Transfer to the refrigerator 30 minutes before serving to soften. Serve in scoops in individual glasses with sweet biscuits.

Serves 6.

MOCHA ESPRESSO ICE CREAM

450 ml (16 fl oz/2 cups) milk
150 ml (5 fl oz/²⁄₃ cup) double (thick) cream
25 g (1 oz/¹⁄₃ cup) medium ground espresso coffee
85 g (3 oz) plain (dark) chocolate, chopped
6 egg yolks
175 g (6 oz/³⁄₄ cup) sugar
chocolate shavings, to decorate

Place the milk, cream, coffee grains and 55 g (2 oz) of the chocolate in a small saucepan and heat slowly until almost boiling. Remove from the heat and set aside for 30 minutes for the flavours to infuse.

Beat the egg yolks and sugar together in a large bowl until thick and pale. Gradually beat in the mocha mixture and transfer to a clean saucepan. Heat gently, stirring, until the mixture thickens, but do not allow to boil. Leave to cool.

Transfer the mixture to a plastic container and freeze. Beat to mix and break up ice crystals after about 1 hour and again at hourly intervals until almost firm. Stir in the remaining chocolate, cover and allow to freeze completely. Remove from the freezer for 20 minutes before serving to allow ice cream to soften. Decorate with chocolate shavings, if wished.

Serves 4.

STRAWBERRY SORBET

250 g (9 oz/1¼ cups) caster sugar
450 g (1 lb) fresh sweet strawberries
1 tablespoon balsamic vinegar

Pour 250 ml (9 fl oz/1 cup) water into a saucepan and add the sugar. Heat gently to dissolve sugar, then bring to boil and boil for 1 minute. Cool then chill in refrigerator. Meanwhile, wash and hull the strawberries. Purée in a blender or food processor until smooth, and pass through a sieve, if liked. Chill the purée.

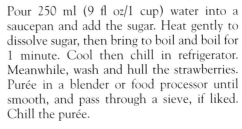

Stir the syrup into the chilled strawberry purée and add the balsamic vinegar. Freeze in an ice cream maker for the best results.

Alternatively, pour mixture into a shallow freezer tray and freeze until the sorbet is frozen around the edges. Mash well with a fork, beat and refreeze until almost solid. Repeat this twice more. Serve in chilled glass dishes.

Serves 6.

ORANGE SORBET

10 juicy oranges
200 g (7 oz/1 cup) caster sugar
2 tablespoons orange flower water

Pare the rind from the oranges with a potato peeler avoiding any white pith. Chop roughly. Squeeze the juice from the oranges and strain through a sieve.

Pour 200 ml (7 fl oz/¾ cup) water into a saucepan, add the sugar and heat gently to dissolve. Stir in the pared orange rind, juice, and the orange flower water. Boil rapidly for 1 minute. Cool, then chill in refrigerator. Strain the syrup.

Freeze in an ice cream maker for the best results. Alternatively, pour into a shallow freezer tray and freeze until the sorbet is frozen around the edges. Mash well with a fork, beat and refreeze until almost solid. Repeat this twice more. Serve in chilled glass dishes.

Serves 4.

NUTTY BROWN BREAD CREAM

55 g (2 oz/½ cup) hazelnuts
70 g (2½ oz/1¼ cups) fresh brown breadcrumbs
25 g (1 oz/2 tablespoons) demerara sugar
2 egg whites
85 g (3 oz/⅓ cup) caster sugar
300 ml (10 fl oz/1¼ cups) whipping cream
1-2 drops vanilla essence

Toast hazelnuts evenly, cool, then grind coarsely in a coffee grinder. Mix with breadcrumbs and demerara sugar in a bowl.

Tip crumb mixture onto a baking sheet and spread out evenly. Grill under medium-hot grill, turning and shaking, until brown. Leave to cool. Whisk egg whites in a large bowl, until stiff. Sprinkle in sugar and whisk for a further 2 minutes. In a separate bowl, whip cream with vanilla essence to soft peaks, then fold into egg whites with all but 1 tablespoon of breadcrumb mixture.

Spoon mixture into 6 glasses and chill until ready to serve. Sprinkle with reserved crumb mixture just before serving.

Serves 6.

Note: This mixture makes a delicious ice cream; simply turn the finished cream into a plastic container and freeze.

LARGE CAKES

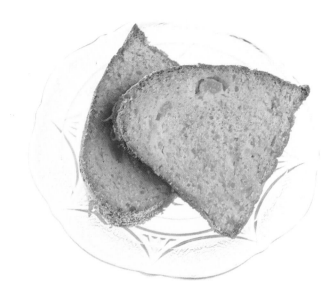

TOFFEE DATE CAKE

225 g (8 oz/1⅔ cups) chopped dates
300 ml (10 fl oz/1¼ cups) boiling water
115 g (4 oz/½ cup) soft butter
175 g (6 oz/¾ cup) caster sugar
3 eggs, beaten
225 g (8 oz/2 cups) self-raising flour, sifted
½ teaspoon ground cinnamon
1 teaspoon bicarbonate soda
few drops vanilla essence
TOPPING:
85 g (3 oz/½ cup) soft brown sugar
55 g (2 oz/¼ cup) butter
9 teaspoons double (thick) cream

Cover dates with the boiling water.

Preheat oven to 180C (350F/Gas 4). Grease a 22.5 cm (9 in) spring-release tin. In a bowl, beat butter and sugar until light and fluffy. Gradually beat in eggs. Fold in flour and cinnamon. Add bicarbonate of soda and vanilla essence to dates and water. Pour onto creamed mixture; stir until thoroughly mixed. Pour into prepared tin. Bake in oven for 1-1¼ hours until well risen and firm.

To make topping, put soft brown sugar, butter and cream in a saucepan. Heat gently until sugar is melted. Bring to the boil and simmer for 3 minutes. Pour over cake and put under the grill until topping is bubbling. Leave to cool in tin until toffee is set. Remove to a wire rack to cool completely.

Makes 8-10 slices.

PEACH & ORANGE CAKE

130 g (4½ oz) can peach slices or halves
175 g (6 oz/¾ cup) butter
225 g (8 oz/1¼ cups) caster sugar
grated rind 1 orange
4 eggs, beaten
150 ml (5 fl oz/⅔ cup) thick sour cream
225 g (8 oz/2 cups) plain flour
½ teaspoon bicarbonate of soda
icing sugar and zest of 1 orange, to decorate

Preheat oven to 180C (350F/Gas 4). Grease a kugelhof mould and dust with flour. Drain peach slices and roughly chop.

In a bowl, beat butter and sugar until light and fluffy. Add orange rind and gradually beat in eggs. Fold in peaches and thick sour cream. Sift flour and bicarbonate of soda onto mixture. Fold in gently and spread into prepared tin. Bake in the oven for 45-50 minutes until well risen and golden brown.

Leave in the tin for 10 minutes, then turn out onto a wire rack to cool completely. Sift icing sugar over cake. Decorate with orange zest.

Makes 8-10 slices.

HONEY SPICE CAKE

150 g (5 oz/⅔ cup) butter or margarine
115 g (4 oz/¾ cup) soft light brown sugar
175 g (6 oz/½ cup) clear honey
200 g (7 oz/1¾ cups) self-raising flour
1½ teaspoons ground mixed spice
2 eggs, beaten
ICING:
350 g (12 oz/2¼ cups) icing sugar

Preheat oven to 180C (350F/Gas 4). Grease an 850 ml (30 fl oz/3¾ cup) fluted ring mould. Put butter or margarine, sugar, honey and 3 teaspoons water into a saucepan.

Heat gently until butter has melted and sugar has dissolved. Remove from heat and cool for 10 minutes. Sift flour and mixed spice into a bowl. Pour in melted mixture and eggs; beat well until smooth. Pour batter into prepared tin. Bake in the oven for 40-50 minutes until well risen and a skewer inserted into the centre, comes out clean. Leave to cool in the tin for 2-3 minutes, then remove to a wire rack to cool completely.

To make icing, sift icing sugar into a bowl. Stir in about 9 teaspoons water to make a smooth, flowing icing. Spoon carefully over cake so that it is evenly covered in icing.

Makes 8-10 slices.

CHOCOLATE MARBLE CAKE

55 g (2 oz) plain (dark) chocolate
3 teaspoons strong coffee
225 g (8 oz/2 cups) self-raising flour
1 teaspoon baking powder
225 g (8 oz/1 cup) soft margarine
225 g (8 oz/1¼ cups) caster sugar
4 eggs, beaten
55 g (2 oz/½ cup) ground almonds
6 teaspoons milk
FROSTING:
130 g (4½ oz) plain (dark) chocolate
25 g (1 oz/6 teaspoons) butter

Preheat oven to 180C (350F/Gas 4). Grease a 1.7 litre (60 fl oz/7½ cup) ring mould. Put chocolate and coffee in a basin. Set over a pan of simmering water; heat until melted. Leave to cool. Sift flour and baking powder into a bowl. Add margarine, sugar, eggs, ground almonds and milk. Beat well until smooth. Spoon half the mixture evenly into prepared tin. Stir cooled, soft chocolate into the remaining mixture, and spoon into tin. Draw a knife through mixture in a spiral. Smooth the surface.

Bake in the oven for 50-60 minutes until well risen and a skewer inserted into the centre, comes out clean. Leave in tin for 5 minutes, then turn out onto a wire rack to cool, completely. To make frosting, put chocolate, butter and 6 teaspoons water in a bowl, then set over a pan of simmering water until melted. Stir and pour over cake, working quickly to coat top and sides. Leave to set before serving.

Makes 10-12 slices.

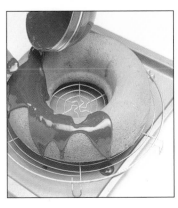

LEMON CRUNCH CAKE

115 g (4 oz/½ cup) butter or margarine, softened
175 g (6 oz/¾ cup) caster sugar
2 eggs, beaten
finely grated rind 1 lemon
175 g (6 oz/1½ cups) self-raising flour
55 ml (2 fl oz/¼ cup) milk
TOPPING:
juice 1 lemon
115 g (4 oz/½ cup) granulated sugar

Preheat oven to 180C (350F/Gas 4). Grease and line a shallow oblong tin measuring 17.5 x 22.5 x 2.5 cm (7 x 9 x 1 in) and line with non-stick paper. In a bowl, beat together butter or margarine and sugar until light and fluffy.

Gradually beat in eggs. Stir in lemon rind. Fold in sifted flour, alternately with milk. Turn mixture into prepared tin and level surface. Bake in the oven for about 50 minutes until well risen and pale golden.

While cake is baking, make topping. In a bowl, mix together lemon juice and sugar. Spoon topping over hot cake. Leave in tin until completely cold, then turn out and cut into squares or diamonds.

Makes 12 squares or diamonds.

GINGER CAKE

225 g (8 oz/2 cups) self-raising flour
3 teaspoons ground ginger
1 teaspoon ground cinnamon
½ teaspoon bicarbonate of soda
115 g (4 oz/½ cup) butter or margarine
115 g (4 oz/¾ cup) light soft brown sugar
2 eggs
5 teaspoons gold syrup
5 teaspoons milk
TOPPING:
3 pieces stem ginger
115 g (4 oz/¾ cup) icing sugar
4 teaspoons stem ginger syrup

Preheat oven to 160C (325F/Gas 3). Grease a shallow oblong tin measuring 27.5 x 17.5 cm (11 x 7 in) and line with non-stick paper. Sift flour, ginger, cinnamon and bicarbonate of soda into a bowl. Rub in butter, then stir in sugar. In a bowl, whisk together eggs, syrup and milk. Pour into dry ingredients and beat until smooth and glossy. Pour into prepared tin. Bake in the oven for 45-50 minutes until well risen and firm to the touch. Leave in tin for 30 minutes, then remove to a wire rack to cool completely.

Cut each piece of stem ginger into quarters and arrange on top of cake. In a bowl, mix together sifted icing sugar, ginger syrup and sufficient water to make a smooth icing. Put icing into a greaseproof paper icing bag and drizzle over top of cake. Leave to set. Cut cake into squares.

Makes 12 squares.

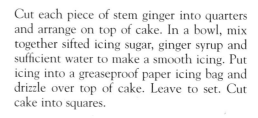

JEWEL-TOPPED MADEIRA CAKE

225 g (8 oz/1 cup) butter, softened
225 g (8 oz/1¼ cups) caster sugar
grated rind 1 lemon
4 eggs, beaten
300 g (10 oz/2½ cups) self-raising flour
2-3 tablespoons milk
TOPPING:
8 teaspoons clear honey
225 g (8 oz) crystallised fruits and angelica

Preheat oven to 160C (325F/Gas 3). Grease
and line a 20 cm (8 in) deep, round cake tin.
In a bowl, beat together butter, sugar and
lemon rind until light and fluffy.

Gradually beat in eggs. Fold in sifted flour,
alternating with sufficient milk to give a soft
dropping consistency. Spoon mixture into
prepared tin. Bake in the oven for 1½-1¾
hours, until a skewer inserted into the centre
of cake comes out clean.

Leave to cool in tin for 5 minutes, then
transfer to a wire rack to cool. Gently heat
honey. Brush over cake and arrange fruits
and angelica on top.

Makes 8-10 slices

Variation: A traditional Madeira cake has a
thin slice of candied peel on top. This should
be placed on cake after it has been cooking
for about 1 hour.

COCONUT & CHERRY CAKE

225 g (8 oz/1 cup) butter, softened
225 g (8 oz/1¼ cups) caster sugar
4 eggs, plus 1 egg yolk
225 g (8 oz/2 cups) self-raising flour, sifted
55 g (2 oz/⅔ cup) desiccated coconut
175 g (6 oz/1 cup) glacé cherries, rinsed and
   quartered
TOPPING:
1 egg white
85 g (3 oz/½ cup) icing sugar, sifted
55 g (2 oz/1¼ cups) shredded coconut

Preheat oven to 180C (350F/Gas 4). Grease
a 20 cm (8 in) loose-bottomed cake tin and
line with non-stick paper.

In a bowl, beat butter and sugar until light
and fluffy. In a bowl, whisk together eggs and
egg yolk. Gradually beat into creamed mixture. Fold in flour, desiccated coconut and
cherries. Spoon mixture into prepared tin
and bake in the oven for 45-50 minutes until
just firm.

To make the topping, whisk egg white in a
bowl until stiff; gradually whisk in icing
sugar. Spread over top of cake. Scatter over
shredded coconut. Return to the oven and
cook for a further 20 minutes until golden
brown and a skewer inserted into the centre
of cake comes out clean. Cover lightly with
foil if topping is browning too quickly. Leave
to cool in tin for 10 minutes; transfer to a
wire rack to cool completely.

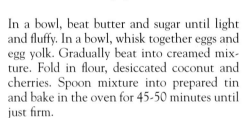

Makes 8-10 slices.

RUM TRUFFLE CAKE

200 g (7 oz) plain (dark) chocolate
115 g (4 oz/½ cup) unsalted butter
70 ml (2½ fl oz/⅓ cup) dark rum
3 eggs, separated
115 g (4 oz/½ cup) caster sugar
85 g (3 ox/¾ cup) plain flour
55 g (2 oz/½ cup) ground almonds
ICING:
200 g (7 oz) plain (dark) chocolate
300 ml (10 fl oz/1¼ cups) double (thick) cream
3 teaspoons dark rum
55 g (2 oz) white chocolate, grated

Butter and flour a 20 cm (8 in) round cake tin and line base with greaseproof paper.

Preheat oven to 180C (350F/Gas 4). Place chocolate and butter in a bowl over a saucepan of hand-hot water. Stir occasionally until melted. Add rum and stir well.

Place egg yolks and sugar in a bowl over a saucepan of simmering water. Whisk until thick and pale, remove bowl from pan and continue to whisk until mixture leaves a trail when whisk is lifted. Stir in chocolate mixture until evenly blended. Mix together flour and ground almonds, add to mixture and fold in carefully using a spatula.

Whisk egg whites until stiff, fold in ⅓ at a time until all egg white has been incorporated. Pour mixture into tin and bake in the oven for 45-55 minutes until firm to touch in centre. Turn out of tin and cool on a wire rack.

To make the icing, melt 115 g (4 oz) of the chocolate with 55 ml (2 fl oz/¼ cup) cream in a bowl over a pan of hot water. Stir in rum until well blended. Leave to cool Whip 115 ml (4 fl oz/½ cup) cream in a bowl until thick, add ½ chocolate rum mixture and fold in to make a smooth icing.

Cut cake in half, sandwich together with the chocolate icing and spread remainder over top and sides. Chill cake and remaining ½ of chocolate rum mixture until firm. Melt remaining chocolate and cream in a bowl, stir until smooth; cool and pour mixture over cake to cover evenly. Shape firmed chocolate rum mixture into 16 truffles, coat in grated white chocolate. Arrange on top of cake; chill to set.

Makes 10-12 slices.

LEMON-POPPY SEED CAKE

4 eggs, separated
115 g (4 oz/½ cup) caster sugar
freshly grated zest and juice 1 lemon
85 g (3 oz/¾ cup) ground almonds
85 g (3 oz/¾ cup) dried breadcrumbs
15 g (½ oz/3 teaspoons) poppy seeds
2 tablespoons brandy
RASPBERRY SAUCE:
225 g (8 oz) fresh raspberries
1 tablespoon clear honey
½ teaspoon ground cinnamon

Preheat oven to 180C (350F/Gas 4) and grease and base-line a 20 cm (8 in) spring-release tin. Beat the egg yolks, sugar and lemon zest and juice together until pale and creamy. Whisk the egg whites until stiff. Fold in with the almonds, breadcrumbs and poppy seeds until evenly combined. Transfer to the prepared tin and bake for 40 minutes until golden and firm to the touch. Remove from the oven and spike all over with a cocktail stick. Pour over the brandy and leave to cool.

Make the sauce. Reserve 12 raspberries for decoration and purée the rest in a blender or food processor until smooth. Pass through a fine sieve to remove the pips and whisk in the honey and cinnamon. Serve the cake cut into wedges, topped with the reserved raspberries and the sauce.

Serves 6.

Note: Frozen raspberries can be substituted for fresh, if more convenient.

OLIVE OIL & APPLE CAKE

250 g (9 oz/2 cups plus 2 tablespoons) self-raising
  flour
¾ teaspoon ground cinnamon
85 g (3 oz/⅓ cup) caster sugar
finely grated rind and juice 1 lemon
2 eggs, beaten
3 tablespoons sweet sherry
160 ml (5½ fl oz/⅔ cup) olive oil
450 g (1 lb) crisp apples

Preheat oven to 180C (350F/Gas 4). Grease an 18 cm (7 in) cake tin. In a bowl, stir together flour, cinnamon, sugar and lemon rind. Make a well in centre and gradually add eggs, sherry, olive oil and lemon juice, stirring to make a smooth mixture.

Peel, core and chop apples. Fold into cake mixture and turn into prepared tin. Bake for 40-45 minutes until golden brown and firm to the touch in centre. Leave for a few minutes before turning onto a wire rack to cool.

Makes 8 slices.

WALNUT GÂTEAU

150 g (5 oz/1 cup) stoned dates, chopped
225 ml (8 fl oz/1 cup) boiling water
115 g (4 oz/½ cup) butter, softened
1 egg
200 g (7 oz/1 cup) caster sugar
few drops vanilla essence
185 g (6 oz/1½ cups) plain flour
1 teaspoon each bicarbonate of soda, baking powder
 and salt
55 g (2 oz/½ cup) walnuts, chopped
BUTTERSCOTCH ICING:
2 tablespoons whipping cream
knob butter
2 tablespoons soft brown sugar

Preheat oven to 180C (350F/Gas 4). Grease and line a 20 cm (8 in) cake tin or 1 kg (2¼ lb) loaf tin. Put dates in a bowl with boiling water. Leave to cool. In a bowl, cream butter, egg, sugar and vanilla essence together until light and fluffy. Sift dry ingredients together into mixture and fold in with the dates and soaking liquid. Fold in chopped walnuts and pour mixture into a prepared tin. Bake in the oven for 1-1½ hours, until spongy to touch. Turn out of the tin.

The gâteau can be served warm or cold, covered with the icing. To make icing, put cream, butter and brown sugar into a small saucepan and stir over medium heat. Bring to boil and pour over cake. Serve at once.

Serves 6-8.

Note: To prevent dates sticking when chopping them, dip the knife in hot water.

ORANGE & ALMOND CAKE

115 g (4 oz/½ cup) butter
grated rind 1 orange
115 g (4 oz/½ cup) caster sugar
2 eggs, beaten
175 g (6 oz/1 cup) semolina
100g (3½ oz/scant 1 cup) ground almonds
1 teaspoon baking powder
3 tablespoons orange juice
strips of pared orange rind, to decorate
SYRUP:
250 ml (9 fl oz/1 cup) orange juice
115 g (4 oz/½ cup) caster sugar
2 teaspoons orange-flower water

Preheat the oven to 180C (350F/Gas 4). Butter and base-line a 20 cm (8 in) cake tin.

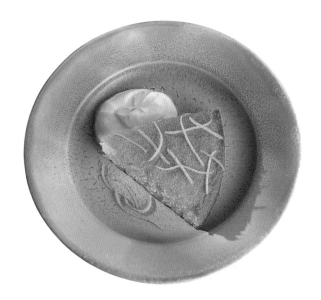

Beat together the butter, orange rind and caster sugar until light and creamy. Gradually beat in the eggs. Mix together the semolina, ground almonds and baking powder and fold half into the creamed mixture with half the orange juice. Fold in the remaining semolina mixture and orange juice. Spoon the mixture into the prepared tin and bake for 30-40 minutes until well risen – a skewer inserted into the centre should come out clean.

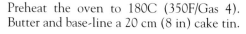

Leave to cool in the tin for a few minutes. Meanwhile, make the syrup. Put the orange juice and sugar in a saucepan. Heat gently until the sugar has dissolved. Bring to the boil and simmer for 4 minutes. Stir in the orange-flower water. Turn the cake out onto a deep serving plate and spoon over the syrup. Decorate with orange rind and serve warm or cold.

Serves 8.

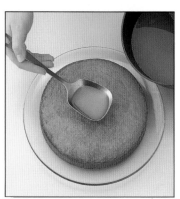

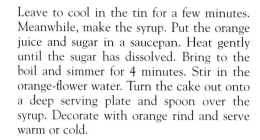

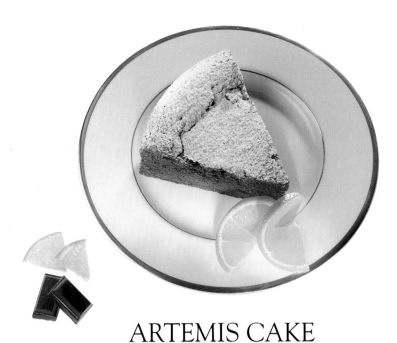

ARTEMIS CAKE

400 g (14 oz) plain (dark) chocolate
5 eggs, separated
225 g (8 oz/1 cup) butter, softened
115 g (4 oz/¾ cup) icing sugar, sifted
6 teaspoons plain flour, sifted
1 teaspoon ground cinnamon
icing sugar, to decorate

Preheat oven to 180C (350F/Gas 4). Butter and line a 20 cm (8 in) cake tin (preferably a loose-bottomed tin). Break chocolate into a bowl and stand bowl over a pan of hot water until melted. Leave until almost cold.

In a bowl, whisk egg whites until stiff. In a bowl, beat butter and icing sugar until light and creamy. Beat in egg yolks. Add chocolate; stir in lightly. It does not need to be thoroughly mixed.

Stir in flour and cinnamon and then fold in whisked egg whites. Pour mixture into prepared tin. Bake in the oven for 45 minutes until well risen and firm to the touch. Leave in tin until almost cool, then transfer to a wire rack. Sift icing sugar over the top and place on a serving plate.

Serves 8.

VICTORIA SPONGE

115 g (4 oz/½ cup) soft tub margarine or butter, softened
115 g (4 oz/½ cup) caster sugar
2 large eggs
115 g (4 oz/1 cup) self-raising flour
milk, if needed
whipped cream and fresh fruit, to serve

Preheat oven to 180C (350F/Gas 4). Grease two 17.5 cm (7 in) round sandwich tins or a 20 cm (8 in) square tin.

In a bowl, cream margarine or butter and sugar together until light and fluffy. Beat eggs in a separate small bowl, then beat into mixture a little at a time. Sift flour into mixture and fold in using a metal spoon. Mixture should be a soft dropping consistency – add a little milk if necessary. Spoon into prepared tin(s). Bake in the oven for about 15 or 20 minutes, depending on tin size, until top is golden and spongy to touch. Turn out and cool on a wire rack.

To serve, spread whipped cream on one round cake and arrange fruit on top. Sandwich with other cake. Spread a square cake with whipped cream mixed with some fruit, and arrange remainder on top.

Serves 6.

Variations: Beat a few drops of vanilla essence or 1 tablespoon grated orange or lemon peel into mixture before adding flour. Ice the cake with water icing, or flavoured butter icing, if desired.

GLACÉ FRUIT CAKE

300 g (10 oz) mixed glacé fruit, chopped
115 g (4 oz/1 cup) dried apricots, chopped
115 g (4 oz/1 cup) chopped pecan nuts
finely grated peel and juice 1 lemon
375 g (12 oz/3 cups) plain flour
1 teaspoon baking powder
1½ teaspoons ground mixed spice
175 g (6 oz/1⅔ cups) ground almonds
350 g (12 oz/1¾ cups) caster sugar
350 g (12 oz/1½ cups) butter, softened
4 eggs
TOPPING:
55 ml (2 fl oz/¼ cup) apricot jam
mixed glacé fruit and nuts

Line a 20 cm (8 in) square cake tin, or a 22.5 cm (9 in) round tin, with double thickness greased greaseproof paper. Tie a double thickness band of brown paper around tin and stand tin on double thickness lined baking sheet. Preheat oven to 140C (275/Gas1). Mix glacé fruit with apricots, nuts, lemon peel and juice; stir. Sift flour, baking powder and mixed spice into a bowl, add almonds, sugar, butter and eggs. Mix, then beat for 2 minutes. Stir in fruit and nuts.

Put in tin; smooth top. Bake in oven for 2¼-2½ hours, or until the cake feels firm and springy when pressed in centre. Cool in tin; turn out and wrap in foil. Place jam and 2 teaspoons water in a pan, bring to boil, stirring; sieve. Brush top of cake with glaze, arrange fruit and nuts over top; brush with remaining glaze. Leave to set, tie with ribbon. Decorate with holly.

Makes 30 slices.

APPLE STREUSEL CAKE

450 g (1 lb) cooking apples
a little lemon juice
175 g (6 oz/1½ cups) self-raising flour
1 teaspoon baking powder
115 g (4 oz/½ cup) soft margarine
115 g (4 oz/½ cup) caster sugar
2 eggs, beaten
1-2 tablespoons milk
STREUSEL TOPPING:
115 g (4 oz/1 cup) self-raising flour
1 teaspoon ground cinnamon
85 g (3 oz/⅓ cup) butter
85 g (3 oz/⅓ cup) caster sugar
icing sugar, to finish

Preheat oven to 180C (350F/Gas 4). Grease a 22.5 cm (9 in) spring-release tin. To make streusel topping, sift flour and cinnamon into a bowl. Rub in butter until mixture resembles coarse crumbs. Stir in caster sugar; set aside. Peel, core and thinly slice apples. Toss in a little lemon juice.

Sift flour and baking powder into a bowl. Add margarine, sugar and eggs. Beat well until mixture is smooth, adding just enough milk to give a soft dropping consistency. Spoon into prepared tin. Cover with apple slices and sprinkle with streusel topping. Bake in the oven for 1 hour until firm and golden brown. Cool in tin before opening sides. Dust with icing sugar.

Makes 8-10 slices

Note: Keep cake for 24 hours before serving.

DUNDEE CAKE

225 g (8 oz/1 cup) butter
225 g (8 oz/1½ cups) soft brown sugar
4 eggs, beaten
300 g (10 oz/2½ cups) plain flour, sifted
a little milk
55 g (2 oz/½ cup) ground almonds
115 g (4 oz/¾ cup) currants
115 g (4 oz/¾ cup) sultanas
115 g (4 oz/¾ cup) raisins
55 g (2 oz/⅓ cup) chopped mixed citrus peel
55 g (2 oz/⅓ cup) glacé cherries
grated rind 1 small orange and 1 small lemon
½ teaspoon bicarbonate of soda, dissolved in 1
   teaspoon milk
55 g (2 oz/⅓ cup) blanched almonds

HALVA CAKE

115 g (4 oz/½ cup) butter
115 g (4 oz/½ cup) caster sugar
grated rind 1 orange
juice ½ lemon
2 eggs, beaten
175 g (6 oz/1 cup) semolina
2 teaspoons baking powder
100 g (3½ oz/1 cup) ground almonds
1 teaspoon ground cinnamon
SYRUP:
175 g (6 oz/¾ cup) caster sugar
juice ½ lemon
juice ½ orange
6 teaspoons candied orange peel, to decorate

Preheat oven to 170C (325F/Gas 3). Grease
and line a 20 cm (8 in) round cake tin. In a
bowl, beat butter and sugar until light and
fluffy. Gradually beat in eggs. Fold in flour to
give a soft dropping consistency. If necessary,
add a little milk. Carefully fold in ground
almonds, currants, sultanas, raisins, peel,
rinsed, dried and halved cherries and orange
and lemon rind. Add bicarbonate of soda
dissolved in milk. Stir to mix.

Preheat oven to 220C (425F/Gas 7). Butter
a ring mould. In a blender or food processor,
put butter, sugar, orange rind, lemon juice,
eggs, semolina, baking powder, ground
almonds and cinnamon. Process until well
mixed. Turn mixture into prepared tin. Bake
in the oven for 10 minutes, then reduce heat
to 180C (350F/Gas 4) and bake for a further
25 minutes or until a skewer inserted into
the cake comes out clean. Leave to cool in
the tin for a few minutes, then turn out into
a warm, deep plate.

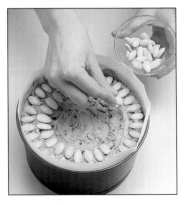

Turn mixture into prepared tin. Smooth the
top. Arrange blanched almonds in circles
over top of cake. Bake in the oven for 2½-3
hours until a skewer inserted into the centre
of the cake comes out clean. Leave to cool in
the tin for 30 minutes, then transfer to a wire
rack to cool completely.

Makes about 12 slices.

Meanwhile, make the syrup. In a pan, put
sugar, lemon juice, orange juice and 115 ml
(4 fl oz/½ cup) water. Heat gently until sugar
has dissolved, then bring to the boil and simmer for 4 minutes. Stir in candied peel. As
soon as cake is turned out, bring syrup to the
boil; spoon over cake so that peel is arranged
decoratively over the cake.

Serves 8.

CHRISTMAS CAKE

1 kg (2¼ lb/6¾ cups) mixed dried fruit
175 g (6 oz/¾ cup) quartered glacé cherries
85 g (3 oz/¾ cup) flaked almonds
finely grated peel and juice 1 orange
115 ml (4 fl oz/½ cup) brandy or sherry
350 g (12 oz/3 cups) plain flour
3 teaspoons ground mixed spice
70 g (2½ oz/⅔ cup) ground almonds
250 g (9 oz/1½ cups) dark soft brown sugar
250 g (9 oz/1½ cups) butter, softened
6 teaspoons black treacle (molasses)
5 eggs
9 teaspoons apricot jam, boiled and sieved
800 g (1¾ lb) marzipan
1 kg (2¼ lb) ready-to-roll fondant icing
red and green food colourings

Preheat oven to 140C (275F/Gas 1). Line a 20 cm (8 in) square or 22.5 cm (9 in) round cake tin with double thickness greased greaseproof paper. Tie a double thickness band of brown paper around tin and stand tin on double thickness lined baking sheet. Place dried fruit, cherries and almonds in a large bowl; stir until well mixed. Add orange peel and juice and brandy or sherry; mix well together.

In another bowl, put flour, spice, ground almonds, sugar, butter, treacle (molasses) and eggs. Stir all ingredients together using wooden spoon to mix, then beat until smooth and glossy. Add fruit mixture to cake mixture; stir until evenly mixed.

Spoon mixture into prepared tin, level top with back of metal spoon, making a slight depression in centre. Cook in the oven for 3¼-3½ hours or until a skewer inserted in the centre comes out clean. Leave cake in tin to cool; turn out, remove paper and place on a cake board.

Brush top and side of cake with apricot jam. Knead marzipan, roll out to 0.5 cm (¼ in) thickness and use to cover top and sides of cake; trim to fit neatly at base. Roll out fondant icing on a lightly-sugared surface and use to cover cake; press icing over top and down side of cake. Trim off excess icing at base.

Knead icing trimmings together; colour ⅓ red and remainder green with food colourings. Make tiny berries with some of the red icing; roll and cut out holly leaves from green icing, mark leaf veins with a knife and leave decorations to set. Arrange on top of cake, securing with jam. Cut out 'NOEL' from red icing and place on cake. Tie ribbon around outside of cake. Leave cake to dry overnight.

Makes 30 slices.

SMALL CAKES

QUEEN CAKES

55 g (2 oz/⅓ cup) currants
115 g (4 oz/1 cup) self-raising flour
55 g (2 oz/¼ cup) butter
55 g (2 oz/¼ cup) caster sugar
1 egg
finely grated rind 1 lemon
3 teaspoons double (thick) cream

Preheat the oven to 180C (350F/Gas 4). Thoroughly butter 9 individual brioche tins. Put currants into bases of tins. Stand tins on a baking sheet.

Sift flour into a bowl and set aside. In a bowl, beat together the butter and sugar until creamy. Mix together egg and lemon rind and gradually beat into creamed mixture. Add half the flour and fold in lightly. Add the remaining flour and cream and mix to a smooth consistency.

Spoon mixture into tins on top of currants. Bake in the oven for 15-20 minutes until golden. Turn out of tins while still hot. Leave on a wire rack to cool completely. Serve currant sides up.

Makes 9.

Note: If you do not have brioche tins, use paper cases placed in bun tins.

LEMON BUTTERFLY CAKES

85 g (3 oz/⅓ cup) butter
85 g (3 oz/⅓ cup) caster sugar
1 egg, beaten
115 g (4 oz/1 cup) self-raising flour
grated rind ½ lemon
3-6 tablespoons milk
ICING:
55 g (2 oz/¼ cup) butter, softened
115 g (4 oz/¾ cup) icing sugar, sifted
3 teaspoons lemon juice
few black and green grapes, to decorate

Preheat oven to 190C (375F/Gas 5). Put 12 paper cases into bun tins.

In a bowl, beat together butter and sugar until creamy. Gradually add egg to creamed mixture, beating well after each addition. Add half the flour and all the lemon rind and fold in lightly. Add remaining flour and sufficient milk to give a medium soft consistency. Spoon mixture into paper cases. Bake in the oven for 15-20 minutes until well risen and brown. Allow to cool.

When cakes are cool, cut a shallow cone from the centre of each one; reserve. To make filling, in a bowl, beat together the butter and icing sugar until creamy. Add lemon juice and beat until smooth and well blended. Fill the hollow in top of cakes with lemon butter-cream. Cut the reserved cones in half and arrange in butter-cream to resemble wings. Cut the grapes into quarters and use them to decorate cakes.

Makes 12.

BLACKCURRANT WHIRLS

225 g (8 oz/1 cup) butter
55 g (2 oz/⅓ cup) icing sugar, sifted
few drops almond essence
225 g (8 oz/2 cups) plain flour
55 g (2 oz/2 tablespoons blackcurrant jam
icing sugar, for dusting

Preheat oven to 180C (350F/Gas 4). Arrange 12 paper cases in bun tins. In a bowl, beat butter with icing sugar and almond essence until creamy. Sift flour onto mixture and beat until smooth.

Spoon mixture into a piping bag fitted with a large star nozzle. Pipe whirls into paper cases, to cover bases. Pipe a ring round the edge to leave a slight hollow in the centre.

Bake in the oven for 20 minutes until set and very lightly browned. Transfer from tins to a wire rack to cool. Put a little jam in the centre of each whirl. Dust lightly with icing sugar.

Makes 12.

STRAWBERRY-ROSE MERINGUES

MERINGUES:
2 egg whites
115 g (4 oz/½ cup) caster sugar
FILLING:
150 ml (5 fl oz/⅔ cup) double (thick) cream
55 g (2 oz) strawberries
2 teaspoons icing sugar
12 teaspoons rosewater
12 strawberries, to decorate

Preheat oven to 120C (250F/Gas ½). Line 2 baking sheets with non-stick paper.

To make meringues, whisk egg whites in a bowl until very stiff; whisk in half sugar. Carefully fold in remaining sugar. Spoon meringue into a piping bag fitted with a large star nozzle. Pipe twenty four 7.5 cm (3 in) lengths on to prepared baking sheets. Bake in the oven for 1 hour until meringues are dry. Cool on wire racks.

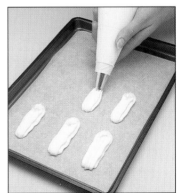

To make filling, whip cream in a bowl, until thick. In a blender or food processor, purée strawberries. Sieve purée into a bowl; stir in icing sugar and rosewater. Add cream and mix well together. Sandwich meringues together with strawberry cream. Decorate with strawberries and serve at once.

Makes 12.

HONEY MADELEINES

55 g (2 oz/¼ cup) butter
2 eggs
55 g (2 oz/¼ cup) caster sugar
3 teaspoons clear honey
55 g (2 oz/½ cup) plain flour
½ teaspoon baking powder
icing sugar, for sifting

Preheat oven to 190C (375F/Gas 5). Lightly butter 12 madeleine tins. In a small saucepan, gently heat butter until melted. Leave to cool.

In a bowl, whisk eggs and caster sugar until thick and pale. Stir in melted butter and honey. Sift flour and baking powder onto egg mixture and fold in gently.

Spoon mixture into prepared tins. Bake in the oven for 10 minutes until light golden brown. Leave in tins for 2 minutes, then transfer to a wire rack to cool. Dust lightly with icing sugar.

Makes 12.

Note: If you do not have madeleine tins, these cakes can be made in tartlet tins.

CHOCOLATE BROWNIES

55 g (2 oz/½ cup) plain flour
25 g (1 oz/¼ cup) cocoa
115 g (4 oz/½ cup) butter
225 g (8 oz/1¼ cups) caster sugar
few drops vanilla essence
2 eggs, beaten
55 g (2 oz/½ cup) chopped walnuts
FROSTING:
115 g (4 oz) plain (dark) chocolate
150 ml (5 fl oz/⅔ cup) thick sour cream

Preheat oven to 160C (325F/Gas 3). Butter a 20 cm (8 in) square cake tin. Sift flour and cocoa onto a plate.

Put butter, sugar and 3 teaspoons cold water into a saucepan. Stir over a low heat to melt butter. Remove from heat; stir in vanilla essence, then beat in eggs, one at a time. Add flour and cocoa; beat to a smooth shiny mixture. Stir in walnuts. Pour mixture into prepared tin. Bake in the oven for 20 minutes until set. Leave in tin to cool.

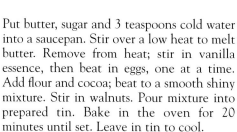

To make frosting, break chocolate into a heatproof bowl. Set bowl over a pan of hot water until chocolate is melted. Stir until smooth; remove from the heat. Stir in thick sour cream; beat until evenly blended. Spoon topping over brownies and make a swirling pattern with a palette knife. Leave in a cool place to set. Cut into squares and remove from the tin.

Makes 9 large or 16 small brownies.

SPONGE DROPS

SPONGE:
55 g (2 oz/½ cup) plain flour
2 large eggs
55 g (2 oz/¼ cup) caster sugar
caster sugar, for sprinkling
FILLING:
150 ml (5 fl oz/⅔ cup) double (thick) cream
4 teaspoons red jam

Preheat oven to 190C (375F/Gas 5). Grease several baking sheets and line with grease-proof paper. Sift flour into a bowl. In a bowl, whisk together the eggs and sugar until pale and thick.

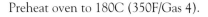

Sift flour again, into mixture and fold in very gently. Put mixture in a piping bag fitted with a 1 cm (½ in) plain nozzle. Pipe mixture onto prepared baking sheets in rounds of 4 cm (1½ in) Sprinkle drops with caster sugar. Bake in the oven for 10 minutes until light golden. Slide the paper with sponge drops still attached off the baking sheet on to a damp tea towel. Leave until cold.

In a bowl, whisk cream until thick. Remove sponge drops from the paper. Sandwich together in pairs with a little jam and whipped cream.

Makes 18.

GINGER BRANDY SNAPS

BRANDY SNAPS
55 g (2 oz/¼ cup) unsalted butter
55 g (2 oz/¼ cup) demerara sugar
55 g (2 oz/2 tablespoons) golden syrup
55 g (2 oz/½ cup) plain flour
½ teaspoon ground ginger
1 teaspoon brandy
FILLING:
300 ml (10 fl oz/1¼ cups) double (thick) cream
3 teaspoons stem ginger syrup
6 pieces stem ginger

Preheat oven to 180C (350F/Gas 4).

Grease several baking sheets. Butter the handles of 3 or 4 wooden spoons. Put butter, demerara sugar and syrup in a saucepan and heat gently until butter has melted and sugar dissolved. Cool slightly. Sift flour and ginger into melted ingredients and stir in with the brandy. Drop teaspoonfuls of mixture, well spaced out, onto prepared baking sheets. Bake in the oven for 7-10 minutes until brandy snaps are golden.

Quickly remove brandy snaps from baking sheets and roll round spoon handles, leaving them in place until set. Slide off spoons; leave on wire racks until completely cold. In a bowl, whisk cream with ginger syrup until thick. Put cream into a piping bag fitted with a small star nozzle. Pipe into each end of brandy snaps. Slice pieces of stem ginger and use to decorate brandy snaps.

Makes about 18.

ICED CUP CAKES

150 g (5 oz/1¼ cups) self-raising flour
115 g (4 oz/½ cup) caster sugar
115 g (4 oz/½ cup) sunflower margarine
2 eggs
2 tablespoons milk
few drops vanilla essence
ICING:
225 g (8 oz/1½ cups) icing sugar
3-4 teaspoons water
few drops food colouring (optional)
tiny sweets, sugar strands, glacé cherries, or other
    cake decorations, to finish

Preheat oven to 180C (350F/Gas 4). In a bowl, mix together all the cake ingredients.

Using a teaspoon, divide the mixture between 20 paper bun cases placed in a tartlet tin. Bake in the oven for 15 minutes until golden. Transfer the cakes to a wire rack to cool before icing them.

To make the icing, sift the icing sugar into a bowl and mix in enough water to give a smooth coasting consistency. Tint some of the icing with a small amount of colouring, if liked. Spread the icing over the tops of the cakes and decorate as wished while the icing is still soft. Leave to set before serving.

Makes 20.

CHERRY NUT ROCKIES

115 g (4 oz/⅔ cup) glacé cherries
55 g (2 oz/½ cup) walnuts
225 g (8 oz/2 cups) plain flour
2 teaspoons baking powder
½ teaspoon mixed spice
175 g (6 oz/1 cup) soft brown sugar
175 g (6 oz/¾ cup) butter
1 egg, beaten
3-6 teaspoons milk (optional)

Preheat oven to 190C (375F/Gas 5). Grease a baking sheet. Cut cherries into quarters; coarsely chop walnuts.

Sift flour, baking powder and mixed spice into a bowl. Stir in sugar. Rub in butter until mixture resembles breadcrumbs. Stir in cherries and nuts. In a bowl, whisk egg lightly and stir into flour mixture to form a stiff dough. Add a little milk if necessary.

Using 2 forks, pile the mixture in rocky heaps on prepared baking sheet. Bake in the oven for 15-20 minutes until golden brown and firm. Leave to cool on baking sheet for 2 minutes, then transfer to a wire rack to cool completely.

Makes 10-12.

WELSH CAKES

225 g (8 oz/2 cups) self-raising flour
pinch salt
55 g (2 oz/¼ cup) white cooking fat
55 g (2 oz/¼ cup) margarine
85 g (3 oz/⅓ cup) caster sugar
85 g (3 oz/⅔ cup) currants
1 egg, beaten
3 teaspoons milk (optional)
caster sugar, for dusting

Sift flour and salt into a bowl. Rub in white fat and margarine until mixture resembles breadcrumbs. Stir in sugar and currants.

Add egg and a little milk, if necessary, to make a soft, but not sticky dough. On a floured surface, roll out dough to 0.5 cm (¼ in) thickness. Cut into rounds with a 6 cm (2½ in) plain or fluted cutter.

Heat a greased griddle or heavy frying pan. Cook the cakes, over a low heat, for about 3 minutes on each side until golden brown. Dust with caster sugar.

Makes about 16.

BRAMBLE MUFFINS

300 g (10 oz/2½ cups) plain flour
3 teaspoons baking powder
115 g (4 oz/½ cup) caster sugar
1 egg
300 ml (10 fl oz/1⅓ cups) milk
85 ml (3 fl oz/⅓ cup) sunflower oil
few drops vanilla essence
175 g (6 oz) blackberries
6 teaspoons demerara sugar, to finish

Preheat oven to 200C (400F/Gas 6). Grease a 12-hole muffin or deep bun tin. Sift flour and baking powder into a bowl, then stir in the caster sugar.

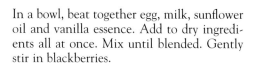

In a bowl, beat together egg, milk, sunflower oil and vanilla essence. Add to dry ingredients all at once. Mix until blended. Gently stir in blackberries.

Spoon batter into prepared muffin tin. Sprinkle with demerara sugar. Bake in the oven for 15-20 minutes until well risen and golden brown. Cool in the tin for 5 minutes, then transfer to wire racks to cool completely.

Makes 12.

SCONES

225 g (8 oz/2 cups) self-raising flour, plus extra for
    dusting
1 teaspoon baking powder
55 g (2 oz/¼ cup) butter
25 g (1 oz/5 teaspoons) caster sugar
150 ml (5 fl oz/⅔ cup) milk
butter or whipped cream and jam, to serve

Preheat the oven to 220C (425F/Gas 7).
Dust a baking sheet with flour. Sift the flour
and baking powder into a bowl and stir to
mix. Rub in butter and stir in sugar.

Make a well in the mixture and pour in milk.
Using a knife, mix together until dough is
soft, but not sticky. Turn onto a floured surface and knead lightly. Pat dough out to a
thickness of 1 cm (½ in).

Using a 5 cm (2 in) round cutter, cut out 12
scones. Arrange on prepared baking sheet
and dust the tops with flour. Bake in the
oven for 10-12 minutes until well risen and
light brown. Remove to a wire rack and
cover with a cloth while cooling. Serve with
butter or whipped cream and jam.

Makes 12.

Variation: For Cheese Scones, omit caster
sugar and stir in 55 g (2 oz/½ cup) grated
Cheddar cheese instead.

CHOCOLATE-NUT MUFFINS

115 g (4 oz) plain (dark) chocolate
225 g (8 oz/2 cups) plain flour
3 teaspoons baking powder
½ teaspoon ground cinnamon
55 g (2 oz/⅓ cup) soft brown sugar
115 g (4 oz/1 cup) roughly chopped walnuts
225 g (8 fl oz/1 cup) milk
55 ml (2 fl oz/¼ cup) sunflower oil
few drops vanilla essence
1 egg

Preheat oven to 200C (400F/Gas 6). Grease
a 12-hole muffin or deep bun tin.

Break chocolate into pieces and put in a
bowl over a pan of simmering water until
melted. Remove from heat.

Sift flour, baking powder and cinnamon into
bowl of chocolate. Add sugar and nuts. In a
bowl, mix together milk, sunflower oil,
vanilla essence and egg, add to dry
ingredients and stir until blended. Spoon
mixture into prepared tin. Bake in the oven
for 15-20 minutes until well risen and firm.
Cool in the tin for 5 minutes. Remove to a
wire rack to cool completely.

Makes 12.

NUTTY BROWNIES

150 g (5 oz/1¼ cups) self-raising wholemeal flour
175 g (6 oz/1 cup) light soft brown sugar
85 g (3 oz/¾ cup) lightly toasted and chopped
  hazelnuts
115 g (4 oz/½ cup) butter
115 g (4 oz) plain (dark) chocolate, broken into
  small pieces
2 eggs, beaten
70 ml (2½ fl oz/⅓ cup) milk
few drops vanilla essence

Preheat oven to 180C (350F/Gas 4). Grease
a 20 cm (8 in) square shallow baking tin. In
a bowl, mix together the flour, sugar and
three-quarters of the nuts.

In a saucepan, melt the butter and the
chocolate over a low heat. Cool slightly.

Beat the eggs, milk and vanilla essence
together and add to the flour mixture with
the melted butter and chocolate; beat until
smooth. Pour into the prepared tin, scatter
the remaining nuts over the top and bake in
the oven for 25-30 minutes until firm. Cool
on a wire rack, then cut into 12 pieces.

Makes 12.

CHOC & ORANGE MUFFINS

300 g (10 oz/2½ cups) plain flour
3 teaspoons baking powder
pinch salt
85 g (3 oz/½ cup) light soft brown sugar
grated rind and juice 1 orange
2 eggs
250 ml (8 fl oz/1 cup) milk
55 g (2 oz/¼ cup) butter, melted
115 g (4 oz) milk chocolate drops

Preheat oven to 200C (400F/Gas 6). Grease
10-12 muffin or deep patty tins or line with
paper bun cases. Sift the flour, baking powder
and salt into a bowl; stir in the sugar and
orange rind.

Beat together the orange juice, eggs, milk
and melted butter. Pour onto the dry ingredients, add the chocolate drops and stir
together to form a batter. Do not overmix.

Spoon the mixture into the prepared tins or
paper bun cases so they are two-thirds full.
Bake in the oven for 20-25 minutes until
golden brown and risen.

Makes 10-12.

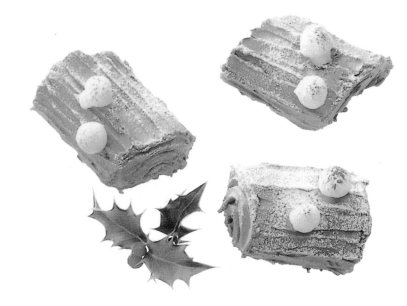

STRAWBERRY SHORTCAKE

SHORTCAKE:
225 g (8 oz/2 cups) plain flour
3 teaspoons baking powder
25 g (1 oz/5 teaspoons) caster sugar
85 g (3 oz/⅓ cup) butter
85 ml (3 fl oz/⅓ cup) milk
FILLING:
700 g (1½ lb) strawberries
55 g (2 oz/¼ cup) caster sugar
300 ml (10 fl oz/1¼ cups) double (thick) cream

Preheat oven to 220C (425F/Gas 7). Grease a baking sheet. Sift flour and baking powder into a bowl.

Stir in sugar; rub in butter until mixture resembles breadcrumbs. Pour in milk and mix to form a soft dough. On a floured surface, roll out dough to 0.5 cm (¼ in) thickness. Cut into eight 7.5 cm (3 in) rounds. Place on prepared baking sheet. Bake in the oven for 10-12 minutes until golden brown. Slice most of strawberries, reserving a few for decoration. In a bowl, mix together sliced strawberries and sugar. In a bowl, whip cream until thick.

Split shortcakes in half while still warm; spread bottom halves with two-thirds of cream. Cover cream with sliced strawberries and top with other halves of shortcake. Add a swirl of cream to each one and decorate with reserved strawberries.

Makes 8.

TINY CHOCOLATE LOGS

3 eggs
45 g (1½ oz/8 teaspoons) caster sugar
25 g (1 oz/¼ cup) plain flour
3 teaspoons cocoa
FILLING AND DECORATION:
300 ml (10 fl oz/1¼ cups) double (thick) cream
115 g (4 oz) plain (dark) chocolate
marzipan toadstools

Preheat oven to 200C (400F/Gas 6). Line a 30 cm (12 in) baking tray (with edges) with non-stick baking paper. Place eggs and sugar in a bowl over a saucepan of simmering water and whisk until thick and pale.

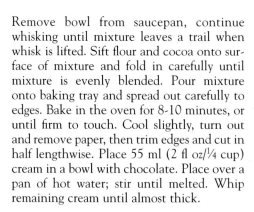

Remove bowl from saucepan, continue whisking until mixture leaves a trail when whisk is lifted. Sift flour and cocoa onto surface of mixture and fold in carefully until mixture is evenly blended. Pour mixture onto baking tray and spread out carefully to edges. Bake in the oven for 8-10 minutes, or until firm to touch. Cool slightly, turn out and remove paper, then trim edges and cut in half lengthwise. Place 55 ml (2 fl oz/¼ cup) cream in a bowl with chocolate. Place over a pan of hot water; stir until melted. Whip remaining cream until almost thick.

When chocolate has cooled, fold it carefully into whipped cream. Using ⅓ chocolate cream, spread over each strip of sponge. Roll each into a firm roll from the long edge. Wrap in plastic wrap and chill until firm. Cut each roll into 6 lengths, spread each with remaining chocolate cream, mark cream into lines. Decorate with marzipan toadstools. Keep the rolls cool until ready to serve.

Makes 12.

BISCUITS

ALMOND MACAROONS

2 egg whites
85 g (3 oz/¾ cup) ground almonds
115 g (4 oz/½ cup) caster sugar
2 teaspoons ground rice or cornflour
few drops almond essence
12 split, blanched almonds

Preheat oven to 180C (350F/Gas 4). Line 2 baking sheets with rice paper or non-stick paper. Reserve 2 teaspoons egg white. Put remaining egg white in a large bowl and whisk until standing in soft peaks.

Fold in ground almonds, caster sugar, ground rice and almond essence until mixture is smooth. Put 6 spoonfuls of mixture onto each baking sheet and flatten slightly. Place a split almond in the centre of each round. Brush lightly with reserved egg white.

Bake in the oven for 20 minutes until very lightly browned. Allow to cool on baking sheets. When cold, remove macaroons from baking sheets and tear away excess rice paper or all the non-stick paper from each one.

Makes 12.

LINZER HEARTS

115 g (4 oz/½ cup) butter
55 g (2 oz/¼ cup) caster sugar
1 egg, beaten
few drops almond essence
200 g (7 oz/1¾ cups) plain flour
25 g (1 oz/3 tablespoons) cornflour
½ teaspoon baking powder
6 tablespoons raspberry jam
icing sugar, for sifting

In a bowl, beat butter and sugar together until creamy. Gradually beat in egg, then beat in almond essence, to taste.

Sift flour, cornflour and baking powder into bowl and blend together with a spoon, then work by hand to form a soft dough. Chill for 30 minutes. Preheat oven to 180C (350F/Gas 4). Butter several baking sheets. Roll dough out on a floured surface to 0.3 cm (⅛ in) thick. Using a 5 cm (2 in) heart cutter, cut out heart shapes from dough. Using a smaller heart cutter, cut out hearts from the centre of 20 of the hearts. Re-knead and re-roll trimmings and cut out more shapes to make 40 in total, half with the centre cut out.

Bake in the oven for 15 minutes until very lightly browned. Remove from baking sheets to wire racks to cool. Dust biscuits with cut-out centres with icing sugar. Spread whole hearts with raspberry jam and top with cut-out biscuits.

Makes 20.

JUMBLES

150 g (5 oz/²⁄₃ cup) butter
150 g (5 oz/²⁄₃ cup) caster sugar
1 egg, beaten
225 g (8 oz/2 cups) plain flour
55 g (2 oz/½ cup) ground almonds
grated rind 1 lemon
GLAZE:
6 teaspoons clear honey
6 teaspoons demerara sugar

In a bowl, beat butter with caster sugar until creamy. Gradually beat in egg.

Sift flour onto creamed mixture; add ground almonds and lemon rind. Mix well to make a firm dough. Knead lightly, wrap in plastic wrap and chill for 30 minutes. Preheat oven to 180C (350F/Gas 4). Grease several baking sheets. Divide dough into 32 pieces. Roll each piece into a pencil thin strip 10 cm (4 in) long. Twist into an S shape and place on a baking sheet. Bake in the oven for 15 minutes, until very lightly browned.

To glaze, brush the warm jumbles with honey and sprinkle with demerara sugar. Return to the oven for 2 minutes. Allow to cool on baking sheets for a few minutes, then remove to wire racks to cool completely.

Makes 32.

COFFEE WALNUT COOKIES

225 g (8 oz/2 cups) plain flour, sifted
225 g (8 oz/1 cup) butter, softened
150 g (5 oz/1 cup) icing sugar, sifted
1 egg yolk
few drops vanilla essence
150 g (5 oz/1¼ cups) coarsely chopped walnuts
2 tablespoons medium ground fresh coffee
115 g (4 oz/1¼ cups) walnut pieces

Preheat oven to 180C (350F/Gas 4). Butter several baking sheets.

Sift flour into a bowl, add butter, icing sugar, egg yolk and vanilla essence. Mix well, then mix in the chopped walnuts and the ground coffee by hand.

Place heaped teaspoonfuls of mixture on prepared baking sheets. Flatten slightly and top each mound with a piece of walnut. Bake in the oven for 12-15 minutes until just starting to colour. Allow to cool on baking sheets for a few minutes, then remove to wire racks to cool completely.

Makes 28-30.

SPICED APRICOT SQUARES

225 g (8 oz/2 cups) plain flour
1 teaspoon mixed spice
115 g (4 oz/1¼ cups) ground almonds
1 egg, beaten
225 g (8 oz/1½ cups) caster sugar
175 g (6 oz/¾ cup) butter
115 g (4 oz/⅓ cup) apricot jam
icing sugar, for sifting

Sift flour and spice into a bowl. Add ground almonds, egg, sugar and butter. Beat well until thoroughly combined. Knead lightly. Wrap in plastic wrap and chill for at least 30 minutes.

Butter a shallow 27.5 x 17.5 cm (11 x 7 in) oblong tin. Press half the dough into tin. Spread apricot jam over dough. On a floured surface, lightly knead remaining dough. Roll out and cut into thin strips. Arrange the strips over the jam to form a close lattice pattern. Chill for 30 minutes. Preheat oven to 180C (350F/Gas 4).

Bake in the oven for 30-40 minutes until lightly browned. Leave the biscuits to cool in the tin, then sift icing sugar over the top. Cut into 24 squares or bars.

Makes 24.

FLORENTINES

55 g (2 oz/¼ cup) unsalted butter
85 ml (3 fl oz/⅓ cup) double (thick) cream
85 g (3 oz/⅓ cup) caster sugar
finely grated rind 1 lemon
1 teaspoon lemon juice
55 g (2 oz/½ cup) plain flour, sifted
85 g (3oz/½ cup) slivered blanched almonds
115 g (4 oz/¾ cup) chopped mixed candied citrus peel
55 g (2 oz/⅓ cup) chopped glacé cherries
25 g (1 oz/2 tablespoons) sultanas
25 g (1 oz/2 tablespoons) chopped angelica
TO FINISH:
85 g (3 oz) plain (dark) chocolate, chopped
85 g (3 oz) white chocolate, chopped

Preheat oven to 180C (350F/Gas 4). Grease several baking sheets. Line with non-stick paper. Put butter, cream, sugar, lemon rind and juice into a large saucepan and stir over a moderate heat until melted. Remove from heat and stir in flour, almonds, mixed peel, cherries, sultanas and angelica. Drop teaspoonfuls of mixture onto baking sheets; space well apart. Using a fork dipped in cold water, flatten each round to a circle about 6 cm (2½ in) in diameter.

Bake in the oven for 10-12 minutes until lightly browned around edges. Cool on baking sheets for a few minutes, then remove with a palette knife to wire racks to cool completely. Melt plain (dark) and white chocolate in bowls placed over pans of hot, not boiling, water. Spread flat sides of half the florentines with plain (dark) chocolate, and the remainder with white chocolate. Using a fork, mark chocolate into wavy lines. Leave to set, chocolate uppermost.

Makes 28.

LEMON SHORTBREAD

115 g (4 oz/½ cup) butter
55 g (2 oz/¼ cup) caster sugar
150 g (5 oz/1¼ cups) plain flour
¼ teaspoon ground nutmeg
25 g (1 oz/2 tablespoons) ground rice or cornflour
grated rind 1 lemon
caster sugar and nutmeg, for sprinkling

In a bowl, beat butter with sugar until creamy. Sift flour and nutmeg into bowl, then add ground rice and lemon rind. Blend in with a spoon, then work by hand to form a soft dough.

Knead dough lightly on a floured surface until smooth. Roll out to a smooth round, about 15 cm (6 in) in diameter. Very lightly flour a 17.5 cm (7 in) shortbread mould. Place shortbread, smooth side down, in mould. Press out to fit mould exactly. Very carefully unmould shortbread onto a baking sheet. Refrigerate for 1 hour. (If you do not have a shortbread mould, shape dough into a neat round. Place on baking sheet, prick well with a fork, then pinch edge to decorate).

Preheat oven to 160C (325F/Gas 3). Bake shortbread in the oven for 35-40 minutes until cooked through , but still pale in colour. Immediately shortbread is removed from the oven, sprinkle lightly with caster sugar and nutmeg. Allow to cool on baking sheet for about 20 minutes, then very carefully transfer to a wire rack to cool completely.

Makes 1.

ORANGE-GLAZED SHORTIES

225 g (8 oz/1 cup) butter
55 g (2 oz/⅓ cup) icing sugar, sifted
grated rind 1 orange
½ teaspoon ground coriander
225 g (8 oz/2 cups) plain flour
GLAZE:
2 teaspoons apricot jam, heated and sieved
9 teaspoons icing sugar, sifted
3 teaspoons orange juice

Preheat oven to 180C (350F/Gas 4). Butter several baking sheets and dust them lightly with flour.

In a bowl, beat butter with icing sugar until very light and creamy. Stir in the orange rind. Sift the coriander and flour into a bowl, then work into creamy mixture with a wooden spoon to form a soft dough. Put mixture into a piping bag fitted with a large star nozzle. Pipe rings of mixture onto prepared baking sheets. Chill for 30 minutes, then bake in the oven for 20 minutes until biscuits are very lightly browned.

To glaze, brush each shortie with a little heated and sieved apricot jam. In a small bowl, mix together the icing sugar and orange juice and brush over biscuits. Return shorties to the oven for 2-3 minutes until glaze is set. Cool on baking sheets for a few minutes, then transfer to wire racks to cool.

Makes 25-28.

DOUBLE CHOCOLATE COOKIES

115 g (4 oz/½ cup) butter
55 g (2 oz/¼ cup) granulated sugar
55 g (2 oz/⅓ cup) soft brown sugar
1 egg, beaten
few drops vanilla essence
130 g (4½ oz/1 cup plus 6 teaspoons) plain flour
15 g (½ oz/2 tablespoons) cocoa
½ teaspoon bicarbonate of soda
150 g (5 oz) white chocolate chips

Preheat oven to 180C (350F/Gas 4). Butter several baking sheets.

In a bowl, beat butter with granulated and soft brown sugar until creamy. Gradually add egg and vanilla essence. Sift flour, cocoa and bicarbonate of soda into bowl. Mix well, then stir in chocolate chips.

Drop teaspoonfuls of mixture, well spaced out, onto prepared baking sheets. Bake in the oven for 10-12 minutes until firm. Allow to cool on baking sheets for a few minutes, then remove to wire racks to cool completely.

Makes about 48.

EASTER BISCUITS

55 g (2 oz/⅔ cup) walnuts
115 ml (4 fl oz/½ cup) sunflower oil
55 g (2 oz/¼ cup) caster sugar
25 g (1 oz/2 tablespoons) currants
1 egg
175 g (6 oz/1½ cups) plain flour
1 teaspoon baking powder
¼ teaspoon vanilla essence
icing sugar

Preheat oven to 180C (350F/Gas 4). Grease 2 baking sheets. In a food processor, chop walnuts finely. In a bowl, mix walnuts, sunflower oil, sugar, currants and egg.

Stir in flour and baking powder. Add vanilla essence. Stir together to form a firm paste, adding more flour if necessary.

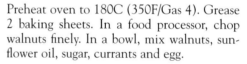

Roll mixture into small walnut sized balls, flatten slightly and place on prepared baking sheets. Bake in the oven for 10 minutes or until crisp and golden. Transfer to wire racks to cool. Dust with icing sugar as they cool.

Makes about 14.

FESTIVAL CRESCENTS

DOMINO BISCUITS

130 g (4½ oz) hazelnuts
250 g (9 oz/1¼ cups) unsalted butter, softened
55 g (2 oz/¼ cup) caster sugar
1 egg yolk
2 tablespoons brandy
55 g (2 oz/½ cup) cornflour
300 g (10 oz/2½ cups) plain flour
orange flower water
icing sugar

In a food processor, chop nuts finely, without reducing to ground hazelnuts. Preheat oven to 180C (350F/Gas 4). Butter 2 or 3 baking sheets.

In a bowl, cream butter and caster sugar until pale and fluffy. Beat in egg yolk and brandy. Stir in hazelnuts. Sift cornflour and flour over mixture. Stir in, adding more flour, if necessary, to make a firm dough. With floured hands, break off small pieces of dough and roll into 7.5 cm (3 in) lengths, tapering into pointed ends. Shape into crescents; place on baking sheets. Bake for 20-25 minutes until firm; reduce heat if browning. Cool on wire racks.

Pour orange flower water into a small bowl and icing sugar into a large one. Dip crescents very briefly into orange flower water, then into icing sugar, to coat completely. Pack loosely in a tin to avoid biscuits sticking together.

Makes about 40.

225 g (8 oz/2 cups) self-raising flour
115 g (4 oz/½ cup) butter or block margarine
115 g (4 oz/½ cup) caster sugar
finely grated rind 1 lemon
1 small egg, beaten
115 g (4 oz) packet plain (dark) chocolate drops

Preheat oven to 180C (350F/Gas 4). Sift the flour into a bowl and rub in the butter until the mixture resembles breadcrumbs. Stir in the sugar and lemon rind, then mix to form a dough with the egg. Turn onto a floured surface and knead until smooth.

Roll the dough out to a rectangle about 0.5 cm (¼ in) thick. Cut into bars about 7.5 x 4 cm (3 x 1½ in) and transfer to greased baking sheets.

Mark each bar in half with a knife and arrange chocolate drops on each one to resemble domino dots. Bake in the oven for 12-15 minutes. Cool slightly before transferring to a wire rack to cool completely.

Makes about 20.

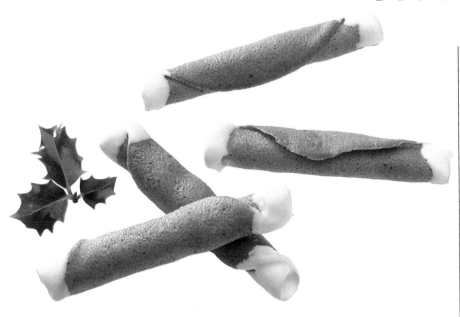

CHOCOLATE CIGARETTES

2 egg whites
100 g (3½ oz/⅓ cup plus 3 teaspoons) caster sugar
50 g (1¾ oz/¼ cup plus 9 teaspoons) plain flour
2 teaspoons cocoa
55 g (2 oz/¼ cup) unsalted butter, melted
55 g (2 oz) white chocolate, melted

Preheat oven to 200C (400F/Gas 6). Line 2 baking sheets with non-stick baking paper. Place egg whites in a bowl and whisk until stiff. Add caster sugar gradually, whisking well after each addition. Sift flour and cocoa over surface of mixture, add butter and fold in carefully until mixture is evenly blended.

Place 3 spoonfuls of mixture onto each baking sheet, well spaced apart. Spread each into a thin round. Bake, one sheet at a time, in the oven for 3-4 minutes, loosen each round with a palette knife, then return to the oven for 1 minute.

Take out one chocolate round at a time and quickly roll around a greased chopstick, or wooden spoon handle, to form a tube. Slip off and cool cigarette on a wire rack. Repeat with remaining rounds. Cook second tray of mixture, then repeat to make about 25 cigarettes. Dip both ends of each cigarette into melted chocolate. Leave to set on a paper-lined baking sheet. Store in an airtight container until required.

Makes 25.

VANILLA RINGS

115 g (4 oz/½ cup) butter
85 g (3 oz/⅓ cup) caster sugar
½ teaspoons vanilla essence
1 egg yolk
175 g (6 oz/1½ cups) plain flour
½ teaspoon baking powder
1½ teaspoons ouzo
6 teaspoons chopped almonds

Preheat oven to 180C (350F/Gas 4). Grease 2 baking sheets. In a bowl, cream together butter and sugar until light and fluffy.

Beat in vanilla essence and egg yolk. Sift flour and baking powder over mixture, then add ouzo, or other aniseed-flavoured spirit, and mix to a smooth dough. Break off walnut sized pieces of dough.

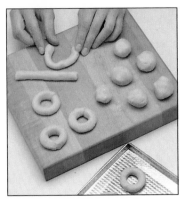

Roll the pieces into short ropes and join the ends to make rings. Place on prepared baking sheets and scatter chopped almonds over the rings. Bake in the oven for 15-20 minutes until pale gold. Transfer to wire racks to cool.

Makes about 16.

CINNAMON COOKIES

225 g (8 oz) soft margarine
115 g (4 oz/½ cup) caster sugar
1 teaspoon vanilla essence
350 g (12 oz/3 cups) plain flour
2 teaspoons ground cinnamon
salt
225 g (8 oz/1½ cups) icing sugar

Preheat oven to 180C (350F/Gas 4).

Grease 2 baking sheets. Beat together margarine, sugar and vanilla essence. Stir in flour and 1 teaspoon cinnamon to make a soft dough. Cover and refrigerate for 1 hour.

Form mixture into 2.5 cm (1 in) balls and place on a prepared baking sheet, leaving space between each one. Bake for 15 minutes. Remove from the oven, leave on the baking sheets for a few minutes, then transfer to a wire rack to cool. Mix together the icing sugar and remaining cinnamon; sieve over the cookies.

Makes 24 cookies.

CRÈME DE MENTHE BISCUITS

225 g (8 oz) plain (dark) chocolate
25 g (1 oz/6 teaspoons) butter
200 g (7 oz/2 cups) digestive biscuit crumbs
85 g (3 oz/¾ cup) plain cake crumbs
caster sugar for sprinkling
FILLING:
55 g (2 oz/¼ cup) unsalted butter
115 g (4 oz/¾ cup) icing sugar, sieved
2 teaspoons crème de menthe

Make filling first. Place butter in a bowl and beat with a wooden spoon until soft and smooth. Gradually beat in icing sugar and crème de menthe until light and fluffy.

Break up chocolate and place in a bowl. Add butter and place over a saucepan of hand-hot water. Stir occasionally until melted. Add biscuit and cake crumbs and stir until evenly mixed and mixture forms a ball. Sprinkle a 25 cm (10 in) square of foil with caster sugar.

Roll out chocolate mixture on the foil to a 20 cm (8 in) square. Spread crème de menthe mixture evenly over chocolate square to within 1 cm (½ in) of edges. Roll up carefully into a neat roll using the foil to help. Wrap in foil and chill until firm. Cut into thin slices as and when required.

Makes 20 slices.

COCONUT CRISPS

150 g (5 oz/²⁄₃ cup) butter or margarine
1 egg
few drops vanilla essence
115 g (4 oz/½ cup) brown sugar
85 g (3 oz/1 cup) desiccated coconut
55 g (2 oz/²⁄₃ cup) rolled oats
115 g (4 oz/1 cup) self-raising flour
55 g (2 oz/2 cups) cornflakes, lightly crushed

Preheat oven to 170C (325F/Gas 3). Grease 2 baking sheets. Put the butter, egg, vanilla essence and sugar into a bowl and beat together until creamy.

Stir in the coconut, oats and flour and mix to form a dough. Roll the mixture into about 25 balls about the size of a large walnut.

Put the crushed cornflakes on a plate. Lightly press the balls in the cornflakes to coat all over, then place on the baking sheets. Cook in the oven for about 15 minutes until lightly browned. Remove from the oven and cool on a wire rack.

Makes about 25.

CHEESE THINS

115 g (4 oz/1 cup) plain flour
½ teaspoon salt
½ teaspoon pepper
½ teaspoon dry mustard
115 g (4 oz/½ cup) butter
115 g (4 oz/1 cup) grated Cheddar cheese
4 teaspoons fine oatmeal
1 teaspoon cayenne pepper
1 egg white

Preheat oven to 220C (425F/Gas 7). Lightly butter 2 baking sheets. Sift flour, salt, pepper and mustard into a bowl. Cut butter into pieces, add to bowl and rub in finely until mixture begins to cling together.

Using a fork, stir in cheese and mix to a soft dough. Knead on a lightly floured surface and roll out very thinly. Using a 2.5 cm (1 in) oval cutter, cut out 80 oval shapes. Arrange on baking sheets, spaced apart.

Mix together oatmeal and cayenne. Brush each oval with egg white and sprinkle with oatmeal mixture. Bake in the oven for 5-6 minutes until pale in colour. Cool on baking sheets, then remove carefully with a palette knife.

Makes 80.

FOOD FOR CHILDREN

PLAYING CARD SANDWICHES

4 slices wholemeal bread, crusts removed
4 slices white bread, crusts removed
sunflower margarine
SALMON FILLING:
1 tablespoon mayonnaise
2 teaspoons lemon juice
90 g (3½ oz) can red salmon
½ carton mustard and cress
EGG FILLING:
2 eggs, hard-boiled
1 tablespoon mayonnaise
2 spring onions, finely chopped

ANIMAL EGGY BREADS

6 slices bread
1 large egg
3 tablespoons milk
45 g (1½ oz/ 9 teaspoons) butter

Cut bread into animal shapes using a variety of biscuit cutters.

Cut each slice of bread into 4. Using half the squares, cut out playing card symbols from the centre of each one. Make the salmon filling. In a small bowl, beat the mayonnaise and lemon juice together. Discard the bones and skin from the salmon, add to the bowl and mash together; stir in the trimmed cress. Lightly spread margarine over the 8 whole squares of wholemeal bread. Spread over the salmon filling, then cover with the cut out wholemeal squares.

Beat the egg and milk together and put into a shallow dish.

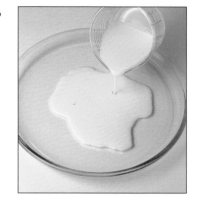

Make the egg filling. In a small bowl, mash the eggs finely; stir in the mayonnaise and onion. Make up the egg sandwiches in the same way as for the salmon sandwiches using the white bread.

Makes 16 sandwiches.

Melt the butter in a large frying pan. Dip the bread shapes in the egg mixture, coating each side, then place in the frying pan and cook on each side until golden. Serve at once.

Makes about 12 pieces.

FUN FISH CAKES

CHEESY MICE

225 g (8 oz) potatoes, peeled
25 g (1 oz/6 teaspoons) butter
1 egg yolk
1 tablespoon chopped chives
200 g (7 oz) can tuna in brine, drained
1 egg, beaten
85 g (3 oz/¾ cup) dry golden breadcrumbs
6 peas
1 small tomato
chives, to garnish

Preheat oven to 200C (400F/Gas 6). Cut the potatoes into even pieces, put into a pan of water and boil until just tender.

Drain the potatoes, return to the pan and dry over a low heat for a few moments. Add the butter and egg yolk and mash together. Stir in the chives and tuna. Divide the mixture into 6 equal portions and, with floured hands, shape into flat pear shapes. Shape the thinner end of the cakes to form a 'V' shape like the tail of a fish.

Put the beaten egg into a shallow dish. Place the fish cakes in the egg and brush with egg. Coat in breadcrumbs, then place on a greased baking sheet. Brush with a little oil and bake for 20-25 minutes until crisp and golden. To serve, place a pea on each fish for an 'eye' and add a small sliver of tomato for the mouth. Garnish with chives and serve hot.

Makes 6.

4 eggs, hard-boiled and shelled
25 g (1 oz/¼ cup) finely grated Cheddar cheese
25 g (1 oz/6 teaspoons) low fat soft cheese
8 radishes
16 currants
55 g (2 oz) Edam cheese, cut into small chunks
salad cress

Carefully halve the eggs lengthways and scoop out the yolks into a bowl.

Add the grated cheese and low fat cheese and mix together until smooth. Spoon into the egg whites and smooth the surface.

To assemble each mouse, cut slits at the pointed end of the eggs, and insert small slices of radish for 'ears', currants for 'eyes', and small pieces of radish for a 'nose'. Attach the radish roots for 'tails'. Place the egg mice on serving plates and arrange small chunks of cheese in front and little bunches of salad cress on each plate.

Serves 4.

PEPPERAMI PASTA

2 tablespoons olive oil
1 onion, finely chopped
1 clove garlic, crushed
1 red pepper (capsicum), seeded and finely sliced
400 g (14 oz) can chopped tomatoes
½ teaspoon sugar
½ teaspoon dried oregano
salt and pepper
225 g (8 oz/4 cups) pasta shapes
115 g (4 oz) pepperami (salami stick), sliced
55 g (2 oz/½ cup) grated Cheddar cheese

Heat the oil in a saucepan, add the onion and cook over a medium heat until softened.

Add the garlic and red pepper (capsicum) and cook briefly. Add tomatoes, sugar and oregano, then season with salt and pepper. Cover and simmer for 10 minutes.

Cook the pasta in a large pan of boiling, salted water for 12 minutes until *al dente* (tender but still with some bite). Drain and return to the pan. Stir in the pepperami and the tomato sauce and heat through. Serve sprinkled with the cheese.

Serves 4.

SURPRISE BEEFBURGERS

575 g (1¼ lb) lean minced beef
1 small onion, finely chopped
1 teaspoon dried mixed herbs
55 g (2 oz/⅔ cup) rolled oats
1 egg, beaten
salt and pepper
85 g (3 oz) piece cheese (such as Gouda)
1 tablespoon oil
lettuce and grated carrot salad and onion rings, to serve

Put the beef, onion, herbs and oats into a bowl and mix together to break up the beef. Add the beaten egg and seasoning to taste and bind together.

With floured hands, divide the mixture into 6, then flatten each piece on a board or work surface. Cut the cheese into 6 and place a piece in the middle of each round of meat.

Carefully enclose the cheese in the meat mixture and form into a burger shape. Brush with oil, place under a medium hot grill and cook for about 4-5 minutes on each side until golden. Serve with lettuce and carrot salad and onion rings.

Serves 6.

FLUFFY JACKET POTATOES

4 potatoes
vegetable oil, for brushing
25 g (1 oz/6 teaspoons) butter
3 eggs, separated
85 g (3 oz/¾ cup) grated Cheddar cheese
salt and pepper
parsley, to garnish

Preheat oven to 200C (400F/Gas 6). Prick the potatoes all over with a fork and brush the skins lightly with oil. Bake in the oven for 45-60 minutes or until the potatoes are cooked.

Cut off the tops of the potatoes and scoop out the cooked flesh and put into a bowl, making sure the skin is not pierced. Mash the potato flesh with the butter, then beat in the egg yolks, cheese and seasoning to taste.

Whisk the egg whites until stiff, then fold into the potato. Spoon back into the potato skins and return to the oven for a further 10-15 minutes. Garnish with parsley.

Serves 4.

Variation: Stir in 55 g (2 oz) chopped cooked ham, or 1 tablespoon sweet pickle, if wished.

CHICKEN FRIED RICE

225 g (8 oz/1½ cups) long-grain brown rice
3 tablespoons sunflower oil
1 egg
1 small onion, finely chopped
1 red pepper (capsicum), seeded and chopped
225 g (8 oz) cooked chicken, shredded
55 g (2 oz) frozen peas, thawed
55 g (2 oz) frozen sweetcorn, thawed
3 teaspoons soy sauce
4 spring onions, to garnish

Cook the rice in boiling, salted water for about 20 minutes until just tender. Drain.

Heat 2 teaspoons oil in a medium frying pan. Beat the egg with 1 tablespoon water, add to the pan and cook until set. Turn onto a board, roll up and cut into thin strips; set aside. Heat the remaining oil in a large frying pan, add the onion and pepper (capsicum) and cook for 2-3 minutes.

Stir in the rice and fry over a low heat for 3-4 minutes. Add the chicken, peas, sweetcorn and soy sauce and stir fry for 3 minutes. Add the omelette strips to the fried rice and toss together before serving, garnished with spring onions.

Serves 4.

FUNNY FACE PIZZAS

2 teaspoons oil
½ small onion
200 g (7 oz) can chopped tomatoes
3 teaspoons tomato purée (paste)
350 g (12 oz/3 cups) self-raising flour
1 teaspoon salt
85 g (3 oz/⅓ cup) sunflower margarine
115 g (4 oz/1 cup) grated milk Cheddar cheese
1 egg
150 ml (5 fl oz/⅔ cup) milk
24 peas
3 large button mushrooms
small piece red, orange or yellow pepper (capsicum)
lollo rosso lettuce, to garnish

Heat oil in a small pan, add the onion and cook until soft. Stir in the tomatoes and purée (paste) and cook over medium heat for 10 minutes until thickened. Preheat oven to 200C (400F/Gas 6). Grease 2 baking sheets. Sift flour and salt into a bowl, rub in margarine, then stir in half the cheese. Beat the egg with the milk; add to the bowl and mix to form a smooth ball of dough. Divide dough into 12 pieces and roll out each one to 7.5 cm (3 in) round and place 6 on each of the baking sheets.

Divide the tomato sauce between the rounds. Place the remaining grated cheese on one edge to resemble 'hair'. Add the peas to look like 'eyes'. Slice the mushrooms, discard the stalks and place a slice on each pizza to resemble a 'mouth'. Cut the pepper (capsicum) into strips and arrange on each pizza to look like a 'nose'. Bake the pizzas in the oven for 12-15 minutes until the edges are golden. Garnish with red lollo rosso lettuce to resemble 'hair'.

Makes 12.

RAINBOW LOLLIES

115 ml (4 fl oz/½ cup) orange juice
85 g (3 oz) fresh raspberries or strawberries
1 teaspoon caster sugar
8 tablespoon blackcurrant cordial

Pour the orange juice into the compartments of a plastic lolly maker. Place in the freezer and leave until hard.

Put the raspberries or strawberries into a blender with the sugar and 4 tablespoons cold water and blend to form a purée. Pass the mixture through a sieve, then pour over the frozen orange layer. Return to the freezer for about 1 hour until almost frozen.

Mix the blackcurrant cordial with 4 tablespoons water, then pour over the raspberry layer. Insert the holders and put into the freezer and leave until solid. To unmould, dip the lolly maker in a bowl of hot water for a few seconds and turn the rainbow lollies out. Serve at once.

Makes about 4, depending on size of lolly maker.

TEDDY BEAR FOOL

225 g (8 oz) strawberries, wash and hulled
300 ml (10 fl oz/1¼ cups) thick Greek yogurt
2-3 teaspoons clear honey
8 thin finger biscuits
8 seedless grapes
2 glacé cherries, halved
2 slices kiwi fruit, halved

In a bowl, mash the strawberries slightly (do not make them completely smooth).

Whisk the yogurt with the honey until smooth and creamy. Add to the mashed strawberries and mix well. Divide the mixture between 4 serving dishes. Decorate by placing the biscuits in position to resemble the 'ears'.

Position the seedless grapes for 'eyes', a cherry half for the 'nose' and finally press one halved slice of kiwi fruit into each fool to resemble a 'mouth'.

Serves 4.

Variation: Cook 115g (4 oz) ready-to-eat dried apricots until soft; purée and mix into the yogurt. Or mash 2 small, ripe bananas and add to the yogurt.

JELLY WOBBLES

4 oranges
55 g (2 oz/¼ cup) sugar
150 ml (5 fl oz/⅔ cup) water
15 g (½ oz/5 teaspoons) powdered gelatine
150 ml (5 fl oz/⅔ cup) natural yogurt
312 g (11 oz) can mandarin segments in natural juice, drained

Using a vegetable peeler, pare the rind from 2 oranges and put into a saucepan with the sugar and water. Bring to the boil and simmer until the sugar has dissolved. Allow to stand for a few minutes. Squeeze the juice from all of the oranges and reserve.

Strain the sugar, water and orange rind liquid into a bowl. Measure 3 tablespoons cold water into a small heatproof bowl, sprinkle over the gelatine and leave for a few minutes to become spongy. Stand bowl in a pan with a little simmering water until the gelatine has dissolved, then add to the strained liquid. Allow to cool, then add the orange juice and refrigerate until beginning to set.

Whisk in the yogurt and pour into 4 or 5 small moulds. Return to the refrigerator for 2-3 hours to set. To serve, turn out into small dishes and decorate each portion with mandarin orange segments.

Serves 4-5.

OWL MADELEINES

115 g (4 oz/½ cup) soft margarine
115 g (4 oz/½ cup) caster sugar
115 g (4 oz/1 cup) self-raising flour
2 eggs, beaten
few drops vanilla essence
4 tablespoons strawberry or raspberry jam
55 g (2 oz/⅔ cup) desiccated coconut
25 g (1oz/6 teaspoons) butter
55 g (2 oz/⅓ cup) icing sugar
16 chocolate buttons
2 glacé cherries

Grease 8 dariole moulds. Put margarine, sugar, flour, eggs and essence into a bowl and mix until smooth.

Preheat oven to 180C (350F/Gas 4). Spoon the cake mixture into the moulds, to come halfway up each one. Place on a baking sheet and bake in the oven for 15-18 minutes until cakes feel firm on top. Remove from the oven, run a knife round the sides of the moulds and turn onto a wire rack to cool. Trim the wider bases so the madeleines are all the same height.

Melt the jam with 1 tablespoon water. Push a skewer into each cake, brush with jam then roll in the coconut until well coated. Put the cakes, narrower ends up, on a plate. Beat the butter and icing sugar together and use a little to attach 2 chocolate buttons to each cake for 'eyes' and pipe a spot in the middle of each. Complete the 'owls' with a piece of cherry to resemble the beak.

Makes 8.

MERRY MICE CAKES

115 g (4 oz/1 cup) self-raising flour
25 g (1 oz/¼ cup) cocoa
115 g (4 oz/½ cup) sunflower margarine
115 g (4 oz/¾ cup) light soft brown sugar
2 eggs, beaten
2 tablespoons milk
DECORATIONS:
175 g (6 oz/1 cup) icing sugar
85 g (3 oz/⅓ cup) butter, softened
chocolate buttons
jelly sweets
liquorice strands and sweets

Put all the ingredients for the cakes into a bowl and beat until smooth.

Preheat oven to 180C (350F/Gas 4). Divide the cake mixture evenly between 20 paper bun cases placed in a tartlet tin. Bake the cases in the oven for about 15 minutes until risen and firm to the touch. Cool on a wire rack. Trim the tops if they have peaks.

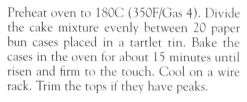

To decorate, beat the icing sugar and butter together until light and fluffy. Spread over the tops of the cakes. Attach 2 chocolate buttons on each cake for 'ears', and place a jelly sweet in position for the 'nose'. Cut slices of liquorice sweets to make 'eyes'. Cut lengths of liquorice strand to make 'whiskers' and insert three on each side of the 'nose'.

Makes 20.

PARTY PIECES

DEEP-FRIED FISH BALLS

450 g (1 lb) firm white fish fillet, skinned
115 g (4 oz) potato flour
55 ml (2 fl oz/¼ cup) coconut milk or water
salt and freshly ground black pepper
1 tablespoon chopped fresh coriander leaves
½ teaspoon minced garlic
1 egg, beaten
flour for dusting and oil for deep-frying
lettuce leaves, to garnish
Spicy Fish Sauce (see page 311)

Remove bones from fish, then cut into small pieces. Using a pestle and mortar, pound to a paste with potato flour and coconut milk, adding the coconut milk a little at a time.

In a mixing bowl, mix the fish paste with the salt, pepper, chopped coriander, garlic and egg. Blend well, then shape the mixture into about 20-24 small balls, dusting with flour.

Heat the oil in a wok, frying pan or deep-fat fryer to 180C (350F) and deep-fry the fish balls, in batches, for 3-4 minutes or until golden brown. Remove and drain. Serve on a bed of lettuce leaves with the Spicy Fish Sauce as a dip.

Serves 8-10.

Variation: Other types of seafood such as prawns, squid and crabmeat can be cooked in the same way.

PEARL PATTIES & SHERRY DIP

175 g (6 oz/¾ cup) long grain white rice
350 g (12 oz) lean minced beef
2 spring onions, finely chopped
1 clove garlic, crushed
1 tablespoon dark soy sauce
1 tablespoon dry sherry
2 teaspoons cornflour
DIP:
2 tablespoons dry sherry
2 tablespoons dark soy sauce
1 teaspoon caster sugar
1 clove garlic, crushed

Place the rice in a bowl, cover with water and soak for 1 hour. Drain well and dry on a clean cloth. Mix together the beef, spring onions, garlic, soy sauce, sherry and corn-flour. Bind together to form a firm mixture. Divide into 16 portions and shape into 4 cm (1½ in) diameter patties.

Press each patty into the rice to coat on both sides. Bring a wok or large saucepan of water to the boil. Arrange the patties on a layer of baking parchment in a steamer, making sure they don't overlap – you will probably need 2 steamers. Place over the water, cover and steam for 20 minutes. Mix together ingredients for dip and serve with the patties.

Serves 4.

CHICKEN APRICOT FILOS

½ tablespoon oil for frying, plus extra for brushing
½ onion, finely chopped
55 g (2 oz/½ cup) dried apricots, finely chopped
115 g (4 oz) cooked chicken, finely diced
4 tablespoons Greek yogurt
2 tablespoons chopped fresh coriander
salt and pepper
3 sheets filo pastry

Preheat oven to 190C (375F/Gas 5). In a small pan, heat the oil, add the onion and cook gently for 3-4 minutes without browning. Add the dried apricots and cook for a further 2 minutes.

Put the onion mixture into a bowl, add the chicken, yogurt, coriander and salt and pepper and mix well. Cut each sheet of filo pastry in half, then cut each half into 4 to form sixteen 10 cm (4 in) squares.

Brush each square with a little oil and place a spoonful of the chicken mixture in the centre. Gather up the corners of the filo pastry and pinch together to form a loose bag. Place the filo bags on 2 greased baking sheets and bake for 10-12 minutes or until the pastry is crisp and golden. Serve warm.

Makes 16.

OLIVE PASTE TOASTS

4 large thick slices country bread
3 tablespoons extra virgin olive oil
½ clove garlic, crushed
red pepper (capsicum) strips and fresh thyme sprigs, to garnish
OLIVE PASTE:
175 g (6 oz/1¼ cups) stoned black olives
2 tablespoons extra virgin olive oil
few drops balsamic vinegar
salt and freshly ground black pepper

Preheat oven to 200C (400F/Gas 6). To make olive paste put ingredients in a food processor or blender and process until fairly smooth. Transfer to a bowl and set aside.

Cut each slice of bread into 3 fingers. Place on a baking sheet and bake in the preheated oven for 10-12 minutes until golden and crisp. Meanwhile, warm oil with garlic in a saucepan.

Trickle oil and garlic over bread. Serve at once spread with olive paste and garnished with red pepper (capsicum) strips and thyme sprigs.

Serves 4-6.

Note: Olive paste can be made in advance or in larger quantities. Put into jars, pour over olive oil to cover and seal and keep in refrigerator for up to 1 month.

PARMESAN BEIGNETS

55 g (2 oz/¼ cup) butter
70 g (2½ oz/½ cup plus 6 teaspoons) plain flour, sifted
2 eggs, beaten
1 teaspoon chopped parsley
55 g (2 oz/½ cup) Parmesan cheese, grated
25 g (1 oz/¼ cup) grated Cheddar cheese
salt and pepper
oil, for deep frying
parsley sprigs, to garnish

In a large pan, melt butter, add 150 ml (5 fl oz/⅔ cup) water and bring to the boil.

Add flour, all at once, and beat thoroughly until mixture leaves the side of the pan. Cool slightly, then vigorously beat in eggs, a little at a time. Stir in parsley, cheeses and salt and pepper to taste. Continue beating until cheese has melted.

One-third fill a deep fat fryer with vegetable oil and heat to 180C/360F. Carefully drop 4 or 5 walnut-sized spoonfuls of mixture into hot oil. Deep fry for 2-3 minutes until puffed and golden brown. Drain on absorbent kitchen paper and keep warm until all the beignets are fried. Serve garnished with parsley sprigs.

Makes about 16.

DEVILLED HAM TOASTS

115 g (4 oz) lean ham
3 teaspoons Worcestershire sauce
cayenne pepper, to taste
2 teaspoons French mustard
6 slices bread
55 g (2 oz/¼ cup) butter
TO GARNISH:
3 stuffed olives, sliced
watercress sprigs

Chop ham very finely, or mince. In a bowl, mix together ham, Worcestershire sauce, cayenne pepper and mustard.

Toast bread. Using a 5 cm (2 in) plain cutter, cut 2 circles from each slice of bread. Butter each circle of toast using 25 g (1 oz/6 teaspoons) of the butter and keep warm. In a saucepan, melt remaining butter. Add ham mixture. Cook, stirring, over a low heat until mixture is hot.

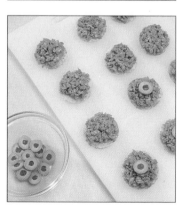

Spread ham mixture over toast circles. Garnish with stuffed olives and arrange on a serving plate with watercress sprigs. Serve at once.

Makes 12.

BACON AIGRETTES

4 rashers streaky bacon, rind removed
3 teaspoons chopped fresh parsley
½ teaspoon ground black pepper
½ teaspoon Dijon mustard
vegetable oil, for frying
CHOUX PASTRY:
55 g (2 oz/¼ cup) butter
70 g (2½ oz/¼ cup plus 6 teaspoons) plain flour
2 eggs
DIP:
150 ml (5 fl oz/⅔ cup) Greek yogurt
3 teaspoons chopped fresh chives
3 teaspoons mango chutney

ASPARAGUS WITH CHICORY

225 g (8 oz) asparagus spears, trimmed
3 heads of chicory
225 g (8 oz/1 cup) cream cheese
3 slices prosciutto or Parma ham
MARINADE:
1 tangerine
½ clove garlic, crushed
¼ teaspoon salt
¼ teaspoon ground black pepper
½ teaspoon Dijon mustard
2 teaspoons clear honey
4 teaspoons olive oil
2 teaspoons chopped fresh tarragon

Grill bacon until crisp; chop finely.

Mix bacon in a bowl with parsley, pepper and mustard. To make choux pastry, in a saucepan, heat 155 ml (5 fl oz/⅔ cup) water and the butter until melted. Bring to boil, remove pan from heat and immediately add all flour, beating vigorously to form a paste. Return to heat for a few seconds, stirring until paste forms a ball. Add eggs one at a time, beating until paste is very smooth and glossy. Stir in bacon mixture until well blended.

Half-fill a shallow flameproof dish or frying pan with water and bring to the boil. Add asparagus and cook for 3-4 minutes until spears are tender, then drain and cool in a shallow dish. To make marinade, using a zester, cut tangerine peel into fine strips, squeeze juice from fruit and place in a bowl with garlic, salt, pepper, mustard, honey, oil and tarragon. Beat with a wooden spoon until thoroughly blended. Pour over asparagus; cover and chill for at least 1 hour.

Half-fill a deep fat pan or fryer with oil. Heat to 180C (350F), or test by dropping a small piece of paste into oil: if it sizzles on contact, the oil is hot enough. Take teaspoonfuls of mixture (a little at a time) and drop into hot oil. Fry for 3-4 minutes, turning once, until puffed and golden brown. Drain on absorbent kitchen paper. Fry remaining mixture in same way. Mix together yogurt, chives and chutney. Serve with hot Bacon Aigrettes.

Makes 35-40.

Separate chicory leaves and cut into 2.5 cm (1 in) lengths. Spread or pipe a little cream cheese onto each leaf. Cut asparagus spears into 2.5 cm (1 in) lengths and place a length onto each chicory leaf. Cut prosciutto or ham into thin strips and wrap a piece around each chicory leaf. Garnish with strips of tangerine peel, reserved from marinade.

Makes 48.

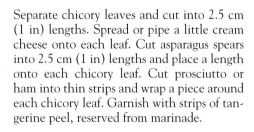

439

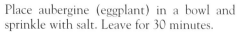

VEGETABLE CURRY ENVELOPES

55 g (2 oz) puff pastry, thawed
1 egg, beaten
1 teaspoon cumin seeds
FILLING:
15 g (½ oz/3 teaspoons) butter
1 leek, finely chopped
1 clove garlic, crushed
1 teaspoon ground cumin
1 teaspoon garam masala
2 teaspoons mango chutney
½ teaspoon finely grated lime peel
2 teaspoons lime juice
55 g (2 oz) cooked, diced potato

Melt butter for filling in a small saucepan. Add leek and garlic to pan.

Cook quickly for 1 minute, stirring. Add cumin, garam masala, chutney, lime peel and juice. Stir well, cook gently for 1-2 minutes, then add potatoes, mix well and cool. Preheat oven to 220C (425F/Gas 7). Roll out puff pastry very thinly to an oblong measuring 30 x 20 cm (12 x 8 in). Cut into twenty-four 5 cm (2 in) squares. Brush edges with beaten egg and place a little filling in centre of each.

Draw all corners to centre and seal joins to form a tiny envelope. Repeat to seal all pastry envelopes. Arrange on a baking sheet, brush with egg to glaze and sprinkle with cumin seeds. Cook in the oven for 5-8 minutes until well risen and golden brown.

Makes 24.

OYSTERS WITH AUBERGINE

115 g (4 oz) aubergine (eggplant), diced
salt
6 large slices white bread
55 g (2 oz/¼ cup) butter
6 teaspoons chopped fresh chives
2 teaspoons chopped fresh oregano
4 button mushrooms, finely chopped
½ teaspoon ground black pepper
2 teaspoons fromage frais
12 fresh oysters in shells
45 g (1½ oz/¾ cup) soft breadcrumbs
oregano sprigs, to garnish

Place aubergine (eggplant) in a bowl and sprinkle with salt. Leave for 30 minutes.

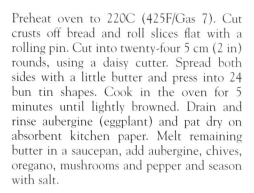

Preheat oven to 220C (425F/Gas 7). Cut crusts off bread and roll slices flat with a rolling pin. Cut into twenty-four 5 cm (2 in) rounds, using a daisy cutter. Spread both sides with a little butter and press into 24 bun tin shapes. Cook in the oven for 5 minutes until lightly browned. Drain and rinse aubergine (eggplant) and pat dry on absorbent kitchen paper. Melt remaining butter in a saucepan, add aubergine, chives, oregano, mushrooms and pepper and season with salt.

Fry quickly, stirring occasionally, until aubergine is tender. Stir in fromage frais. Scrub oyster shells, then open and remove oysters. Cut each in half and place ½ an oyster into each bread case. Top with aubergine (eggplant) mixture and sprinkle with breadcrumbs. Return to oven for a further 10 minutes until breadcrumbs are lightly browned. Arrange on a serving plate and garnish with oregano sprigs.

Makes 24.

OATIE BRIE CUBES

85 g (3 oz/1½ cups) soft breadcrumbs
25 g (1 oz/¼ cup) fine oatmeal
½ teaspoon salt
½ teaspoon ground black pepper
½ teaspoon dry mustard
2 eggs
225 g (8 oz) firm Brie or Camembert cheese
vegetable oil, for frying
lime wedges, bay leaves and cranberries, to garnish
DIP:
85 g (3 oz/¾ cup) cranberries
finely grated peel and juice 1 lime
15 g (½ oz/3 teaspoons) caster sugar

In a bowl, mix together breadcrumbs, oatmeal, salt, pepper and mustard.

Beat eggs in a small bowl. Cut cheese into bite-sized cubes, dip one cube at a time in beaten egg, then coat evenly in oatmeal mixture. Repeat to coat cheese cubes a second time in egg and oatmeal mixture. Chill until required. To make dip, place cranberries, lime peel and juice in a saucepan, bring to boil, cover and cook for 1-2 minutes until tender. Place in food processor fitted with a metal blade, add sugar and process until smooth. Place in a small serving dish.

Half-fill a deep pan or fryer with oil, heat to 180C (350F), or until a cheese cube sizzles immediately. Fry about 6 cheese cubes at a time until pale golden in colour. Drain on absorbent kitchen paper and cook remaining cheese cubes in the same way. Arrange on a serving dish with cocktail sticks. Garnish with lime wedges, bay leaves and cranberries and serve with cranberry dip.

Makes 20.

CRAB & FENNEL PUFFS

1 quantity Choux Pastry (see Bacon Aigrettes, page 439)
1 egg yolk
2 teaspoons sesame seeds
fennel sprigs and radish slices, to garnish
FILLING:
15g (½ oz/3 teaspoons) butter
9 teaspoons finely chopped spring onions
9 teaspoons finely chopped fennel
85 g (3 oz) white crabmeat
55 g (2 oz) dark crabmeat
½ teaspoon finely grated lemon peel
¼ teaspoons ground black pepper
3 teaspoons thick sour cream
cayenne pepper

Preheat oven to 220C (425F/Gas 7). Grease 2 baking sheets. Make pastry, see page 439. Place mixture in a piping bag fitted with a 1 cm (½ in) plain nozzle. Pipe about 40 small rounds of mixture, spaced apart, on baking sheets. Brush with egg yolk. Sprinkle with sesame seeds. Cook in the oven for 15-20 minutes until crisp and golden brown. Cool on a wire rack. To make filling, melt butter in a small saucepan, add onions and fennel and cook for 1-2 minutes until tender.

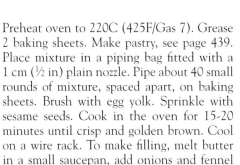

Remove pan from heat, stir in white and dark crabmeat, lemon peel, pepper and thick sour cream until well blended. Cut each choux ball across the top and fill each with crab mixture. Dust with cayenne pepper, arrange on a serving plate and garnish with fennel sprigs and radish slices.

Makes 40.

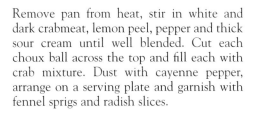

SESAME PRAWN TOASTS

225-300 g (8-10 oz) raw peeled prawns, chopped
½ teaspoon minced garlic
½ teaspoon finely chopped fresh root ginger
2 shallots or 1 small onion, finely chopped
1 egg, beaten
salt and freshly ground black pepper
1 tablespoon cornflour
1 French baguette
3-4 tablespoons white sesame seeds
oil, for deep-frying
chopped fresh coriander leaves, to garnish

In a bowl, mix the prawns, garlic, ginger, shallots, egg, salt, pepper and cornflour and chill in the refrigerator for at least 2 hours.

Cut the bread into 1 cm (½ in) slices and spread thickly with prawn mixture on one side, then press that side down onto the sesame seeds so that the entire surface is covered by the seeds, making sure the seeds are firmly pressed into the prawn mixture.

Heat the oil in a wok or deep-fat fryer to 180C (350F) and deep-fry the toasts, in batches, spread-side down, for 2-3 minutes until they start to turn golden brown around the edges. Remove and drain on absorbent kitchen paper. Serve hot, garnished with chopped coriander.

Serves 6-8.

CRISPY PESTO PRAWNS

12 Mediterranean (king) prawns, peeled
6 large slices white bread
55 g (2 oz/¼ cup) butter
1 clove garlic, crushed
4 teaspoons pesto sauce
1 teaspoon finely grated lemon peel
¼ teaspoons salt
¼ teaspoon ground black pepper
lemon triangles, basil leaves or parsley sprigs, to garnish

Cut each prawn in ½ across width. Cut crusts off bread and, using a rolling pin, roll each slice flat.

Place butter in a small bowl, beat until soft and smooth. Stir in garlic, pesto sauce, lemon peel and salt and pepper. Beat together until smooth and well blended. Spread both sides of each slice of bread with butter mixture, then cut each slice into 4 triangles.

Place a prawn in centre of each bread triangle, fold 2 side points to centre and secure with a cocktail stick. Arrange on a grid in a grill pan and cook under a moderately hot grill until bread is lightly browned. Serve hot, garnished with lemon triangles, basil leaves or parsley sprigs.

Makes 24.

FESTIVE DIP SELECTION

CURRY WHIRLS

1 small aubergine (eggplant)
2 cloves garlic
115 ml (4 fl oz/½ cup) thick sour cream
salt and freshly ground black pepper
3 teaspoons chopped fresh rosemary
225 g (8 oz/1 cup) cream cheese
6 teaspoons fromage frais
25 g (1 oz/¼ cup) chopped fresh mixed herbs
   (parsley, basil, thyme, oregano and chervil)
115 g (4 oz/⅔ cup) red lentils, cooked in 430 ml
   (15 fl oz/1¾ cups) water
150 ml (5 fl oz/⅔ cup) Greek yogurt
mixed vegetable sticks such as courgettes (zucchini),
   peppers (capsicums), celery, cucumber and carrots;
   baby sweetcorn, cherry tomatoes and radishes, to
   serve

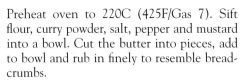

150 g (5 oz/1¼ cups) plain flour
1 teaspoon curry powder
½ teaspoon salt
½ teaspoon pepper
½ teaspoon dry mustard
115 g (4 oz/½ cup) butter
6 teaspoons grated Parmesan cheese
a little beaten egg
1 teaspoon coriander seeds

Preheat oven to 220C (425F/Gas 7). Sift flour, curry powder, salt, pepper and mustard into a bowl. Cut the butter into pieces, add to bowl and rub in finely to resemble bread-crumbs.

Preheat oven to 220C (425F/Gas 7), or use a hot grill. Bake or grill aubergine (eggplant) until skin has charred and flesh is tender, turning once. Cut aubergine (eggplant) in half, scoop out flesh; cool. Using a food processor fitted with a metal blade, add aubergine (eggplant), 1 clove garlic, thick sour cream, salt and pepper to taste and rose-mary; process until mixture is smooth and creamy. Place in a serving bowl. Place cream cheese, fromage frais, mixed herbs and salt and pepper in a bowl and beat until soft and well blended. Spoon into a serving dish.

Using a fork, stir in Parmesan cheese and egg until mixture clings together. Mix to form a soft dough. Place mixture in a nylon piping bag fitted with a star nozzle. Pipe 40 swirls of mixture onto lightly greased baking sheets, spacing them apart.

Cool lentils. In a food processor, place remaining garlic, salt and pepper to taste, lentils and yogurt and process until creamy and smooth. Place in a serving bowl. Serve dips accompanied by mixed vegetable sticks, baby sweetcorn, cherry tomatoes and radishes.

Each dip serves 6-8.

Sprinkle each swirl with coriander seeds and cook in the oven for 10-15 minutes until lightly browned at edges. Cool on a wire rack. Arrange on a plate to serve.

Makes 40.

PEPPER-FILLED LEAVES

10 small spinach leaves
10 small lettuce leaves
10 small radicchio leaves
FILLING:
25 g (1 oz/2 tablespoons) long-grain rice
5 rashers streaky bacon
4 teaspoons chopped pickled vegetables
55 g (2 oz/¼ cup) curd cheese
1 teaspoon Dijon mustard
½ teaspoon salt
½ teaspoon ground black pepper
1 small red pepper (capsicum), seeded
1 small yellow pepper (capsicum), seeded

Bring a saucepan of water to the boil. Add spinach leaves, bring back to boil; remove leaves quickly and refresh leaves in cold water. Drain thoroughly and pat dry on absorbent kitchen paper. Repeat this process with remaining leaves. To make filling, cook rice in boiling salted water until tender; drain and cool. Grill bacon until crisp, then chop bacon and pickled vegetables finely. Place curd cheese in a bowl and beat until smooth. Add rice, bacon, pickled vegetables, mustard and salt and pepper; stir until well blended.

Spread leaves out flat on a board, place a teaspoonful of mixture on each. Roll up neatly and secure each with a cocktail stick. Cut peppers (capsicums) into thin rings, then cut rings into 4 and use to garnish filled leaves. Arrange on a serving plate and serve with a spicy sauce, if desired.

Makes 30.

FETA CHEESE KEBABS

200 g (7 oz) feta cheese
¼ red pepper (capsicum)
¼ yellow pepper (capsicum)
1 courgette (zucchini)
¼ aubergine (eggplant)
thyme sprigs, to garnish
MARINADE:
6 teaspoons olive oil
3 teaspoons raspberry vinegar
1 teaspoon pink peppercorns, crushed
1 teaspoon clear honey
½ teaspoon Dijon mustard
2 teaspoons chopped fresh thyme
¼ teaspoon salt
½ teaspoon ground black pepper

To make marinade, place oil, vinegar, peppercorns, honey, mustard, thyme, salt and pepper in a large bowl. Stir mixture together with a wooden spoon until thoroughly blended. Cut feta cheese, peppers (capsicums), courgette (zucchini) and aubergine (eggplant) into bite-sized pieces. Add to marinade, stir well to coat evenly, cover with plastic wrap and leave in a cool place for at least 1 hour.

Thread one piece of each ingredient onto wooden cocktail sticks. Just before serving, cook under a hot grill for 2-3 minutes until vegetables are just tender. Arrange on a serving plate, garnished with sprigs of thyme.

Makes 24.

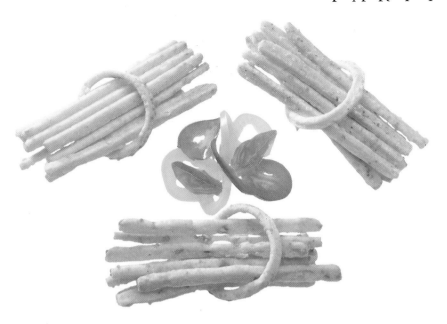

CHEESE STRAWS

225 g (8 oz/2 cups) plain flour
½ teaspoon salt
½ teaspoon cayenne pepper
½ teaspoon dry mustard
115 g (4 oz/½ cup) butter
115 g (4 oz/1 cup) grated Cheddar cheese
1 egg, beaten
4 teaspoons finely chopped red and yellow peppers
  (capsicums)
1 clove garlic, crushed
4 teaspoons chopped fresh basil and parsley
peppers (capsicums), basil and parsley, to garnish

Preheat oven to 200C (400F/Gas 6). In a bowl, sift flour, salt, cayenne and mustard.

Cut butter into pieces, add to bowl and rub in finely to resemble breadcrumbs. Using a fork, stir in cheese and egg until mixture clings together. Knead to form a smooth dough. Cut pastry into 4 pieces. Flavour one piece with peppers (capsicum), one with garlic and one with herbs, kneading each piece lightly. Roll out one piece at a time to a strip measuring 10 cm (4 in) wide and 0.5 cm (¼ in) thick.

Using a long-bladed knife, cut into 0.5 cm (¼ in) strips. Arrange in straight lines on greased baking sheets. Knead each of the flavoured trimmings together, re-roll and cut out circles using a 5 cm (2 in) and 4.5 cm (1¾ in) plain cutter. Place on baking sheets. Cook in the oven for 5-8 minutes until pale in colour. Cool on wire racks. Serve straws in bundles threaded through pastry rings, garnished with peppers (capsicum), basil and parsley.

Makes 100 straws plus rings.

COCKTAIL BISCUITS

350 g (12 oz/3 cups) plain flour
½ teaspoon salt
½ teaspoons cayenne pepper
1 teaspoon dry mustard
175 g (6 oz/¾ cup) butter, diced
115 g (4 oz/1 cup) grated Cheddar cheese
1 egg, beaten
FLAVOURINGS:
1 teaspoons sesame seeds
1 teaspoon poppy seeds
1 teaspoon curry paste
2 teaspoons tomato purée

In a bowl, sift flour, salt, cayenne and mustard. Add butter and rub in finely.

Using a fork, stir in cheese and egg until mixture clings together. Knead to form a smooth dough. Cut pastry into 4 pieces. Knead sesame seeds into one piece and poppy seeds into another. Form both into 15 cm (6 in) rolls. Wrap separately in plastic wrap. Roll remaining 2 pieces of pastry into 20 x 15 cm (8 x 6 in) rectangles. Spread one piece with curry paste and the other with tomato purée. Roll up each from a long edge to form 2 firm rolls. Wrap in plastic wrap. Chill all the rolls until firm, or freeze until required.

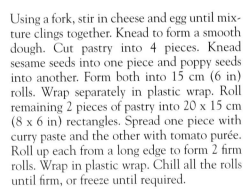

Preheat oven to 200C (400F/Gas 6). Line several baking sheets with non-stick baking paper. Cut each roll into thin slices and arrange a little apart on baking sheets lined with baking parchment. Bake for 6-8 minutes until pale in colour. Cool, then transfer to wire racks.

Makes 96.

445

HERBED CRÊPE PINWHEELS

55 g (2 oz/½ cup) plain flour
¼ teaspoon salt
¼ teaspoon ground black pepper
1 egg
115 ml (4 fl oz/¼ cup) milk
3 teaspoons chopped fresh basil
vegetable oil, for frying
cherry tomato wedges and herb sprigs, to garnish
FILLING:
8 large spinach leaves
115 g (4 oz/½ cup) soft cheese with herbs and garlic
8 thin slices prosciutto or Parma ham

Sift flour, salt and pepper into a bowl. Add egg and half the milk; beat until smooth.

Stir in remaining milk and basil and beat until well blended. Heat a little oil in a small frying pan, add a spoonful of batter and swirl pan to coat thinly. Cook until crêpe is pale golden on both sides, turning once. Place on absorbent kitchen paper. Repeat to make 8 crêpes in total.

To make filling, cook spinach leaves for 1 minute in boiling salted water; drain and cool. Take one crêpe at a time and cover with a spinach leaf, then spread with a little cheese and cover with a slice of prosciutto or Parma ham. Roll up firmly and wrap in plastic wrap. Repeat with remaining ingredients to make 8 crêpe rolls. Just before serving, cut each roll into 1 cm (½ in) slices. Arrange on a serving plate and garnish with tomato wedges and sprigs of herbs.

Makes 48.

PARTY QUICHES

PASTRY:
55 g (2 oz/½ cup) plain flour
¼ teaspoon salt
25 g (1 oz/6 teaspoons) butter
FILLING:
1 egg
6 teaspoons single (light) cream
¼ teaspoon salt
¼ teaspoon pepper
¼ teaspoon dry mustard
2 teaspoons each finely chopped peppers
  (capsicums), chopped button mushrooms, crisp
  crumbled bacon and fresh herbs

Sift flour and salt into a bowl. Cut the butter into small pieces.

Add butter to bowl and rub in finely until mixture resembles breadcrumbs. Using a fork, stir in 2-3 teaspoons water until mixture begins to bind together. Knead to form a firm dough. Roll out pastry thinly on a lightly floured surface and use to line 24 tiny pastry boat moulds or tiny round tartlet tins. Prick bases and chill for 1 hour. Preheat oven to 220C (425F/Gas 7). Bake pastry moulds for 5 minutes, then remove from oven.

To make filling, put egg, cream, salt, pepper and mustard in a bowl. Whisk until well blended. Half-fill each pastry case with egg mixture, then fill 6 with chopped peppers (capsicums), 6 with mushrooms, 6 with bacon and the remainder with herbs. Return to the oven for a further 5-6 minutes until filling has set. Cool slightly, then slip pastry cases out of moulds. Serve warm or cold.

Makes 24.

CRISPY BACON PINWHEELS

85 g (3 oz/¾ cup) grated Cheddar cheese
¼ teaspoon salt
¼ teaspoon pepper
½ teaspoon Dijon mustard
6 teaspoons Greek yogurt
6 large slices white bread
45 g (1½ oz/9 teaspoons) butter
6 rashers streaky bacon
celery leaves and radish leaves, to garnish

In a bowl, mix together cheese, salt, pepper, mustard and yogurt. Cut crusts off bread and roll slices flat with a rolling pin.

Spread each slice with butter and invert. Spread unbuttered sides evenly with cheese mixture and roll each slice into a firm roll. Remove rinds and bones from bacon; stretch each rasher with a knife and cut into 3 pieces. Cut each bread roll into 3 rolls and wrap a piece of bacon around each one; secure each roll with a cocktail stick. Cover with plastic wrap and chill until required.

Just before serving, remove plastic wrap and grill bacon-wrapped rolls under a hot grill until bacon is crisp and golden brown. Cool slightly, remove cocktail sticks and then cut each roll into 3 slices. Arrange on a serving plate and garnish with celery leaves and radish slices.

Makes 54.

MUSHROOMS & GRAPEFRUIT

225 g (8 oz) button mushrooms
fresh mint leaves or chives, to garnish
MARINADE:
1 large pink grapefruit
90 ml (3 fl oz/⅓ cup) ginger wine
2 teaspoons mint jelly
½ teaspoon salt
½ teaspoon ground black pepper
1 teaspoon Dijon mustard

To make marinade, cut away grapefruit peel and white pith from flesh, allowing juice to fall into a small saucepan. Cut out segments between membranes and place on a plate.

Squeeze remaining juice from membranes into saucepan. Add ginger wine, mint jelly, salt, pepper and mustard; bring to the boil and stir in mushrooms. Pour into a bowl and leave until cold.

Cut grapefruit segments into bite-sized pieces. Thread 2 mushrooms and a piece of grapefruit onto each cocktail stick and garnish with mint leaves or chives.

Makes 24.

AVOCADO SALMON ROLLS

85 g (3 oz) sliced smoked salmon
3 slices rye bread
25 g (1 oz/3 teaspoons) butter
dill sprigs and lemon twists, to garnish
FILLING:
55 g (2 oz/¼ cup) full fat soft cheese
½ avocado, mashed
2 teaspoons chopped fresh dill
1 small tomato, skinned, seeded and chopped
¼ teaspoon ground black pepper

To make filling, put cheese in a bowl and
beat until soft. Add avocado and stir until
blended.

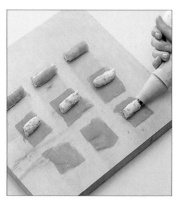

Add dill, chopped tomato and pepper and
stir gently. Place in a piping bag fitted with
1 cm (½ in) plain nozzle. Cut smoked
salmon into 20 oblongs measuring about
4 x 2.5 cm (1½ x 1 in). Pipe a length of
cheese mixture across top of a short edge of
each salmon oblong. Roll up each one
neatly.

Spread rye bread with butter, then cut into
20 rectangles to fit salmon rolls. Place a
salmon roll on each piece and garnish with
sprigs of dill and lemon twists.

Makes 20.

FILLED BUTTON RAREBITS

55 g (2 oz/1 cup) soft white breadcrumbs
55 g (2 oz/¼ cup) chopped ham
3 teaspoons chopped fresh parsley
3 teaspoons fromage frais
24 button mushrooms
4 large slices white bread
25 g (1 oz/6 teaspoons) soft tub margarine
3 teaspoons cider
85 g (3 oz/¾ cup) grated Cheddar cheese
1 teaspoon Worcestershire sauce
¼ teaspoon salt
¼ teaspoon ground black pepper
¼ teaspoon dry mustard
fresh herbs, to garnish

Preheat oven to 220C (425F/Gas 7). In a
bowl, mix together breadcrumbs, ham,
parsley and fromage frais. Remove stalks
from mushrooms, chop finely and add to
bowl; stir thoroughly. Press this mixture into
centre of each mushroom. Cut out rounds of
bread to match size of mushrooms, using a
plain cutter. Spread both sides with margarine and sit a mushroom on top of each
bread round. Arrange on a baking sheet and
cook in the oven for 5 minutes, then remove
and keep on one side.

Place cider in a saucepan and bring to the
boil. Remove pan from heat, stir in cheese,
Worcestershire sauce, salt, pepper and
mustard; beat well together. Spoon a little
cheese mixture over top of each filled mushroom. Return to oven and cook for a further
3-4 minutes until cheese has melted and
browned slightly. Arrange on a serving dish
and garnish with fresh herbs.

Makes 24.

DRINKS

STRAWBERRY YOGURT WHIZZ

225 g (8 oz) strawberries
300 ml (10 fl oz/1¼ cups) cold milk
300 ml (10 fl oz/1¼ cups) natural or strawberry yogurt
2 scoops vanilla or yogurt ice cream
1 kiwi fruit (optional)

Reserve 4 strawberries for decoration; wash and hull the remainder.

Put the milk, yogurt, strawberries and ice cream into a blender and blend until smooth, or put them into a jug and blend with a hand blender.

Pour into glasses. Decorate with the reserved strawberries and slices of kiwi fruit, if using.

Serves 3-4.

MALTED MILKSHAKES

410 g (14½ oz) can evaporated milk
450 ml (16 fl oz/2 cups) chilled milk
3 tablespoons cocoa
2 teaspoons light soft brown sugar
3 tablespoons malt extract
8 scoops vanilla ice cream
4 chocolate flakes

Put 4 glass tumblers in the refrigerator to chill for 30 minutes.

Depending on the size of blender available, either blend in 1 or 2 batches. Put the milks, cocoa, sugar, malt extract and half the ice cream into a jug or blender and blend for 2 minutes until frothy.

Pour into chilled glasses, top each drink with a scoop of ice cream and a chocolate flake. Serve with straws.

Serves 4.

Variation: Use powdered malted chocolate drink instead of cocoa, if preferred, and reduce the amount of sugar.

APPLE ZING

2 ripe pears, peeled and cored
450 ml (16 fl oz/2 cups) pure apple juice
crushed ice
550 ml (20 fl oz/2½ cups) chilled ginger ale
apple slices or mint sprigs, to decorate

Put the pears and apple juice into a blender and process until smooth, or put them into a jug and blend with a hand blender.

Spoon some crushed ice into 4 tall glasses and pour over the apple juice mixture.

Top up the glasses with the ginger ale and decorate with the apple slices or mint sprigs. Serve immediately.

Serves 4.

SPANISH HOT CHOCOLATE

85 g (3 oz) plain (dark) chocolate, broken into
  pieces
450 ml (16 fl oz/2 cups) milk
cinnamon sticks and orange rind, to decorate

Put chocolate in top of a double boiler or a bowl placed over a saucepan of hot water. Leave chocolate to melt.

Heat milk to boiling point. Using a wooden spoon, slowly stir a little boiling milk into chocolate.

Using a wire whisk, whisk in remaining milk and continue to whisk until mixture is frothy. Pour into heatproof glasses or cups and decorate with cinnamon sticks and orange rind.

Serves 2.

Variation: Rub 2 sugar cubes over a whole orange to extract the zest, then add the sugar to the hot milk. Sprinkle cinnamon on the top of the hot chocolate.

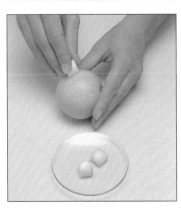

OLD-FASHIONED LEMONADE

3 lemons
115 g (4 oz/½ cup) sugar
TO FINISH:
ice
sprigs of mint
lemon slices

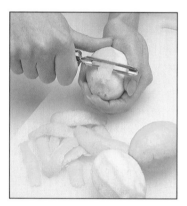

Using a potato peeler, thinly pare the rind from the lemons and put in a bowl or large jug with sugar. Squeeze juice from lemons into a bowl and set aside.

Boil 850 ml (30 fl oz/3¾ cups) cold water and pour over lemon rind and sugar. Stir to dissolve sugar and leave until completely cool. Add lemon juice and strain into a jug. Chill well. Serve in ice-filled tumblers, decorated with mint and lemon slices.

Serves 6.

Variations: To make Pink Lemonade, add just enough pink grenadine syrup to each glass to give lemonade a pale pink colour. Omit the mint and lemon slices and decorate each glass with a cherry.

To make Orangeade, use 3 oranges and 1 lemon instead of 3 lemons. Omit the mint and lemon slices and decorate the glasses with orange slices.

GRAPEFRUIT BARLEY WATER

55 g (2 oz) pearl barley
55 g (2 oz/¼ cup) sugar
2 pink grapefruit
TO DECORATE:
mint leaves

Put barley into a saucepan. Just cover with cold water and bring to the boil. Tip barley into a colander and rinse thoroughly under cold running water.

Return barley to the saucepan, add 550 ml (20 fl oz/2½ cups) cold water and bring to the boil again. Cover and simmer for 1 hour. Strain liquid into a jug, stir in the sugar and leave until completely cold.

Squeeze juice from grapefruit and add to cooled barley water. Chill well. Serve decorated with mint leaves.

Makes about 550 ml (20 fl oz/2½ cups)

Variation: To make Lemon Barley Water, use 2 lemons instead of grapefruit.

FRAGRANT LEMON SHERBET

grated peel and juice 2 lemons
55 g (2 oz/¼ cup) caster sugar
handful lemon balm leaves
crushed ice
about 1 litre (35 fl oz/4½ cups) iced water
spirals lemon peel and lemon balm leaves, to decorate
 (see Note)

Put lemon peel and juice, sugar and lemon balm leaves in a blender or food processor and process until smooth. Strain into a jug and chill.

Fill glasses with crushed ice, pour over a little lemon concentrate and top up with iced water. Serve, decorated with spirals of lemon peel and lemon balm leaves.

Makes about 1.2 litres (2 pints/5 cups).

Note: To make lemon spiral decoration, cut a long strip of peel using a cannelle knife. Wind round a skewer or chopstick, fasten securely and blanch in boiling water for a few seconds. Rinse in cold water and remove skewer or chopstick.

SPICED TEA

5 teaspoons black peppercorns
3 teaspoons cardamom seeds
3 teaspoons cloves
4 cm (1½ in) cinnamon stick
25 g (1 oz/⅓ cup) ground ginger
Indian tea leaves
boiling water
sugar and milk, to taste

Put peppercorns, cardamom seeds, cloves and cinnamon in a mortar and grind to a fine powder with a pestle. Add ginger and grind again for a few seconds to mix.

Make a pot of tea and add about ½ tablespoon of spice mixture and leave in a warm place for 1-2 minutes to brew. Serve hot, with sugar and milk.

Makes about 8 tablespoons spice mix, enough for 16 pots tea.

Note: Store remaining spice mixture in a screw-topped jar in a dark cupboard to preserve its flavour. It will keep for 2-3 months.

CAFE DE OLLA

1.2 litres (2 pints/10 cups) water
2.5 cm (1 in) piece cinnamon stick
2 cloves
55 g (2 oz/¼ cup) muscovado sugar
4 tablespoons freshly ground coffee

INDIAN SUMMER PUNCH

3 teaspoons fennel seeds
seeds from 6 green cardamom pods
3 cloves
4 black peppercorns
55 g (2 oz/½ cup) ground almonds
25 g (1 oz/¼ cup) shelled pistachio nuts
55 g (2 oz/½ cup) sunflower seeds
300 ml (10 fl oz/1¼ cups) boiling water
115 g (4 oz/½ cup) caster sugar
850 ml (30 fl oz/3¾ cups) cold milk
apple slices and fennel sprigs, to decorate

Put fennel and cardamom seeds, cloves and peppercorns in a mortar and grind to a fine powder with a pestle.

Put the water, cinnamon and cloves into a saucepan and bring to the boil. Lower the heat, add the sugar and stir until dissolved. Stir in the coffee and simmer for 2 minutes.

Put almonds, pistachios and sunflower seeds in a small bowl and pour over 90 ml (3 fl oz/⅓ cup) boiling water. Leave to soak for 20 minutes, then drain. Put in a blender or food processor fitted with a metal blade and add remaining water and process until smooth.

Turn off the heat and allow to stand, covered, for about 5 minutes until all the coffee has settled. Strain into individual mugs.

Serves 4.

Add spices and sugar and process again. Strain through a cloth or 2 layers of muslin, squeezing paste to extract as much liquid as possible. Discard paste and chill liquid for at least 1 hour, then mix with milk. Serve in tall glasses over ice, decorated with apple slices and fennel sprigs.

Makes about 1.7 litres (3 pints/7½ cups).

Note: If preferred, grind spices in a coffee grinder.

ICED ROSE TEA

45 g (1½ oz) Ceylon breakfast tea
1 litre (35 fl oz/4½ cups) lukewarm water
sugar, to taste
few drops rosewater, to taste
12 ice cubes
6 sprigs of mint
fresh rose petals

Put tea in a bowl, pour over warm water and leave to stand overnight.

Strain tea into a large jug. Stir in sugar and rosewater to taste and add ice cubes. Place a sprig of mint and a few rose petals in each of 6 glasses and pour the tea on top.

Serves 6.

Variations: For Vanilla Iced Tea, omit rosewater. Put a vanilla pod in the bowl with tea to soak overnight. Remove it before serving.
For Mint Tea, omit the rosewater and rose petals. Put a sprig of mint in the bowl with tea to soak overnight. Remove it before serving. Place a small sprig of fresh mint in each glass.

SUMMER TEA CUP

1 Lapsang Souchon tea bag
550 ml (20 fl oz/2½ cups) boiling water
4 teaspoons soft brown sugar
300 ml (10 fl oz/1¼ cups) pineapple juice
70 ml (2½ fl oz/⅓ cup) white rum
550 ml (20 fl oz/2½ cups) ginger ale
ice cubes
pieces fresh pineapple, to decorate

Place tea bag in a bowl and pour over the boiling water.

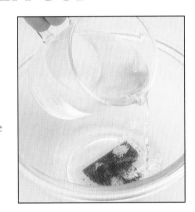

Leave tea to infuse for 5 minutes, then remove tea bag. Stir in brown sugar and leave until cold. Stir the pineapple juice and rum into the cold tea.

Just before serving, pour ginger ale into tea. Add ice cubes. Place a few pieces of pineapple in each glass and pour in the chilled tea.

Makes about 1.5 litres (2½ pints/6 cups).

TEQUILA SUNRISE

55 ml (2 fl oz/¼ cup) tequila
150 ml (5 fl oz/⅔ cup) fresh orange juice
1 tablespoon grenadine
1 teaspoon fresh lime juice
crushed ice
cocktail cherry, to decorate

Pour tequila, orange juice, grenadine and lime juice into a blender or food processor; mix well. Put crushed ice into a tall, chilled glass.

Strain tequila mixture over the ice. Decorate with a cocktail cherry on cocktail stick.

Serves 1.

MARGARITA

1 lime, halved
salt
crushed ice
55 ml (2 fl oz/¼ cup) tequila
1 tablespoon Triple Sec or Cointreau
wedge lime to serve

Rub the rim of a chilled cocktail glass with one of the lime halves then dip into salt. Add crushed ice to a cocktail shaker or mixing glass. Squeeze the juice from the remaining lime half.

Pour into the shaker or glass with the tequila and Triple Sec or Cointreau. Shake or stir well. Strain into the glass. Serve with a wedge of lime to squeeze into drink.

Serves 1.

TENNIS CUP

225 g (8 oz/1 cup) granulated sugar
1 lemon
2 oranges
2 bottles red or white wine
550 ml (20 fl oz/2½ cups) soda water
TO DECORATE:
thin slices cucumber and orange
borage flowers or violets, if available

Put sugar in a saucepan with 150 ml (5 fl oz/
⅔ cup) cold water. Heat gently until sugar
has dissolved. Bring to the boil and boil
gently until syrup reaches 105C (220F).

With a potato peeler, thinly pare rind from
lemon and oranges. Add to syrup and simmer gently for 10 minutes. Set aside until
completely cold.

Squeeze juice from lemon and oranges and
strain into syrup, then pour in the wine and
chill. Just before serving, add soda water.
Pour into glasses. Decorate with slices of
cucumber and orange and sprigs of borage or
violets.

Makes about 2 litres (3½ pints/9 cups).

CHRISTMAS EVE MULL

1 bottle white wine
1 bottle red wine
300 ml (10 fl oz/1¼ cups) sweet red vermouth
3 teaspoons Angostura bitters
6 strips orange peel
8 whole cloves
1 cinnamon stick
8 cardamom pods, crushed
3 teaspoons raisins
115 g (4 oz/½ cup) caster sugar
lemon, lime, orange and apple slices, to decorate

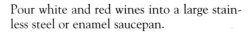

Pour white and red wines into a large stainless steel or enamel saucepan.

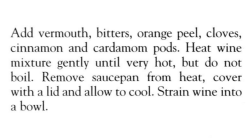

Add vermouth, bitters, orange peel, cloves,
cinnamon and cardamom pods. Heat wine
mixture gently until very hot, but do not
boil. Remove saucepan from heat, cover
with a lid and allow to cool. Strain wine into
a bowl.

Just before serving, return wine to a clean
saucepan, add raisins and sugar. Heat gently
until sugar has dissolved and wine is hot
enough to drink. Decorate with fruit slices
and serve in heatproof glasses or mugs.

Serves 18.

HOT BUTTERED RUM

ROSÉ GLOW

4 cinnamon sticks
4 teaspoons light soft brown sugar
115 ml (4 fl oz/½ cup) dark rum
550 ml (20 fl oz/2½ cups) cider
25 g (1 oz/6 teaspoons) butter
1 teaspoon ground mace
4 lemon slices

55 ml (2 fl oz/¼ cup) sweet red vermouth
55 ml (2 fl oz/¼ cup) cherry brandy
55 ml (2 fl oz/¼ cup) brandy
1 kiwi fruit, peeled and sliced
8 maraschino cherries, halved
orange, lemon or lime slices
1 bottle rosé wine
ice cubes
sprigs mint and borage and rose petals, if desired, to decorate
1 bottle sparkling white wine

Divide cinnamon sticks, sugar and rum between 4 warm, heatproof glasses or mugs.

Pour vermouth, cherry brandy and brandy into a large punch bowl.

Place cider in a saucepan and heat until very hot, but not boiling. Fill each glass or mug almost to the top with cider.

Add kiwi fruit, cherries and orange, lemon or lime slices. Stir to mix well. Just before serving, pour in rosé wine and add ice cubes. Decorate with mint, borage and rose petals, if desired.

Add a knob of butter, a sprinkling of mace and a lemon slice to each glass or mug. Stir well and serve hot.

Serves 4.

Add sparkling wine and serve at once in punch glasses or cups, including some fruit and ice with each serving.

Serves 10.

CHOCOLATES & CANDIES

CHOCOLATE TRUFFLE CUPS

450 g (1 lb) white chocolate
55 g (2 oz/¼ cup) unsalted butter, softened
6 teaspoons whipping cream
4 teaspoons cherry brandy
pink, green and yellow food colourings
4 teaspoons Chartreuse
4 teaspoons apricot brandy
6 pistachio nuts, chopped

Break up chocolate and place in a dry bowl over a saucepan of hand-hot water. Stir occasionally until melted; remove bowl from pan and cool. Place 36 foil cases on a tray, spoon a little chocolate into each one.

Using a fine brush, coat inside of each case; leave to set. Add soft butter and cream to remaining chocolate; stir until smooth. Divide mixture between 3 bowls. Flavour one with cherry brandy and tint pink; flavour another with Chartreuse and tint green, and the other with apricot brandy and tint with yellow and pink colouring to give an apricot colour.

When chocolate mixtures are set enough to peak softly, place each in a separate piping bag fitted with a small star nozzle; pipe swirls of each flavour into 12 chocolate cases. Sprinkle with pistachio nuts and leave to set. Pack in pretty containers.

Makes 36.

CHOCOLATE DECORATIONS

115 g (4 oz) plain (dark) chocolate
225 g (8 oz) white chocolate
pink, green and yellow oil-based, or powdered, food colourings
pink, green and yellow ribbon

Break up each chocolate and put in separate bowls over saucepans of hand-hot water. Stir occasionally until melted. Divide ½ white chocolate between 3 bowls and colour pink, green and yellow with food colourings.

To make novelty shapes, draw around biscuit or cookie cutters on non-stick baking paper. Invert paper and place on a baking sheet. Half-fill 2 greaseproof paper piping bags with melted plain (dark) chocolate. Snip a small point off one bag and pipe a fine outline of chocolate following the drawn shapes. Snip a larger point of end of remaining piping bag and pipe chocolate into shapes to give an over-filled and rounded appearance.

Repeat to make different shaped chocolate decorations, using white and some coloured chocolate. Leave to set hard, then carefully peel off paper, taking care not to mark surfaces. Sandwich matching shapes together with remaining melted chocolates, placing ribbon loops in-between. Decorate shapes with piped coloured chocolate using a greaseproof paper piping bag. Allow all decorations to dry before hanging up with different colour ribbons.

Makes about 20.

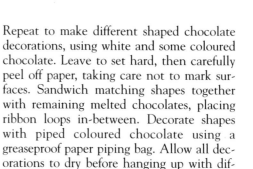

FONDANT SWEETS

225 g (8 oz) ready-to-roll fondant icing
pink, green, yellow, mauve and orange food
    colourings
FLAVOURINGS:
3 marrons glacés
3 pieces crystallised ginger
few drops peppermint oil
1 teaspoon each finely grated orange, lemon and lime
    peel

Cut fondant icing into 6 pieces. Keep one piece plain and, using food colourings, tint remaining 5 pieces a very pale pink, green, yellow, mauve and orange.

Cut 2 marrons glacés and pink fondant into 8 pieces, wrap each piece of marrons glacés in pink fondant and shape into a neat ball. Repeat with mauve fondant and 2 pieces of crystallised ginger to make oval-shaped sweets. Decorate tops with remaining marrons glacés and ginger.

Flavour white fondant with peppermint oil and roll out to 0.5 cm (¼ in) thickness. Using a small round or crescent-shaped cutter, cut out 8-10 shapes. Knead orange peel into orange fondant, lemon peel into yellow fondant and lime peel into green fondant. Shape each piece into tiny pinwheels, squares, diamonds or trefoil shapes. Or press small pieces of fondant into plastic sweet moulds. Dry out completely on a paper-lined baking sheet.

Makes about 40.

HAND-MADE CHOCOLATES

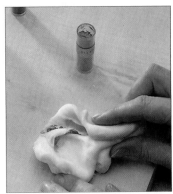

85 g (3 oz) ready-to-roll fondant icing
rose and violet flavourings
pink and mauve food colourings
55 g (2 oz) white marzipan
6 maraschino cherries
6 crème de menthe cherries
6 Brazil nuts
6 whole almonds
175 g (6 oz) plain (dark) chocolate
175 g (6 oz) white chocolate
175 g (6 oz) milk chocolate
crystallised rose and violet petals

Cut fondant into 2 pieces: flavour ½ with rose flavouring and colour pale pink.

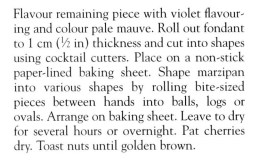

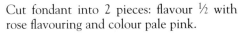

Flavour remaining piece with violet flavouring and colour pale mauve. Roll out fondant to 1 cm (½ in) thickness and cut into shapes using cocktail cutters. Place on a non-stick paper-lined baking sheet. Shape marzipan into various shapes by rolling bite-sized pieces between hands into balls, logs or ovals. Arrange on baking sheet. Leave to dry for several hours or overnight. Pat cherries dry. Toast nuts until golden brown.

Melt each type of chocolate in separate bowls over hand-hot water and stir until melted. Using a fork, dip one prepared centre at a time into chocolate; tap to remove excess, and place chocolate on a paper-lined baking sheet. Leave plain, or mark top with a fork or with piped chocolate. Decorate rose and violet centres with crystallised petals. Continue to dip all centres, giving a variety of white, plain (dark), or milk chocolate.

Makes about 30.

THAI SWEETMEATS

55 g (2 oz) split mung beans, rinsed
45 g (1½ oz/½ cup) desiccated coconut
1 egg, separated
115 g (4 oz/½ cup) palm sugar, crushed
few drops jasmine essence

Put mung beans into a medium saucepan, add sufficient water to cover by 4 cm (1½ in). Bring to the boil, then simmer for about 30-45 minutes until tender. Drain through a strainer, then mash thoroughly.

Using your fingers, mix in coconut and egg yolk to make a firm paste. Divide into pieces about the size of a small walnut and shape into egg-shaped balls using a spoon. Put sugar into a saucepan, add 175 ml (6 fl oz/¾ cup) water and heat gently, stirring, until sugar has dissolved. Bring to the boil. Add jasmine essence to taste and keep hot.

Using a fork, well beat egg white in a bowl. Using 2 forks, dip each ball into egg white, then lower into syrup. Cook for 2-3 minutes. Using a slotted spoon, transfer to a plate. When all sweetmeats have been cooked, spoon over a little syrup. Leave until cold.

Makes about 16.

PISTACHIO HALVA

175 g (6 oz/1¼ cups) shelled pistachio nuts
250 ml (8 fl oz/1 cup) boiling water
2 tablespoons milk
115 g (4 oz/½ cup) sugar
22 g (¾ oz/4½ teaspoons) butter or ghee
few drops vanilla essence

Put pistachio nuts in a bowl, pour over boiling water and leave to soak for 30 minutes. Grease and base-line an 18 cm (7 in) square tin.

Drain pistachio nuts thoroughly and put in a blender or food processor fitted with a metal blade. Add milk and process until finely chopped, scraping mixture down from sides once or twice. Stir in sugar. Heat a large non-stick frying pan, add butter or ghee and melt over a low to medium heat. Add nut paste and cook for about 15 minutes, stirring constantly, until mixture is very thick.

Stir in vanilla essence, then spoon into prepared tin and spread evenly. Leave to cool completely, then cut into 20 squares using a sharp knife.

Makes about 20 squares.

Note: This halva will keep for 2-3 weeks, stored in the refrigerator.

TOASTED ALMOND TOFFEE

450 g (1 lb/2 cups) sugar
150 g (5 oz/2 cups) low-fat milk powder
few drops vanilla essence
25 g (1 oz/¼ cup) flaked almonds, toasted

Grease and base-line an 18 cm (7 in) square tin. Put sugar in a large heavy-based saucepan with 225 ml (8 fl oz/1 cup) water and heat gently, stirring occasionally, until sugar is dissolved.

Bring to the boil, then boil over a medium-high heat until a few drops of mixture will form a soft ball in cold water. Stir in milk powder and cook for 3-4 minutes more, stirring constantly, until mixture begins to dry on spoon. Stir in vanilla.

Pour into prepared tin and spread evenly. Scatter almonds over top and press into surface. Leave to cool slightly, then cut into 25 squares with a sharp knife while still warm. Leave in tin until cold and firm.

Makes 25 squares.

CASHEW NUT FUDGE

225 g (8 oz/1½ cups) unsalted cashew nuts
350 ml (12 fl oz/1½ cups) boiling water
6 teaspoons milk
150 g (5 oz/⅔ cup) sugar
15 g (½ oz/3 teaspoons) butter or ghee
few drops vanilla essence
few sheets silver leaf (optional)

Put cashew nuts in a bowl, pour over boiling water and leave to soak for 1 hour. Grease and base-line an 18 cm (7 in) square tin.

Drain cashew nuts thoroughly and put in a blender or food processor fitted with a metal blade. Add milk and process until smooth, scraping mixture down from sides once or twice. Stir in sugar. Heat a large non-stick frying pan, add butter or ghee and melt over a low to medium heat. Add nut paste and cook for about 20 minutes, stirring constantly, until mixture is very thick.

Stir in vanilla essence, then spoon into prepared tin and spread evenly. Leave to cool completely, then press silver leaf onto surface, if desired. Cut fudge into about 25 diamond shapes using a wet sharp knife.

Makes about 25 pieces.

Note: This fudge will keep for 2-3 weeks if stored in an airtight tin.

PEANUT BRITTLE

175 g (6 oz) skinned, unsalted peanuts
350 g (12 oz) granulated sugar
3 tablespoons golden syrup
25 g (1 oz/6 teaspoons) butter
pinch bicarbonate of soda

Lightly oil a 17.5 cm (7 in) shallow square tin. Spread the peanuts on a baking sheet and warm in the oven at 140C (275/Gas 1) for about 15 minutes.

Put the sugar into a heavy, medium saucepan with 4 tablespoons cold water and the golden syrup and heat until the sugar dissolves. Stir in the butter and boil rapidly until the mixture reaches 149C (300F) on a sugar thermometer, or a small amount of syrup forms a brittle strand when dropped in a cup of cold water.

Remove from the heat, stir in the bicarbonate of soda and the peanuts. Pour into the tin and leave to cool. When almost set, mark into squares with an oiled knife. Break into pieces once set and wrap them in coloured cellophane, if wished.

Makes about 25 pieces.

CHOCOLATE BALLS

115 g (4 oz/½ cup) butter
3 tablespoons golden syrup
115 g (4 oz) plain (dark) chocolate
85 g (3 oz) ready-to-eat apricots, chopped
175 g (6 oz) muesli-style cereal
drinking chocolate powder

Put the butter and golden syrup into a saucepan and heat gently until melted.

Break the chocolate into pieces, add to the pan and leave to melt. Beat together until smooth, then add the apricots and muesli; mix well. When cool, chill in the refrigerator for about 1 hour.

Take teaspoons of the mixture and roll into balls. Toss in the drinking chocolate, then place in petit fours cases. Return to the refrigerator until firm.

Makes about 20.

PRESERVES

LEMON CURD

4 lemons
350 g (12 oz/1¾ cups) caster sugar
115 g (4 oz/½ cup) butter
4 eggs

Finely grate rind from all 4 lemons into a heatproof bowl. Squeeze lemons and pour juice into the bowl. Stir in sugar. Cut butter into small pieces and add to other ingredients in bowl.

Set bowl over a saucepan one-quarter filled with simmering water, until butter has melted and sugar dissolved. In a bowl, break up eggs with a fork and strain into lemon and butter mixture.

Cook gently, stirring frequently, for 10-15 minutes until mixture is thick and creamy. Pour into clean warm jars and seal while hot. Keep in the refrigerator.

Makes about 700 g (1½ lb).

Variations: For Lime Curd, use limes instead of lemons.

For Lemon & Elderflower Curd, add 2 handfuls of elderflowers, well shaken and flowers removed from stems, after adding the butter to the bowl.

APPLE BUTTER

1.2 litres (2 pints/5 cups) dry cider
1 kg (2¼ lb) dessert apples
450 g (1 lb) cooking apples
granulated sugar
grated rind and juice ½ orange
grated rind and juice ½ lemon
½ teaspoon ground cinnamon
½ teaspoon ground cloves

Put cider in a large saucepan. Boil rapidly until reduced by one-third. Peel, core and slice apples and add to pan.

If necessary, add sufficient water to just cover apples. Half-cover the pan and simmer gently until apples are very soft and pulpy and well reduced. Stir occasionally and crush pulp down in the pan as it cooks. Measure pulp and process to a purée if it is lumpy. Return to saucepan. Add 300 g (10 oz/1¼ cups) sugar for every 550 ml (20 fl oz/2½ cups) of apple pulp. Stir in the orange and lemon rind and juice and cinnamon and cloves.

Cook gently until sugar has dissolved. Simmer, stirring frequently, until most moisture had been driven off. The mixture is ready when a spoon drawn across the surface will leave an impression. Pot in clean, warm jars and store in the refrigerator. Once a jar is opened the apple butter should be consumed within 3-4 days.

Makes 4 or 5 small jars.

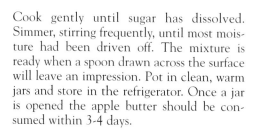

CUMBERLAND RUM BUTTER

115 g (4 oz/½ cup) butter, at room temperature
225 g (8 oz/1½ cups) soft dark brown sugar
¼ teaspoon ground cinnamon
6 teaspoons dark rum
hot toast, muffins or crumpets, to serve

Put butter into a bowl and beat until soft. Gradually beat in sugar.

Gradually beat in the cinnamon and rum. Pile mixture into a small dish. Cover and leave in a cool place until firm. Serve with hot toast, muffins or crumpets.

Serves 6-8.

Variation: For Anchovy Butter, instead of sugar, cinnamon and rum, work 45 g (1½ oz) drained, canned anchovies into butter. Serve on toast.

ROSE PETAL JAM

225 g (8 oz) red, fragrant rose petals
450 g (1 lb/2 cups) granulated sugar
juice 2 lemons

Cut off white area from base of each petal. Put petals in a bowl and sprinkle with enough of the sugar to cover them. Leave overnight.

In a saucepan, put remaining sugar, 1 litre (35 fl oz/4½ cups) water and the lemon juice. Heat gently until sugar has dissolved. Stir in rose petals and simmer for 20 minutes. Bring to the boil and boil for 5 minutes until mixture thickens.

Pour jam into clean, warm jars. Cover and label. Store in a cool place.

Makes about 450 g (1 lb).

SPICED CITRUS SLICES

3 thin-skinned oranges
4 thin-skinned lemons
5 limes
550 ml (20 fl oz/2½ cups) white wine vinegar
1.15 kg (2½ lb/4½ cups) granulated sugar
2 cinnamon sticks
7 g (¼ oz/2 teaspoons) whole cloves
6 blades mace

Scrub fruit thoroughly, then cut into 0.3 cm (⅛ in) thick slices. Lay slices in a stainless steel or enamel saucepan and just cover with water. Bring to boil, then cover and cook very gently for about 15 minutes until peel is tender. Drain slices and reserve liquor.

In another saucepan, gently heat vinegar, sugar and spices, stirring occasionally, until sugar has dissolved. Bring to the boil, then add fruit slices. Add reserved liquor to cover fruit if necessary, then cook very gently for 15 minutes until peel looks transparent.

Arrange fruit slices in small, clean, hot jars, alternating slices, or packing each separately, as desired. Bring syrup to the boil, discard cinnamon and immediately fill each jar to top. Cover with airtight, vinegar-proof lids. When cold, label and store in a cool place for up to 6 months.

Makes 4 small jars.

FRUITS IN CHARTREUSE

10 fresh lychees or 425 g (15 oz) can lychees
225 g (8 oz/2 cups) cherries or 425 g (15 oz) can cherries
225 g (8 oz/1 cup) granulated sugar
300 ml (10 fl oz/1¼ cups) Chartreuse or Benedictine liqueur

Peel fresh lychees and carefully remove stones, keeping fruit whole, or drain and stone canned lychees. Remove stalks and wash fresh cherries, or drain canned cherries, and dry on absorbent kitchen paper. Pierce skins of cherries all over with a clean needle or fine skewer.

Have ready 3 or 4 very small, clean, dry, sterilised jars with well-fitting lids. Arrange a layer of cherries in one clean jar and sprinkle with about 1 tablespoon sugar. Arrange a layer of lychees on top and sprinkle with more sugar. Continue to layer cherries, sugar and lychees until jar is loosely filled to neck of jar, do not pack fruit in tightly. Sprinkle with a final layer of sugar.

Fill jar to the top with Chartreuse or Benedictine and seal with a clean lid. Repeat to fill remaining small jars with fruits, sugar and liqueur. Store in a cool, dry place for up to 6 months. Gift wrap for presents.

Makes 3 or 4 small jars.

SATSUMA & PINE NUT CONSERVE

1 kg (2¼ lb) satsumas
1 kg (2¼ lb/4 cups) granulated sugar
55 ml (2 fl oz/¼ cup) orange flower water
55 g (2 oz/½ cup) pine nuts

Scrub satsumas well, then using a potato peeler or sharp knife, pare peel from satsumas, not including white pith. Cut peel into fine strips and place in a large saucepan with 150 ml (5 fl oz/⅔ cup) water. Bring to the boil, cover and cook gently for 1 hour, or until tender.

Cut satsumas in half, squeeze juice into a jug and make up to 470 ml (15 fl oz/1¾ cups) with water, if necessary. Reserve all pips, place in a piece of muslin and tie securely with string. Place in a saucepan with satsuma shells and 470 ml (15 fl oz/1¾ cups) water. Bring to boil, cover and simmer for 1 hour. Strain liquid into saucepan containing strips of peel. Stir in sugar and juice and bring to boil, stirring, until sugar has dissolved.

Boil rapidly for 5-10 minutes until setting point is reached. To test, spoon a little conserve onto a cold plate, leave for a few minutes, then push with your finger: if surface wrinkles, setting point has been reached. Add orange flower water and pine nuts, bring to boil and boil for 2 minutes. Cool for 30 minutes, stir, then pour into warm, dry, sterilised pots. Cover with wax discs; seal. Store in a cool, dry place.

Makes 1.3 kg (3 lb).

BRANDIED MINCEMEAT

450 g (1 lb/3 cups) raisins
450 g (1 lb/3 cups) sultanas
450 g (1 lb/3⅓ cups) currants
115 g (4 oz/1 cup) dried apricots
115 g (4 oz/¾ cup) stoned dates
175 g (6 oz/1 cup) candied peel
125 g (4 oz/¾ cup) whole almonds
450 g (1 lb) cooking apples, peeled and cored
finely grated peel and juice 2 lemons
350 g (12 oz/2¼ cups) light soft brown sugar
225 g (8 oz/1 cup) unsalted butter, melted
3 teaspoons ground mixed spice
150 ml (5 fl oz/⅔ cup) brandy

In a bowl, put raisins, sultanas and currants.

Chop or mince apricots, dates, candied peel, almonds and apples. Add to bowl with lemon peel and juice and mix well together. Stir in sugar, butter, mixed spice and brandy. Stir the mixture until evenly blended, cover bowl with plastic wrap and leave in a cool place for 2 days.

Preheat the oven to 200C (400F/Gas 6). Thoroughly wash and dry six 450 g (1 lb) jam jars, stand them on a paper-lined baking sheet and place in the oven until hot. Stir mincemeat thoroughly, then spoon into hot jars, filling each to the top. Place a wax disc on top of each and cellophane covers over the jars, securing each with an elastic band. Label clearly and store in a cool, dry place for up to 6 months.

Makes 3 kg (7 lb).

MANGO CHUTNEY

1.8 kg (4 lb) green mangoes, peeled and cubed
2 limes, sliced into semi-circles
3 fresh red chillis, cored, seeded and finely chopped
685 ml (24 fl oz/3 cups) white wine vinegar
1 tablespoon ground toasted cardamom seeds
1 teaspoon ground toasted cumin seeds
1 teaspoon ground turmeric
1½ teaspoons salt
450 g (1 lb) light brown sugar

Put mangoes, limes, chillies and vinegar into
a nonreactive pan. Bring to a boil then lower
heat and simmer, uncovered, for 10-15
minutes until mangoes are just tender.

Add spices, salt and sugar. Stir until sugar
has dissolved, then increase heat and bring
to a boil. Lower heat again and simmer,
uncovered, for 50-60 minutes, stirring
occasionally, until most of the liquid has
evaporated and the chutney is quite thick.

Ladle chutney into hot, very clean jars.
Cover top of each jar of chutney with a disc
of waxed paper, waxed side down. Close jars
with nonreactive lids. Leave chutney for
1 month before using.

Makes about 1.3 kg (3 lb).

LIME PICKLE

12 limes
55 g (2 oz/¼ cup) coarse sea salt
3 teaspoons fenugreek seeds
3 teaspoons mustard seeds
6 teaspoons chilli powder
3 teaspoons ground turmeric
225 ml (8 fl oz/1 cup) vegetable oil, such as
   sunflower or peanut
coriander sprigs, to garnish

Cut each lime lengthwise into 8 thin
wedges. Place in a large sterilised bowl,
sprinkle with salt and set aside.

Put fenugreek and mustard seeds in a frying
pan and dry roast them over a medium heat
for 1-2 minutes, until they begin to pop. Put
them in a mortar and grind them to a fine
powder with a pestle.

Add chilli powder and turmeric and mix
well. Sprinkle spice mixture over limes and
stir. Pour over oil and cover with a dry cloth.
Leave in a sunny place for 10-12 days, until
softened. Pack into sterilised jars, then seal
and store in a cool, dark place. It can be kept
for 1-2 weeks. Serve at room temperature,
garnished with coriander.

Makes about 1.3 kg (3 lb).

Variation: To make Lemon Pickle, substitute
8 lemons for the limes.

SPICY OLIVES

450 g (1 lb) green or black olives
1 sprig oregano
1 sprig thyme
1 teaspoon finely chopped fresh rosemary
2 bay leaves
1 teaspoon fennel seeds, bruised
1 teaspoon finely crushed cumin seeds
1 fresh red chilli, seeded and chopped
4 cloves garlic, crushed
olive oil, to cover

MARINATED FETA CHEESE

350 g (12 oz) feta cheese
2 cloves garlic
½ teaspoon mixed peppercorns
8 coriander seeds
1 bay leaf
oregano and thyme sprigs
olive oil, to cover
hot toast, cut into squares, to serve

Cut feta cheese into cubes. Cut garlic into thick slivers.

Using a small sharp knife, make a lengthways slit through to stone of each olive. Put olives into a bowl Stir in oregano, thyme, rosemary, bay leaves, fennel seeds, cumin, chilli and garlic.

In a mortar and pestle, lightly crush peppercorns and coriander seeds.

Pack olive mixture into a screw-top or preserving jar. Pour over sufficient oil to cover, close the lid and leave for at least 3 days, shaking jar occasionally, before using.

Serves 6.

Pack cubes of cheese into a preserving jar with the bay leaf, interspersing layers of cheese with garlic, peppercorns, coriander and oregano or thyme. Pour in enough olive oil to cover cheese. Leave for 2 weeks. Serve on hot toast, sprinkled with a little of the oil from the jar.

Serves 6.

471

MEDITERRANEAN INGREDIENTS

Balsamic vinegar: This Italian vinegar is more expensive than wine vinegars but has a rich, sweet, aromatic flavour so is used much more sparingly. The more mature vinegars, which can be very expensive, are more concentrated and often a few drops are all that are required to flavour a dressing.

Bresaola: Sold thinly sliced, bresaola is raw beef that has been salted and airdried in the same way as prosciutto (see below).

Bulgar wheat: Also spelled bulghar and burghul, this is made from wheat grains that are cracked by boiling, then dried. It only needs to be rehydrated by soaking in water for 10-20 minutes before it is ready for use.

Cous cous: A staple in North African countries, cous cous is really a form of pasta, not a grain. Fine grains of semolina are dampened then rolled in flour. Most of the cous cous now sold has already been cooked and only needs to be moistened and reheated, usually by steaming, and the grains separated.

Dolcelatte: This is a factory version of gorgonzola (see below). It has a creamier flavour.

Feta cheese: A white, salty cheese, stored in brine. Traditionally, feta comes from Greece and Cyprus and is made from unpasteurised ewes' milk, but today it is often made elsewhere from cows' milk.

Filo (phyllo) pastry: When using filo pastry it is important to keep the sheets in a pile between two tea towels or closely covered with plastic wrap and to work with one piece at a time, otherwise the pastry will become dry and brittle.

Garlic: The smell and taste of garlic is one of the most characteristic features of the food of the Mediterranean. For the best flavour, use garlic that is as fresh as possible and if there is a green shoot in a clove, discard the shoot. Buy garlic bulbs loose, rather than in cardboard boxes, or woven into a string. Store in a cool airy dry place away from direct light.

Gorgonzola cheese: A mild, blue-veined Italian cheese with a pleasantly sharp flavour.

Haloumi cheese: A Greek soft to semi-soft goats' milk cheese that is quite salty, yet mild. It is generally served toasted or fried.

Kefalotori cheese: A strong Greek cheese that is good for grating. If you can't find it, use Parmesan or mature, well-flavoured Cheddar instead.

Mascarpone cheese: A very rich, thick velvety Italian cheese that is often served sweetened and flavoured with liqueurs as a dessert but its luxurious flavour and texture are very good in savoury dishes as well.

Mortadella: The largest Italian sausage. The best are made from pure pork but others may contain some beef or offal.. The spices and flavourings can vary, the most usual being black peppercorns, coriander seeds and pistachio nuts.

Mozzarella cheese: Today most of the mozzarella we buy is made from cows' milk. This is fine for cooked dishes, but for salads or for eating on its own it is worth paying for the authentic full-flavoured, more creamy textured mozzarella di bufala.

Olives: These come in many different varieties and colours and may be cured in brine, packed in oil or flavoured with herbs, spices or lemon. Colour differences are linked to the degree of ripeness – a progression from green through yellow or greeny-brown to red, violet, then purple and black.

Olive oil: Each country, even regions within a country, have their own olive oils and these give the dishes in which they are used their distinctive flavour. Extra virgin oils have the strongest, finest flavour and are usually used for dressings; virgin oils are one step down in the hierarchy and can be used in special dishes; olive oils are the everyday cooking oil.

Orange flower water: A clear, delightfully scented liquid that is distilled from orange blossoms. It is widely used to flavour sweet dishes around the southern Mediterranean, Turkey and Greece, and in southern France. It is particularly good with its own fruit, the orange, whether in sweet or savoury dishes.

Parmesan cheese: The most famous matured hard cheese of Italy, Parmesan is most often used for grating over pasta, risottos, sauces and other cooked dishes, but it is also superb as a table cheese. Always buy Parmesan in a piece to be cut or grated as needed. The drums of ready-grated Parmesan cheese that are available simply do not compare in flavour.

Pasta: Unless you are going to prepare your own pasta, dried pasta is usually preferable to commercial "fresh" pastas, which can be starchy and rather heavy. If making pasta at home, try to buy special "type 00" flour, which is available in Italian delicatessens and some large supermarkets. Alternatively, use strong bread flour.

Pine nuts: These are not really nuts but are the kernels from the cones of the stone pine. They are expensive but have a distinctive almost resinous flavour for which their really is no substitute.

Prosciutto: Salted and air-dried raw ham. Parma ham is the most famous, but other regions have their own versions.

Rice: Locally grown short grain rice gives a characteristic texture to Spanish paellas, Turkish pilaus and Italian risottos. Risotto, or arborio, rice is now widely available and is the only one to use for a genuine risotto; it can also be used for paellas. For pilaus and other Mediterranean rice dishes, use long grain rice, or basmati rice.

Ricotta cheese: This is a fresh, soft Italian cheese that is made from the whey that is the by-product of other cheeses. Ricotta has a mild, delicate flavour and should be used soon after purchase.

Rose water: Made from distilled fragrant rose petals, rose water is used in many North African, Middle Eastern, Turkish and Greek pastries and sweet dishes, particularly milk-based desserts. In North Africa, rose water is also sometimes added to savoury dishes.

Saffron: For preference, use pure saffron threads rather than powder as this may be adulterated. A mere pinch of saffron is all that is needed to flavour a dish for four to six people.

Tahini: This a paste made from ground toasted sesame seeds. Tahini separates if left to stand for a while and must be stirred thoroughly before using; the jar can be inverted for a while to make blending easier. Keep tahini in a cool place, but preferably not the refrigerator, because this makes blending more difficult.

EASTERN INGREDIENTS

Bean curd: Low in fat and high in protein, bean curd is made from yellow soya beans and has a mild flavour.

Chinese beef stock: Put into a large saucepan 900 g (2 lb) lean stewing beef, trimmed and cut into 5 cm (2 in) pieces, 2.5 cm (1 in) piece fresh root ginger, peeled, 1 garlic clove, 2 shallots, 1 stick celery, 2 carrots, 2 tablespoons dark soy sauce, a large pinch of salt and a large pinch of freshly ground black pepper. Add 2 litres (3½ pints/9 cups) cold water. Bring to the boil. Skim scum from surface, cover pan and simmer gently for 2 hours. Leave to cool. Line a sieve with clean muslin and place over a large bowl. Ladle stock through sieve and discard beef and vegetables. Cover and chill. Skim fat from surface. Refrigerate for up to 3 days or freeze for up to 3 months. Makes 1.7 litres (3 pints/7½ cups).

Chinese vegetable stock: Put 1 lemon grass stalk, broken, 2 slices fresh root ginger, 1 garlic clove, 2 spring onions, 115 g (4 oz) carrots, sliced, 2 sticks celery, 115 g (4 oz) bean sprouts, a large pinch of salt and a large pinch of ground white pepper in a large saucepan. Add 2 litres (3½ pints/9 cups) cold water and bring to the boil. Skim scum from the surface then cover pan and simmer gently for 45 minutes. Leave to cool. Line a sieve with clean muslin and place over a large bowl. Ladle stock through sieve and discard vegetables. Cover and refrigerate for up to 3 days or freeze for up to 3 months. Makes 1.5 litres (2½ pints/6 cups).

Coconut milk and cream: This is not the liquid from inside a coconut, but is extracted from shredded coconut flesh that has been soaked in water. Soak the shredded flesh of 1 medium coconut in 300 ml (10 fl oz/1 1/4 cups) boiling water for 30 minutes Tip into a sieve lined with muslin or fine cotton and

squeeze this fabric hard to extract as much liquid as possible. Coconut milk can also be made by putting 225 g (8 oz/22/3 cups) desiccated coconut in a blender with 300 ml (10 fl oz/11/4 cups) boiling water. Mix for 1 minute then soak and strain as above. Home-made coconut milk should be stored in the refrigerator. Ready prepared coconut milk is sold canned (which affects the flavour) and in pouches. Coconut cream is the layer that forms on top of the coconut milk.

Coriander: Fresh coriander looks like fine flat-leaf parsley but it has a more pungent, distinctive smell and taste.

Dried mushrooms: There are several types of Eastern dried mushrooms, all of which add a distinctive flavour and aroma, but the most commonly used is the Chinese black mushroom. They need to be soaked in hot water for about 20 minutes then drained and the tough stalks discarded.

Fish sauce (nam pla): A clear brown liquid, rich in protein and B vitamins, this is South East Asia"s answer to soy sauce and the essential Thai seasoning. It enriches without tasting too fishy or salty when mixed with other ingredients or when cooked.

Five-spice powder: The Chinese spice mixture made from ground star anise, Szechuan peppercorns, fennel, cloves and cinnamon. Five-spice powder adds a warm, spicy, fragrant flavour to recipes.

Galangal (galangale, laos): A root that is similar in appearance to ginger but the skin is thinner, paler and more translucent. The flavour is also similar to ginger but with distinctive, seductive citrus-pine undertones. A whole root can be kept wrapped in paper in the refrigerator for up to two weeks, or it can be frozen. Allow to thaw just enough for the required amount to be sliced or grated off, then return the root to the freezer.

Hoisin sauce: A reddish brown sauce based on soya beans and flavoured with garlic, chillies and a combination of spices. Brands vary in flavour, but hoisin sauce is usually quite sweet and can range from the thickness of a soft jam to a runny sauce.

Kaffir limes: These are slightly smaller than ordinary limes and have dark green, knobbly rind. The smell and taste of the peel resemble aromatic limes with a hint of lemon. The peel of ordinary limes can be substituted.

Kaffir lime leaves: The smooth, dark green leaves give an aromatic, clean, citrus-pine flavour and smell. They keep well in a cool place and can be frozen. Use 1½ teaspoons grated ordinary lime rind if kaffir lime leaves are unavailable.

Lemon grass: A long, slim bulb with a lemon-citrus flavour. To use, cut off the root tip, peel off the tough outer layers and cut away the top part of the stalk. Then chop the remaining bulb very finely. Lemon grass can be kept in a cool place for several days, or it can be chopped and frozen. If lemon grass is unavailable, use the grated rind of half a lemon in place of one stalk.

Lily buds: Also known as golden needles, these are dried buds of the tiger lily flower. Soak them in warm water for 30 minutes or so, then rinse in fresh water and discard the hard tips before use.

Noodles: There are many varieties and thicknesses. Egg noodles, whether fresh or dried, need to be cooked in a similar way to pasta before using. Rice noodles are also known as rice sticks and come in three different widths, large, medium and small. There are also fine strands of rice vermicelli. Rice noodles only need to be soaked in hot water to separate and soften them.

Oyster sauce: Used in Chinese cooking this thick brown sauce is made from concentrated oysters, soy sauce and brine. Nowadays, cornflour and colouring are also often added.

Plum sauce: A thick, sweet condiment made from plums, apricots, garlic, vinegar and seasonings. It is used in cooking and as a dip.

Preserved vegetables: Mixed pickled mustard greens and root vegetables are available in cans and jars and have a crunchy texture and hot, spicy flavour. They are salty and need to be rinsed before use. Once opened, jars should be covered and stored in the refrigerator and canned vegetables should be transferred to a glass or pottery container.

Rice: For authentic-tasting savoury Thai dishes, use Thai fragrant, or jasmine, rice; for other savoury eastern recipes use long grain rice for everyday meals. Short grain glutinous rice is used for particular desserts.

Rice vinegar: This is fermented from rice and is much less acidic than Western vinegars. Chinese rice vinegar many be "black" with a rich, smoky, complex flavour and is usually used for dips; clear pale red, when it is slightly tart; and white and mild. Japanese rice vinegar is subtle, with a clean, elegant flavour. Cider or sherry vinegar can be substituted for rice vinegar.

Rice wine: Chinese rice wine is similar to sherry in colour, bouquet and alcohol content (18%). It is made from glutinous rice, yeast and spring water. Dry sherry can be substituted.

Sesame oil: A thick, rich oil made from toasted sesame seeds with a strong nutty flavour. The darker the oil, the stronger the flavour. Lighter oils can be used for cooking but full-flavoured ones are reserved for use as a seasoning when the cooking is complete.

Shrimp paste: Made from fermented dried shrimp with salt, this highly pungent paste is used sparingly.

Soy sauce: The essential ingredient in Chinese cooking, soy sauce is made from soya beans, flour and water, fermented together and aged for several months. Light soy sauce is more full flavoured and quite salty; dark soy sauce, which has caramel added, is thicker and sweeter. Additional salt is often unnecessary.

Fragrant curry paste: This Indian mix is often described as mild as well as fragrant and is available in jars. Fragrant curry powder can be substituted if liked.

Garam masala: A prepared mixture of Indian spices, garam masala can be bought readily in jars and packets.

Tamarind: Sold in sticky brown blocks, tamarind provides a sharp, slightly fruity taste. To make tamarind water, break off a 25 g (1 oz) piece and pour over 300ml (10 fl oz/1¼ cups) boiling water. Break up the lump then leave for about 30 minutes, stirring occasionally. Strain off the tamarind water, pressing on the pulp, and discard the remaining debris. Keep the water in a jar in the refrigerator. Ready-to-use tamarind syrup is sometimes available and is usually more concentrated than homemade tamarind water.

Thai curry pastes: Red and green Thai curry pastes are readily available in jars and sachets from supermarkets. The red varieties are more mild than green pastes, and have a more mellow flavour, but brands vary in their strengths so add cautiously.

INDEX

A

Afelia 172
Almond macaroons 418
Amaretti-stuffed peaches 352
Anchoïade 24
Anchovy and Parmesan salaad 266
Anchovy-stuffed mushrooms 51
Animal egg breads 428
Apples
  and olive oil cake 401
  baked 357
  blackberry and apple cobbler 356
  butter 466
  charlotte 385
  French tart 334
  pancakes 363
  Peking 363
  streusel cake 404
  tarte tatin 336
  zing 451
Apple sauce with mint 308
Apricopita 350
Apricots
  and chicken filos 437
  and chicken curry 111
  and hazelnut galette 347
  dessert 375
  pudding 366
  sauce 313
  spiced squares 420
  Arabian poussins 112
Aromatic duck 120
Artemis cake 403
Artichokes
  and broad beans 291
  baked stuffed 52
  char-grilled 300
Asian fried rice 230
Asparagus
  and egg salad 262
  niçoise 35
  parmesan 48
  rice with asparagus and nuts
    220
  risotto 234
  with chicory leaves
Aubergine
  and olive salad 265
  caponata 36
  crab and aubergine noodles 215
  fritters 54
  funghetto 302
  Imam bayaldi 54
  in spicy sauce 296
  baked layers 49
  macaroni with 206
  Moroccan casserole 191
  Napoletana 53
  oysters with 440
  pizza 239
  stuffed 200
  Szechuan 292
Austrian curd cheesecake 380
Avocado

B

  and red currants 35
  salmon rolls 448

Bacon
  aigrettes 439
  crispy pinwheels 447
Baked aubergine layers 49
Baked Basque cod 80
Baked eggs in nests 189
Baked eggs with ricotta 46
Baked lamb with vegetables 162
Baked mixed vegetables 299
Baked mushrooms 52
Baked demelza apples 357
Baked stuffed artichokes 52
Baklava 350
  nectarine 349
Bananas
  and rum ice cream 392
  caramel sesame 361
  with rum and lime 355
Barbecue sauce 310
Barbecue spareribs 177
Barbecued spareribs 166
Basic white sauce 304
Bass with ginger and lime 72
Beans
  and mushroom noodles 218
  and onion salad 262
  and sweetcorn chilli 198
  black-eyed and rice 228
  broad and artichokes 291
  broad in tomato sauce 289
  broad with dill 291
  broad with goat's cheese 47
  fasoulia 199
  fennel and bean casserole 189
  green with onion 290
  lentil and bean chilli 194
  mushroom and bean chilli 183
  soupe au pistou 13
  three bean salad 277
  tomato and bean tian 185
  Tuscan bean soup 21
Bechamel sauce 305
Beef
  cubes and strips
    Belgian hotchpotch 144
    boeuf bourguignon 131
    chilli with peppers 141
    curry 138
    dry-fried strips 140
    garlic casserole 132
    ginger with pineapple 140
    goulash with chilli 144
    in oyster sauce 142
    light satay 137
    mango with cashews 139
    mulligatawny 20
    Provençal beef daube 130
    shredded with ginger 136
    spicy sesame 139
    spicy with peppers 141
    stir-fried 133
    stir-fried with leeks 132
    stroganoff 142
    Szechuan 133

    teriyaka 141
    Thai with noodles 138
    with water chestnuts 136
  ground
    bobotie 143
    chilli with nachos 145
    Italian meatballs 147
    meatballs in tomato sauce 143
    minced meat fingers 257
    stuffed cabbage 134
    surprise beefburgers 430
  pot roast of brisket 145
  roast in barolo wine 147
  steaks
    deviled 146
    with Béarnaise sauce 130
    spicy braised 131
    with tomato and olives 146
    with tomato sauce
Beef-stuffed cabbage 134
Beet soup, clear 8
Belgian hotchpotch 144
Blackberry and apple cobbler 356
Black currant whirls 409
Black-eyed peas and rice 228
Blue cheese and broccoli soup 14
Bobotie 143
Boeuf bourguignon 131
Braised lamb and vegetables 158
Bramble muffins 413
Brandied mincemeat 469
Bread and butter pudding 359
Bread and cheese pudding 186
Bread pudding, savoury 190
Broccoli
  and blue cheese soup 14
  and cheese sauce 306
  and tomatoes 293
  and turkey flan 244
  caponata 184
  noodles 217
  pasta 202
  with chillis 293
Brussels sprouts, gingered 294
Bucatini siciliana 202
Butternut squash crumble 186

C

Cabbage
  beef-stuffed 134
  spiced 297
  stuffed leaves 179
Cabinet pudding 367
Café de olla 454
Cajun crabcakes 65
Cajun-style red snapper 79
Candied fruit tarts 341
Capellini, with snapper 209
Caper sauce 304
Caponata 36
Caramel oranges 372
Caramel sesame bananas 361
Caraway kugelhopf 328
Caraway pot roast 175
Carrots
  and coriander soup 13
  and ginger soufflés 48
  and sultana pudding

  carottes Vichy 285
  puréed ginger 284
  Oriental salad 265
Cashew nut fudge 463
Cauliflower
  in coconut 296
  insalata 263
  spicy 294
  with peppers 295
Celeriac rémoulade 29
Chapati 318
Charlotte russe 385
Char-grilled artichokes 300
Cheese
  and chive plait 326
  and herb triangles 28
  and honey triangles 340
  Austrian cheesecake 380
  blue cheese and broccoli soup 14
  bread and cheese pudding 186
  buns 322
  cream cheese strudel 349
  cream with herbs 26
  dolcelatte mini pizzas 242
  fennel and dolcelatte 33
  feta and herb popovers 47
  feta cheese kebabs 444
  filled button rarebit 448
  goat's cheese and fig tart 247
  goat's cheese on broad beans 47
  goat's cheese soufflés 46
  goat's cheese tarts 249
  gratin savoyard 284
  herb and feta balls 27
  marinated feta 471
  parmesan asparagus 48
  ricotta and coffee dessert 379
  ricotta moulds 28
  Roquefort veronique 104
  straws 445
  stuffed tomatoes 199
  thins 426
Cheese sauce 304
Cheesy mice 429
Chelsea buns 329
Cherry clafouti 356
Cherry-nut bread 328
Cherry-nut rockies 412
Chicken
  and mushroom rice 231
  and mushroom soup 17
  Arabian poussins 112
  biryani 220
  breasts
    chow mein 218
    crumble 110
    fajitas 102
    grilled with herbs 104
    in black bean sauce 101
    in vinegar sauce 103
    kiev 103
    layered country terrine 44
    lemon 100
    Mexican salad 274
    mozzarella 110
    nutty goujons 61
    peppered kebabs 102
    Roquefort veronique 104

    satay salad 274
    spicy patties 112
    stir-fried 100
    tikka kebabs 105
    with green sauce 41
    with salsa verde 107
  cooked
    and apricot filos 437
    and corn fritters 106
    and ham mousse 44
    apricot bags 437
    coriander 109
    coronation 275
    fried rice
    rich country soup 17
  cubed
    and ham potpie 250
    Flemish braised 108
    garlic chicken 99
  jointed
    lemon and chilli 107
    Moroccan-style 107
    poulet basquaise 97
    poulet provençal 97
    with sherry 106
  liver
    pâté 43
    crostini 60
  pasties 257
  pieces
    apricot and chicken curry 111
    chicken chasseur 98
    Chinese barbecue 99
    cock-a-leekie 18
    coq au vin 96
    farmhouse pie 250
    grilled drumsticks 101
    lemon and coriander 111
    poulet au vinaigre 98
    spicy wings 109
    tandoori 105
  poussins with watercress 113
  thigh meat
    steamed with rice 232
  with tarragon 96
Chickpeas
  and pepper tortilla 182
  curried 198
  hummus 25
  rice with 230
  salad 275
  spicy soup 19
Chilli beef with nachos 145
Chilli beef with peppers 141
Chilli shrimp balls 62
Chinese barbecued chicken 99
Chocolate
  and orange muffins 415
  balls 464
  brownies 410
  cherry slice 390
  cigarettes 424
  decorations 460
  double chocolate shorties 422
  hand-dipped 461
  marble cake 397
  profiteroles 390
  Spanish hot 451

INDEX

terrine, white and dark 391
tiny Christmas logs 416
truffle cups 460
Chocolate-nut muffins 414
Chow mein 218
Christmas cake 406
Christmas Eve mull 457
Christmas pudding, round 370
Chunky fish casserole 84
Cinnamon cookies 425
Clam
  chowder, New England 16
  Malay curried 91
Clear beet soup 8
Clementines
  and date salad 374
  tartlets 346
Cock-a-leekie 18
Cocktail pinwheels 445
Coconut
  and cherry cake 399
  crisps 426
  custards 366
  layer cake 389
  pork with lime 172
Cod
  baked Basque 80
  roast with lentils 69
Coffee-brandy cake, spicy 388
Coffee-walnut cookies 419
Coffee brulée 367
Coeurs à la crème 384
Cold spicy noodles 216
Coq au vin 96
Coriander and lime dressing 316
Coriander chicken 109
Coronation chicken 275
Coulibiac 246
Courgette
  and tomato salad 264
  and tomato soup 10
  gougère 190
  gratin 288
  spicy sauce 306
  stuffed rings 55
  timbales 51
  with cheese 301
  with garlic 302
  with ginger 292
Couscous salad 278
Crab
  and avocado salad 272
  and aubergine noodles 215
  and fennel puffs 258
  and ginger triangles 258
  and ricotta tarts
  Cajun crabcakes 65
  curried 90
  fried rice 223
  spicy 90
Cream caramel, orange 384
Cream cheese with herbs 26
Cream cheese strudel 349
Creamy fish soup 15
Creamy paprika turkey 114
Crème de menthe cookies 425
Crêpes, hazelnut with spinach 182
Crispy bacon pinwheels 447

Crispy fish hotpot 83
Crispy noodles 213
Crispy pesto prawns 442
Crispy won tons 57
Crumpets 330
Crunchy peaches 354
Cumberland rum butter 467
Cupcakes, iced 412
Currants, mixed sensation 377
Curried chickpeas 198
Curried crab 90
Curried lamb with raita 157
Curried parsnip soup 10
Curried vegetable envelopes 440
Curry
  apricot and chicken 111
  beef 138
  mixed vegetable 196
  mushroom 295
  red lamb and almond 156
  Thai pork 165
  vegetable and fruit 185
Curry sauce 310
Curry wheels 443

D
Dark chocolate sauce 312
Deep-fried fish balls 436
Devilled ham toasts 438
Devilled steaks 146
Devonshire splits 330
Dim sum 58
Dolcelatte mini pizzas 242
Domino biscuits 423
Double chocolate cookies 422
Duck
  breasts
    with apples and prunes 119
    with kiwi fruit
    with orange 118
    with plums 120
  Peking duck 121
  pieces
    aromatic 120
    Vietnamese roast 119
  with turnips 118
Dried fruit salad 377
Dry-fried beef strips 140
Dundee cake 405
Dutch pea soup 22

E
Easter bread 327
Easter biscuits 422
Egg fried rice 224
Eggs
  and anchovy mayonnaise 32
  and spinach cups 50
  baked in nests 189
  baked with ricotta 46
  cheese and egg strata 186
  chickpea and pepper omelette 182
  fresh herb frittata 196
  oeufs à la neige 386
  prawn-stuffed 32
  soufflé omelette 362
  Spanish omelette 193
  English trifle 383

F
Farmhouse chicken pie 250
Fasoulia 199
Feather-light tiramisu 380
Fennel
  and bean casserole 189
  and dolcelatte 33
  and Parmesan gratin 288
  siciliano 289
  soup 9
Festival crescents 423
Festive dip selection 443
Feta cheese
  and herb popovers 47
  and shrimp purses 62
  kebabs 444
  marinated 471
Fideua 208
Figs
  and orange tart 335
  with cinnamon cream 354
  roast 352
Filled button rarebit 448
Fish
  and pesto parcels 68
  and tomato gratin 286
  avocado salmon rolls 448
  baked Basque cod 80
  bass with ginger and lime 72
  Cajun-style red snapper 79
  chunky fish casserole 84
  coulibiac 246
  creamy soup 15
  crispy fish hotpot 83
  deep-fried fish balls 436
  fideua 208
  fish cakes 71
  five-spice salmon 80
  fun fish cakes 429
  goujons with piquant dip 64
  gratins 70
  Greek seafood casserole 84
  grilled fish and coriander 73
  grilled flat 81
  haddock and salmon pie 83
  herrings in oats 76
  hot fish loaf 71
  layered fish terrine 40
  lime grilled fish skewers 82
  mackerel and gooseberries 77
  mackerel with mustard 76
  Mediterranean soup 15
  Middle Eastern monkfish 72
  roast cod with lentils 69
  salmon millefeuille 39
  salmon with herb sauce 75
  salt and sour baked trout 82
  sea bass roasted with fennel 77
  seafood and coconut soup 16
  skate with brown butter 78
  smoked trout mousse 38
  snapper with capellini 208
  sole meunière 74
  sole with chive sauce 79
  steamed 81
  tandoori trout 43
  trout with almonds 74
  tuna Basquaise 75

tuna pâté 38
tuna salad 272
turbot parcels 68
  with mushroom crust 69
  with ginger 78
  yogurt-topped halibut 70
Flemish braised chicken 108
Florentine roast pork 166
Florentines 420
Fluffy jacket potatoes 431
Focaccia 321
Fondant sweets 461
Fragrant gammon 178
Fragrant lime sherbet 453
Frangipane tarts 346
Frankfurter risotto 227
French apple tart 334
Fresh herb frittata 196
Fresh tarragon dressing 316
Fruit and elderflower cream 373
Fruit-filled white crêpes 364
Fruit fritters 364
Fruits in Chartreuse 468
Fruity cheese coleslaw 270
Fruity filo parcels 338
Fruity gammon steaks 178
Fudge, cashew nut 463
Fun fish cakes 429
Funghetto 302
Funny face pizzas 432

G
Gammon
  fragrant 178
  fruity steaks 178
Garlic and lemon prawns 61
Garlic and olive oil mash 282
Garlic beef 135
Garlic beef casserole 132
Garlic chicken 99
Garlic-roasted potatoes 282
Gâteau Grenoble 388
Gazpacho 9
Gingered Brussels sprouts 294
Gingerbread snaps 411
Ginger cake 398
Gingered melons 33
Ginger beef with pineapple 140
Ginger turkey and cabbage 113
Glacé fruit cake 404
Glazed baby onions 285
Goat's cheese and fig tart 247
Goat's cheese soufflés 46
Goat's cheese tarts 249
Gooseberry sauce 308
Gooseberry-yogurt snow 378
Grapefruit barley water 452
Gratin of vegetables 183
Gratin savoyard 284
Greek seafood casserole 84
Green beans with onion 290
Green and gold roulade 34
Green fried rice 222
Green rice 233
Grilled butterfly prawns 64
Grilled chicken and herbs 104
Grilled chicken drumsticks 101
Grilled flat fish 81

Grilled fish and coriander 73
Grilled pepper salad 261
Grilled quail 124
Grilled radicchio 55
Grilled vegetable pizza 242
Grilled vegetables 56
Grissini 323
Guinea fowl, pan-fried 123

H
Haddock and salmon pie 83
Halibut, yogurt-topped 70
Halva, pistachio 462
Halva cake 405
Ham, devilled toasts 438
Hand-dipped chocolates 461
Harira 19
Harvest casserole 177
Hazelnut crêpes with spinach 182
Herb and feta balls 27
Herbed crêpe pinwheels 446
Herbed pea soup 12
Herby cheese dressing 315
Herby peas 286
Herby yellow pepper sauce 307
Herrings in oatmeal 76
Honey madeleines 410
Honey spice cake 397
Hot and sour prawn soup 18
Hot buttered rum 458
Hot chocolate soufflé 369
Hot fish loaf 71
Hot lemon sauce 313
Hot orange cake 365
Hummus 25

I
Iced cupcakes 412
Iced rose tea 455
Imam bayaldi 54
Individual pear puffs 344
Indian summer punch 454
Indonesian-style pork 173
Italian meatballs 147
Italian meat platter 42

J
Jambalaya 221
Jelly
  port 381
  strawberry milk 383
  wobbles 433
Jewel-topped Madeira cake 399
Jumbles 419

K
Kadaifi 339
Kedgeree 221
Kiwifruit ice 392

L
Lamb
  chops
    braised with vegetables 158
    tarragon noisettes 150
  cubes
    chilindron 159
    curried with raita 157

harira 19
in green sauce 155
Moroccan 152
navarin 152
red-cooked fillet 154
sage cobbler 156
souvlakia 160
spice-coated 153
stir-fried sesame 154
with black olives 153
with lemon and garlic 158
yogurtlu 160
minced
moussaka 162
stir-fried meatballs 155
stuffed aubergine 157
leg
baked with vegetables 162
boulangère 151
roast with wine 161
with rosemary 150
neck
Scotch broth 20
shanks and flageolet beans 151
shoulder with onions 156
spiced rack 161
steaks
en papillotte 159
parcels 258
with pasta 212
Lasagne, seafood 207
Layered country terrine 44
Layered fish terrine 40
Leche frita 362
Leeks
and bacon knots 322
and cheese pie 249
and mushroom pilaf 226
stew with dumplings 181
tart 244
vinaigrette 30
Lemon
and chilli chicken 107
and coriander chicken 111
and currant brioches 329
Belvoir pudding 369
butterfly cakes 408
chicken 100
curd 466
custard slices 348
crunch cake 398
fragrant drink 453
hot sauce 313
shortbread 421
tarte au citron 333
vegetable rice 234
Lemonade, old-fashioned 452
Lemon-orange cups 382
Lemon-poppy seed cake 401
Lentils
and bean chilli 194
roast cod with 69
salad 277
spicy soup 22
stuffed peppers 197
Lettuce and egg salad 266
Light beef satay 137
Lime

grilled fish skewers 82
pickle 470
pudding, saucy 358
Linzer hearts 418
Lobster with basil dressing 89

M
Macaroons, almond 418
Macaroni
pastitsio 211
rainbow cheese 211
with aubergine 206
Mackerel
and gooseberries 77
with mustard 76
Madeira cake 399
Madeleines, owl 434
Maids of honour 342
Malay curried clams 91
Malted milkshakes 450
Mango
and lychee turnovers 339
chutney 470
mousse 378
with sticky rice 360
Mango beef with cashews 139
Margarita 456
Marinated feta cheese 471
Marinated mushrooms 31
Marinated mushrooms with grapefruit 447
Marinated spiced pork 167
Meatballs
in tomato sauce 143
Italian 147
stir-fried 155
Mediterranean fish soup 15
Mediterranean potato salad 276
Melba sauce 312
Melon
and chilled berries 373
gingered 33
Merry mice cakes 434
Mexican chicken salad 274
Mexican rice 225
Middle Eastern monkfish 72
Mild curry dressing 314
Milkshakes, malted 450
Mincemeat crêpe gateau 365
Mincemeat jalousie 345
Minestrone 14
Minted seafood salad 271
Minty apple sauce 308
Minty chocolate mousse 379
Mixed currant sensation 377
Mixed vegetable rösti 192
Mixed vegetables 298
Mocha espresso ice cream 393
Oeufs à la neige 386
Monkfish, Middle Eastern 72
Moroccan casserole 191
Moroccan lamb 152
Moroccan-style chicken 108
Mortadella salad 273
Moussaka 162
Mozzarella chicken 110
Muffins
blackberry 413
chocolate and orange 415

chocolate-nut 414
Mulligatawny 20
Mushrooms
à la Grecque 30
anchovy-stuffed 51
and barley broth 21
and bean chilli 183
and bean noodles 218
and cheese pies 253
and chicken rice 231
and rice patties 227
baked 52
brioches 57
curry 295
gratin 195
marinated 31
marinated with grapefruit 447
polenta with 188
soup, cream of 12
tart 251
Mussels
in tomato sauce 92
in white wine 92
stuffed 65
with basil 91

N
Naan 318
Navarin of lamb 152
Nectarine
baklava 349
meringue nests 382
New England clam chowder 16
Noodles
bean and mushroom 218
chow mein 218
cold spicy 216
crab and aubergine 215
crispy 213
pork and noodle parcels 214
pork and prawn 215
Singapore 217
Thai beef with 138
Thai fried 214
sesame salad 280
with broccoli 217
with chop suey 216
with spinach 207
Nut bake with tomatoes 193
Nutty brown bread ice cream 394
Nutty brownies 415
Nutty chicken strips 61
Nutty goujons 61
Nutty filo fingers 338

O
Oatie Brie cubes 441
Oeufs à la neige 386
Okra and tomatoes 287
Old-fashioned lemonade 452
Olive and mozzarella puffs 255
Olive bread 324
Olive oil and apple cake 401
Olive paste toasts 437
Olives, spicy 471
Omelette
soufflé 362
Spanish 193

Onions
and anchovy pizza 238
glazed baby 285
soup 11
Orange
and almond cake 402
and cinnamon dressing 315
cake, hot 365
cream caramel 384
meringue pie 332
muffins 415
sorbet 394
Oranges, caramel 372
Orange-glazed shorties 421
Oriental carrot salad 265
Owl madeleines 434
Oysters with aubergine 440

P
Pacific prawns 88
Paella, wok-style 228
Palmiers 342
Pancakes
apple 363
Szechuan 197
Pan-fried guineafowl 123
Panzanella salad 267
Parathas 327
Parma ham
baskets 60
with figs 42
Parmesan asparagus 48
Parmesan beignets 438
Parsley sauce 304
Parsnip
pear and almond sauté 184
curried soup 10
Partridge, Spanish 126
Party quiches 446
Pasta
bolognese 204
bucatini siciliana 202
carbonara 203
fideua 208
macaroni with aubergine 206
marinara 209
napoletana 204
pastitsio 211
penne, vodka and tomatoes 210
penne with leeks and ricotta 205
pepperami 430
primavera 212
rainbow macaroni cheese 211
seafood lasagne 207
snapper with capellini 209
spaghetti with garlic 203
tagliatelle with beetroot 206
tuna, tomato and penne 210
tortelloni salad 280
vegetarian spaghetti 205
warm salad 279
with broccoli 202
with lamb steaks 212
Pastitsio 211
Pâté
chicken liver 43
de campagne 36
pork and liver 43

tuna 38
Peaches
amaretti-stuffed 352
crunchy 354
and orange cake 396
rice pudding with 358
trifle 387
Pea soup
Dutch 22
herbed 12
Peas
herby 286
tabbouleh 278
Peanut brittle 464
Pearl patties and sherry dip 436
Pears
and cinnamon crumble 357
and date slices 347
individual puffs 344
in red wine 374
toffee and pecan 355
with chocolate sauce 372
with Stilton sauce 27
Pecan pie 332
Peking apples 363
Peking duck 121
Penne
tuna and tomato 210
penne, vodka and tomatoes 210
with leeks and ricotta 205
Peperonata 300
Pepperami pasta 430
Peppered chicken skewers 102
Peppers
grilled salad 261
herby yellow pepper sauce 307
lentil-stuffed 197
peperonata 300
pizza 239
pizzettes 240
red hot, and onion tart 252
red pepper vinaigrette 29
soup 11
spice rice and 229
with cauliflower 295
Peppered chicken kebabs 102
Petits pots au chocolat 386
Pheasant
in parsley sauce 124
with sultanas 125
Pigeon with crisp polenta 122
Pineapple Alaska 353
Pissaladière 325
Pistachio halva 462
Pitta bread 324
Pizza
aubergine 239
dolcelatte mini 242
funny face 432
grilled vegetable 242
margherita 238
onion and anchovy 238
pepper pizzettes 240
potato 241
roasted pepper 239
swirls 241
Playing card sandwiches 428
Plum-custard tart 335

Plum sauce 309
Polenta
 pigeon with 122
 with mushrooms 188
 with vegetables 298
Pork
 and liver pâté 43
 chops
  harvest casserole 176
  Provençal 176
  ratatouille-style 174
  with apple balls 176
  with cider 168
  with herb sauce 164
  with prunes 167
 cubes and strips
  and prawn noodles 215
  satay 171
  stir-fried 171
  Thai curry 165
  with basil 169
  with pears 168
  with water chestnuts 169
 cutlets, coconut with lime 172
 fillet, spicy with lemon grass 174
 leg, marinated spiced 167
 loin
  Florentine roast 166
  in cider and orange 164
  spicy 165
 minced
  and noodle parcels 214
  dim sum 58
 sausages
  and peppers 180
  Chinese stir-fry 180
  toad in the hole 179
 shoulder
  caraway pot roast 175
  stuffed 175
 spareribs
  barbecue 177
  barbecued 166
 stuffed cabbage leaves 179
 tenderloin
  afelia 172
  Indonesian-style 173
  prune medley 173
  with chilli and peas 170
Port jelly 381
Potatoes
 and onion flan 255
 baked eggs in nests 189
 fluffy jacket 431
 forestière 283
 garlic-roasted 282
 gratin savoyard 284
 Mediterranean salad 276
 pizza 241
 potato cakes and mango sauce 187
 salad 276
 vegetarian hash 187
 with chorizo 283
Pot roast of brisket 145
Potted prawns 39
Poulet au vinaigre 98
Poulet basquaise 97
Poulet provençal 97

Poussins with watercress 113
Prawns
 and feta purses 62
 and feta tarts 248
 and pork noodles 215
 chilli balls 62
 crispy pesto 442
 crystal rolls 31
 garlic and lemon 61
 grilled butterfly 64
 hot and sour soup 18
 in coconut sauce 86
 Pacific 88
 potted 39
 rice with tofu 231
 salt and pepper 87
 sesame prawn toasts 442
 sizzling 66
 spicy king 66
 stir-fried 89
 stuffed eggs 32
 with Asian sauce 87
 with garlic 86
 with lemon grass 88
Provençal beef daube 130
Provençal pork chops 176
Provençal rabbit 127
Prune and almond tart 337
Punch, Indian summer 454
Puréed ginger carrots 284

Q
Quail
 grilled 124
 spicy grilled 123
 with figs and oranges 125
Queen cakes 408
Queen of puddings 359

R
Rabbit
 in mustard sauce 128
 Provençal 127
 stifado 128
Radicchio, grilled 55
Rainbow macaroni cheese 211
Rainbow lollies 432
Raspberries
 and apple strudel 348
 eclairs 343
 roulade 387
Ratatouille 301
 in olive tarts 254
 terrine 37
Ratatouille-style pork 174
Red berry soufflé 353
Red-cooked lamb fillet 154
Red-hot pepper and onion tart 252
Red fruit tart 334
Red lamb and almond curry 156
Red pepper vinaigrette 29
Red snapper
 Cajun-style 79
 with canellini 209
Rhubarb meringue 375
Rice
 and black beans 229
 and black-eyed beans 228

and fruit mould 381
and mushroom rice 231
Asian fried 230
asparagus 234
chicken and mushroom 231
chicken biryani 220
chicken fried 431
crab fried 223
egg fried 224
frankfurter risotto 227
green 232
green fried 222
leek and mushroom pilaff 226
lemon vegetable 234
mango with sticky 360
Mexican 225
mushroom and rice patties 227
pearl patties and sherry dip 436
pudding with peaches 358
seafood fried 232
shrimp paste 222
spiced rice and peppers 229
spicy fried 232
spinach risotto cake 235
steamed chicken and 232
summer risotto 235
sun-dried tomato risotto 235
sweet saffron 226
vegetable biryani 235
vegetable fried 223
wild and brown salad 279
with asparagus and nuts 220
with chickpeas 230
with shrimp and tofu 231
wok-style paella 228
Yang Chow fried 224
Rice-filled tomatoes 225
Rich country chicken soup 17
Ricotta
 and coffee 379
 moulds 28
Roast cod with lentils 69
Roast figs 352
Roast leg of lamb with wine 161
Roast stuffed turkey 116
Roasted pepper pizza 239
Roasted pepper soup 11
Roquefort salad 267
Roquefort veronique 104
Rosé glow 458
Rose petal jam 467
Round Christmas pudding 370
Rum butter, Cumberland 467
Rum, hot buttered 458
Rum truffle cake 400

S
Sage lamb cobbler 156
Salade niçoise 270
Salami puffs 245
Salmon
 avocado salmon rolls 448
 coulibiac 246
 five-spice 80
 haddock and salmon pie 83
 with herb sauce 75
 millefeuille 39
 terrine 40

Salsa fresca 311
Salt and sour baked trout 82
Salt and pepper prawns 87
Saltimbocca 148
Satsuma and pine nut conserve 469
Sauces
 Asian 87
 barbecue 310
 basic white 304
 Béarnaise 130
 Bechamel 305
 black bean 101
 broccoli and cheese 306
 caper 304
 cheese 304
 chive 79
 chocolate 372
 curry 310
 dark chocolate 312
 green 41, 155
 herb 75, 164
 herby yellow pepper 307
 hot lemon 313
 mango 187
 mustard 128
 oyster 142
 parsley 124, 304
 plum 309
 salsa fresca 311
 spicy 296, 299
 spicy courgette 306
 spicy fish 311
 Stilton 27
 sweet and sour 309
 tarragon 305
 tomato 143, 289, 307
 vinegar 103
 white 304
 yellow 86
 yellow bell pepper 307
Saucy lime pudding 358
Sausages
 and peppers 180
 Chinese stir-fry 180
 toad in the hole 179
Savoury bread pudding 190
Savoury pastries 321
Scallops
 stir-fried 94
 with cashews 93
 with vegetables 93
Scones 414
Scotch broth 20
Sea bass roasted with fennel 77
Seafood
 and coconut soup 16
 fried rice 232
 lasagne 207
 parcels 248
 salad, minty 271
 Thai curried 94
 Serpent cake 341
Sesame noodle salad 280
Sesame prawn toasts 442
Shredded beef and ginger 136
Shrimp paste rice 222
Singapore noodles 217
Sizzling prawns 66

Skate with brown butter 78
Smoked trout mousse 38
Snapper with capellini 209
Sole
 meunière 74
 with chive sauce 79
Soufflés
 carrot and ginger 48
 goat's cheese 46
 hot chocolate 369
 red berry 353
Soufflé omelet 362
Soup
 blue cheese and broccoli 14
 carrot and coriander 13
 chicken and mushroom 17
 clear beet 8
 cock-a-leekie 18
 courgette and tomato 10
 cream of mushroom 12
 creamy fish 15
 curried parsnip 10
 Dutch pea 22
 fennel and pear 9
 gazpacho 9
 harira 19
 herbed pea 12
 hot and sour prawn 18
 Mediterranean fish 15
 minestrone 14
 mulligatawny 20
 mushroom and barley broth 21
 New England clam chowder 16
 onion 11
 rich country chicken 17
 roasted pepper 11
 seafood and coconut 16
 Scotch broth 20
 soupe au pistou 13
 spiced lentil 22
 spicy chickpea 19
 Tuscan bean 21
 vichyssoise 8
Soupe au pistou 13
Souvlakia 160
Spaghetti
 marinara 209
 vegetarian 205
 with garlic 203
Spanakopitta 245
Spanish country bread 326
Spanish hot chocolate 451
Spanish omelette 193
Spanish partridges 126
Spice rice and peppers 229
Spice-coated lamb 153
Spiced apricot squares 420
Spiced citrus slices 468
Spiced cabbage 297
Spiced lentil soup 22
Spiced rack of lamb 161
Spiced tea 453
Spicy braised beef 131
Spicy cauliflower 294
Spicy chicken patties 112
Spicy chicken wings 109
Spicy coffee-brandy cake 388
Spicy courgette sauce 306

Spicy crab 90
Spicy fish sauce 311
Spicy fried rice 232
Spicy grilled quail 123
Spicy king prawns 66
Spicy olives 471
Spicy pork and lemon grass 174
Spicy pork loin 165
Spicy sesame beef 139
Spicy Thai salad 273
Spicy tofu 200
Spinach
    and egg cups 50
    green and gold roulade 34
    noodles with 207
    roulade 41
    salad 261
    spanakopitta 245
    stir-fried with tofu 188
    risotto cake 236
    warm salad 268
    with raisins 290
Sponge drops 411
Spotted Dick 368
Spring rolls, Vietnamese 59
Squid
    salad 271
    stuffed 63
Steak with béarnaise sauce 130
Steaks with tomato and olives 146
Steamed chicken and rice 232
Steamed fish 81
Steamed fruit dumplings 368
Stir-fried beef steak 133
Stir-fried beef with leeks 132
Stir-fried chicken 100
Stir-fried meatballs 155
Stir-fried pork and beans 170
Stir-fried prawns 89
Stir-fried sesame lamb 154
Stir-fried scallops 94
Stir-fried spinach and tofu 188
Stir-fried vegetables 297
Strawberry
    mille-feuille 344
    shortcake 416
    sorbet 393
    yogurt milk jelly 383
Strawberry-rose meringues 409
Strawberry-yogurt mix 450
Stuffed aubergine 157
Stuffed cabbage leaves 179
Stuffed courgette rings 55
Stuffed leaves 444
Stuffed pork shoulder 175
Stuffed mussels 65
Stuffed squid 63
Sultana and carrot pudding 370
Summer fruit gratin 260
Summer fruit tartlets 343
Summer puddings 376
Summer risotto 236
Summer tea cup 455
Sun-dried tomato risotto 235
Surprise beefburgers 430
Sweet and sour sauce
Sweet and sour turkey 115
Sweet pepper chilli 194

Sweet saffron rice 226
Szechuan aubergine 292
Szechuan beef 133
Szechuan pancakes 197
Szechuan turkey 115

T
Tagliatelle with beetroot 206
Tandoori chicken 105
Tandoori trout 73
Tangerine syllabub 376
Tapénade 24
Taramasalata 26
Tarragon dressing, fresh 316
Tarragon lamb noisettes 150
Tarragon sauce 305
Tarte au citron 333
Tarte tatin 336
Teddy bear fool 433
Tennis cup 457
Tequila sunrise 456
Teriyaki steaks 141
Terrine
    layered country 44
    layered fish 40
    ratatouille 37
    salmon 40
    white and dark chocolate 391
Thai beef with noodles 138
Thai curried seafood 94
Thai fried noodles 214
Thai pork curry 165
Thai sweetmeats 462
Thousand island dressing 314
Three bean salad 277
Tia Maria choux 337
Tikka kebabs 105
Tiny Christmas logs 416
Tiramisu, feather-light 380
Toad in the hole 179
Toasted almond toffee 463
Toffee, toasted almond 463
Toffee date cake 396
Toffee pears and pecans 355
Tofu
    rice with shrimp and 231
    spicy 200
    stir-fried with spinach 188
Tomato
    and aubergine gratin 286
    and bean tian 185
    and okra 287
    and onion bread 319
    and red onion salad 263
    cheese stuffed 199
    gazpacho 9
    rice-filled 225
    salsa fresca 311
    sun-dried risotto 235
    with garlic crust 287
Tortelloni salad 280
Tricolor salad 264
Tropical salad 260
Trout
    baked with ginger 82
    salad 272
    smoked mousse 38
    tandoori 73

with almonds 74
Tuna
    Basquaise 75
    croquettes 63
    pâté 38
    salad 272
    tomato and penne 210
Tunisian orange salad 260
Turbot parcels 68
Turkey
    boneless pieces
        sweet and sour 115
        Szechuan 115
    breasts
        and broccoli flan 244
        ginger and cabbage 113
    cutlets
        creamy paprika 114
        with broccoli 114
    roast stuffed 116
Tuscan bean soup 21
Tzatziki 25

V
Vanilla rings 424
Veal
    saltimbocca 148
    scaloppine 148
Vegetables, mixed
    and cheese bake 190
    and fruit curry 185
    baked mixed 299
    biryani 235
    cobbler 192
    crostini 56
    curry 196
    filo parcels 253
    fricassée 195
    gratin 183
    grilled 56
    in spicy sauce 299
    mixed 298
    rösti 192
    salad 269
    Spanish salad 261
    stir-fried 297
    winter vegetable pie 254
Vegetarian Caesar salad 268
Vegetarian hash potatoes 187
Vegetarian spaghetti 205
Venison ragoût 127
Vichyssoise 8
Victoria sponge cake 403
Vietnamese spring rolls 59
Vietnamese roast duck 119
Vine fruits gateau 389

W
Walnut
    bread 320
    coffee-walnut cookies 419
    Easter cookies 422
    gâteau 402
    pastries 340
Warm pasta salad 279
Warm spinach salad 268
Watercress custards 50
Welsh cakes 413

White and dark chocolate terrine 391
White sauce 304
Wild and brown rice salad 279
Winter vegetable pie 254
Wok-style paella 228
Won tons, crispy 57

Y
Yang Chow fried rice 224
Yogurt-topped halibut 70

Z
Zabaglione 361